I shall pass through
this world but once.
Any good therefore
that I can do or any
kindness that I can
show to any human
being, let me do it now.
Let me not defer or
neglect it for I shall
not pass this way
again.

EX LIBRIS

WHAT THE BIBLE SAYS SERIES

WHAT THE
BIBLE SAYS
ABOUT

SALVATION

by

Virgil Warren

College Press Publishing Company, Joplin, Missouri

Library of Congress Catalog Card Number: 82-73345
International Standard Book Number: 0-89900-088-6

IN GRATEFUL DEDICATION TO

MY DAD

ERVIN WARREN

MY FIRST THEOLOGY PROFESSOR

ABOUT THE AUTHOR

Virgil Warren is currently Professor of Theology at Manhattan Christian College, Manhattan, Kansas. In 1977 he received his Ph.D. in systematic theology from The Southern Baptist Theological Seminary. Previous work includes the M.Div. (1971) and M.A. (1973) from Wheaton College with undergraduate studies at The Cincinnati Bible Seminary (A.B.; Th.B.). Dr. Warren is a member of several societies including the Society of Biblical Literature, the American Academy of Religion, the Evangelical Theological Society, and the International Council on Biblical Inerrancy.

Table of Contents

PART VI: PERSEVERANCE IN SALVATION

PART VII: INDICES

PREFACE

A book is never the product of the immediate author alone. Accordingly, gratitude becomes the appropriate attitude with which this enterprise is begun and consummated. I wish to thank those whose previous contributions to my own development have helped to shape my conclusions on the several issues treated in the present volume. It is doubtful that much contained herein is truly new even where there is no conscious dependence on former writers. Nevertheless the volume may make some positive contribution to the study of the themes it treats.

To my colleagues and students at Manhattan Christian College I owe a word of appreciation for the constant encouragement to complete this year-long project. Their patience along with that of my family is much appreciated since my involvement in this effort has probably detracted from the performance of my regular responsibilities both in school and at home. Hopefully these written notes will enhance the quality of my future instruction in salvation and related fields.

A special word of thanks goes to my wife Ruth Ann for her diligence in preparing the first and final drafts of the manuscript. Her tenacious efforts in reference verification, galley-proof reading, and other meticulous operations have significantly increased the accuracy of the end product. I am grateful as well to College Press for offering opportunity to put down these thoughts in more organized and permanent form. The book is sent out in the hope that it will edify the reader and elucidate the great theme that it treats: man's reconciliation to God.

Introduction

What the Bible Says about Salvation covers a rather broad sweep of subjects that belong to the study of reconciling men to God. It goes without saying that our presentation implicitly distinguishes between "what the Bible says" and what we understand it to mean. Our efforts have not necessarily exhausted the biblical materials relevant to each sub-topic, but we have endeavored to place before the reader those passages and those interpretations of them that warrant serious reflection. Often in the interests of conserving space, we have simply given references to other verses with similar import. Frequently we have fully listed the pertinent texts even though they may not all be necessary for establishing the point at hand.

We hope to speak to as wide a readership as possible, while realizing that this presentation will be more suitable for some than for others. The study is neither overly advanced nor merely introductory. Technical jargon has been minimized, but where it seemed indispensable we have tried to explain unfamiliar terms and concepts. Consequently, ministers, church leaders, and teachers will presumably find these notations helpful in their ministry. Perhaps the book could serve as collateral reading in college courses or even as a text, course structure permitting. We do not pretend to address trained theologians although concepts as concepts are comprehensible and useful to all minds regardless of their level of doctrinal maturity.

One major concern has been to describe conclusions other than our own. Knowing the main alternatives enables better understanding of the position deemed correct because ideas become clearer when set in contrast to alternatives. Knowing other positions and the arguments for them also prepares for more beneficial discussions with other people. We have attempted therefore to set forth alternate views in their best light and to avoid short cuts in responding to them. Although proliferating interpretations and the arguments for them runs the risk of confusing someone, we have preferred that risk to leaving a person unprepared for unforeseen options. Hopefully we have struck a happy balance between breadth and depth in so doing.

Another concern has been to present fundamental concepts and principles, because proper interpretation depends on a sufficient inventory of concepts to match those expressed and presupposed by biblical authors. This general requirement applies as much to biblical interpretation as it does to any other usage of human language. Deficiency in this inventory can result in equating the wrong idea with a writer's words when they are sufficiently ambiguous to allow it to happen. An error of equivocation can flow by undetected until it creates a "log jam" farther downstream. To change the figure, the "domino effect" in exposition forces one for consistency's sake to twist other passages in unlikely ways. Proper interpretation procedure is a total program that requires sensitivity and humility because no one is exempt from the pitfalls involved.

In this connection it may be well to state the format for what we will call a "biblical-systematic hermeneutic." Interpretation involves more than reading a text in its immediate context—*the law of harmony.* Interpretation works back and forth between text, concept, and text again. Specific passages are often not clear except on the general background they presuppose, yet general backgrounds must come from specific passages. The solution to this apparent circularity is that one specific passage will express the general concept that clarifies another specific passage. The combination of texts may further elaborate the conceptual background for yet another specific passage, and so on. Moving from general concept to specific passage must be done on the basis of *the nature of the case.* Consequently, at each point along the way clear thinking and prior understanding will necessarily shape biblical interpretation as much as it does other interpretation. Accuracy depends on the rigorousness with which the enterprise is conducted. Interpretation is "systematic" because we are dealing with the whole picture, and it is "biblical" in that the whole picture grows out of the specifics of scripture.

In order to carry out the program outlined above, we adopt a view of scripture that we believe it claims for itself: the accuracy of scripture is such that we may add an insight in one author to an insight in another one in order to make an inference not necessarily verbalized by either one. Scripture harmonizes to the extent that we may properly suppose compatibility between individual writers so that the parts of the whole to which they give expression are indeed parts of the same whole. No biblical writer systematically sets forth the whole picture on any subject; consequently, combining different writers' testimony is necessary for gaining systematic understanding. Since Romans, Galatians, Hebrews, and other New Testament books exhibit this method of interpreting Old Testament materials, we consider it an appropriate method of interpreting scripture generally.

2

Experience has shown that a book this size serves more as a reference tool than as a text to be read straight through. For that reason we have written groups of chapters in each part as more-or-less self-contained units. This procedure has not created undue repetition, yet it avoids excessive cross references. The topical index may always be used in case incidental remarks need clarification. The book moves naturally through the whole subject, but the parts should be independently understandable.

Deficiencies in the body of the book will perhaps be alleviated by the indices at the end. A classified bibliography lists many modern studies of salvation as viewed from several different traditions. More advanced students can move beyond our work here by consulting these entries. The bibliography should go a long way toward making up for weaknesses inherent in not using footnotes. We have taken special pains to prepare scripture and subject indices that will facilitate the location of all our materials on each passage and each topic. A glossary of salvation terms assembles much of the vocabulary used in salvation studies. Frequently, technical terms limited to a specific discipline do not find their way even into unabridged dictionaries; if they do, the brevity of the entries does not always satisfy the reader's needs.

One difficulty in writing a book like this one is making space allotments. Our arrangement has allowed practical rather than theoretical considerations to dictate procedure. Sometimes central issues do not require so much discussion as other ones do because there is greater unanimity on them in the Christian community. Furthermore, some subjects bear more directly on practice and so they call for special attention on that account.

We have therefore assigned significant space to the meaning and scope of the atonement, the concept of salvation by faith, several issues on baptism, and the question of perseverance. Atonement has practical importance because we must articulate clearly the connection between Jesus Christ and the forgiveness of sins; otherwise, non-Christians will have added difficulty making sense of the gospel. Salvation by faith carries considerable importance in that it couples divine grace with human response; that connection must be properly expressed in order to avoid merit on one side and determinism on the other. Baptism has caused significant difficulty in modern unity movements, and it happens to be a practical matter where several salvation issues surface. Since

3

baptism involves obedience, it cannot be held in abeyance. Apostasy, perseverance, and eternal security deal with the combination of human responsibility and divine assistance in the continued Christian status. These topics the reader will agree are constant subjects of discussion among believers; perchance the treatment given them here will help clarify the issues.

The natural breadth of our subject and the necessary limitations of our presentation require us to restrict our study to a descriptive and conceptual approach. No effort has been made to interact with specific authors and their distinctive contributions to the topics. We have not traced the historical development of sub-topics in our study. Names, dates, places, and movements have remained unlabeled throughout as a safeguard against confusion and misrepresentation. Cross-fertilization in the modern theological scene often makes traditional categories inappropriate and misleading anyway.

In our estimation the nature of man greatly affects the whole reconstruction of salvation. In particular the question about natural ability or inability to accept the gospel crops up again and again. Although we have treated "natural depravity" in various places throughout the book, the reader may want to consult the author's doctoral dissertation for a more systematic presentation: *The Implication of Divine Self-Consistency for the Doctrine of Natural Depravity: A Biblical-Systematic Approach* (Ph.D. dissertation, The Southern Baptist Theological Seminary) Ann Arbor, Michigan: University Microfilms (#77-23, 835), 1977. This work may serve as a companion volume to our present study.

The author takes responsibility for biblical quotations used in the book. New Testament passages have been rendered from the third edition of the United Bible Society's Greek text edited by Kurt Aland and others: *The Greek New Testament* (1975). Old Testament references come from *Biblia Hebraica Stuttgartensia*, edited by R. Kittel and others (1977).

4

Part I—The Nature of Salvation

Chapter One

THE NATURE OF SALVATION

The Central Issue

"Salvation" labels several matters in scripture, but for our purposes (1) *salvation has centrally to do with restoring interpersonal relationship*. The role of Christianity in the world is *reconciliation*. The primacy of reconciliation in salvation can be inferred from the fact that (a) both *God and men are persons* constituted for fellowship by virture of sharing the same image (Gen. 1:26-27); restoring what has been ruined by sin centers on saving from separation.

(b) Scripture uses *interpersonal imagery* to describe the divine-human relationship—father, son, friend, marriage; coming into those relationships describes salvation. From the nature of the case what constitutes personhood and personal relationship constitutes the governing principles for salvation.

(c) Scripture and *experience* show that a new quality of interpersonal relationship is the only benefit that necessarily comes from Christian faith during this life. Christians may not have stronger health, greater wealth, more attractive physical appearance, higher community status, greater fame, and the like. They do have available in all cases an abundance of life not found anywhere else. Therefore since a quality of relationship is the only consistent benefit, fellowship is the central category for life, and reconciliation becomes the primary goal in salvation. Only what is uniform can be central.

(d) *Scripture* itself summarizes the life of man in interpersonal terms. Salvation thus returns a man to his intended form of existence. Love occurs between persons and the great love commands are the pegs for God's revelation both new and old. The *First Great Commandment* is to love God and the *Second Great Commandment* is to love your neighbor as yourself: Matthew 22:34-40; Mark 12:28-31; Luke 10: 25-28; John 13:34-35; Romans 13:8-10; Galatians 5:13-15. James calls the Second Great Commandment the *Royal Law* (2:8) and Jesus rewords it in the Golden Rule (Mt. 7:12). The First Great Commandment is called the *Shema* (Deut. 6:4-5). Micah 6:8 summarizes the central matter of life when he says, "What does Yahweh require from

5

you but to do justly and to love kindness and to walk humbly with your God?" Habakkuk 2:4 provides the foundation for all the main New Testament teaching on faith: "The just shall live by faith." In every instance the nature of life is interpersonal; therefore salvation is interpersonal because it brings men into life.

We experience this relationship in two directions—vertically with God and horizontally with other people. Our sense of fulfillment relates to how we imagine reality to be, where it is going, and how we fit into it; that is, authentic existence derives from world view. The intangible aspects of life have more real bearing on long-term happiness than the material environment does. Christianity speaks particularly to the intangibles of the human predicament, offering faith, hope, and love from God to all men through Jesus Christ.

Since a new quality of interpersonal relationship is the *only* necessary benefit of Christianity, the Christian religion analyzes the human predicament as resulting primarily from faulty social interaction. Therefore salvation deals fundamentally with correcting estrangement, alienation, and separation between persons. In saying that proper relationship *always* comes from Christianity, we presuppose correct practice by adherents of the Christian system.

Personal relationship deals with interaction between persons. Therefore, (2) *salvation has to do with correcting interpersonal behavior.* Christianity calls for *conversion* because it assigns the cause of alienation to misbehavior (Isa. 59:2); alienation is overcome through change in behavior that leads to reconciliation. Righteousness, or right behavior, is a preliminary concern of salvation.

More exactly, however, since sin has already occurred by the time salvation enters the picture and since we have no more practical hope of living perfectly in the future than we did in the past, perfect righteousness cannot be the decisive basis for reconciliation. Reunion with God must result from a righteousness the sinner is viewed as having instead of a righteousness he has. Specifically then, (3) *salvation has to do with the manner in which God comes to view us as righteous.* Reconciliation does not come directly from conversion, but from *justification.* The sinner has faith that God has grace; he believes God is gracious because he went so far as to send his Son to model righteousness unto death by crucifixion. God has offered to view men in terms of Jesus Christ if they will identify themselves with the ideal personalized in him. Conversion leads to justification which leads to reconciliation. Salvation is interpersonal, functional, and gracious.

Derivative Benefits of Salvation

Although salvation begins with personal relationships, it does not stop there. *Psychological* benefits also arise from association with God and fellow believers: security, love, freedom, meaningfulness, innocence, spiritual strength. Sin creates inner conflict because men are not constituted to live in certain ways God has designated sinful. Salvation calls for turning from such behaviors so that the changed life style brings improved self-image, peace, and psychological power. Even as salvation brings a quality of interpersonal relationship without necessarily changing the environment, so also it can change the way a person feels about his circumstance without altering the circumstance.

The psychology of grace means that we no longer have the feeling of being considered guilty (Heb. 9:9, 14; 10:2, 22). The grace of salvation also removes us from the pressure of the perfection requirement so that we do not *have* to be righteous; we can relax and concentrate on improving our weaknesses without fear that failure will destroy something ultimate. People always perform better when they sense they are accepted. Furthermore, salvation by grace removes competition as a basis for self-esteem. Grace effectively removes the past from having any bearing on the present and creates an atmosphere of acceptance in the present to enhance self-image and stimulate spiritual growth.

Physical effects of faith may be found as well, not only in the sense that God may miraculously or providentially heal the body, but because many physical ailments have a psychological origin. Because man is a psychosomatic whole, "mis-behavior" in one aspect of his being sends off negative effects into other aspects of his self. Correcting that behavior tends to reverse its effects on the body. Moreover, Christianity affirms this world by granting salvation *in* it rather than *from* it; interest in physical health comes naturally from conceiving of the body as the temple of God's Spirit (I Cor. 6:12-20). Bodily exercise does profit a little although in comparison such activity is prompted by the godliness that is profitable for all things and for all time (I Tim. 4:7-8).

7

Even *material* benefits may result from salvation, not because God has promised monetary blessings in return for righteousness, but because honesty, willingness to work, self-discipline, and frugality affect financial stability, all other factors being equal. It would be a mistake, however, to make material advantage a motive of righteousness or an expectancy of the Christian faith.

Beyond personal rewards of righteous living, there are *social* implications of the gospel. The general character of a whole culture is shaped by values that govern its functioning at all levels. Salvation has a place here inasmuch as the humanitarianism in Christianity militates against the organized evil that can inhere in the very structures of society. In that sin alienates people from each other because it is a self-orientation, salvation through Christ creates a new united mankind (Eph. 2:15). Properly applying the gospel makes for peace between social classes by bringing individuals together into a new, common identity through Christ. Previous distinctions based on race, nationality, wealth, sex, social status, and vocation can no longer serve as a basis for measuring worth (I Cor. 7:18-24; Gal. 3:28). There is a new society within society at large that leavens the world toward righteousness. Even *political* applications may arise as outgrowths of social implications if a nation becomes permeated with the attitude of mutual respect, human worth and dignity, responsible freedom, and the like.

The *cosmic* dimension of salvation refers to the "restoration of all things" (Acts 3:21; cp. Rom. 8:19-25; Heb. 2:5-9). Man's sin has affected all aspects of his self and his relations because the effects of sin are universal and pervasive. Included among these corruptions is his relationship to the world over which God originally gave him dominion. Instead of serving responsibly as caretaker for the world, sin exploits nature for selfish ends so that wholeness and harmony are destroyed. At Christ's return proper order will be restored between man and that over which God gives him responsibility.

Finally, *eternal* life means that the meaningful existence already begun in this age will develop into higher forms of divine fellowship according to the promises of God. Salvation amounts to retrieval from endless meaninglessness because it puts a person into permanent association with the creator, sustainer, and director of history and eternity.

8

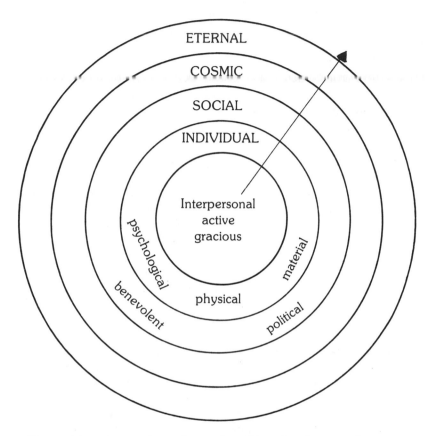

Up to this point we have been describing the theoretical structure of salvation. The structure of the system, however, is often the reverse of the sequence of presenting the system. Effectively proclaiming the Christian world view and program will often have to follow the demonstration of love that helps fulfill physical, psychological, and social needs of the spiritually disoriented. By giving the "cup of cold water" in Jesus' name, ambassadors for Christ may have to win the right to speak to people who as yet have little appreciation for the intangible realities of life. The sequence used in the proclamation of salvation does not necessarily follow the *structure* of salvation. In the living situation the central and the less central are equally present, but they are not therefore equally important.

In order of importance Christian living begins with personal relationship to God; and when that happens, other matters do come in and take their places. If men seek first the kingdom of heaven, all these other things will be added unto them (Mt. 6:33). What is true about the *structure of life* determines what is true about *entering back into life* —which is salvation. Since everything in a sense falls under the concerns of salvation, the study of this subject would ideally include everything that needs to be remedied.

Other Formulations

Properly understanding salvation means that nothing be omitted, that foreign concepts be avoided, and that the components be kept in proper relationship. Subtle errors can come from pushing secondary aspects into primary positions; what is true as a part becomes false if made into the whole. Every conscientious student of special revelation wants to avoid such mistakes even though it is much more difficult to do so than it might appear. For the sake of clarification by contrast, we survey below some reconstructions of salvation that in different ways misconstrue its character in our estimation.

Formulations based on misemphasis

Misemphasis occurs in Christian salvation when through *mysticism* spiritual concerns eclipse physical matters. Jesus directed his ministry to salvation from sin, but he made compassion for the sick a bridge to that larger concern. Proper salvation theory affirms this world and the individuality presupposed in interpersonal relations. Christian salvation does not countenance the absorption of self into an unidentifiable One or encourage flight from this-worldly affairs. The other-worldliness of some approaches to Christianity conceives of salvation as escape from this manner of existence and flight into an intangible realm.

The opposite, this-worldly extreme crops out in the *social gospel,* where benevolence is an end instead of a natural approach to eternal, vertical, and spiritual reconciliation. Jesus exemplified a holistic approach to the human condition by blending compassion for physical needs with compassion for spiritual welfare and used the first to authenticate his avowed concern for the second.

Morality is also not salvation. Although men are called to obedience and moral consciousness, sonship with God does not rest on attaining

10

moral excellence. Christianity is not ethics even though it has an ethic. Since salvation comes from the offended party, the offender is in no position to restore the relationship, having been the cause of its dissolution in the first place. Salvation sees God taking the initiative in reconciliation and presents him as doing it out of grace, because our present behavior no more warrants his kindness than our past behavior did. Although it can be appreciated, basic morality does not satisfy the ideal life God holds up before men; for good moral living is not ideal living.

Formulations based on foreign concepts

Impersonal thinking has been perhaps the greatest plague of Christian thought over the centuries. Salvation has often been interpreted and applied mechanistically as in the sale of indulgences to sin, treasury of merit of the saints, inherited salvation, inherited damnation, changed status without changed behavior, and changed behavior without loss of status. In these matters *legal transaction* has replaced interpersonal process and has made salvation into so much paper work.

Sacramentalism perverts the nature of salvation by bringing in the concept of the automatic flow of grace so that the free decision of God in salvation and blessing fades from view. It operates as if impersonal processes were at work in salvation without any necessary awareness and direct involvement on God's part. In sacramentalism the properties of the matter signified are at least psychologically attributed to the sign performed by the person rather than attributed to God who grants the benefits.

Another problem has been the substitution of *natural process* for personal relationship. A misunderstanding of the nature of evil broadened sin from "mis-action" to "mis-being," and out of that single move has grown the concept of natural depravity with its far-reaching implications for the manner in which salvation occurs and continues. Miracle preempts forgiveness as the decisive act inasmuch as salvation would not be possible without the "ontic" regeneration that enables men to believe.

In *gnosticism* the knowledge of secret information became the means by which "salvation" occurred, and salvation consisted in deliverance from the confining and perverting presence of matter. Remnants of this Greek mentality surface in the church when correct doctrine rather than personal relationship becomes psychologically the ultimate frame of

11

reference. Salvation is more than corrected understanding because Christ did more than teach.

Lastly, *political theology* attempts to accomplish by compulsion what presumably does not happen by conversion. Instead of transformation from within, liberation movements short-cut the dynamics of change by compelling it from the outside and short-circuit the transformation in the process. God has ordained civil government to operate from the outside to restrain self-centered behavior, but positive conversion from within must be the domain of salvation preached by the church. Salvation does not center in the political kingdom of Jewish expectation, but in the interpersonal kingdom of Jesus the Messiah (Lk. 17:20-21; Jn. 18:36).

Salvation is ultimately a matter of solving a person's identity, and identity is the sum total of all acts and relationships. Relationship between persons pre-empts all other considerations in reflecting on the nature of salvation. We infer the further truth that all processes associated with the *manner of bringing about salvation* are to be interpreted in harmony with the dynamics of interpersonal relationship. Finally, the *characteristics of persons* must be remembered when attempting to arrive at the truth about restoring relationship between persons.

Part II—The Need for Salvation

Chapter Two

THE HOLINESS OF GOD

Introduction

Isaiah represents all scripture by centering on a basic conflict between the holiness of God and the sinfulness of Israel. What epitomizes his message (1:2-31) characterizes revelation through all God's prophets, the scripture, and the incarnation. Individual events, specific commands, and general teachings center around this conflict like petals on a daisy;

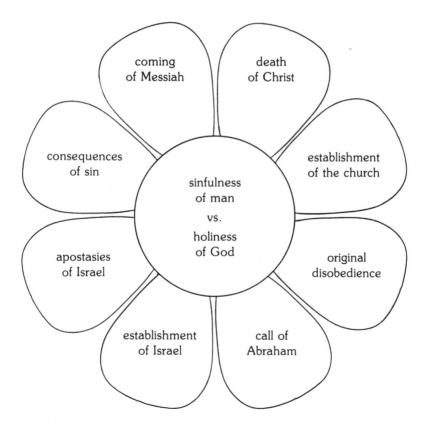

they form the components of redemptive history. Since a holy God created man for fellowship, his love impelled him to establish a long-range program by which the estrangement caused by sin could be overcome.

In preparation for the sending of his own Son, God called Abraham and developed a nation that was to become a preliminary light of holiness to the other nations. In due time the Jewish Messiah came, and the primary witness for righteousness through him went out to all men beginning at the capital of Israel. The good news of reconciliation means that through Christ there has been established in historic reality the means by which the conflict between human sinfulness and divine holiness can be overcome.

Fact of God's Holiness

Consistency

More than any other book Isaiah emphasizes the holiness of Yahweh, God of Israel. In addition to related expressions, the distinct title "The Holy One of Israel" occurs some twenty-five times (1:4; 5:19, 24; 10:20; 12:6; 17:7; 29:19; 30:11, 12, 15; 31:1; 37:23; 41:14, 16, 20; 43:3, 14; 45:11; 47:4; 48:17; 49:7; 54:5; 55:5; 60:9, 14). Although the great prophet of the Southern Kingdom may be credited with popularizing the designation for Yahweh, the characteristic itself was affirmed of the Lord from the earliest times. Abraham interceded for Lot with the question, "Shall not the Judge of all the earth do right?" (Gen. 18:25). Elihu vindicated the justice of God when he said to Job, "Far be it from God that he should do any wickedness and from the Almighty that he should commit iniquity" (Job. 34:10; cp. 34:12). Moses said of him, "All his ways are justice, a God of faithfulness and without iniquity; he is just and right" (Deut. 32:4). The terminology varies, but the message remains the same: Yahweh is ethical deity.

The stress on the holiness of Yahweh in the Hebrew scriptures contrasted him with deities of surrounding nations. They were gods of power rather than gods of principle. Their behavior did not rise above the depraved actions of those who conceived them; even in their worship appeared the lowest forms of debauchery and human degradation. Men feared them because of their might and served them for fear and favor. Such gods were guided by whim instead of values. Saying that

14

God is a God of principle, not just a God of power, means that he conducts himself by values instead of drives. God is a spirit, who does not possess the human vices based on flesh.

Selflessness

In contrast to the carnal character of pagan deities, Yahweh is a selfless God. Not only is he "wholly other" from sinful man, but he is wholly for man. Whereas holiness describes his self-consistency, love describes the manner of his self-consistency—the interpersonal character of his holiness.

Criteria for God's Holiness

Positively speaking

In logical sequence the criteria for divine holiness are God's (a) *nature*, his (b) *purposes*, and his (c) *promises*. Out of the nature of God arise his purposes, and from his purposes arise his promises. Relative to various amounts of this total truth cluster, scripture speaks of God's holiness. He is unable, for example, to "deny himself" (II Tim. 2:13); he operates by principles internal to himself. He cannot "lie" (Tit. 1:2; Heb. 6:18; Num. 23:19); his word is his bond. Whatever God freely promises can always be believed because God can be trusted to be himself and to act consistently with his nature, purposes, and promises.

Negatively speaking

If the foregoing facts hold true, several erroneous ideas may be set aside, including the notion that (1) *there are no criteria for his holiness* because God is sovereign. Sovereignty does not excuse inconsistency or capriciousness because sovereignty only describes his lack of *external controls*. Unlike ancient gods controlled by the Fates, Yahweh embodies the highest level of authority and power; but he subjects himself to his own *internal controls* in not denying himself or lying.

Another false conception takes it that (2) *his holiness is subject to external abstract rules.* Although sovereignty does not eliminate criteria for evaluation, it does eliminate external ones. Needless to say the principles we hold up in measurement of him come not from us but from his own self-determined patterns of conduct revealed in scripture. We have no authority or power to enforce them and no right to criticize

15

him on the basis of them since we are ignorant of what informs his total operation. Nevertheless we recognize them in him. His word is his bond, but it is *his* word that is his bond. Any evaluating we may do is for being encouraged to trust him for ourselves and to commend him to other people. Neither freedom nor pattern creates any difficulty for divine action, for God freely patterns himself and is true to his principled freedom.

We also must not suppose that (3) *his holiness allows for self-centeredness.* God's righteousness does not exist separate from other attributes, especially not apart from love, which draws attention to the interpersonal dimension, sphere, scope, and basis of divine activity. Since salvation incorporated both God and man, holiness in salvation means consistency with love. Love gives of itself out of concern for the needs of others; consequently, God's holiness involves consistency within the qualification that love for others makes on abstract principles and personal decisions. Any decision or requirement takes into consideration man's nature and purpose. Because God's character is loving holiness, he does not self-centeredly make requirements without regard for man's need, condition, or capacity. God's consistency includes his concern for us.

Right and wrong, good and evil derive from purpose. The purpose in creating man, Paul says, was "to the praise of the glory of his grace" (Eph. 1:6, 12, 14). Whether creation for his own glory is self-centeredness depends on how the glory comes from creation. The key point is that God made man "to the praise of the glory of his *grace.*" Grace derives from love so that glory results from God's first giving himself. God did for man first (I Jn. 4:19b); as a result of his doing for the creature, the creature responds to God in love (I Jn. 4:19a), which glorifies him. The heavenly Father enjoys seeing man take his gifts and derive joy and abundance from them. In that respect he is like an earthly father who enjoys seeing a grateful son delighted by his present. God is glorified when a man properly uses his gifts; his honor comes indirectly from the free response of love in those first loved by him.

By implication we set aside any notion of divine dependence on man. God, for example, did not make man because he was "lonely" in a "needing" sense. Paul describes the God of his fathers by saying he was not "served by human hands as if he needed anything since he gives to all life and breath and all things" (Acts 17:25). Men's sacrifices do not feed him; men's praises do not feed his ego; their presence does not keep him from feeling useless. Loosely speaking, God created man from something of the reason parents want children—as offspring in their likeness on whom they can bestow love, and with something of the same results—the implicit limitation love for offspring puts on parental freedom.

Scripture also does not allow the idea that (4) *holiness excludes love.* While ancient philosophers argued for the apathy of the gods, Christianity has always taught that the Holy One of Israel loves his people. Apathy was defended because being able to appeal to God's "emotions" would afford a certain amount of control over him who was supposed to be sovereign. Being able to affect God is not, however, to control him.

Another perversion of biblical holiness in God occurs when (5) *holiness is allowed to stand parallel to love* rather than in sequence with it in salvation. God does not extend love to some and holiness to others. "Distinguishing love" does not pass over some in the saving of others. Men do come into their lost state because of their own sins so that from the standpoint of sheer justice no charge could be brought against God for unconditionally selecting a remnant for salvation. Consequently, anything God might do to avert man's chosen destiny would be an act of grace that goes beyond the call of justice. Although nothing can be criticized in regard to justice in the above reconstruction, we question whether love is there in the sense scripture represents God as having it.

An alternative formulation of love and holiness puts love first. From love comes the salvation possibility. If men refuse salvation provided by love, justice then comes about in the form of judgment, condemnation, and destruction. Holiness is brought to bear when love is refused, a procedure hardly able to be faulted either from the standpoint of love or holiness.

On this last perversion of the love-holiness relationship, a final comment needs to be made in anticipation of a clearer description under atonement. God's love did not override his holiness even *in* the process of providing the salvation possibility; in fact, holiness is stressed there. He did not abandon his requirements for ideal men or withdraw the death penalty. Instead, he provided through his Son a source of motivation to righteousness, identity for it, and hope for resurrection. In effect, he bought time for men to be transformed into the image of his Son.

17

Chapter Three

The Nature of Sin

The Biblical Concept

Active

Scripture defines sin first as action. "Little children, let no one deceive you; he who does righteousness is righteous even as *he* is righteous. He who does sin is of the devil because the devil sins from the beginning. For this purpose the Son of God was manifested: that he might destroy the works of the devil" (I John 3:7-8). That sin is action is also shown by the repeated statements of scripture that God will render judgment and reward according to the deeds done in the body whether good or bad (Job 34:11; Ps. 62:12; Mt. 16:27; Rom. 2:6; II Cor. 5:10; Eph. 6:8; Col. 3:25; I Pet. 1:17; Rev. 2:23; 20:12; 22:12). Sin is something a person does even as righteousness is doing something.

Relational

Scripture defines sin secondly as relationship. By putting cause for effect, biblical writers call separation sin: "For we previously accused both Jews and Greeks of all being under sin" (Rom. 3:9). Since a person's actions affect more than himself, they can create estrangement. Sinful actions remove the common ground with people who share our values and identity: the prodigal confesses, "I am no more worthy to be called your *son*" (Lk. 15:18-19, 21). Sins normally express self-centeredness so that they alienate those used and manipulated for the sinner's self-interest. Separation from God is a state of sin called "bondage" in Romans 8:15 because it is a state from which the sinner cannot free himself. Sin is therefore a state as well as an act.

Legal

Sin is defined relative to an objective standard. Again I John provides the definition: "Everyone that does sin also does *law*lessness, and sin is lawlessness" (3:4). On several occasions Paul comments in a similar vein: "Where there is no law neither is there transgression" (Rom. 4:15); "Wherefore out of works of law no flesh will be justified before him, for through law comes knowledge of sin" (3:20); "However, I did not know sin except through law . . . for without law sin is dead" (7:7-8). "Sin is not reckoned when there is no law" (5:13). Even Jesus looked to the

18

Father for the definition of good (Jn. 8:29; 4:34, etc.). Sin is not a matter of ineffective vs. effective, but of right and wrong as measured by a standard. To the extent that God's will exists sin exists (cp. Ezek. 18:5-9).

Sin figured relative to a standard applies to (1) *both written and unwritten will.* The legal aspect actually extends from the personal because it means nothing more than the *expressed* will of God for human activity. Whether he has simply explained his desires or enacted them in the form of a written code matters little inasmuch as statements or statutes guide behavior.

God's law means God's will in much the same way the "law" of a parent means his will and authority. Ideally, a parent could write down everything he wanted his children to do and not to do; it would not differ from telling them orally. The amount and exactness of the requirements would be the same theoretically. Christians need to bear in mind that New Testament writers object to the Mosaic Law, not because of its high standards, but because it lacked any real provision for saving infractors from its curse. The followers of Messiah stand as much under divine regulation as any Jew did under the law and prophets. The different "feel" in the "law of Christ" (Gal. 6:2; cp. 1 Cor. 9:21; James 1:25; Rom. 8:2) comes from the stronger emphasis on personal concern, the significant reduction in ceremonial and civil regulations, and the removal of the curse.

Much objection to "legalism" stems from factors not essentially in view at this point. A written code often carries (a) an impersonal implication that does not decisively stress personal qualities like love, caring, and concern. But the law of God should not be viewed in abstraction from him.

A second problem grows out of (b) the difficulty of adapting a written code to peculiar circumstances not contemplated when the legislation was enacted. Officers have problems executing some laws because occasions arise where the offender did nothing morally wrong; yet he stands in conflict with the letter of the law. It is practically impossible to set forth in written form a provision for every conceivable situation. "Legalistic" mentalities fail to understand the "rule-of-thumb" nature of law and refuse to allow extenuating circumstances to alter application of the principle. (c) From the strict wording of a statute it may be hard to know what the intent of the law really was.

19

"Legalism" in modern usage tends to regard (d) outward action as what falls under the scrutiny of law. A legalist does not let attitude, motive, and intent qualify the character of an act. In practice, laws are often written in terms of somewhat artificial concerns because inner thoughts are hard to evaluate objectively and consistently. A related point is that law often operates from the outside in, rather than vice versa, so that force instead of influence characterizes law in people's minds.

In the will of God and the law of Christ, however, many of these deficiencies disappear because of the character of the Lawgiver and Judge. Since he knows the heart, he takes motives into consideration. The impersonal element is overridden by the realization that this law-giver never ceases to be present and aware of us; consequently, we can live consciously unto him rather than to an abstract standard of ethics. Peculiar circumstances are avoided by not giving culture-specific legislation or situation-specific laws in close detail.

The legal nature of sin means primarily that it has an objective component. It will not allow executive privilege; no one stands above the will of God (James 4:11b) because God is no respecter of persons. It calls for moral absolutes and sets aside any ethic that is keyed only to circumstance aside from divine purpose.

The concept that sin is relative to an objective standard applies even to (2) *the unevangelized*—those who have never received special revelation of the standard. First, (a) sin is sin irrespective of knowledge. Sin is defined by God's purpose, not by the hearing of that purpose made known by proclamation (Rom. 2:13-15; Lev. 5:17-19). Sin does not go against the record of someone who does not know it (Rom. 5:13), but it is still sin definitionally. Paul implied this fact when he told the Epicurean and Stoic philosophers, "Having therefore overlooked the times of ignorance, God is now commanding men that they should all everywhere repent" (Acts 17:30). There is no repentance for what is in fact not wrong; consequently, the call for repentance in light of judgment to come shows that sin is sin aside from knowledge.

Second, (b) sin is sin on the basis of conscience. Although the content of conscience is itself subjective and did not develop from revelation, the conscience is objective insofar as it corresponds with the actual intents of God. That area wherein conscience has properly led serves as the foundation for defining and imputing sin. The part of the law

law   conscience

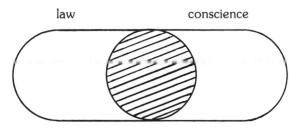

that conscience does not duplicate is disregarded for judgment purposes. This overlap of law and conscience explains why Paul can say on Mars' Hill that God overlooks ignorance (Acts 17:30), while saying in Romans 2:12 that as many as have sinned without the law will perish without the law. The law in these cases reduces to an area congruent with conscience so that the objective principle for evaluation remains decisive.

Right and wrong measured by a standard applies also to (3) *God himself*. Obviously in his case the standard is not beyond him and therefore objective, but he maintains a code of personal behavior. Even his holiness is defined relative to a standard of principles that came from himself without being self-centered. Generally, however, sin is an act measured by an objective standard.

Personal

Sin and consequently its guilt and penalty are not transferable from one person to another. Paul exhorts the Galatians as follows: "Let each person prove his own work and then he will have grounds for boasting for himself alone and not for the other person. For each one will bear his own burden" (6:4-5). From the very beginning of national Israel this principle of jurisprudence obtained: "The fathers shall not be put to death for the children; neither shall the children be put to death for the fathers. Each man shall be put to death for his own sin" (Deut. 24:16; cp. 2 Kg. 14:6; Prov. 9:12; Jer. 31:30; Ezek. 18:4, 19-20; 33:20; see also Ex. 32:30-35; Rom. 9:3). When personal guilt and penalty combine with judgment according to knowledge, then guilt and penalty correspond with the extent of responsibility. Therefore "each person will receive his own reward according to his own labor" (1 Cor. 3:8). Sin is a personal act measured by an objective standard.

Psychological

Human nature includes bodily appetites and abilities not in themselves wrong, but capable of being perverted by abuse. Previous actions establish characteristic ways of doing, thinking, and feeling so that they become habits difficult to break; they may begin to occur unconsciously.

Even without previous misuse the will may not overcome temptation from the outside, as the sin of Adam and Eve illustrates. Beyond the act of sin itself there is psychological weakness that keeps us from coping perfectly with the internal and external challenges raised against our wills.

In light of this psychological weakness, Romans 7:14-25, we believe, gives inspired testimony to the frustration all men feel when they dwell on their failure to do what they know:

> For we know that the law is spiritual, but I am fleshly, sold under sin. For I do not know what I am accomplishing for I do not do what I want but I do what I hate. And if I do what I do not want to do, I consent to the law that it is good. So now *I* am no longer accomplishing it, but sin dwelling in me is doing it. For I know that in me—that is, in my flesh—no good thing resides; for desiring is present with me, but doing good is not. For I do not do good, which I want to do; but I do evil, which I do not want to do. But if I do what I do not want to do, *I* am no longer accomplishing it, but sin residing in me does it. With respect to the law I find then for me who want to do good that evil is present with me. For I delight in the law of God according to the inner man, but I see in my members another law fighting against the law of my mind and making me captive to the sinful law that is in my members. I am a wretched man! Who will deliver me out of the body of this death? But thanks be to God—through Jesus Christ our Lord. So then I myself serve the law of God with my mind, but with my flesh I serve the law of sin.

Paul does not explain how we become the way we are, but in the next chapter he does explain how we overcome in it and that the gospel removes the fear and despair in that struggle (8:15). In Christ we have made commitment to live according to the spirit rather than according to the flesh (8:12). By the power and influence of the Spirit we "put to death the deeds of the flesh" (8:13; cp. Col. 3:5). By the motivational strength his presence supplies (Phil. 2:13), we buffet our bodies daily and bring them into subjection (1 Cor. 9:27).

Our lack of total success in this process (1 Jn. 1:6-10) witnesses to our humanness, and the phenomenon can be called "indwelling sin" (Rom. 7:17, 18, 20, 23). Consequently, there is not only the *state of bondage*, but also a *psychological bondage* akin to the power of habit.

In summary, we venture to define sin as a personal, self-centered act measured by an objective standard and leading to social alienation and psychological conflict.

Other Concepts

Natural

When I John 3:7-8 indicates that righteousness and sinfulness have to do with action, it evidently does so in order to offset the influence of Greek dualism in the Asian churches. An underlying presupposition in much Greek philosophy was the idea that matter is evil and spirit is good. Applied to man, this notion meant that flesh is itself evil and spirit is good. Salvation called for release of the soul from bodily imprisonment, hence the foolishness of resurrection for Greeks (I Cor. 1:23-25; Acts 17:31-32).

Greek dualism tended to undercut the high ethical standards of the Christian faith because "salvation" sought deliverance from the contaminating presence of flesh, not the change from improper ways of acting. Because evil and good were substances, then the problem was the *presence* of flesh, not its *performance*. Therefore, as far as salvation was concerned, it did not matter what a person *did* with his body; it mattered perhaps what he *knew*, such as the secret knowledge needed for one's journey through the successive levels of existence toward the realm of pure spirit. John needed to emphasize that being considered good correlated with behavior, not with being (cp. Rom. 2:25; 3:1; Heb. 4:2).

Paul does say in Romans 8:3, "God, having sent his own Son in the likeness of sinful flesh and concerning sin, condemned sin in the flesh." "Sinful flesh" does not mean naturally sinful as in Greek dualism, but experientially and psychologically sinful. When a person lets his flesh determine his needs, he adopts an ingrown life style because flesh desires for itself. Flesh is not itself sinful, but unless some spiritual value system curbs the fulfillment of its appetites, life in general has a self-centered pattern when lived according to the flesh.

Natural depravity. Under the influence of Greek dualism traditional Christian thought has formulated the concept of natural depravity, which commonly goes under the term "original sin." This view has not considered flesh itself evil, but postulates a correlation between man's

23

being and his behavior. Here evil is not a *substance*, but a deficient *form in the substance*. Sin results from deficiency, or privation, or lack of form in man. Because of Adam's sin human nature has been disordered in comparison with its pristine form so that the human constitution inherited from Adam does not "work right" until the Spirit "fixes" it by regeneration. Not "working right" is called "sin." A person cannot avoid sin because he inherits the depraved nature that produces sin. In this view sin is not just evil *action* and estranged *state*, but fallen *nature* also.

Other observations will be made later when we discuss the impossibility of self-salvation, but we affirm now the lack of support for natural depravity in biblical writings. It is not evident, for example, from Romans 7:14-25 or Galatians 5:17 that Paul believed this idea when he said that the flesh wars against the spirit so that we cannot succeed as we want in holiness. Romans 8 describes the full experience of life in the Spirit so that the interpretative task is to discover what missing element causes the experience presented in the previous chapter.

Romans 7 gives classic expression to the typical human struggle between resolve and accomplishment. Interpreters defending natural depravity typically understand Romans 7 as a statement of Paul's preChristian experience that exemplified the presence of "indwelling sin," "inborn sin," "inbred sin"; Romans 8 presumably describes the postconversion experience. This interpretation of Romans 7, however, does not do justice to the Christian experience as we know it, and it is not a necessary reconstruction of Paul's thought in the two chapters taken conjointly. Romans 7 does not mean pre-Christian experience particularly if pre-Christian exempts the Christian life from this struggle.

Our conviction is that Paul describes his present experience contemplated aside from salvation through Christ. In the following chapter he adds that dimension, but here he views himself under the Mosaic perfection requirement struggling against the weaknesses of the flesh. He looks at the actual Jewish situation from the Christian perspective, and pictures himself under a holy God and bereft of the benefits of grace. The full Christian experience involves a struggle, although it is not a struggle that ends in despair; consequently, Romans 7 does not talk about "unregenerate" vs. "regenerate" even though it does not describe the Christian experience completely.

Everyone agrees that man is depraved, but the reason for this depravity does not necessarily reside in the nature that a person receives by

24

birth. "Depraved" describes the way people act. Why they act this way goes beyond scripture at this point. Rather than speak about natural, or ontic, depravity we prefer to speak of psychological depravity. The powerful pull of sin comes from amoral bodily drives plus previous experience that produces "habitual" ways of behaving; if that pull has resulted from previous action, it may be reversed by personal influence instead of supernatural miracle on the structures of human nature. There is no adequate reason for supposing that the structural givens in Adam before his sin differed after he sinned or differed from those in a Spirit-led Christian. Adam sinned; non-Christians sin; Christians sin: there is no need for natural explanations for any one of these more than for any other. We are satisfied to say that unfallen, fallen, and saved man have the same fundamental nature. Such a view, of course, allows for pull of bodily drives and the drag of previous sin on present resolve, as discussed above in connection with the psychological definition of sin.

Functional depravity. Greek dualism considered matter evil (nature itself); traditional Christian theology has considered evil to be a form in matter (form in nature). A biblical view needs to take one more step away from Greek philosophy and consider evil as function of mind in reciprocation with function of body (act of nature). Fundamental perversion of nature comes from a man's own actions, not from heredity. Should there be hereditary perversion of being, it does not figure into a man's eternal destiny.

Hereditary

When I John 3:8 defines sin as doing, it also sets aside the idea that physical descent contributes to acceptableness with God. Jews in the day of John the Baptist tended to feel—if not to think—that their ancestral connection with the Jewish forefathers also gave them spiritual relationship with the God of their fathers, hence John's warning: "And do not think to say in yourselves, 'We have Abraham as our father'; for I say to you that God is able to raise up children to Abraham from these stones" (Mt. 3:9). Circumcision for identification with Abraham, national Israel, and the law profits nothing unless the person keeps the law, which has not happened (Rom. 2:17-29; 3:1; Gal. 6:13; Heb. 4:2). Since righteousness is the opposite of sinfulness, then race, nationality, birth, or political relationship neither justifies nor condemns any person before God.

Commenting above on the personal character of sin, guilt, and penalty, we cited several Old and New Testament references to the effect that God imputes sinfulness only to the sinner himself: "If you are wise, you are wise for yourself; and if you scoff, you alone shall bear it" (Prov. 9:12). Nevertheless, for hundreds of years many theologians in Christendom have taught that everyone is liable to eternal damnation because of Adam's sin, including newborn infants that know nothing about sin or righteousness. Not only does birth transmit "original sin" by passing on the fallen nature that leads necessarily to sinful action; birth also transmits "original guilt" by putting the newborn person into the human race, which is damned because the original man Adam disobeyed God. By virtue of his temporal priority God figures lostness in relation to him; because of his biological primacy natural depravity is inherited from him.

Psalms 51:5. Psalms 51:5 occupies a prominent place in the foundation for this doctrine: "Behold I was brought forth in iniquity and in sin my mother conceived me." Instead of understanding this statement as a hyperbole to express David's disgust with himself over the Bathsheba incident, defenders of original sin take it as a sober literalism. That it is figurative should be obvious from (a) the contradiction it otherwise implies with several references on the personalness of guilt. To be born in something means simply to be totally characterized by it (Isa. 48:8). In this way evidently the Jewish leaders referred to the man born blind as "altogether born in sin" (Jn. 9:34; cp. 9:2). They subscribed to the notion of poetic justice and the moralizing view of history in which sin causes calamities and righteousness brings blessing. Figurativeness must be the case in (b) the similar statement in Psalms 58:3: "The wicked are alienated right from the womb; they go astray as soon as they are born, speaking lies." Babies are no more sinful by conception and birth than they are liars on the birth stool.

Romans 5:12. Romans 5:12 is probably the cornerstone for the doctrine of original guilt: "Therefore as through one man sin entered into the world and death through sin, so also death passed into all men on account of whom [the one man] all have sinned." One key point comes in the expression "on the basis of whom," which could be translated "on account of whom" or "because of whom." Advocates of original sin understand the phrase in a more restricted sense: "in whom

26

all sinned." The latter concept makes all men federally involved in the single sin of the federal head—Adam. "On account of whom all sinned," however, does not specify the exact manner of connection between his sin and ours. The more restricted notion does not well translate the original Greek here. Another key point is the word "have sinned"; it is the same expression in Romans 3:23, where translators commonly render it "have sinned" so as to refer to the whole process of sinning that has included each man personally. Often that word is translated "sinned" in 5:12 in keeping with a narrowed understanding of "on the basis of whom."

Whatever we decide positively about the teaching in Romans 5:12-21, original guilt is eliminated ahead of time by the fact that (a) other, clear passages teach the personalness of guilt and penalty. Original guilt is also eliminated because (b) universalism would be implied by 5:18: "So then as through one transgression judgment came unto all men unto condemnation, even so through one act of righteousness the free gift came to all men unto justification of life." Many theologians have not kept Christ and Adam sufficiently parallel. Unless potentiality enters the picture on both sides, it becomes most difficult to avoid the inference that all men are in fact as eternally saved in Jesus Christ as they are eternally damned in Adam.

We suggest that the main intent of this text is (a) *destiny by identification*. Romans 5:12-21 as well as I Corinthians 15:22-23, 45-47 contrasts Adam and Christ as representative heads of alternative groups and systems. Point by point Paul distinguishes in broad contours their ideal characteristics and main principles of operation. In Adam everybody dies; in Christ everyone resurrects. In Adam all are unrighteous; in Christ all are righteous. All men have gotten into Adam by sin (12), and all men get into Christ by receiving the abundance of grace; but the manner of those entrances does not receive exact treatment. The "citizens" of the group share the characteristics, states, and destinies of their respective heads. For all practical purposes death is coextensive with sin. Since all would sin, it was appropriate that death be set up to pass on all men; infants and unevangelized elect would form exceptions that Paul does not stop to elaborate.

The passage does not *say* all men get into Adam by birth; we infer that it does not *mean* that, because entrance into the other side is not by birth, but by rebirth. Men do not enter Adam by birth either, as far as anything that Paul means is concerned. "What is born of flesh is flesh; what is born of spirit is spirit" (Jn. 3:6). All men *do* get into Adam and Christ by an act of identification. In the case of Adam it is an act of distrust (sin) while in the case of Christ it is an act of trust (obedience). Consequent to identification with either, the person thus identified receives justly the punishment or blessing of the group he has in effect chosen. We have supplied potentiality on both sides by seeing Adam and Christ entered by disobedience and faith respectively; the entrance is not of necessity on either side. Thus entrance is by identification in either case, by birth in neither case.

We may possibly add another dimension on top of the personal identification already described. (b) *Objective condemnation and justification* could also be in Paul's mind. What all men lost in Adam through no fault of their own they regain in Christ through no virtue of their own. First, physical death came upon all men in Adam, but was replaced by the resurrection of both just and unjust in Christ. Second, corporate, or federal, condemnation came on all men in Adam, but was neutralized by corporate or federal justification in Christ. This second aspect would not mean actual salvation for all any more than it means actual condemnation for all. The idea would only be Paul's way of stating the replacement process in which Christ theoretically (here) as well as actually (above) stands opposite to everything for which Adam stands. The advantage of this conceptualization is that it makes easier the co-extensiveness between sin and death. Under the previous dimension infants and unevangelized elect were accounted for by supposing that Paul used "Adam" and "Christ" only as general representatives of their respective systems without reference to the exceptional aspects of the real situation, which are taken care of by another principle—not imputing personal sins of ignorance. Whether one wants to add this second dimension may be a matter of taste, but under no reconstruction is it acceptable to consider guilty to eternal damnation those who have no active part in their own destiny; the divine principles of justice stated elsewhere prevent such an interpretation of Romans 5.

Our concept of corporate guilt differs from original guilt by the manner of entering the lost group. Under original guilt the person enters the group passively by physical birth, and automatically stands condemned unless infant baptism cleanses him unconsciously from Adam's guilt. Original sin will later make him guilty also of his own sins. Under corporate guilt the person enters the group actively by personal sin at the age of accountability, and thus identifies himself implicitly with Adam and his destiny. God does not impute his sins against him until he becomes responsible for himself (Rom. 7:9 11). Hereditary guilt represents a legal model for an interpersonal reality and thus beclouds the concept of salvation as a whole.

Generally speaking, a person is not responsible for what he cannot help doing or at least he is not held responsible for it in the sense of eternal condemnation. Such a generalization does not intend to omit acts done by those who first got themselves into a condition where they could not then help doing what they did later. They can be responsible for a sin over which they have no direct control because they had indirect control over it by being able not to get drunk or destroy their minds with drugs.

Racial solidarity. The concept of racial solidarity also underlies the argument for racial guilt under Adam. Of the several supposed examples of this concept we look at two. (a) In Hebrews 7:4-8 the writer describes the interaction of *Melchizedek and Abraham* in Genesis 14 and makes some applications to his exegesis of Psalms 110:4. Abraham tithed the spoils of war to Melchizedek and so the Hebrew writer comments that, so to speak, Levi paid tithes to Melchizedek because he was in the loins of Abraham when the two met.

Nothing about this exchange implies that racial solidarity supports racial guilt. The goal of Hebrews is to elucidate the statement of Psalms 110:4 that the one appointed to priesthood in that Psalm was after the order of Melchizedek. Aaronic priesthood in Israel descended from Levi and so from Abraham. Inasmuch as the Aaronic priesthood operated on heredity principles, it is not surprising that the Hebrew writer's comments take the form they do. He only points out that the priesthood of Psalms 110:4 falls, not within the Levitical priesthood, but parallel to it. That parallel position is seen clearly in the occasion when the ancestor of Aaron met Melchizedek at ancient Salem. Admittedly the Levitical priesthood operated by racial and familial connections; the point to be proved is that righteousness and sinfulness function that way.

Shortly after entering upon the conquest of Canaan (b) *Achan* disobeyed (Josh. 7) the injunction to destroy "devoted things" and to bring all precious metals into the treasury of the Lord (Josh. 6:17-19). Achan took a "mantle of Shinar" together with some gold and silver and hid it in the floor of his tent. When Joshua discovered the deed, he had Achan, his whole family, and his cattle stoned and burned. Supposedly Joshua legitimately punished the whole family for the father's guilt.

Such a reconstruction evidently does not represent what transpired. Since the spoil was buried in the family tent, the rest of Achan's family probably did not escape involvement in the incident. Sins by other family heads did not involve execution for the whole family. The clear passages in the law of Moses would have forbidden what in fact occurred here according to the solidarity concept (Deut. 24:16). Precedent shows Yahweh not destroying the righteous with the wicked (Gen. 18: 22-23). In the Achan case the stolen object involved the worship of pagan deities, which made it all the more important not to allow that influence to spread in Israel. Achan may have had more interest in this devoted thing than just as a treasure of art or as a momento of the war; favorable attitudes toward the gods of the Canaanites could—and would—undercut everything Yahweh intended to do in Palestine through Israel. At any rate the clear must interpret the unclear and enough unknowns exist in the Achan episode to remove it from supporting a concept at direct odds with the clearer statements of the law of Israel.

Conceiving of the human race as an organism has served as a model for solidarity. The act of one member like the hand is blamed on the whole person; the act of one member of humanity makes the whole guilty. Such analogy is pointless, however, because it remains to be shown that humanity compares with an organism in this respect. That it does not should be evident from the fact that a hand or ear does not operate out of its own will, but out of the same brain that controls all the rest of the body. Furthermore, the illustration would prove too much because it would make all men guilty of the sins of every man in society, a notion obviously false from scriptures that eliminate the transfer of guilt and penalty. The illustration does not fit the referent.

30

Chapter Four

THE SINFULNESS OF MAN

Need for Man's Holiness

The holiness of God

Ultimately the need for the holiness of man comes from the holiness of God; his nature and character set the standard for human conduct. God makes himself holy by setting himself apart *from* acting in just any fashion; he sets himself apart *to* acting consistently; with propriety he calls upon his rational and moral creations to the same. They need to set themselves apart to his standards and thereby sanctify themselves to their sanctified God.

Therefore, in the origination of the chosen nation God set forth in the constitution itself that the citizens of national Israel were to "be holy *for* I am holy" (Lev. 19:2; cp. 11:44-45; 20:7, 26; 21:8; cp. Deut. 18:13). The theme in Leviticus establishes the rationale for holy living also in the holy nation of Christians: "But even as the one that called you is holy, you yourselves also be holy in all manner of life style, because it is written, 'Be holy because *I* am holy'" (I Pet. 1:15-16; cp. Mt. 5:48).

The purpose of man

Fellowship with God. Man's need for holiness comes secondly from being created for fellowship with God: ". . . even as he chose us in him [Christ] before the foundation of the world that we might be holy and blameless before him in love" (Eph. 1:4). Scripture uses a number of pictures to get at the personal association between creature and Creator: "walking with God" (Gen. 5:24; 6:9; 17:1), being a friend of God (Isa. 41:8; II Ch. 20:7; James 2:23; Jn. 15:13-15; Lk. 11:5-13), collectively being a bride for Christ (Eph. 5:21-32; II Cor. 11:1-2; Rev. 19:6-9; Jer. 3:14). The same idea appears in brotherhood with the Son (Heb. 2:10-13) and sonship with the Father (Mt. 6:9; Jn. 14:2, etc.).

Glorification of God. Being created for fellowship leads to glorification of God, for Paul proceeds from Ephesians 1:4 to say in 1:6, 12, 14 that we are for "the praise of the glory of his grace." Jesus combines fellowship with glory when he says, "The one who sent me is with me and has not left me alone because I always do the things pleasing to him" (Jn. 8:29; cp. Gen. 6:9; 17:1). We cannot be characterized by

31

what God dislikes and fulfill this natural reason for our existence. God is holy so that man needs to be holy in order to relate to him and glorify him forever.

The Fact of Man's Sinfulness

History

A familiar summary of man's condition before God appears in Romans 3:23: "All have sinned and fall short of the glory of God." This statement climaxes everything Paul has said so far in the letter. The overview of history in Romans 1 traces the recurring pattern of apostasy in the human race. In general, divine-human estrangement results from abandoning previous knowledge of the Creator (1:19, 21, 28) in order to worship the creation instead (1:23, 25). Man's folly consists in leaving an adequate explanation of the world in order to espouse an inadequate one. The consequences are dishonor (1:24), disfellowship (1:24a, 26a, 28a), and disillusionment (1:27).

Experience

The apostle also notes in Romans 2 the specific experience of each man and its indictment that he is sinful. Whereas the historical verdict centered on special and general revelation, the experiential indictment centers on conscience. Even where conscience has not been informed by knowledge of God revealed from the outside, it testifies to each person from the inside that, regardless of his ideals or their source, he never lives up to them.

Scripture

Finally, in Romans 3 Paul highlights the uniform witness of scripture by a series of citations from Psalms and Isaiah; their joint verdict on man is that "There is none righteous, no, not one" (Ps. 14:1-3 = 53:1-3; cp. 5:9; 10:7; 36:1; 140:3; Isa. 59:7-8; cp. also I Kg. 8:46; II Ch. 6:36; Job 14:4; 15:14; 25:4; Ps. 130:3-4; 143:2; 20:9; Eccl. 7:20; Mt. 19:17; Mk. 10:18; Lk. 18:19; Jn. 7:19; I Jn. 1:8).

Criteria for Man's Sinfulness

Biblical criteria

Nature, purpose, commandments of God. In other connections we have already observed that (1) *the nature of God* establishes the final measure of human behavior. Jesus restated the Levitical concept by saying, "You shall be perfect as your heavenly Father is perfect" (Mt. 5:48). Similarly, (2) *the purposes of God* become guidelines for man. Collectively we are not to have "spot or wrinkle or any such thing" (Eph. 5:25b-28), and individually we are to "glorify God in our bodies" (I Cor. 6:13-20). Divine purpose leads to (3) *the commandments of God*, including the several commissions given to men in the Bible (Gen. 1:26-31; 3:23; 9:1-7; Mt. 28:18-20). The whole of man is to "revere God and keep his commandments" (Eccl. 12:13; cp. I Jn. 3:4; 5:17).

Nature of man. Beyond previously noted matters we may say that (4) *the nature of man* determines his actions. With profound insight Paul tells the Corinthians that fornication is unique; it sins against the person's own body in contrast to other sins that are "outside the body." We take him to mean that fornication disrupts one's very sense of identity, an internal conflict made possible by our psychological constitution. In a different way doing drugs is sin because among other things drugs destroy our bodies and therefore interfere with our potential for happiness, fellowship, and responsibility.

(5) *The conscience of man* supplies another guide for human action. In Romans 2:12-15 the apostle to the Gentiles explains briefly how God deals with people outside the scope of previous special revelation:

> For as many as have sinned without law shall also perish without law, and as many as sinned inside law will be judged by law. For not the hearers of law are just with God, but the doers of law will be justified. For when Gentiles, who do not have law, do naturally the things of the law—they, because they do not have law, are a law for themselves, who show the work of the law written in their hearts, their conscience bearing witness with them and their thoughts accusing or else excusing one another.

Men living beyond the witness of God's special revelation have at least a built-in factor that assists them in maintaining principled living.

Conscience of fellowmen. Social relationships require the intermingling of consciences so that right action depends also on (6) *the conscience of fellowmen.* In Romans 14 and I Corinthians 8 Paul furnishes guidelines for interaction between Christians whose moral sensitivities do not always vibrate at the same frequency. Preferences on diet and high days, for example, may be tolerated in Christian brotherhood because they do not necessarily involve matters germane to Christian faith. Particularly with believers susceptible to being misled, Paul stresses the principle that one person's actions are not determined by his own feelings and beliefs alone even if Christian teaching is not at stake. Love and expediency must prevail lest misunderstanding lead to misbehavior in the weaker brother.

Of course, limits need to be placed on the extent to which the conscience of others restricts personal choices. The apostle limits concession to considerations short of doubtful distinctions; legalistic mentalities could virtually immobilize the Christian community if the brethren conceded everything they called for (Rom. 14:1; cp. Tit. 3:9). Primarily the concession principle applies to cases where a brother could be disillusioned, confused, or led into "mis-belief" and misbehavior because he misunderstands the intents behind a stronger brother's deeds. In such cases, "None of us lives to himself and none dies to himself" (Rom. 14:7); moral choices include more than individual preferences.

Insufficient criteria

Human nature. Although human nature goes a long way in providing guidelines for human behavior, human nature stands among the insufficient measures for right action. Scientific research is an important but insufficient basis for ethics. From personal and race experience, we can see that in most cases there are physical and psychological reasons for what God commands. Many practices are wrong, not only because God forbids them, but because we are not happy—at least on the long haul—when we do them. Careful investigation can usually discover adverse effects from disobedience.

Nevertheless we do not necessarily assume one-to-one correlations between divine purpose in creation and the human nature created. We would then be locked into determinism, where all right action would be genetically encoded into our being. To a great extent in place of animal instinct man has reason and learning so that what is instinctive in animals is learned in man. This fact sets up (a) *a broad variability potential in man,* which is often wider than the will of God for him. The human race could continue in polygamous form even if polygamy does not provide the most abundant form of life and does not reflect in man the image of God he intended in the husband-wife relationship. Over time society might discover that aberrant family structures do not

34

provide the best arrangement, but by that time the situation may be irreversible. The trouble with the scientific basis for morality is that society will settle for less than the ideal because man can exist under less than ideal conditions.

Beyond the broad variability in human nature there is such a thing as (b) *positive commandment in God's will.* "Positive commandment" means that the required action does not come from the necessities of the purpose in view, but from the will of God directly. There are several ways by which a person could be initiated into Christ, for example, but baptism in water has been the one specified. Any specification more particular than purpose dictates is a positive commandment and cannot be experimentally discovered since nothing in human nature necessitates it.

Conscience. A second insufficient measure for right action is conscience. Since it is an educated thing (a) *it is subject to original errors.* By birth men have the capacity of conscience (nature), but by experience they put content into it (nurture). The values in terms of which conscience operates come through learning and personal reflection; social mores and theological education establish the norms conscience uses. Heredity combines with environment to produce the conscience. As a result Paul cautioned his readers to consider the feelings of others; their conscience may bother them on matters that do not bother everyone. "Let your conscience be your guide" is better than nothing, but it is not an adequate guide for the whole will of God.

Conscience is also insufficient because (b) *it is subject to defilement* (Acts 10:9-16; I Cor. 8:7, 10, 12; I Tim. 4:2; Tit. 1:15). Conscience can be influenced in the wrong direction by a change of beliefs or hardened from continued disregard. People reared in godly homes may grow up later to practice habits that would have pricked their moral sensitivities before; but because they kept grating against them, the conscience became callous enough to stop sending its guilt signals. A well-trained conscience enhances the power of Christian morality, but its formation and continuation is often subject to environmental influences opposed to God's will for human existence.

Harmlessness for others. Right action cannot be determined by what does not hurt other people. (a) *It is doubtful whether there are in fact "victimless crimes."* Some sins may not physically hurt anyone else, but they may do psychological damage by creating a sense of disillusionment

35

and betrayal. In secular law enforcement it is understandably difficult to administer laws dealing with factors not easily quantifiable. Much of God's law, however, addresses "spiritual" concerns that play such an important role in the sense of self-image, self-worth, identity, and abundant living. "No one lives to himself or dies to himself" (Rom. 14:7).

(b) *The Christian ethic stresses positive action* as shown by the New Testament form of the Golden Rule: "Do to others as you would have them do to you" (Mt. 7:12). Galatians 6:2 reiterates the positive stance: "Bear one another's burdens and so fulfill the law of Christ." Likewise the apostle says in I Corinthians 10:24, "Let no one seek his own good, but the welfare of the other person" (cp. Rom. 15:1-2; I Cor. 10:33; Phil. 2:4). Society needs more than restraint from hurting other people; God therefore wills for men to hold each other up so that their enmeshed lives will have greater strength for coping with problems bigger than any one person can handle. What does not hurt others does not provide for the social dimension.

Since we have been created by God and redeemed by his Son (I Cor. 6:20), (c) *even damaging or destroying ourselves is not our prerogative.* We are not finally a law unto ourselves because we belong to God by creation and redemption. What does not hurt other people heads in the right direction, but it does not take a person to the destination.

Majority opinion. In keeping with the remnant doctrine majority vote gives no satisfactory basis for ethics. "Strait is the gate and narrow is the way that leads to life and there are few that find it" (Mt. 7:14; cp. Lk. 13:23-30). Much of what society approves does fall within the horizons of divine guidance, but Christians cannot expect culture to reinforce their ideals if as a matter of fact most people travel the broad road to destruction. The narrow way represents exception to majority vote.

Erroneous criteria

Might makes right. The idea that might makes right is obviously no ethic for men created in the image of God, because Almighty God himself refuses to stoop to the self-centeredness implicit in that principle. Man's orientation is from above, not only in his destiny (Phil. 3:20; Col. 3:1-4), but in his origin (Eccl. 12:7). He does not espouse the behavior of animals from whom God dissociates him (Gen. 2:18-25; Ex. 22:19; Lev. 18:23; 20:15), but adopts the ethics of him whose image and likeness he bears (Gen. 1:26-27; 5:1; 9:6). Therefore he conducts himself according to love, not competition. Paul applied this principle even to apostolic rights lest he would be counterproductive in the work of reconciliation and edification (II Cor. 12:9-10, 14-21; 10:8; 13:10, etc.). Being able to do something does not justify doing it.

Machiavellianism. Christianity also rejects the notion that the end justifies the means. Paul opposes it when he says in Romans 3:7-8:

> But if God's truth abounds in my life unto his glory, why am I still condemned as a sinner? And why not say—as we are slandered and as some affirm that we do say, "Let's do evil in order that good may come"? whose condemnation is just.

There are wrong ways to do right things; therefore, the sons of a holy God cannot subscribe to this criterion for behavior.

Origin of Man's Sinfulness

Fall of Satan

In John 8:44 Jesus calls Satan a liar and the father of lying (cp. I Jn. 3:8; Gen. 3:4, 13; II Cor. 11:3; Rev. 12:9; 20:2-3). Sin had its absolute origin outside humanity. It did not, however, originate in God, but in the free will of God's creatures; evil in a holy God's universe is due to the choice of secondary agencies. God himself never *did* a sin, and he could not have *created* it because it is not something. He originally *defined* it, but that does not make him guilty of it because sin becomes real, not at the point of definition, but at the point of choice to do it.

God could perhaps be counted guilty for allowing sin to continue in his universe if he never met his responsibility for dealing with it. But he has done many things in preparation for the destruction of sin, such as putting a boundary on how much and how long evil can oppose him. Additionally, he provided opportunity for retrieving sinful men from sin and its effects. Though perhaps by origin a "son of God" (Job 1:6), Satan along with his followers has been dismissed from the presence of the Almighty and in due time their opposition to him and his people will fully end (II Pet. 2:4; Jude 6: Rev. 20:10). Yahweh therefore maintains his holiness by curbing and then defeating sin; he expresses his love by providing opportunity and allowing time for reconciliation,

Fall of man

Sin entered the human race through temptation by the Father of Lies. When Adam sinned in the beginning he set an example that has been

37

individually followed in varying degrees by everyone since then. Moreover, mankind *corporately* became alienated from full fellowship with God because Adam and Eve at the time of their disobedience were the human race. By his own disobedience each person in effect identifies himself with Adam and consequently shares his fate (Gen. 3; Rom. 5:12-21; I Cor. 15:20-22). Those other consequences that came down to all men through no act of their own may be thought of as removed by Second Adam through no act of their own. In these matters what men lost in Adam they will regain in Christ.

Consequences of Sinfulness

Genesis mentions several consequences of Adam's sin that applied to *Adam himself:* a sense of nakedness (3:7), fear of God and separation from him (3:8), labor for food from the ground and thorns to encumber his labor (3:17-18), knowledge of good and evil (3:22), and removal from Eden and the tree of life (3:22-24). *Eve* would have pain in childbirth (3:16). The *serpent* was to go on his belly (3:14) and enmity would exist between his seed and the woman's seed (3:15). All *men* would experience physical death (3:19; Rom. 5:12, 14; I Cor. 15:21-22) and perhaps "representative guilt" (Rom. 5:12). Some of these effects recur in each person's experience while others not clearly involved here need to be added from elsewhere in scripture.

Personal perversion

Romans 1:18-32 comments on departures from knowing God and indicates several inherent consequences visited on men. Instead of forcing obedience, God "gives them up" to the consequences of disobedience (1:24, 26, 28). Even in their bodies they receive recompense for transgression so that personal experience confirms the sinfulness of sin revealed in scripture. The integration of the human person means that deeds done in the body variously affect all aspects of the self. Therefore, sin pervades the whole person and his relations.

Affective disorientation. (a) Affective disorientation exemplifies personal perversion because of sin. The apostle mentions particularly the *sexual disorientation* so prevalent in his own day (1:24-27); homosexuality epitomizes human degradation in the Bible and led to the destruction of Sodom and Gomorrah among the Canaanites. Paul

38

speaks of *inordinate affections* (Col. 3:5) and of people *bereft of natural affection* (Rom. 1:31; Eph. 4:17-19; II Tim. 3:3; II Pet. 2:14). Since sin reinforces the tendency to turn in on one's self (II Tim. 3:2), accumulating things for self perverts affections from loving people to loving things (I Tim. 6:10), which do not satisfy (Eccl. 5:10 12; Gal. 6:8). Likes, dislikes, and interests affect actions and are in turn affected by them (Mt. 6:21) so that the end result is a downward spiral of deterioration.

Perverted drives. Closely akin to the above are (b) perverted drives, corrupt not only as to their *object*, but in their *degree*. Sin is self-centered so that "flesh," especially in Paul's usage of the term (cp. Rom. 7:14— 8:17), stands for a pattern of living that takes outside things toward the self to satisfy it; fleshly drives receive satisfaction by taking something to themselves instead of giving of themselves for the needs of others. When the whole thrust of life takes this format, the dulling of the senses results from overuse; consequently, it takes increasingly bigger "doses" of pleasure to achieve the same effect. The stronger the drive for fulfillment, the lower the fulfillment by a given degree of stimulus. The law of diminishing returns leads to more extreme measures for self-satisfaction and the process eventually ends in self-destruction. Rangling, clamor, aggressive and violent behavior appear in Paul's vice lists (Gal. 5:19-21; II Tim. 3:2ff.) in testimony to the total chaos brought about by perverted appetites.

Weakened will power. Yielding to the pull of unwholesome activities creates (c) weakened will power. Some sins create psychological as well as physical dependence on the continued practice. Drunkenness, overeating, and drugs work to engulf the participant till he finds himself under bondage. Giving in to anger and greed makes it harder to handle those temptations the next time. The power of habit increases with the length and depth of previous involvement. One virtue of fasting is that it exercises the will in a tangible way, and success with controlling food intake empowers self-control in other areas.

Intellectual confusion. God also abandons men to (d) intellectual confusion when they refuse to have him in their thinking. If the ultimate frame of reference is missing, secondary realities move into the primary slot called "God." But the pieces do not go together right when the biggest one is thrown away and replaced by another one:

> . . . knowing God, they did not honor him as God nor were thankful, but became vain in their reasonings and their foolish heart was darkened.

Claiming to be wise they became fools and changed the glory of the incorruptible God into the likeness of corruptible man and birds and fourfooted animals and creeping things. Wherefore God gave them up . . . to a reprobate mind (Rom. 1:21-24a, 28).

Nothing observed in this universe requires any different explanation than revelation has previously given about its origin, nature, and destiny. Forsaking the revealed explanation in order to adopt a lesser view raises a question about the motives for choosing a view that has no God like Yahweh the Father of Jesus Christ. Men evidently turn away in order to remove God from their thinking because that truth lays primary claim on their lives and actions. This reconceptualization of reality necessarily misunderstands the place of everything else, particularly man, who fancies himself either the apex of cosmic processes or a thing like everything else; neither view properly assesses him. When a man is confused about ultimate reality and when the knower is confused about himself, intellectual confusion reigns all the way down the line in his self and his associations.

Insensitive conscience. The practice of sin grates against the conscience and dulls it so that a man ends up with an (e) insensitive conscience on matters that should cause discomfort. People who know "the ordinance of God that they who practice such things are worthy of death, not only do them, but also approve of those who practice them" (1:32). Paul predicted that in the last times some would fall away from the faith ". . . through the hypocrisy of liars seared in their own conscience with a hot iron" (I Tim. 4:2). There comes a time when a person *knows* his acts are sinful and knows the consequences of them and yet does not *feel* conscience stricken; he can get to a point where he cannot repent (Heb. 6:4-6).

God's purposes set the standard for human action. The very nature of nature including human nature may be regarded as an approximate expression of God's will. Living against nature constitutes sin against the will of God expressed in nature, for the creation arose from his purposes and will.

Personal guilt

God's will expressed in nature is also expressed in special revelation. Therefore sin against nature is also sin against the will of the Creator. Viewed in this respect personal perversion becomes (f) personal guilt, a sixth consequence of sin. Beyond nature itself special revelation alone calls men to acts and attitudes more explicit than nature is designed to show them clearly. Disobedience in matters peculiar to special revelation is measured by the word revelation of God's prophets.

Social alienation

The personal perversion that equals personal guilt also becomes personal affront against the Creator himself. (g) Social alienation results in the vertical when sin as disobedience occurs; alienation on the horizontal results when sin as selfishness takes place. "Your sins have separated me and you" (Isa. 59:2; cp. Amos 3:3). In elaborating the effects of being given up to a reprobate mind, Paul presents a vice list in Romans 1:29-31 that includes a number of items related to social alienation: maliciousness, envy, murder, deception, whisperings, backbiting, hatred toward God, disobedience to parents and other authority figures (cp. II Pet. 2:10), covenant breaking, unmercifulness, and argumentativeness (II Pet. 2:12; Tit. 3:9-11). Society cannot exist when each person tries to manipulate everyone else to his own ends. The home disintegrates and with it social relationship; all that remains is a series of individuals wanting what they cannot have and what does not satisfy.

Cosmic dysfunction

Psalms 8:3-8 asks why God is mindful of man and then answers that it is because he received dignity and honor by being made caretaker of creation. The Hebrew writer acknowledges in 2:8-9 that man does not satisfactorily have everything under control and so Messiah became a man to qualify for taking over this work. Because of sin and selfishness men cannot even take care of the ground much less the earth or the universe; hence, sin has brought about (h) cosmic dysfunction and chaos. He must wait now for the time of the restoration of all things (Acts 3:21). Modern concern about ecology belongs under this item in the list of effects of sin. Erosion, extinction, pollution and the like normally result from selfishly and thoughtlessly exploiting the earth for personal profit without regard for future generations. Adam's labor for food from ground that has thistles and does not yield its strength represents nature's control over *man* in place of man's responsibility for *it*.

41

Perpetuation of Man's Sinfulness

Sin originated ultimately in the free choice of God's creatures and entered the human race when our first parents yielded to the influence of Satan. The subsequent question deals with the origin of sin in each individual's life as history proceeds. The New Testament guideline is that the mechanisms proposed for the perpetuation of sin must yield the conclusion in Romans 3:23: "All have sinned and fall short of the glory of God."

Ignorance

What we do not know will hurt us if it lets us wander into sinful behavior from which we find it difficult to escape later. Whether we are children too young to understand readily or heathen people that have not received special revelation, ignorance brings men into ways of living that do not give lasting abundance and whose consequences may not be reversible.

Subjective viewpoint

The subjective viewpoint is another form of ignorance, because each person sees the world from his own position and perspective. As a result he does not automatically see it the way it really is, and his actions may not then be proper. Although there is no sin in seeing the world from some point, self-consciousness is potential for self-centeredness. When that slip occurs, a person has adopted the fundamental posture of sin. There is not a big difference between seeing from somewhere and acting from there. Seeing and wanting naturally happen from the viewpoint of consciousness so that a correction factor must be found for this ignorance because of viewpoint.

Correction is by way of love. Men are not born with an instinct that compels right behavior; they are born with a capacity to learn right behavior. This learning comes, of course, through teaching and modeling the values of the faith; but more importantly for our purposes here, the learning process builds on the innate ability to project consciousness over behind the eyes of other people and thereby to discover how to relate to them in their situation (Mt. 7:12). Transferring viewpoint enables the socialization process to take place so that the individual person becomes the relational person. In this sense perhaps there is

42

a modicum of truth in the idea that a person does not have to learn to sin, but he has to learn to do good.

It is natural to assume that the time when a person developmentally passes into the period of socialization is approximately the time when he reaches the age of accountability, reason, puberty, and the like; it is likewise the appropriate time for formal identification with Christ unto forgiveness of sins because this is the time when the commandment can come alive for him (Rom. 7:9-11). Christianity teaches that the commandment is love, that salvation is restoring loving relationship, and that the gospel is the news that it is possible. The subjective viewpoint is a structural given that contributes significantly to the need for this salvation for everyone.

God's absence

Although God sees us, we do not see or sense him. "Out of sight, out of mind" applies to invisible things and therefore to God. Kids will not misbehave nearly so much when parents are around. Students behave better when the teacher is in the room. Men drive more circumspectly when a patrolman is in sight. Similarly God's open presence among men could have significant effect on the conduct of life by putting restraint on sin. Nevertheless, God's withdrawn presence is an act of grace. By withdrawing, (a) he treats us responsibly, respectfully, and maturely; he does not continually police us, but trusts us to do his will when we "feel" he is absent. In this way (b) he also develops a greater potential for free obedience; the less the compulsion the greater the *self-control*. By invisibility (c) he protects us from psychological destruction —if Isaiah's self-conscious reaction in the temple is any indication of how a sinner normally feels in the presence of a holy omnipotent God (Isa. 6); it is harder to love someone we inordinately fear. Finally, (d) God's visible absence enhances his glory potential. As parents, teachers, and patrolmen are more pleased with the people they are responsible for when they voluntarily do what is right, so God is more greatly glorified the less restraint he exercises on us. But in the meantime being out of sight removes a certain deterrent from sin and incentive to righteousness, even though it is done, we suppose, in order to establish a higher kind of righteousness in the end.

43

Sinful example

Our first three items for perpetuating sin could be grouped together as various forms of *ignorance*. The next four items can be classified as *social sources* of sin. Society, not biology, is the main mechanism for transferring sin from one generation to the next. Modeling plus mimicking is the basic educational process in any society. The values for living are caught, if not taught, from the actions of others. Human behavior is largely learned rather than instinctive, social rather than innate.

Social pressure

Peer pressure is sinful example consciously aimed at us; the model is not simply out there to follow or set aside. Social pressure implies threat of ostracism and lack of acceptance by the group. Our social nature tends to make us recoil from doing anything not acceptable to those we love and respect; that is the reason "evil companions corrupt good morals" (I Cor. 15:33). Once we break the barrier into a new way of living, we become increasingly accustomed to it, and sin has had its way with us because the influence of others has pressured us to conform.

Misunderstood example

When Paul advised the Corinthians about meat offered to idols, he cautioned them not to mislead weaker brothers who might misread their actions. Their example might be all right, but other people who did not know their motives might eat the meat with religious associations in mind. The very fact that love and expediency are commended in matters of opinion shows that some acts are not right or wrong in themselves but according to what is meant and understood in them, hence, the possibility of misunderstanding them and bringing sin into one's life in consequence.

Social reinforcement

Praise and acceptance reinforce behavior so that it tends to recur. In raising children, parents soon learn that directing the way they act is usually accomplished by stroking what is acceptable and not rewarding the other. Positive rejection like withdrawing privilege is often not necessary; the sheer absence of recognition often curtails misconduct. The same principles operate for reinforcing sin; they become powerful mechanisms used to induce and perpetuate sins in the oncoming generation.

Physical constitution

People have bodily drives that are neither good nor bad in themselves, but they become the occasion for sin. Although there are acceptable ways of fulfilling all these needs, there are also irresponsible and selfish ways of fulfilling them. Satan made his approach to our first parents by tempting them with food; he tempted Jesus by urging him to use his miraculous powers to turn the stones into bread and satisfy his hunger. Temptation traces a familiar route when it lures the flesh to sin and cultivates that sin to extremes that ultimately lead to self-destruction (James 1:14-15).

The combined interaction of these eight contributors to sin leads to the practical conclusion that no one has or will pass through the human experience untouched by personal sin. We consider it unnecessary to add natural depravity to this list of perpetuating *causes* for sin in order to guarantee the criterion established in Romans 3:23. In previous topics we have also not included it among defining *characteristics* of sin, nor among the *consequences* of Adamic sin. We would distinguish natural depravity from bodily drives and viewpoint of consciousness because they are not bad in themselves. Likewise among the reasons against self-salvation we regard the notion of natural depravity an example of "overkill." The hopelessness of "man on his own" and "man come of age" is tragically obvious from the factors already enumerated.

Chapter Five

THE IMPOSSIBILITY OF SELF-SALVATION

Whatever we understand about the processes at work in salvation, we must conclude that a person cannot save himself. If he could do so, there would really be no reason for Messiah (Gal. 2:21). At least a fourfold reason exists for deciding that no one can deliver himself from condemnation.

Interpersonal Reason

The first reason we cannot save ourselves is that forgiveness is always done by the other person and forgiveness cannot be forced. If a person never sinned against another, the second party could not withdraw fellowship without becoming unholy himself; he "owes it" to a good man to treat him like a friend. But if sin occurs, then the offender has no recourse. No moral compulsion requires positive relationship to a sinner. A change of the sinner's views or feelings does not effect a change of his state. On the basis of love the offended may forgive if the offender repents, but legally he could "hold it against" him indefinitely.

Legal Reason

Relative to the law

Secondly, we cannot save ourselves because imperfection cannot be overcome by the nature of the case. Perfect righteousness is God's requirement. That he requires perfection is evident from (1) Galatians 3:10, where Paul quotes Deuteronomy 27:26 as saying, "Accursed is everyone who does not continue to do all the things written in the book of the law." An alternate translation is "abide by all things." Either way *continuing* to do *all* states the perfection concept. If he breaks perfection, he creates a situation that cannot be remedied; he is under a curse. (2) "And I testify again to every circumcised man that he is debtor to do the whole law" (Gal. 5:3). (3) One sin dismissed the first pair from the Garden (Gen. 3; see also Num. 15:22; Jn. 8:7, etc.).

(4) James 2:10 says it clearly as well: "Whoever keeps the whole law, but offends in one point, has become guilty of all." Not only is it true that if a person can do one he probably can do them all; but if he is guilty of one he is as good as guilty of them all inasmuch as perfection is broken by one or one hundred. The sinner has broken the commandment to keep them all. One sin is as bad as another for becoming

unrighteous even though James agrees that there are degrees of sin, degrees of sinfulness, and degrees of punishment: "Do not many of you be teachers, my brothers, knowing that we will receive greater condemnation" (3:1). Jesus told Pilate, "On account of this the one who delivered me to you has greater sin" (Jn. 19:11). At the mission of the twelve Jesus told his disciples regarding a city that rejected them, "It will be more tolerable for the land of Sodom and Gomorrah in the day of judgment than for that city" (Mt. 10:15; cp. Mk. 6:11; Mt. 11: 22-24; Lk. 10:12-14). Some sinners are beaten with many and some with few stripes (Lk. 12:47-48; cp. Mt. 12:45; Lk. 11:24-26; Heb. 10:28-29; 12:25; II Pet. 2:20-21). There is sin unto death and sin not unto death (I Jn. 5:16-17). Degrees of sinfulness can exist relative to results and amount of disobedience, but as to perfection there is only one "degree."

Relative to the lawgiver

The perfection requirement is also evident from Romans 3:21-22, where Paul describes two sources of righteousness—law and faith. "The righteousness of God" could mean the righteousness he has or the righteousness he gives, but either way it yields the inference that God commands perfection. Therefore, when scripture talks about righteousness, holiness, and justice, it speaks of perfection.

A legitimate standard

It is not surprising that perfection should be the standard. A person's own conscience requires him to follow it perfectly; it does not prick him just most of the time. Furthermore, in principle if not in practice we hold up the ideal for both ourselves and our fellowmen, and plan on making up the difference by repentance and forgiveness; the degree of failure correlates with the lowered degree of self-worth or the weakness of relationship. Neither God nor man removes the ideal as the goal of life; the ideal persists and certain procedures are used to bridge the gap between performance and perfection; in the case of positive penalty pronounced on sin, "taking care of" the penalty must happen as well.

Corporate Reason

The third reason a person cannot save himself is that, as part of a lost group, he cannot rise above the status of the group. He becomes part

47

of the Adam group by sinning as Adam sinned, and consequently participates in Adam's state and destiny. There is no way to avoid the destiny of one's own group. Students from unaccredited colleges, for example, cannot get credits transferred to accredited universities if the latter institutions by policy do not accept credits from such schools. Since the policy is directed against the classification of schools, it does not even matter that the student has demonstrated good scholarship; his credits will not transfer. So to speak, "You can't beat the system."

Functional Reason

The fourth reason against self-salvation is that a person needs the influence of others to conquer the practice of sin. Here we speak of the functional or behavioral conquest of sin rather than its forgiveness or acquittal; functional inability deals with breaking the power of sin as habit more than overcoming sin as penalty. Actions leave behind the tendency to repeat themselves. In the legal, personal, and corporate reasons a person *cannot* save himself because they are logical and natural impossibilities; in the functional reason he *will not* save himself because it is a behavioral impossibility.

A common delusion is that knowing the truth about God, Christ, the universe, and what the Bible says is tantamount to salvation instead of preliminary to it. To believe there is one personal God is not to be a Christian: "The demons believe and shudder" (James 2:19). "Not the hearers of the law are justified before God, but the doers of the law will be justified" (Rom. 2:13; cp. James 1:22-25; 2:14-26; Mt. 7:24-27; 23:3; Lk. 6:47-49; Jn. 5:45). As in the definition of sin so also in the definition of salvation, the issue is what must we *do* (Acts 2:37; 16:30) more than what must we *know*.

Education, therefore, does not solve the world's internal problems, nor does Christian education solve its problems in relationship to God. Technology levels have continued to escalate, but man's relationship with fellowmen has not comparably improved. Greater know-how only increases the capacity for greater evil if man's sensitivities to God and other men do not keep pace. Impersonal information does not confront men and call them into question sufficiently; so refining information does not necessarily change behavior. Men are surrounded by increasingly complex machinery, but their lives deteriorate from within

48

because they have not learned first the spiritual values by which they themselves should operate for maximum efficiency in experiencing joy and abundance. Sin is not just because of ignorance, which can be corrected by education; it is also due to egotism, which must be overcome by conversion, that is, by projection of consciousness, by love, by a change to God-centered and "other-centered" living. Motivation to do what they know, righteousness to annul their alienation, and resurrection to replace the grave still need to have their ultimate source from outside the human circumstance.

Natural Reason

In addition to the four reasons given above, traditional Christian orthodoxy has formulated the doctrine of natural depravity. According to this view man cannot save himself because he cannot respond to God; his lack of ability eliminates the possibility of self-salvation. He has biologically inherited from Adam a fallen nature needing supernatural regeneration by the Holy Spirit prior to any possibility of response to salvation. We do not present this concept sympathetically for the reasons given below.

Systematically unnecessary

Natural depravity is not necessary for explaining the universal and pervasive effects of sin. (a) The reasons already given for the origin and perpetuation of sin sufficiently undergird the verdict of history, experience, and scripture that all men fall short (Rom. 3:23). (b) The reasons previously listed against self-salvation adequately show that Christ did not die for nothing (Gal. 2:21). (c) Conditionality satisfactorily safeguards against salvation by works (Rom. 3:28). Although acting faith does logically precede righteousness, it is not the kind of thing that can produce righteousness by forgiveness. To precede is not to cause. Acting faith only meets the condition on which God has freely offered to "give" the righteousness that leads to fellowship with him. By contrast, in Pauline usage works inherently, directly, and by themselves produce the perfect righteousness requisite for divine fellowship. (d) There seems to be no convincing reason for God's "depravitizing" man and then "undepravitizing" him later for salvation. Natural depravity is unnecessary on the legal and corporate side because of conditionality and on the interpersonal side because of love. Systematically speaking, natural depravity is unnecessary for explaining and safeguarding grace.

Biblically unwarranted

While a truth may not be necessary systematically, it may be true positively because God decided to have it be the case. Our affirmation here is that depravity is also not a positive doctrine. Scripture does mention several consequences of Adam's sin, but (a) among them it does not specifically include inability to respond to the gospel. (b) Natural depravity is inferred needlessly from a combination of points: man was created in the image and likeness of God (Gen. 1:26-27); through Christ men are renewed to the image of God's Son (Rom. 8:29); therefore, in the Fall man lost the image because Adam and Christ are said to stand for the lost and the saved respectively (Rom. 5:12-21; I Cor. 15:20-22). The loss and renewal envisioned here need not include more than the holiness Adam lost when he sinned and the righteousness each man loses when he sins like Adam. Natural inability does not have to enter the picture because a man's "fall" can be his own.

(c) Specific passages usually come up in discussions about natural depravity. Without being exhaustive, we take notice of a few references. "No one is able to come to me unless the Father who sent me draws him, and I will raise him up in the last day" (Jn. 6:44). "Drawing a person" need not mean a direct, irresistible operation on his nature. Furthermore, applying this verse to depravity assumes the wrong set of contrasts. The statement does not contrast with "not drawing him" so as to imply his inability to respond without special divine assistance; rather it contrasts with someone else drawing him. The religious leaders whom Jesus addresses here opposed his ministry and claims; consequently, they were not going to be drawn to Jesus because they had already committed themselves to an opposing view of the Messianic kingdom. Jesus simply affirms that God is on his side of the controversy. They cannot come to him because the Father is not drawing them; something else is drawing them in an opposite direction. So to speak, the statement needs to be read with a stress on "Father." "No one can come to me unless the *Father* draws him; your being drawn is not by the Father as you may suppose."

Romans 8:7-8 says, "The mind of the flesh is enmity toward God, for it is not subject to the law of God; for neither is it able to be. And those who are in the flesh are not able to please God." The mind of the flesh stands in opposition to the mind of the spirit and as such opposes God. A person in this mindset cannot be subject to God because the system he has espoused is not subject to God. Being in the one, he cannot satisfy the requirements of the other. That poses a different question from whether he has the ability to change systems. A similar point needs to be made on I John 3:9; John 15:5. "You cannot drink the cup of the Lord and the cup of demons; you cannot partake of the table of the Lord and of the table of demons" (I Cor. 10:21). Even Jesus could not do anything of himself alone and at the same time please the Father: "Truly, truly I tell you: the Son is not able to do anything of himself . . ." (Jn. 5:19, 30). Natural inability should not be confused with "circumstantial inability."

"Create in me a clean heart, O God; and renew an upright spirit in me" (Ps. 51:10) does not have to mean that God must do something supernatural on the heart before it can be cleansed. God tells the Israelites, "Make for yourselves a new heart and a new spirit" (Ezek. 18:31). The Jerusalem church leaders rejoiced and glorified God because he had given repentance to the Gentiles (Acts 11:18; cp. II Tim. 2:25; Mt. 11:27), but "giving repentance" need not mean more than allowing the opportunity for repentance unto salvation as an option for Gentiles.

Paul describes the Ephesians as previously "dead in trespasses and sins" (2:1). Interpreters allegorize the comparison, however, if they infer that spiritually dead means *insensible* to spiritual things. The comparison between death and their condition does not have to be carried beyond being *insensitive* to spiritual concerns. This passage stands aside from how someone can become sensitive.

As a last example, Paul says in I Corinthians 2:14, "The natural man does not receive the things of the Spirit of God, for they are foolishness to him; and he is not able to know them because they are spiritually discerned." In 1:18—2:16 the apostle depreciates wisdom as a means of knowing God (1:20). Revelation has only recently made known the truth of the gospel (2:7-9), but people accustomed to operating by human wisdom do not readily receive revelation. Additionally, part of their reluctance comes from erroneous presuppositions that make resurrection foolish to Gentiles and a crucified Messiah foolish to Jews (1:22-24). "Philosophical method" uses reason on experience to find truth, but the truth of the gospel comes by revelation. Understanding

51

revelation comes from using reason on revelation in terms of experience. This "exegetical method" for Jews would have been fine if they had properly understood the law and the prophets and had properly appreciated the signs of Christ's ministry (1:22). In that they did not, they, too, were unable to know what must be spiritually discerned. The passage states a general rule to which there are exceptions (1:26), but on the whole the gospel makes no living sense to people who fancy themselves wise. All this is quite aside from whether it takes supernatural benefits to change such men or whether the reason for their insensitivity is natural inability to perceive spiritual matters. The inability here is in the functioning and circumstance, not necessarily in the nature.

Experientially unverified

Examples cited in verification of hereditary depravity of nature do not require the interpretation placed on them by theologians favorable to the doctrine. Several causes for sin have been described in the previous chapter; they seem sufficient for explaining what we see in ourselves and others. The *crying* of an infant has nothing necessarily to do with self-centeredness; crying serves as his only means of communication and self-expression. Having no alternative, he uses the only technique available to him.

Selfishness in young children likewise may be understood in other ways. It may be behavior learned through bad example or misperceived good example. Sometimes what adults read as selfishness may amount to fear, distrust, or misunderstanding as when a toy is taken and given to another child. Some interesting examples of selflessness could be laid alongside examples to the contrary so that one suspects there is an interaction of influences on the innocence of young minds. Seeing the world as they do from behind their own eyes, they do not perform in light of the viewpoint of others; developmentally they have not reached the socialization stage.

Since we do not know very clearly the mind of the young child we are observing, reticence should characterize our explanation of his motives. We have no desire to discount the effect of diet, sleep, the weather, space, individual biological constitution, etc., upon behavior; but we do not infer from these things that there is a one-to-one relationship between body and behavior so as to conclude that inheritable factors explain sin and thus favor natural depravity. There is no more reason to suppose that a baby has inherited a depraved nature from Adam than there is to believe he will inherit his father's scar. Generally speaking, we operate on the principle that acquired characteristics are not inherited. Sin is an acquired characteristic.

Self-contradictory

According to II Peter 3:9 (a) the Lord "does not want any to perish, but all to come to repentance." On the other hand, (b) he decides to save only some: "These will go away into eternal punishment, but the righteous into eternal life" (Mt. 25:46). Finally, (c) God is consistent inasmuch as he is "the same yesterday, today, and forever" (Heb. 13:8). The explanation for the difference between the "all" he desires to save and the "some" he decides to save must lie outside himself or he would be inconsistent. The solution must lie in man because he is the outside person involved. Man must have the ability to respond to God or the variable would be put back inside God: he would become the chooser of who was saved by becoming the chooser of whom he enabled to respond. The end result would be inconsistency in God.

This particular difficulty could be answered by supposing that God enables all men equally to the point of ability to respond rather than to the point of necessity to respond. Even then, systematic and biblical inadequacies leave the doctrine without support so that it ought not be presented as Christian doctrine. At any rate, the doctrine of natural depravity falls beside the way because the interpersonal, legal, corporate, and functional reasons sufficiently show that man cannot save himself.

Part III—The Basis for Salvation

Chapter Six

GUIDELINES FOR UNDERSTANDING THE ATONEMENT

Introduction

The first great principle in salvation is the Christian doctrine of grace. God's unmerited favor toward man surpasses the mercy that withholds just punishment and goes on to bestow positive good. Whatever may be said for man's responsibility in salvation, his faith responses have value only because they fall within a previous framework made possible by grace. God took the initiative to change man's irretrievable condition. The atonement through Christ represents the culminating event of God's redemptive history.

In the next two chapters we seek to understand the meaning of Christ's work for redemption from sin and reconciliation to God. At this point we attempt to lay down the ground rules for understanding the connection between his work and man's righteousness. The principles enunciated here restrict the field in which the significance of his atonement must be positively formulated.

Elements of the guilt problem

Statement of the problem. Several difficulties present themselves when guilt is examined at close hand. One difficulty stems from (a) *the nature of time.* Guilt arises from an act of irresponsibility or disobedience, and action happens in the realm of time. Once it occurs that point in time has passed forever. No one can turn back the relentless flow of history in order to relive a certain moment to erase some deed. If the past cannot be undone, it would appear that sin cannot be removed.

A second difficulty lies in (b) *the nature of man.* By virtue of *conscience* there is an innate drive for innocence. That inability to feel comfortable with guilt poses the question of how to admit guilt without self-destruction. Furthermore, by virtue of *practical inability,* performance and aspiration create internal conflict for each person so that he experiences a sinfulness from which he finds insufficient power of will to extricate himself, not so much from past sin as from present sinning, all the while accused by conscience.

54

Another problem derives from (c) *the nature of righteousness*. Righteousness cannot be transferred from person to person any more than unrighteousness can (Ezek. 18:19-20). If all men have lost righteousness, there would seem to be no way to obtain righteousness from someone else. If we have no way to "unload" our own unrighteousness or to "load" someone else's righteousness, there is neither escape from guilt nor attainment of guiltlessness.

A fourth complication comes from (d) *the nature of perfection*. Once imperfection has become the case, there is no way to change it back into perfection. Even living perfectly thereafter would only be perfection from then on; past imperfection would still remain. God requires the same perfect holiness of us that he has in himself.

Unsatisfactory responses to guilt. Because there is no escape from the past and no living with present guilt feelings, it is unsatisfactory to suppose that (a) *no solution* exists. We must do something with those behaviors that we and others dislike in us. Self-pity, for example, tries to act as if nothing can be done because the system is out to get us or whatever; secretly we realize that using self-pity is a way of removing the call to change. At the other extreme it is unsatisfactory to hold that (b) *no problem* exists. Rationalization tries to define sin out of existence by making values totally relative. Although conscience sometimes pricks when it ought not, making evil an illusion disregards its effects and ignores the accusations of the moral instinct. Guilt can neither be denied nor endured.

As a result other unsatisfactory responses are attempted, including (c) *projection*, which shifts blame elsewhere. Making society responsible for sin, for example, only moves guilt to the environment, where it remains to be eradicated still. (d) *Lying* seeks to hide faults from other people, but it does not eliminate those faults or their consequences. (e) *Hardheartedness* attempts to dull the pangs of conscience by willing not to care, but it worsens the situation by perpetuating the behavior along with its results. (f) *Withdrawal* looks for solace in solitude, but by so doing creates a void of fellowship; thus it compounds and prolongs the problem in an effort to solve it. (g) *Hyperactivity* keeps the mind occupied with work or pleasure, but escapism merely delays the solution till we no longer have enough energy to run from contemplating life. (h) *Compensation* tries by "penance" and "works" to make up for the "absence" of good by doing more good than "normal"; but when we have done everything, "we are [still] un*profitable* servants; we have done [only] what we ought to have done" (Lk. 17:10).

(i) *Self-punishment* makes conscious or unconscious attempt to "balance the books" by inflicting self-deprivation, emotional stress, or even physical pain in order to achieve a semblance of self-salvation. (j) "*Letting it blow over*" acts as if time *per se* weakens an act's power to destroy. Mind may forget and feelings may subside without gaining positive restoration. Finally, (k) *finding fault with others* seeks to relieve the sense of guilt by pointing out that other people sin, too. We find ourselves trying to soothe conscience by not being so bad as others. The effects of fewer sins, however, are no less real because they are fewer. Guilt must be dealt with, but how to be delivered from this one-way, dead-end street remains a "problem fit for God."

Preliminary Solutions to Guilt

Fact of revelation

From the beginning God has revealed his will so men could know how to conduct themselves properly before him. Because of the oracles of the Father, we know the *definition* of sin. We are not dependent simply on nature for the foundation of moral behavior; consequently, we are not restricted to the scientific method as a basis for ethics.

Science is also transcended by revelation in creating *sensitivity* to sin. Aside from the fact that guilt is not reckoned without knowledge, revelation seeks to avoid guilt by making clear what sin is and what is sin. Guilt comes in breaking that revealed standard of behavior.

General process of reconciliation

Revelation is inadequate, however, because knowledge is not virtue; it has been in knowing God that men have not glorified him as God (Rom. 1:19, 21, 25, 28, 32). Therefore, in addition to revelation they need reconciliation; sin brings guilt, the feeling of it, and the effects of it. Although *guilt* comes from breaking the standard, the *sense of guilt* comes even more from personal considerations. Sin breaks the standard, affronts the author of the standard, and alienates someone. Feeling conscience stricken emphasizes the last two effects. Serious attention must be given to overcoming the sense of guilt that issues from sin, because knowledge does not eliminate sin.

56

We can grasp the dynamics of *relationship* with God by observing the principles of relationship between men. Both associations take place between persons and for that reason function similarly. *Restoring fellowship* with God uses the formula for restoring fellowship between men. This affirmation reiterates our underlying conviction that salvation—and therefore the atonement—operates in the realm of persons. Scripture confirms our expectancy by commanding in religion what is practiced in society. Revelation relates to atonement so as to *avoid guilt*; reconciliation relates to atonement so as to *rid from guilt*; both are necessary because the knowledge of revelation does not guarantee the practice of virtue.

The first problem for guilt was that once the sinful act occurs its guilt cannot be undone because the act cannot be undone. This analysis, however, misconstrues the situation, because it is not so much the past, but the present, that matters in the present. Guilt is not just a characteristic of an act; it is also a characteristic of the transgressor in the eyes of the one he has sinned against. Even as time carries the act away forever, it can also remove it from relevance forever. The past is no longer important in the present except insofar as it continues to affect it. Therefore, the need is not to get rid of the past, but to get rid of its effect on the present. Removing the sense of guilt calls for removing the displeasure of the offended one who keeps the past relevant to the present through memory and alienation.

Repentance. Our repentance separates us from our past. In repentance we change our minds about what we should be, our feelings about who we are, and our resolve about future behavior. In effect repentance says, "That is not me; I repudiate such a deed; what I *did* is no longer who I *am*. It has no more bearing on the way I will act." *Repentance removes our past from us as far as we are concerned.*

Ezekiel enunciates the principle that the way a man *is* amounts to being the way God relates to him:

> If the wicked person turns from his sins that he has committed and keeps all my statutes and does what is lawful and right, he will surely live and not die. None of his transgressions that he has committed will be remembered against him: in his righteousness that he has done he will live. Do I have any pleasure in the death of the wicked, says the Lord, and not rather that he should turn from his way and live? But when the righteous person turns away from his righteousness and commits iniquity and does according

57

to the abominations the wicked man does, will he live? None of his righteous deeds that he has done will be remembered: in his trespass that he has trespassed and in his sin that he has sinned—in them he will die (18:21-24; cp. Jer. 18:7-10).

Past goodness or wickedness does not dictate present relationships; God has determined that present conduct governs dealings with men in the present.

Apology. Apology admits to the offended party that the offender has separated himself from his past. Scripture uses "confession" as a rough equivalent for admitting sin to the other person. Candidates for John's baptism came "confessing their sins" (Mk. 1:5). Among men James commands, "Confess your sins therefore one to another" (5:16); likewise with God John says, "If we confess our sins, he is faithful and righteous to forgive us our sins" (I Jn. 1:9). Confession or *apology helps bridge the gulf between offender and offended by expressing repentance from the past.*

Forgiveness. Finally, forgiveness by the offended person separates us from our sin. In forgiveness the one sinned against agrees that our sin is no longer who we are; he begins to view us the way we are now. Forgiveness says, "That is not you; what you *did* is no longer who you *are*. It has no more bearing on the way I will relate to you." *Forgiveness removes our past as far as the other person is concerned, too.* When the past no longer affects the present subjectively because of repentance or objectively because of forgiveness, then reconciliation has swallowed up alienation, and life begins again.

Groundwork for Understanding Christ's Atonement

As stimulating and clarifying as these preliminary solutions are, a moment's reflection reveals that they include no necessary role for Jesus of Nazareth. Furthermore, having revelation and understanding reconciliation have not proved sufficient for avoiding or removing guilt. If these mechanisms already available in the Abrahamic-Mosaic covenant could have brought about reconciliation, then Christ would have died for nothing (Gal. 2:21); but his ministry built atop these foundations the provision called "the atonement." Our task consists in verbalizing the need for that additional something Messiah supplied. Among the basic dynamic factors of reconciliation we must insert aspects of the atonement. In working out the meaning of the atonement, we offer some guidelines for interpretation.

Concepts underlying the atonement

The interpersonal framework. The atonement is to be understood within the framework of interpersonal relationship. Distinctively *personal elements* take precedence in the "at-one-ment" of men with God and with one another. We start here because (a) the nature of the atonement equals the nature of salvation—restoring personal relationship with God and men. Consequently, we do not treat the atonement as if it functioned like *natural cause.* Jesus' ministry does not cause our salvation in the same way gravity causes a tree to fall. Nothing "comes between" gravity and a tree, but between the work of Jesus Christ and our salvation comes personal operations like those of divine and human will. This lack of rigid connectedness in the aspects of the atonement

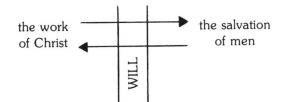

imageries is explained, we propose, by personal characteristics like love and choice that exist in the reality these pictures point to. (b) All impersonal models of the atonement begin to break down when examined closely.

The incarnational mode. Another primary fact is *the incarnation.* Atonement takes place through incarnation inasmuch as the Word became flesh (Jn. 1:14); Jesus partook of flesh and blood for the express purpose of giving help to seed of Abraham, not to angels; he was in fact made lower than the angels in order to sanctify men (Heb. 2:4-18): "For both the sanctifier and the sanctified are all of one [*nature*/Father?]" (Heb. 2:11). After quoting Psalms 40:6-8 to the effect that God was dissatisfied with animal sacrifice, the Hebrew writer explains that the offering of Messiah's body did fulfill the will of God (Heb. 10:1-13). God did not speak to us directly from heaven, but spoke to us on earth in his Son (Heb. 1:2).

As we hope to show when positively presenting the meaning of the atonement, Christ's work for our salvation does not have the rigid nature of *law* even though it fulfills the requirements of the Father. There are no artificial moves for satisfying the letter of written requirements without taking care of the real problem.

The event character. Inasmuch as the atonement takes place through the incarnation, it takes place through someone acting in history. The life, death, and resurrection of Messiah can therefore have *multifaceted significance,* because it has several components standing at the crossroads of converging historical patterns. By contrast, the meaning of language is single; that is, a word or statement carries one idea rather than several parallel ones. Consequently, atonement does not operate in terms of the principles of metaphysics, language, mathematics, or abstract *logic.* Although it makes sense, the atonement does not work like a syllogism. We might not arrive at what God would do to bring about atonement even if we understood all the facets of the problem. We hesitate, then, to speak of the necessity of the cross, for example, in any sense except that something had to be done; given the circumstances, man could not save himself; we presume not to say that what was done was the only option for what could have been done.

In fact, lack of necessity may even enhance the meaning of the cross. Christ endured crucifixion more because of impulsion than compulsion. If no inherent connection exists between the cross and the Christian, then it necessarily demonstrates love more than duty.

The "event of Jesus Christ" contains both apologetic and theological values. In the one case its supernatural element verifies the claims of Jesus, God's approval of him (Rom. 1:4), and the truthfulness of the Christian faith; in the other case it bears at least three major thrusts as we will show in the following pages. This possibility of multifaceted meaning exists because of what the nature of an event is.

The appropriateness nature. So far we have drawn attention to the interpersonal framework, the incarnational mode, and event character of the atonement, inferring that salvation through Christ is not like causal determinism, legal requirement, or logical necessity. Here we affirm that the atonement is not merely symbolic either: "For such a high priest was *appropriate* for us—holy, without deceit, undefiled, separated from sinners, and made higher than the heavens, who did not need daily . . . to offer sacrifices first for his own sins and then for those of the people . . ." (Heb. 7:26-27; cp. Heb. 2:10; Lk. 24:26). Atonement through the crucified and resurrected Son of God is more than a suggestive figure into which we intuitively read various meanings. The work of Christ actually did something instead of just symbolizing something. What it did was appropriate to the personal, material, historical realm where it occurred.

Its appointment connection. The value of Calvary was one God *chose to appoint;* what Christ did there, who he was, and how he benefited us did not therefore have inherent value. His life and death were not causally atoning, but appointedly atoning. As to (1) *who he was,* Paul told Gentiles on the Aereopagus, ". . . inasmuch as he appointed a day in which he intends to judge the world in righteousness in the man whom he *designated,* having provided assurance to all men by resurrecting him from the dead" (Acts 17:31). Hebrews 3:2 speaks of Jesus as "faithful to the one who *appointed* him . . ." (cp. 1:3). Matthew 12:18 quotes Isaiah 42:1: "Behold, my servant whom I have *chosen* . . ." (cp. Lk. 23:35). Peter testified before the Sanhedrin, "And there is no salvation in any other, for neither is there another name *given* among men in whom we must be saved" (Acts 4:12).

As to fact, of course, no one else possessed the qualifications appropriate to the atonement, "for all have sinned and fall short of the glory of God" (Rom. 3:23); but as to theory someone else that possessed them could have been designated; otherwise there is no reason to speak of "appointing" him as the measuring stick of men.

On (2) *what he did* Hebrews comments, "It was appropriate for him, on account of whom are all things and through whom are all things, in bringing many sons into glory to make the pioneer of their salvation perfect through suffering" (2:10). On the road to Emmaus, Jesus explained to the two travelers, "Did it not behoove the Messiah to suffer these things and to enter into his glory?" (Lk. 24:26).

As to (3) *how he benefited us* the words of Paul to the Corinthians include the following insight on (a) removing our sins from us:

But all things are from God who reconciled us to himself through Christ and gave us the ministry of reconciliation; that is, in Christ God was reconciling the world to himself, not *reckoning* [*logizomai*] their sins to them, having placed in us the word of reconciliation (II Cor. 5:18-19).

Even as *sins* are *not* reckoned, counted, or imputed against us, so also (b) *righteousness* in Christian salvation *is* reckoned to us: "Even as David also pronounces blessing on the man to whom God reckons righteousness without works" (Rom. 4:6). There is a difference between sins and reckoned sins: "Blessed is the man to whom God does not reckon iniquity" (Ps. 32:2; cp. 32:1; Rom. 4:6-8; 5:13). Sins are "detached" by reckoning and righteousness is "attached" by reckoning. Both "unsinfulness" and righteousness result from the way we are *regarded*, not the way we *are*.

In regard to (c) *status* Peter tells his readers, "You are a *chosen* [*eklegō*] race, a royal priesthood, a holy nation, a people for God's own possession . . ." (I Pet. 2:9; cp. Mt.20:16; 22:14; Mk. 13:20; Rom. 16:13; Eph. 1:4; II Th. 2:13; I Pet. 2:4; Rev. 17:14). To these passages may be added all cases where God's people in Christ are called "elect," or "chosen ones," and where their state is called "election" (Mt. 24:22, 24, 31; Mk. 13:20, 22, 27; Lk. 18:7; Rom. 8:33; 9:11; 11:5, 7; Col. 3:12; I Th. 1:4; II Tim. 2:10; Tit. 1:1; I Pet. 1:2; 5:13; II Pet. 1:10). The connection between the cross and the Christian comes about through personal choice, not impersonal causation.

On the one hand, since salvation comes from God's (a) *personal choosing,* not only do we not save ourselves, but Christ's sacrifice does not itself save us inherently, logically, or necessarily. His work and our benefit join together because of personal choice and appointment by the Father. On the other hand, since salvation comes through the (b) *incarnation* in (c) *history,* the correlation between Christ's sacrifice and our salvation is (d) *appropriate,* not artificial, legal, or symbolic. The balance between non-necessity and realness is kept, we feel, by making interpersonalness the primary category of the atonement. How that interpersonalness operates, we will endeavor to show later under "the benefits of the atonement," but here we affirm that the atonement operates personally on the principle of appropriateness.

Messiah's sinlessness. A fifth principle in the atonement is the *sinlessness* of the incarnate one. To atone for sin requires sinlessness. Paul says, "Him who did not know sin [God] made sin on our behalf that we might become the righteousness of God in him" (II Cor. 5:21). The Hebrew writer declares unequivocally, "For we do not have a high priest who cannot be touched by the feeling of our weaknesses, but one that has been tempted in all things like those we are tempted by without sin" (4:15); "Being a son he learned obedience by the things that he suffered; and having been made perfect, he became the author of eternal salvation to all them that obey him" (5:8-9; cp. 2:10); "For such a high priest was also appropriate for us—devout, without evil, without deceit, separated from sinners and made higher than the heavens—who did not need daily like those high priests to offer sacrifices first for his own sin then for those of the people" (7:26-27). Peter cites the Suffering Servant Poem at Isaiah 53:9, ". . . who did no sin; neither was deceit found in his mouth" (I Pet. 2:22; cp. 1:19). John records Jesus' challenge, "Which of you proves me guilty of sin?" (Jn. 8:46); in his first epistle he declares, "And you know that he was manifested that he might take away sins and there is no sin in him (3:5; cp. 2:29; 3:3, 7). With perhaps less precision Luke records Peter as designating Jesus "the Holy and Righteous One" (Acts 3:14; cp. 2:27; 4:27; 7:52; Mk. 1:24; Lk. 1:35; 4:34; Jn. 6:69). We so perceive the paramount importance of this truth for the atonement that we could in theory sooner give up the deity of the Messiah than dispense with his sinlessness.

Non-transferability of guilt. By the nature of the case, guilt cannot be transferred from one person to another. Since guilt arises from action and an act cannot be transferred, its guilt cannot be transferred. What derives from the nature of the case scripture also directly declares to be so in Ezekiel 18:19-20. The prophet says expressly that in divine jurisprudence one person does not bear the iniquity of another: "he shall not die for the iniquity of his father" (18:17; see 18:14-19).

What applies to guilt applies equally to righteousness. Since righteousness arises from acts, it cannot be transferred from one person to another because the acts cannot be transferred. Again Ezekiel confirms by statement what inheres in the nature of things: "The righteousness of the righteous shall be upon himself" even as "the wickedness of the wicked shall be upon himself" (18:20). The implications for the atonement are all too obvious. Strictly speaking, the atonement does not involve transfer of sins to Christ nor transfer of righteousness to sinners. The harmony of scripture requires treating righteousness like unrighteousness—as untransferable.

WHAT THE BIBLE SAYS ABOUT SALVATION

Harmony of scripture and consistency of thought also require interpreting the Fall and the atonement alike. Even as we reject the idea that descendants of First Adam are guilty to hell for his act, so also we must reject the idea that descendants of Second Adam are righteous to heaven for his act. All this must allow for the indispensableness of Messiah's work and must legitimately understand passages that could mean his righteousness is transferred to us or our guilt is projected onto him.

Non-transfer of penalty. Since our *act* does not move from one person to another and since *the guilt or righteousness of an act* cannot be transferred, *the penalty for guilt* cannot be transferred. Although *suffering* may be brought on innocent people because of the nature of social relationship, nevertheless it seems contrived to suppose punishment was transferred at Calvary. One man may volunteer to pay his neighbor's speeding ticket. Societies have developed ideas like the whipping boy, sin eaters, and the like; but executing a substitute for a murderer, for instance, does not seem appropriate even if society could somehow count on the murderer's sincere pledge to reformed living. If society could do that, it would not need to execute the substitute. As said above, then, the atonement evidently has to do ultimately with real interpersonal relationship.

This expectancy about penalty also seems verified by Ezekiel: *"The soul that sins is the one* that shall die" (18:20). The prophet does not mean that the soul that sins shall die rather than be fined, as if the contrast were between kinds of punishment: "For the wages of sin are death, but the free gift of God is eternal life in Christ Jesus our Lord" (Rom. 6:23). The prophet does not say, "The soul that sins shall *die*"; but "The soul that sins *he* shall die." In the previous verses 10-18 he declares that fathers do not bear the sins of sons or vice versa; consequently, his contrast is between that denied alternative and the one affirmed. Afterward in 18:20 he goes on to say, "The righteousness of the righteous shall be upon *himself*." This same proposition appears to be Paul's teaching in Galatians 6:5: "For each person shall bear his own burden" (cp. Prov. 9:12; Rom. 14:12; I Cor. 3:8).

In spiritual-salvation matters the non-transferability of punishment does not seem to be altered by voluntariness on the part of the one who would help; that is to say, the reason punishment does not transfer is not because a second person cannot be *forced* to bear punishment for another man. When Israel offended Yahweh by making the golden

64

calf in the wilderness, Moses went before the Lord and said,

> "Surely this people has sinned exceedingly and have made for themselves gods of gold. Yet now, if you will forgive their sin—; and if not, pray blot me out of your book that you have written." And Yahweh said to Moses, "Whoever has sinned against me—him I will blot out of my book" (Ex. 32:32-33; cp. Rom. 9:3).

Of course, Moses did not constitute a sinless substitute that would have been necessary in a stand-in mechanism, but the Lord's answer to him expressed a different reason for refusing the offer: God punishes the guilty for spiritual disobedience.

Unless this premise on the non-transferability of guilt creates difficulty later, we lay it down as another preliminary principle that Christ's atonement did not in precise terms include putting our penalty upon him in the sense of causal, legal, or logical transfer.

Interpreting atonement passages

Imageries of the atonement. Christ's atonement is set forth in scripture under several widely diverse and unrelated *imageries.* First among them is that of (a) *ransom:* "For even the Son of Man did not come to be served but to serve and to give his life as a ransom [*lytron*] for many" (Mt. 20:28; Mk. 10:45; cp. Lk. 24:21; Tit. 2:14; I Pet. 1:18). In this analogy sinners occupy the position of slaves whose freedom Jesus buys with his life as if in payment to Satan, who owns them. Similarly Paul says to the Ephesians, ". . . in whom we have our redemption [*apolytrōsis*] through his blood . . ." (1:7; cp. Jn. 8:34-36; Rom. 3:24; 6:16-18; I Cor. 1:30; Eph. 1:14; Col. 1:14; Tit. 2:14; Heb. 9:15; I Pet. 1:18-19; cp. Heb. 9:12). As the freedom of a slave was brought about by someone else's payment, so the sinner is freed from the bondage of sin and death by the blood of Christ.

In John 3:14-15 Jesus compares salvation by faith in the crucified Christ with (b) *the brazen serpent* held up on a standard by Moses during the plague of vipers: "And as Moses lifted up the snake in the desert, thus the Son of Man must be lifted up in order that the one who believes in him may have eternal life" (cp. Num. 21:4-9). Putting faith in Messiah on the cross for the healing of the soul roughly corresponds with looking at the brazen serpent on the standard for the cure from snake bite.

Isaiah depicts the atonement under the picture of (c) *healing:* ". . .

and by his stripes we are healed" (53:5; cp. I Pet. 2:24; Heb. 12:13; cp. Jn. 3:14-15). That same Messianic poem uses a kind of (d) *"whipping boy"* model when it says, "He was wounded for our transgressions and bruised for our iniquities, and the chastisement of our peace was on him, and with his stripes we are healed" (53:5; cp. 53:4, 7, 8b).

Probably the most frequent model is that of (e) *animal sacrifice* in its various Mosaic institutions. Hebrews dwells at length on this theme, especially in 10:1-12 as based on Psalms 40:6-8. Parallels with the passover lamb are particularly suggestive: "Behold, the Lamb of God that takes away the sin of the world; (Jn. 1:29; cp. 1:36; Isa. 53:7; Acts 8:32; I Pet. 1:19; Rev. 5:6, 8, 12, 13, etc.). Instituting the Lord's Supper during the passover meal draws attention to this same connection with the paschal lamb (Mt. 26:26-29; Mk. 14:22-25; Lk. 22:14-20). Scapegoat imagery may be involved in I John 3:5: "And you know that he was manifested to carry sins away" (cp. Lev. 16:1-28). Other substitutionary and sacrificial passages include Romans 3:21-26; Galatians 3:13; Hebrews 9:26; I Peter 2:24.

Hebrews 1:3 combines with other texts in using the idea of (f) *purification:* ". . . when he had made purification of sins, he sat down on the right hand of the majesty on high." Often related to sacrificial and priestly work, purification had to do with removing the taint of real or ceremonial defilement by the offering of a sacrifice with attendant ritual washings over which the priest officiated (Num. 19). Cleansings of this sort included rites for forgiveness of sin (spiritual), for the healing of disease (fleshly), and for the removal of taboos (social), all of which are analogous to cleansing the heart and conscience through Messiah (Jn. 8:9; Acts 15:9; 23:1; 24:16; I Tim. 1:5, 19; 3:9; II Tim. 1:3; Tit. 2:14; Heb. 9:9, 13-14; 10:2, 22; 13:18; I Pet. 2:19; 3:16, 21; I Jn. 1:7-9; Rev. 7:14). Cleansing imagery appears also in descriptions of appropriating the atonement, even to the point of calling baptism a washing away of sin (Acts 22:16, etc.).

On two occasions the role of Jesus falls under the label of (g) *founder,* or perhaps captain, pioneer, or author, depending on what best translates *archēgos:* "It was appropriate for him on account of whom and through whom are all things, in bringing many sons into glory, to make the founder of their salvation perfect through sufferings" (Heb. 2:10; cp. 12:2; Acts 3:15; 5:31). Perhaps "pioneer" comes closest to the derivational meaning of the word in Hebrews; if so, the writer pictures him as the "first-leader" of the lost into the safety of salvation. He is a kind of trail blazer through death and the grave into incorruptible, eternal life.

The atoning work of Christ is compared to that of a (h) *conqueror who removes barriers or destroys opponents*. New Testament writers often speak of conquering *death:* "Since the children share in blood and flesh, he also in like manner partook of the same in order that through death he might bring to nothing the one who has the power of death, that is, the devil, and might deliver these as many as by fear of death were subject to bondage" (Heb. 2:14-15; cp. Mt. 16:18; Mk. 3:27; Jn. 8:34; Rom. 6:16; 8:37-39; I Cor. 15:55-57; II Tim. 1:10; I Jn. 3:8).

On other occasions the writers spoke of delivering from the *law.* Since the law is for flesh-and-blood people, death becomes a way out from under its jurisdiction; and resurrection ushers in a new era of living unto God in primarily personal terms. Like a widow separated from her husband by his death, Christians have joined themselves to Messiah and have died to the law with him so that they are taken out from under the law: "So then, my brothers, you also died to the law through the body of Christ unto your becoming joined to another who was raised from the dead that we might bear fruit unto God" (Rom. 7:4; cp. 1-6; 6:1-14). In a related figure Christians are delivered from the law by having it taken away from over them, either by its being nailed to the cross (Col. 2:14; cp. Rom. 10:4; Gal. 3:13; 5:1) or by its being abrogated (Heb. 8:7-13; 10:15-18).

At still other times Christ conquers *Satan* and his cohorts. He triumphs in the temptations (Mt. 4:1-11; Lk. 4:1-13), exorcizes demons (Mt. 12:28; Lk. 11:20), and casts out Satan (Jn. 12:31).

Another imagery may be (i) *propitiation,* which views the work of Christ as placating God's wrath at our sin (Rom. 3:25; Heb. 2:17; I Jn. 2:2; 4:10; cf. Rom. 5:10; 11:28).

Jesus is viewed as an (j) *example* for us to follow: ". . . because Christ also suffered for you, leaving you an example that you should follow in his steps, who did no sin neither was deceit found in his mouth, who when he was reviled, did not revile in return; when he suffered he did not threaten, but committed himself to him who judges righteously" (I Pet. 2:21-23). He is a moral influence upon all who follow him (Lk. 7:47; Jn. 15:13).

67

Hebrews 2:5-18 develops from Psalms 8:4-6 the idea that as a (k) *representative* of the race Jesus saves us from failure in exercising dominion over the earth. Jesus is the one "crowned with glory and honor" because he became lower than the angels in order to taste of death and then be exalted as Lord of creation.

The work of intercession falls within the function of (l) *priest,* and Jesus serves as a go-between on man's behalf (Heb. 5-10). The work of communication makes Jesus a (m) *prophet* to the people of God (Heb. 1:1-4). The Messiah is pictured as a (n) *testator* who mediates a new testament wherein men's sins are remembered no more. By analogy his death puts the will into effect (Heb. 9:15-22).

He also fulfills the role of (o) *primogenitor,* not only because he is firstborn over creation, but firstborn from the dead, so that God reconciles all things to himself through the Son of his love (Col. 1:13-24). Not only did the firstborn son receive the double portion, but had responsibility over the family and for it. Similarly, Christ bears responsibility for the identity of the Christian family in its reconciliation to the Father.

We must handle this variety of pictures sensitively in order to accord to them the function intended by the authors who used them. Along with basic concepts, atonement imageries form the data out of which understanding the work of Christ comes.

Interpreting atonement imageries. (1) Interpreting the atonement allows the possibility of figurative language. The first reason for this conviction is that (a) New Testament writers describe the atonement several different ways. They do not consistently use sacrificial language, or conquest descriptions, or ransom metaphors. All their pictures cannot then individually represent *a model of the whole.* Either each picture represents *an aspect of the whole,* or one picture must be the reality while the others stress aspects of it. The analogies do not form one continuous whole, but present several distinct images. When some models are looked at closely, they begin to break down. Understanding them as models rather than as realities can eliminate this difficulty.

Analogy must also be involved because (b) some imageries contain elements foreign to what they represent. The ransom idea, for instance, raises the question of who receives the payment. If Satan receives the payment, he has some legitimate right of control over sinners—as if he obtained them "fair and square." Propitiation may not adequately picture God the Father as initiating reconciliation; his anger at sin had to be placated by someone more merciful than himself. Because of the harmony of scripture, appeal to figurativeness is legitimate in cases where literal interpretation creates difficulties.

(2) Interpreting the atonement requires the use of first principles in order to separate figurative from literal. The non-transferability of guilt, etc., enables us to see whether a certain description is the reality or a metaphor for the reality, to determine what aspect of a metaphor corresponds with the reality, as well as to be alerted to the very fact that figurativeness exists in biblical presentations of the atonement. Basic principles protect us from the extremes of reducing biblical models to meaningless symbols on the one hand or from treating them as necessarily stark literalisms on the other.

(3) Interpreting the atonement involves the possibility of more than one meaning. Because of its event character and personal framework it is a mistake to attempt to reduce the work of Christ to one significance; events may be multifaceted and persons may recognize this fact. Therefore the incarnational medium must not be read as causality, and the legal imagery based on the Old Testament should not be read as ultimately definitive for understanding the ministry, death, and resurrection of the Savior.

Chapter Seven

BENEFITS OF THE ATONEMENT

Introduction

Previously we laid the groundwork for understanding the atonement. Observations noted there were *restrictive* in that they established a limiting framework within which to interpret specific passages and models bearing on the death of Christ. In this chapter we seek to present within those restrictions the *positive* meaning of his life, death, and resurrection.

Motivation for Repentance

The first reason salvation comes through Jesus Christ is that *his example provides a unique source of motivation to repent.* Men need motivation for repentance. God could not just forgive men *without* repentance because there would be no distinction between his relationship to evil and his relationship to good; consequently, there would be little practical difference between evil and good themselves. Without the repentance requirement God would be exerting no influence toward correcting man; his only other options would be to destroy mankind or to forfeit control of the creation over which he had responsibility by virtue of creating it. The very option to repent, then, amounts to grace. Forgiveness *with* repentance, however, presupposes that the sinner will repent. Consequently, with or without repentance there is a need for Christ above and beyond previous revelation and reconciliation efforts.

Besides revelation and an understanding of reconciliation process, sinners need motivation to *do* the repenting and apologizing they *understand.* Jesus' contribution to revelation comes distinctively in the *affective* dimension rather than in the cognitive one. If God was willing to send

his Son from heaven to here and if his Son was willing to come, some things are implied that enhance repentance and confession above any previous revelation from God.

The distinctive role of Messiah in the atonement does not set aside previous revelation or the reconciliation process; it confirms revelation in a new dimension and works within the pattern of repentance, confession, and forgiveness. In keeping with this fact, Hebrews presents communication as the first reason for the incarnation: ". . . God spoke to us 'son-wise'" (Heb. 1:1-4). In the imagery of *prophet* the Son provided a perfect example, which did not exist with previous revelations. His communication was *demonstration* instead of ideas and words only. The "son-wise" revelation was also *holistic* instead of a progressive unfolding of prophetic revelation over several centuries. Furthermore, God's speech through him was *personal* since God himself became incarnate.

Unique among the world's religions, the incarnation of the Logos incorporated the whole range of human experience from birth to death and beyond. He did not assume flesh-and-blood existence for just a time, but for a lifetime. His incarnation went beyond some brief skirmish in defeating an enemy on the battlefield; it included physical pain, emotional strain, and social rejection. Divine identification with man extended even to the point of sin itself in the sense that as a physical human being he had to cope with human temptation: ". . . one who was tempted in all points as we are, without sin" (Heb. 4:15). Through the Messiah God's full identification with the human condition demonstrates six truths that move us to repentance.

God's love

No longer can we suspect God of not knowing what it is like to be a man with its frustrations, failures, and weakness; it is not appropriate now to withhold repentance as if to say that God might not fare so well either if our plight were his lot. There is no room left for feeling that we have a "high priest who cannot empathize with our weaknesses" (Heb. 4:15); "In that *he* has suffered being tempted, he can help those who are being tempted" (Heb. 2:18).

We doubt that, strictly speaking, an omniscient God learned anything from the incarnation, but Christ can help us now because *we* have learned something from it and are moved by his love to let him help us. The appropriate response to God's identification with man is man's identification with God by boldly "drawing near to the throne of grace to receive mercy and find grace in time of need" (Heb. 4:16; cp. 7:19, 25; 10:1, 22).

Identification with the human order compares favorably with a mother who, after repeated promptings, finally tells her daughter she will get no supper until she cleans up her room. The daughter does not get it cleaned by suppertime; so she does not get supper yet. But to make sure the discipline is not read as hate, the mother eats no supper either. A father may punish irresponsibility by telling his son to work all day on the yard; and then, to avoid overly discouraging him, he may help with the job. In such cases the parent enters into the appointed "suffering." By incarnation unto death God entered into the suffering he specified for men so the limitations of their condition would be read as discipline and not as hate or fate; hopefully we will be motivated to "clean up" our lives as a result (cp. Heb. 12:4-11; Prov. 3:11-12).

Through the incarnation we know God loves us. In Romans the apostle Paul gives his classic statement on the divine love manifested by the ministry of Jesus:

> . . . God's love has been poured out in our hearts through the Holy Spirit that was given to us; for while we were still weak, in due season Christ died for the ungodly. For scarcely for a righteous person will anyone die, for perhaps for the good man someone would even dare to die. But God commended his own love toward us in that while we were still sinners Christ died for us (5:5-8; cp. Jn. 3:16; Eph. 1:3-7; Tit. 3:4-7; I Jn. 4:9-10).

Love demonstrated by voluntary death begets love in flesh-and-blood men and moves them to repentance.

Sin's sinfulness

Messiah's atonement sensitizes to sin. If God has condescended to share our experience from manger to grave, we infer something about how sinful sin is. The amount of attention given to a problem shows its importance and the importance of its negative consequences. Incarnation shows the sinfulness of sin.

God's holiness

The gift of his Son balances the love of God with his holiness. Holiness could not deal with sin lightly; love would not allow not dealing with it at all. Having required personal perfection from men, he could not haul down that standard; having prescribed death for imperfection, he could not reverse himself without being inconsistent and therefore unholy. His holiness first prompted the holiness requirement for men: "You shall be holy because I am holy" (Lev. 11:44, 45; 19:2; 20:7; I Pet. 1:16), and prompted the death limitation (Gen. 3:22-24). Sending his Son to live the holy life as a man meant that God could in appearance and in fact avoid compromising his principles and his word. He could transcend personal perfection by requiring commitment to his ideal Son; he could transcend death by resurrection.

Man's worth

From the extreme to which God went to bring about reconciliation, we can tell what a premium he puts on fellowship with men, and hence, how much he values his human creation. Man's first commission was to serve as caretaker of the creation (Gen. 1:26-31); in that respect God crowned him with glory and honor and set him over the works of his hands (Ps. 8:5-8). Not only is a man more valuable than many sparrows (Mt. 10:31; Lk. 12:7); not only is a man's life worth more than the whole world (Mt. 16:26; Mk. 8:36-37; Lk. 9:25); he is important enough for God to let men crucify his Son in an effort to reconcile men to himself.

Death's demise

Divine identification has extended unto death, but atonement did not end there. The atonement includes the resurrection: the Lord "was delivered up for our trespasses and was raised for our justification" (Rom. 4:25). Passing through death via resurrection, he has delivered "all them who through fear of death were all their life subject to bondage" (Heb. 2:15). Henceforth, we are moved to cry out, "Abba, Father" (Rom. 8:15), because he "begot us again to a living hope by the resurrection from the dead" (I Pet. 1:3). Repentance comes more easily when the hope of resurrection transforms death from a psychological "dead end" into a doorway to eternal fellowship with a forgiving God. In that God raised Jesus up, he furnished a reason for trust that leads to hope for all men (Acts 17:31).

Sin's forgiveness

The apologetic implication of the resurrection has to do with more than the truth of Jesus' claim about his *person*—deity, Messiahship,

divine sonship; it also pertains to the truth of his claims about his *work*
—the forgiveness of sins and the conquest of death. When four men
lowered a paralytic through the roof and Jesus forgave his sins, he
answered the murmuring in the audience by healing the cripple:

> "Which is easier, to say to the paralytic, 'Your sins are forgiven you'; or to
> say 'Get up and pick up your pallet and walk'? But in order that you might
> know that the Son of Man has authority on earth to forgive sins"—he says
> to the paralytic, "I say to you, 'Get up, pick up your pallet and go to your
> house'" (Mk. 2:9-11).

The man looked no different after his sins were forgiven; the subsequent
miracle had the effect of making visible that invisible truth about his
forgiveness. In like fashion the resurrection makes our forgiveness
visible. By neither perception nor products can the believer tell whether
his sins have in fact been removed, but the resurrection makes clear
what feelings and reformed living can only confirm. Since it is a miraculous event, the resurrection aspect of the atonement actually has the
general effect of making visible several invisible truths: God's love and
holiness, the future demise of death, and the present forgiveness of sins.

The motivational value of Christ's atoning death lies in the extent of
its identification with humanity. Adopting the full degree of the human
situation demonstrates that God himself is willing to do what he calls
upon men to do so that they are without any rational or emotional
excuse for continued estrangement from the Father. It is not just Messiah's
death, but his whole life that figures into the foundation of the atonement; death resulted from his consummate devotion to the Father.

His *incarnation* unto death serves as a divine (a) word about God's
love, our sinfulness, our worth, and our eternal hope. His *obedience*
unto death serves as (b) an example for our emulation. As (c) moral
influence it elicits the high resolve to go and do likewise (Phil. 2:1-8).
He is more than a symbol of total commitment; he is an example of it.
In Christ God took his strongest initiative to bring us to the repentance
and apology conditional for forgiveness. If we were to wonder why
God could not simply forgive because of repentance, we could say
that in some respects perhaps he could have, but the atonement supplies
antecedent motivation to repent unto that forgiveness.

In regard to the motivational benefit of the atonement, the mode of
connection between Christ's work and our profit today is *perceived*

74

demonstration mediated by the words and deeds of his body the church. Even in this most elementary benefit of the cross and empty tomb, man cannot imagine that he is saving himself by responding to the example and moral influence of the cross because forgiveness is always done by the other person in an expression of mercy; but God in an expression of grace even went farther and took the initiative to love men back to himself.

Righteousness by Identification

Perfection as the object

The second reason salvation comes through Jesus Christ is that *his sinlessness qualifies him to be the divinely appointed object of identification unto perfection.* Men need to commit themselves to future righteousness as part of the condition for forgiveness of past sins. God could not just forgive men on repentance because in the reconciliation process repentance from sin implies commitment to departure from sin.

motivation to repent	repentance	confession	commitment to perfection	forgiveness

Christianity, however, does not call for commitment to perfection in the abstract, but to righteousness personalized in the concrete example of the ideal person—Jesus of Nazareth. Personalizing perfection in Jesus Christ helps focus the desire for sinlessness. Commitment to a person and his values is easier and more appropriate than commitment to impersonal principles. Here again God's provision comes from grace. In Christ he offers to accept aspiration for achievement and commitment to the Perfect One in place of personal perfection.

Because of his righteousness God appointed him (Heb. 5:1-10) to be the one with whom we identify for righteousness in God's eyes. Since "all men have sinned and fall short of God's glory" (Rom. 3:23), the ideal man needed to come from outside humanity; incarnation enabled deity to become the ideal representative of a righteous humanity. Perfected as a man through the things he suffered, Messiah was chosen to stand for the goal of righteous men.

This object of identification is set forth under *representative* imagery in Hebrews 2:5-18. Because of sin mankind cannot fulfill even his first

75

responsibility in the creation, but we do behold Jesus made lower than angels to establish residency in this creation so he could hold office over men because he was from among them.

This object of identification is likewise set forth under *priesthood* imagery in the New Testament, chiefly again in Hebrews. On the background of Psalms 110:4 the Hebrew writer discusses at length Messiah's priestly role (chapters 5-10): "The Lord swore and will not retract it: 'You are a priest forever after the order of Melchizedek.' " From this verse the writer elaborates the permanent ("forever") appointment ("the Lord *swore*"; "you *are*") of his priesthood ("a priest") in place of the Aaronic order ("after the order of Melchizedek"). By ascension he entered, not a temple made with hands, but heaven itself to appear before the face of God for us (9:24).

Being released from the personal-perfection requirement amounts to being released from the legal basis for relationship with God. Paul pictures this release from law as accomplished by death. Given for a nation of people, the Mosaic law addressed those living in the world. Under this circumstance if a person dies, he is released from the jurisdiction of the law (Rom. 7:1-6, 24-25; Gal. 2:19; cp. Rom. 6:2, 11; I Cor. 1:20; 15:54-57; cp. also II Cor. 5:14; I Pet. 4:1b). Jesus died, was therefore released from the law, and rose again to live unto God (Rom. 6:9-10). By becoming united with him and his death, we too in God's eyes pass from under the law, and its personal-perfection requirement, and its death penalty for any sin (Rom. 6:8, 11).

Christ died to sin by dying to the law that defined sin. Though born under the law (Gal. 4:4), he passed from under it, from under the sin circumstance created by it, and from the potential state of bondage issuing from any disobedience to it. "Dying to sin" is said of Christ as contemplated in his role for us (Rom. 6:10). Though still alive physically, we psychologically die to sin with him who actually died to sin and the law and rose again (Heb. 12:2-4).

God established this procedure because he is willing to release men from the personal-perfection achievement through personal identification with perfection personalized in Messiah. By so doing, God has returned to his more original and fundamental manner of relating to men—the one operative before the law, when Abraham was justified by faith (Gal. 3:17-18). The law did not represent the primary or ultimate framework of divine-human relationship. God only added it temporarily to interpersonal processes in order to define sin, increase sensitivity

76

to sin, and restrain sinning (Rom. 5:20; Gal. 3:19). The only objection the New Testament ever raises against the law is as a basis for relationship with God. As a *definition of righteousness* it was holy, just, and good (Rom. 7:12, 16; I Tim. 1:18); as a *basis for divine fellowship* it proved destructive because no one could measure up to its demands (Rom. 7:9-11, 24-25; I Cor. 15:56-58; Acts 15:10). On the one hand, under law there was no real provision for reversing an infraction of it; it offered no redemption or rehabilitation. On the other hand, all were accursed who did not continue to do all that was commanded (Gal. 3:10). Animal sacrifices could not remove sin because animals are not perfect moral beings; consequently, identification was not really a relevant mode of perfection.

In theory, during the law perfection was held up as the ideal, but there was no perfect exemplar with whom to identify for that perfection. Prior to the law there was the same ideal, but fellowship with God took place in terms of interpersonal principles of reconciliation. *After the law* the ideal is still held up, but Jesus Christ serves as the object of identification unto perfection.

In actuality, of course, the benefits of Christ's perfection unto death are retroactive to the previous age as well as perpetual for coming ages because his death "took place for the redemption of transgressions that were *under the first covenant*" (Heb. 9:15). Even though the first covenant required personal sinlessness, all those saved during its time of operation were saved by faith rather than by works (Hab. 2:4; Rom. 5:20-21?). Even for people *in the pre-Mosaic era* salvation and lostness are figured in relation to Christ from the standpoint of theory. Therefore, the gospel was preached even to the saved dead in confirmation of an eternal status judged relative to him (I Pet. 4:6); it was also announced to the lost dead from, for example, the antedeluvian world as a basis for confirmation of their destiny (I Pet. 3:18-20).

Those *outside the first covenant* and the *unevangelized after Christ* also have their judgment conducted in terms of the gospel (Rom. 2:12-16). Just as by our disobedience we classify ourselves with First Adam though we may not have realized it, so also by intent to obey conscience and limited revelation the pre-Christian saints and unevangelized elect have classified themselves with Second Adam unto salvation. This classification is a new state viewed as being upon us by way of our self-classification with Christ and because of intent and attitude to be like him.

77

Inner intent corresponds to external state while actions only tend in a growing way to be congruent with both. Acts may not always reflect basic commitments; but as people overlook them in each other in marriage, etc., so God will overlook them until such time as the invisible line is crossed and the relationship becomes void.

Perfection has always been God's requirement, whether under law or not. In the beginning it was one sin that expelled Adam from the Garden. On the other side of the coin, the law was also an expression of the will of God. The problem with the law was not its demand for perfection, but its theoretically irreversible penalty for *imperfection*. Law or the law could not therefore be an ultimate frame of reference for righteousness even during the time of its jurisdiction. Law only represents one half of the total picture for God's dealings with men. His will, or law, together with its penalties ideally set up the guidelines for human life; these matters envision total righteousness and derive from his holiness. His salvation represents the second half of the picture; it envisions a program of correction and derives from his love. In total perspective God will bear with our failures (grace) as long as we are concerned about overcoming them toward the righteousness he requires (law). The atonement bridges the gap between the goal and the present development. It allows the "now" to *become* the "not yet."

In Christ, then, there has been a transition from legal to personal bases for relationship to God. Salvation changed from the impersonal realm of legal perfection to the personal realm of faith and grace. Love in response to his love replaces fear of failure and fear of death for having failed.

Identification and forgiveness as the mode

The general proposal is that since atonement operates in the medium of interpersonal relationship, it occurs in the mind—the mind of God and in the mind of men. On the positive side the actual perfection of Jesus is connected with us by God, who identifies Jesus' righteousness with us after we identify our ideals with him completely, permanently, and exclusively. On the negative side, our sins are separated from us by our repentance and apology plus his forgiveness. "Identification" is our word for part of what we feel New Testament writers have in mind when they use the word "faith." Men "trust" that being "identified" with Jesus Messiah will have the effect of being acceptable to God. Identification and

78

forgiveness occur on the principle of appropriateness,not legal manipulation, natural causation, logical necessity, or symbolic representation.

When we seek to find in scripture the connection between Christ's
work and man's righteousness, we discover that many passages do
not in fact use very precise words to express the idea. For example,
several scriptures say that he gave himself "on behalf of" (hyper) us
(Mk. 14:24; Lk. 22:19, 20; Jn. 6:51; 10:15; 11:50, 51, 52; 18:14;
Rom. 5:6, 8; 8:32; 14:15; I Cor. 5:7; 11:24; II Cor. 5:14, 15^2, 21;
Gal. 2:20; 3:13; Eph. 5:2, 25; I Th. 5:10; Tit. 2:14; Heb. 2:9; I Pet.
2:21; 3:18; 4:1; I Jn. 3:16; cp. Jn. 13:37, 38; Acts 21:26; I Cor. 1:13)
and "on behalf of" our sins (I Cor. 15:3; Gal. 1:4; Heb. 5:3; 7:27;
10:12; cp. Heb. 5:1; 9:7). Other texts make him an offering and propitiation "concerning" (peri) our sins (Rom. 8:3; I Pet. 3:18; I Jn. 2:2^3;
4:10; cp. Heb. 10:6, 8, 18, 26). The above references talk about the
purpose of Christ's atonement, but Romans 4:25 speaks of the need
for it by saying that the Lord "was delivered up 'on account of' [dia +
acc.] our transgressions and was raised 'on account of' [dia + acc.] our
justification." With similar indefiniteness Daniel predicted generally
that seventy "hebdomads" were decreed on Israel and Jerusalem to
finish transgression, make an end to sins, make reconciliation for iniquity, and then to bring in everlasting righteousness (9:24). The indefinite
references on mode of connection speak negatively as getting rid of sin
rather than positively as receiving righteousness.

Legal manipulation. Regardless of what the authors may have had
in mind in such texts, we affirm that it was not *legal manipulation.* We
take this position despite several legal imageries used for the atonement
in the Bible. Jesus spoke on one occasion about giving his life as a
ransom "in return for" (anti) many (Mt. 20:28; Mk. 10:45). Sacrificial
language also uses legal framework to connect Christ's work with man's
profit. Substitution appears in several elements of the prediction from
Isaiah 53:5-12 as well as in Galatians 3:13: "Christ redeemed us from
the law, having become a curse for us" (cp. again Mt. 20:28; Mk. 10:45;
see also Rom. 3:21-26). The Hebrew writer says, ". . . we have been
sanctified through the offering of the body of Christ once and for all"
(10:10; cp. II Cor. 5:21). "Bearing sin" has legal sacrificial imagery,
too: "Behold, the Lamb of God who 'takes away' the sin of the world"
(Jn. 1:29). I John 3:5, ". . . he was manifested to take away sin";
similarly I Peter 2:24, ". . . who himself bore our sins in his body on the

tree." A related legal expression is Paul's statement, "The one who knew no sin he made sin for us" (II Cor. 5:21; Gal. 3:13; cp. Rom. 8:3).

Repentance, apology, identification, and forgiveness are interpersonal processes that operate on the principle of appropriateness and therefore transcend these legal manipulations. Transferring our guilt or his righteousness does not, and indeed cannot, happen strictly speaking. When literal interpretation produces such incongruities, figurativeness offers a legitimate technique for avoiding unnecessary contradictions. Consequently, we infer that scripture describes atonement under legal terms as an approximate way of saying what is really an interpersonal occurrence; that is to say, "transfer" roughly corresponds to a process occurring in God's mind. It is a way of "looking at" the sin problem and a way of "regarding" us. We are "viewed" by him as like Christ because we want to be associated with him in God's eyes. Identifying with him says something about who *we* are in the inner man and what we want to become outwardly (Rom. 7:11-25); it does not make us individually righteous by proxy. The reality set forth under the imagery of transfer is that God has offered to treat us according to our intents, aspirations, motives, commitments, and goals to be like Messiah rather than according to our achievements. Such an approach is an interpersonal one.

New Testament writers probably explained the atonement as they sometimes did because legal and sacrificial concepts already existed particularly in the minds of their Jewish readership; Jews would feel a kinship with these categories even though they were only approximate categories. They served as a psychological point of contact for communicating the Messianic good news.

Hebrews 9:22 does characterize the law as providing cleansing on a legal substitution model: "And according to the law almost all things are cleansed in blood, and without bloodshed there is no forgiveness." The law did not, however, have any means by which any real salvation could be offered, not only because it had no perfect sacrifice, we take it, but because even a perfect sacrifice could not make perfect ultimately. Christ's work could perhaps be substitutionary in terms of the Mosaic law, but that law did not establish an ultimate framework for divine-human relations. Besides, it did not establish a universal framework for divine-human relations; it applied only to a small portion of the human race. Any legal aspect of the atonement therefore must yield to the more ultimate category of personal relationship during the present age of non-legal basis for fellowship with God.

That legal categories are not ultimate is implied, not only by the primarily interpersonal nature of relationship with God and by the secondary character of law vs. faith and grace (Gal. 3:17-19); it is also implied by the omission of legal matters in presenting Christianity to Gentile audiences (Acts 14.15-10, 17.22-31). We should not then feel obligated to entertain as our ultimate conclusion the idea of legal substitution regardless of how much favorable to that model may be said in a preliminary study of the atonement or how often that model is used; it is a model still. Having given the law, God needed to provide a release from its perfection requirement; therefore, for Jews, legal release from sin was appropriate expression because they had previously become legally bound by sin.

Substitution is involved in the sense that (a) Second Adam replaced First Adam as the object of man's identity. Jesus died *for* sin as a "last measure of devotion" in establishing the perfection that qualified him to replace Adam, who died *from* sin.

Substitution is involved also in the sense that (b) Christ's personal perfection replaces necessity for our own perfection as requisite for divine fellowship. The "Christ ideal" (law) corresponds with divine holiness and justice while the "identification principle" (faith) corresponds with divine love and grace. Christ's personal perfection reaffirms God's ideal so that commitment to him and aspiration to be like him can be offered to man "in place of" being what he is. Commitment to Christ in his righteousness and aspiration to become righteous like him replace present accomplishment of righteousness in ourselves.

(c) From the standpoint of the Mosaic law, Christ's death may be regarded as functioning vicariously after the likeness of animal sacrifice. The Mosaic law does not represent an ultimate frame of reference on salvation matters, but Jesus Christ did come in the train of the law. He came of woman, that is, to redeem flesh-and-blood human beings (Gal. 4:4; Heb. 2:14-16); he came under the law to redeem men under the law (Gal. 4:5). Even though the law did not operate in terms of ultimate principles, Christ's death on the cross fulfilled its demands in the lesser plane of legal process. Because it is an event, Christ's death can have multifaceted significance so that it can accomplish the demands of the law on a penal substitutionary model while at the same time accomplishing the real and ultimate basis for righteousness through identification in the interpersonal realm. Therefore Calvary sufficed for saving Jews as Jews but also sufficed for saving Gentiles as Gentiles. In other words, it satisfied the real requirements of the Mosaic law while at the same time it satisfied the real requirements of personal relationship with a holy God.

(d) For affective purposes Christ's death may be viewed as a substitute for my death even though in cognitive terms substitution does not really happen. In substitutionary atonement the event on Golgotha is described "phenomenologically"; that is, to the sinner Christ's death has the appearance of standing instead of his own death. Substitution can be the way the execution of a sinless man looks. As long as we do not carry this beyond the affective way the event looks, regarding him as a substitute provides a way of helping our feelings get hold of the love he demonstrated toward us in maintaining for our benefit his righteousness to the point of death.

In respect to salvation Christ's death carries two thrusts: the *preliminary thrust* comes in the Old Testament mold of substituting an animal's death for the sinner's death; inasmuch as physical death ends probation, personal death for sin would amount to eternal death under law. In terms of the law Christ comes in and takes the sinner's place. The more *ultimate thrust* comes, not in the negative withholding of *penalty for sin* by putting it on another, but in the positive establishment of an *object of righteousness* identified with by the sinner.

Besides penal substitution as an ultimate frame of reference, our stricture on legal manipulation includes the idea of sinfulness or righteousness by birth—a concept contrary to the nature of guiltiness or guiltlessness. We do not get into Adam, or Satan, legally by physical birth, nor do we get into Second Adam that way. We enter both Adam and Christ by active, personal identification. By our behavior we say in effect, "That's the kind of person I am, too"; consequently, God regards us in terms of our implicit ideals in either direction. By disobedience (distrust) we identify with First Adam who disobeyed unto death, and therefore we share his penalty, state, and destiny. By obedience (trust) we identify with Second Adam who obeyed unto death, and therefore we share his blessing, state, and destiny. Our standing and state before God, both as to lostness and salvation, come by the appointment of the Father relative to our deeds; and Adam and Messiah serve as representative heads of their respective "kinds of mankind."

Distrust identifies with Adam; trust identifies with Christ. Therefore lostness and salvation in the larger sense lie at the corporate level. Because

Adam began the race and was the race, he stands by appointment as representative of all who become part of him by conducting themselves as he did. Because Messiah began the new race and was the race, he stands by appointment as representative of all who put trust in him.

Consequently, we can speak of substitutionary atonement in that by appointment the Messiah "replaces" Adam as representative head of the race. Representatively the obedience of one can justify many even as representatively the disobedience of one can constitute many as sinners (Rom. 5:18-19, cp. 12-17). Not only then can this one man "die for many" *men*, but by his one act of righteousness can many *sins* be overcome (Rom. 5:18). Identification with either primary representative establishes the state of the one who identifies with him. Strictly speaking, Jesus Christ did not die for anyone's sins directly or specifically; he died for them inclusively by dying to sin as such (Rom. 6:10). His refusal to compromise his calling led to the death that climaxed his sinlessness. Because of that, God designated him as the replacement for Adam. Faith puts trust in Messiah; it believes that God has appointed him the new representative of the race so that repentance amounts to renouncing identification with Adam.

Natural causation. If atonement operates in the medium of interpersonal relationship, not only do salvation and lostness not operate in the legal realm; they do not operate in the realm of natural causation. Sin is not the sort of thing that can be washed away with *water* even though Ananias told Paul to be baptized and wash away his sins (Acts 22:16). Water only symbolizes the invisible reality that takes place in the mind of man and God.

Similarly the *blood of Jesus* does not wash away, dissolve, or absolve sin even though Hebrews says that it cleanses our conscience from dead works (Heb. 9:14; Rev. 1:5). We mean this not simply in the obvious sense that washing in blood cannot make garments white (Rev. 7:14) or clean consciences literally, but in the sense that natural causality is not involved at all in connecting Christ to us. Sin is not "something"; therefore it cannot be removed causally, but must be removed by reckoning. "Blood" atonement means that our reconciliation to God entails unnatural death. Jesus did not die of old age, disease, or malnutrition; he experienced violent death—the shedding of blood. That incarnate obedience unto violent death qualified him in the Father's mind for appointment as the Sinless One with whom men are called to identify as a condition for forgiveness. Atonement derives from Christ's obedience to the extent of bloodshed, not from the blood shed.

Old Testament *animal sacrifices* stressed the shedding of blood for the same reason the New Testament antitype did. Although temporally they preceded the reality they foreshadowed, logically they succeeded the obedience-unto-bloodshed that eventuated in the cross and empty tomb. The Levitical sacrifices anticipated the Messianic self-sacrifice, and Messiah's crucifixion is cast in the imagery of those Levitical offerings; hence, the common element of blood receives considerable attention, but this emphasis should not obscure the reality itself, which is only being set forth under approximate models used prior to it. Therefore the death of Christ is not the whole basis of atonement, but epitomizes it as the highest expression of Messiah's sinlessness. It is then sinlessness unto bloodshed that establishes the basis of atonement.

Logical necessity. Because atonement operates interpersonally according to the principle of appropriateness, Christ's death does not have to be a mathematical equivalent, or logical necessity, at least in regard to motivation and perfection. It is at least conceivable that Jesus of Nazareth would not have had to die even though it is *most* appropriate that his obedience be demonstrated to this extent in order to become a complete opposite of what it antithesized and in order to demonstrate in the basis for atonement the extent of obedience his followers are called upon to perform. Jesus does pray in the Garden that, if possible, the crucifixion might be avoided (Mt. 26:39; Mk. 14:35-36; Lk. 22:42; cp. Jn. 18:11). That impossibility is sufficiently understood as an impossibility given the Father's will for him instead of an impossibility based on the nature of the case. The reason for the Father's will that he die came, we infer, from the added appropriateness of appointing Jesus as Messiah; it also set the stage for resurrection in proof of his claims.

Some advantages can be seen in not having logical necessity for the death of Jesus. For one thing (a) there is no excuse for supposing then that Judas Iscariot was tricked into denying Christ or fated beyond his control to betray him and then to suffer the consequences of self-destruction for his remorse (Mt. 27:3-10; Acts 1:18-19) and to "go to his place" (Acts 1:25).

Likewise (b) there is no reason to think that the Jews were unconditionally predetermined to reject their Messiah in order to make sure that atonement came about for them and for the Gentiles. Both facts were predicted, but prediction is as much after the fact logically as any gospel account of what happened. His death would certainly happen, but it did not have to happen of necessity. Had the Jews accepted him, the program of world wide reconciliation to God could have gone forward without his death. Had the Jews accepted their Messiah, the preceding prophecy would have been worded otherwise and the system of animal sacrifice would not have been divinely instituted in anticipation of his death.

(c) Jesus' freedom in self-giving is also accentuated so that his obedience unto death for us can be all the more appreciated. He was not forced by fate or logic, but drawn by the will of the Father and his love for men (Mt. 26:39, 42, 44; Mk. 14:35-36, 39; Lk. 22:42); for he lay down his life "of himself"; he had "the *right* to lay it down" (Jn. 10:17-18). He told Peter in Gethsemane that even at that late date he could call more than twelve legions of angels to his rescue (Mt. 26:53). The number of times he did not let the leaders take him (Lk. 4:28-30; Jn. 8:59; 10:39; 18:6; cp. 19:10-11) confirms that his offering was free will. Jesus' perfect obedience short of death might have sufficed for appropriateness, but in that he obeyed to the point of death by crucifixion he is a most appropriate source of our salvation.

Symbolic representation. Our point here has been to show that Christ's work and our need are not connected by legality, necessity, or causation, but by correlation because of the choice of God. Lack of logical necessity for Jesus' death must, of course, be differentiated from lack of necessity for the atonement itself. If in our imperfection we could have commended ourselves to God by any means, Christ died for nothing (Gal. 2:21). For that very reason salvation is by grace (appointment), not by works (causation).

This last distinction leads us to reaffirm our rejection of *symbolic representation* as the essence of the atonement. Jesus did not just represent something; he provided something: he provided the personal object of identification unto righteousness and the subsequent transcendence of physical death. Though we do not wish to theorize on whether God could have accomplished salvation some other way, we do wish to emphasize that it was necessary to do something, given the nature and condition of man who needs motivation, the nature of God who requires righteousness, and the fact of death that he had pronounced on mankind in order to maintain control over sin.

Baptism as the event

Identification describes the mode of connection between Christ's perfection and ours. In keeping with this fact, God established baptism for expressing formally the desire for this identification. Immersion in water re-enacts pictorially in the experience of each believer the distinctive and epitomizing act of the Sinless One—his death, burial, and resurrection. By implication it commits the candidate to the resurrected life:

> Or are you ignorant that as many of us as were baptized into Christ Jesus were baptized into his death? Therefore we were buried with him through baptism into death that as Christ was raised from the dead by the Father's glory, we also should walk in newness of life. For if we have become united with the likeness of his death, we shall on the other hand also be united with the likeness of his resurrection (Rom. 6:3-5).

The Father appointed Messiah as the object of identity; we culminate initial identification with Messiah by obedience in baptism, and God regards us under that identity unto forgiving our sins. Instead of being baptized unto Moses (I Cor. 10:2), unto Paul (I Cor. 1:13), or unto John's baptism (Acts 19:3), we are baptized unto the Christ. Even as faith involves identification with Christ, so baptism is an act of faith because it is an act of identification. Natural causality, logical necessity, and legal requirement have no place here. Communion, we may add then, reidentifies the communicant with that death and expresses continued participation in that commitment.

Sacrificial concepts, satisfaction of God's honor, ransom to Satan for his slaves, manifestation of divine justice, cleansing, healing, and the like are several approximate models capturing aspects of human righteousness on the basis of Jesus' blood atonement. They are *post facto* interpretations of the Christ event in terms of analogous events and functional equivalents. Nevertheless, even though the law was not an ultimate frame of reference, having established the personal perfection requirement in the law as well as in the beginning, God needed to provide a way to transcend the personal perfection requirement or he could not maintain his self-consistency and at the same time save anyone. Similarly, God needed to provide a way to transcend the death penalty prescribed by the law and in the beginning or he could not maintain his self-consistency and at the same time save anyone from death. The atonement process centers in the righteousness provision

86

because righteousness results from the motivation engendered as the first benefit and leads to resurrection which overcomes death that results from sin.

In regard to the righteousness benefit of the atonement, the mode of connection between Christ's work and our profit is mutual identifica tion comprised of repentance, apology, and commitment on the one side and acceptance plus forgiveness on the other; in other words, grace from God and faith from man. Man cannot imagine that he is saving himself by identifying himself with the Sinless One because only by God's prior appointment does identification with Christ have anything to do with his relating to us differently. Salvation is by grace before it is by faith.

Triumph over Death

The third reason salvation comes through Jesus Christ is that *he is the one by whom God chose to overcome death in men.* Obviously, men need death removed, but God could not just forgive sin on repentance because in consequence of human sin he had already determined that death would be the experience of all men: ". . . it is appointed to men once to die and after this, judgment . . ." (Heb. 9:27; cp. Gen. 3:19; Rom. 5:12, 14, 19; I Cor. 15:22). Having pronounced a penalty upon disobedience (Gen. 2:16-17; Rom. 6:23; James 1:15), he could not maintain his holiness without exacting the penalty. He would have become unholy by inconsistency if he had "gone back on his word." Since the penalty is death, an impossible situation is created for man because death also ends man's probation for eternal life.

Purposes of death

In the nature of things death and its accompanying experiences became a way of *maintaining control over men* by limiting the extent of their disobedience. Had God relied simply on dynamic processes for restoring man to fellowship, he would have had no recourse against those who would not repent. If God did not righteously visit wrath on sin, he would not be judge of the world (Rom. 3:6); mankind would not be under his direction. Since Yahweh is a God of principle, not just a God of power, he revealed beforehand the consequence of distrusting him: "In the day that you eat from it you shall surely die" (Gen.

2:17). Human death does not just establish a framework for the progress of the race; it limits the expression of evil:

> And Yahweh God said, "Behold, man is become like one of us [by exercising autonomy while at the same time?] knowing good and evil. And now lest he put forth his hand and partake of the tree of life and live forever—"; therefore Yahweh God sent him out of the Garden of Eden to till the ground from which he was taken. So he drove the man out and placed cherubs at the east of the Garden of Eden and the flame of a sword that turned every way to keep the way of the tree of life (Gen. 3:22-24).

Communication. At the same time, death and associated weaknesses have the function of *communicating the need for right relationship with God.* They show unequivocally a person's secondary status in the universe so that along with other factors they prepare him for seriously hearing the good news about reconciliation.

The stark reality of pain and death function like corporal punishment of a child. Without perceiving the importance of the "spiritual" values that govern his discipline, he may not see how—or care how—misconduct has antisocial effects. Spanking symbolically substitutes more perceptible experiences for the real effects unacceptable behavior brings on a person and his relationships. Punishment is not for venting a parent's anger, but for enhancing the quality of the child. Similarly, suffering and death do not have the character of hate, but of discipline. They force the human consciousness to perceive more keenly the importance of intangible verities for authentic existence. Pain quickens the will out of its spiritual lethargy; fear produces practical motivation to ask ultimate questions and hear ultimate answers; restraint gives perspective for appreciating the hope of resurrection and the removal of this-worldly limitations. Thus death and related events control the creature and communicate God's truth to him.

Penalty. Death also functioned for *exacting penalty on Adam for his guilt.* This function must be stated carefully because punishment implies correction that leads to future behavior, which in Adam's case may imply more than revelation warrants; but "penalty" leaves open the possibility of irreversible consequence. We have not said that death is the penalty for sin as a general truth, because (a) two men did not die, whom we doubt were perfect (cp. Rom. 5:14), and because (b) death occurs in infants against whom God does not reckon sin (Rom. 7:9-11).

Physical death as penalty for sin also does not, strictly speaking, plague each man because of Adam's sin since (c) God does not punish one person for another person's guilt (Ezek. 18:4, 19-20; Deut, 24:16; II Kg. 14:6; II Ch. 25:4; Jer. 31:29-30; cf. Lam. 5:7). *Guilt* is personal; therefore penalty and punishment for guilt are personal. Consequently, the uniform experience of death does not have the quality of punishment for Adam's guilt but at best for our own. The nature of society does mean that many others experience *suffering* because of the sin of one. Similarly death has come upon all men either because they themselves have all sinned, practically speaking (Rom. 5:12; cp. 2:12), and therefore share death with Adam, or because natural and social vehicles transmit death even to those who have not sinned, including children and forgiven men. "The fathers ate sour grapes and the children's teeth are set on edge" (Jer. 31:29-30; Ezek. 18:2) does describe suffering, but not punishment. Death is penalty to the sinner, but simply pain to the sinless. In general, then, suffering and death serve the divine purposes as restraints and motivators.

God has chosen in Jesus Christ not to remove death and suffering, but to transcend them. Death and suffering are remedied by resurrection so that the control factor still operates in human existence. God does

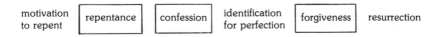

not become inconsistent in transcending death because he did not say death for sin was necessarily permanent or irreversible. Death has been the lot of every man except Enoch and Elijah (Gen. 5:24; II Kg. 2:1-12); it will continue to be the case except for the generation of saints alive at Christ's return (I Cor. 15:51-54). We understand that divine appointment establishes the connection between Christ's death-resurrection and our resurrection at the last trump. Since Christ is the one with whom men are identified unto resurrection, Christ is the *first*fruits of the dead followed at his coming by those who are his (I Cor. 15:23). Being the first to rise never to die again, he is the author of eternal salvation to all who obey him (Heb. 5:9; cp. 2:10; 12:2). Death is not *removed* by living eternally or *replaced* by translation into a higher realm, but it is *overcome* by resurrection.

Purposes of Christ's resurrection

Physical death. From a negative standpoint, the purpose of Christ's death-resurrection was evidently not to substitute for the *physical* aspect of human death because obviously (a) the saved still die and (b) sinless children sometimes die, too. (c) Death reigned even where no law required the death penalty (Rom. 5:12-14). Therefore death is a race experience irrespective of personal guilt so that sinlessness is not necessarily implied by the cases of Enoch and Elijah. (d) Christ's death cannot substitute for permanent death either, because he did not die permanently. Moreover, (e) only one man died on Calvary, yet millions have died since the origin of the race. Messiah's physical death could at best have substituted only for the first representative's death, but (f) Christ's death in substitution for Adam's death would mean that the second death canceled out the first; apparently in that case no one would ever have died because Christ's death had retroactive force (Heb. 9:15). In other words, from what actually happens to men and from what actually happened to Christ, by the nature of the case the Sinless One cannot be a substitute for the sinner. As to physical death he did not die in our place, but simply on behalf of us so that death is overcome in resurrection.

Spiritual death. Evidently the purpose of Christ's death-resurrection was also not to substitute for the *spiritual* aspect of death. From any approach a paradox admittedly exists: in one respect Jesus was carrying perfection to the ultimate; in another respect, he was separated from the Father according to precise substitutionary theory. We might try to explain this by (1) his *two positions*: as to himself he was united with God because he accomplished the Father's will, but supposedly the Father's will was for him to bear sinners' penalty, which was separation from the Father. It would seem hard to spank an older child for a younger one's disobedience and at the same time be feeling united with the older one for his own goodness in accepting the spanking. That Jesus was both accepted because he had no sin and rejected because he bore our sins seems artificial and contrived because of the interpersonal medium in which the atonement primarily operates. Even if this reconstruction makes sense in terms of the legal structure of Mosaic sacrificial theory, it does not make sense in terms of the more ultimate framework that lies beyond the approximations of legal constructs.

There would be awkwardness also into appealing to (2) *two viewpoints,* as if from Jesus' point of view he was separated from God but from the Father's he was united with him. This arrangement does not accomplish a substitution since the original penalty was separated in the Father's eyes as well. Similarly we would run into difficulty by referring to (3) his *two natures*: as deity he was related to God, but as humanity he was separated from him. But Jesus was one person, one consciousness, one entity, however the divine-human relationship within him is to be conceived.

The cry of dereliction presses home this difficulty all the more if the words of Jesus meant spiritual as well as physical abandonment when he cried out, "My God, my God, why have you forsaken me?" (Mt. 27:46; Mk. 15:34; Ps. 22:1). The paradox does not disappear by supposing (4) *two events*, as if Jesus quoted the Psalm to call attention to the fact that this event fulfilled the one predicted by the Psalm; for as a prediction the Psalm still refers to Jesus' future experience. Psalm 22, however, does not require a forsaking of the speaker in any sense beyond physical death. Consequently, Jesus' quotation of it does not have to mean more than being forsaken unto physical death, and does not therefore lend support to the idea of Jesus' estrangement from the Father. For the benefit of those who witnessed his death, we may suppose that he used the first line of the Psalm in order to express his own feelings and connect the Psalm with the present event.

The cry from the cross better reveals (5) *two aspects* of his person. In our own experience we sometimes know the truth but do not feel that way. It is not difficult to imagine that in his dying moments he knew he had done what the Father sent him to do: "It is finished" (Jn. 19:30); yet he felt abandonment in his agony: "Why have you forsaken me?" The scene in Gethsemane depicts a similar situation: he knows he has come for this very reason, yet he feels overwhelming emotional stress from the prospects at dawn. We infer from the cry of dereliction that there is inadequate reason for believing that anything more than abandonment to physical death was objectively involved in Christ's death.

This conclusion only brings us back, however, to the original question of how one obedient man's death relates to removing death for other, disobedient men. Our proposal is simply that this paradox, like any other, is solved by distinguishing words from realities—seeing substitution words as models instead of realities.

From a positive standpoint, then, Christ's resurrection as a triumph over death was directed toward us. Its meaning was not directed toward the Father as if Jesus proved himself to God by conquering death, because God was the one who raised Jesus from the dead (Acts 2:24, 32; 3:15, 26; 4:10, etc., yet contrast Jn. 10:17-18). From the *physical standpoint* the message to us speaks unequivocally for (a) the certainty of life after life. From the *spiritual standpoint* resurrection says that (b) the sting of death has been removed because it is not permanent and because guilt has been removed through Christ; guilt is what makes death especially hard to take. Jesus' resurrection by the power of the Father is something like a drama acted out to the human audience; it is like the brazen serpent to which we can look and be healed from the physically and psychologically fatal effects of sin.

From Christ's death and resurrection also comes (c) the reversal of uncorrectable effects of previous sin. Forgiveness, etc., take care of the interpersonal effects of sin; restitution as part of repentance can undo many damages. Resurrection will need to rectify many other irreversible effects of sin from drug abuse, brutality, and the like. In the loss of a murdered father, no specific, one-for-one correction is possible, given the nature of the world God has made; but the generally higher quality of the incorruptible realm will more than "make up for" the sufferings of this present age (Rom. 8:18; Heb. 11:24-26).

The problem of physical death is overcome through Christ, but the manner in which it is overcome is not by strict substitutionary process. In his own death he did not substitute for every sin specifically or for every man individually, nor did he substitute for Adam and thus for every man corporately. Rather than being a *substitute* for Adam, he was a *replacement* for Adam and then not directly in the case of physical death, but directly as an object of identification unto righteousness and then unto resurrection. Conquering death comes indirectly from being "in (the category of) Christ." Instead of taking Adam's or our punishment on himself when he died, he suffered unto death as the culminating act of obedience to the Father, thus establishing his perfection to that degree so that our righteousness and our resurrection come by appointment (grace) because of identification (faith) with him who was righteous and rose again. The precise "cause" of righteousness and resurrection is an act of the divine *will* on the principle of *appropriateness* through *identification* in such a way that divine *consistency* is maintained in a framework of *interpersonal dynamics.*

In regard to the resurrection benefit of the atonement, the mode of

92

connection between Christ's work and our profit is again *mutual identification* comprised of obedience unto death and our commitment to Christ unto death. Here most clearly salvation comes by grace through faith in him who raised up Jesus from the grave.

Summary and Conclusion

Elements of the atonement are supplied by God primarily and man secondarily. Because of love and holiness God designed to provide salvation for men through Jesus Christ. (1) The Son qualified himself to be an appropriate savior by completely identifying with the human circumstance and perfectly obeying the Father to the extent of violent death. (a) *Motivation* to righteousness comes most particularly through his perfect example. (2) God appointed him as the basis for the other benefits men need: (b) *righteousness* and (c) *resurrection*. Application of these benefits comes by appointment as well. The life, death, and resurrection jointly contribute to atonement. Death consummates Christ's righteousness and his motivating power so as to transcend personal perfection; resurrection actualizes and demonstrates the transcendence of death. (3) Men identify themselves with Christ by repentance, confession, and commitment. (4) God forgives sin and appoints resurrection on the principle of appropriateness in that he regards men in terms of their identity with Christ. Repentance, apology, and forgiveness constitute the orienting pegs of reconciliation operating horizontally among men and vertically with God. Motivation, righteousness, and resurrection are the additional elements involved in the Christian application of this process to divine-human reconciliation.

Connectors in the atonement are primarily personal. Instead of natural causality, logical necessity, and legal transfer we understand that personal connectors tie the process together: identification (faith) and appointment (grace). Identification with the perfect person transcends the requirement for personal perfection. Appropriateness and correlation describe the nature of relationship between man's need and God's benefits.

Interpersonal relationship is the primary category in the atonement. Reconciliation is the aim. Divine appointment and human identification are the connectors. Motivation, righteousness, and resurrection are the benefits. Repentance, confession, and commitment are the conditions. Salvation is reconciliation and Christ is the "source" of man's identity with God.

Part IV—The Scope of Salvation

Chapter Eight

LIMITED UNIVERSALISM

Introduction

No more familiar passage of scripture can be found than the classic statement on salvation given in John 3:14-18:

> Even as Moses lifted up the serpent in the wilderness so it is necessary for the Son of Man to be lifted up, in order that everyone who believes in him may have eternal life. For in this way God loved the world, so that he gave his only Son in order that everyone who believes in him may not perish but have eternal life. For God did not send the Son into the world in order that he might condemn the world, but in order that the world might be saved through him. The one who believes in him is not condemned, but the one who does not believe stands condemned already because he has not believed in the name of the only Son of God.

These verses introduce some great truths about salvation, including (a) the sequence of love and holiness (cp. 12:47), (b) the nature of divine love, and (c) the relationship of the universal and the limited in atonement. The last item is the subject of the next three chapters. "Universal" and "limited" refer to the scope of the atonement. They deal with whether God intended to establish salvation as a possibility for all people or for some, and with how the "all" and the "some" relate in the atonement.

Intent of the Atonement: Universal

The following pages survey the evidence for what may be called "limited universalism." In this view salvation is "universal" insofar as God intended to establish it and make it available for everyone; salvation is "limited" because not everyone will accept it. The work of Christ produces a universalism that is limited because God intended in the atonement to save *all* that *believe.*

For everyone after Christ

Three passages in Paul's writings describe the overall scope of salvation. After discussing the role of Jews and Gentiles in the divine plan,

Paul sums up his treatment by saying, "For God has imprisoned them all in disobedience in order that he might have mercy on them all" (Rom. 11:32). The apostle's concern does not lie at a general class level so as to say simply that both Jews and Gentiles benefit from God's mercy. (a) He does not say "that he might have mercy on *both*," but "that he might have mercy on *all*." (b) As surely as all were "disobedient" and "imprisoned," "all" are objects of God's mercy unto eternal salvation.

Near the end of his missionary career, Paul wrote to Timothy, "For to this end we work and strive because we have set our hope on the living God, who is the Savior of all men, specifically of faithful ones" (I Tim. 4:10). At about the same time he instructed his co-worker Titus in the truth he should exhort everyone to follow: "For God's grace has appeared, bringing salvation to all men, instructing us . . . to live seriously and righteously and piously in the present age" (Tit. 2:11-12). The exhortation applies to older men and women, younger men and women, and even to slaves (2:1-10). In all these representative classes "God's grace" instructs "us" on life conduct, whoever we are. As surely as God's grace is for instructing all men, it is for saving them all; and that grace is for "all" in the same sense—individually, not just some out of all (kinds of) men.

Prompting the atonement. Stated positively, salvation means that God wants all men to be saved. His love for the world prompts concern for all men according to John 3:16. Especially in John's writings the "world" stands for men separated from the Father: 15:19; 16:8, 11, etc.; yet God "loved" the world in sending his Son. What the love of God is like may be seen from the kind of love men are to have for one another in order to be like him. Therefore the apostle John writes in his first epistle:

> Beloved, let us love one another because love is of God and everyone who loves has been begotten by God and knows God. The one who does not love does not know God because he is love. In this the love of God was manifested among us because God has sent his only Son into the world in order that we might live through him. In this is love, not that *we* have loved God, but that *he* loved us and sent his Son as a propitiation for our sins. Beloved, if God in this way loved us, we also ought to love one another (4:7-11).

This love of God is a saving love for all men, not just for the elect as shown by (a) the parallel between "world" and "us." The last sentence

95

of the quotation bears close resemblance to John 3:16, where it also speaks of God *in this way* loving the world. Here in 4:11 it speaks of God *in this way* loving us. The parallelism between "us" and "world" seems apparent so that one equals the other. Even within I John 4:7-11 parallelism exists between "the love of God *manifested* among *us*" and "sending his *Son* into the *world.*" Paul confirms by saying, "God commended his love toward us in that while we were still sinners Christ died for us" (Rom. 5:8; cp. II Cor. 5:14a + 19; Eph. 2:4-6; II Th. 2:16-17; Rev. 1:5).

That God's saving love reaches out to all men is also apparent from (b) the ones men are to love when loving as he did. Although the quotation from I John 4 calls for love among Christian brothers, it obviously does not mean to limit love to those *already saved.* Taking "brothers" as excluding non-Christians would be the same kind of error the Jews made on the commandment "love your neighbor as yourself." God did not mean neighbor vs. non-Jew (Lk. 10:25-27), or neighbor vs. personal enemy (Mt. 5:43-48). In contrast to such weakening of the law, Jesus commands his followers to be perfect as the heavenly Father is perfect (5:48). "If you love those that love you," you are doing no more than anyone else does—publicans and Gentiles included. Therefore "love your enemies" (Lk. 6:27-36; cp. 23:34; Acts 7:60).

It would likewise be meaningless to limit love to those we believe will respond to the gospel later—the *future saved*, as if to say that God loves only those unsaved who will later become part of the saved. I John 3:17 defines the love of God: "But whoever has the world's possessions and sees his brother having need and closes his compassions from him, how does the love of God dwell in him?" "When Jesus saw the multitudes, he was moved with compassion because they were worried and scattered like sheep having no shepherd" (Mt. 9:36). Paul therefore tells the Romans, "If your enemy is hungry, feed him. If he is thirsty, give him something to drink. For by doing this you will heap coals of fire on his head. Do not be conquered by evil, but conquer evil with good" (Rom. 12:20-21; cp. Prov. 25:21-22; II Kg. 6:8-23).

What governs interpersonal relationships like these also governs ministry. The "love of Christ" constrained Paul to preach the gospel to all men inasmuch as in Christ God was reconciling the *world* to himself; the ministry he gave Paul therefore was a ministry of reconciliation to all men (II Cor. 5:14-19). God has compassion on the lost unto the

96

fulfillment of their needs so that he calls on his servants and ministers to do the same. We have then no reason to believe that God's love and compassion are any less in salvation than in other matters of need.

According to I Timothy 2:4 God our Savior "wants all men to be saved and to come to a knowledge of truth." All kinds of men come within the scope of his interest including Gentiles (2:7) as well as Jews, and rulers (2:2) as well as commoners. Christianity is not a race religion, a poor man's faith, or an elitist cult for the upper classes. It is for all men because God wants all men to be saved.

Stated negatively, salvation means that God does not want any man to perish. In the Old Testament the prophet Ezekiel expresses God's attitude toward the wicked when he says, "'Do I have any pleasure in the death of the wicked,' says the Lord Yahweh, 'and not rather that he turn from his way and live?'" (18:23). After he tells transgressors to throw away all their transgressions and to make for themselves a new heart and a new spirit, he says, "'Why will you die, O house of Israel? I have no pleasure in the death of the one who dies,' says the Lord Yahweh. 'Therefore turn and live'" (18:32; cp. 33:11). The difference between dying and living depends on whether the transgressor will turn from his way of acting. God loves the wicked; so he wants them to repent, or "turn from their way." He loves the righteous, too; so he does not allow the unrepentant wicked to go on endlessly ruining life for the righteous; consequently, God assigns death to the wicked even though he has no pleasure in their death.

In the New Testament, II Peter 3:9 makes one of the clearest statements on God's compassion for all men: "The Lord is not slow of promise as some reckon slowness, but is patient toward you, not desiring any to perish, but all to come to repentance." Three features of this text and its context make it important for our present discussion. (a) *The ancient flood and the future fire* show that the author is not thinking about "all" the elect, but all men generally. God's destruction of the ancient world involved everyone living at the time; the future destruction of the present world will do the same.

(b) *The delay of the consummation* implies further that natural depravity is not the reason people fail to repent. Divine patience could not then contribute to avoiding destruction; consequently, the lack of universal salvation is not due finally to divine choice, but human disbelief. Delaying the consummation to allow for repentance indicates God's desire for the salvation of all men.

(c) *No desire for "any" to perish* makes clear, of course, that "all" does not mean a general rule with untold exceptions. More importantly "any" also indicates that God's "desiring" is not a neutral willingness, but a positive wanting. He is not passively willing to let people come while not caring whether they stay away and perish. Not desiring that "any" perish equals desiring that all repent. God does not "actively-desire" for "any" to perish; hence, he does "actively-desire" all to repent. The meaning of desire has to be the same *for* repentance as it is *against* perishing: ". . . he is patient toward you, not actively-desiring any to perish, but [actively-desiring] all to come to repentance." It is not therefore possible to understand God's wanting as a complacent thing that withholds love by not supplying whatever is needful for men to repent. The love of God would not abide in a God like that (cp. I Jn. 3:17).

A final passage about not wanting any to perish comes from the lips of Jesus when he takes a little child in his arms and teaches his disciples about greatness in the kingdom of heaven: "Thus it is not the will of your Father who is in heaven that one of these little ones should perish" (Mt. 18:14). What holds true for all little children must hold true for all people regardless of age.

Establishing the atonement. Prompted by love for all men and a desire that none perish, God sent his Son to establish the basis for salvation. Obviously, the scope of salvation for which Christ's death laid a foundation would be as broad as the love that prompted him to lay it. Accordingly, John 3:14-18 correlates the breadth of God's love and the Son's salvation when it says both that "God loved the world" (3:16) and that "the world should be saved through him" (3:17). As surely as the brazen serpent was lifted up for all Israelites to look on and be cured from snake bite, the Son of man was lifted up for all the world to see and be cured from sin.

Hebrews 2 explains the Messianic work in conjunction with the role of mankind described in Psalms 8:4-6. The writer explains that since mankind has not succeeded as caretaker of the creation, the incarnation of the Son serves, among other things, to qualify him for holding this office conjointly with his work of sanctifying men from sin: "We do see Jesus, made a little while lower than the angels on account of the suffering of death, crowned with glory and honor in order that by the grace of God he might taste death on behalf of every person" (2:9).

98

Immediately after saying "every person," the writer adds a word about "bringing many *sons* into glory" (2:10) and about "sanctifying" them (2:11).

Having made some comments about Psalms 22:22 and Isaiah 8:17-10, the author returns to comment further on the Son's death:

> Since then the children have shared blood and flesh, he also in like manner partook of the same things in order that through death he might bring to nothing him who has the power of death, that is, the devil; and might deliver these as many as were enslaved by fear of death through all their living (2:14-15).

The obvious purpose of his death extended as widely as those enslaved by fear of death. Inasmuch as all men die (cp. 9:27), his death was on behalf of all men.

In a central prediction on the work of Christ the Suffering Servant Poem says, "We all have strayed like sheep; everyone of us has turned to his own way, and Yahweh has made to land on him the iniquity of us all" (Isa. 53:6). The extent of the iniquity put on the Servant corresponds with the extent of those who have strayed away. To press farther, the prophet declares in the two preceding verses that the griefs and sorrows he bore included those belonging to people who "esteemed him smitten by God and afflicted" (cp. Mt. 27:39-44; Mk. 15:27-32; Lk. 23:35). He died for the very ones that mocked his rejection by God.

The apostle Paul writes in II Corinthians 5:14-19 a significant passage on the universal meaning of Christ's death unto reconciliation:

> For the love of Christ constrains us because we reckon this: that one died on behalf of all; hence, they all have died. And he died on behalf of all in order that the living might no longer live to themselves but to him who on their behalf died and arose. Therefore we from now on know no one according to the flesh. Even though we have known Christ according to the flesh, we however now no longer know him. Therefore if anyone is in Christ he is a new creature. The old things have passed away; behold, things have become new. And all things are from God who reconciled us to himself through Christ and gave us the ministry of reconciliation; that is, in Christ God was reconciling the world to himself, not reckoning their trespasses to them and having committed to us the message of reconciliation.

Although the text may be interpreted differently depending on some prior understandings, 5:14 must mean by "Christ died for all" some idea that can yield the inference that "all died," or "all have died." At least four reconstructions can be put on the verse, but we prefer the following: if Christ died for all, then all have died by virtue of their sin; in other words, that all are sinners may be inferred from the fact that Christ died for them all. Therefore the love of Christ constrained Paul to make known to all men that Christ died for them all to reconcile them to God. The apostle no longer knew men or Christ himself in terms of their flesh (Joel 2:28)—as to whether they were Gentiles or Jews because that distinction no longer exists in God's mind: "The old things have passed away; things have become new" (II Cor. 5:17).

Regardless of how correct the above explanation is, "all who *died* means died spiritually, and Christ's death was for the purpose of bene- fiting them all. Christ did die for all (14, 15); the "all" is as inclusive as "the living" (15) and as those who should "stop living to themselves" (15). The "all" is as broad as those who are not to be known according to the flesh (16). It includes as many as are in the world (19). As far as God at least is concerned, the work of reconciliation through the death of Christ includes everyone.

A similar text is found in Romans 5, where Paul contrasts the respec- tive effects of Adam and Christ for human kind.

> So then as through one transgression judgment came to all men to con- demnation, so also through one act of righteousness the free gift came to all men to justification of life. For as through the disobedience of one man the many were made sinners, so also through the obedience of the one the many will be made righteous (5:18-19; cp. I Cor. 15:20-22).

The free gift covers as much of humanity as was affected by the condem- nation. Paul does not expressly declare how the sin of the one makes the others sinners or how the righteous act of the one makes the others righteous, but he does make evident that the scope is the same in some sense. We prefer to think that the one-to-many relationship in both cases is potential as far as personal lostness and salvation are concerned. The potentiality between all men and Adam has in fact become a reality; the potentiality between all men and Second Adam could in theory become a reality as well, but we know from elsewhere in scripture that such will not be the case. Paul speaks descriptively of the two groups and their representative heads and does not at this point stop to talk about practical proportions; he is talking about theoretical operation, that is, how the systems work. The two systems work coextensively.

II Peter 2:1 offers another statement relevant to the intent of Christ's death: "And false prophets also appeared among the people as also there will be false teachers among you, who will bring in destructive heresies under false pretenses, denying even the master who bought them, bringing upon themselves swift destruction." Several interpretations have arisen which in varying degrees relate the verse to the scope of atonement. The Lord may have bought them prior to their denial, in which case apostasy is presupposed. Conceivably the statement is made in terms of the false teachers' claim that the Lord had bought them, even though they were denying him in practice and doctrine. Peter may mean, however, that Christ had bought them as to intent, but they were denying him.

Earlier we quoted I Timothy 2:4 in connection with God's compassion for all men. That verse leads into a comment about the death of Christ: "For there is one God and one mediator between God and men—the man Jesus Christ, who gave himself as a ransom for all" (2:5-6a). In the beginning John the Baptist introduced Jesus to the multitude by saying, "Behold, the Lamb of God, that takes away the sin of the world" (Jn. 1:29). The Samaritans confessed, "We have heard for ourselves and know that this is truly the Savior of the world" (Jn. 4:42). Jesus himself affirmed, "And if I am lifted up from the earth, *I* will draw all men to myself" (Jn. 12:32). John the apostle also said, "And we have seen and testify that the Father has sent the Son as Savior of the world" (I Jn. 4:14); "He is the propitiation for our sins and not for ours only, but also for the whole world" (2:2). On Solomon's porch Peter told the multitude after healing the impotent man, "To you first God, having resurrected his Servant, sent him to bless you in turning away each of you from your sins" (Acts 3:26). To the Stoics and Epicureans Paul said, "Because he has appointed a day in which he will judge the world in righteousness in the man whom he appointed, furnishing assurance to all, having raised him from the dead" (Acts 17:31). These passages together with Hebrews 2:9; Romans 5:18; and II Corinthians 5:14-15 make it abundantly clear that the death of Christ establishes a universal atonement option.

Availability of the atonement. John 3:14-18 speaks, not only to the prompting and establishing of the atonement; it speaks as well about its availability: "whoever believes in him may have eternal life" (3:15; cp. 16, 18). The frame of reference is the world, not Jewry, even though during his ministry that truth did not dawn on even those disciples who heard him most. Curiously, universal availability did not dawn on them in a practical sense until at least the time of Cornelius' conversion in Acts 10-11. Peter himself quoted Joel's prophecy on the day of Pentecost: "Everyone who calls on the name of the Lord will be saved" (Joel 2:32; Acts 2:21; cp. Rom. 10:12-13), but did not see all its implications immediately. The Great Commission had also indicated a world-wide proclamation (Mt. 28:18-20; Mk. 16:15-18; Lk. 24:46-47; Jn. 20:21-23). Nevertheless, Peter had his Cornelius experience and the conference on circumcision took place so that he knew the universal availability of the gospel was God's will.

Next to the Commission itself Paul's comments cited earlier from II Corinthians 5:14-19 probably carry the strongest sense of compulsion to preach the gospel to every person regardless of race or nationality. The availability is to every person; the possession is to everyone who comes to Christ (Lk. 6:47), believes (Jn. 12:46; Acts 10:43; 13:39; Rom. 1:16; 10:4), and confesses Jesus as the Son of God (I Jn. 4:15). There should therefore be no hesitancy to affirm that God intended the death of Christ to be the basis of salvation for everyone from that time forward. The question remains, nonetheless, whether salvation has even a greater scope, and so we proceed to other groups of men needing reconciliation to God.

For faithful Israelites

One group needing reconciliation was pre-Christian Jews. Salvation does not come one way for Christians after Christ and another way for Israelites. Relationship to God during the Mosaic period did not actually result from offering animal sacrifices for sin (Ps. 40:6-8; Heb. 10:1-11), but from the subsequent offering of Christ. Righteousness did not really come from keeping the law, but from faith (Hab. 2:4; Rom. 1:17; Gal. 3:11; Heb. 10:38). Fellowship with the Father came for Jews and Christians alike—by faith and through Messiah:

> And on account of this he is the mediator of a new covenant, in order that, a death having taken place for the redemption of transgressions under the first covenant, they who have been called may receive the promise of the eternal inheritance (Heb. 9:15).

102

In one way of looking at it, the blood of Jesus Christ worked retroactively to cleanse sinners who lived before him and was perpetually active to those who come later. More exactly, it is not a legal jurisdiction or dispensation that is at issue, but an ideal person in terms of whom God regards those who identify themselves with him (explicitly) or would have done so had they known about him (implicitly).

For non-Israelite elect

Hebrews 9:15 *establishes the basis* for saving the Old Testament worthies; I Peter 3:18—4:6 *makes it known* to them and others. Although Hebrews speaks only of those under the Mosaic covenant, I Peter extends the idea to patriarchal times. Not only is it true that Christ has been appointed judge of the living and the dead (Acts 10:42; II Tim. 4:1; I Pet. 4:5; cp. Jn. 5:22, 27; Acts 17:31), but his atoning work has become the reference point for judgment. For people in any time salvation and lostness are figured in relation to the death-resurrection of the Sinless One. It was only appropriate, then, that the dead should have made known to them the basis of their salvation or condemnation: "For to this end the gospel was preached even to the *dead* in order that they might on the one hand be judged according to men in the flesh, but on the other hand might live according to God in the spirit" (I Pet. 4:6). The previous dead can thus be judged the same way as men who heard the gospel *in the flesh,* even though it was announced to them *in the spirit* that they might have life there in that state.

To the *saved* Christ's preaching the gospel (4:6) made known the basis of redemption and, perhaps we can say, allowed those to accept it who would have accepted it on earth. Luke's account of the transfiguration mentions that at that time Moses and Elijah talked with Jesus about his "exodus," or death. Peter refers, however, to preaching that Jesus did after his death. When he died, it is natural to assume that he too went to the abode of the dead (3:18-19). He evidently did not spend that time in heaven because he says to Mary Magdalene, "Don't keep hanging on to me, for I have not yet ascended to the Father" (Jn. 20:17). We do not mean to affirm that he offered salvation to the unsaved dead, but that he made a confirmation and clarification of a status already determined. Christ's death was a preaching of good news to the saved worthies of old (*euangelizomai*).

An alternative understanding of I Peter 4:6 takes "dead" to refer to spiritually dead people still physically alive on earth. Such a meaning for the word "dead" itself has precedent in the New Testament (Col. 2:13; I Pet. 2:24, etc.), but that significance does not seem appropriate here. In 4:5 the word "dead" appears in the statement ". . . who shall give account to the one who is ready to judge the living and the dead." The last expression occurs in Acts 10:42; Romans 14:9; and II Timothy 4:1, clearly meaning those physically alive and dead. We would expect the meaning to stay the same in the next verse. Preaching the gospel "even," or "also," to the dead sounds a little unusual if spiritually dead is meant because they are the very ones for whom the gospel is designed; in fact, they are the only ones there are to hear it. It might be possible for Peter to mean that the gospel is to be preached even to such as those who are persecuting his readers. With the mention of Christ's descent to hades in I Peter 3, the statement of 4:6 appears most naturally to teach that Christ preached the good news to the dead in hades in order to let them know the real ground of their relationship to the Father.

To the *lost* Christ made an announcement (*kēryssō*; 3:18-20). Peter only mentions going to those who had been disobedient at the time of the flood. The "spirits in prison" were presumably not some order of supernatural beings (Gen. 6:1-4), but members of the human race destroyed by the cataclysm; Jesus himself is likewise said to be "in the spirit" after he was put to death in the flesh. Peter may have chosen Noah's contemporaries in anticipation of the loose comparison he intended to make between the flood that saved Noah's family and the baptismal flood that saves the sons of God now (3:20-21). More fundamentally Peter chose this group of disobedient men because they so greatly outnumbered the eight obedient ones; their destruction should encourage readers surrounded by infidels that mock and revile them for obeying God.

For unevangelized elect

Even some two thousand years after the Great Commission more people in the world have *not* heard the gospel than *have* heard it. The secret things do belong to God, but Christians and non-Christians alike cannot help wondering about the justice as well as the compassion of a God who assigns to eternal torments people who for reasons beyond their control never heard about fellowship with him through Jesus Christ. The question here is fundamentally the same as the one about non-Israelites during the Mosaic era or about anyone else beyond the

104

circle of special revelation. Our opinion is that scripture does not automatically assign the unevangelized to endless hell; the question about their destiny is not altogether among the secret things that belong to God.

As a *basis* for our opinion we turn to Paul's thoughts about the conscience in his letter to the Romans. In 2:11-16 he reasons that hearing the law is not righteousness, but doing it. Therefore, doing God's will without hearing it satisfies God and is evidently a possibility in Paul's mind. The source of leading outside of special revelation is the conscience of a man. Consequently, with or without special revelation condemnation can happen because God can use alternative measures of sin. At the same time the apostle talks about alternative criteria for sin, he speaks of Gentiles doing the things of the law and of being judged by Jesus Christ according to the gospel.

Peter perhaps harbors a like conception when he addresses the household of Cornelius, where he says after his experience in Joppa, "Truly I perceive that God is not a respecter of persons, but in every nation the one who reverences him and works righteousness is acceptable to him" (Acts 10:34-35). Here again Gentiles as Gentiles have access to God (10:28). The difference may be that Peter contemplates non-Jews who know the true and living God and therefore fear him.

With a couple additional observations from experience, the picture Paul contemplates begins to come into focus. Men do not always live up to the leading of their own consciences; therefore condemnation on that basis becomes possible. Experience also demonstrates that many fundamental moral values appear universally among ethnic groups with no acquaintance with Judaeo-Christian heritage. Since all normal men can project consciousness over behind the eyes of someone else, they all have access to an approximate definition of right behavior in social relations. Therefore conscience will contain many correct guidelines. Conscience will not, however, provide a complete guide for human behavior because cultural influences along with incorrect perception may mislead the conscience.

For the unevangelized during the Christian era or for men outside the province of special revelation in any age, conscience will not supply everything God expects, but neither will it always mislead. We assume that revealed matters not accessible by conscience fall among those sins God does not reckon against people. The overlapping areas of revelation and conscience furnish the basis for judging Gentiles.

On the proposition that God does not reckon sins of ignorance, we may observe that he has often allowed people to walk in the ignorance of their own way (Acts 14:16) even to the point of crucifying the Messiah: none of the rulers of this world had known the hidden wisdom of God, "for if they had known it, they would not have crucified the Lord of glory" (I Cor. 2:8; cp. Acts 3:17; 13:27). Because of ignorance sins may be forgiven or not reckoned: "Forgive them because they do not know what they are doing" (Lk. 23:34; cp. Acts 7:60). Paul confirms this point in Romans: ". . . to show his righteousness because of the passing over of sins done previously in the forbearance of God" (3:25; cp. Acts 17:31). Paul even says he received mercy for persecuting Christ and his disciples because he "did it ignorantly in unbelief" (I Tim. 1:13). At least he received the mercy when he later repented upon enlightenment (Acts 2:36 + 38; 3:17 + 19; 17:31; Lev. 5:17-19). His experience seems to include under ignorance those matters of revelation earnestly misunderstood (cp. Acts 13:27; I Cor. 2:8). Earnest misunderstanding requires proper motivation and brings up the difference between ignorance and willful ignorance: "If you were blind you would have no sin; but now you say, 'We see'; therefore your sin remains" (Jn. 9:41; 15:22, 24). James 4:17 summarizes, "To him that knows to do good and does not do it, it is sin." Part of ignorance qualifying for forgiveness is an honest effort to search out the truth from the material available, which includes a willingness to reconsider an understanding of scripture and excludes ignorance from neglect. Withholding punishment for ignorance presupposes unintentional ignorance and willing repentance upon enlightenment.

The foregoing schematic does not as yet authorize the conclusion that an unevangelized person could be saved. No one ever lives up to his conscience even in that restricted area where it properly leads him. No one lives up to his conscience any more than any Jew lived up to the law. Since perfection is God's universal, eternal standard, the conclusion appears to be that no one can be righteous by his own deeds; consequently, no unevangelized person would ever be saved.

Further reflection, however, reminds us that all Israelites did not perish simply because none ever obeyed the law fully. Those under the law did not achieve righteousness by it; they were reckoned righteous in terms of Christ; so also then for the "noble pagan." God can exercise as much consistency in saving the unevangelized who fail to achieve the correct ideals of conscience as he can in saving a Christian who fails to achieve the ideals of revelation. In either case aspiration is reckoned for achievement; the spirit of the law stands instead of the letter of the law. As in all cases such salvation would not come from a person's own doings, but only from Christ. The Father has already appointed him as the one with whom he will identify this kind of person. His not knowing about Christ does not preclude God's identifying him with Christ because such a person would himself seek that identification if he knew to do so. Although Romans 2 applies particularly to non-Israelites, we have adopted from it principles applicable to like situations. Consequently, we summarize by saying that the scope of Christ's atonement includes Christians, faithful Israelites, pre-Mosaic saints, and unevangelized elect despite their ignorance of Christ. There may be salvation outside the awareness of Christ even though there is no salvation outside of Christ.

Among the *objections* to possible salvation outside the hearing of faith, we note the following arguments. (1) II Thessalonians 1:7-9 may seem to pose an objection to having unevangelized elect. The Thessalonians afflicted for their allegiance Paul commands to rest with him "at the revelation of the Lord Jesus from heaven with his mighty angels in flaming fire, rendering vengeance to those that do not know God and to those that do not obey the gospel of our Lord Jesus, who will suffer justice, eternal destruction from the face of the Lord and from his mighty glory." Not only does Christ take vengeance on those disobedient to the gospel—disbelievers, but also on those ignorant of God—unbelievers. Consequently, no salvation can occur without evangelistic endeavor.

A couple other reconstructions, however, may be placed on these verses: First, (a) not knowing God and not obeying the gospel may demonstrate synonymous *parallelism;* not knowing means not obeying. It could also be synthetic parallelism in which the second description elaborates the first one. Not knowing God amounts to being out of fellowship with him because of disobedience to his word. Knowing would not be an intellectual awareness made possible through evangelism, but a personal relationship made possible through conversion. Under this interpretation there are not two groups, but two descriptions of one group.

Secondly, even if two groups are in view (b) the statement makes note of a *practical generality* when it speaks of taking vengeance on

107

those not knowing God. If "know" means "to be aware of by special revelation," Paul need not be indicating more than that heathen peoples have grossly sinful lives without the restraining influence of Christ and his word. Paul charges the Ephesians,

> This then I say and testify in the Lord that you no longer walk even as the Gentiles walk in the vanity of their mind, being darkened in their understanding, alienated from the life of God on account of the ignorance that is in them because of the hardening of their heart, who being past feeling, have delivered themselves over to lewdness unto the working of all uncleanness with covetousness (4:17-19).

Yet Paul might not have classified Sergius Paulus with the majority Greek life style of his day (Acts 13:7, 12). We hesitate to consider bound for hell men like the proselytes and God-fearers, or "sebomenoi," who were Greeks attached to Jewish synagogues (Acts 13:43; 16:14; 17:4, 17; 18:7). We hesitate to affirm that, had such people died before the Gentile mission extended to their location, they would have been lost automatically. Paul's general impression of Greek morality put such exceptions aside: ". . . that each one of you know how to control his own vessel in sanctification and honor, not in lustful passion as also the Gentiles that do not know God" (I Th. 4:4-5; cp. I Pet. 1:14). The apostle may therefore be putting aside exceptional Gentile devoutness when he affirms that Christ will take vengeance on those who do not know God, because that ignorance characteristically leads to a life guided by passion, lewdness, and lust.

(2) Luke 12:47-48 also appears to controvert the proposition laid out above. In the parable of the faithful and unfaithful servants Jesus says,

> And that servant who knew his master's will and did not prepare or do according to his will will be beaten with many blows. But the one who did not know and did things worthy of blows will be beaten with few blows. And to whomever much is given much will be sought from him, and to whom they commit much, they will ask more.

In this passage ignorance did not remove punishment, but reduced it. The application to salvation would be that eternal punishment is less severe for the ignorant and disobedient person, but eternal punishment is not removed.

Jesus' parable falls somewhat aside from our inferences from Romans 2, because in Romans Paul agrees that as many as have sinned without law shall perish without law (2:12). Sin is still measurable aside

108

from law because it is measured at least by conscience. There can be a "not knowing" that stems from no revelation without denying a knowledge by conscience, which leads to destruction. Presumably Jesus is talking about cases where the servants should have been able on general grounds to "guess" what they had not in fact been told.

(3) Paul tells the Ephesians that in their former condition they had no hope and were without God in the world (2:12). But we may ask (a) whether he means this as to fact or relative to their previous vantage point outside the official people of God. Their framework of life had to do only with this world, and they were excluded from any express promises from the God of Israel. Positive promises to the chosen nation did not include Gentiles; alternative possibilities and "back up systems" God could make, but they are not necessarily known. Only that to which God positively commits himself can serve as a basis for hope, even though he may elect other options for those outside his field of attention in making specific promises.

Furthermore, (b) the statement is made from the vantage point of salvation. An act is sinful regardless of ignorance; the question is whether it is reckoned against the sinner. To sin and to have sin reckoned are two different things: "Blessed is the man to whom the Lord does not reckon sin" (Ps. 32:2; Rom. 4:8; II Cor. 5:19). Therefore, if and when awareness comes, the sinner is called upon to repent even for his sins done in ignorance. Addressing a Jewish audience in the temple, Peter says of their crucifying the Messiah, "And now, brothers, I know that you acted according to ignorance as did also your rulers. . . . Repent therefore and turn again that your sins may be blotted out" (Acts 3:17, 19). On Pentecost after saying, "This Jesus whom you crucified God has appointed both Lord and Messiah," Peter answers their question about what to do by commanding, "Repent and be baptized each of you in the name of Jesus Christ unto remission of sins . . ." (2:36, 38). Likewise Paul tells the Athenian philosophers, "Having overlooked the times of ignorance, God now commands men that all everywhere should repent" (Acts 17:30; cp. Lev. 5:17-19). Measured by their present awareness, their previous ignorance meant condemnation if repentance did not occur.

Perhaps more importantly, (c) as a general rule those outside the scope of special revelation are lost because their ignorance of authoritative spiritual values means from a practical standpoint that those

109

values break down in the face of competing influences. Without the power of objective authority, even the correct inclinations of the conscience are more easily overrun by the pull of the flesh and environment. Men are thus hardened by the deceitfulness of sin and alienated from God (Col. 1:21; cp. I Pet. 4:3-6).

(4) Another objection is that if salvation is possible without knowing Jesus, he need not have come to die on the cross for our sins (cp. Gal. 2:21). Even Jesus himself said, "Unless you believe that I am the one, you will die in your sins" (Jn. 8:24). In the conclusion of Mark's gospel Jesus is represented as telling his disciples, "The one who believes and is baptized will be saved, but the one who disbelieves will be condemned" (16:16). A distinction, however, must be made between the necessity of atonement and knowing about the atonement. The Old Testament saints received salvation on the basis of Christ's death that took place for sins under the first covenant (Heb. 9:15). If Abraham could be justified by faith without knowing Christ, then in principle nothing prohibits salvation without a knowledge of the real basis for it.

A distinction exists between *disbelief* and *unbelief*. It is one thing not to believe because of rejecting what has been heard; it is another not to believe because of not hearing. Jesus' charge against the religious leaders and the future hearers had to do with rejection, not complete ignorance. Even as men by their sin identify themselves in effect with Adam whom they may not be knowingly trying to emulate, so by their longing after righteousness God can identify them with Christ. That real basis for their destiny can be made known to them later (I Pet. 4:5-6).

(5) If it is possible to be saved without knowing Jesus, there is no urgency for fulfilling the Christian mission to the unreached. We submit, however, that the conclusion does not follow from the premise because proclaiming the gospel to the unsaved affects more than their eternal destiny. Our concern is not just about their eternal destiny, but (a) their lack of abundant life in the present. Paul reminds the Christian Gentiles in Galatia, "But at that time, not knowing God, you were enslaved to those which by nature were not gods" (Gal. 4:8). By turning to Christ, they had received freedom from things that held them in bondage. The same apostle tells the Ephesians that before their conversion they were "without Christ, alienated from the commonwealth of Israel and strangers of the covenants of promise, having no hope and without

110

God in the world" (2:12). Hope appears in anticipation of the resurrection when Paul speaks to the Thessalonians: "But we do not want you to be ignorant, brothers, concerning those who have fallen asleep, that you not sorrow as also the rest who have no hope" (I Th. 4:13). We are inclined to understand both of these hope passages to be from the standpoint of the Gentile's perception of his situation in contrast to the way he feels about life now that Christ has come. That there was no hope for him could conceivably be true without detracting from this benefit of the gospel to Gentiles. Without fear of contradiction we can affirm that "there is no one who has left house or wife or brothers or parents or children on behalf of the kingdom of God that will surely not receive much more in this time and in the coming age eternal life" (Lk. 18:29-30; cp. Mk. 10:29-30). The healing, spiritual, psychological, and motivational benefits of the gospel begin on this side of eternity. In fact, the good news of the gospel is primarily designed for this realm insofar as this realm was what God first gave mankind as his ideal habitat.

(b) A greater number will be saved through proclamation. To leave open the possibility of salvation to an unevangelized person does not mean that anywhere near so many will be saved without the gospel as by it. The warnings of Ezekiel need to be heard in this connection because the prophet presents God as saying, "When I say to the wicked, 'You shall surely die,' and you give him no warning nor speak to warn the wicked from his wicked way to save his life, the same wicked man will die in his iniquity, but his blood I will require at your hand" (3:18; cp. 3:10; 33:6, 8). Wicked men will die in their sins under any circumstance unless they respond to warnings of prophets willing to fulfill their commissions.

In Peter's first epistle he encourages the readers by saying, ". . . set your hope perfectly on the grace brought to you at the revelation of Jesus Christ, like obedient children not patterning yourselves according to the lusts you formerly had in your ignorance" (1:13-14; Eph. 4:17-18; I Th. 4:5; Heb. 9:7). The ignorance the heathen experience leaves them with less restraint on their conduct of life so that they more easily become hardened in heart and turn themselves over to lewd practices (Eph. 4:17-19). After speaking about thieves, extortioners, revilers, and drunkards, Paul observes, "Such were some of you" (I Cor. 6:11). Men of the sort he envisions were changed by the gospel from a condition that precludes inheriting the kingdom of God with or without

111

revelation (6:10). Appealing to ignorance of special revelation as a basis for mercy does not remove a man's responsibility for living up to the light of conscience wherein it agrees with God's will.

Evangelism does not simply benefit the convert; (c) spreading the gospel is for the glory of God. When men conceive of God falsely and serve him ignorantly, God does not receive the honor and glory he would if he were known in his true character and served appropriately on that basis. Although God has elected to forgive ignorance in those who worship him ignorantly, he sends men like Paul to set God forth to people of all cultures and stations of life (Acts 17:23) that they may know his nature, his deeds, his purposes, his promises, and his aspirations for men (17:24-31). The passion for souls is not as ultimate as a passion for praising God; the motive of missions is the glory of God.

(6) Another objection to mercy based on ignorance is that such a view leads to lack of growth in order to avoid additional responsibility. In our statement about ignorance we have distinguished willful and unintentional ignorance because they differ in intent. Even among men a differentiation is made between mistakes of innocence and mistakes of negligence. To a man with ready access to the scripture in written or oral form, the appeal to ignorance is an excuse; to a noble pagan with only a partially enlightened conscience to guide him, ignorance is much more a reason. Someone might do as good a job living up to the correct leading of his conscience as a Christian did living up to special revelation. God would be as consistent and justified in saving such a person in terms of Christ as he would in saving a professing Christian. It is not the hearer but the doer that is justified.

Results of the Atonement: Limited

John 3:14-18 has served as the beginning point in our presentation on the universal intent for salvation through Christ. It serves also as the beginning point in our presentation on the limited result of that salvation. The limitation factor comes in because of disbelief: "The one who does not believe stands condemned already because he has not believed in the name of the only Son of God" (3:18).

Christ's work of atonement was sufficient for all men, appropriate for them all, and to be proclaimed to them all. Nevertheless, not all will in fact receive salvation. There are two destinies for men, not just

112

one. Biblical teaching about *final* judgment makes evident that not all will be reconciled to God because they refuse the terms of pardon and the basis of reconciliation.

The judgment

Revelation 20:11-15 describes the final judgment of every man according to his works. Two destinies are represented here and elsewhere in consequence of this judgment process. Besides those given eternal life, "If anyone was not found written in the book of life, he was cast into the lake of fire." The herald of Messiah depicted the consummating work of Messiah as twofold: wheat into the granary or chaff into the fire (Mt. 3:7-12; Lk. 3:7-9). Messiah himself predicted that there were two patterns of life and that the saved would form a minority: "Wide is the gate and narrow is the way that leads to destruction and there are many that enter in through it; how narrow the gate is and straitened the way is that leads into life and there are few that find it" (Mt. 7:13-14; cp. 22:14; Lk. 13:22-30; Rom. 9:27; 11:4; I Pet. 3:20). Paul enjoins the Philippians not to be "afraid of the adversaries, which is for them an evident indication of destruction, but of your salvation, and this from God" (1:28). The uniform testimony on this point in the New Testament includes references to destruction and lostness in Matthew 13:24-30, 36-43; 12:32; 25:41, 46; Mark 9:44-48; Luke 12:4-5; John 17:12; Romans 2:5, 8-9; 5:9; 9:22-23; I Corinthians 16:22; II Corinthians 2:15-16; 11:15; Galatians 1:8-9; 3:10; Philippians 3:19; Colossians 3:25; I Thessalonians 1:10; 4:6; II Thessalonians 1:6-8; 2:3, 8; I Timothy 6:9; II Timothy 2:12; 4:18; Hebrews 10:26-27; II Peter 2:3-4, 14, 17; 3:7, 16; Jude 4, 6-7, 13 and a number of references in Revelation (2:11; 11:18; 14:9-12; 17:8, 11; 18:6; 19:20; 20:10-15; 21:8; 22:12, 15). There would seem to be no doubt that God divides human destiny into two groups instead of rewarding everyone alike or having everyone start all over again.

The eternal verdict

Not only are there two fundamental destinies, but the verdict given at the "Great White Throne Judgment" is an eternal verdict both for the saved and for the unsaved. In Matthew 25:46 Jesus unites in one sentence the permanence of both conditions: "And these will go away into eternal punishment, but the righteous into eternal life." Since the

113

same word for "eternal" describes both destinies in direct comparison, one reward has the same duration as the other. The certainty for eternal heaven is no greater than the certainty of eternal hell. Since no one wants to defend a temporary heaven, the eternality of hell must be accepted with equal certainty.

Other texts confirm the summary stated in Matthew 25:46. In regard to eternal *life* Mark 10:30 records Jesus' promise that those who had put Christ ahead of family and possessions would receive eternal life in the world to come (cp. Mt. 19:21; Mk. 10:21, etc.). Permanent *death* is described in Revelation 14:11: "The smoke of their torment goes up forever and ever, and they have no rest day or night who worship the beast and his image and receive the mark of his name." In a statement limited to the devil, the beast, and the false prophet, Revelation 20:10 speaks of their being "tormented day and night forever and ever." While some passages only say explicitly that the instrument of punishment is eternal (Isa. 66:24; Mt. 3:12; 18:8; 25:41; Mk. 9:43, 48; Jude 7), the parable of the rich man and Lazarus makes clear that no one can cross over from either state to the other (Lk. 16:19-31). Those who do not obey the gospel will suffer eternal destruction from the face of the Lord when Christ comes again (II Th. 1:8-9). The Hebrew writer calls eternal judgment, in fact, an elementary rudiment of the faith (6:2). He who blasphemes the Spirit commits an eternal sin (Mk. 3:29). Sins committed in this world will not be forgiven in the next (Mt. 12:32). It seems clear from these considerations that not all will be saved even though salvation through Christ is open to all.

Because scripture teaches that not all will in fact be saved, we understand all passages about universalism in a potential rather than an actual sense. By "potential" we do not mean to say that the texts about universal atonement are *grammatically* potential, but *actually* potential. They speak of the atonement descriptively and so say that its intended scope is universal; the conditional element involved in the application does not form part of the author's attention in the immediate statement. Many texts themselves include the limitation factor by observing that not all men will accept salvation. Others like Romans 5:18-19 do not particularly stress limitation because they speak descriptively about how the system works and how broadly atonement considerations operate. God intended the basis of salvation to be for *all* men *who would accept it;* hence, it is respectively universal and limited.

Chapter Nine

UNIVERSALISM

Introduction

In the previous chapter we surveyed the evidence for *limited univer-salism*. It was "universal" inasmuch as God meant for salvation to be available for everyone to accept; it was "limited" because not everyone will accept. In the present chapter we look at the doctrine of *universalism*, which teaches that reconciliation actually occurs between God and all his creatures.

Different authors formulate universalism differently. (a) Restora-tionism projects eternal option for salvation and may combine eternal option with a purification process (*apokatastasis*). (b) Another view considers earthly existence to be "hell" so that everyone subsequently passes into the heavenly state. (c) A third position divides salvation into objective and subjective sides. Objectively all men are reconciled to God as far as he is concerned, but subjectively not all men feel united with God from their side of the relationship; evangelism announces their acceptance by God and encourages them to accept their acceptance by the way they feel and live.

Universalism moves the study of salvation into the area of "escha-tology," the study of last things. Personal experience shows that not all men come into practical relationship to God during this life; hence, the future realm offers opportunity for completing the reconciliation program. The above formulations of universalism appeal in different ways to the future state in solving a presumed problem of eternal separ-ation between Creator and created.

Much of the impetus for universalist thinking comes from considera-tions that we too perceive to be unworthy of the God and Father of our Lord Jesus Christ. We would not expect him to (1) send to eternal torture unborn infants, innocent children under the age of practical accountability, the unevangelized, the erroneously evangelized with no access to correction, or the mentally handicapped. Along with this expectancy we have set aside (2) the concept of an original guilt that leads to eternal hell, because we understand that guilt lies at the point of responsibility, knowledge, and choice. A person does not go to damna-tion simply because he has descended from someone else who sinned.

Although eschatology does not form a central concern in our subject, we express our conviction that (3) hell is not a literal fire by which God tortures men eternally. (a) God exterminated the Canaanites because of gross forms of worship like live human sacrifice; we see little consistency in objecting to that kind of abominable insensitivity while prescribing eternal torments to the disobedient, especially since it appears that it accomplishes no purpose because we do not consider subsequent restoration a possibility scripture presents. (b) After death and resurrection we will not necessarily have a form of existence that can be tortured by fire. The "intermediate state" between death and the judgment day is what the parable of the rich man and Lazarus pictures with its flames, finger, tongue, eyes, and water in a very corporeal fashion; yet Jesus after his death went in the *spirit* to the intermediate abode of the dead, where he preached to the *spirits* in prison. At least in the intermediate state between death and resurrection it appears that men do not have the kind of existence in which they can be tortured with fire. Even in the resurrection, where people do not marry because they are like the angels in heaven (Mt. 22:30), it is not necessary to suppose that men have a flesh-and-blood existence; the general assembly and church of the firstborn is comprised of the spirits of just men made perfect (Heb. 12:23). Furthermore, (c) literal interpretation on eternal states creates contradiction within scripture. Flaming fire presumably involves light, yet the unsaved occupy a place of outer darkness (Mt. 8:12; 22:13; 25:30; II Pet. 2:4, 17: Jude 6, 13; cp. Rev. 16:10-11 + 8-9). Rather than seeing these representations as sober literalisms, we prefer to think that whatever hell is, it involves separation from God in such a way that the sinner receives there what he sought in turning away from God.

Finally, a less crucial criticism we seek to avoid is (4) the idea that everyone is rewarded equally. Although such a procedure could be more easily justified than the other objectionable matters above, we agree that it is not likely. Postulating a common destiny is inferior to believing that degrees of reward come to people in relation to the manner of fulfilling their responsibilities. On the negative side the parable of the faithful and unfaithful servants speaks of being beaten with few or many stripes (Lk. 12:41-48). Jesus tells those of his own day that their lack of repentance would make it less tolerable for them in the day of judgment than for Sodom, Gomorrah, Tyre, and Sidon (Mt. 10:15; 11:22, 24; Lk. 10:12-14). On the positive side the parable of the pounds rewards God's servants with varying levels of responsibility (Lk. 19:12 -27). Having degrees of reward and punishment relieves whatever perceived injustice exists in divine economies on either side of the eternal state.

Nevertheless when all legitimate refinements are made, a difference persists between potential universalism and actual universalism; consequently, the reasons for this difference must be investigated.

Evidence for Universalism

The Christ-Adam parallel

In Romans 5:12-21 and I Corinthians 15:20-22, 45-49 the apostle Paul draws a parallel between Adam and Christ. In these passages two verses especially relate to the extent of atonement through the Messiah: "So then as through one transgression judgment came to all men to condemnation, so also through one act of righteousness the free gift came to all men to justification of life" (Rom. 5:18). "For as in Adam all die, thus also in Christ all will be made alive" (I Cor. 15:22). According to universalist interpretation the scope of atonement is as broad as humanity and death, and the nature of atonement is as actual in Christ as death and condemnation is actual in Adam.

As far as it goes we have no objection to the preliminary observations about scope and nature of atonement, but the universalist inference does not follow. Of the two passages I Corinthians has less importance because strictly speaking (a) Paul only comments on resurrection. Since resurrection applies to good and evil alike (Dan. 12:2; Jn. 5:28 -29; Acts 24:15), eternal life does not necessarily come into view.

Furthermore, (b) the text does not clearly affirm that all are in Christ, but only that "in Christ all will be made alive." In fact, the following verse proceeds to define a limitation for what Paul contemplates: "But each in his own order: Christ the firstfruits, then *those of Christ* at his coming" (I Cor. 15:23).

Romans 5, however, clearly envisions justification, not just resurrection. If the passage is taken to mean actual salvation automatically upon Christ's atonement, the interpreter has failed to remember (c) the interpersonal character of both lostness and salvation. *Automatic universalism forgets that sin is what separated man from God in the first place;* it is not appropriate, then, for reconciliation to set aside the cause of division or attempt to solve the problem in some other plane besides the one in which it occurred—personal action. Legal maneuvers are

117

foreign, artificial, and contrived both in lostness and in salvation. Therefore, an act by a third party cannot by the nature of the case effect the reunion of opposed parties. We have denied that man's predicament stems from ancestral sin because on God's own avowed principles of operation personal *acts* are what bring personal *guilt* and subsequent *punishment* (Ezek. 18:1-20). It is as unlikely that all men receive automatic salvation because of Christ as it is that they all receive automatic damnation because of Adam. Since we refuse the inference about Adam, we likewise refuse the inference about Christ. Legal manipulation relative to automatic destinies is replaced by personal activity relative to potential destinies. In Romans 5 we understand Paul to be talking, not about actual universalism, but about how the Christ system works and what effects it produces. How a person gets into Christ or Adam is not definitively addressed by Paul's remarks there.

If Romans 5:18 is taken to mean actual salvation eventually upon acceptance of Christ's atonement, the interpreter has again failed to remember the nature of interpersonal relationship and personal character. *Eventual universalism* must remember that interpersonal relationship does not allow for overcoming estrangement from just one side of the relationship so that more is involved in reconciliation than *God's* desire for unity with men. Not only has he laid down conditions for fellowship with him, but freedom of choice in *man* eliminates necessary uniformity in reconciliation. To suppose that, given enough time, all men will eventually repent sounds too much like the tantalizing idea that knowledge is virtue; it says that if a person is really convinced that something is true he will act accordingly. To this kind of mentality Abraham seems to be speaking in the parable of the rich man and Lazarus, "If they do not hear Moses and the prophets, neither will they be persuaded if a person arises from the dead" (Lk. 16:31). There tends to be a general relationship, but not a one-to-one correlation between sufficient knowledge and satisfactory response because the reason for sin and separation is more than ignorance. Even if eternal opportunity *could* produce universalism, *scripture* not only lends no support to the idea, but speaks elsewhere in ways that preclude such an inference from Romans 5.

In Christ

Ephesians 1:4 makes use of a favorite Pauline expression when it says that God "chose us *in him* before the foundation of the world that we should be holy and without blemish before him in love." As in I Corinthians 15:22 certain benefits apply to those "in Christ": every spiritual blessing, election, sonship, redemption, forgiveness, revelation, inheritance, the earnest of the Spirit (Eph. 1:5-14). Paul writes to Christians in this letter; consequently, his frame of reference stops with them when he says "us." In order for "in Christ" to yield the universalist conclusion, all men would first have to be in Christ; but as we said earlier the texts carrying the expression do not say all are in Christ, but that all in him are chosen, blessed, etc. Our treatment of the atonement concluded that a person gets into Christ by identifying himself with Christ. He is not born into him or arbitrarily assigned into him, but chooses to put faith in the promise that identification with Christ serves as a basis for being regarded as righteous. Not all men are in Christ because some refuse to enter him. Before the foundation of the world God did choose to bless all those in Christ, but not all have chosen to be in Christ in order to be chosen in him as God's sons.

Reconciliation of all things

A cluster of New Testament texts affirm the restoration, reconciliation, and subjection of all things to God through Christ: ". . . whom [Jesus] it is necessary for heaven to receive until the times of restoration of all things that God spoke through the mouth of his holy prophets from of old" (Acts 3:21); "And when all things are subjected to him, then also will the Son himself be subjected to the one who subjected all things to him in order that God may be all in all" (I Cor. 15:28); ". . . unto the dispensation of the fulness of times to sum up all things in Christ, things in the heavens and things on the earth" (Eph. 1:10); ". . . in order that at the name of Jesus every knee should bow of heavenly things/ones, of earthly things/ones, and subterranean things/ones and every tongue should confess that Jesus Christ is Lord to the glory of God the Father" (Phil. 2:10-11); ". . . because it was well pleasing that in him should all the fulness dwell and through him to reconcile all things to him, making peace through the blood of his cross whether things on the earth or things in the heavens" (Col. 1:19-20).

These passages unite in affirming the restoration of "all things." The word "all" belongs to a group of universal words. (a) Seldom do such words have absolutely universal application; they usually stand within an implicit limitation such as what the subject at hand naturally includes.

This principle of interpreting universal words finds acceptance with all interpreters, including universalists inasmuch as they also invoke the concept of implicit limitation when discussing the meaning of "forever" in regard to the duration of hell. The question is not about the principle, but when and how to apply it.

A related matter for interpreting "all" has to do with (b) the difference between actual and potential. Without claiming application to the specific citations above, we remind ourselves that descriptions of how the system operates may include references to all because potentially all could be affected by the system; nevertheless, practical factors unaddressed by such passages may cause the system actually to produce less than all it could produce; in this case the practical factor is the freedom of human choice granted and honored by the Creator. Whether potentiality comes into the discussion must be determined by the nature of the case as evaluated by more fundamental considerations or by other related passages that give clearer expression to the issue.

Finally, (c) "all things" may represent a general rule or significant examples with unspecified amounts of exception. In this sense "all the Judaea territory and all the Jerusalemites" were going out to John's baptism (Mk. 1:5). Likewise the Pharisees said of Jesus' popularity toward the end of his ministry, "Behold, the world has gone away after him" (Jn. 12:19). Because they are conventional expressions, we do not force such statements into unqualified literalisms.

The five references under consideration vary in the possibilities for restricting the universals in them. Acts 3:21 has an element of ambiguity because the lack of punctuation in the original Greek manuscripts leaves it uncertain whether a comma should appear after "things," thus transforming it into a non-restrictive clause. The difference in meaning is whether Peter speaks of "the restoration of all things that the prophets predicted" or whether he means "the restoration of all things, which is a matter the prophets predicted." Even if the latter alternative seems preferable, the restoration of all things may point to a reconciliation subsequent to the eradication of all foreign matters that have come in since the beginning to draw the creation away from its Creator. The times of restoration may refer to the restoration of all things that will be restored. At any rate, the chapter proceeds to warn that every soul who does not hearken to God's prophet "will be utterly destroyed from among the people"(3:23).

120

The I Corinthians 15 reference has all things subjected to Christ, but it does not affirm willingness or reconciliation in that subjection. In 15:25 Christ has all his enemies put under his feet in conquest over them, including the enemy death. Enemies that are put underfoot are enemies still, albeit subjected (cp. Ps. 110:1; Mt. 22:44; Mk. 12:36; Lk. 20: 42-43; Acts 2:34-35; Eph. 1:20-23; Heb. 1:13). The imagery of the conquering sovereign expresses final subjugation of all things presently intruding upon the happiness and hope of God's people. An exhortation underlies the point because the present condition of God's patience will not endure forever: this is the patience and faith of the saints (Rev. 13:10; 14:12). Since it is a model instead of a prediction of a reality, its wording may not be pressed beyond its intended use and what the nature of the reality allows.

The passages in Ephesians, Philippians, and Colossians may be taken together since their import is the same. In all three Paul affirms that in *Christ,* rather than in someone else, God has chosen to bring everything to completion. Especially does this emphasis seem obvious in Colossians, where Paul is evidently battling the teachings of gnosticism. This religious philosophy of Greek extraction had tried to syncretize Christianity into its scheme of delivering men from the evil material universe by a series of aeons, or levels, between the world and the realm of pure spirit, which was pure good. This series taken as a whole was called the *plērōma,* or "fulness"; gnostics tried to make Jesus into a ruler over one of these aeons, or ages/levels. Paul declares, however, that Jesus Christ is, so to speak, the whole series; and that in his flesh he alone reconciled men to God. Referring to his body and flesh (Col. 1:22) opposes the belief that all matter is evil; enmity with God because of evil deeds contrasts with the gnostic idea that good and evil consisted in kinds of substances rather than in ways of acting. Several other considerations in Colossians 1 make clear that Paul affirms the lone sovereignty of Christ as redeemer in order to deny these speculations in Greek dualism. Since the contrast lies between Christ and others both in Colossians and the other two books, then "Christ" receives the emphasis instead of "all"; consequently, the "all" can naturally be limited to all those in view rather than all those things absolutely. "All" may be understood simply as all in God's program of reconciliation. Everything (he reconciles) will be reconciled through Christ.

It may be worthy of note as well to contrast the heavenly, earthly, and subterranean ones who confess on the one hand (Phil.) with the heavenly and earthly things summed up in Christ (Eph.) and reconciled to him in peace (Col.). Those still in the nether world may refer to the lost; hence, they are not said to be reconciled. The confession of every tongue (Phil.) need not be more than an admission about who Christ is as in the case of conquered subjects. That confession does not have to refer to acknowledgement unto salvation.

Other universal passages

John 1:9 says, "He was the true light that enlightens every man coming into the world." Since enlightenment can designate the condition of the saved person (II Cor. 4:4, 6; Heb. 6:4; 10:32), it seemingly teaches the eventual salvation of everyone. We affirm, however, that such is not the case because the writer goes on to say that his own did not receive him. The enlightenment discussed here occurs in the world so that eternal option to be enlightened falls outside the scope of this passage. The light enlightens all men as to intent, but some men refuse the light because their deeds are evil (Jn. 3:19-20).

God "wants all men to be saved and to come to a knowledge of the truth" (I Tim. 2:4). God "is the Savior of all men, especially of believers" (I Tim. 4:10). "For the grace of God appeared bringing salvation to all men" (Tit. 2:11). "And he is the propitiation of our sins, and not of ours only but also of the whole world" (I Jn. 2:2). None of these texts need to mean more than that potentially all men could be saved because God wants them all to be reconciled to him and has made adequate provision in Christ to make reconciliation appropriate for everyone. In all these epistles as elsewhere texts speak of rebellious spirits who will not in fact make potential into real by acceptance. No interpretation of such references can set aside the requirement of acceptance known from elsewhere because reconciliation requires assent from both parties, and holiness has also established terms for reconciliation.

A series of statements in Romans 11:25-32 offers another approach to the universalist position. "All Israel will be saved" (11:26); "a hardening has in part befallen Israel until the fulness of the Gentiles is come in" (11:25). "The gifts and the calling of God are not repented of" (11:29). "God has shut up all unto disobedience in order that he might have mercy on all" (11:32). The combination of "all Israel" and "the fulness of the Gentiles" makes universalism. More exactly Paul says, "*In this way* all Israel will be saved," that is, subsequent to a period of insensitivity to the Christian message and after the fulness of the Gentiles has come in. "All Israel will be saved" means then "all Israel that will be saved will be saved in this manner." "All Israel" would not mean every Jew that ever lived because Paul refers to those alive after the fulness of the Gentiles has come in. Furthermore, in Paul's mind "Israel" means spiritual Israel: "They are not all Israel that are of Israel" (9:6).

The "fulness of the Gentiles" is sufficiently understood as the full number of Gentiles converted during "the times of the Gentiles" (Lk. 21:24). Not changing his mind about calling the Israelites means, we take it, that God has not turned his back on Israel in turning his face to the Gentiles. He has instead expanded his theater of operation to include them along with Jews (cp. Acts 11:18). Israelites as well as Gentiles have been categorized as disobedient, but mercy is open to them all. Whether mercy becomes effective unto actual salvation, however, depends on its acceptance because God designed salvation to include assent on the part of the disobedient.

The nature and character of God

The real beginning point for the universalist conclusion is the nature of "the God and Father of our Lord Jesus Christ." Particular texts on the atonement admittedly could bear another significance besides universalism. Therefore some more primary factor must help the interpreter select among the possible meanings of atonement texts. Aspects of God's character establish that selection principle for universalism.

His love. The character of God appealed to by universalism centers around his love so as to suggest that love, in order to be love, must always allow reconciliation. Such an approach takes a naive view of evil creatures as if love were irresistible and free will cannot be irrational. It also absolutizes love to the exclusion of holiness. Men become rather impossible in their demands upon God, arguing on the one hand against the idea that a holy, omnipotent God could allow evil in his universe and arguing on the other hand against his overthrowing evil decisively and finally in that universe. In order for God to be loving to the rest of his creation he exerts his holiness against the disobedient.

Many times the Old Testament repeats the standard acclamation, "His lovingkindness endures forever" (Ps. 118:1, etc.). Such expressions, however, do not require "eternal" option for salvation, for (a) this same idea universalists argue stands within implicit limitations when

123

it describes eternal destruction (Mt. 25:46). The limitation of God's lovingkindness in texts like Psalms 118 pertains to those in covenant relationship with him. They extol the endless expressions of grace God extends to his own (I Ch. 16:41; II Ch. 5:13; 7:3); that eternal lovingkindness to Israel nevertheless meant death and destruction to the enemies of Israel and was in fact much of the reason for developing that interjection of praise in the first place (I Ch. 16:34; Ps. 107; 118; 136; 138). The generalized application would appear to be that God always keeps his promises to protect and bless his own, which includes the permanent destruction of their enemies.

(b) Other passages show that God's lovingkindness has its boundaries, as when he says before the flood, "My Spirit will not strive with man forever" (Gen. 6:3). Nevertheless, it is claimed, if God *does* display his wrath he does not continue it forever; when the inhabitants of Judah went away into exile, God eventually brought them back after their chastisement. He only brought back, however, those that would come back. Moreover, what God does during a process does not dictate what he will do when he completes the process. The nature of God's dealings with Israel (Lev. 26:25, 38-45; Deut. 30:4) derives from his purpose for Israel beyond these events; eternal option does not follow from such temporal procedures. Mercy must come to an end eventually or evil never gets eradicated from the holy God's universe. Eternal opportunity would appear to bring sovereignty as well as holiness into question.

His fatherhood. The fatherhood of God is also understood to imply universal reconciliation. In the Sermon on the Mount Jesus taught his audience to emulate their heavenly Father, who sends rain on the just and on the unjust and makes the sun to rise on the evil and on the good (Mt. 5:43-48; cp. Lk. 15:11-32; Jn. 4:23; Acts 14:15-17; 17:28). The fatherhood of God implies the brotherhood of men and thus their salvation—at least eventually. We submit, on the contrary, that God's behaving in a fatherly way toward disobedient men does not make him their ethical Father or make them his ethical sons. Sons of God by creation do not equal sons of God by behavior. By creation all men are constituted for spiritual sonship, and so God relates to them in terms of their potential; but when time has made evident that they refuse to have him in their knowledge, he justly gives them up to the consequences of refusing the Father's love.

His freedom. Divine sovereignty forms another basis for the universalists' case. Since God has the freedom to do as he sees fit, no man has a right to deny that God can offer eternal opportunity. But the objection does not come from human denial; it comes from God's revelation. Freedom does not allow God to do other than what his promises and commitments already indicate. Having said that evil people will perish eternally, he does not have freedom to grant endless opportunity for reconciliation. At this point arises a major difficulty with universalist groups: they usually hold a relatively low view of scripture, which enables them to deny its accuracy if no interpretative technique can legitimately handle a passage like Revelation 14:10-11. Evidently this view of scripture is reinforced by its overall testimony against the universalist viewpoint.

Arguments Against Limited Universalism

Eternity as limited

According to universalists the Hebrew word *'ōlam* and its approximate Greek equivalent *aiōn* do not refer to absolutely endless duration. Examples abound where these words speak about matters known to be restrictive. Most absolute words—all, never, always, endless, permanent, no, none—are limited to a framework. The words translated "forever" and "eternal" are no exception, being used of the following items:

(1) the lifetime of a slave (Ex. 21:6; Lev. 25:46; Deut. 15:17);
(2) the lifetime of a tree (Mt. 21:19; Mk. 11:14);
(3) ten generations of a Moabite or Ammonite (Deut. 23:3-6; Neh. 13:1);
(4) a son's stay in a household (Jn. 8:35);
(5) the rainbow covenant (Gen. 9:16);
(6) the memorial stones in the Jordan River (Josh. 4:7);
(7) the duration of the hills (Gen. 49:26; Deut. 33:15; Ps. 78:69);
(8) Israel's possession of Canaan (Gen. 13:15; 17:8; 48:4; Ex. 32:13; Josh. 14:9; Ezra 9:12);
(9) David and Jonathan's covenant (I Sam. 20:23, 42);
(10) the sword's presence with the house of David (II Sam. 12:10);
(11) Samuel's appearance before Yahweh as priest (I Sam. 1:22);
(12) leprosy on the descendants of Gehazi (II Kg. 5:27);
(13) God's dwelling in Jerusalem (II Kg. 23:25; II Ch. 33:4; Ps. 61:4);

(14) the duration of Jerusalem (Ps. 48:8);

(15) Israel as God's people (II Sam. 7:25, 26, 29; I Ch. 17:22);

(16) Solomon's temple (I Kg. 8:13; 9:3, 5; II Ch. 7:16; 30:8);

(17) the ordinance of circumcision (Gen. 17:7 + 9-14);

(18) the observance of the sabbath (Ex. 31:16, 17);

(19) the annual atonement (Lev. 16:29, 31, 34; 23:31, 41);

(20) the passover sprinkling (Ex. 12:14, 17, 24);

(21) various offerings (Lev. 3:17; 6:18, 22; 10:9, 15; 23:14, 31);

(22) matters associated with the Aaronic priesthood (Ex. 28:43; 29:9; 30:21; 40:15; Lev. 7:34, 36; 10:9; 24:8, 9; 25:32, 34; Num. 18:8, 11, 19, 23; 25:13; I Ch. 15:2; 23:13);

(23) rules on uncleanness (Num. 19:10, 21);

(24) the sounding of trumpets at the solemn assemblies (Num. 10:8);

(25) the burning of a lamp in the temple court (Ex. 27:21; 24:3).

In addition to this formidable list, non-biblical references from Jewish and Greek authors confirm that the words involved often describe matters not absolutely endless.

Full weight should be given to data of this sort, especially in biblical interpretation because modern interpreters must work across language barriers. Despite this acknowledgement three points reduce the ambiguity seemingly present in these words. (a) *Scripture uses the same words to describe both good and evil destinies.* If no consideration but word usage applies here, eternal blessing has no more positive foundation than eternal banishment of the wicked. It might be conceivable that Matthew 25:46 could speak of eternal life and eternal punishment without meaning equal duration for both; in that case "eternal" would not indicate something absolutely eternal in either case, but would mean permanent without further elaboration. We would then have to distinguish the duration of each destiny by factors not specified in the Olivet Discourse. First principles could be invoked so that eternal life is endless because God's redemptive purposes are endless as implied by his holiness. But if we return to first principles, we also need to do so for condemnation; in our opinion there are no decisive first principles that would reduce the eternity of the negative destiny. In fact, eradicating evil permanently could also be argued from God's holiness; evil must be removed from a holy God's universe.

Another line of thought could develop out of supposing a potential character for these destinies. Some theologians teach the doctrine of

126

"confirmation in holiness" by which they mean that after the final judgment no possibility remains for revolting against God. Admittedly a speculative matter, "confirmed in holiness" does raise the question of whether a saved person could apostatize in the afterlife and lose his "eternal" life. On the surface of it, such rebellion would be very foolish, but then Satan's rebellion against a holy, loving God would also seem foolish. If a person believes in the possibility of apostasy after genuine conversion, he advocates something again that would appear most foolish; nevertheless, probable examples of that very thing come to mind all too readily. If a person can apostatize in heaven, then eternal life is potential instead of actual. By parity of reason eternal destruction could be potential instead of actual so that "eternal destruction" could countenance the possibility of salvation subsequent to death or the judgment. Even if the point were granted, however, universalism has not become the case, but only a potentiality.

A second response to a restricted meaning for "forever" is that (b) *on three occasions the fuller expression "forever and ever" comes into descriptions of destruction for men, Babylon the Great, the devil, the beast, and the false prophet.* We wonder how much more explicit the writer of Revelation could have been in these cases. It matters little, of course, whether the references apply to men or angels, because the underlying objection is that a loving God would not consign someone to an unremedial state.

The most important consideration against the limited eternity argument is that (c) *an absolute word is absolute if it is not in an inherently limiting situation.* Much of what can be discovered statistically from the usage of '*ōlam, aiōn,* and *aiōnios* becomes indecisive because it merely points up the necessity of determining duration from the nature of the situation. A proper analysis must recognize that these words cover the whole of any remarkable time period; that is, they do carry an absolute meaning, but they usually carry it as reduced by an implied limitation. Of course, the Aaronic priesthood or the Solomonic temple was not absolutely eternal, but they were eternal within the confines of the potentialities of the first covenant. The meaning of the words is not at issue, but their proper context. The real question becomes whether any legitimate bases exist for putting a boundary on eternal destruction. Our conviction leads us to affirm that no revealed principle establishes a positive reason for imposing boundaries on eternal separation from

God. If in fact there is one, it might be possible to bring the biblical witness into conformity with such an option; but until that reason is revealed, we cannot affirm the idea of *continued opportunity*. Regarding *universalism*, nevertheless, we must be more emphatic and say that not all will be saved because those who blaspheme the Spirit do not receive forgiveness "either in this age/world or in the one to come" (Mt. 12:32). If exceptions to universalism occur, it does not in principle matter how many of them there are.

Judgment as myth

A "myth" takes recurring processes and casts them in story form. Jesus and the New Testament writers speak of final judgment in the gospels, Acts, epistles, and Revelation. Universalists often contend that these descriptions do not picture a historical event, but a myth. "Final judgment" is really an eternal process based on permanent principles of evaluation. New Testament descriptions for the coming age commonly employ apocalyptic imagery and highly figurative language so that the use of myth would not be surprising.

On the other hand, (a) to agree that judgment can be a dynamic process does not eliminate it from being also a culminating, specific occasion. (b) If we adopt the principle of sliding-scale judgment, we avoid a great deal of the reason for wanting to make salvation an eternal possibility and judgment an ongoing process; in other words, the concerns behind making judgment a myth can be alleviated by a judgment that gathers up in itself the inequities of life.

Hell as purification

In reaction to biblical presentations on hell several views have grown up that attempt to remove the image of a loveless fiend torturing men eternally. *Annihilationism* teaches the natural immortality of the human soul with the result that hell-fire represents God's positive act of annihilation so that the person ceases to exist. *Conditional immortality* teaches that the human soul is not immortal so that God does not need to destroy man as a positive effort; he simply withdraws his sustaining power from the wicked so that they cease to exist. *Absolute universalism* avoids the problem by making all men actually saved so that, at most, hell-fire and brimstone answer to a subjective self-condemnation that "gnaws at" a person psychologically for varying lengths of

128

time till he accepts his acceptance. *Restorationism* projects an unspecified time limit on the "mental suffering" of the unrighteous and regards hell-fire as a purifying process for all sinners much like purgatory for the marginally sinful. These views all contrast with *eternalism*, which sees no deliverance from the state of estrangement. Since restorationism has had more advocates than absolute universalism, the problem of hell in relation to "second probation" warrants more attention.

Divine failure. I John 3:8 is one point of departure for restorationism: "The Son of God was manifested in order to destroy the works of the devil." It would be a strange destruction of the devil's works if he retained eternal possession of a majority of the human race. The argument gets its cogency from playing on the word "destroy." Destruction conjures up a situation where the acting party accomplishes the result by his own action alone. Destruction, however, represents rather loosely some of the aspects of the Son's manifestation. Overcoming Satan's power involves more than the action of the Son; it involves acceptance by the other party. Salvation destroys Satan's power in the sense that it establishes a possibility of deliverance (Lk. 10:18?). Christ's manifestation also destroys the works of the devil by bringing Satan's program to an end; evil organized and operating against God will cease. Therefore, in the restoration aspect of that destruction, potentiality, not actuality, is the case because reconciliation involves both parties. Failure to establish reconciliation represents, not divine failure, but human disregard.

Forgiveness later. When the scribes suggested that Jesus' exorcisms came by the power of Beelzebub, he warned that such an accusation tended toward blasphemy of the Holy Spirit, a sin unpardonable in this age/world and in the age/world to come. Universalists have reasoned that forgiveness in the next age must represent a possibility or Jesus would not have made the remark (Mt. 12:32; cp. Mk. 3:29). Since other reconstructions can be supposed, however, restorationism does not gain anything from the Lord's comment. For one thing, (a) the translation of *aiōn* could be "age" or "world"; if age properly reflects his intent, he may mean the Christian era rather than the eternal state. Perhaps more likely, (b) not forgiven in the coming age may indicate that at the judgment blasphemy of the Holy Spirit will not be included in sins overlooked or not figured in the verdict. Such blasphemy does not qualify as a sin of ignorance because it is not attitudinally appropriate to that class of sins. Finally, (c) the proposed interpretation does

129

not lead to universalism unless no one were ever to commit blasphemy of the Holy Spirit.

Figurative language. Surely, it is said, God has a higher goal for hell than vengeance (II Th. 1:8). Furthermore, punishment is always remedial elsewhere; so it must be remedial after the judgment (Mt. 25:46). We infer, however, that both vengeance and punishment are ways of looking at hell and the intermediate state between death and the judgment; similarly we regard destruction and imprisonment as models (I Pet. 3:19; II Pet. 2:4, 9; Rev. 20:2-3). Perhaps they form aspects of the condition experienced there, but these several imageries do not mix, nor do all their elements fit the reality they name. Punishment does not equal revenge because discipline lacks the spirit of revenge nor does it involve destroying the person. To argue the remedial nature of hell from its punishment label allegorizes the comparison between hell and punishment much as annihilationism argues from the destruction label. Parts of these concepts apply to hell, but not all the parts of each concept.

Handling vengeance, punishment, destruction, and imprisonment as figurative expressions only adopts a procedure used by all interpreters including universalists themselves. The inseparable gulf between Abraham's bosom and hell (Lk. 16:19-31) looks away from changes in state after death has occurred. Since this point occurs in a parable, however, universalist interpreters do not regard it as necessarily significant. All agree that figurativeness inheres in these matters so that it is really more a matter of choosing when to invoke the principle rather than whether to invoke it.

Eschatological limit. Scripture cannot express the true nature of eternal times because they participate in a spiritual dimension beyond our experience. Since language meanings develop from experience, we have no way to receive a description of future existence we have not experienced. Consequently, words about eternity cannot signify perceivable truth. The inference is that scripture is written from and for this present age, and its endeavors to describe the future realm only intend to engender hope and provide strength for us here and now so we will remain faithful till we can experience the hereafter. Almost invariably statements on the intermediate and eternal states are couched in apocalyptic imagery so that by the very form of extreme expression we should understand that they lie beyond our ken. Eternal time may be used

130

simply to indicate extreme degree as in the statement "He scared me to death" or "I'll never do it again." Actual endless hell is removed from the picture on the basis of first principles like the love of God and his previous manner of operating in the world. Eternal opportunity, then, derives from first principles, and eternal hell falls out under the figurativeness principle all because the anticipations of scripture are from the limited perspective of this age.

Although we can agree with some points in the notion of eschatological limit, we contend that the general truth it expresses becomes false by making the future utterly different from today. The future states cannot be wholly different from our own present age or human kind could not even participate in them. Sequence, separation, fellowship, love, and other equally fundamental concepts we have no reason to discard. Trying to get rid of all information about the afterlife constitutes an overreaction to unnecessary literalism. It is one thing to say, for example, that the great gulf of separation between Lazarus and the rich man does not have to be literally an expanse of space people can see across but cannot traverse; it is quite another to say that no case can be made out for any form of separation between the saved and the lost. Being limited to this universe does not preclude understanding something about the future "worlds." Scripture can communicate to the reader something as basic as a lack of further opportunity for positive relationship to God.

The very least we could say to the doctrine of universalism is that it could possibly avoid being disproved, but the positive arguments for it fall short of being convincing. More realistically, however, universalism will never come true because eternal opportunity will not be extended to those guilty of utter rejection (Mt. 12:32), the only possibility being that no one ever commit blasphemy of the Holy Spirit. Finally, we feel the emphasis on biblical ambiguity about future states has been overdone. Conceiving of hell as what man sought in his disobedience seems clear enough and fair enough. Refused love brings condemnation that is self-justified and, in a way, self-inflicted.

Chapter Ten

PARTICULARISM

Introduction

Under *limited universalism* we combined universal and limiting factors in the number of people covered by the atonement; it was universal as to who may accept it and limited as to who will accept it. *Universalism* made the unlimited factor dominant over the limited one so that all people are saved at least eventually. To finish the list of possibilities, this present chapter discusses *particularism*, which makes the limited factor dominant. The limitation, however, does not come so much from men's unwillingness to accept as from God's not intending the atonement for them all. Instead, God has chosen, or "elected," a definite number to benefit from the blood of Christ. Within this basic structure two variants have been developed. The one supposes that (a) God first chose whom he would save and then planned to send Christ to save them; the other supposes that (b) God first planned to provide salvation through Christ and then chose whom he would save. Either way a one-to-one correlation exists between those for whom Christ died and those whom God chose to save. God intended only to save some rather than to make salvation possible for all.

Particularism is not a separate doctrinal item, but stands in a context that requires it or at least harmonizes with it. Traditionally the total doctrinal system has been described in six sequential points: inscrutable sovereignty plus "TULIP," an acronym for *T*otal depravity, *U*nconditional election, *L*imited atonement, *I*rresistible grace, and *P*erseverance of the saints. (a) *Inscrutable sovereignty* means not only that "God's ways are past finding out" and do not have to appear consistent to men, but that in salvation he directs his will without reference to considerations in one lost person as compared to another. (b) *Total depravity* means that by virtue of Adam's original act of disobedience his nature was changed in such a way that all his descendants have inherited a fallen nature with no ability to choose God without miraculous assistance. (c) *Unconditional election* refers to the lack of any condition, act, or choice as a basis for being chosen. (d) *Limited atonement* is a synonym for "particularism," in which the work of Christ intentionally pertains only to selected individuals; "definite atonement" is another synonym for it. (e) *Irresistible grace* indicates that the elect cannot refuse to believe and repent when the Spirit quickens them to respond to the gospel. Finally, (f) *perseverance* signifies unfailing faithfulness till death.

Obviously if a person possesses no capacity for response to Christ (total depravity), no act on his part can logically precede Christ's atonement for him (unconditional grace). If grace is unconditional, the atonement would have no reason to be intended in any sense for more than the ones God actually chose to save (limited atonement). Likewise those chosen could not refuse to be saved or the intended scope of atonement would fail (irresistible grace). Particularism shares with universalism the conviction that grace is irresistible; the difference lies in whether the grace is universal.

Arguments for Particularism

Model for atonement

A special understanding of Romans 9 furnishes the model for limited atonement. Paul's discussion includes four background elements for his theme that God's program is not of man, but of himself (9:11, 16, 18): (a) the choice of Isaac over Ishmael (9:6-9); (b) the choice of Jacob over Esau (9:10-13); (c) the choice to have mercy or harden (9:14-18); (d) the choice to make a vessel of honor or dishonor (9:19-24). In all four instances God supposedly chooses without reference to any quality or any act in the one chosen; therefore, by comparison the number of those actually saved cannot be altered by any quality or act in the ones needing salvation. In keeping with the idea that salvation is unconditional, atonement is specific. God has the *right* (inscrutable sovereignty) to *choose* aside from factors in the chosen ones (unconditional election) whom he will *save* (specific atonement).

Choosing Isaac. According to the particularist reconstruction of Romans 9, God chose Isaac to be the one through whom the lineage would be counted in developing a promised nation. Abraham's surrogate son by Hagar was set aside from fulfilling the role of heir even though in Near Eastern custom he would legitimately have received the inheritance. God simply exercised his sovereignty and annulled that procedure because he decided for inscrutable reasons to give Sarah a son after natural fertility had passed. There was nothing about Isaac personally that qualified him above Ishmael for this favor except perhaps that God himself miraculously brought about the birth of Isaac. Similarly, children

133

of God are reckoned according to promise instead of reckoned according to their own doing, and Christ died for those God reckoned to make his children.

In this illustration, however, unconditionality is clearly not Paul's reason for citing the event, because co-operation is demonstrated in it. The birth of Isaac was miraculous, but it was not a virgin birth. His parents co-operated with God both with their wills (inner) and their bodies (outer). God's power established the decisive factor for bringing about this child of promise so his sovereignty could elect him as official heir; nevertheless, prior to the choice came the acceptance and co-operation of Abraham and Sarah. In relation to salvation, however, inner or outer acts of men do not produce the result in whole or in part. Paul obviously does not appeal to the Isaac-Ishmael differentiation in order to teach unconditional, and therefore limited, atonement because the illustration does not demonstrate unconditionality. Rather it demonstrates sovereign right to choose even contrary to human expectancy. We conclude that sovereignty of divine choice exhausts Paul's reason for referring to the incident; unconditionality in salvation would have to come from other evidence.

Choosing Jacob. Before Jacob or Esau had done anything good or bad, God decided to set aside the right of primogeniture—the right of the older son to govern the family: "The older will serve the younger" (Gen. 25:23; Rom. 9:11-12). "Jacob I loved, but Esau I hated" (Mal. 1:2; Rom. 9:13). Loving the one and hating the other appears to contrast positive love with a neutral attitude rather than with a negative one. Despite the command to love father and mother, Jesus says on one occasion, "If anyone comes to me and does not hate his father and mother . . . , he cannot be my disciple" (Lk. 14:26). Positive vs. neutral may be the point in Jacob's loving Rachel and "hating" Leah (Gen. 29:31) and in the teaching about loving a neighbor while "hating" an enemy (Mt. 5:43-48; Lk. 6:27-38; 16:13). God told Samuel that he had "rejected" Eliab, David's brother, from the kingship when all that was meant is that he had passed over Eliab in choosing David as the future king (I Sam. 16:6-7). Applied to salvation, the concept is often described as passing over some (hating) in the saving of others (loving). All men justly deserve condemnation; God's holiness operates on many as he passes over them and lets them face their appointed destiny; God's love operates on the others he chooses to redeem.

134

The notion of passing over some to help others reminds us of the ancient pagan concept of "the impassibility of the gods." Evidently, it was argued, the gods do not have feelings or emotions because men could exercise a certain amount of control over them by appealing to their feelings; hence, the gods would not be sovereign if they could love. But love is not just an emotion; it is a manner of giving one's self for the needs of others. Neither is love God's lone characteristic. His love is bounded by his holiness so that his compassionate response to human need always stands within the confines of self-consistency.

Passing over some in *blessing* others can operate in this-worldly affairs like the formation of a special nation through Jacob rather than Esau. To apply such a procedure without qualification to situations of *need* is not natural to what scripture means by "love." If all men need salvation from sin and death, it might be legally proper to help some without helping others (justice); but it would not be loving to pass over six starving children to feed two—unless, of course, the benefactor had resources inadequate for them all. Christians should follow the example of God and love their enemies by feeding them and giving them something to drink when needed (Mt. 5:43-48; Lk. 6:27-38; Rom. 14:12-21). How can divine love reside in a man who sees need without having compassion (I Jn. 4:17-21)? How then could divine love reside in a God who sees the need of the lost without having compassion on them? Passing over a majority in order to save some is not what we would expect Paul to be teaching about the God who calls men to be like him in meeting the needs of brothers and enemies alike. Romans 9 therefore cites the Jacob-Esau differentiation as an example of sovereign right to choose, not as an example of sovereign right to choose unconditionally as in the theory of limited atonement. Passing over Esau in order to bless Jacob is not a model for salvation because it is not a situation of *need*, but of *blessing*. The atonement applies to a situation of need.

A similar distinction applies to Deuteronomy 7:7-8:

> Yahweh did not set his love upon you or choose you because you were more in number than any people, for you were the fewest of all peoples; but because Yahweh loves you and because he would keep the oath that he swore to your fathers. Yahweh has brought you out with a mighty hand and redeemed you out of the house of bondage from the hand of Pharaoh king of Egypt.

Again the passage is not talking about an eternal need, but a temporal blessing. Statements about blessing should not be combined with statements about eternal need and used as the model for salvation; otherwise a contradiction is created between what God's offspring are called upon to do and what God himself does.

Choosing to have mercy. In having mercy or in hardening, God says he will act on whom he chooses. The original quotation about having mercy comes from Exodus 33:12-23. After the golden-calf incident Yahweh threatened to withdraw his presence from the Israelites; but because Moses found favor with God, he granted his request to continue with the nation. Moses then proceeded to ask to see God's glory, whereupon the reply in question was given. Having mercy upon whom he would evidently meant that Moses should not suppose that just because he asked, Yahweh would automatically grant his request. The Lord processes prayers through his sovereignty; they are not like prescriptions he automatically fills on demand. Perhaps the statement originally was meant to grant Moses his request while at the same time curbing any tendency toward familiarity and curiosity.

Paul's application of Exodus 33:19 would be a misapplication if he intended to suggest by it that nothing in the person affected the dispensing of grace. The original context says repeatedly that Moses found favor in God's sight (Ex. 33:12, 13, 16, 17). That favor obviously included his innocence in the golden-calf incident and his holy indignation at it when he found it out. When Moses told God to blot him out of his book if he would not forgive their idolatry, God replied, "Whoever has sinned against me I will blot out of my book" (Ex. 32:31-33). Moses sinned in other respects, but he had not sinned in this incident. There was then something in him that underlay the favor he had in God's eyes. Here as elsewhere the character of the person did affect the granting of a request: "The supplication of a *righteous* man avails much in its operation" (James 5:16; cp. Jn. 9:31). Since this principle resides in the Exodus context from which Paul quotes, his reason for quoting it cannot be to deny that principle. Therefore, the relevance of Exodus 32-33 is the sovereignty God has in such matters. Whether sovereignty operates conditionally or unconditionally becomes a further consideration determined by the nature of the case, but unconditionality in salvation is not a point that originates from Romans 9:14-16. God wills to have mercy sovereignly, but he wills to express his mercy sovereignly to

136

those who meet his conditions for receiving it. There is no contradiction in sovereign action conditioned on response because the Sovereign has specified the acceptable conditions and is the only actor when he does it.

Hardening. As with the mercy quotation, the Pharaoh reference also lacks any implication that divine favor in salvation operates unconditionally. Nowhere in Exodus does scripture require or even suggest that God hardened Pharaoh in any way that circumvented free choice. In passages like Deuteronomy 29:4; Isaiah 29:10; and Romans 11:8 biblical interpretation must let the conventions of a language operate, including the "streamlining" of a cause-effect series. For example, when the Father gave the Israelites the "true bread out of heaven" (Jn. 6:32), he did not do so in a way that circumvented the Son's free choice to come (Jn. 6:38). When things are given, the receiver is not passive but responds in acceptance. When Jesus told the woman with an issue of blood, "Your faith has saved you," he did not mean that mind succeeded over matter; Jesus saved her from her condition (Mt. 9:22; Mk. 5:34; Lk. 8:48; cp. Mk. 10:52; Lk. 7:50; 17:19; 18:42). When in Romans 11:6-8 Paul quotes Isaiah 29:10 and Deuteronomy 29:4 to the effect that God gave the Israelites a spirit of stupor, he does not mean that God irresistibly made them so they could not see or hear; if God had made them sin irresistibly, he would have been the author of sin. According to Acts 14:27 God opened a door of faith to the Gentiles, but the previous chapters show that the mode of that opening was through human proclamation. What a person does through another he does himself.

In Hebrew idiom especially, God can be said to do what in fact he only originates, allows, or oversees: the *mariners* threw Jonah overboard (Jonah 1:15), but *God* is also said to have thrown him overboard (Jonah 2:3). To suppose that God nullified the will of those sailors is gratuitous; to suppose that he canceled Pharaoh's choice is likewise arbitrary; to suppose therefore that election is unconditional is unnecessary. Pharaoh hardened his own heart in response to events that should have opened his heart; God hardened his heart inasmuch as he mediated to him miraculous events that were the occasion of hardening. Strictly speaking, it is the deceitfulness of past sinfulness that hardens the heart (Heb. 3:13; Eph. 4:22), not the intentional will of the Holy God of Israel.

Forming a vessel. Paul closes out his set of examples in Romans 9 by comparing God's choice to making a vessel of honor or a vessel for menial tasks (Rom. 9:19-24; cp. II Tim. 2:20-21). As the potter has a right to make either kind from a given lump, so God has the right—according to particularism—to choose unconditionally whom to save and whom to destroy.

As with the other three examples, however, Paul's point is not unconditional election, but the right to elect according to principles he deems appropriate. It is not said that his election is capricious, arbitrary, or unconditional, but that it is sovereign. (a) No one makes vessels for the sheer purpose of destroying them. (b) Particularly, no one makes vessels for destruction that involve him in enduring them with "much long-suffering." (c) Conditional vs. unconditional is completely foreign to making pottery anyway, if that in fact were to explain the reason for using the illustration. Actually, (d) Paul elsewhere adjusts the pottery illustration so it can apply to people who have wills to meet conditions for being honored by God: "In a large house there are not only gold and silver vessels, but wooden and earthen ones, and some are for honor and some are for menial use. *If then anyone cleanses himself from these things,* he will be a vessel for honor, sanctified, useful for the master, prepared for every good deed" (II Tim. 2:20-21). (e) The classical potter's passage in Jeremiah 18:1ff. may lie behind the Romans reference; if so, it too involves conditionality because it says that God will reverse his decision to destroy or benefit a nation if the nation changes. In making a vessel, the potter demonstrates his sovereignty by making it however he pleases since it can have no choice in the matter; in making a son, God demonstrates his sovereignty first by establishing the conditions for being reckoned a son, for people can choose to cleanse themselves and to accept God's cleansing; secondly, he expresses his sovereignty by actually doing the reckoning.

Besides objections raised against the five illustrations singly, two general observations prevent a particularist interpretation of Romans 9. (1) Only what is common to all four illustrations can be included in Paul's reason for citing them. There is *co-operation* in the Isaac-Ishmael illustration, *unconditionality* in the pottery and Esau-Jacob examples, and *mediation* in the Pharaoh episode. Unconditionality in salvation cannot be the point of the illustrations even though unconditionality may be exhibited in one or two of them; the application to salvation must be kept at the more general level of sovereign choice instead of narrowing it to unconditional sovereign choice; otherwise the reader is guilty of "allegorizing the comparison" by making too many parallels between the examples and the thing they exemplify.

(2) The interpreter should claim Paul's authority only for the application Paul makes of the examples: (a) that it is not the children of the flesh, but the children of promise whom God reckons as the seed (9.8), (b) ". . . that the purpose of God according to choice might stand, not of works, but of him who calls" (9:11); and (c) that receiving mercy is from him who does or does not show it (9:16, 18). For something to be "not of works" does not mean that doing something is not required for the result, but that such "doing something" does not produce the result or necessitate it. The purpose of him who calls may or may not be conditioned on the deeds of the chosen; the point is that those deeds do not of themselves determine the outcome. God decides the result and he decides whether there are conditions and what deeds he will honor in relation to his gift.

In Romans 9 Paul infers from his illustrations the seemingly obvious point that being chosen is done by the chooser, not the chosen. The application is to Israel, who had been favored by God's choices before (in contrast to Ishmaelites, Edomites, and Egyptians), and should not object to God's choice now to include Gentiles in his favor (9:24-33; Hosea 1:10; 2:23). After all, it was not because the Jews were such holy people that God selected them (Deut. 7:7-8). Despite having the law, they exhibited (Rom. 9:30-32) many of the same sins found among the heathen. Thus they deserved a full cutting off like Sodom and Gomorrah (9:27-29) instead of the remnant God brought back from the exile (Isa. 1:9; 10:22-23).

Paul deals then with the question of how many the special people-of-God privilege is overtly open to, not particularly with the question of how many believe and actually become special people of God (Rom. 9:24-26, 33; Isa. 28:16). Strictly speaking, Paul is discussing the general range of people God is openly dealing with in the *Christian era*, not the number of individuals benefiting from it unto *eternal salvation*. Whereas there may be unconditionality in selecting the range of people, conditionality still applies to whether he continues to deal with that people or how many of them will reap eternal salvation out of those dealings.

God plays the decisive role in all his affairs with people. *Sovereignty* applies to all relationships corporate or individual, eternal or temporal, in selecting a task force or continuing to work through it. The *mode*

139

of sovereignty—conditional or unconditional—varies between each of these pairs and operates according to circumstance. Unconditionality in individual, eternal salvation is too restricted a matter to present as an apostolic model undergirding the doctrine of particular atonement. The atonement model implied by Romans 9 is not unconditional atonement, but sovereign atonement, which may be conditional if the rest of scripture so teaches.

Efficacious results

According to the doctrine of particularism the rest of scripture does not teach conditional atonement. Instead it teaches that God always accomplishes what he purposes and the will of men cannot frustrate his designs: "If while we were enemies we were reconciled to God through the death of his son; much more, being reconciled, we will be saved by his life" (Rom. 5:10; cp. 8:32; II Cor. 5:21; Gal. 1:4; 3:13; Eph. 1:7; etc.). Accordingly, since God purposed in Jesus Christ to save men, he will certainly bring about their salvation. Under conditionality God would not certainly be bringing to pass the salvation of those choosing not to meet the conditions; he would not be saving those he planned to save.

Students of scripture agree that God always accomplishes what he purposes, but particularism does not properly state the purpose of God in the work of Christ. His purpose in Christ was not to bring about the salvation of men; his purpose in Christ was to bring about the possibility of salvation for all men and to bring about the actual salvation of all men who accept it. That purpose he has accomplished and will accomplish. In those passages that speak of an accomplished reconciliation, the accomplishment pertains to those who have accepted Christ. For them the potential reconciliation did become actual reconciliation. Becoming actual for them does not eliminate being potential for others.

Particular sacrifice

According to particularism the rest of scripture also does not teach conditional atonement because Christ died for his own: "Take heed to yourselves and to all the flock in which the Holy Spirit has made you overseers to feed the church of God that he purchased through his own blood" (Acts 20:28; cp. Mt. 1:21; Jn. 10:11, 15; 11:51-52; 15:13; Rom. 8:32; Eph. 5:25-27; Tit. 2:14).

The list of texts about Christ's dying for the saved does nothing to establish particularism. Dying for all men obviously includes dying for all who accept his death. Of course, those who do accept his death are distinguishable because his potential atonement for all has become his actual atonement for all who accepted him. Paul does not mean that Christ died only for Paul just because he speaks of "the Son of God who loved me and gave himself for me" (Gal. 2:20). The angel did not mean that Christ died only for the Jews when he told Joseph in a dream, "You shall call his name Jesus because *he* will save his people from their sins" (Mt. 1:21; cp. Acts 13:23). Likewise statements about laying down his life for the church do not restrict its potential range to its actual range.

Particular intercession

Jesus limits his intercessory role in the highpriestly prayer: "I am praying for them; I am not praying for the world, but for the ones whom you have given me" (Jn. 17:9). But intercession operates more narrowly than atonement because intercession in the sense of John 17 occurs only with those actually redeemed. Intercession could also be viewed as universal if it were considered in a potential sense; Christ is potential intercessor for all even as he is the potential atonement for all. It was not of the elect that Jesus said, "Father, forgive them because they do not know what they are doing" (Lk. 23:34). He actually intercedes for some even as he actually atones for some.

Arguments Against Limited Universalism

All classes of men

Particularism has used various techniques for reinterpreting passages favoring limited universalism. One method employs the class idea so that "all men" means all men as to kind rather than all men as to number. "All kinds of men" does not necessarily include *every* individual within each class. I Timothy 2:4, 6 may conceivably refer to all kinds of men because the apostle has just enjoined prayer for "all men—for kings and all who are in high places" (2:1-2). God's wanting all men to be saved (2:4) and Christ's giving himself as a ransom for all men would not have to contradict the concept of limited atonement; the gospel benefits more than commoners, slaves, or Jews (2:7).

Titus 2:11 talks about "bringing salvation to all men," but it does so immediately after a series of comments regarding aged men (2:2), aged and younger women (2:3-5), younger men (2:6-8), slaves and slave owners (2:9-10). While on I Timothy 2:4, 6 and Titus 2:11 the class idea may be possible, it is obviously not at all necessary unless a person first has an external reason for such a limitation. Unless Romans 9 can establish that reason, nothing needs to qualify the universal import of passages like these.

Passages about Christ's death for the world receive similar treatment by particularists. John 3:17 says that God sent his Son into the world that the world might be saved through him. "The world" does not mean everyone in the world, but all classes of men in the world; he died for the world, not just for Jews (Rom. 11:12, 15), and not just for those already in the fold (I Jn. 2:2?).

According to John 3:18, disbelief is a sin, yet disbelief could not be a sin in those for whom Christ did not die. When standards do not apply, they cannot condemn.

In John 1:29; 6:33, 51; I John 2:2; and II Corinthians 5:19, nothing particularly in the context suggests that the authors meant "kind" rather than "extent" when they talk about the work of Christ. Moreover, John 3:16 and 6:33-35 individualize the atonement by saying that whoever in the world believes on Christ may have eternal life. Finally, if God loved the world even as to kind only, we wonder why he would love one sinner in it and not another. If he can love the extreme sinners that have actually come to Christ, he can love any sinner; yet according to particularism he does not love them in the sense of John 3:16.

The counterresponse is that God's reason, if any, for loving one rather than another is simply unrevealed, which seems plausible; but that answer amounts to an appeal to silence for preserving an interpretation of these passages that they do not require. No external basis for limiting the atonement has previously been found. Using silence or divine sovereignty to defend selective love is illegitimate when the difficulty with limited love is created by the theory of limited atonement, not by the direct statement of scripture itself. The person responsible for a viewpoint bears responsibility for answering questions created by it. If he cannot at least postulate answers, he must proclaim the concept as an opinion, not as a doctrine of scripture. Relying on silence puts the interpreter in a position where his misunderstanding escapes correction. He operates as if his understanding of scripture equals scripture so

142

as to avoid critique. Invoking silence is not an answer; it is an admission that there is no answer to remove inconsistency between interpretation and scripture. To put it differently, appealing to silence is a tacit claim not to have to answer.

Our critique on this matter relates to a principle of thought that the burden of proof rests on the affirmative. Others are not obliged to accept a position just because they cannot disprove it. Appealing to silence shirks the responsibility for providing evidence; such a procedure is not valid elsewhere and has no place in religious studies. If scripture and religious studies are not subject to the appropriate laws of thought, these studies have put themselves not only beyond refutation, but beyond validation as well. Should the objection be raised that these concerns are not matters of human reason, then we must object that human reason has created the difficulty by an inadequate use of reason in the interpretation process. Truth is not originated by reason, but it is recognized by reason. The need to make use of silence ought to signal the need to re-examine previous conclusions reached in the work of interpretation.

Saying that "reconciling the world" in II Corinthians 5:19 must involve some restriction to avoid universalism does not require restriction in the intended extent of the atonement; it may involve restriction in its actualization. There is more to the intent of the atonement than its scope; in the intent of the atonement there is also the conditional manner in which it is applied to individuals. Both universal scope and conditional actualization participate equally in the divine intent; consequently, there is no reason to fear that sovereignty would be lost if free will prevented someone from accepting the atonement who was intended to receive it. Such a case would not happen, not because the person has to "accept," but because the intent is conditional. Definite atonement as well as universalism incorrectly supposes an effective atonement instead of a conditional one. If atonement is truly interpersonal, it must be conditional in order to involve both sides of the relationship.

All the elect

Different authors of particularist persuasion handle differently the passages that underlie the position of limited universalism. II Peter 3:9 says that God wants all to come to a knowledge of the truth. Should it be proposed that the reference is only to all the elect, three objections apply: (a) the statement is in a context with universal emphasis because it talks about the flood and the consummation. (b) Wanting all to come to a knowledge of the truth parallels not wanting any to perish. (c) No mechanism in the passage suggests a limitation on God's desire to have men avoid perishing.

All in God's complacent will

The concept. Usually II Peter 3:9, Hebrews 2:9; Ezekiel 33:11 are handled by a different mechanism. Traditionally particularism has distinguished between the "will of preterition" and "the will of complacency." The former means what God has decided in eternity past and has retained as his hidden will; the latter means that God is willing to let everyone come and so offers the gospel to all people according to his revealed will.

The hermeneutical objection. Differentiating preterite will and complacent will does not satisfy the requirements of these texts because (a) the passages talk about God's *desire* that no one be lost, not just universal *offer* of the gospel. God does go ahead and offer salvation to those whom he knows will not accept it. He operates with men honestly in letting them refuse his offer; their refusal removes the excuse that they would have accepted salvation if they had only known about it. But there is no reason to offer salvation to people God has already appointed not to be able to respond to it. His secret will only contains the verdict that he has reached on the basis of foreseen rejection or acceptance. The proclamation logically preceded that hidden will. Not just universal offer, but universal concern is God's revealed will.

(b) Complacent will does not fit with the structure of thought in II Peter 3:9. Either way the "willing" in II Peter is read, the complacency idea creates difficulties: ". . . not actively-willing that any should perish, but [actively-willing] that all would come to repentance"; ". . . not complacently-willing that any should perish, but [complacently-willing] that all come to repentance." The first alternative denies the particularist view that God is complacently willing to let all come; the second denies the context because "not complacently-willing" means "actively willing" so that God actively wills the death of those for whom he is patiently waiting to repent (cp. 3:15; I Pet. 3:20; Rom. 2:4; 9:22; I Tim. 1:16; Rev. 2:21; Ex. 34:6; Prov. 3:12). The previous verse declares that God is longsuffering unto the repentance of the wicked; consequently, he does not actively will their death in the same sense and at the same time. Furthermore, Ezekiel 33:11; 18:23, and 18:32 declare that God

144

has no pleasure in the death of the wicked. In Ezekiel 33:11 he says with an oath, "As I live, says the Lord Yahweh, I have no pleasure in the death of the wicked, but [I have pleasure] that the wicked turn from his way and live" (cp. Hosea 11:8-9). Complacency does not fit with the demands of the immediate and distant contexts of II Peter 3:9, for God does not take a passive attitude toward the condition of the lost.

Under the concept of complacent will, love again gets misdefined as distinguishing love, a concept in scripture clearly applied to temporal blessings only (Deut. 7:7-8; Mal. 1:2-3; Rom. 9:13). The love God calls upon his servants to have is one that fulfills the needs of those in need. Complacently letting men pass into eternal condemnation hardly represents the kind of concern God's messengers are to have in presenting the good news of salvation to *every* creature.

The philosophical objection. (c) Differentiating preterite and complacent will also creates a contradiction between the message and the fact. In the presentation the evangelist is presumably free to include anything taught in the Bible. Consequently, he will say that God desires the salvation of all sinners, that Christ died for *every* man, and that he has no pleasure in the death of the wicked but wants them to turn and live; yet the truth is that he has appointed a majority of them to hell.

Our comments here reflect a long-standing criticism of particular atonement: the difference between revealed and hidden will means that the proclamation of the gospel does not present a bona fide invitation to salvation. Whether it is an offer in "good faith" may be a problem of terms, but the realities are these in the particularist system of thought:
1. in consequence of Adam's sin, God "depravitized" our common ancestor either directly by decree or indirectly by intentionally creating him in such a way that an act of sin would make him unable to do good;
2. God passed that depravity biologically onto all Adam's descendants;
3. God offers the gospel to men whom he made unable to respond to it.

Offering implies "may accept"; depravitizing means "cannot accept." The proclaimed message not only *differs* from the hidden decree; it *contradicts* it. When free will does not reside in the creature, only the Creator has it. Whether the will is hidden or revealed is immaterial because God is the only essential actor; whether the depravity is direct or indirect is also immaterial because God is the only cause.

We affirm that this system of thought implicates God in two unacceptable ways: (a) he mocks the sinner to offer him what he cannot want, but is sent to hell for refusing, all the while making him unable to want it. (b) He causes him to sin further by commanding the man to do something he has made him unable to do, yet God does not tempt any man with evil (James 1:13). The hidden-revealed, or preterite-complacent, distinction in the divine will needs to be replaced with actual-potential. In his own "hidden will" God has *actually decided* to save some men on the basis of foreknown free response to the gospel; in his "revealed will" he provides *potential acceptance* to all men.

Particularism attempts to retain the preterite-complacent distinction without making God blameworthy. A use is made of the difference between compulsion and necessity. "Compulsion" means being forced from the outside; "necessity" means being forced from within. Man's own internal depravity causes his sin and refusal of salvation; God does not force him from the outside to sin and refuse reconciliation.

The inner-outer distinction becomes impertinent, nevertheless, because according to particularism itself the inner depravity that necessarily produces sin originated outside in God who irresistibly depravitized our common ancestor in such a way that depravity is transmitted into each of us by birth. The situation *is not* one in which each man has chosen a nature that produces subsequent actions he cannot avoid; admittedly a drunk who kills someone is guilty of murder even if he could not help himself, for he was responsible for getting into a condition where he could not help himself. The situation *is* one in which each man has supposedly received aside from choice a nature that produces subsequent actions he cannot avoid. At the point of choice lies the point of guilt; God's depravitizing man is the point of choice; therefore God is guilty if anyone is guilty.

Human inability

According to definite atonement there can be no potentiality in salvation because a man has no ability to meet the conditions for making potential salvation into actual salvation in his own case. Therefore salvation established is no broader than salvation applied. The change in man's capacity for faith must be accomplished supernaturally by divine agency: ". . . neither does anyone know the Father except the Son and the one to whom the Son wants to reveal him" (Mt. 11:27b;

cp. Jn. 6:44). In accordance with the number of those God plans to save and enable to believe, Christ died only for the elect.

We have simply denied that scripture teaches the doctrine of natural depravity. Further, we have denied that God grants faith and repentance in the sense that the person receives by that grant a capacity for faith and repentance. The references used to prove this idea have nothing necessarily more in view than the *opportunity* to believe and repent.

Even if men needed supernatural aid to accept the gospel, it would not necessarily make atonement definite, or particular, rather than potentially universal. God could empower all men to respond and then allow them to refuse salvation or meet the conditions upon which Christ's universal atonement becomes actual for them individually. According to scripture God sent his Son to establish salvation, and according to all interpreters of scripture the atonement he wrought was *sufficient* for all men. It would have added no more to his sufferings to have made it *applicable* to all. God has sent his Son; he has gone to great lengths in calling all men; he commands his ministers to present it to them all; he does not want anyone to die, yet presumably the one thing needful he knowingly withholds. If God did not spare his own Son, we would expect him to give freely whatever is needful for salvation through him.

Granted conditions

Not only did the atonement establish the salvation possibility; it secures the fulfillment of the conditions that would have to be met to have it if meeting conditions were possible. Of *repentance* the Jerusalem leaders said, "Then to the Gentiles also God has given repentance unto life" (Acts 11:18). Peter had earlier told the Sanhedrin, "God exalted him at his right hand to be a prince and a savior, to give repentance to Israel and remission of sins" (5:31). Paul told the Romans, "Do you despise the goodness of his riches and forbearance and longsuffering, not knowing that the goodness of God leads you to repentance?" (Rom. 2:4). The apostle writes in II Timothy that the servant of the Lord needs to correct "them that oppose one another if perhaps God may give them repentance unto the knowledge of the truth" (2:25).

The statement made in Acts 11 responds to the conversion of Cornelius and his household, the first Gentile converts in the Christian age. "Giving repentance" does not mean giving the act of repentance or the ability to repent, but giving the opportunity to repent. Salvation

147

through Messiah is epitomized under the concept of repentance. "Giving an act" in Jewish idiom can mean to allow the act, make it possible, or even supervise its being caused. Revelation 2:7 promises, "To him that overcomes I will give to him to eat of the tree of life that is in the paradise of God" (cp. Gen. 20:6; Ex. 3:19; Num. 20:21; 21:23; Deut. 18:14; Job 9:18; II Ch. 20:10). The Hebrew writer says, "If Joshua had given them [the Israelites] rest, he [David] would not have spoken afterward of another day" (4:8; cp. Acts 22:14). The Israelites helped conquer Canaan, yet Joshua "gave" them the land. The passage in Romans 2 does not mean that God is leading the readers to repentance in some irresistible way. If men could not repent, being patient with them would do no good (cp. II Pet. 3:9; Rev. 2:21). Rather, Paul means that delay in the judgment needs to be read as grace that gives the sinner more chance to repent.

In regard to *faith* Paul tells the Philippians, "To you it was granted on behalf of Christ, not only to believe on him, but to suffer for him" (1:29). To the Galatians he also says, "Christ redeemed us from the curse of the law, having become a curse for us . . . that upon the Gentiles might come the blessing of Abraham in Christ Jesus, that we might receive the promise of the Spirit through faith" (3:13-14). Luke 10:22 says in the mouth of Jesus, "No one knows the Father except . . . him to whomever the Son wills to reveal him." Apollos helped the Achaians much "who had believed through grace" (Acts 18:27). James declares, "By his will he brought us forth by the word of truth that we might be a kind of firstfruits of his creatures" (1:18). In a classic text he writes to the Ephesians, "By grace you have been saved through faith and that not of yourselves; it is the gift of God" (2:8).

As with repentance, "giving" faith means giving the opportunity or the basis for believing. The Galatians passage is talking about giving the promise, not giving the faith. Ephesians 2:8 does not really belong to the idea of "securing the fulfillment of the conditions" because it does not say that faith is not of ourselves, but that salvation is not of ourselves. "Saved through faith and that not of yourselves" is constructed in the Greek text so the word "that" refers to the idea in the verb "saved" instead of referring to "faith." The "gift of God" and the thing "not of ourselves" is salvation: "By grace you have been saved through faith and that [*salvation*] is not of yourselves; it is the gift of God." Another apparent interpretation could take the whole idea of saved by faith as

148

the reference of "that": "By grace you have been saved through faith and that [*salvation by faith*] is not of yourselves; it is the gift of God." "Saved by faith," however, is evidently not the antecedent of "that" in 2:8 because "that" must refer to something that can be the subject of the implied verb in 2.9. "[*Salvation by faith* is] not of works lest anyone should boast." It is more natural, we feel, to say, "[Salvation is] not of works . . . ." At any rate, either way the verse is taken it does not teach that the *faith* is given, but that salvation is given and is not caused by faith. Consequently, we must deny the proposition that scripture anywhere means to say that the atonement of Christ accomplishes the fulfillment of the very conditions upon which salvation would be granted if it were conditional.

Works

Inability to meet the conditions for a "potential" salvation has been invoked by particularism because of the more fundamental idea that if a man could respond to the gospel, he could save himself. Natural depravity serves to prevent salvation by works.

When Paul teaches against salvation by works, however, he does not by "works" mean "*doing* something," but "*producing* something." Romans and Galatians argue that salvation cannot come from doing "works of the *law*"; works of the *law* are those which do what the law commands so that righteousness results from "doing" what the law commands. If a person "*continues* to do *all*" the commandments in God's law (Gal. 3:10-11), clearly he is righteous as the direct, inherent result of his own deeds alone. Since everyone has disobeyed the law, no one has the righteousness requisite to divine fellowship. Once righteousness is broken it cannot be achieved again under a law that puts a curse on everyone who does not continue to do everything. Therefore, the reason a sinner cannot save himself is not necessarily because he cannot "do" anything good, but because doing even *every*thing good cannot save him. The problem stems not from the nature of man, but from the nature of imperfection. Once perfection has been lost, imperfection cannot be overcome. "Salvation" means being brought into personal relationship with a righteous God; righteousness is the appropriate quality needed for relationship with a righteous God. Salvation therefore involves becoming righteous; but since righteousness is perfection, the unrighteous cannot become perfect; unrighteousness

149

cannot be overcome because imperfection cannot be overcome. Guarding against salvation by works via the concept of natural depravity is unnecessary because "salvation by *works*" is impossible by the nature of the case. A person's responses in salvation by faith have only the significance of meeting God's conditions for regarding him in terms of the righteousness of Christ. Faith means believing and trusting that identification with Christ and commitment to him serve as an adequate basis for being considered righteous.

Divine sovereignty

The problem posed. Natural depravity has been used unnecessarily to protect against self-salvation, but it has been invoked for yet a more basic reason: the ability to respond to God would eliminate divine sovereignty. The person would be determining his own eternal destiny; that is, free will negates sovereignty. By this time we have traced backwards the line of reasoning outlined above in the introduction. Limited atonement rests on Unconditional grace, which in turn derives from Total depravity under inscrutable Sovereignty.

Philosophical objection. Two main objections militate against this line of thought issuing in limited atonement. Philosophically, absolute determinism, total depravity, and unconditional election demonstrate overkill. Sovereignty only requires that God retain control of his universe; it does not necessitate retaining that control by eliminating freedom of choice from his creatures. Because he is all-powerful, he can establish boundaries on the exercise of any freedom; he grants movement within the boundaries allowed for that freedom. Meeting conditions for God's restoring a person to fellowship can occur without precluding sovereignty because God himself established what those conditions would be. Meeting them only identifies with Christ because the Sovereign has said so, and that identification itself has value only because God so decreed. God is sovereign in deciding (a) to make creatures who could sin, (b) to provide a salvation possibility after they sinned, (c) to choose the conditions for that salvation, (d) to have the destinies that there are, (e) to limit the expression of evil against himself both as to degree and length. *Absolute* free will would eliminate sovereignty, but *limited* free will retains sovereignty by putting a boundary on the expression of the actions that issue from free will. Limited free will also retains the priority of God who gave the free will and allowed it to operate in the area of eternal destiny.

Behind the particularist system of thought stands a presupposition that invalidates the operation of the whole system: determinism is the only means to certainty. Conditionality and free choice mean uncertainty and therefore lack of sovereignty. A free choice, however, is as certain as anything determined, because the reason for certainty lies in the nature of space-time reality, not just in the nature of the thing acting. By the very occurrence of any act—free-choice or otherwise—all parallel possibilities are eliminated. Certainty therefore exists, and what is certain can be known, hence, foreknown. What can be foreknown provides no surprises. As in staying Abraham's hand, God can always enter in between the choice and the act in order to stop any act he wants to prevent. For God to be in control means he is sovereign.

Determinism as the only means to certainty has generated the expression "definite atonement," another designation for particular atonement. Unless God determines atonement, conversion, reconciliation, or redemption, it is supposedly not certain and affords no comfort. In place of the certainty that comes from legal or natural determinism, however, we have put the certainty of faith: God is one whom we can trust to be and do as he has revealed and promised. As for ourselves we need no absolute confidence in becoming or remaining faithful. First, from the nature of things we have no reason to ask for protection against our own wills either to refuse God in the offer of salvation or to desert him afterwards.

Second, from the standpoint of our feelings about things, we would not have concern about our redemption prior to it, but after it. In that case our present certainty about present salvation is sufficient for the present. When the future arrives, we can experience the future's certainty at that time, knowing he is dependable always. We do not need absolute certainty now about our salvation later; it is sufficient to remember now that *God* commits himself to our nurture (I Cor. 10:12-13) as assuredly as to our redemption. Eternal rewards call for temporal responsibility; consequently *we* have the responsibility now to strengthen ourselves under God's mighty hand (I Pet. 5:6-7) in anticipation of future temptation (Heb. 10:19-25) because continued growth in the present safeguards against apostasy in the future. Asking for protection against ourselves sounds like the self-centeredness that is supposedly removed by conversion; asking for protection against free will stands contrary to desiring to have the dignity free will affords. We take it that more abundance of life comes from being able to accept salvation freely than from having no ability to do otherwise; we also take it that God is more greatly glorified by sons who can choose not to reject him.

If freedom of the will precludes divine sovereignty, Adam and Satan could not have possessed the power of choice before they fell or God would not have been sovereign then either. If God's creatures do not have free choice, evil could not have originated in their free choice. God therefore must be the cause of sin if free will precludes sovereignty.

Hermeneutical objection. Hermeneutically, the interpretation of the core passage in Romans 9 does not require a view of sovereignty in which God chooses the elect without reference to their responses. Romans 9:13 does speak about passing over the oldest twin to show love to Jacob, but that passing over pertains to bestowing a positive blessing, not to fulfilling a need. It has to do with choosing a special nation to work through, not the eternal salvation of men needing divine fellowship.

In 9:20-23 Paul compares his topic to pottery making, but it allegorizes the comparison to consider unconditional God's decision about the station of a man or nation just because making a vessel glorious or menial is done unconditionally. Pottery passages elsewhere in scripture involve conditionality despite its absence in the image itself. God has the right to do everything he does but whether he does it conditionally depends on what it is. Paul's subject in Romans 9 is sovereignty, not unconditionality.

For something to be of "promise" (9:8) means only that those people involved did not bring about the result. Not to be "of works" (9:11) requires only that the actions do not produce the result or put God under obligation. "Having mercy on whom God wills" (9:16) need not mean more than that a request for mercy does not automatically receive affirmative answer. "Hardening whom he wills" (9:18) allows for Pharaoh's free response to signs presented through Moses. The family of Job "comforted him concerning all the evil that *Yahweh* had brought upon him" (Job 42:11), yet *Satan* initiated and brought about the plagues he endured (1:6—2:3). In biblical idiom what Yahweh *permits* may be said to be what Yahweh *does.*

The hypothetical respondent in Romans 9:19 is not quoted because he correctly evaluates the situation by saying, "Why does he still find fault,

152

for who is withstanding his will?" Because Pharaoh's hardening is called God's will does not mean that his obstinacy was God's *positive will.* Instead, Pharaoh's hardening was God's *permissive will* in the sense that he would be allowed to refuse Yahweh's directive to let the Israelites go. God does not tempt men with a view to making them sin (James 1:13-15); their sin may be the result, but not the purpose. Consequently, the respondent is quoted in order to be corrected; he has put an incorrect reconstruction on divine hardening by making it positive instead of permissive, the same reconstruction particularism puts on the divine purpose of the Egyptian plagues. The Lord found fault with Pharaoh because he resisted his positive will to let the people go, not because he was hardened in response to an intent of God to harden him.

Therefore when Paul retorts, "No but, O man, who are you to reply against God?" he does mean the critic should acquiesce to what he properly represents. He rebukes him because he is replying against God with impertinence. By his question he demonstrates his lack of a right to question.

A final matter comes in connection with the "vessels of wrath fitted for destruction." Particularism takes "fitted" as a *passive participle* so as to mean that by creation men are "fitted" by God for destruction. The Greek word may be analyzed as a *middle participle,* in which case men "fit themselves" for destruction. Inasmuch as it is a *perfect participle,* perhaps it is best taken in a stative sense: vessels of wrath "fit" for destruction. At any rate the passage furnishes no reason to think that the atonement is limited because God created some people for the purpose of destroying them.

Universalism

A common accusation against limited universalism is that if Christ did die for all men, the result would be universalism instead of limited universalism. Therefore some kind of limitation is justified on passages like Romans 5:12-21; I Corinthians 15:20-22; and Hebrews 2:9.

The problem poses a false issue because limited universalism believes that Christ died potentially for all, not effectively for all. Since not all are saved, we infer that such passages talk about how many people atonement is possible for, not how many it is actual for. The choice to accept the atonement *potential for all* is what makes the atonement *actual for some.* Conditionality bridges the gulf between a possibility and an actuality. Particularism reads limited universalism as actual universalism because it does not itself have the conditionality concept present in limited universalism. Particularism lacks a conditionality concept because it cannot conceive of an act preceding a result without causing the result.

In reality, one important objection to definite atonement is its own inability to handle satisfactorily the Christ-Adam parallel in Pauline teaching. In Romans 5:12-21 and I Corinthians 15:20-22 particularism does not make Christ coextensive with Adam despite the clear parallel between them, especially in Romans 5:18 and I Corinthians 15:22. (a) *Universalism* honors the parallelism by making all men actually lost in Adam and actually saved in Christ. (b) *Potential universalism* is also consistent in making all men potentially lost in Adam and potentially saved in Christ. Paul is describing how the systems work. A third view, (c) *objective justification*, makes all equally lost and saved in Adam and Christ, but not in a manner bearing on eternal life. Men are representatively lost and saved by Adam and Christ respectively; what is lost in one through no fault of our own (death) is gained in the other through no virtue of our own (resurrection). (d) *Definite atonement,* however, teaches from Romans 5 that all men are lost in Adam, but then draws back from affirming the corresponding statement that "through one act of righteousness the free gift came to all men unto justification of life."

Conclusion

Primarily three views have held sway in Christendom on the intended scope of the atonement. We have defended (a) *limited universalism,* which understands Christ's atonement as potential for all but actual for some. The two other views weight one side or the other of this balance. On one side (b) *universalism* makes Christ's atonement actual for all: if not now, at least eventually. (c) *Particularism* takes the opposite extreme by making his salvation intentionally actual for some.

Scripture contains many passages that employ universal words like "all" and "everyone" in connection with salvation, and a number of options have been generated for understanding them: (a) actual all, (b) potential all, (c) all kinds, (d) all the elect, (e) all in the will of complacency, (f) sufficient for all, (g) offered to all, (h) appropriate to all, and (i) generally all. As interpreters move through the passages in question, they use different ones of these mechanisms at different places in

154

order to arrive at their different conclusions. Legitimacy in using them must finally rest with the honest mind of each person as he interacts with the components of each passage.

As to general method, *limited universalism* notices the unlimited character of passages like John 3:16ff.; II Peter 3:9; Romans 5:18; and Ezekiel 18:30-32. On the other side of the ledger appear references on the final lostness of some people. The inference is that atonement is possible for all but actual for some.

In method, *universalism* stresses the love of God in order to make secondary those passages that seem to require belief in the eternal lostness of disbelievers. *Particularism*, on the other hand, stresses the holiness of God and takes its starting point with a sovereignty that operates through total depravity and unconditional election in order to arrive at limited atonement. As universalism overdoes the love of God, particularism overdoes his holiness. Hopefully in defending *limited universalism*, we have kept love and holiness in proper balance.

In the course of our interaction with particularism, we have raised several conceptual objections in addition to the hermeneutical ones for individual passages.

(1) *Definite atonement misdefines God's love by making it selective.* The Godlike love enjoined on his sons does not shut off compassion to those in need whether friend or foe.

(2) *Definite atonement depersonalizes salvation.* It does not retain the *personal* character of salvation because it makes man operate in terms of nature, or being, and makes God operate like a legal process or a logical syllogism. Love, choice, and power are replaced by mechanical procedures. Limited atonement also does not retain the *interpersonal* character of the God-man relationship because it makes reconciliation one-sided. Since persons have choice, willingness must operate from both sides or the process is person-thing instead of person-person.

(3) *Definite atonement makes God the author of evil.* It denies free will in order to preserve sovereignty so that free will in secondary agencies (Satan, Adam, men) cannot be responsible for the origin of sin.

(4) *Definite atonement does not offer a bona fide call to all sinners.* By God's own appointment they cannot respond to an offer in which he requires response.

(5) *Definite atonement presents a contradiction between God's revealed will and his hidden will.* In the revealed will he has no pleasure

in the loss of any sinner, but in the supposed hidden will he withholds the power to believe from men he knows cannot believe because he has depravitized them.

(6) *Definite atonement does not parallel Adam and Christ coextensively* as Paul requires in Romans and I Corinthians.

The six foregoing objections derive from two philosophical presuppositions: (a) definite atonement cannot conceive of an act logically preceding an effect without causing the effect and thus creating a works situation; thus particularism must affirm total depravity in order to avoid merit. A condition, however, can also logically precede a result and can do so without causing it, thus not creating a works situation. (b) Definite atonement cannot conceive of a free act without relinquishing sovereignty. Free choice, however, functions within a framework maintained by divine omnipotence.

(c) These philosophical presuppositions are supposedly validated by the teaching of Romans 9, but passing over Esau to choose Jacob describes a model for bestowing *blessing*, not a model for fulfilling *need*. Therefore the impersonal, implacable God pictured in definite atonement is set aside in favor of the God and Father of our Lord Jesus Christ, "Who is the Savior of all men, especially of them that believe."

Part Five—The Application of Salvation

Chapter Eleven

THE FOREKNOWLEDGE OF GOD

Introduction

Under the general heading of God's *grace* comes the *basis for salvation* established by the death-resurrection of Jesus Christ. Once the possibility for salvation has been set up, there is an *application* of salvation to the lost. The process involves two things: the *activity of God* and the *response of man*. God's grace expressed in creation, revelation, and the work of Christ involved nothing on man's part, because men had nothing to do with God's acting in these ways. In applying the benefits of Christ's work to the individual, however, God has allowed each person to help determine whether he will be benefitted by God's grace. There is a selection made among the all who need grace to choose the some that receive it. Establishing the principle of salvation does not automatically save everyone any more than establishing the principle of private property makes everyone a landowner. Such processes require an additional act of application, and in salvation that application involves in differing ways the activity of both God and man within the general framework of grace.

In Romans 8:29-30 applying salvation is summarized chronologically under foreknowledge, foreordination (predestination), calling, justification, and glorification: "For the ones he foreknew he also foreordained to be conformed to the image of his Son, that he might be the firstborn among many brothers; the ones he foreordained he also called; the ones he called he justified; and the ones he justified he also glorified." These acts of God need to be examined individually beginning with foreknowledge.

Foreknowledge

That God knows the future is *declared* in Romans 8:29 as well as in passages like Psalms 139:16, where the psalmist says, "Your eyes saw my unformed substance and in your book they were written, even the days that were ordained for me when as yet there were none of them."

Foreknowledge, or prescience, is *implied* by all predictions that God enabled his prophets to give. Isaiah records God as saying, "I am God and there is none like me, declaring the end from the beginning and from ancient times things that are not yet done . . . saying, 'My counsel will stand, and I will do all my pleasure . . . yes, I have spoken; I will also bring it to pass. I have purposed; I will also do it'" (Isa. 46:9-11).

Foreknowledge and Free Will

As regards salvation the primary question is whether God's knowledge of the future precludes man's freedom to choose in the future. If God knows ahead of time that a given person will accept salvation through Jesus Christ, can that choice be free?

Compatibility of foreknowledge and free will
Biblical evidence. If there is one biblical case of foreknowledge and free will, the two in theory are compatible even if our limited perspective does not allow us to understand how these things can be. One such case seems unmistakable: Jesus freely gave his life and God foreknew that he would. The freedom of Jesus' self-giving is implied in John 10:17-18a, "Therefore the Father loves me, because I lay down my life that I may take it up again. No one takes it away from me, but I lay it down of myself. I have the right to lay it down, and I have the right to take it again" (cp. 19:11; 18:37).

On the other hand, Peter says regarding God's foreknowledge of the sacrifice of Christ, ". . . you were redeemed . . . with precious blood, as of a lamb without blemish and without spot, even the blood of Christ who was foreknown before the foundation of the world, but was manifested at the end of the times for your sake . . ." (I Peter 1:18-20; cp. Isa. 52:13—53:12; Acts 2:23; 4:28; Rev. 13:8). The "Lamb was slain from the foundation of the world" (Rev. 13:8; cp. 17:8), yet Christ chose to give his life as the struggle in Gethsemane confirms. The prophecy of Isaiah 53 did not eliminate the freedom in John 10.

A second case of foreknowledge plus free will apparently exists in the case of Adam's original act of disobedience. Before he ever sinned God had already planned to make provision for sin. Adam's transgression was a free choice since, as admitted by most, Adam had the ability not to sin before the Fall; otherwise God is found to be punishing him for what he could not help doing and that before any hereditary depravity or race condemnation could have been part of the picture.

A final case of foreknowledge and freedom is God's awareness of his own future acts. If knowing ahead of time eliminates free will, God himself would not be free with respect to anything he knows he will do, and he would not be free for the very reason that he himself knows his future deeds.

Proposed view. Understanding foreknowledge and free will carries us into the use of sanctified reason for suggesting unrevealed ideas that can show how revealed truths are in fact part of a consistent whole. We begin by distinguishing *knowledge and reality* because the knowledge of an event differs from the event itself. It does not matter whether it is past, present, or future; the knowledge of an occurrence is in the knower's mind, but the event happens in the realm of reality outside the knower's mind.

A distinction must also be maintained between *certainty and the reason for certainty.* In order for there to be knowledge there must be certainty. We do not mean certainty on the part of the *knower,* but certainty in the sense that the *thing known* cannot be other than what it is if we are going to know it. But even as a past or present act is not certain because we know it, so also a future one is not certain because God knows it. Correct knowledge only corresponds with reality; it does not bring it about. Certainty leads to knowledge, not the other way around. God's foreknowledge does not cause a man's choice and thus eliminate freedom.

Not only is knowledge not the cause of certainty, but there may be *more than one cause of certainty.* For example, it is not correct to say, "If God knows what I *will* do, I *cannot* do otherwise." Rather, "If God knows what I *will* do, I *will* not do otherwise." In the first sentence the conclusion goes beyond what the if-clause implies and adds a reason for the certainty, the reason being the inability or impossibility of doing otherwise. The error comes from supposing that certainty demands what is called "determinism," where things have to be the way they are because they cannot be any other way. To show that such is not the case here, one must explain the structure of things that guarantees certainty, but allows free will.

As an alternative to determinism we propose that *certainty is based on the space-time nature of reality itself.* Although an infinite number of parallel possibilities may exist for what may happen in any given time and place, by the very nature of reality only one will actually occur. If someone throws a rock, an infinite number of possibilities exists for exact directions in which it could go, particular places where it could land, the side it might land on, how many bounces it could take, how fast it would go, how many rotations it might make, etc. When the rock is thrown, however, all this happens only one way. *The other possibilities are eliminated by the very occurrence itself*; or, to be more accurate, only one possibility becomes an actuality. Likewise with free will; in a given instance several choices may be possible, but when one of them is made all the rest are eliminated. If only one thing will actually happen, there is certainty for knowing anything regardless of the time relative to the knower and regardless of whether it is a free choice or a determined event.

The real issue in this chapter is not the compatibility of free will and foreknowledge by direct sight. The real issue is "contingency" and "certainty." "Certain" means that an event is one way rather than other ways; "contingent" means that an event could be other ways from the way it is. "Unnecessitated" means that an event is not determined to be the way it is by previous causes. A choice is unnecessitated because it is not determined by *previous* causes, yet it is certain because *in its happening* other alternatives are eliminated; it can also be contingent because there may have been other alternatives. In our subject certainty correlates with foreknowledge and contingency correlates with free will. Solving the problem occurs by finding a way to have an event that is both contingent and certain. This we propose can be done by the space-time nature of reality so that we can deny any form of determinism and still affirm knowledge.

The main consideration not addressed by the above "construct" is *how* God can come to know certainly a future free choice. We can conceive of knowing certainly the present and the past because we know them through senses and memory, but we have only two models for knowing the future, neither of which combines certainty and freedom. Predictions may be made on the basis of current trends as in the case of the stock market. This model allows for freedom of choice on the part of investors, but it yields probability, not certainty, as investors discover when economists prove to be wrong. On the other hand, astronomers can predict with great accuracy the time and place of a solar eclipse, but they do it on the basis of built-in physical laws, which do not include freedom of choice. Neither model shows how God can foreknow choices.

160

A proper inference seems to be that God can know intuitively, that is, without means. The concept may be expressed by saying that God stands above the flow of time and so is not bound by it like men, who live in it. Though there is sequence with him, time is not a limitation. Being a spirit, he is also not restricted by physical means of knowing. Direct foresight is an imagery used of God's foreknowledge in Acts 2:31 concerning the resurrection and in Galatians 3:8 concerning the universal proclamation of salvation. *That* God foreknows all kinds of events seems clear from scripture; *how* he foreknows them remains a mystery. We must be satisfied with affirming that such knowing is theoretically possible because of the space-time nature of physical reality and because of God's unbounded power and authority.

In affirming the possibility of foreknown choice, we are not appealing to proof by default; that is, we are not claiming it is true because it cannot be disproved; it is affirmed because scripture gives positive evidence for it. Our lack of experience with it does not provide decisive evidence against God's being able to do it.

Other views

The supposed incompatibility of divine knowledge and human free will has prompted the denial of foreknowledge, free will, or both. In philosophical circles these options have been taken simply because of the perceived power in one or another of these ideas themselves. In theological circles championing one or another of them has had the added task of reinterpreting the relevant texts of scripture in order to bring them into harmony with any given view.

Limited divine foreknowledge. One view allows for (1) *no foreknowledge.* Cicero, Roman statesman and philosopher (106-43 B.C.), arguing against the Stoic concept of fate, proposed that divine foreknowledge does not exist. In order to avoid the notion that the future is programmed for man at a relatively detailed level, he postulated the opposite extreme. Complete denial of foreknowledge assumes that knowledge must come timewise after the event as it does with men. It conceives of God's knowledge on the analogy of man's—that he knows through sense perception and mental reflection on sense perception. It also may assume that nature does not function in a highly regular way so that one cannot even make predictions based on physical processes. Since foreknowledge constitutes a view of God that finds no parallel

161

in man, a position like Cicero's is not capable of formal refutation aside from a prior acceptance of divine revelation in scripture. About all that can be done is to show, as we have done earlier, that certainty does exist even in freedom, and to assert that with sufficient power and authority foreknowledge is a possibility that cannot be denied.

Another view calls for (2) *naturally limited foreknowledge.* God in his own nature lacks the ability to foreknow at least certain kinds of events. Positive affirmations are that he knows all possibilities; that he knows his own general plan for creation; and that he knows important things and generalities, but not necessarily unimportant particulars.

In regard to the last concept two examples may clarify. We know that a gas released in a vacuum will diffuse evenly throughout the container, but we cannot predict where a particular molecule will locate. There is fixity at the general level and randomness at the particular level. Likewise, a sample of radioactive carbon 14 will "decay" into stable carbon 12 at a given rate under uniform conditions, but the order in which the different atoms lose their two extra electrons is unpredictable. The decay rate is a "statistical thing" measurable at the mass level, but not able to be known at the atomic level. Similarly God is said to know general contours of the future.

The formulations of limited foreknowledge use omnipotence to make up for lack of omniscience. Since God has all power he can intervene to control movements contrary to his will despite prior ignorance of them. He can handle all particulars as they come along, and he foreknows all the possibilities of what can come along. In this manner God's supremacy and direction of his universe are maintained.

In defense of limited omniscience, it is often urged that Jesus' knowledge did not include the time of his return (Mt. 24:26; Mk. 13:32). Jesus was deity; deity is omniscient; therefore, Jesus was omniscient. Since he did not know the time of his own return, omniscience need not be absolute. He must have stopped knowing it or never knew it. While the observation bears reflection, it is not decisive because the mystery of the incarnation involves too many unknowns. It may not be legitimate to compare incarnate and non-incarnate deity. Furthermore, the mystery of the trinity comes into play. To say that God knows all things does not require each member of the Godhead to know all things; Jesus said the Father knew the time of Christ's return so it is *not* an example of something God did not know. Admittedly, such questions

162

surpass human ken and outdistance biblical revelation, but some special explanation may be supposed about this passage because it is the only one that says a member of the Godhead did not know something.

A second defense of limited foreknowledge is that when scripture speaks of God's knowing all things (omniscience), it may be taken as a sufficient rule rather than an absolute statement. Peter believed Jesus knew all things (Jn. 21:17; cp. 16:30), but he did not know the time of his return (Mt. 24:36; Mk. 13:32). While human language is such that an absolute statement may have some exceptions, we prefer not to take a position that *must* put boundaries on God's knowledge when scripture in its universal statements puts none, especially when it does teach—as we will see later—that God foreknew the very kinds of things limited foreknowledge would omit.

A third defense of limited foreknowledge is that omniscience is like omnipotence. Even as God's power is not being exercised at all times, so omniscience is only potential, not actual. We agree that omnipotence is potential, but it is an ability; knowing all things is the result of an ability. Christians believe in the omniscience of God because scripture reveals that God *knows* all things, not because scripture teaches he has the ability to *learn* all things. Admittedly, ability to learn all need not mean knowing all. The God of the Bible evidently knows all.

A fourth defense of limited foreknowledge might be to question whether scripture necessarily means what we have interpreted our original three examples of foreknowledge and freedom to mean. God's foreknowledge of Jesus' voluntary death may not be the certainty of sight, but the certainty of faith. The Father knew the Son would give himself, not because he could foresee the sacrifice (*scienta visionis*), nor because the Son was merely a being who *could* not do otherwise (*scienta media*), but because he had faith in him that he was the kind of person who *would* not do otherwise (*scienta fide*). Similarly he foreknew man's sin because he knew Satan's character and man's weakness so that it would be only a matter of time before man needed redemption. His foreknowledge of his own choices were certain and free by his own irresolute commitment to his program plus his confidence in his own power.

The three clear instances of free choices we gave originally were calculated to offset the argument against free choice plus certainty. They can still serve that function whether certainty is by sight or faith since it is not by determinism. We prefer, however, not to adopt any form of limited foreknowledge because of the following considerations.

(a) *Limited foreknowledge does not adequately cover the data of scripture.* Quite a number of rather *precise predictions* appear in the prophetic and apostolic records. Jesus predicted Peter's threefold denial before the second cock crow (Mt. 26:34-35). He told his disciples they would see a man carrying a waterpot on his head (Mk. 14:13-15). Isaiah predicted the Messiah's virgin birth (7:14; cp. Mt. 1:23); Micah predicted his place of birth (5:2; cp. Mt. 2:6); Zechariah prophesied the spear thrust on Calvary (12:10; cp. Jn. 19:37). The prophets, says Peter, testified beforehand of the sufferings of Christ and the glories that would follow them (I Pet. 1:10-12). At least as the text now reads, Isaiah 44:28 specifies by name that "Cyrus" would allow the rebuilding of Jerusalem after the exile; according to conservative scholarship Isaiah himself penned the verse 150 years before its fulfillment. If such specifics were foreknown, God could in principle know any and all future specifics. When it comes to dealing with the whole range of biblical phenomena, certainty by sight needs to be retained as one option to call upon when lesser options fail to satisfy the requirements of the case.

(b) *Limited foreknowledge does not protect against anthropomorphism;* that is, it does not safeguard against reducing God's characteristics to man's capacities. Perhaps the disinclination of many to accept direct foresight stems from a lack of that possibility in human experience; but, in principle, with God it is better to allow the higher affirmation since God is higher than man.

(c) *Limited foreknowledge does not protect against natural depravity in man.* Usually, limited divine foreknowledge is advocated in the interest of human free will. Natural depravity means that man's nature lacks freedom of choice. Certainty by faith cannot suffice to explain how men's names have been in the Lamb's Book of Life "from the foundation of the world" (Rev. 13:8; 17:8; cp. II Th. 2:13). God the Father knew himself and the Son before time and thereby could make a "character judgment" about future trustworthiness. He could perhaps be "sure" Adam would eventually sin under Satan's negative influences, but knowing which men would later believe would have to be knowledge by sight or knowledge by determinism because there would have been no pre-creation relationship to provide a basis for knowledge by faith or judgment based on character. Limited foreknowledge is usually adopted in the interest of preserving human freedom; therefore certainty by determinism is not an option, while certainty by faith does not work here. The Lamb's-Book-of-Life imagery in effect, then, eliminates the limited foresight theory as the highest affirmation about God's knowledge.

(d) *Naturally limited foreknowledge is not coherent.* Limiting foreknowledge to generalities involves one such inconsistency because general and specific are relative matters. Reality has more than two levels of specificness. What is specific in relation to the more general level is itself general relative to more specific levels. A person may communicate (general) by talking, using sign language, or transmitting Morse code (specifics); but he may talk (general) hurriedly or slowly, in German or English, loudly or quietly (specifics). "General" in one instance would mean that God could foreknow that his servant would communicate, but not that he would communicate by talking; in another instance "general" would mean that he could foreknow his servant would talk, but not that he would speak in German. Knowing only the general level presupposes making a comparison between the levels, which in turn presupposes knowing them both in the first place.

The example of diffused gas in a vacuum seems to be irrelevant to our question. Men know that the gas will diffuse evenly by assuming the uniformity of nature, and past experience has led them to this observation. Such a model will not provide the requirements of a free-will situation because free will means precisely that uniformity is not the case with men. Inasmuch as generalities arise from particulars, there would seem to be no way to know a generality other than through determinism or being taught; but God has not been taught: "Who has directed the Spirit of God; or, being his counsellor, has taught him? With whom did he take counsel, and who instructed him, and taught him knowledge, and showed him the way of understanding?" (Isa. 40:13-14).

A final version of limited foreknowledge is (3) *self-limited foreknowledge.* This concept intends to differ from the previous ones by allowing for God's ability to foreknow choices, but it proposes that he voluntarily limits himself from coming to know salvation choices because he wants them to be free. The self-limitation must somehow precede the knowing because under the original assumption subsequently "repressing" the

165

knowledge would allow determinism to have occurred already through the previous knowledge, if indeed God can cease knowing what he knows. As to limitation *before* knowing, the question is how one can choose not to know something without first knowing it enough to decide against knowing it.

The real question, though, is how it can be a coherent idea that God limits himself so man could have free choice. If God can know free choices, he does not have to limit himself to make them free. If he cannot know them, he will not be limiting himself to make them free. There is no need for the concept of self-limitation. If foreknowledge of free will is impossible, limiting himself will not make choices free. A future choice is already free or not, prior to knowing it, even as a past choice is free or not, prior to knowing it. Self-limitation is therefore irrelevant.

The Lamb's-Book-of-Life imagery (Rev. 13:8; 17:8) also becomes seemingly inappropriate if God keeps himself from knowing the identity of the elect. Of course, God does not need to keep a literal list, but surely the figure includes at least knowing who they are, especially since he is also pictured as removing people from it (Rev. 3:5). All that would otherwise remain of the meaning is that there is a real number which increases and decreases with conversion and apostasy. The element "from the foundation of the world" would have to be explained as an absolute time reference used to mean the absolute certainty of a person's status with God. Such exegesis is perhaps possible as a last resort, but it seems to be such an unlikely notion, particularly when there is no reason to resort to it. If God wills not to know free choices, then he does not know those matters that issue from them, in this case the list of the saved.

Limited free will. The previous viewpoints stemmed from attempts to harmonize foreknowledge and free will from the divine side of the issue. Harmonization has been attempted from the human side as well. These efforts have centered on a denial of free will both together with, and apart from, a concern to protect divine omniscience. Man's depravity has been understood to be such that he has no ability to respond to God's love proffered in Christ.

The concept has often been combined with understanding "foreknow," not so much as knowing about someone ahead of time, but as setting

166

regard upon someone ahead of time. Some scholars take "know" to mean "have personal relationship with" rather than simply "to be aware of." The more pregnant understanding of foreknow accords well with I Corinthians 8:3: "If anyone loves God, he stands known by him" (cp. I Jn. 4:7-8). Inasmuch as God first loved us (I Jn. 4:10, 19), "foreknow" amounts to "forelove." Romans 11:2 may be particularly associated with this meaning, ". . . his people whom he foreknew." On the other hand, Acts 2:23 would not readily fit with the idea of setting regard upon. Of course, the relational meaning includes the informational one so that for present purposes a choice between them is unnecessary. Freedom of the will allows for either interpretation. If free choice is denied on any ground other than incompatibility with foreknowledge, freedom must be discussed in terms of that other ground. If freedom is denied because of omniscient foreknowledge, then the following comments are in order.

Certainty could be based on (1) *direct determinism*. Under this view God directly "decrees," or wills, what will happen in each time and place as a kind of divine programming. His foreknowledge of events unfolding in history grows out of his decrees. No other possibilities exist because nothing comes between God and the future. *Other possibilities are eliminated by not being decreed.* Cause and effect in nature may even be an illusion. The patterns of nature do not result from a cause-effect mechanism within nature, but from God's choosing to decree in patterns. God would know the future by predestining the future whereas Paul, in describing salvation, places foreknowledge before predestination in Romans 8:29. As regards other more general matters such as his purpose in creation and the fact that there would be the *establishment* of the possibility of redemption, direct determinism by eternal decrees is true; but it is not the mode of foreknowledge in the *application* of salvation as far as who receives it is concerned.

There is also a certainty based on (2) *indirect determinism*. God knows the future perfectly because he knows the nature of all things perfectly. The concept may be likened to a break at the beginning of a billiard game. If a person knew everything about the cue stick, the balls, the table they were on, the air pressure in the room, the power of the strike, etc., he could predict exactly where each ball would be at any microsecond after the break. The knowledge is indirect because it comes from the nature of the components themselves. *Other possibilities are eliminated by the built-in nature of reality.* On the basis of God's perfect understanding of human nature, he can predict how a man will react to his environment in much the same way as he can predict the movements of the heavenly bodies whose governing laws he knows perfectly as Creator. Who would be converted, when, and where are all predictable because God knows enough about men to predict it.

Salvation under this construct sees God either as directly decreeing a man's conversion or manipulating circumstance to bring it about. For the system to provide certainty, a given response has to correspond with a given stimulus; hence, there is no freedom of the will to choose between alternatives. There is only the ability to respond to the one alternative implicit in the stimulus. There is an ability to act, but not a freedom to choose.

Freedom of choice, however, must be aside from a stimulus-response framework. Choice requires ability to refrain from acting when all requisite conditions for acting are present, and it requires an ability to choose between alternatives as distinguished from the ability merely to act (rather than not be able to act) when a stimulus for good is present. Freedom of the will looks beyond the notion of responding to the strongest stimulus or influence in the environment, and places within the person a capacity for operating in terms of values more than drives.

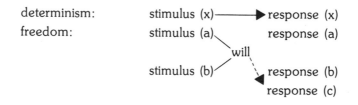

Everyone agrees that God uses a restricting determinism to keep men from doing just anything they please, but the objection here is to a positive determinism that makes men do everything they do. Indirect determinism means that the sense of freedom is an illusion.

168

In our positive statement on foreknowledge and free will, we proposed that foreknowledge and free choice are compatible because certainty unto foreknowledge can be based on (3) *the nature of space-time reality itself.* Certainty exists because *other possibilities are eliminated by the very occurrence of the choice itself.* Consequently, denying free will because of foreknowledge is unnecessary.

Advocating direct foresight does not eliminate statements revealing characteristic behavior of men which can serve also as a general basis of foreknowledge: "If I tell you, you will not believe" (Lk. 22:67; cp. 22:68; 10:13; Mt. 11:21); "If they are not listening to Moses and the prophets, neither will they be persuaded if someone arise from the dead" (Lk. 16:31); ". . . he himself knew what was in man" (Jn. 2:25; cf. 2:24). Direct foresight does not contradict also knowing what a person will do on the basis of character, as men often do with each other (I Sam. 22:22); direct foresight is simply the more powerful way of knowing with God.

Although we have discussed direct and indirect determinism under solving the foreknowledge problem from man's side, it should be obvious that these solutions do not just reduce the nature of man in order to achieve consistency; they reduce God as well. A God who can foreknow free choices certainly outclasses one who cannot. Were a person to suppose it better to degrade man in order to exalt God, he would fail in this instance to exalt him because God becomes more like man in these views.

There is truth in all three bases for certainty. Our only contention has been that direct and indirect determinism do not pertain decisively to the question about who will be saved. Direct determinism may be seen in God's decision to create a universe with men in it who should be "to the praise of the glory of his grace" (Eph. 1:6); God, of course, would thus know the future he would do. Indirect determinism may be seen in the overall operation of natural physical processes; God can thus know their future by way of their characteristics. In salvation, nevertheless, scripture leads us to believe both that God knows ahead of time and that man has free moral agency. To make sense of these facts we have supplied the notion of certainty through the space-time nature of physical reality and have left unanswerable the question of *how* he can intuitively foreknow free choice.

Summary

The main question created by foreknowledge is whether it allows for free moral agency. Assuming that it does not, thinkers have adjusted their conception of either or both issues in the problem. Foreknowledge has often been viewed in Christendom as limited or self-limited. We have argued, however, that limited foreknowledge lacks scriptural approval, recreates God in the image of man, requires natural depravity, and is incoherent in itself. Limiting human will, on the other hand, means natural depravity, which is unacceptable on separate grounds and unnecessary in that no real problem exists between foreknowledge and freedom.

By distinguishing knowledge and reality, certainty and the reason for certainty, we propose a way of having certainty and choice simultaneously. Certainty is created by the very occurrence of any event because the occurrence eliminates all other possibilities. From this construction it is inferred that God knows without means, but *how* he can do so remains a mystery that should not be denied on the grounds of human experience because God is higher than man and his ways higher than man's ways.

God knows his own future acts by direct determinism; he can know the future of his impersonal creation by indirect determinism; but he knows the elect on the basis of direct foresight of faith.

Chapter Twelve

THE PREDESTINATION OF MAN

Introduction

Following the outline in Romans 8:29-30 takes us from foreknowledge to predestination. The sequence traces the *chronological* order of acts on *God's side* of *salvation* in those places that appear *subsequent to the atonement*. Approaching the study of predestination from this guide text calls for a reminder that Paul's subject is salvation particularly, not history generally. Although some theologians may identify salvation history with the whole of history, we prefer to consider salvation history at least a secondary process in the unfolding of time inasmuch as sin plus its remedy is not an essential part of creation, because it entered subsequent to an ideal relationship between man and God. There is more to life in history than the process of redemption even if the whole of history is the arena and object of renewal.

Since Paul's subject is not history generally, the motif he sketches does not necessarily apply beyond salvation. Predestination as an aspect of God's plan for the ages does not have to apply in the same manner to all levels of creation. Neither determinism nor freedom automatically establishes itself as a monolithic principle. Paul might reverse the order of foreknowledge and predestination were he addressing the doctrine of creation and providence and speak instead of predestination and foreknowledge. Freedom at the level of individual salvation does not require freedom at the general level, and determinism at the general level does not necessitate determinism in the redemption of sinners.

Proposed View of Predestination

Terminology

The biblical doctrine of predestination is set forth in the New Testament under words related to the verb *proorizō*, which is translated "predestinate," "predetermine," or "foreordain" depending on the version (Acts 4:28; Rom. 8:29-30; I Cor. 2:7; Eph. 1:5, 11; cp. Acts 2:23; 17:26). *Proorizō* is comprised of *pro*, meaning "before," and *horizō*, meaning "to set a boundary" (cp. "horizon"). Accordingly by derivation the word picture is that of "determining the boundary ahead of time."

Predestination is set forth conceptually under other terms as well, particularly those related to *tithēmi*, meaning "to put, place, appoint, or ordain" (Acts 1:7; 13:48; 17:31; I Th. 5:9; I Pet. 2:8). Other miscellaneous expressions include "raised up" (Judges 2:16, etc.), "chosen from the beginning unto" (Eph. 1:4), "separated from my mother's womb unto" (Job 10:18; Ps. 22:8-10; Is. 46:3-4; 49:1; Jer. 1:5; 20:18; Gal. 1:15), "written unto" (Jude 4), "laid up for" (*apokeimai* in Col. 1:5; II Tim. 4:8; Heb. 9:27).

Objects of predestination

Organizing the specifics of scripture presents the difficulty of keeping foreknowledge, election, and predestination separate because given passages mix them, because the concepts themselves are coextensive in salvation, and because they imply one another. The following list is not strictly complete, but organizes the objects of predestination that relate to salvation.

Predestination of history. Although a word equivalent does not appear in Isaiah 46:9-11, the prophet evidently has in mind the predestination of history as well as a foreknowledge of it as a whole when he says, ". . . I am God . . . declaring the end from the beginning . . . My counsel shall stand and I will do all my pleasure . . . I have spoken; I will bring it to pass. I have purposed; I will also do it." In light of the rest of the passage, "declare" comes to mean decree more than predict.

When questioned about restoring the kingdom of Israel, Jesus told the apostles, "It is not for you to know the times or seasons that the Father has appointed by his own authority" [or ". . . the Father set in his own authority"; Acts 1:7]. Given in answer to a question associated evidently with the return of Christ, the answer itself expresses a much broader truth about the future.

Paul explains to the Epicurean and Stoic philosophers that God "made of one every nation of men to live on all the face of the earth, having determined their appointed seasons and the bounds of their habitation" (Acts 17:26).

Predestination of redemption. The mystery and wisdom Paul talks about in I Corinthians 2:7 seems to amount to the scheme of redemption through Christ: "We speak God's wisdom in a mystery, even the wisdom that has been hidden, which [wisdom] God foreordained before the worlds to our glory."

172

Predestination of Christ. At least twice in Acts the death of Christ is considered determined beforehand by God: "Him, being delivered up by the determinate plan and foreknowledge of God, by the hand of men without the law, you crucified and killed" (2:23); ". . . against your holy Servant Jesus . . . Herod and Pontius Pilate with the Gentiles and the peoples of Israel were gathered together to do as many things as your hand and your plan predestined to happen" (4:27-28). The better translation of Revelation 13:8 speaks of "the Lamb that was slain from the foundation of the world."

Predestination in Christ. In Ephesians Paul describes Christians generally as chosen and foreordained "to adoption as sons" (1:5) and to being a heritage for God (1:11). Likewise to the Thessalonians he gives a reminder, "God appointed us . . . to the obtaining of salvation through our Lord Jesus Christ" (I Th. 5:9). Lastly, he tells Timothy, "[God] . . . saved us and called us with a holy calling . . . according to his own purpose and grace, which was given to us in Christ before times eternal" (II Tim. 1:9). Benefits from being in Christ come from a process of election and predestination and are regarded as given in consequence of identity in Jesus Christ.

Predestination into Christ. Paul constantly thanked God for the Thessalonians because "God chose [them] from the beginning unto salvation in the sanctification of the Spirit and the belief of the truth" (II Th. 2:13). The election and predestination were not just in Christ, but into him. Similarly Peter singles out his readers personally, calling them elect according to foreknowledge (I Pet. 1:1-2). Acts reports the response to the gospel in Antioch of Pisidia by saying, "As many as were appointed to eternal life believed" (Acts 13:48). These hearers are not contemplated as being in Christ with salvation regarded as a consequence. They are outside of Christ and are thought of as having been appointed to eternal life from that position. Predestination applies to individual salvation.

Pattern of Christian living. The guide verse in Romans 8:29 even brings in the kind of lives Christians need to live: "The ones he foreknew he also predestined to be conformed to the image of his Son."

Predestination of human activites. Clearly, not only was the fact of Christ's death predetermined, but more specifically the acts of men who did "as many things as your hand and your counsel predestined to happen" (Acts 4:28). Peter says of disbelievers, "They stumble at the word, being disobedient, unto which [stumbing/disobedience] they were also appointed" (I Pet. 2:8). Jude seems to have a like notion in mind when he writes, "There are certain men crept in secretly, even they who were of old written unto this condemnation—ungodly men, turning the grace of God into licentiousness and denying our only Master and Lord Jesus Christ" (Jude 4). "This condemnation" apparently means the creeping in secretly, turning grace to licentiousness, and denial of the Lord.

On the evil side God raised up Pharaoh in order to show his power in him (Rom. 9:17 and a host of passages that speak of God's raising someone up for good or evil). These passages come close to the even more extreme statements about God himself doing evil (Ex. 4:21; Deut. 2:30; Judges 14:4; I Sam. 16:14; 18:10; II Sam. 12:11-12; Ps. 105:25; II Cor. 7:7; II Th. 2:11-12; Rev. 17:17). On the good side Jeremiah was appointed a prophet to the nations before God separated him from his mother's womb (Jer. 1:5).

Physical death. The Hebrew writer says, ". . . it is appointed to men to die once and after that comes the judgment" (9:27).

Final judgment. In parallel passages between II Peter and Jude the authors speak of angels being destined to condemnation: ". . . God did not spare angels when they sinned, but cast them down to hell and committed them to pits of darkness to be reserved unto condemnation" (II Pet. 2:4); "angels that did not keep their own position, but left their proper dwelling have been kept by him in eternal chains under darkness unto the judgment of the great day" (Jude 6). It is evident from the context that judgment will not be lenient for them so that eternal condemnation is surely in view. On the Areopagus Paul indicates that God has appointed a day to judge the world in relation to Christ (Acts 17:31; cp. Heb. 9:27).

Eternal state. Paul speaks of the hope and the crown that is laid up for the Christian (Col. 1:5; II Tim. 4:8).

The concept of foreordination is applied then to history as a whole and to all its parts, to the redemption possibility, to the basis of it in the death of Christ, to the blessings from being in Christ, to the entrance into that status, to the life style expected of those who are in him, to the good and evil activities of men, and to the judgment and eternal state of both men and angels. Although not everything has been listed in the previous headings, enough has been given to show that predestination is a general idea that in principle can be applied to any event.

Manner of predestination

Our task is to understand and distinguish, if necessary, the modes in which this determination of the future takes place in the mind of God insofar as that mystery has been disclosed through his word and insofar as it can be imagined through creative thought. In order to present a total picture, we retain the same breakdown of action as applies to foreknowledge.

Direct predestination. Many matters of the future may be directly willed by God, namely those actions that (1) *he himself* will do both aside from and in response to the choice of persons. These actions are the creation, express miracles and special providence, and the consummation, that is, all the acts of God that are not more precisely attributable to blind force or the agency of secondary creatures.

Indirect predestination. In matters that pertain to (2) *the non-rational universe* the future may be indirectly decreed by virtue of the processes God built into nature. The movements of the heavenly bodies, the weather patterns, the laws of heredity, and the like may be conceived of in this way.

Permissive predestination. For (3) *the rational creation,* however, models of determinism give way to permission as the decisive factor especially for *who* is saved. Predestination is not fate but choice here. (a) *Willful acts are permissively willed by God* within boundaries prescriptively willed. Permissive will has to do with what God allows someone else to do; prescriptive will means what God alone determines must happen. Central to understanding the predestination of volitional acts—acts arising from the will—is the fact again of foreknowledge. In contrast to the previous two models, God does not know the future from predestination, but predestines the future from foreknowledge.

The permission-prescription model in salvation takes its cue from the word picture in *proorizō.* Setting the boundary ahead of time suggests prescription as to where the boundaries lie and permission as to movement within them (cp. Acts 17:26; Deut. 32:8). Ability sets the most outlying limitation and providence narrows it. Gamaliel has this second limitation in mind when he advises the Sanhedrin concerning the witness of the apostles about the promised Messiah, "If it is from God, you will not be able to overthrow it lest you be found to be fighting God" (Acts 5:39).

At a still more restricted scope is the range of behavior acceptable

175

for righteousness. Permissive predestination describes God's ratification of an intention to act in a way he will allow. Freedom and certainty *at*

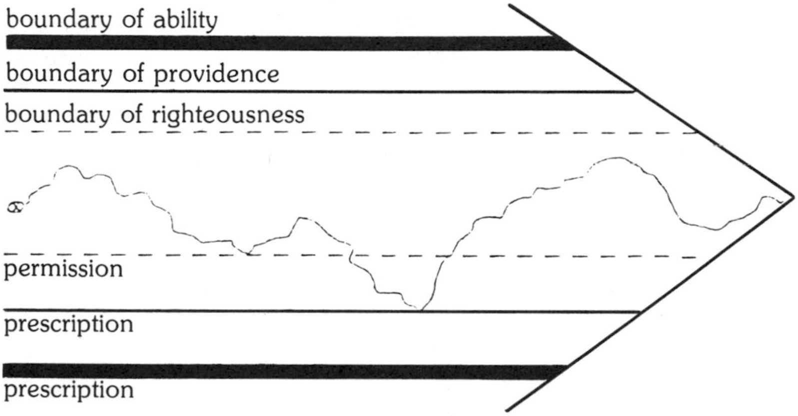

boundary of ability

boundary of providence

boundary of righteousness

∞

permission

prescription

prescription

the level of a specific have been combined under foreknowledge by the space-time nature of reality. Freedom and certainty *between* levels of specificness are combined under predestination by the framework concept. God foreknows all things. Under the present model whatever is capable of being foreknown is capable of being predestined, which is the very thing data in scripture requires.

In salvation the willful acts of response are predestined permissively; but because these are acts of faith, not works, they identify us with Christ only as far as *we* are concerned. *God,* however, has taken the initiative in prescribing what acts are required and in offering to identify us with Christ on these terms. Through foreknowledge of these acts of faith, (b) *the identification with Christ is itself prescribed by God* (predestination *into* Christ).

Moreover, (c) *any temporal or eternal benefits consequent to identification with Christ are prescribed by God* in keeping with his previous free promises. In *election* a person's faith does not itself establish his relationship with God, strictly speaking, because the salvation is by grace, not as of debt (Rom. 4:1-5). Had he never sinned, it would be "of debt" in that God would owe a person sonship or whatever other

176

blessing he offered to perfectly righteous men. But in salvation the righteousness itself must first be given so that subsequent rewards for righteousness can only be of grace, too. The strict discontinuity between act and destiny can be seen even more clearly in *reprobation* because the reprobate goes to hell despite his desire perhaps to go to heaven.

God foresees the will to act (foreknowledge) and allows the will to become an act (permissive predestination). Christ freely gave himself in response to the will of the Father so that he made Jesus the head of all things to the church (prescriptive predestination *of* Christ). On the basis of men's acts of response, God gives identification with Christ (prescriptive predestination *in* Christ).

Frequent discussions about predestination seek to avoid determinism by speaking of conditional vs. unconditional predestination. The terminology works well in speaking of destinies such as entrance into Christ or the privilege of heaven; but unlike "predestine" the usage of *proorizō* covers more than "destinies," which can be conditional; it describes the very conditions themselves, which are not likely to be called "conditional." When condition terms are used exclusively, no expression remains for talking about the predestination, predetermination, or foreordination of the conditional acts themselves—an important concern because of passages like I Peter 2:8 and Jude 4. The freedom of the acts themselves under both foreknowledge and predestination is the crux of the whole issue. Nevertheless, permission-prescription and conditional-unconditional can serve well as complementary terminologies. The former has the advantage of being able to describe the predetermination of free acts as permissive while the latter has the advantage of being able to describe the relationship of destiny to act as conditional. God prescribes destinies, permits acts, and conditions destinies on the acts.

We must show reason now for shifting to a different mode of predestination for rational creatures. It is one thing to show that an idea like permissive predestination is meaningful, but it is another to show that it is indeed the truth of the matter. In order to explain the shift, we call first upon a line of reasoning basic to a number of subjects in the Christian faith. Three facts lie at the foundation: God's desire to save all (II Pet. 3:9), his decision to save some (Rev. 14:11), and his self-consistency (James 1:17). Whatever explains the difference between the "all" he desires to save and the "some" he decides to save must lie outside himself or God becomes inconsistent. That variable lies in man because he is the only other one involved in this relationship. Man must have the ability to choose to accept God or God would have to enable him to make that choice. If God had to enable him, the variable would be back in God by virtue of the fact that he would be choosing who would be saved by choosing whom to enable to respond unto salvation. All are not enabled despite God's desire to save all. God cannot, therefore, be the chooser of which ones are saved; so men must have the ability to choose. Direct and indirect determinism leave no room for choice; hence, predestination *into* Christ must be permissive rather than prescriptive.

We call secondly upon the fact that in an obvious series Romans 8:29 places foreknowledge before predestination. Peter agrees when he writes to ". . . the elect . . . according to foreknowledge" (I Pet. 1:1-2; cp. Acts 2:22-23; 4:28). What is foreknown is the faith of the individual. From elsewhere we know that faith is given by God through the hearing of the word (Rom. 10:17; cp. II Th. 2:13).

Corporate before individual. Lostness and salvation both occur first at the corporate level and then at the individual one. First Adam because of sin separated himself from God and became the head of a spiritual race in exile from the Creator. Thereafter each man by his own sin has identified himself with First Adam, thus joining "the company of the condemned." Second Adam because of his righteousness is in fellowship with God, and has become the head of a spiritual race enjoying sonship with the Father. Second Adam is a substitute, a replacement, an alternative for First Adam. By acting faith each man identifies himself with Second Adam, thus joining "the company of the committed."

A systematic approach to salvation naturally expects predestination to correlate with the work of Christ. In Ephesians 1:3-14 such is practically the situation because Paul speaks of our predestination as being through Christ unto adoption (1:5) and in Christ to God's glory (1:11-12); this part corresponds to identification in the group (Christ). Paul also speaks of God's purposing in Christ to sum up all things (1:9-10); this part corresponds to the group. This two-level approach has been called the predestination *of* Christ and the predestination *in* Christ. The Ephesians passage stops short of saying predestination *into* Christ, an element that can be supplied from elsewhere.

178

Effects of predestination

Divine sovereignty. Predestination operates to the fulfillment of the will of God. The concept goes beyond that of foreknowledge by emphasizing God's role in the events that transpire at all levels. He is not simply aware of them, but his will is decisive in their occurrence. This decisiveness about their occurrence is the element common to predestination in its various modes and therefore is most particularly what predestination means. Predestination is not a mode, but a fact. In the case of volitional acts predestination adds ratification to foreknowledge. Foreknowledge is aware of the act; predestination puts a stamp of approval on its occurrence. Finally, omnipotence comes in to execute predestination and maintain sovereignty. The framework concept exalts God above what he would be if he could only control through built-in forces.

Divine glory. "The heavens do declare the glory of God" (Ps. 19:1), but man can glorify him more by using his freedom potential for that end. God is more greatly glorified by someone who does it by choice than by something that could not do otherwise. Who would want to be married to a wife who could not do other than love him?

Human freedom. The framework concept also gives dignity to man by allowing him the right to initiate action. He is allowed to move in a higher realm than the stars; consequently, he gets more out of life than they do.

Assurance. Predestination comforts the believer because he is assured that good will triumph over evil. The certainty of that triumph is such that it can already be announced as a fact in waiting, even to the point of the salvation of the individual. "Nothing can separate us from the love of God," including "the things to come" (Rom. 8:35-39). In our opinion it is for assurance of the elect that scripture speaks of God's appointing men unto disobedience (I Pet. 2:8; cp. perhaps Prov. 16:4; Rom. 9:22). All is in hand; God knew wicked men would stumble over the stone rejected by the builders. If he has ratified their disobedience, he knows it will not overthrow his rule or frustrate his plans. Let the elect race know they are the people of God.

Meaningfulness. Predestination guarantees the meaningfulness of history inasmuch as history is going somewhere. Because men can be part of God's history, predestination guarantees the significance of human existence. *Meaning is measured by purpose* and can be stated

179

in terms of purpose. A man has value and worth if he operates within the purposes of God that predestination guarantees will come to pass. With predestination history does not just eventuate wherever randomness takes it.

Man has *objective* worth under predestination because foreordination guarantees that meaning can be *in* events rather than just *read into* them by people. Prediction makes the predetermination known to us and does it in an apologetic way. We have access to the purposes of God through such revelation. Prediction implies that an event has the meaning assigned to it in the prophecy because prediction can only come from God, and he is the one who predestines. Jerusalem did not just fall to the Babylonians, for example; its fall had the meaning of punishment for disobedience to the Mosaic covenant. That meaning was known to be *in* the event because God spoke through Isaiah generations before it happened. The same line of thought applies to Messiah's death for forgiveness of sins, which was by "the determinate counsel and foreknowledge of God" (Acts 2:23; 4:27-28; Lk. 22:22). We know it had that meaning because it was prophesied (Isa. 52:13—53:12), and it could be prophesied because it was foreknown and predestined. Prediction of an event reveals the meaning in such a way that it guarantees that meaning.

Objections considered

With foreknowledge as prerequisite to the predestination of rational creatures, there is a guarantee of meaning and assurance without loss of moral freedom. Nevertheless in the history of Christian thought certain objections have been raised against the construction of foreknowledge and foreordination outlined above.

No divine control. One objection is that God cannot be controlling the future if his creatures are choosing their own behavior. A necessary reminder has to do with what free will means; it does not mean absolute freedom. Predestination as understood here provides for freedom within a framework; consequently, God maintains control by virtue of boundaries and allows man freedom to move inside them. The limitations include (a) natural boundaries in the abilities rational creatures have for opposing God and (b) providential boundaries on the expression of their capacities because God can intervene in history along the way. There is also (c) practical bondage to sin originated by ignorance, ingrained by past failures, and reinforced by social pressure so that the resolve for noble living is harder than it would otherwise be. In salvation God chooses (d) whether a scheme of redemption exists, (e) what destinies there will be, (f) what behaviors correspond to each destiny, and (g) which destiny each person has. God does not have to maintain his supremacy by doing all the deciding; he has only to put limits on the extent to which his creatures can decide against him. Omnipotence guarantees sovereignty.

A related matter is *how* God maintains his control. If God must "wait" to see what happens in order to know the future, the future has already happened before he can decide whether he wants it to occur. Thus foreknowledge precludes predestination.

The problem, however, is soluble because in the case of willed action, the volition precedes the act that fulfills it. In the *rational creation*, where permissive predestination obtains, God can intervene during the "time between" the intention and the fulfillment and prevent whatsoever he does not want to come to pass. A striking example occurred when the angel stayed the hand of Abraham between the intent of his mind and the act of his hand in sacrificing Isaac (Gen. 22:9-12). God confused the languages at Babel and the people left off building the tower to heaven (Gen. 11:1-9). God destroyed the Egyptian army in the Red Sea (Ex. 14:15—15:21). The two angels struck the Sodomites with blindness (Gen. 19:1-11).

In the *non-rational universe*, where prescriptive predestination operates, God can intervene between the cause and the effect. In his own action no intervention, of course, is necessary so that the categories addressed in foreknowledge coincide appropriately with the manner of foreknowing and the mode of predestining.

Faith as a gift. In the interest of combining free will and predestination, much has been made of divine foreknowledge as a basis for predestination. A question, however, is often asked: "How did the person get the foreknown faith?" The answer is that God gave it to him. If so, God has become the primary actor again, not in predestining directly, but in giving the faith on which predestination rests. Foreknowledge therefore becomes immaterial.

A further question, however, needs to be raised: "How did God give the person that faith?" Paul says in Romans 10:14, 17 that faith comes by hearing the word of Christ. The "give" terminology has

181

nothing particularly to do with eliminating acceptance by the hearer. Before the fact God promised the Israelites from the time of Abraham forward to give them the land of Canaan. The fact that it was a gift had nothing to do with their not having to fight the Canaanites to conquer it (Ex. 6:4). In fact, the first generation did not possess the land because they did not do their part. "Surely you shall not come into the land, concerning which I swore [lifted up the hand] that I would make you inhabit" (Num. 14:30; cp. Josh. 24:13). "You" does not mean the Israelite nation in general, but the ones who would not be going into Canaan. The Semitic idiom tended to omit intermediate and secondary causes (cp. Jn. 3:22 and 4:2; Ps. 51:10 and Ezek. 18:31; Ex. 10:1 and 8:15; Jonah 1:15 and 2:3; Acts 21:27—22:29 and 26:21-23; Eph. 2:1 and 5:14; II Cor. 8:16-18). The divine activity of giving, granting, or making has implication for response, acceptance, or co-operation. God gives faith by making it possible to have faith: he commissions the proclamation of the gospel so men have opportunity to believe it. Their belief is then foreknown.

Man's depravity. Foreknowledge also becomes immaterial because man does not have free will. God supposedly must perform an invisible miraculous operation directly on the person's very nature in parallel to the proclamation of the good news to him. If God does not regenerate his abilities, the person will not believe because he cannot believe. Predestination ends up being without reference to the man in the end, not because God does not know, but because what he foreknows he alone does.

At this point it is simply denied that scripture teaches the notion of a human inability that needs to be corrected miraculously. The objection is handled below in responses to other views of predestination.

Other Views of Predestination

Calvinistic predestination. This type of predestination gets its name from John Calvin (1509-1564), influential reformer in Geneva, who developed the system of theology known as Calvinism. Predestination in this system is unconditional with respect to men as well as the impersonal universe. Nothing in a man or his response to the gospel serves as a condition for God's choosing him while passing by others. All men are viewed as "depraved," having inherited biologically Adam's fallen nature. The result is that no one can answer the call unless God miraculously enables him to do so. There cannot be the meeting of any conditions because the person has no ability to meet them.

The objections to this view are the same as the reasons given earlier for shifting to permissive predestination for the rational creation. Natural depravity is not a necessary inference from the teaching of scripture about man. The accompanying view of God makes him inconsistent if, while desiring to save all, he saves only some instead of "doing all his pleasure" (Isa. 46:10; Num. 23:19; I Cor. 1:21; Gal. 1:15; Eph. 1:11; Phil. 2:13; Col. 1:19). In effect Calvinism reverses the order from foreknowledge and predestination to predestination and foreknowledge, or makes them synonymous.

Barthian predestination. Karl Barth, world-renowned theologian of the twentieth century, has influenced much of Christian scholarship in Europe and America. In the doctrine of election Barth began his thought with a special approach to election that made Jesus Christ both reprobate man and elect man. Mankind is viewed as incorporated in him with objective universalism resulting from God's acceptance of Jesus Christ. The election and predestination of Christ is a double predestination, but it is in series, not in parallel. Christ (and mankind in him) is first reprobate and then elect. Christian teaching has always made double predestination parallel with some lost and some saved. Needless to say, Barthian universalism is unconditional.

With Barth a new variable appears to come into the picture because salvation gets split between the objective and subjective sides. Theoretically, it would seem, Barth's theology issues in the actual salvation of all men; but since a man might never be able to bring himself to accept his acceptance, Barth never affirmed universalism positively, but only potentially. A man could eternally be filled with a sense of separation from the Father even though the Father does not so regard him. Insofar as he represented sinful humanity he was first rejected, and insofar as he did the will of the Father he was secondly accepted.

The fundamental difficulty in his view is that in Ephesians 1 and elsewhere Paul does not say that all men are in Christ, but that those who are in Christ have been predestined to special blessings as sons and heirs of the Father. With this primary matter confused, consequent inferences naturally do not fit with New Testament teaching about final judgment and eternal death.

Class predestination. Sometimes it is said that God predestined the plan, not the man. Under this view the Father decided that he would save everyone who identified with his Son, but he did not know or predestinate who would identify themselves with him. The benefits of salvation are then regarded as logically subsequent to being in Christ. Such a construction might satisfy the requirements of a passage like Ephesians 1:3-14, but it does not cover all the examples wherein predestination is *into* Christ rather than just *in* him (Acts 13:48; II Th. 2:13; I Peter 1:1-2). Some passages do not refer to an indefinite group, but speak of specific individuals and identifiable groups, as does the Lamb's-Book-of-Life imagery in Revelation 13:8 and 17:8. Class predestination is not wrong in what it affirms, but in not affirming everything scripture seems to require on this subject. It appears from the above passages that God has predestined both the plan and the man. Predestination *of* Christ and predestination *in* Christ is accompanied by predestination *into* Christ together with a switch from prescriptive to permissive, conditional predestination in the last case.

Single predestination. Predestination in our construct for rational creatures is a type of "double predestination." It contrasts with any view that sees only the saved as predestined while the lost are considered to have brought their fate upon themselves. We see no reason for restricting the mechanisms of providence to one group on the other because a choice on God's part always stands between the life of a man and whatever destiny is involved. Behavior does not by itself automatically produce the destiny even in reprobation, or lostness. God assigns it to the person. There is no impropriety in speaking even of predestining the sinful behavior itself since it is a ratifying, permissive act subsequent to the free intention to sin.

Summary

Predestination emphasizes the control that God exercises over every aspect of his creation by previous determination or ratification. In biblical usage "predestinate" and its equivalents apply to any occurrence including free-will choices and eternal destinies.

Direct determinism applies to God's own future acts, indirect determinism to the processes in the natural order, and permissive predestination to volitional acts. Permissive foreordination refers to what God allows;

prescriptive foreordination refers to what he himself does. *Permissive* predestination provides the mechanism for human freedom under divine sovereignty. Since salvation pertains to men, who are able to choose, the concept occupies a prominent place in predestination theory. Permissive predestination combines with *conditional* predestination, which emphasizes the connection between men's acts and the *prescriptive* predestination of their resulting status with God in time and eternity.

Permissive predestination pictures fixed boundaries in which men move freely by choice. Our reasons for shifting from positive determinism to restrictive determinism with rational creatures are that (a) positive determinism creates inconsistency in God and that (b) in Romans 8:29 foreknowledge precedes predestination in salvation. Permissive predestination shows how divine sovereignty and human freedom can fit together in such a way as to guarantee assurance and worth to all men.

The most significant effect of predestination is that it guarantees the objective meaningfulness of history because time is going somewhere specifically.

Chapter Thirteen

GOD'S CALL TO MEN

Introduction

After foreknowledge and foreordination Paul lists calling as the third step in the chronological order of salvation on the divine side (Rom. 8:29-30). Whereas the first two entries occurred before time (Eph. 1:3-14), calling represents the first divine activity carried on in history as far as the individual application of salvation is concerned. Either the apostle does not mean to be exhaustive or he subsumes under calling the providential preparation of the heart before and during God's call to justification and glorification.

Calling to salvation is to be distinguished from calling to ministry (Mk. 1:20; Rom. 1:1; I Cor. 1:1; Gal. 1:15-16; Heb. 5:4), from calling as one's situation in life (I Cor. 7:15, 17, 20), and from calling as naming (Mt. 1:21, etc.). Calling is God's invitation to salvation through the gospel.

A Biblical Description of Calling

Divine initiative

Romans 10:6-21 gives a classic description of the calling situation, which Paul identifies with faith by making faith the acceptance in the same situation where calling is the offer. Men did not ascend to heaven to bring Christ down or descend into the abyss to raise him up (10:6-7). Man's quest for God succeeds God's quest for man. Not only Paul, but all the New Testament writers characteristically treat calling to salvation as an essentially divine activity (Mt. 9:13; Mk. 2:17; Lk. 5:32; Rom. 8:30; I Cor. 1:9; Gal. 1:6, 15; 5:8; I Th. 2:12; 4:7; 5:24; II Th. 2:14; I Pet. 1:15; 2:9; 5:10; II Pet. 1:3). By the very nature of what it is, calling comes from beyond us. "And no one takes the honor to himself, but [he receives it] by being called by God as also Aaron [was]" (Heb. 5:4).

Calling never involves our taking the initiative and then asking God to help us fulfill our plans. It is not a matter of successfully feeling after God and finding him, but a matter of a spokesman offering the invitation in God's name (Acts 17:26-27); it is not simply a case of coming to know God through nature (Rom. 10:18; Ps. 19:4),

186

but a word directed to us from above (Isa. 65:1; Rom. 10:19-20; 8:30). Calling contrasts with seeking God by wisdom, "for . . . the world through its wisdom did not know God" (I Cor. 1:21). In calling the effect is not produced by the hearer: ". . . not of works, but of him who calls . . ." (Rom. 9:11-12; 10:6-8). God initiates the process, determines the agenda, and grants the results.

Human proclamation

Although calling is an essentially divine activity, it is carried out through the direct agency of men who preach the gospel: "Wherefore he called you through our gospel unto the obtaining of the glory of our Lord Jesus Christ" (II Th. 2:14). We understand that faith comes by hearing the word of Christ (Rom. 10:17), and the word of Christ is borne in the *proclamation* of a preacher sent by God (Rom. 10:8, 14-16).

Divine initiative eliminates from the calling framework any discovery process based on *reason* and *experience*. Calling through proclamation likewise stands distinct from *direct implantation* of concepts. There is no evidence that God directly plants the knowledge of salvation in anyone's mind; the knowledge of salvation through Christ exists only where the message has been verbally conveyed and personally demonstrated. Parapsychology supplies models like clairvoyance and clairaudience where seeing and hearing distant events are said to happen through extrasensory perception, but neither scripture nor experience finds such "mystical" operations at work in conversion and salvation before God.

Learning through belief of testimony also contrasts with innate awareness of the gospel message. Preaching does not amount to a stimulus for *recollection*, or anamnesis. Neither is calling equal to *intuition* as if salvation resulted from an automatic understanding of salvation. Instead of all these inter-related notions, scripture describes the initiation of reconciliation in terms of preaching.

Interpersonal operation

Denying recollection, reason, intuition, and conceptual implantation reaffirms interpersonalness as the primary consideration in calling. Miracle is inherently unnecessary to this program of God in history. Persons stand on both sides of the transaction; consequently, calling and faith are correlative realities performed by persons in I-you relationship.

187

Other possibilities either eliminate effectively one side or the other, or they reduce calling to an I-it process.

Included under interpersonalness is the lack of determinism in calling. If personhood means anything distinctive, choice must appear in the structure of calling and faith. Personness must reject stimulus-response reactions or other forms of necessary causation. Although acceptance of testimony correlates with its quality of presentation, there is no hard and fast connection between calling and faith. Calling is something one person does to another person.

Universal scope

Finally, calling is universal because the Great Commission has a universal thrust. God's theater of special operation has moved from Jewish circles to all nations. Various social categories have no bearing on preaching whether rich or poor, bond or free, male or female (Gal. 3:28). They are all called to become sons of Abraham by faith in Christ.

The Doctrine of Effectual Calling

Description of effectual calling

Many theologians have divided calling into general and effectual calling. The distinction involves more than the difference between a call extended to all and a call accepted by some (Mt. 20:16; 22:14; cp. Isa. 45:22; Mt. 11:28; Jn. 7:37). Effectual calling is not only effective, but irresistible.

Through a secret operation of the Spirit parallel to the proclamation the hearer is supernaturally rendered capable of answering the invitation and is positively caused to answer it. Previously the sinner had no innate *ability* to answer gospel invitations; now he can and must do so. *Supernatural agency* brings about enablement directly by a miracle performed on the being of the person or perhaps through heightened environmental stimulus that indirectly guarantees the desired response. At any rate, no capacity for choice resides in the person himself.

The operation is a *secret operation* inasmuch as God keeps secret his election and timing. The human messenger does not know who will answer or when God will act to bring the sinner into faith. It is a *parallel operation* because it is not through the message but in addition to it and of a different sort; there is more at work than content, communication,

188

influence, and motivation. Strictly speaking, effectual calling is not so much a kind of calling as it is a separate act that makes calling necessarily fruitful.

Evidence for effectual calling

Biblical grounds. (1) Most passages make calling and conversion coextensive by virtue of identifying the call with Christians (Rom. 1:6-7; 8:28; I Cor. 1:2, 9, 24, 26; 7:15; Gal. 1:6, 15; 5:13; Eph. 1:17-18; 4:1, 4; Phil. 3:14; Col. 3:15; I Th. 2:12; 4:7; I Tim. 6:12; II Tim. 1:9; Heb. 3:1; I Pet. 1:15; 2:9; 5:10; II Pet. 1:10; Jude 1: Rev. 17:14). In Romans 8:29-30 Paul equates the scope of foreknowledge, foreordination, calling, justification, and glorification.

This type of evidence, however, does not yield the conclusion sought in it. Obviously since all the saved have been called, Christians may all be described as called. The doctrine of effectual calling does not distinguish positive and restrictive affirmation at this point. To say that all the saved are called does not restrict calling to saving.

(2) Romans 11:29 is a special passage made to do service for the doctrine in question: "For the gifts and the calling of God are not repented of." The inference is that since an effectual call is not withdrawn, it insures the intended purpose.

Some qualification must be made on the notion that God's decisions are irrevocable or he could never change from doing something one way to doing it another. Paul does not necessarily state in Romans 11:29 a universal principle of divine operation. He may have in mind only "the gifts and calling" God directed to Israel as a special people (cp. 3:1-4; 9:1-5). God called Saul and his dynasty to be the royal house in Israel: ". . . Yahweh would have established your kingdom over Israel forever, but now your kingdom will not continue" (I Sam. 13:13-14; cp. 15:11). After Saul's ill-advised sacrifice, the prophet Samuel anointed David and his lineage to be the permanent dynasty in Israel (I Sam. 16:1-13; II Sam. 7:12-16). Several scriptures speak of God's repenting (Gen. 6:6; Ex. 32:14; Judg. 2:18; Ps. 106:45; Jer. 18:7-10; 26:3, 13, 19; Joel 2:13-14; Jon. 3:9-10). If God changes his mind in these and other instances, his not repenting in Romans 11:29 cannot be lifted from the specific case to which Paul applies it and used without qualification as a general principle of divine operation in other areas like spiritual calling unto salvation. *From the standpoint of the passage of time,* God does repent, or change his mind, because the circumstances of his operation change even though Romans 11:29 says that the gifts and calling of God are not repented of.

From the standpoint of omniscience and consistency God does not repent, or change. Even if Romans 11:29 is generalized and then applied to salvation calling, it does not yield the conclusion of irresistible calling.

The original decision to call includes within it any implicit limitations of time or extent. God decided to call national Israel, but he did not thereby eternally lock himself into a national structure for his kingdom; he implicitly called Israel for as long as he had planned to use a political kingdom for his base of operation. An irrevocable calling can therefore be (a) *temporary.*

An irrevocable calling can also be (b) *conditional,* but the conditionality resides in the original calling itself. We may legitimately speak of never revoking a conditional call so that irreversibility does not create necessary response. Inasmuch as Paul appears to argue his point on the basis of divine character, we understand him simply to mean that God does not abandon his purposes without accomplishing them and he does not make promises without fulfilling them.

In the specific case of Romans 11:29 Paul evidently means that God has not cast off his people (cp. 11:1); he has not set aside the essential reason for which he called them. The gospel opportunity for salvation and the concern for righteousness through Israel still operate as always. Blessing all the families of the earth is still figured in terms of faithful Abraham. The national base has been discarded according to plan, but that aspect was never essential to Israel anyway: "They are not all Israel that are of Israel" (9:6). Paul conceives of the sons of God by faith as being spiritual Israel, which is comprised of righteous Jews together with faithful Gentiles grafted into the Jewish tree (11:16-24). God has not taken a different people by accepting Gentiles, but he has looked on his people as Jews purged of sinners and enlarged by Gentiles. The identity is conceived of historically (11:28) in regard to its Jewish roots. God has not revoked his calling, but that calling is still conditional; branches without faith are removed whether Jewish or Gentile in origin.

Dogmatic grounds. We are persuaded that effectual calling is not at all required or even suggested by passages about calling. The real basis for the doctrine lies in the requirements of the theological system in which it stands. If divine sovereignty is incompatible with free will or if

190

total depravity is the case, conditionality cannot exist either because it would contradict divine sovereignty or because a man has no ability to meet the conditions. Being depraved, a person must have something done to him parallel to the proclamation, or he cannot accept the call issued through the gospel. That added operation of the Spirit makes the calling effectual. Effectual calling really rests on dogmatic grounds, not on biblical ones. Inasmuch as we do not espouse the theological system that implies it, we do not affirm the distinction between effectual and general calling.

Equivalent of effectual calling

There is a reality that answers to the concept of a secret operation of the Spirit parallel to the proclamation. Although it fills the same functional slot in the total process of evangelism, it differs significantly in its nature. God has structured in humanness and in the human situation those characteristics and experiences that render a person susceptible to the gospel. These capacities and experiences are roughly "parallel" to the proclamation, and the experiences may in a sense be assigned to the agency of the Spirit. The *content* of the Christian faith comes

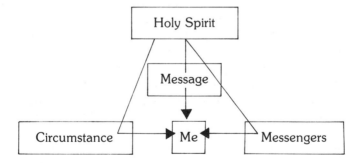

through the message. *Motivation* to accept the content comes also through circumstance and the influence of human messengers—Christians who already embody and personalize the word of Christ. The *nature* of each person already corresponds to the content of the message in that what the gospel offers corresponds to the needs and capacities of the hearer.

Some of the primary givens in human nature are the desire to be loved, the drive for meaningfulness, the concern for security, and the need for innocence. The gospel itself addresses each of these basic needs, but natural circumstance and personal influence increase the motivation to receive it. If a little boy is playing with his friends and his mother calls him for supper, he is more likely to come if he is hungry. Parallel to calling, Mother may open the window to let out the aroma from the French fries and hamburgers. In connection with circumstance we may observe that God has placed in human experience events that push men toward recognizing their dependent position in the universe—natural catastrophies, sickness, suffering, death. They function not only to curb sin by putting a boundary on the expression of it (Gen. 3:22-24), but by moving men away from the practice of it (Heb. 12:4-8). Need awareness creates greater openness to the gospel answer for the human predicament (I Cor. 4:10; II Cor. 12:10; 13:9). The greater the awareness the more likely the acceptance.

When Paul says, "Now I . . . complete in my flesh the things that are lacking in the afflictions of Christ . . ." (Col. 1:24), he does not refer to some deficiency in the basis of atonement, but to his role as a messenger for the atonement. The *manner of the witness* affects the quality of the response to it: ". . . but we put up with all things in order that we may not give any hindrance to the gospel of Christ" (I Cor. 9:12; II Cor. 6:3). Experience shows that ministers and congregations reap a harvest proportionate to the *quality of their life*. Circumstance and demonstration prepare the heart for reception.

Therefore, the Spirit of God may be said to work (a) *parallel* to the proclamation so as to create readiness. Normally his operation is (b) *ordinary* instead of special, although the conversions of Cornelius (Acts 10-11) and of Saul (Acts 9:1-18; 22:1-21; 26:2-23) show that in principle God may intervene supernaturally either to perform a visible or invisible act tending toward conversion of sinners. Even here the intervention is (c) *circumstantial* rather than a miraculous alteration of the being of the person himself. Generally speaking, however, we have no reason for affirming more than an (d) *indirect* operation through the built-in processes of the (e) *natural* order and the inherent power of the gospel message. Finally, the work of the Spirit through circumstance, the message, and through human agency is (f) *resistible*. If we ask why God operates ordinarily, indirectly, resistibly, etc., in calling men to be his sons when other methods would guarantee more uniformly men's coming to his call, we may answer that he wants sons, not offspring.

192

No man wants to be the father of someone who cannot be other than his son.

Tendencies toward acceptance are different from one-to-one correlations between stimulus and response. When the conversion process retains its personal character, influence replaces stimulation, motivation replaces causation, and choice replaces necessity. The doctrine of effectual calling represents one of several outgrowths of the concept of natural depravity along with its depersonalization of the Christian enterprise. Calling, however, by its very name places its operation within the framework of interpersonal relationship.

Chapter Fourteen

JUSTIFICATION BY FAITH: CONDITIONALITY

Introduction

Everything pertaining to salvation thus far is *grace* because it expresses God's unmerited favor toward us. Creation endowed us with capacity for fellowship with him in ways more meaningful than his relationship to stars or animals. Revelation guided us to know him and to know how to be in fellowship with him. Redemption laid a foundation for overcoming broken fellowship and for renewed blessing. God initiated and completed all these blessings aside from any input on man's part.

After the acts of God comes the act of *faith*, which is our unmeriting response to him. In coming to the doctrine of faith, we have not left the subject of grace. Indeed we have only come to consider what lies within the framework of grace and stands secondary in it. Were there no grace, faith would not only have no value, it would not exist, because the previous acts of God open up the possibility of salvation by faith and prompt men's subsequent trust in him.

Since scripture uses "faith" to describe the manner of man's return to righteousness and divine fellowship, the next chapters seek to define the relationship of faith to grace so as not to contradict grace or make it void and unnecessary in salvation. Grace summarizes the initiating activity of God toward man while faith summarizes the responsive activity of man toward God, but each in its own order and in its own domain so as not to dishonor him or degrade us.

The Terms "Faith" and "Works"

Much can be learned about the meanings of "faith" and "works" by looking at the positive statements in which they occur independently, but terms are clearest when used in contrast with one another. Following is a formal analysis of three ways the New Testament distinguishes these words in discussing salvation through Christ.

Faith as a work

Perhaps the most surprising combination occurs in John 6:29, where Jesus answers the multitude's question, "What shall we do in order that we may be working the works of God?" "This is the *work* of God: that you *believe* on him whom he sent." In this usage faith falls within the category of works; it is an example of a work. "This" looks forward to

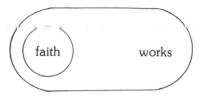

"the work of God," which equals "believing."

Some translations of John 6:29 could allow the reader to suppose that "this" refers to 6:27: "This [giving of the food that abides for eternal life] is the work of God in order that you might believe on him whom he sent." Such an understanding skips over the immediate question and ties into a more distant part of the discussion. It fails to recognize a standard construction in John's writings: "This is the will of the one who sent me: that I should lose nothing of what all he has given me, but should resurrect it in the last day" (Jn. 6:39); "For this is the message that you heard from the beginning: that we should love one another" (I Jn. 3:11); "And this is his commandment: that we should believe the name of his Son Jesus Christ and love one another as he gave us commandment" (I Jn. 3:23; cp. Jn. 6:40; 15:12, 13, 17; 17:3; I Jn. 3:8; 4:21; 5:3; II Jn. 6a, 6b as well as James 1:27; I Jn. 2:25; 5:4; Jn. 3:19; I Jn. 1:5; 4:9; 5:9b, 11, 14; Lk. 10:20; I Jn. 5:2). Clearly, then, "that" does not mean "in order that," but serves as a colon pointedly introducing the matter of concern. Thus Jesus classifies believing as a work in his statement here.

When Jesus identifies faith as a work in John 6:29, he is answering a question about "doing": "What shall we *do* in order that we may be working the works of God?" (6:28). John 3:36 contains a parallelism with similar implications: "The one who *believes* on the Son has eternal life, but the one who *disobeys* the Son will not see life, but the wrath of God remains on him." The Philippian jailer asked Paul and Silas, " 'Sirs, what must I *do* in order that I may be saved?' And they said, '*Believe* on the Lord Jesus, and you and your house will be saved' " (Acts 16:30-31). In Hebrews 3:18-19 the same association occurs: "And to whom did he swear that they would not enter into his rest except to the *disobedient?* And we see that they were not able to enter

195

on account of *disbelief.*" In such texts belief and works interchange as different kinds of doing.

Faith and works

A more familiar combination of faith and works appears in the epistle of James. "Even so faith, if it does not have works, is dead by itself" (2:17); ". . . faith apart from works is ineffective" (2:20); ". . . by works faith was made complete" (2:22); "You see that by works a man is justified, and not by faith only" (2:24); "even so faith apart from works is dead" (2:26). In this usage faith leads to works, and the two together make up the whole picture of man's response in salvation.

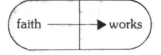

Faith without works

Traditionally, the Christian doctrine of salvation by faith has centered around the writings of Paul. In his distinctive terminology he says that men are saved by faith, *not* by works of law.

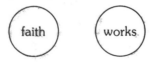

(a) Where then is boasting? It is excluded. By what kind of principle/law [is it excluded]? [Is it excluded by the principle/law] of works? No, but [it is excluded] by the principle/law of faith (Rom. 3:27);

(b) We reckon that a man is justified by faith apart from works of law (Rom. 3:28);

(c) What shall we say then? that Gentiles, who were not straining after righteousness, attained righteousness, but [it was] a righteousness that [comes/is] out-of/by faith. But Israel, straining after a righteousness principle/law, did not arrive at the principle/law. Why? because [they did] not [seek it] by faith, but as if [they could attain it] by works (Rom. 9:30-32a);

(d) Knowing that a person is not justified by works of law, but through faith in Jesus Christ, we also believed on Christ Jesus in order that we might be justified by faith in Christ and not by works of law, because by works of law no flesh will be justified (Gal. 2:16);

196

(e) This only do I want to learn from you: Did you receive the Spirit by works of law or by hearing of faith? Are you this foolish? Having begun with spirit, are you trying to bring yourselves to completion with the flesh? Did you suffer so many things for nothing? if indeed it was for nothing. Does then the one who supplies you the Spirit and works powers among you [do it] by works of law or by hearing of faith? (Gal. 3:2-5).

In three other passages Paul contrasts faith and works without specifying works "of law":

(f) But to the one who does not work but believes on him who justifies the ungodly person, his faith is reckoned unto righteousness, even as David also pronounces blessing on the man to whom God reckons righteousness without works, "Blessed is the one whose iniquities are forgiven and whose sins are covered; blessed is a man whose sin the Lord does not reckon at all" (Rom. 4:5-8).

(g) But if [election] is by grace, it is no longer by works; otherwise grace is no longer grace (Rom. 11:6; cp. II Tim. 1:9; Tit. 3:5)

(h) For you have been saved through faith and this [salvation is] not of yourselves; [it is] a gift of God. [Salvation is] not of works lest anyone would boast (Eph. 2:8-9).

In another passage Paul simply denies salvation by works:

(i) For the children having not yet been born neither having done anything good or bad, in order that the purpose of God might stand not by works but by the one who calls, he said, "The older shall serve the younger" (Rom. 9:11-12).

Observations

Three inferences may be made from the purely formal way in which New Testament writers employ "faith" and "works" in regard to salvation. (1) They obviously do not use them to mean the same thing. (2) What Jesus means by works correlates with what Jesus means by faith and works and with what Paul means by faith only. (3) Evidently the individual concerns of each author are not the same even though they address the same general topic. If the authors of scripture do not employ the expressions uniformly, the reader is immediately warned to expect an interpretation process more complex than he might suppose initially.

197

The Meanings of "Faith" and "Works"

In John

Not much specific can be said about faith and works in John 6:29 and related passages. From the context of John 6 "works" appears to equal "doing." (a) Faith is one kind of doing that summarizes the basis for righteousness and salvation. (b) Faith here is saving faith. (c) Faith to eternal life harmonizes with being given eternal life (Jn. 6:27). (d) It is something done, rather than something given. (e) Faith logically precedes the eternal life; faith-for-life compares with work-for-bread.

In James

James 2 agrees with John in making both faith and works something a person does, but he is more specific in making faith an inner act and works an outer act that expresses faith. Faith includes (a) *understanding* and (b) *assent* that a brother needs food and clothes. Since, however, the demons have what James means by "faith," commitment and trust fall under the label of works, and encompass such activities as would solve the problem. (c) Faith is not a saving degree of faith, being something that even the demons have (2:19; cp. Jn. 12:42-43). (d) It is something the person himself does which (e) serves as that out of which acceptable works are performed. The one without the other is unsatisfactory in either case because love is what transforms.

In Paul

Whereas James is concerned with *what* men should do, Paul is concerned with *why* they do. James urges his readers to outward expression of inward conviction; Paul urges his readers to recognize that they do not produce their standing with God. James deals with the relationship between inner and outer action; Paul deals with the relationship between personal action and divine grace in salvation. James speaks of the identity of human responses required in salvation; Paul speaks of the meaning of them.

Works. In order to arrive at this generalization in Paul, it is best to begin with his usage of "works" and then conclude what he means by "faith." First, (1) *Paul means works "of law" when he denies salvation by works.* For him "works" means not just doing something, but doing something that has to do with law or is in the context of law. He does

198

not, therefore, mean something as broad as John 6:29, nor does he mean something so narrow as James 2.

Second, (2) *"works of law" means perfection.* Galatians 3:10 quotes Deuteronomy 27:26 to the effect that "everyone who does not continue to do all the things written in the book of the law is accursed." *Continuing* to do *everything* amounts to perfection. James agrees in this assessment when he says, "Whoever keeps the whole law and yet stumbles in one point is guilty of all" (2:10). Perfection has always been God's standard for men (Mt. 5:48; Gen. 17:1; Deut. 18:13), and the Mosaic law required no less.

In Romans 3:21-23 Paul speaks of the "righteousness of God" when he says,

> And now apart from law a righteousness of God has been made manifest, witnessed to by the law and the prophets, but it is a righteousness of God through faith in Jesus Christ to all those who believe; for there is no distinction, for all have sinned and fall short of the glory of God.

The "righteousness of God" could indicate a righteousness God has or perhaps a righteousness he gives, but either way perfection is the concept involved.

"Righteousness" and other related terms then mean perfection in Paul; they indicate the idea of being characterized by everything God's law stipulates: ". . . God . . . condemned sin in the flesh in order that the *righteousness of the law* might be fulfilled in us who walk, not according to the flesh, but according to the spirit" (Rom. 8:3-4). "But when the kindness of our Savior God and his love toward man appeared, he saved us—not by *works in righteousness* that we ourselves did but according to his mercy—through the washing of regeneration and renewal of the Holy Spirit whom he 'poured out' richly on us through Jesus Christ our Savior" (Tit. 3:4-6). "Works of the law" corresponds with "righteousness of the law," "works in righteousness," and "righteousness of God."

When Paul concludes in Romans 3:23 that "all have sinned and fall short of the glory of God," he teaches that no one has lived up to the divine standard of excellence. Consequently, he means earlier in the same chapter that no one is *perfect* when he declares that not one is *righteous* or does *good.* The citations from Isaiah and the Psalms he understands to mean that no person does everything he should do.

Therefore the apostle does not affirm that the unsaved do not, or cannot, do a *good* but that they cannot do *good,* that is, perfect goodness. He does not intend to intimate that a sinner's every act is tainted with sinful, self-centered, ulterior motives; but that, standing in a context of imperfection, good qualities do not suffice to make a man good in God's eyes.

Paul's concern is simply this: salvation by works is inherently impossible because renewing perfection is inherently impossible. Perfect obedience to God's will revealed in his law is what constitutes righteousness. Under law *being righteous* is necessary for *being regarded as righteous* in God's eyes. Since no one ever lives up to the perfection standard for righteousness, legal righteousness means that in theory everyone lives under the curse of separation from God, which comes from that unrighteousness. Salvation removes separation from God; imperfection caused the separation; therefore perfection is required before restored fellowship can exist. A blemished record cannot be removed. It is not that a sinner cannot do anything good, but that he cannot do everything good after he has failed once. We re-emphasize that salvation by works of law is impossible because overcoming imperfection is impossible.

Assumed in this line of reasoning is the ineffectiveness of Old Testament animal sacrifice. In 10:1-14 the writer of Hebrews makes explicit this segment of the total argument when he concludes from Psalms 40:6-8a that the blood of bulls and goats cannot take away sin. God prepared a body for the new Melchizedekian priest of Psalms 110:4 so that he might accomplish in his flesh what was lacking in the Levitical offerings for sin. Since the law provided no real basis for removing guilt after disobedience, the loss of perfection theoretically and legally amounted to a one-way, dead-end street.

Third, (3) *"works of law" means inherent result.* Because of foregoing observations, we may now say that "works of law" indicates a situation where the righteousness results directly and inherently from one's own obedience to the law. Paul uses "works" in a way similar to a related verb form in James 1:3: ". . . the testing of your faith *produces* patience." In the theory of law a person's *acts* of obedience produce his record whether good or bad. Only *perfect* obedience qualifies the person for being defined as righteous. Imperfection cannot be overcome; therefore works of the law provide no solution to unrighteousness and consequent disfellowship from God. That works—as well as faith—do not particularly refer to acts is implied in Romans 3:27, where Paul speaks of the "law of works" and the "law of faith." "Law" evidently means "principle." If works and faith are principles, they are not acts but patterns—in this case, patterns of connection with the resultant righteousness.

From among the several elements involved in a working situation, Paul selects the cause-effect, or purpose-result aspect, to communicate his point that the law does not serve as a practical basis for fellowship with God. Ordinarily, when a person does something he causes something; so when he does everything God commands, he causes righteousness. But causing perfect righteousness is no longer possible after sinning. Works are works of law; works of law are perfection; works of law are perfection inherently resulting from our obedience to the law.

Fourth, (4) *"works of law" means personal perfection.* We conclude that if works of law produce righteousness inherently, then righteousness is produced personally. One's only claim to righteousness and divine fellowship rests on his being everything he ought to be. Such an arrangement is devastating to all interpersonal relationships because no one fully lives up to any value system. Under law the situation must be that he *is* righteous; it cannot be that he is *regarded* as righteous either by overlooking his faults or by viewing him in terms of the perfect model with whom he identifies.

This personal character of righteousness under law does not come just as an inference from the nature of the case; it comes also in repeated declarations of scripture and in Paul's own presentation against salvation by works. In Galatians 3:12 he cites Leviticus 18:5: "He that does them shall have life in them" (cp. Neh. 9:29; Ezek. 20:11, 13, 21; Mt. 19:17; Lk. 10:28; Rom. 10:5). Ezekiel emphasizes the personal character of both righteousness and wickedness by saying, "The soul that sins is the one that shall die; the son shall not bear the iniquity of the father, neither shall the father bear the iniquity of the son. The righteousness of the righteous shall be upon himself, and the wickedness of the wicked shall be upon himself" (18:20; cp. I Kg. 8:32; Isa. 3:10-11; Mt. 16:27; Rom. 2:6-9; 14:12; II Cor. 5:10; Eph. 6:8; Col. 3:25; Rev. 2:23; 20:12; 22:12). Deuteronomy 27:26 requires perfection; Leviticus 18:5 specifies personalness in that perfection. In Paul therefore "works" refers to the principle of personal perfection.

Faith. Galatians 3:10-12 specifies that theoretically the Old Testament system of things stands antithetical to faith. In practice, as Habakkuk

2:3-4 declares, there is and has always been another basis for life. "The just shall have life by faith" undergirds all the main New Testament materials on salvation: Romans 1:17; Galatians 3:11; Hebrews 10: 37-38. Consequently, that other basis for life Paul calls "faith."

If "works" means the principle of personal perfection, "faith" refers to the principle of non-personal perfection; that is, it indicates a righteousness of God that comes from some other source. The conclusion that "faith" refers to trust in an alternate source of righteousness accords with Paul's teaching in Romans 3:21-24, where he speaks of (1) *a righteousness of the law* and (2) *a righteousness apart from the law.* The former is (1) *works;* the latter is (2) *faith.* The same contrast between sources of righteousness comes in Philippians 3:9: ". . . not having my own righteousness, which is of the law, but [having righteousness] through faith in Christ, the righteousness which is of God by faith." Here (1) *my own righteousness* equals righteousness of the law as in Romans 3:21 and contrasts with (2) *righteousness of God through faith in Christ.* In Romans 9:11 Paul contrasts (1) *election out of works* with (2) *election out of him who calls.* Faith is righteousness (a) from the one who calls, is (b) apart from the law, and is (c) put in Jesus Christ.

If "works" in Paul addresses the relationship between action and righteousness, faith also addresses that relationship so as to make the two parallel alternatives. Paul illustrates the positive nature of faith by recalling Genesis 15:6: "Abraham believed God and it was counted to him for righteousness" (Rom. 4:3, 5, 9, 21-22). Although believing was a righteous thing to do, it was not righteousness because it was counted *for* righteousness; believing did not produce Abraham's righteousness because it was *counted* for righteousness.

Therefore the subject for Paul is not receiving a blessing based on righteousness, but receiving righteousness itself. Righteousness comes by reckoning; hence, it exists in the eyes of the beholder, not in the believer. Regarding Abraham as righteous was not a matter of "debt." If he had been perfect, God would have "owed it to him" to regard him as such (Rom. 4:4); but since his faith was "counted for" righteousness, the righteousness he had was only in the way God viewed him. All this transpired prior to the covenant of circumcision, and Paul reinforces by this fact his point that righteousness by obedience to the law signified by circumcision did not serve as an ultimate framework for righteousness and divine fellowship.

The Genesis 15 episode gives more positive content to the second means to righteousness. The first way perfect righteousness could come was (a) *through perfect obedience to the revealed will of God.* This option has no practical value for righteousness because no one can live up to his own ideals, much less the exalted standards of a holy God. The New Testament never depreciates the Mosaic law except as a means to righteousness: "The law is holy, and the commandment is holy and righteous and good" (Rom. 7:12, 16; I Tim. 1:8). The law was holy, but it could not make holy (Heb. 7:19; 10:1; Acts 13:39; Rom. 3:20; Gal. 2:16). This difficulty lies not in the Mosaic law, but in law as such; for "if there had been a law given that could make alive, truly righteousness would have been of the law" (Gal. 3:21). Consequently, even the Israelites, who had the law, were to understand that their righteousness and life did not come thereby, but by faith (Hab. 2:4). Law was only added to promise in order to define righteousness, sensitize men to it, and restrain unrighteousness until there should come the promised object of identification unto righteousness (Gal. 3:19; Rom. 5:20). With the coming of Messiah as perfect model, the second way of righteousness fully arrived; it is a righteousness (b) *through being viewed as righteous by God because of trust in his provisions and promises.*

We may summarize by saying that in Paul "works" means the principle of personal perfection, and "faith" is the principle of trust in another to regard us as perfect. For him works are not doing something, doing something outward, doing token acts, doing something after salvation, or doing something not germane to Christ in salvation. In Paul "works" is *accomplishing something.* In John and a few other passages "works" is *doing something,* and faith is a prime example of it. According to James faith is inner action and "works" is *doing something outward.*

The Concept of Salvation by Faith

The second way to righteousness is *trusting in another to regard us as righteous* in distinction from *being righteous.* It remains for us to determine what value human obedience has in a faith situation, that is, in the situation of simply being regarded as righteous.

In their respective discussions of salvation both James and Paul refer to Genesis 15:6 and to the general flow of events in which it stands.

Paul uses it to illustrate justification by faith while James uses it to illustrate justification by faith and works. Mutually exclusive ideas could not, of course, be legitimately drawn from the same circumstance. Consequently, the work of offering up Isaac that James cites must come under the heading of faith in Pauline usage.

This phenomenon presses us to ask what real meaning such obediences have in salvation. Clearly Paul would say that they do not produce the salvation, yet James declares them necessary for salvation inasmuch as he says a man is justified by works (2:21, 24). Both the believing and the working in James logically precede the resultant justification so that the reader must find a positive way of understanding the significance of inner and outer response in justification.

Conditionality

Conditionality is a traditional term we have adopted for this purpose. Precision is a must at this juncture if we are to avoid confusion and self-contradiction in setting forth this delicate issue. On the one hand, we must avoid the concept of *merit,* which sees the human act as causing the righteousness. On the other hand, for reasons given shortly we are not satisfied with the concept of *recognition,* which puts all human responses logically subsequent to justification; such an arrangement means that God would be choosing to save few despite the fact that he wants no one to be lost (II Pet. 3:9). On all hands, it is agreed that Christianity cannot countenance *antinomianism,* which sees no connection whatever between status with God and personal behavior.

Logically prior. Conditionality as one aspect of faith refers to the circumstance where human acts logically precede the result involved. Logical priority inheres in acts that (1) *result* in salvation: "Repent therefore and turn again unto the blotting out of your sins" (Acts 3:19). "Repent and be baptized . . . unto the remission of sins . . ." (Acts 2:38). "With the heart man believes unto righteousness" (Rom. 10:10). "Godly sorrow works repentance unto salvation" (II Cor. 7:10; see also Rom. 4:5).

Logical priority also inheres in the concept of (2) *means.* We have already noted James' contention that Abraham was justified by works (2:21) and that "by works a man is justified and not by faith only" (2:24). "For we reckon that a man is justified by faith apart from works of law" (Rom. 3:28). "Therefore having been justified by faith, we have peace with God through our Lord Jesus Christ" (Rom. 5:1; see also

Gal. 2:16, 3:8, 24; Eph. 2:8; 5:26; Tit. 3:5; I Pet. 3:21). When one thing is a means to another, it logically precedes the other.

(3) *Conditions* also precede the results given: "If you will confess with your mouth Jesus Christ as Lord . . . you will be saved" (Rom. 10:9). (4) *Purpose is logically before a result.* "What must I do in order that I may be saved" (Acts 16:30). (5) *Sequential listing of human obediences prior to salvation* confirms the above points. "Believe and be saved" is never reversed to "be saved and believe." Evidently human responses precede righteousness, but it is not yet clear how they do so.

Non-causal. However responses logically precede righteousness they do not causally precede it. The fact that salvation has to do with (a) *interpersonal relationship* means that restoring interpersonal relationship does not happen from just one side of the relationship. James 2:21-24, in discussing Abraham's justification by *faith*, stresses this *interpersonal truth* when he adds to Genesis 15:6 the point that Abraham was called a *friend* of God (Isa. 41:8; II Ch. 20:7). On the one side, atonement and salvation are not done wholly by God without reference to human response. On the other side, renewed fellowship cannot be produced by the human response; otherwise God would not be involved even in accepting the person's company.

But more must be said because salvation has to do with (b) *interpersonal relationship between unequals*; therefore we must add that the human responses leading to fellowship have been defined, specified, and commanded by God instead of being originated by men.

This admission is still not enough because salvation has to do with (c) *restoring interpersonal relationship between unequals.* The topic is not originating a relationship, but restoring a broken one. Since imperfection has already set in, God does not have to consider a person righteous as a result of the responses with which we are concerned in salvation: believing, repenting, trusting, committing, confessing, being baptized, continuing steadfastly.

Not only do such acts by one party not produce a two-party relationship; such acts in the state of imperfection cannot even produce the perfect righteousness prerequisite to acceptance by the second party. Salvation then has to do with (d) *restoring the righteousness prerequisite to restoring interpersonal relationship between unequals.* Human obedience does not even produce a quality of character such that God would for self-consistency's sake owe it to a person to regard him as righteous and therefore make him his friend (James 2:23; Gen. 15:6

+ Isa. 41:8; II Ch. 20:7). Not only are acts of faith not causal because they cannot produce the interpersonal relationship; they are not causal because they cannot produce the righteousness either. Acts of obedient faith logically precede the righteousness, yet they do not cause it.

For greater precision in defining conditionality we turn to Jesus' own description of salvation by faith in John 3:14-15: "And as Moses lifted up the serpent in the wilderness, thus it is necessary for the Son of man to be lifted up in order that everyone who believes on him may have eternal life." According to Numbers 21 when poisonous snakes came among the Israelites, God told Moses to fashion a brazen serpent and put it on a standard; if the person bitten by a viper would look at the brazen serpent, he would be cured. Jesus makes a suggestive comparison between that event and salvation. Looking on the brazen serpent correlates with believing on the crucified Christ.

The event shows five characteristics of any conditionality construct. A man bitten by a snake represents (a) *a dependent first person*. He occupied a position from which he lacked the wherewithal to deliver himself. Similarly, the unrighteous person lacks the wherewithal to overcome imperfection.

In the Numbers 21 episode God stands as (b) *a sovereign second person*. No moral or ethical compulsion caused him to deliver the victims from deadly snake bite; after all he himself had sent the adders among them in punishment for blaspheming him and Moses. On the other side of the analogy sinners have alienated themselves from God so that he bears no legal obligation to make provision for renewed fellowship with them.

God offered (c) *a free promise* to overcome the effects of his plague on the people. The promise was free, not because it cost them nothing, but because it was freely given. A promise always anticipates a future benefit; consequently, at the time of giving it, the object of it has not been realized. In salvation the promise again arises freely from the love of God, which puts restraint on his holy wrath even as his holiness puts restraint on his fatherly love. God took the initiative in laying a foundation for his promise of renewed relationship with men. Therefore, under free promise belongs the understanding and feeling that God is approachable and that men do not have to agonize before him to obtain his concern and favor.

Looking on the brazen serpent illustrates (d) *a predicated obedience*.

206

Many blessings poured out upon his people have no prerequisites, but in conditionality the benefactors must obey the commandments pursuant to the benefit. This obedience they themselves do as distinguished from something done to them or through them by God himself or other men. Believing in the crucified Christ correlates with looking on the brazen serpent. Believing is something sinners do as distinguished from something done to them or through them by God or human proxies. The act of obedience is predicated on the person in need, and it logically precedes the result in question.

Cure from snake bite came in (e) *a bestowed result*. By no stretch of the imagination would one ever suppose that looking at a snake on a standard could neutralize the venom of a viper. Such an action cannot cause the cure. Clearly God gave the result. In like fashion, eternal life comes to the person by the sole agency of God. He alone acts in giving that result as well as the righteousness precedent to it. The predicated obedience does not figure into the bestowed result because the kind of obedience required cannot contribute to the kind of result needed. There is discontinuity between response and result in conditionality.

Other situations abound in scripture to illustrate the non-causal nature of conditionality. Naaman (dependent) besought Yahweh (sovereign) to cure him from leprosy (result). He was told (promise) to dip himself (obedience) in the Jordan River seven times (II Kg. 5). Dipping in the Jordan or the Pharpar any number of times has nothing to do with curing leprosy. Jesus put clay on the eyes of the man born blind (Jn. 9) and told him to wash it off in the pool of Siloam in order to receive his sight. Again the clay, the spittle, and the water were not the effective agents in producing his sight. By definition all "miracles" requiring acts by those in need have their consequences disjoined from their antecedents.

In *conditionality* the predicated obedience does not cause the result in whole or in part because it is not directed to the result but to the sovereign. The person does what he does because he is commanded to obey, not because he has decided to produce. He does the act because it is commanded, not because it is effective. In *merit* situations there is no dependent first person because he can cause his own result. There is no sovereign second person because he owes it to the other to view him as he is. There is no free promise because the sovereign adds nothing to the action of the servant. There is no bestowed result because the

207

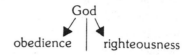

obedience suffices for the effect. All there is is the predicated obedience that creates righteousness on its own.

In regard to the nature of relationship between act and result, conditionality has its own distinctive nature that must not be allowed to slide off into either merit or recognition. Like merit conditionality involves acts logically before the result, but it does not share its *causal* priority; like recognition conditionality does not cause the result, but it does not include the logical *subsequentness* that is in recognition. Conditionality is non-causal like recognition, but logically prior like merit. Therefore it is neither the one nor the other, yet it has characteristics of both.

The value of conditionality in salvation theory is inestimable. It solves the problem between God's desire to save all and his decision to save some without nullifying grace. By virtue of having conditions to meet, it allows men to determine *who* is saved; by virtue of the inability of these conditions to effect the result, *conditionality preserves grace*, which determines *that* men are saved. Consequently, there is no need to postulate total depravity because *conditionality protects sovereignty.*

Appropriate. The question comes as to whether the commanded conditions are arbitrary since there is discontinuity between them and the result. We answer that conditions are appropriate in all conditionality situations, even when miracles are involved because they are at least symbolically associated with the result. Looking on the brazen serpent ties in with the cure from the bites of serpents. Dipping in the Jordan symbolizes cleansing. Washing the spittled clay from the blind man's eyes corresponds with the identity of his problem.

In salvation the conditions specified all partake of the appropriate concerns of the gospel. It is appropriate that a man believe in him who serves as the basis for his righteousness. It is appropriate that forgiveness call for repentance from sins to be forgiven. It is appropriate that a person trust God and commit himself to the one who saved him. Christian baptism is appropriate for symbolically re-enacting in the experience of

208

each believer the distinctive event in the ministry of him who died for sins and resurrected for justification; it pictorially buries the old man and resurrects a new man unto life eternal. The conditions of reconciliation and perseverance do not have a penance character, where the act required for absolution may not necessarily be germane to the end in view. Although the obediences vary in how germane they are to the concern in salvation, they are related to the concern for righteousness and fellowship with God, if not naturally, at least symbolically.

Active. Another question comes as to what degree of faith, belief, trust, and repentance proves satisfactory as a condition for the bestowal of saving grace. We might wonder whether our repentance is serious enough or our faith strong enough to please God. This potential uncertainty could create the very insecurity grace purportedly eliminates when it replaces works.

Although degree questions cannot be answered with categorical precision, the general principle we infer from James 2 is that, to be valid, faith and repentance must be of sufficient degree that they transform themselves into action. We never believe anything strongly enough for practical purposes until we believe it strongly enough to act on it; otherwise it is academic and theoretical. But the kingdom of heaven is not in word and thought, but in deed (I Cor. 4:19-20; 2:1-5). Christian faith calls for a difference that makes a difference. Therefore, the Pauline use of "faith" includes the expression of faith.

Even this statement is deficient because we do not overtly live up to our aspirations. If always living up to our aspirations were the "condition," it would no longer be conditionality but works again. Not only would we not be psychologically free from a "yoke neither we nor our fathers were able to bear"; we would not have any real freedom from it. We would end up labeling the same old thing by a new label, but works by any other name is still works.

In calling for faith to the degree of action, we mean to deny the sufficiency of mental assent, not to affirm the necessity of perfect expression. The idea is not that of filling the gaps in previous righteousness. The good news is that we do not have to remain separated from God because of past sin or to continue in perfect righteousness after salvation. Willingness to identify with Jesus Christ as perfect model is the condition for initial reconciliation; aspiration to live up to his example is the condition for continued reconciliation. Our point here is that aspiration includes the outward expression of inner belief, not the perfect outward expression of it. Attempt is counted for achievement; expressed attitude is counted for perfect accomplishment. Salvation operates in an interpersonal framework (faith, repentance, forgiveness), not in a legal one (works). Grace plus faith shifts relationship from a quantitative to a qualitative base and from a legal to an interpersonal realm.

Thus when Paul speaks about the spirit of the law as opposed to the letter of the law, he talks respectively about the purpose of the law as distinguished from the specific manner in which the law theoretically accomplished that purpose. The Mosaic revelation sought human righteousness, and the means to it was personal achievement. The purpose of the gospel is also righteousness, but now faith is the "means" to it. Since both works and faith have the same purpose (Rom. 3:31; 8:4; Mt. 5:17), faith fulfills the purpose, or "spirit," of the law even though it does not accomplish that purpose by the same specific manner, or "letter," as the law did (Rom. 7:6, 2:27, 29; II Cor. 3:6).

Defining saving faith as faith to the degree of action harmonizes with the mechanics of sanctification, or Christian growth, experienced by the person in Christ. Christian growth takes place in the reciprocation between inner and outer action. "The good man out of the good treasure of his heart brings forth the good thing" (Lk. 6:45a); thus the outer flows from the inner. "Where you treasure is there your heart will be also" (Mt. 6:21); thus the inner is shaped by the outer. Obviously the degree of inner faith must be to the extent of outward expression in order to set in motion the interplay between outer and inner dimensions. Faith like a mustard seed will move mountains because among other things it will trigger the outward behavior that in turn increases the inner dimension unto mountain-moving expression. By seeing genuine faith as being to this degree, we see also how the process of conversion links up immediately with the process of growth.

Conditionality describes the manner in which human response relates to divine gift; it describes the way by which the benefits of the death of Christ are appropriated to the individual. This concept by no means, however, captures everything present in a faith situation. Consequently, we briefly notice four other, less controversial components of the total concept of faith.

210

Identification

Conditionality designates the aspect of faith that deals with the relationship between human response and human righteousness. Identification designates the object of faith; faith is put in Jesus Christ. He is the Sinless One with whom the sinner identifies himself in order to be viewed by God as sinless.

Commitment

Identification with Christ expresses commitment *to live* as he lived. In baptism Paul says the sinner buries the old way of life and resurrects to a new aspiration to carry out in his behavior the pattern of acting that corresponds with the status he has been granted in identification (Rom. 6:1-14). Identification also expresses commitment *to the purpose* of him whose name identification causes us to wear.

Trust

Habakkuk 2:4 undergirds the doctrine of faith in Romans, Galatians, and Hebrews. In that passage faith carries the connotation of trust, which is the assurance and conviction (Heb. 11:1) that promises will be fulfilled, goals can be reached, and hopes can be realized through identification with Christ and commitment to his purposes in the world. Faith is not therefore an abstract trust that "things always seem to work out"; rather, it is a conscious trust in God who calls and gives and saves us. Faith is also not something able to be done by a proxy; each person must trust for himself unto eternal life. Although trust cannot be done by another, it is always placed in another person; faith therefore does not equal the power of positive thinking as if to say, "Believe in yourself." Its message in fact enjoins the very opposite: man is no longer to believe in himself because he has already failed and characteristically so; thus he must trust in God who justifies the ungodly.

Belief is a way to know. It is the most fundamental element in faith since it is the foundation for the aspects already noticed. Belief and sight are two ways to know something (II Cor. 5:7). Salvation requires belief of testimony about events not personally witnessed, about future fulfillments not seen as yet, and about present relationship to God that is not known by sense perception. Faith is not just mental assent, but it is a mental assent that leads to trust, commitment, and identification; it relates to its results by being conditional.

211

Faith in Its Systematic Relationships

Salvation vs. innocence

The concept of conditionality has been used in the context of *salvation* as distinguished from *innocence*. God might choose to relate to a personal unconditionally if he were establishing an original association with him. Parents do this with innocent children who have never done anything good or bad. They relate to them, so to speak, by creation, not by holiness. The idea of unconditional grace applies to principles for initial relationship, but scripture differentiates innocence from forgiveness by treating the former as unconditional and the latter as conditional.

Salvation established and applied

Our previous comments on conditionality in salvation *applied to the individual,* which needs to be differentiated from salvation *established by Christ* as a possibility for all men. Conditionality has to do with the application, but not with the establishment. Asking whether salvation is conditional raises an ambiguous question unless one goes on to distinguish these two stages. God did not require anyone to meet any condition to get him to provide a plan for atonement.

In the accompanying diagram we have attempted to incorporate the main features of salvation as a context for the present distinction. Whether there is a plan of salvation is unconditional. Within the plan

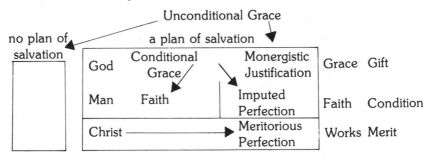

of salvation grace is conditional inasmuch as the required responses do not produce the perfection needed. That perfection is imputed or reckoned to men; they are regarded as perfectly righteous although they are not personally so. At the decisive point salvation is "monergistic"; that is, God is the only one working or acting when he pronounces a

212

man justified from guilt. The change of status is performed in the mind of God only by the free choice of God and in conformity with his prior promise to men. Beneath the divine acquittal lies the perfect righteousness of Christ that was produced by his perfect obedience to the Father's will for him. Our faith *trusts* that *identification* with him and *commitment* to what we *believe* about him is the Father's adequate *condition* for justifying us in grace.

Salvation initial and continued

Salvation by faith means conditionality both in initial and continued righteousness. A man's obedience to God no more keeps him righteous after justification than it makes him righteous unto justification. This particular truth is in fact the very reason Paul wrote Galatians. Although his treatment of faith has most often been applied to modern discussions of bringing men to Christ, Paul wrote that epistle to correct the influence of Judaizing teachers who were following along behind him trying to get the Gentile converts to become Jews by submitting to circumcision. That rite formally brought proselytes under the jurisdiction of the Mosaic law and therefore under the principle of righteousness by works, that is, perfection by personal obedience.

The Judaizing teachers in effect taught that initial salvation comes by grace but continues by works. Paul objected to this misperception of the Christian message by saying,

> O foolish Galatians, who bewitched you before whose eyes Jesus Christ was publicly portrayed as crucified? This only I want to learn from you: did you receive the spirit by works of law or by hearing of faith? Are you so foolish? Having begun with spirit, are you now brought to completion with flesh? Did you suffer so many things in vain, if indeed it has been in vain? Does he then that supplies the Spirit to you and works miracles among you do it by works of law or by hearing of faith? (3:1-5).

From this point the apostle goes on to cite Genesis 15:6; 12:3 along with Deuteronomy 27:26; Leviticus 18:5; and Habakkuk 2:4, which have already entered into our presentation on faith and works. Paul also joins pre- and post-conversion operations under faith and grace in Romans 3:22 24: "for all have sinned [pre conversion] and fall short [post-conversion] of the glory of God." Hebrews 10:36—11:40 likewise speaks to the already saved that they not shrink back but "have *faith* unto the saving of the soul." Galatians, Romans, and Hebrews all derive eventually from the same Old Testament text: Habakkuk 2:4. Continuing steadfastly relates conditionally to continued righteousness as assuredly as faith, repentance, and baptism relate conditionally to initial righteousness.

Righteousness and salvation

We stress again, not just salvation by faith, but righteousness by faith. Since faith includes conditionality, we may say that it is not just a matter of conditions for salvation, but conditions for the righteousness that precedes it. Hopefully, emphasizing this point will help avoid any tendency to suppose that a "condition" refers to some quality or condition of goodness resident in the person. This quality itself is the very thing that is missing and is itself given to each person by reckoning, or imputation, in the mind of God. "Condition" in our usage means always and only a kind of relationship between human response and divine grace.

Righteousness and blessing

Related to the previous observation is the distinction between righteousness and blessing. Righteousness could conceivably serve as a condition for reward or blessing, but the concern of conditionality here is not health, wealth, long life, special privilege; conditionality speaks to the obedience that man renders to God before he justifies the sinner, grants him fellowship, and perhaps blesses him further with temporal or

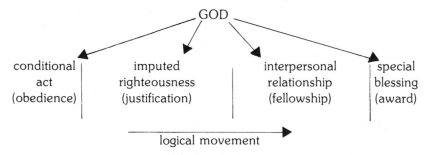

eternal benefits. The horizontal movement of conditionality, righteousness, fellowship, and blessing are not causally connected; they are personally connected by the free choice of God in accordance with his previous purposes and promises.

214

Conditionality and self-interest

Conditionality might appear to avoid merit technically without escaping self-centeredness in people who know their own actions have a decisive bearing on their eternal destiny. We suggest, however, that (1) concern for ourselves is not self centeredness unless it seeks to help self by hurting others or neglecting God's purposes. Furthermore, (2) part of the condition is love responding to love first demonstrated toward us. Love naturally is not self-centered because it gives of itself to meet the needs of others. Consequently, self-centered response does not meet the condition laid down for divine action on our behalf.

To summarize, we may say that in the various aspects of faith there exists a gap—between the knower and the thing known (belief), between the truster and the thing hoped for (trust), between the act and the result (conditionality). A person always stands in that gap to connect the two "sides," thus the appropriateness of this term for defining a relationship and a program that are primarily interpersonal.

Chapter Fifteen

JUSTIFICATION BY FAITH: INNER ACTION

Introduction

Our previous chapter on faith stressed the logical priority of human response to divine application of salvation; hence, it highlighted the conditionality element in faith as contrasted to "recognition." Recognition puts human responses only after reconciliation in appreciation for unconditional election. Especially for the non-elect recognition leads to fatalism and quietism in spiritual matters because men can do nothing about their situation before God.

The present chapter considers a distinction often made within conditionality between inner and outer action. Discussions of salvation frequently proceed as if "faith" refers to a cluster of inner factors so that "works" refers to the consequent outward behavior of saving faith. Under this second concept saving faith is *active faith* in contrast to acting faith. Faith does act, but in salvation—especially in initial salvation—God contemplates only the inner factor as the condition for salvation. If inner faith does not issue in outward expression, it is not genuine. On the other hand, *acting faith* includes the outward behavior that corresponds with belief, trust, and a sense of commitment. What happens under the impetus of faith has the same non-causal character as the faith that generated it.

The problem between these two reconstructions of conditionality is a matter of terms that becomes a matter of concept. Therefore in the ensuing remarks we seek to demonstrate that *terminologically* an act of faith is not a work in the Pauline doctrine of salvation by faith. We are then in a position to reaffirm the last chapter's claim that *conceptually* we may regard the expression of belief and trust as included in what God contemplates when he grants salvation.

The Case for Faith as Inner Action

Lexical meanings of "pistis"

The argument. Presentations on Pauline theology do not always make clear exactly what the apostle means by "faith." Authors evidently assume that he means belief, trust, commitment. In other words, they develop their interpretation of Paul out of (1) *the dictionary meaning of "pistis."* For the Greek word *pistis,* often translated "faith," lexicons

216

list definitions like faithfulness, trust, confidence, belief. For this second view of faith, the investigation seems to stop with dictionary definitions and the doctrinal work begins immediately.

The objections. Studying the meaning of a word must go beyond the use of a dictionary. First, lexicons get their information from investigating circumstances where terms are used. On crucial questions the student may want *personal verification* of the conclusions presented in reference works. Secondly, words occasionally have *technical usage* so that general entries in a study tool do not satisfy the requirements of a specific study. Technical usage covers instances where a writer uses a term to highlight one aspect of the total situation where the word is used. Thirdly, a word has meaning by virtue of *contextualization*; that is, terms do not carry in themselves all their meaning, but depend upon the nature of the subject and the circumstance of usage to "fine tune" the point being made. Meaning "rides on," or "hovers over," the total set of interdependent words and phrases.

These observations on the nature of words and language affect our understanding of Paul because we perceive from the nature of his concern about works of law that he is employing the word technically to express non-causality in the sense of conditionality.

James' meaning for "pistis"

The general procedure. A second reason for understanding faith as inner actions is (2) *the meaning of "pistis" in James.* Customarily theologians appear to get their definition from the book of James and then use that meaning to interpret Pauline literature. Perhaps they do so because James presents his material in more straightforward fashion while Paul's argumentation is more complex. Since the former is more readily understandable, the word meanings found there tend to serve the interpreter elsewhere as well.

Because their formal relationships differ, however, it is not possible to get the meanings for "faith" and "works" from James and then use them in Paul. The procedure forces contradiction between the authors because James *affirms* that both are in salvation while Paul *denies* that both are in salvation. James makes faith and works complementary, but Paul makes them *antithetical.* For James faith *with* works is justification; for Paul faith *without* works is justification. The harmony of scripture dictates the conclusion that the two authors have different concerns

217

and employ terms differently; hence, getting the meanings from one in order to apply them to the other cannot represent sound exposition.

Kind of faith. In order to resolve the formal difficulty, various attempts have been made to bring James and Paul into complementary relationship in their teaching about salvation. Thus commentators (1) *attempt to transform "faith" in James 2 into a "kind of faith."* Accordingly James teaches that "genuine" faith does work, and certain verses in Paul's letters confirm that he occasionally makes the same point under the same terminology. Galatians 5:6 affords one example: "For in Christ neither circumcision nor uncircumcision accomplishes anything, but faith expressing-itself/worked-through love [accomplishes something]." Another comes in Ephesians: ". . . [salvation is] not of works in order that no one should boast, for we are his workmanship created in Christ Jesus for good works which God previously prepared in order that we might walk in them" (2:9-10; cp. I Th. 1:3; Tit. 2:7, 14; 3:8, 14). Paul and James obviously agree that works arise from saving faith or the faith is not genuine.

Further confirmation on active faith is sought in James 2:14: "What is the profit, my brothers, if someone says he has faith, but does not have works? Is that faith able to save him?" In the last clause "that faith" is taken to mean "that kind of faith": a faith that does not have works is not able to save a person. The combined teaching of Paul and James is taken to be that we are *saved* by faith without the works (Paul); nevertheless the kind of faith that we are saved by is a faith that works (James). God does not justify us *by faith and works,* but he does justify us *by a faith that works.* In saving us, God contemplates only the faith, but the faith he contemplates is one that works.

We agree that saving faith is a faith that works. We might even allow that under the influence of Hebrew grammatical patterns "justified by works and not by faith only" (2:24) could mean "justified by a faith that works." Such a reconstruction, however, does not do full justice to everything actually said in James 2. Both faith and works precede justification because justification is both *by* faith and *by* works. If we were to allow 2:24 to mean "justified by a faith that works," we could only do so by including works ahead of justification conceptually.

But, in shifting to the expression "a faith that works," commentators have made an alteration in wording that creates ambiguity: "justified by a faith that works" does not require both works and faith to precede justification. Having made the verbal alteration, commentators go on to conclude that saving faith will work, which, though true, is irrelevant to solving the apparent disparity between James and Paul. Such exegesis skews the testimony of James by advancing "faith" to a "faith that works" and then lifting that definition out of James and inserting it into Paul. The hybrid ends up saying that we are saved by faith that works, not by faith and works. The elemental error here stems from making James discuss "saving" faith. He does not discuss "saving" faith, but faith and works that save; the demons do the faith he is talking about, but they are not saved.

As to the expression "that faith" in James 2:14, the sentence in the original language does not say "that" faith necessarily. It could be satisfactorily rendered, "Faith is not able to save him, is it?" Grammarians occasionally say that the Greek article sometimes assumes a demonstrative force. The article in front of "faith" here can therefore be translated "that" (faith). Irrespective of the propriety of the rule, it does not have to apply to this verse. The article can bear its normal function of marking the *identity* of a thing in contrast to the *nature* of a thing. Interpreting James on his own terms, we find him expressing a perfectly lucid idea: "Faith can't save him, can it?" Of course not; faith can no more save a person (2:14) than it can warm or clothe him (2:16); there is no "profit" in either case because obviously no practical change ever comes from anything but a change in practice.

Even if we were to translate the verse "Such faith cannot save him, can it?" we would still not necessarily be talking about a kind of faith, but about its context: "that faith unaccompanied by works" as distinguished from "that kind of faith that produces works." Demonstrativeness has to do with identity, not necessarily with kind.

We close this point by registering our opinion that the issue over the Greek article here may have more to do with conventions of usage than with meanings of words. Greek is satisfied to use the article in places where other languages conventionally insert demonstrative adjectives. That is a different thing from saying that the Greek article *means* demonstrativeness.

Although we agree that Paul uses "works" in some cases to refer to actions, it is interesting to note that with perhaps one exception (a) he is not talking about salvation but about Christian living when he speaks of the necessity of works. (b) He is also not talking about works "of law," as he is when denying salvation by works of law. In these few cases he highlights a different aspect of the general notion of working than he does in his discussion of salvation by faith. In the former he stresses overt activity, but in the latter he stresses productiveness. The exceptional passage is Ephesians 2:10, but we feel it is satisfactory here to understand Paul as making a play on words by shifting from works as productive action in 2:9 to works as prepared actions in 2:10.

Occasion of faith. A second, related manner of combining James and Paul (2) *supposes that Paul is talking about pre-Christian actions while James talks especially about post-Christian actions.* Ephesians 2:8-10 might be used to undergird this reconstruction of the difference. Our objection here is that responses unto initial salvation must relate to the salvation status in the same way as responses unto ultimate salvation do; otherwise we contradict Galatians, where Paul opposes putting one's self under the law after becoming a disciple of Jesus Messiah. He argues against the Judaizers' position by the line of reasoning modern Christians have grown accustomed to using for initial salvation. According to Galatians 3, then, we *do not* continue in salvation by works either; hence, James cannot be teaching that we *do* continue in salvation by them.

Theologians that move from James to Paul in interpreting salvation by faith usually believe in perseverance of the saints, which means that genuine converts will indeed remain faithful until death. Consequently, they weld together initial and ultimate salvation in a one-to-one relationship because they are coextensive. In a sense, then, these thinkers believe that ultimate salvation likewise rests only on the faith part of the faith-that-works. If this thought pattern is being followed, the earlier objection applies that James puts works logically ahead of justification when he says justified *by* works. This phraseology cannot harmonize with Paul who says justified *not by* works; hence, James and Paul must be talking about different ideas.

As a result of these considerations we return to our own contention that James and Paul harmonize because (3) *Paul deals with why we respond and James deals with what response we should have.* Therefore we do not get the meaning for "faith" or "works" from either writer and plug it into the other's writings; rather, we study each author on his own terms and thus correct our understanding to the view that both inner and outer response can fill the conditionality requirement unto salvation.

The Case Against Faith as Inner Action

Argument from the law

The first reason against defining "works" as outer action is that (1) *the law was not just outward commandments.* Contrasting faith with works of law does not therefore contrast inner with outer action. The first and second great commandments spoke of inner factors conceptually central to the law. When Paul characterizes sin in Romans 7:7ff., he selects coveting, a prohibition contained in the decalog itself. The law repudiated people who honored God with their lips, but their heart was far from him (Isa. 29:13-14). Love, coveting, being faithful, and many other such inner considerations are included in the law. According to Galatians 3:12 Paul taught that the law was not of faith. The Israelites were betrothed to God in "faithfulness" (*'emunah*), the same word used in Habakkuk 2:4 and the one from which Paul draws the conclusion that in his terms the law was not of faith. If the law was not of "faith," yet contained inner requirements including faith, then in Paul's usage "faith" does not particularly have to do with inner actions, and "works" does not have to do with outer ones.

Argument from theory

Secondly, (2) *from the theory of things an inner act is not less objectionable to grace than an outer act would be.* If it were true that an act logically prior to salvation would contradict grace and displace sovereignty, then whether it was inner or outer would be immaterial. One would need to suppose some other reason for the objectionableness besides grace or sovereignty.

Instead of a theological reason one might appeal to a psychological one: an outward act is more tangible and more likely to be considered the cause of some effect, whereas an inner act would not bring about righteousness or reconciliation and therefore would not give anyone grounds for pride and boasting.

On the contrary, however, from a psychological standpoint a person might feel like "taking credit" for at least believing and trusting God, and then set at nought ignorant infidels for not accepting the gospel. Pride from internal acts could be more subtle and consequently even more dangerous to salvation by grace. We doubt that psychological considerations furnish any adequate reason against the conditionality of outer actions.

221

Argument from function

Thirdly, (3) *no hard and fast line can be drawn between inner and outer action*. Prayer combines the attitude of the heart and the outward speaking of the mouth, but the publican went down to his house justified by his audible prayer (Lk. 18:9-14). Confession illustrates another act with inner and outer components; yet Paul connects it with salvation, "If you confess with/in your mouth Jesus as Lord and believe with/in your heart that God raised him from the dead, you will be saved. For with the heart a person believes unto righteousness, and with the mouth he confesses unto salvation" (Rom. 10:9-10). Since the apostle differentiates confession from faith in the heart, confession tends to receive more of an outer stress even though it is placed logically before salvation. As inseparable connections bind together the good tree and its good fruit, so also it is out of the abundance of the heart that the mouth speaks (Mt. 12:33-35). As the inner produces the outer, so also the outer shapes the inner. The *composite character* of some acts and the *reciprocal relationship* between inner and outer behavior eliminates the need and possibility for choosing one but not the other as a condition for salvation.

Summary and Conclusion

Relationships between grace and response

Four theoretical relationships exist between human response and divine grace. The first is (a) *conditionality,* and within it there have developed two views, one that allows for *both inner and outer acts* and another that allows for *only inner acts.* Both contrast with (b) *nonconditionality,* which allows only for responses after righteousness; with (c) *merit,* which sees human acts as causing the righteousness; and with (d) *antinomianism,* which sees no connection at all between human acts and divine grace.

The concept of conditionality is the crucial link between divine and human action in salvation. It joins the grace of God to the need of man. Without conditionality one must espouse the system of thought summarized by inscrutable sovereignty plus TULIP. Unconditionality (a) requires Total depravity in order to avoid merit. The lack of conditionality also (b) eliminates the distinction between potential and actual; hence, a potential death for all could not become an actual death for some. Only Limited atonement or universalism would be possible.

Unconditionality further (c) necessitates *Irresistible* grace or God would not be exerting sovereignty. No conditionality also (d) requires *Perseverance* of the saints. The whole TULIP system becomes unnecessary when conditionality is given its place in the grace-faith system.

Our interpretation of James and Paul comes from the conclusion that they use "faith" and "works" differently. "Works" in Paul means acts that produce the effect; in this case the effect is righteousness. "Works of law" are those acts required by the law in order to be considered righteous, hence, *the principle of personal perfection.* "Faith," then, means *the principle of trusting in another to regard us as perfectly righteous;* hence, in a Christian context, it means trusting that identification with Jesus Christ is adequate for being considered righteous. Paul therefore uses these words to speak about the *relationship* of human responses and divine grace. James, on the other hand, uses them to refer to the *identity* of the human responses required for the application of divine grace. Faith is mental assent while works is the expression of belief in outward behavior. Paul speaks of saving faith but James does not.

Relationship between faith and works

Biblical terms. In treating the concept of righteousness by grace, the New Testament authors relate "faith" and "works" in three ways: (a) faith as a work, (b) faith and works, and (c) faith without works. The second usage appears mainly in James while the third characterizes Paul's presentations. Our presentation has concluded that the authors do not use these words in the same way because they discuss different concerns.

The most crucial question here is with the method of harmonizing the teachings of Paul and James. Some interpreters suppose that (a) Paul is talking about *initial* salvation and James is talking about *continued* salvation. But the mode of relationship between human response and divine grace must be the same because Galatians does not allow beginning with faith and then maintaining with works. Commentators also suppose that (b) James means a *kind* of faith that works (active faith), and that Paul means the works necessarily accompanying faith do not figure in the conditionality basis for counting men righteous. But James cannot be understood in this way if the concept removes works from its logically prior relationship to justification; James puts both faith

223

and works ahead of salvation in that he says justified *by* faith and *by* works also.

Our solution has been that (c) James is talking about *what* we are to do while Paul is concerned with *why* we do it. James says we are not only to believe with our minds, but to act on what we believe in order to receive salvation (acting faith). Paul says we are not to suppose that anything we do has the significance of bringing about our righteousness. Our righteousness exists only in the eyes of God on the basis of our concern for righteousness expressed through identification with Christ; righteousness does not exist in us because we are not perfect.

Modern terminology. The term "works" furnishes the key to the above reconstruction. Instead of taking it to mean (a) *the principle of personal perfection,* many modern students of Paul suppose he employs the word as it is used in James—to refer to (b) *outward behavior.* In John it means simply (c) *doing something.* Since in practice salvation is normally discussed in connection with Paul's formulation of faith without works, it is important not to plug these second and third meanings into his formula.

It is also important not to plug in other modern ideas, one being that works are (d) *acts by which we seek to win God's favor.* Although this more psychological definition does represent an error, it is a different one from what Paul controverts. He concerns himself with the law itself, not with a contemporary perversion of the law in first-century popular theology. Works are also not (e) *outward acts bereft of heartfelt intent.* Even James does not use the word this way although the problem is often discussed in both Old and New Testaments.

Lastly, works are not (f) *special representative acts* that establish the benefits of the covenant. Paul contrasts faith with continuing to do all, not just with special acts like circumcision or baptism. Obviously, tokenism is erroneous, but it is not the problem Paul seeks to solve. Consequently, for him saving faith is not specifically some natural alternative to these concepts. Instead, it is belief and trust in Christ to the point of active commitment to him and his purposes. Saving faith as a condition is not so much a kind of faith—*active faith*—as it is a degree of faith—*acting faith.*

Chapter Sixteen

THE MEANING OF CHRISTIAN BAPTISM

Introduction

Justification as category change

From the nature of the case justification from sin is logically categorical rather than continuous. By this statement we mean that God's pronouncement "Innocent" moves a person out of the guilty category and puts him in the one labeled "Not Guilty." Since moral perfection stands as God's ideal for fellowship with himself, anything less is insufficient. Therefore salvation in the sense of justification is not a matter of degree but of kind; it is not a process but a point. We are not continually being saved as meant here—initial transfer from lost to saved. The concept of salvation as process holds significant truth, but refers to improvement of life quality or continually being cleansed from sins done while in Christ, whose blood continues to save us from all sin (I Jn. 1:5-10). Worshipers that have once been cleansed have no more consciousness of being regarded as sinners (cp. Heb. 10:2b).

Justification as time when

Four statements may be made: *fellowship* with a perfect God requires *perfection;* perfection is a *categorical matter;* since perfection is a categorical matter, justification is a *categorical act;* since justification logically requires a categorical act, justification requires chronologically a *crisis occasion.* Justification looks at salvation from a formal or abstract standpoint. To put this fact in more interpersonal terms, we can say that the act of forgiveness occurs at a specific time and that the relationship is re-established at that same time.

Justification as one time when

Since the concern of justification in salvation is the categorical removal of sin, it follows that there is only *one* time when a person is acquitted and forgiven. Any figure that expresses such categorical riddance from sin is speaking of justification. A person is not at one time forgiven, at another time cleansed, saved, freed, justified, etc. There is one time when a person is saved.

Justification as one standard time when

The next matter is deciding when that time is and whether there is a uniform, or standard, time for justification in all conversions. We have decided that human obediences serve as conditions for salvation, not causes of it. This relationship between our faith and God's grace leaves open the question of when in the series of commanded responses God has promised to count us under the perfection of his Son Jesus Christ and to grant to us the blessings of that status. Since no obedience inherently connects with salvation, there is no inherent reason that salvation should occur at one point in the series rather than at another point.

The following study reaches the conclusion that, formally speaking, *baptism* is the standard time when God forgives our sin by identifying us with the Sinless One. In baptism we identify ourselves with Jesus Christ because God has appointed that act as the one in which we express, culminate, and formalize our identification with the Messiah. Then the Father freely identifies us with the Son and his perfection.

Effects Conjoined with Baptism

Identification with Jesus Christ

At its first level baptism means identification with Jesus Christ. Christian baptism identifies a person with Jesus Christ *rather than with someone else.* We take identification as the most basic point (a) in the expression "baptize into/unto Christ." Paul uses this phrase in Romans 6:3, ". . . all we who were baptized into Christ Jesus were baptized into his death." Similarly he says to the Galatians, ". . . as many of you as were baptized into Christ put on Christ" (Gal. 3:27). Luke recounts the Samaritan mission with the comment, ". . . as yet [the Holy Spirit] was fallen on none of them; they had only been baptized into the name of the Lord Jesus" (Acts 8:16; cp. 19:5). In a somewhat broader connection the Great Commission itself includes "baptizing them into the name of the Father and of the Son and of the Holy Spirit" (Mt. 28:19).

The preposition that follows "baptize" in the above passages is *eis,* whose elemental meaning is "into." It signifies entrance into the sphere of, as well as the associate idea "to" or "unto." Under either nuance of meaning baptism serves as a pledge of allegiance to Christ. In less explicit ways other expressions imply the same idea. Peter tells the crowd at Pentecost, "Repent and be baptized . . . in [*epi*] the name of Jesus . . ."

226

(Acts. 2:38). Later to Cornelius' household "he commanded them to be baptized in [*en*] the name of Jesus Christ" (Acts 10:48). The latter two usages may involve the idea of the authoritative basis on which the act is performed (cp. Acts 4:7); baptism on that authoritative basis, of course, still draws attention to relations with the Messiah. All three sequential prepositions could conceivably translate the one Hebrew-Aramaic inseparable preposition *le* that would have originally been used in Palestine to discuss the meaning of baptism.

What baptism unto Christ means fundamentally can also be seen (b) in cases of baptism unto others than Christ. Paul finds occasion to draw a parallel between Christian baptism and the crossing of the Red Sea. Because the crossing and baptism may be regarded as functional equivalents as well as analogous events, he calls the exodus a baptism, saying, ". . . our fathers were all baptized unto Moses in the cloud and in the sea" (I Cor. 10:1-2). Passing through the Red Sea, the Israelites identified with *Moses* by renouncing the sense of belonging to Egypt.

Similarly when Paul found twelve believers in Ephesus who were baptized into John's baptism, he baptized them "unto the name of the Lord Jesus" (Acts 19:1-7). The contrast between the baptisms suggests there would be propriety in speaking of baptism unto *John* even as unto Christ or Moses. From the negative side the apostle to the Gentiles denies that baptism unto *Paul* was what happened in the beginning of the Corinthian mission (I Cor. 1:13, 15); the Corinthians, therefore, should not identify themselves as being "of Paul," "of Peter," or "of Apollos" (1:12), but "of Christ" (3:22-23). The first level of meaning for "baptize unto" must be such that it could apply to others than Jesus Christ, were that same act done in different connections. We feel that the idea can be conveyed well under the imagery of identification.

Identification occurs (c) in the idea of union with Christ, particularly in his commitment to God to the point of death and resurrection. Paul describes baptism among other things as that in which we "become united with him in the likeness of his death" (Rom. 6:5; cp. II Cor. 4:10; Phil. 3:10-11; Col. 2:12; 3:1). Union with Christ equals identification with him.

We also suggest that the concept of identification is shown (d) in the appropriateness of Jesus' baptism by John even though John's baptism was called a "baptism of repentance unto remission of sins." The Lord thereby identified himself with the work of his forerunner and identified himself with righteousness. Being sinless, Jesus did not need the particular benefit associated with that identification; but, being a man, he did need to identify himself with the divine program for man inaugurated in John's ministry.

Christian baptism identifies us with Jesus Christ *as a pledge of allegiance*. It is first a pledge to the *person*. To identify with a person is also to identify with what he stands for. It becomes an expression of commitment to his *purposes*. Since the pledge of allegiance takes the form of an act specifically linked with Christ's death-resurrection, Paul in Romans 6:4-11 declares that it is a death to sin and a resurrection to a new kind of living (cp. Col. 2:11-15). The pledge means walking as he walked because the old way of walking has "died." In baptism we symbolically die *to* sin after the analogy of Christ's death *for* sin. Baptism pledges allegiance to the *point of death* as Christ did. By submitting to this "rite of passage," we perform the "sign of the covenant" that was founded most centrally on the death-resurrection of the Messiah. Identification is taking a stand.

By its form and purpose baptism becomes an *appropriate* act of identification with the Lord. His death-resurrection distinguishes him from all who went before him or came afterwards. Baptism symbolically re-enacts that event in the life of any person who would have the benefits of being in Christ by committing himself to the resurrected way of life. In consequence of identifying with the distinguishing event in the ministry of the Son of God, a person is made a son of God.

Forgiveness of sins

Identification with Christ. In consequence of identification with Christ comes a series of divine gifts, the first of which is remission of sins. Conversely, the first reason for conceiving of baptism as unto remission of sins is that (1) *baptism is an act of identification with Christ who saves us.* God forgives sin when we express repentant faith to the point of formally espousing Jesus and his life as our ideal. Since baptism identifies us with him, it takes upon itself the significance of bringing us to the consequences of that new identification; as an initiatory rite it is the occasion of, and a condition unto, God's reckoning us according to the character of him with whom baptism identifies us. That One being sinless and that state being sinlessness, baptism may be said to be unto remission of sins. To put it more strictly, salvation from sin comes not particularly from the act of baptism, but in consequence of the identification it marks with Christ. It is not so much that baptism is for remission of sins as it is that baptism is for identification with Christ and God's forgiveness is in consequence of that identification. As far as the sinner is concerned his responses prior to justification culminate in the formal obedience of baptism. He is baptized *into* Christ (Rom. 6:3) *outside of* whom there is no salvation (Acts 4:12) and *in* whom there is no condemnation (Rom. 8:1). Baptism identifies us with Christ by identifying us with his distinctive act. Since that distinctive death, burial, and resurrection is most precisely the event that serves as the basis for forgiveness of sins, it is most appropriate that baptism be viewed as the occasion of appropriating to the individual the benefits made possible by the event it re-enacts.

We belabor the point at this juncture because historically Christian unity has been greatly hindered by the mutually exclusive positions taken on the design of Christian baptism. Furthermore, we must safeguard our description so as not to violate the principle that our acts do not save us even while maintaining the full import of scriptural teaching about this ordinance frought with much controversy even in our own day.

The main thing is that no direct or indirect causal connection exists between baptism and sinlessness any more than between any other human response and salvation—including the responses of faith and repentance. Between baptism and the remission of sins stands God's pronouncement of acquittal because of the new identity he accepts in Christ. The sinner identifies himself with Christ subjectively by obeying

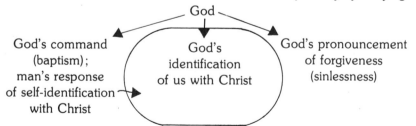

among other things the commandment to be baptized in an attitude of repentant trust. When he so identifies himself, God objectively pronounces him sinless because the Father has appointed the Son as the one in terms of whom he pronounces sinlessness. Men have access to God through Christ. There are two intercedents between the act of baptism and God's act of forgiveness: the state of identification with Christ and God's pronouncement of justification. Baptism is the chronological occasion of salvation, but God's pronouncement of forgiveness is the logical occasion of salvation.

Were there a direct or indirect causal connection between baptism and sinlessness, baptism would have the nature of a work. Not only are there two things in between them; but the act of baptism is an act of obedience, not an act of causation. It is done because it is commanded, not because it is inherently able of itself to produce the result needed. There is nothing about the water, the hands of the administrator, or the form of the act that brings about an automatic flow of grace. Baptism then is not a sacrament nor is it baptismal regeneration, because miracle, law, causation, and other non-personal categories do not apply here. Therefore the relationship between baptism and remission of sins is not only indirect, but also non-inherent.

Stated association with forgiveness. The second reason for conceiving of baptism as unto remission of sins is (2) *its stated associations with being rid of sins.* Ridding from sin is expressed under the concept of *salvation* in I Peter 3:20-21: ". . . wherein few, that is, eight, souls were saved through water, which also after a true likeness now saves you, even baptism, not the putting away of the filth of the flesh, but the appeal of a good conscience toward God . . . ." Peter indicates that the purpose of baptism is not to wash off dirt, but to appeal to God for cleansing. Baptism loosely compares with Noah's flood since water in both cases was connected with salvation of different sorts. The water that was death to all others was by buoyancy salvation to eight souls. That same water was a cleansing of sin from the earth by way of destroying all those sinners. On Pentecost after Peter exhorted the people to "save themselves" from that perverse generation, three thousand were baptized in accordance with his command to "repent and be baptized in the name of Jesus Christ unto remission of sins" (Acts 2:38-41). Paul also says that God "saved us through the washing of regeneration and renewing of the Holy Spirit" (Tit. 3:5).

A related idea is that of *remission*, the throwing away of sin, or *forgiveness,* which appears in Peter's sermon on Pentecost when the gospel possibility was preached for the first time as an accomplished fact. The assembly reacted with a question about what they should do. The answer was to "repent and be baptized . . . unto remission

230

of sins . . ." (Acts 2:38). Of John's baptism forgiveness of sins is also affirmed (Mk. 1:4; Lk. 3:3; cp. 1:77).

When Saul of Tarsus asked the Lord a similar question on the way to Damascus (Acts 22:10), Jesus told him to go into the city and he would be told what to do (22:10, 9.6). Ananias instructed him on that matter by setting forth baptism under the imagery of *washing*: "Arise and be baptized and wash away your sins, calling on the name of the Lord" (22:16; cp. Tit. 3:5). After three days of a new belief about Jesus as the Messiah and the repentance demonstrated in fasting and prayer, his sins were formally remitted when he was baptized, calling on the name of the Lord.

Another imagery appears in Titus 3:4-7 when Paul writes about "the washing of 'regeneration,'" or *rebirth*:

> But when the kindness of God our Savior and his love toward man appeared, not by works done in righteousness, which we ourselves did, but according to his mercy, he saved us through the washing of regeneration and renewing of the Holy Spirit, whom he poured out on us richly through Jesus Christ our Savior that, being justified by his grace, we might be made heirs according to the hope of eternal life.

"Washing of regeneration" has been understood by commentators ancient and modern as a reference to Christian baptism, especially since washing brings to mind the water involved in baptism. Coupling it with renewing of the Holy Spirit is reminiscent of Acts 2:38, where baptism is also combined with the gift of the Holy Spirit (cp. Jn. 3:5).

"Regeneration" reminds us of the imagery used by Jesus in his discussion with Nicodemus:

> . . . "Truly, truly I say to you, unless a person is born again he cannot see the kingdom of God." Nicodemus said to him, "How can a man be born when he is grown? Can he enter into his mother's womb a second time and be born?" [cp. Job 1:21; Eccl. 5:15]. Jesus answered, "Truly, truly I tell you, unless a person is born of water and Spirit he cannot enter the kingdom of God" (Jn. 3:3-5).

Although "born of water" is not always understood as a reference to Christian baptism, we will show later our reasons for preferring that view as the time of spiritual renewal. The following context of John 3 elaborates on this "new birth" as connected with eternal life (3:15, 16) and salvation (3:17).

A fifth imagery for expressing riddance from sin is *resurrection*. According to Romans 6:2-11 baptism may be considered a death to sin (6:2-3) in which the old man is crucified (6:6) and buried, and a new man resurrected to newness of life (6:4). The person is justified from sin (6:7) in baptism, wherein he was also united with Christ. Both rebirth and resurrection emphasize the idea of *renewal*. In the present passage *justification* comes in as imagery subsidiary to resurrection (cp. Col. 2:12-13).

Colossians continues the burial-renewal picture, but associates ridding from sin with the idea of *circumcision*: ". . . in whom you were also circumcised with a circumcision not made with hands in the putting off of the fleshly body in the circumcision of Christ, having been buried with him in baptism . . ." (2:11-12). Baptism is analogous to spiritual circumcision.

Generalizing on the above passages, we may say that separation from sin is communicated more abstractly by the similes of salvation—renewal, justification, and forgiveness, but more concretely by the analogies of washing, rebirth, resurrection, and circumcision. The consistency with which ridding from sin accompanies descriptions and explanations of baptism establishes a significant correlation between baptism and forgiveness.

Prepositions in the previous texts make the same sort of logical connection between baptism and riddance from sin as they do with belief, repentance, and confession. Belief and confession (Rom. 10:10) as well as repentance (Acts 3:19; II Cor. 7:10) *result* in (*eis*) righteousness and salvation; so does baptism (Acts 2:38). Faith (Eph. 2:8, etc.) and baptism (I Pet. 3:21) are *means* to (*dia*) salvation. Our understanding of the significance of baptism must be such that we can make the same logical associations between baptism and forgiveness as we make between faith and forgiveness and yet do it without compromising ourselves on salvation by faith instead of works. This we have proposed can be done under the concept of *identification* with Christ together with the concept of *conditionality*.

Terminal position. The third reason for conceiving of baptism as unto remission of sins is (3) *its terminal position among human acts associated with forgiveness.* Paul's conversion is recorded in more detail than any other in the New Testament: Acts 9:1-19; 22:6-16; 26:12-18. It is also unique in being spread over a three-day period. We adopt it

THE MEANING OF CHRISTIAN BAPTISM

initially as a working model on which the time of justification can be determined when verified against other conversion accounts and other teaching material about faith, repentance, and baptism.

A reading of all three accounts makes evident that Paul believed Jesus who appeared to him on the road to Damascus was indeed the Messiah. The behavior of repentance is unquestionable in the three days of prayer and fasting in the city. Then Ananias arrives, restores his sight, and commands him to wash away his sins. Removal of sin had not occurred by the time Paul had believed and repented. Contrast the statement in the familiar hymn "To God Be the Glory": ". . . The vilest offender who truly believes, that moment from Jesus a pardon receives." The time interval between initial belief and subsequent baptism stresses the association of justification, not with a first moment of believing, but with baptism-washing-calling. The commitment type of faith came later than the believing, but the commitment occurred in his baptism if anywhere. Washing is associated with baptism also in Titus 3:5; I Peter 3:21 (cp. I Cor. 6:11; Eph. 5:26; Heb. 10:22).

As respects the relative order of faith, repentance, baptism, and continuing steadfastly, there is uniformity in all the conversion accounts in the New Testament. A list of the more significant ones includes the three thousand on Pentecost (Acts 2:14-42), conversions in Samaria (8:4-13), the Ethiopian eunuch (8:26-38), Paul (9:3-19; 22:6-16; 26:12-18), the household of Cornelius (10:24-48; 11:15-18); Sergius Paulus (13:6-12), Lydia (16:14-15), the Philippian jailor (16:25-34), the household of Crispus (18:8; I Cor. 1:14), and the twelve at Ephesus (19:7). Not all elements are mentioned in these accounts. Repentance is not mentioned in the eunuch, Lydia, the jailor, etc., and baptism is not included with Sergius Paulus. Though all are not mentioned, they are always in the same order, no pattern existing for other acts after this initial acceptance. Baptism standing last among these acts unto salvation corroborates the teaching of the New Testament generally regarding the meaning of baptism.

Punctiliar character. The fourth reason for conceiving of baptism as the time of justification is (4) *its punctiliar nature.* Baptism happens at a point in time in contrast to faith and repentance which may be a while in coming. It does not admit of degrees whereas faith and repentance are growing realities in the Christian experience throughout the whole of life. Since justification occurs at a given time, baptism as the only punctiliar act in the initial conditions of salvation is well suited for marking the time when our identity in Christ is consummated. Baptism is a crisis occasion, not a process.

General observations. In relation to *viewpoints* baptism may be contemplated from three perspectives: from outside, from inside, and from above. From the *outside* baptism carries a symbolic significance appropriate to the transitions God effects in connection with it. The first of these is washing (Acts 22:16; Tit. 3:5; cp. Eph. 5:26). The second is burial and resurrection (Rom. 6:1-11; Col. 2:12). The third is birth (Jn. 3:3-7; Tit. 3:5). In traditional terminology baptism seals and signifies the invisible acts of God occurring in it and in consequence of its fulfillment.

From the *inside* baptism is an appeal to God (I Pet. 3:21; cp. Lk. 3:21). It is an act of personal commitment (Rom. 6:12-14) and an expression of faith (Col. 2:12).

From *above*, baptism is the time when God saves, regenerates, renews, and justifies the individual (Tit. 3:4-7; Jn. 3:4-7; cp. 1:13; I Pet. 1:23; I Jn. 2:29; 3:9; 4:7; 5:1, 4, 18). Baptism is therefore the standard time of divine justification. While baptism does not convey grace, it does more than signify it inasmuch as baptism serves as a condition for it.

In regard to its *character* baptism may be positively viewed as appropriate. Its appropriateness lies in its *form* as suggestive of burial and resurrection—the lowering into water and the rising out of it; it interestingly pictures even the state of death in that normal bodily functions like breathing and seeing cease to operate. It re-enacts for us the specific event that establishes the forgiveness of sins granted at the time of this re-enactment. Baptism is also a crisis occasion since it occurs at a point in time instead of being a process over time. It is a passive act in keeping with the essential character of justification as something done by another rather than caused in whole or in part by one's self; baptism is a purely volitional act answering to the active-commitment element in saving faith; belief and repentance to a certain extent cannot help themselves, being somewhat automatic in response to the effective proclamation of grace. The appropriateness of baptism shows up in its *nature* since it clearly has no inherent ability to save a man from sin; likewise, human responses in the state of imperfection cannot have anything themselves to do with producing perfection. Finally, the appropriateness of baptism

234

lies also in its *element* because water serves as a cleansing agent.

The appropriateness of baptism may be viewed negatively as well. It is not an *arbitrary* act because it pictures the distinctive act of the Son of God. Baptism is not a *necessary* act in the sense that there could be no such thing as salvation without it. Old Testament saints like Moses, Elijah, and Abraham were not baptized because the ordinance was not instituted then. It is obvious that baptism is not the sort of thing that really washes away sin since sin is not soluble in water. Neither is baptism a *discrete* act that stands disjoined from any context. Since it indicates a desire to be in Christ, faith that such an identification will benefit unto salvation is necessarily implied as is repentance from a former way of life and commitment to obedience to the point of death. Neither is baptism *meritorious* like an act of penance, where the sinner tries to make up on his own for the deficiency of holiness his sin has left on his record. The holiness is all the Lord's. We are only regarded as righteous by virtue of espousing as our ideal the righteousness that he has with whom we identified. By speaking of baptism as an act of identification, we retain interpersonal relationship as the primary concept in salvation.

In respect to *time* baptism pictures *in retrospect* the death-resurrection of Jesus Christ. It thus identifies us with him and commits us to him. *In prospect* it anticipates the purification process in Christian living. It commits us to the process of transformation into the image of him who died for us and commits us to allegiance to the point of death.

The Gift of the Spirit

In consequence of identification with Jesus Christ and forgiveness of sins, we receive the gift of the Spirit as the second one of the divine gifts. The second benefit of repentance and baptism given in Acts 2:38 is this gift. Once sin, which separates from God, has been removed by forgiveness, fellowship with him becomes appropriate. This fellowship with God operates most particularly with the Spirit of God whom Christ promised to be with us and in us after he ascended (Jn. 14:16-18). Therefore the gift of the Spirit is not particularly a gift *from* the Spirit, but the gift is the Spirit. More strictly the gift is the relationship with the Spirit. He is a gift from *Christ*.

Nature of the gift. We understand the essential nature of the gift to be interpersonal because (1) the Spirit is personal in biblical descriptions.

235

He acts like a person in that he is characterized by communication (Jn. 14:26; 15:26; Rom. 8:26; I Tim. 4:1), cognition (Acts 15:28; Rom. 8:27; I Cor. 2:10-11), and affection (Rom. 15:30?). He is treated like a person in that he can be blasphemed (Mt. 12:31), lied to (Acts 5:3), tempted (Acts. 5:9), resisted (Acts 7:51), grieved (Eph. 4:30), and insulted (Heb. 10:29). The personal verbal *paraklētos* is used as his name by the apostle John (Jn. 14:16, 26; 16:7) so that we know him as the Paraclete, a term applied also to Jesus in I John 2:1.

That the Spirit has a personal nature brings significant clarification because it avoids confusing him with his products. The Spirit is not a *power,* but a person who has power. He is not a *feeling,* but a person we feel close to. He is not an *attitude,* but a person who influences our attitudes. The Spirit is not a *principle,* but a person who communicates principles to us. He is not an *atmosphere,* but one who creates among us an atmosphere of love. Thus we distinguish his effects from his "self."

The second reason for understanding the gift of the Spirit as interpersonal is that (2) relationship between persons naturally comes out of removing sin from between persons. Sin severs relationship with the Spirit of God (cp. Gen. 6:3), and the expression "Spirit of God" has primarily to do with emphasizing God in his presence (cp. Gen. 6:3; 4:16; 3:8; 1:2). Therefore, receiving the Spirit means primarily coming back into the presence of God.

Functioning of the gift. Several advantages come from emphasizing the Spirit's interpersonal relationship with us. Generally speaking, it helps us get away from mechanical conceptualizations of matters associated with the Spirit. (a) It keeps us from supposing that he is an energy like electricity that can be transmitted by contact through the laying on of hands in healing or ordination; imposition of hands visualizes his invisible presence, approval, and production. We are also less likely to assume we can sense the Spirit himself (Judges 16:20).

(b) It helps us replace the idea of "deposit" with that of influence in modeling the manner of his primary assistance to us. Rather than capacities inserted, we have responses elicited.

(c) It helps us avoid notions that replace the self with the Spirit. He does not operate in place of us, but through us. The indwelling of the Holy Spirit is not like possession by an evil spirit. Getting the Spirit does not mean getting out of the way. He does not knock us out of

236

our senses, or throw us out of control, but helps us gain control.

(d) Interpersonal relationship reduces the tendency to confuse ourselves with the Spirit. It helps avoid the tendency to confuse feelings that come over us with divine guidance and ideas that pop into our minds with revelation.

(e) Finally, interpersonal relationship qualifies the expectancy of supernatural manifestation of the Spirit's presence by miracle. Miraculous manifestation is not germane to the relationship or the purpose of it particularly. While we believe that he directs and controls in special providence beyond even the laws of nature, *visible* miracle may not be produced by his relationship with a person.

It becomes obvious that the degree of benefit from the gift of the Spirit will correspond to the degree of conscious awareness of his presence so that it behooves us to do those spiritual exercises that will increase our awareness of his real but invisible presence with us.

Benefits of the gift. Under the gift of the Spirit we place three benefits that scripture associates with him. (a) The first benefit is *guidance.* He performs this guidance through scripture (Heb. 3:7-11) inasmuch as his work lies behind that of the prophets and apostles who served as his spokesmen (Jn. 14:26; 16:13). The Spirit performs his guidance through circumstance which he controls to our being directed by his will. He guides through fellow Christians who have absorbed the word of scripture and have their minds saturated with his aspirations for men. The Spirit guides by sheer presence in relationship much as a father's presence affects the way a child acts.

(b) The second benefit of the Spirit is *power.* Power in this connection means personal strength: the strength to cope with conflict, overcome temptation, improve self; and the boldness to evangelize others. "Temptations lose their power when thou art nigh." Because of these empowering benefits the scripture says the Spirit sanctifies (I Cor. 6:11; I Th. 4:7-8; II Th. 2:13; I Pet. 1:2), frees (II Cor. 3:17), supplies (Phil. 1:19), strengthens (Eph. 3:16), comforts (Acts. 9:31), and perhaps also brings fruit (Gal. 5:22, 25). These blessings come from the fact that we have not been left desolate like orphans (Jn. 14:18), but have the earnest, or downpayment, of our inheritance already in the presence of the Spirit (II Cor. 5:5; Eph. 1:13-14; 4:30). Interpersonal power generates motivational strength.

237

(c) The third benefit of the Spirit is *intercession*. We need not worry that the thoughts and intents of our hearts cannot be fully and accurately expressed through words to the Father. Those inexpressible, inner longings Paul says the Spirit carries to the Father by means which are not uttered. He knows the heart and can help our inadequate self-expression according to the will of God (Rom. 8:26-27).

(d) The fourth benefit of the Spirit is *Christian unity*. Through the medium of love believers can "keep the unity of the Spirit in the bond of peace" (Eph. 4:3-4). The same Spirit abides with all believers so that a spirit of oneness characterizes fellowship, edification, and evangelism (I Cor. 12). With this connection between the Spirit's work and the group dimension of the Christian experience, we come to a brief statement of the third blessing scripture associates with baptism: membership in the body of Christ.

Church membership

In consequence of identification with Jesus Christ we share identity with all those who are in him, have their sins forgiven, and have fellowship with the Spirit of God. Therefore church membership is the third one in the series of divine gifts. We speak of baptism as into the church universal, not just into the local church; baptism is into both the visible church and the invisible church. Salvation is individual in that one person is not saved for another and in that God does not save men in groups irrespective of the faith of the individuals within the group. There is nevertheless a strong group emphasis because individuals are brought into fellowship. Identifying themselves with Second Adam brings them into a new united mankind (Eph. 2:15). Associating themselves with the new Lawgiver makes them citizens of a spiritual Israel. They become organs in the body of Christ. There is no such thing as sonship with God aside from brotherhood with the other sons of God.

As with forgiveness and the gift of the Spirit, so here again the interpersonal character of salvation stands at the fore. Men by nature have a social constitution that is part of what it means to be created in the image of God (Gen. 1:26-27). Interdependency of persons requires that being renewed into the image of his Son will involve many brothers (Rom. 8:29). Consequently, when the first three thousand accepted Jesus as Messiah, they not only had their sins forgiven and received the Spirit of God, but they were added together into the church (Acts 2:41, 47).

Summary of Relationships

Baptism and the Structure of Acts 2

The above reconstruction in almost every particular reproduces the pattern of thought found in Acts 2. After the audience *heard* and *believed* (37), Peter said, "Repent and be baptized every one of you / in the name of Jesus Christ / unto remission of your sins, / and you shall receive the gift of the Holy Spirit (38), / . . . And there were added together that day about three thousand souls (41; cp. 47b) . . . . / And they continued steadfastly . . . ." In the first frame (a) baptism in the context of repentant faith is called for; in the second frame stands a correlate identification with Christ. Thirdly comes the remission of sins, followed fourthly by the gift of the Holy Spirit and fifthly by church membership. "Continuing steadfastly" is the sixth item, which refers to the Christian life (42-47a). What has been adjudged the logical sequence of these elements corresponds to the literary structure of Luke's account of Pentecost. Note also that Matthew 28, Romans 6, and Galatians 3 move from baptism to identification with Christ and then move directly to practical considerations in the Christian continuation—observing all that Christ taught (28:20), walking in newness of life (6:4-14), and putting on Christ (3:27).

Baptism as a total event

Baptism in its first level is identification with Jesus Christ. In its second level it is the occasion of the blessings God gives. These three blessings are really the benefits of salvation more than benefits of baptism because they come from the act of God, not even indirectly or partially from the obedience of man in this ordinance. In scripture, baptism *may* serve as label for the whole event because it is visible.

BAPTISM

A	B
Baptism in water	1. forgiveness of sins 2. gift of the Spirit 3. church membership
man's act	God's gifts

239

The divine gifts on this occasion are known to occur because God has promised them, not because they can be seen. In presenting these aspects of salvation, we have associated them with baptism because scripture associates them with the ordinance and because they are the natural elements of initial salvation and the identification with Christ that baptism marks.

Generalizations on Baptism from Previous Considerations

Significant generalizations about baptism

(1) Baptism *formalizes into a point* what in many respects is a process. Belief and trust in the Lord may conceive and grow before this "birth" actually takes place, and a repentant attitude like Saul's may engulf the spirit prior to the rite that expresses commitment to Christ. In this respect baptism is like a wedding ceremony. The man and woman have come to some degree of mutual trust and love before the wedding occurs, but that ceremony formally establishes an identity between them that did not previously exist in the eyes of other people or in their own eyes. Furthermore, that relationship deepens over the years even as appreciation and love for Christ develops throughout life.

Becoming an adult illustrates the same principle. Most cultures have some rite of passage by which a person enters into society as a full-fledged participant even though many developmental matters precede and follow that initiatory rite. Crisis and process are not only compatible, but they together form a total picture of what happens in salvation. Faith as a process grows to the point of willingness to identify with Christ. Baptism is that formal act of identification God instituted to mark the change of category he promises to pronounce on that occasion. Without the personal, interpersonal, and dynamic factors there is no promise that the anticipated blessings are forthcoming.

(2) Baptism is the *time when* God forgives our sin, gives us his Spirit, and adds us to his church. This ordinance culminates the development of the dynamic factors that must be present to the extent that *identification* and *commitment* are willing to be made. If baptism is into Christ (Col. 2:11-13) and if salvation comes only in Christ and his New Covenant (Heb. 8:10-12), then baptism as entrance into Christ is the time of forgiveness of sins.

(3) Baptism is *logically prior* to the forgiveness of sins. Although the forgiveness may be viewed as granted at the *time when* we identify

240

with Christ, the meaning of baptism as identification with Christ requires that it stand *prior to* the benefits bestowed on those who are in Christ. Consequently, baptism is here not regarded just as a *seal* of salvation because a seal may indicate only a previous reality. Only perhaps could it be regarded as a seal proleptically—if such a notion makes sense— because the candidate in his obedience to God believes that God always keeps his promises including the promises made in connection with this obedience. To obey God is "as good as" having the assurance of forgiveness, fellowship with the Spirit, and membership in the body of Christ.

(4) Baptism in its logical priority bears a *condition relationship* to salvation. All human responses stand inside the system of faith. Baptism is the *time when* God grants salvation and is a *condition unto* that salvation. To be logically prior does not mean to be a cause. There is no power in water of any sort to clean off sin; neither is there power in any act to do it in part or indirectly. Only because God has appointed it does it have any relation whatever to his salvation and then only because God has promised the results in connection with the obedience. The act of baptism does not simply *signify* the invisible realities God grants. On the other hand, it does not *cause,* convey, or effect them. Like the faith, repentance, and the commitment it expresses, baptism is an act of self-identification with Christ that serves as a *condition* for God's identifying us with him, in terms of whom God then dispenses his grace.

(5) Baptism has first to do with *salvation,* then the reception of the Holy Spirit and church membership. Church membership is not the first or main association of baptism because there is no ideal or intentional difference between the saved of the body of Christ and the members of the visible church community. The individual logically precedes the group insofar as it is by individual response that the group is entered.

(6) Baptism into Christ addresses *standard procedure* unto salvation. Special cases need not hinder us from giving baptism its full scriptural status. We need not despair over the state of those converted in situations not readily allowing for obedience to this command. "Hard cases make bad law," we say because they are not the ones addressed by standard procedure the terminally ill, the imprisoned, the Eskimo, the desert dweller. Many times problem cases can be solved; but even if not, God will deal with those believers in a fashion appropriate to his holiness and love. A fatal accident en route to baptism presents no

difficulty because God can count the intent for the obedience as he did in the sacrifice of Isaac. In such a case it would not be the faith instead of the act that saved, but the intent to act counted for the act. In his revelation God leaves himself free, we believe, to dispense his grace on conditions other than those to which he has committed himself even though no one has any right to presume on his grace unnecessarily. God is not trying to see how many people he can keep out of heaven. This judge does not have the mentality to condemn on a technicality. He allays that fear by the great lengths to which he has gone to secure our salvation. Furthermore, we have from another dispensation a model of divine grace in a non-standard situation. The thief on the cross was in no position to offer for his cleansing the proper sacrifices required through Moses. Nevertheless, the verbalized attitude of his heart the Lord acknowledged as sufficient in that case for his forgiveness. Like the woman that anointed Jesus in Bethany, he did what he could (cp. Mk. 14:3-9). When the palsied man and his bearers gained entrance through the roof to get Jesus to heal him, Jesus for their faith went beyond their request and forgave the man's sins (cp. Lk. 5:18-24; 7:48). To adopt the sentiment of Jesus in another connection, man was not made for baptism, but baptism was made for man. To say the least in hard cases, "we judge not even our own selves" (I Cor. 4:3), but concentrate on doing what God has commanded. Ritual and form are never the end all and be all of true religion, but whatever under God's grace he requires of our faith is to be obeyed with all readiness to the glory of Christ and it is, of course, to be accorded the significance he attaches to it.

Baptism and its interpersonal context

Throughout our study on salvation we have endeavored to keep interpersonal relations in the center of all that we have had to say because that seems to be the organizing truth in scripture regarding this subject. Baptism therefore has been viewed as an act of identification with the person of Jesus Christ who embodies the ideal way of behaving that contrasts with our previous sinful behavior. The breach between man and God is closed by forgiveness, an interpersonal act. Receiving the Spirit centers around participation in the presence of God, the natural result of forgiveness of sin between persons. Finally, the church is a

242

community of saints separated from sin and united together in the bond of interpersonal peace and love.

Baptism must be contextualized in this interpersonal framework of the Christian system in order for its proper position not to be over-stressed or underestimated. The interpersonal character of that context also protects against making baptism a merely outward ritual that would have validity aside from personal factors like faith, repentance, and commitment. Without these baptism would not be baptism.

For this reason we have not called baptism a "sacrament" because sacramentalism suggests a view of baptism that makes it valid aside from personal and dynamic factors. Automatic flow of grace, baptismal regeneration of an ontic sort, objective efficacy, Levitical holiness, and other concepts traditionally related to this ordinance make it mechanistic, impersonal, heartless, legal, and like paper work. By so regarding it, we would become proper objects of the displeasure God directed against Old Testament worshipers when they presumed on the efficacy of sacrifices offered ritually (Isa. 1:11-13; Jer. 6:20; Mal. 1:6-10). "Going through the motions" has never satisfied our heart-knowing God any more than such things are fulfilling and satisfying to the performers themselves. Baptism in our view is not baptismal regeneration because in baptism the initiate expresses faith rather than receives faith. The fundamental principles that govern the meaningfulness of interpersonal relationships in the horizontal apply significantly to that kind of rela-tionship in the vertical. Their appropriateness stems from the kind of relationship involved, not particularly the direction of it.

Our treatment of baptism has put first the meaning of the ordinance in a treatment of the entire subject. The meaning of baptism establishes the framework for the upcoming discussion on the candidate for baptism, the subject to which we will turn after we have interacted with three other views of the meaning of baptism as discussed in the next two chapters.

Chapter Seventeen

BAPTISM AS A SEAL OF PREVIOUS FAITH

Introductory Description

The first alternative interpretation of baptism is that *baptism is an outward seal of an inward faith*. God's grace precedes man's faith by making it possible, or by "giving" it; the coming of that faith not only logically precedes baptism, but chronologically must be present before baptism can legitimately occur. Therefore it is commonly called believers' baptism. It brings us into membership in the visible church because of previous personal salvation.

This view of baptism shares significant elements with the view we proposed. It is performed for believers only, and the grace received requires prior dynamic factors before it is valid baptism. It differs by placing salvation previous to baptism in such a way that baptism simply pictures what stands logically before it instead of standing as part of the condition for the salvation that follows it.

A prominent tradition in Christian thought furnishes the framework for this view of baptism by defining differently Paul's salvation words in a subtle but significant way. Saving faith is "active faith"; it is the kind of faith that acts rather than faith put into action. True faith, it is emphasized, will act and true faith meets the condition for salvation; but the action that stands inseparable from faith is not contemplated with it in salvation. "Faith" is something inner, so that all the outer things fall into the category called "works." Baptism must then be included in works, but works are what men are saved unto (Eph. 2:10), therefore not what they are saved by. Baptism—a work—is something that men are saved "for," not "by."

Baptism cannot serve as an act of identification with Christ in consequence of which sin is forgiven, etc., because such an understanding puts the "work" baptism logically prior to forgiveness. The present section of this study endeavors to describe the view of baptism that has developed out of this thought and to show how passages are reinterpreted which touch on the purpose of baptism.

Concepts Applied to Baptism Texts

In the following pages four principles, or concepts, appear which are utilized in the interpretation of passages bearing on baptism texts, especially the ones we have felt lead to the understanding of baptism described in the previous chapter. Different authors of the present persuasion utilize different ones of these concepts on given texts, but the principles affect the exegesis of the texts important to the subject of Christian baptism.

Baptism in the state of forgiveness

Baptism *in* remission of sins seeks to solve the perceived problem with works by putting baptism logically *after* the remission. The King James Version renders Acts 2:38, "Repent and be baptized . . . *for* the remission of sins." Instead of taking "for" in the sense of John 1:7, "He came for a witness . . . ," the word has been understood as in the statement, "We imprisoned him for embezzlement." The meaning of the verse becomes, "Repent and be baptized . . . on account of the remission of sins," with the implication that forgiveness precedes baptism. Under this construction our idea falls out. Baptism is reduced to a subsequent outward manifestation of a logically previous inward faith and grace.

Of course, such a treatment only takes advantage of a turn in the English word "for." Other translations substitute "unto" in its place so as to indicate that the thought moves from baptism to forgiveness rather than the reverse. Scholars go beyond the popular manner of presentation for English-speaking audiences and comment on the Greek text as well. "Unto remission of sins" translates *eis aphesin hamartiōn.* The word *eis* has received a great amount of attention and has served as the center of discussion on the meaning of baptism.

Eis meaning "in." It is admitted on all hands that *eis* means "into," but the claim has been that (a) on a number of occasions the word amounts to meaning "in"; examples cited are Matthew 2:23; 4:13; Mark 13:3, 16; Luke 9:61; 11:17; John 1:18; Acts 2:27, 39; 8:40; 19:22; 21:13; 23:11; 25:4; Hebrews 11:9; I Peter 5:12; I John 5:8.

In keeping with these examples is the observation that (b) in the history of the Greek language *eis* developed out of the word *en*, meaning "in." Bringing these points to bear on Acts 2:38 can yield the conclusion that baptism is done *in* remission of sins; if so, forgiveness has already occurred by the "time" baptism is administered.

As an elaboration of the "in" idea for *eis*, (c) occasions arise in first-century Greek literature where *eis* is said to have a causal force and may be translated "because of." Luke 11:32 illustrates this other usage when Jesus says, "They repented at [*eis*] the preaching of Jonah, and behold a greater than Jonah is here" (cp. Mt. 12:41).

Countering considerations. Several matters warrant consideration in light of this approach to Peter's words in Acts 2:38. The first has to do with (1) the total expression *eis aphesin hamartiōn* as meaning purpose-result. It occurs three other times in the New Testament, twice with reference to John's baptism (Mk. 1:4; Lk. 3:3) and once in reference to the shedding of Christ's blood (Mt. 26:28; cp. Heb. 9:15). The two usages with John's baptism involve the same question we are seeking to solve and therefore must be set aside for now. Christ's blood, however, was not poured out for many because remission of sins already existed. It was "poured out for many unto remission of sins," that is, "in order that" sin could be forgiven or "with the result that" sin could be forgiven. This unquestionable example of purpose is not simply a matter of the meaning of the one word *eis*, but of the whole expression *eis aphesin hamartiōn* and of that expression in the context of salvation.

Maintaining that *eis aphesin hamartiōn* addresses purpose-result matters in both Matthew 26:28 and Acts 2:38 is not to say that the *same* purpose-result is in view. In Matthew it is the *basis* of salvation; in Acts it is the *appropriation* of the basis. As the purpose of shedding Christ's blood was to establish the basis for remission of sins, the purpose of baptism is to be part of the human response commanded for appropriating remission of sins.

Other combinations of "baptize" and *eis* occur besides *eis aphesin hamartiōn*. (2) In none of these other associations do we feel an urge to translate *eis* so baptism is logically after it: "on account of" (causal), "in the state of" (stative), etc. The usages with persons would seem strained: "baptized *on account of* the name of Paul," etc. (I Cor. 1:13, 15; 10:2; Gal. 3:27; Mt. 28:19; Acts 8:16; 19:5; Rom. 6:3). "Baptized *because of* John's baptism" would be meaningless in Acts 19:3 as well as in I Corinthians 12:13: "We were all baptized in one body in one Spirit *on account of* one body."

Baptism in Galatians 3:27 simply must stand logically prior to what *eis* governs: "As many of you as were baptized *into* Christ have put on Christ." Not only would it seem unnatural to say baptized "on account of" Christ, but the parallelism sets the direction of thought flow by

246

saying "put on Christ." One clear example of baptism for entrance shows that the idea of entrance in connection with it has biblical approval. If we conclude that baptism is unto identification with Christ, we are surely bound to conclude that it precedes forgiveness; otherwise we find ourselves advocating the perplexing proposition that forgiveness of sins precedes identification with the One on the basis of whom that forgiveness comes. Christ would then have died for nothing. If forgiveness is on the basis of Jesus Christ, obviously forgiveness must come after the act that establishes the identification. If there has been no contact with Christ and his blood, there can be no benefits of that contact. Baptism is unto that contact because baptism is into Christ.

(3) Other acts followed by *eis*-plus-salvation are regularly taken to mean purpose-result by those concerned to adopt another meaning in Acts 2:38. The frame may be laid out as follows:

Christ's death			forgiveness of sins
faith			saving of the soul
repentance	} *eis* {		salvation
confession			righteousness
baptism			life

We have already noticed *the death of Christ* in Matthew 26:28: "This is the blood of the covenant, which is poured out for many *into* remission of sins." *Repentance* appears in this same frame in II Corinthians 7:10: "For godly sorrow works repentance *unto* salvation . . ." (cp. Acts 3:19; 11:18; II Tim. 2:25). In Romans 10:10 Paul combines *faith* and *confession* when he says, "With the heart a person believes *unto* righteousness, and with the mouth he confesses *unto* salvation." Unless something forbids it, we would expect *eis* to carry the same meaning with baptism as with the other human responses unto salvation.

One proposed exception to this generalization is the description of John's baptism in Matthew 3:11: "*I* baptize you in water *unto* repentance." The rendering in a causal sense would be "*I* baptize you in water *because of* [*eis*] repentance." While this translation expresses a clear idea, we must remember that a word does not necessarily mean what makes sense in its place. Other ideas may make sense in place of *eis* here. Although the passage could be satisfactorily rendered with the general expression "in regard to" repentance, the notion of identification gives an even more precise explanation in this usage. John's baptism identified its recipients with repentance as the framework of access to righteousness in contradistinction to privileged birth in the line of Abraham (3:9).

When Peter explained his preaching to Cornelius' house (Acts 11:1-18), he told the apostles and brethren in Jerusalem that the descent of the Spirit on them reminded him of Jesus' last reference to the baptism of John (Acts 1:5): "John baptized in water, but *you* will be baptized in the Holy Spirit" (11:16). The brethren and apostles responded, "Then also to the Gentiles God has given repentance unto life" (11:18; cp. Heb. 6:6?). We take the answer to mean that God has opened up the repentance-to-life possibility to Gentiles even though they were not from the privileged line. Salvation is not tied to Abraham's descendants either as a guarantee of their salvation (Mt. 3:9) or as an exclusion of others' salvation (Acts 11:18). One cannot help thinking that their labeling the salvation possibility as "repentance" stemmed from the prominence of that concept in the work of John the Baptist and in the description of his baptism (Mk. 1:4; Lk. 3:3; Acts 13:24; 19:4). In their statement, "repentance" stood for the system of salvation based on dynamic factors in contrast to the system of salvation based on ancestral origins. John's baptism identified men with the approach to salvation that was based on personal conversion in opposition to physical descent. Thus it was a forerunner to the further refinement in Messiah's baptism that identifies men with Jesus of Nazareth as the Messiah in terms of whom personal conversion takes place. Under John's baptism the candidate gave up the notion of ancestry and accepted personal responsibility, and under Jesus' baptism the candidate further gives up the notion of personal righteousness to accept salvation through personal identification with the righteous Messiah. If this analysis of Acts 11 is correct, it provides a parallel to Matthew 3:11 that does not require a causative force for *eis*. Instead, it is translated, "*I* baptize you in water *with respect to* repentance."

Prepositions like "in" or "unto" tend to display a range of ideas, especially in abstract settings. For this reason we regard the above observations as a more solid foundation on which to build a theological distinction because they look at total expressions related to our subject. Nevertheless some observations on *eis* itself are in order.

Whereas there are occasions where "in," "at," "to," or "with respect to" may be a satisfactory translation of *eis*, (4) "into" is the predominant and underlying signification of the word, while "in" is the predominant and underlying signification of another Greek preposition—"*en*." Matthew 2:11 says, "And going into [*eis*] the house, they saw the child with Mary his mother . . ." (cp. 2:20, 21, etc.). *Eis* is in fact the only word that distinctively carries the notion of entrance. As a result Greek dictionaries consistently define it primarily with reference to entrance and so say it means "into" (cp. Mt. 3:10, 12; 4:1, 5, 8, 12^2, 18; 5:20, 25, 29, 30; etc.).

The underlying idea of entrance may be mentally adjusted to related ideas. One such manipulation *abstracts* the concrete picture in the word.

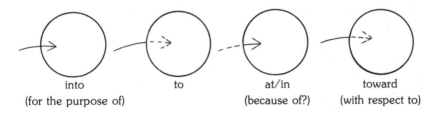

into	to	at/in	toward
(for the purpose of)		(because of?)	(with respect to)

By "concrete" we mean a situation like "He went into the house." "Abstract" means a statement like "He went into a rage." Prepositions tend to be concrete pictures that are then adapted for expressing abstract relationships. In our example "rage" is conceptually regarded as a sphere. When a person "gets mad," we speak of his going "into a rage." Abstract relationships are commonly pictured in concrete terms.

Forgiveness is an abstraction pictured as a sphere. Our understanding has been that Peter meant baptism *into* the sphere, or state, of forgiveness, not baptism *in* that sphere. The reason for our preference is that entrance cannot be expressed with any other Greek preposition. Had Peter meant "in the state of," one would certainly expect him to have used *en*, the regular word for location inside.

Further mental adjustments pictured by the diagrams highlight different parts of the original picture so that other parts are not held in sharp focus. In some places "up to" instead of "into" seems more to be the point. "Toward" gives a proper sense in the preferred reading of II Peter 3:9, ". . . but he is longsuffering toward [*eis*] you." On other occasions "at" or "in" appear to be adequate translations: "For as you have testified the things concerning me in [*eis*] Jerusalem, thus it is necessary for you to bear witness also in [*eis*] Rome" (Acts 23:11). When there is movement in the verb—going, traveling, etc., *eis* will normally be translated "into," "unto," or "toward"; but where movement is missing, "at" or "in" may appear in the translation.

At this juncture we must draw a line between the meaning of a word and the idiom of a language. Occasions arise where translating a word "literally" according to its elemental meaning will not make a natural expression in the new language because there is between the languages a difference in idiom, or customary way of speaking. Good translation work must take into account both meaning and idiom.

An example of this phenomenon is Greek's tendency to let the article suffice in places where English expects to use a possessive adjective. John 3:16 says that God "gave his only Son," but the word "his" is actually the Greek article. To say "God gave the only Son" would not be idiomatic in English. Strictly speaking, the Greek article does not sometimes mean "his." Rather, English custom expects "his" in places where Greek custom can be satisfied with using the article.

Keeping this phenomenon in mind reduces by a large percentage the number of places in which *eis* might appear to mean "to," "toward," or "in." Acts 11:25 may seem more natural if rendered "Then Barnabas departed to [*eis*] Tarsus" even though Greek seems to conceive of the movement as ending up inside Tarsus as an area rather than at Tarsus as a point.

After making adjustments for the difference in language custom, we nevertheless find occasional usages of *eis* that make possible, at least in theory, the claim made for this alternate view of Acts 2:38. On occasion Greek does use the conceptual notion of "into a sphere" where English is content to speak of being "in the sphere of." Even a case like Mark 13:16 does not set aside this principle entirely: "Let not the one in [into] the field turn back [*into the thing behind*] to get his coat" (cp. Mt. 2:23; 4:13; Mk. 10:10; 13:3, 9; Lk. 4:23; 9:61; 11:7; Acts 2:5, 39; 7:4; 8:40; 21:13; Heb. 11:9; I Pet. 5:12). Current English idiom displays a similar usage when people say, "He is really *into* classical music." The statement is not exactly synonymous with something like "He is really *in* classical music." "Into music" includes the idea of having entered as well as the idea of being in. For all practical purposes a translator could take this English expression into another language by using a word that means "in," but he would not be justified in saying on the basis of this example alone that the English word "into" on occasion means "in." Nevertheless, a usage of *eis* like Mark 13:16 would for Acts 2:38 end up having the notion of location inside instead of just direction only, because it would mean "forgiveness being-into Christ."

By applying this discussion to Acts 2:38, we do not mean to suggest that "be baptized being-into remission of sins" is an impossible idea in and of itself. Whether *eis* here means "entrance into" or "state of being entered into" will finally have to be settled on grounds other than the word *eis* itself. The real purpose for which others have noted that *eis* can mean "being into something" is to defend against using Acts 2:38, as we have, to demonstrate a purpose-result relationship between baptism and remission of sins. On the other hand, their argument does not, of course, require that *eis* mean "in" at this point either, because there are too many clear cases of its meaning "into."

As for the proposed causal usage of *eis*, we feel that a rare meaning does not receive first option unless pressing considerations warrant; a disputed meaning becomes all the more suspect when it cannot be understood consistently even in the usages pertinent to the subject. Only four out of the approximately 1,750 times *eis* occurs in the New Testament could conceivably bear the meaning "because of." One of these (Mt. 3:11) has already been shown to be inconclusive. A second one has a similar uncertainty about it: ". . . yet *eis* the promise of God he did not waiver in unbelief but was enabled by faith, giving glory to God" (Rom. 4:20). A sufficient translation would be "with respect to" the promise of God. The same holds for the other two passages, parallel accounts about the Ninevites repenting "*eis* the preaching of Jonah." They "repented with respect to the preaching of Jonah." All four of these statements may be handled satisfactorily in this way.

On the surface of things we would not expect *eis* to mean "because of" in Acts 2:38. A meaning witnessed four times is rare and somewhat unconvincing even in the passages cited. Furthermore, it reverses the a-*eis*-b direction of movement in the word, making it into b-*eis*-a. All the other usages of *eis*, including its mental adjustments diagrammed above, maintain a left-to-right sequence. Likelihood cannot therefore stand on the side of a causal usage in Acts 2:38, it being preferable to translate it "in" if a person feels theologically compelled to place baptism logically after salvation.

Furthermore, (5) according to Acts 2:38 repentance accompanies baptism in its associations with forgiveness and receiving the Holy Spirit.

251

Putting baptism after remission of sins would seem to be no more likely than putting repentance after it, but faith and repentance are viewed as previous to salvation by those who put baptism after forgiveness. As far as this particular text is concerned, there is no self-evident reason for making baptism after forgiveness while leaving repentance before it.

(6) Mark 16:16 does not support this view of baptism. Mark 16:9-20 is now generally regarded as lacking in the original edition of the gospel. Nevertheless, it may be worth noting that in 16:16 the text says, "The one who believes and is baptized shall be saved," which is hardly synonymous with the idea, "The one who believes and is saved shall be baptized."

In consideration of the argument that *eis* derived from *en* (meaning "in"), it is to be remembered that (7) usage, not derivation, is more primarily determinative for word meanings. Where a term came from a hundred or more years ago is not always known by later speakers of a language. Even if they could explain the derivation when asked, they would probably not consciously think of it when using the term. A "secretary" keeps "secrets," but no one thinks of that when he uses the word today.

When all is said and done, the interpretation of Acts 2:38 will depend on our prior understanding of works and faith in Paul's thought. We interpret works to be that which themselves produce righteousness, not particularly that which is an outward act. "Faith" we understand as trusting in someone else for the needed effect righteousness, not particularly that which is an inward act. Consequently, we sense no problem in incorporating baptism under the concept of faith. Baptism has not meant for us something that is an outward work whose efficacy stems from the one who administers it, or from the element used, or from the form of the action performed, or from any such basis for validity other than what it pictures about Christ's death and what it expresses about the candidate's attitude toward that death. Baptism as naturally comes before salvation as does believing or repenting without thereby contradicting the doctrine of salvation by faith. The character and significance of any act cannot rise above the category in which it stands. Baptism stands in the category of faith because it is expression of trust in another; so it cannot be a work in the Pauline sense.

We have so far argued that the meaning of Acts 2:38 cannot be settled decisively without first settling the meaning of "faith" and "works" in Paul. In Acts 2:38 itself we have gone ahead to assume the negative burden of proof, arguing that likelihood looks away from baptism in consequence of remission of sins. (a) The total phrase *eis aphesin hamartiōn* has a purpose-result meaning in Matthew 26:28. (b) Other "baptism-into" expressions must construe baptism ahead of the object of "into," especially in Galatians 3:27. Surely identification (by baptism) with Christ must precede the forgiveness of sins in Christ, or the forgiveness would be coming from somewhere other than Christ's death-resurrection. (c) In all other acts preceding *eis*-plus-salvation, the preposition is understood as result. (d) Even in cases aside from a salvation context *eis* carries a uniformly left-to-right logical sequence in that it governs what logically succeeds rather than what logically precedes. (e) Repentance is joined with baptism in Acts 2:38 so that a judgment in favor of causal *eis* would seem also to require putting repentance after forgiveness.

We feel that these observations, though not individually decisive, have cumulative effect, creating expectancy that baptism precedes remission of sins. An unusual meaning is not opted for in similar settings unless prior considerations require them—considerations like the nature of the case and the harmony of scripture. Our contention is that the Pauline doctrine of faith and works is fundamentally misunderstood by those who take at best an uncertain meaning for *eis* in Acts 2:38.

Faith of the sacrament

Description of the view. A concept prevalent in Christian thought since at least the fourth century is that it is not the "sacrament" that saves, but the faith of the sacrament. In other words, it is not baptism itself that saves and not even faith plus baptism, but faith only. The outward obedience must be there, not as part of the condition for salvation, but because true faith will express itself in obedience. If obedience were not forthcoming, it would indicate a false kind of faith. God does not regard the expression of faith in saving us, but only the faith behind the expression, although the two are necessarily welded together by the nature of what acceptable faith is. We are saved by the right kind of faith—active faith, rather than by the right degree of faith—acting faith. "Faith only" does not at all mean that only faith is *necessary*, but that only faith is *reckoned* in salvation. Obedience in baptism will necessarily follow as an outward expression of a previous inward faith. Faith is also not merely believing, but carries the more pregnant sense of trusting and putting trust in, or committing one's self to, Christ.

Salvation by the faith of the sacrament has molded the interpretation of Acts 2:38 in a way different from the one previously discussed. Instead of maintaining that baptism is *in* remission of sins here, it puts repentance in immediate connection with remission and goes ahead to translate *eis* as "into." Baptism is mentally subordinated to repentance in order to allow that direct connection. Baptism is still placed in the state of forgiveness as to the truth of the matter, but not as to the point of this verse.

Grammatically, of course, repentance and baptism are parallel in Acts 2:38, but conceptually they are not in this interpretation of the verse. Peter's statement teaches that repentance is unto remission of sins. The first step is to view repentance as the negative side of faith; repentance is being sorry that you did not trust. The second step is to view baptism as a derivative of faith-repentance; baptism expresses faith. The third step is to read Acts 2:38 with "repent" immediately connected with "unto remission of sins": "Repent—and be baptized in the name of Jesus Christ [as an expression of repentance]—unto remission of sins . . . ." The section between the dashes is conceptually subordinated to "repent," so that repentance is free to stand in direct relationship with forgiveness; and baptism, while subordinate to repentance is subsequent to the forgiveness because it is the faith of the sacrament that saves rather than the expression of faith by the sacrament.

There is no denying that natural and grammatical relationships do not have to be the same. For example, in the statement "I went to town to buy groceries," "buy" is grammatically subordinate to "went," but naturally (from the standpoint of the nature of things) going and buying are two separate acts in series. We might tell about that same trip to town by saying, "I went to town and bought groceries." Now admittedly the two sentences do not strictly mean the same thing, but they are referring to the same event. If a person by some other way knew that the speaker went to town with the purpose of buying groceries (rather than buying them as an afterthought once he was there), he would then understand the second statement in a way that included the idea expressed by the first. Confusion does not result when the natural

254

and grammatical relationships are different because the hearer can understand the relationship from the nature of the case rather than from the form of this statement about the case.

Observations on the view. First, in this reconstruction of Acts 2:38 avoiding salvation by merit again establishes the point of departure. Even in our own view we have conceptually subordinated baptism to faith in the sense that baptism is in the context of personal faith and therefore relates to the effect forgiveness as faith does—conditionally. We have not, however, adopted the principle that act-producing faith is the *kind* of faith that saves, but that faith to the *degree* of producing acts is (along with those products) what saves. The faith together with its expression is as a cluster regarded as the condition for salvation. The point of salvation by faith is the *relationship* of human response to the result righteousness, not the *identity* of an act as inner rather than outer.

Secondly, under the "faith only" construction the ordinance is observed as surely as it is under our view of baptism. No necessary difference exists from a practical standpoint. All the same elements are present; the difference lies in understanding what the scripture means their theoretical relationship is in God's eyes. For that reason we have no desire to deny the validity of baptism administered and received under the alternative reconstruction. In both cases the candidates realize that forgiveness of sins is the object in view. They also realize that God has promised to dispense his grace only when men obey his commands. Both views understand that by baptism or any other act the person is not saving himself. They also agree that baptism pertains to initial identification with Christ so that it is not an act that falls among the general observances of the Christian life. It remains distinguishable then from the Lord's Supper in which, among other things, the communicant continues to reidentify himself with Jesus Christ. The difference is not one that necessarily makes a difference.

Certain cautions nevertheless are in order. Baptism after the fact has sometimes led to delaying it and thus separating it actually and psychologically from its natural place among the elements of conversion. Suffice it to say, the New Testament examples lend no support to waiting six months or a year or two till a person gets settled among a body of believers, the Ethiopian eunuch being perhaps a satisfactory example. Invariably, dissociating baptism from salvation has led to associating it with the visible church, and this conception of its primary meaning

255

relates, not only to delayed baptism, but to infant baptism as well, which is the subject of a following chapter. These practical aberrations need not develop, and as long as they do not there is no practical difference involved in the wake of this or the previous exegesis of Acts 2:38.

Weaknesses of the view. Making these concessions in the interest of practical theology, we are obliged to return to Acts 2:38 in the interest of biblical theology and sound exegesis. Likelihood operates contrary to the exposition proposed in this chapter. (1) In the biblical statement "repent" and "be baptized" are separated from each other so as to receive separate attention and stress. "Repent" is second person plural while "be baptized" is third singular. In a woodenly literal way the verse reads, "You [pl.] repent and let each one of you be baptized in the name of Jesus Christ unto remission of your sins." Some manuscripts offer further disjunction by inserting "he said" between the two verbs. Two finite verbs are joined by "and," rather than even subordinating one of them to another by making one a participle as in Matthew 28:19 (cp. Acts 22:16), which has only one finite verb in the injunction —"make disciples."

(2) Jumping over the nearer element to modify a distant one creates in the case of John's baptism the opposite conclusion from what the alternative exegesis has sought to establish in Acts 2:38. "Baptism of repentance unto remission of sins" appears in Mark 1:4 and Luke 3:3. "Unto remission" would probably be better taken to modify "baptism" than "repentance" because in a frame like this one the closing component more usually modifies the phrase head than the nearer noun. An obvious case is "the blood of the covenant which is poured out . . . ." It is the blood that is poured out, not the covenant. Jumping over the nearer verb in Acts 2:38 will not help the overall discussion since that pattern would have to be abandoned in the other two texts where it would be more likely than it is here.

(3) The baptism and forgiveness are joined together. Perhaps the recurrence of "your" with sins makes stronger connection with the "each of you" that serves as subject of "be baptized."

Baptism as the occasion

Titus 3:5 connects the washing, or laver, of regeneration with salvation: ". . . he saved us through the washing of regeneration . . . ." In order again to separate baptism from salvation some exegetes want to say that baptism saves as the occasion, not as a condition. Baptism in the present verse refers to the event, not the act, as in the statement "At the baptism of Jesus he received the Holy Spirit." By a figure of speech baptism can be said to save us because the container (event of baptism) is put for the contained (faith): ". . . in order that, having been *justified by faith* in him, we might become heirs according to the hope of eternal life" (3:7). Precisely speaking, we are justified by grace (3:7); loosely speaking, we are saved through the washing of regeneration (3:5).

As we have reiterated in each case, so we say again that we really cannot enter effectively into the discussion of the meaning of baptism by entering into it at the level of specific verses about baptism. The immediate signals within every one of these texts prove to be theoretically imprecise enough that only likelihoods and tendencies may be argued for, but likelihoods can always be struck down in favor of seeming unlikelihoods because of larger or more preliminary truths established from elsewhere. If, however, various points in a text point toward the same likelihood, there is a cumulative force that increases exponentially the strength of the likelihood.

A couple of notes may still be helpful on the Titus reference in establishing likelihoods. First, Paul's mind seems to be focused on acts more than events in which acts are done. He begins the verse with an emphasis on acts: ". . . not out of works which *we* did in righteousness, but he saved us through the washing of regeneration . . . ." Instead of saying that washing of regeneration means event, it is at least equally cogent to say that it means an act we do; that is not a work because it is not done in righteousness (perfection). Baptism could not have the significance a work would have of maintaining righteousness because righteousness is the very thing God saves us to. In Paul's usage baptism is not a work because, having said "not of works," he proceeds to say "through baptism." Granted, if baptism meant occasion, then as an occasion it would not be a work, but by his prior comments acts are directly in his thoughts. He is reminding his readers that they are not saved by their acts done in maintained perfection, but by God through their acts done in imperfection.

Second, we know of no clear case in New Testament usage where "baptism" is used as a label for the event, as in the expression "at his baptism." That may be happenstance, but then again it may be that New Testament and Pauline idiom does not include the meaning being

257

advanced for "baptism" and its equivalent "washing of regeneration" in Titus 3:5.

Baptism in the Spirit

Discussions about the meaning of baptism in water often come to a stalemate in regard to some passages because "baptism" is taken to mean baptism in the Holy Spirit as far as any salvation connection is concerned. In effect what has been advocated for the significance of water baptism shifts by this mechanism to Spirit baptism.

Baptism in the Holy Spirit in this view usually means more than we attach to it. Our understanding is that receiving the Holy Spirit in Christian baptism is primarily an establishment of interpersonal relationship with him. Anything more than the relationship itself would not be necessary to what is involved or uniform in the experience of the Christian and would depend on circumstances of need and on God's will. The benefits—guidance, power, and intercession—come through the interpersonal relationship itself.

The other view, however, normally adds to this interpersonal dimension an energizing of the Christian by an unspecified mechanism beyond interpersonal empowerment. It would seem appropriate to designate the mechanism "miraculous" inasmuch as something is evidently done to the very structures of fallen humanness to produce effects not even theoretically possible before. Historically this effect has been called "regeneration," a term variously used to include not only a new beginning of state in justification, but also a new beginning of ability for sanctification.

Baptism in the Holy Spirit according to the alternate view relates to baptism in water in either of two ways. The first way sees them as (1) *simultaneous.* Holy-Spirit baptism happens at the same time as water baptism. According to this view texts that connect baptism with salvation mean baptism *as inclusive of* baptism in the Holy Spirit. Baptism into salvation is a metonymy for baptism in the Holy Spirit unto salvation. Baptism in the Holy Spirit and baptism in water are two aspects of one event—baptism. "Baptism unto remission of sins" is a loose statement meaning in a strict sense that the Holy-Spirit-baptism part is unto salvation, not the water-baptism part; the outer-baptism aspect is logically after the inner-baptism aspect and brings about visible church membership while the inner baptism of the Spirit brings about salvation.

Since the reason for the inner-outer baptism distinction comes from elsewhere, we cannot hope to controvert it from this verse directly. Nevertheless it may be worth noting that the gospels describe John's baptism as "a baptism of repentance unto remission of sins" (Mk. 1:4; Lk. 3:3, cp. Lk. 1.77). The distinguishing feature between the two ministries of John and Jesus lay precisely in the fact that John did not baptize in the Holy Spirit; consequently, the baptism terminology needs no special explanation, and it cannot be explained in John's baptism by appeal to a Holy-Spirit aspect of baptism.

A conceivable response might be that in "baptism of repentance unto remission of sins" the phrase "unto remission of sins" modifies "repentance" rather than "baptism." We have connected the modifying phrase more closely with the phrase head, "baptism," although the other analysis is grammatically possible. But associating forgiveness with the Holy-Spirit aspect of baptism lacks warrant if conditionality means what we have described.

The second way of seeing baptism in the Holy Spirit and water baptism is to view them as (2) *separable*. The former may occur before, at, or after the latter. Cornelius' household was baptized in the Holy Spirit before they were baptized in water (Acts 10). Jesus was baptized and received the Spirit at the same time. The twelve disciples of John discovered by Paul in Ephesus were baptized in water and received the Spirit at about the same time (Acts 19). In Samaria the believers received the Spirit a good while after water baptism. Texts that connect baptism with salvation mean baptism in the Holy Spirit *instead of* baptism in water.

Part of the difficulty in the understanding just outlined lies in not making distinctions natural to the subject. What happened to Cornelius' household does not necessarily equal what occurred with the Samaritan and Ephesian believers. Prayer and the laying on of hands occur in some cases, but not in others. Miraculous manifestation applies to some and not to others. Sometimes apostles were involved, but at other times they were not. Without investigating these matters now, we suggest that (a) "receiving the Spirit" may fluctuate in its precise application depending on the peculiar circumstances involved. It is worth noticing as well that (b) logical and chronological sequence may not coincide if circumstances warrant. Receiving the Spirit may precede the full range of those responses it logically succeeds even as an employer for special reasons might pay a workman for his work ahead of time.

259

A related part of the difficulty with using Cornelius' and the Samaritans' conversions is that events do not have enough clarity to determine the kind of questions that are being raised to them by interpreters. The logical relationships of an event's components are not able to be read off the occurrence itself. For this reason statements of definition and description must take precedence over accounts of events.

For now, whatever may be said for or against receiving the Spirit irrespective of the time of baptism, certain guidelines may be used by which to differentiate water baptism from Holy-Spirit baptism. (a) Any passage that has a resurrection element in it does not mean particularly baptism in the Spirit. There is nothing about baptism in the Holy Spirit that corresponds to resurrection. Baptism in the Holy Spirit is an effect; consequently, it is not something we get over or resurrect from. Water baptism, however, has an end to it because it is not a continuing effect given, but a one-time obedience rendered. Passages like Romans 6 and Colossians 2 that speak in resurrection terms do not mean baptism in the Holy Spirit.

(b) Any passage that contains a command to be baptized is not so likely to mean baptism in the Holy Spirit as it is baptism in water. The presence of the Spirit is an effect, not something done. Moreover, Jesus Christ administers Holy-Spirit baptism as well as forgiveness of sins and church membership. Men only administer baptism in water, not the gifts bestowed by God at conversion. On occasion language does, of course, allow statements like "save yourselves from this crooked generation" (Acts 2:40).

(c) No case where "baptism" occurs alone indicates clearly that baptism in the Holy Spirit is meant. In many such instances context shows that baptism in water is involved. In fact, only when baptism contrasts with baptism in the Holy Spirit do we find the modifying phrase "in water" added (Mt. 3:11; Mk. 1:8; Lk. 3:16; Jn. 1:26, 33; Acts 1:5; 11:16).

Baptism in the Holy Spirit is never said to be "unto remission of sins." In several texts where "baptism" stands unmodified it must mean water baptism, yet it is associated with salvation or forgiveness (Acts 22:16; Rom. 6:1-14; Col. 2:11-15; I Pet. 3:21).

(d) Any context mentioning literal water more likely refers to water baptism, and any context that speaks of cleansing must be at least inclusive of water baptism or the rationale for the cleansing imagery disappears. A passage like I Peter 3:21, "baptism saves," does not

260

mean Holy Spirit baptism because water in the context brought baptism to the mind of the writer.

(e) Finally, in a passage that also mentions the Holy Spirit, baptism does not mean Holy-Spirit baptism (Acts 2:38). When these distinctions are kept in mind Holy-Spirit baptism does not occur as a frequent subject addressed under baptism terminology.

No treatment of Holy-Spirit baptism for remission of sins would be complete without considering John 3:5. Our positive presentation incorporated the passage under baptism in water, but objections and counterproposals have often been made against that interpretation. Besides the perceived problem of works, which need not be reiterated here, the question has been raised whether Nicodemus would have understood what Jesus meant if he was talking about a baptism not yet instituted.

Two answers may be given to the question. First, (a) *the general principle that a teacher cannot mean what his hearers will not understand is not decisive.* Old Testament prophecies were not always fully understandable to the prophets' contemporaries, or even to the prophets themselves (I Pet. 1:10-12). More directly related to the practice of Jesus as a teacher stands his unexplained comment to other religious leaders in the previous chapter a few days earlier: "Destroy this temple and in three days I will raise it up" (Jn. 2:19). As that statement was not understood even by his disciples until after the resurrection three years later, even so "born of water and Spirit" may not have been fully understandable to Nicodemus until the day of Pentecost.

That the case does not stand even so ambiguous as these examples are may be seen from a second consideration: (b) *the central emphasis in Jesus' conversation with Nicodemus was the necessity of the new birth, not the Christian occasion of it.* Granted that the ruler did not know about Christian baptism, he was nevertheless faced with the central proposition of spiritual renewal by rebirth as the proper basis for sonship with God in contrast to sonship by physical birth as a descendant of Abraham. Jesus riveted his attention to that proposition by the striking figure under which he set it forth: rebirth. Jesus expected this teacher of Israel to understand that all men are sinners in need of forgiveness. Water did not pose a problem to Nicodemus; he asked only about rebirth as a spiritual experience and in so doing showed immediate insight into the essential issue at stake.

261

As far as the water part of this conversation is concerned, Nicodemus could understand the idea of symbolizing *spiritual renewal* by the application of water. He was prepared to grasp that idea by his acquaintance with Old Testament ceremonial washings. He could also understand the idea of commitment as joined to that act in water by the current ministry of John the Baptist. The exact form of purification Jesus meant to establish later Nicodemus could comprehend and obey later. At the time his yielding to the baptism of John would be sufficient (cp. Mt. 3:7ff.); the later Christian baptism may be viewed in its components and effects as a combination of John's baptism plus the gift of the Holy Spirit.

Regarding baptism as primarily an act of identification makes Christian baptism completely understandable to Nicodemus. As we have said, the spiritual renewal aspect he could understand. The water part Nicodemus could also understand simply by analogy with (a) John's baptism as an act of identification with his role of preparation for Messiah. If we agree that proselyte baptism was already being practiced by the Jews, another analogy with (b) proselyte baptism becomes basic for Nicodemus' understanding water baptism. Rabbis had to argue for the legitimacy of proselyte baptism even though it was not directly commanded or practiced according to extant Old Testament canonical literature. They reasoned that the Israelites were baptized unto Moses in the crossing of the Red Sea. Paul adapts this thought in I Corinthians 10:1-4 as a comparison with Christian concerns. We believe that both aspects of Christian baptism would be understandable to this ruler of the Jews, and therefore that Christian baptism in water may remain as part of what Jesus had in mind in John 3:3ff.

If Christian baptism were neither for the *purpose* of justification nor were the *occasion* of the gift of the Spirit, we can appreciate the hesitancy to consider "born of water" as a reference to Christian baptism; for in that case nothing understandable to Nicodemus at the time would be left to be associated with Christian baptism; there would be only the act itself, which had not yet been instituted. But as soon as baptism becomes the occasion of remission and renewal, then we can see how Jesus could be teaching him something already relevant and understandable.

Having dealt with objections to our proposal for John 3:5, we need to interact with counterproposals for what Jesus meant by "born of water and Spirit." Interpretations of this phrase fall into two groups

262

depending on whether both parts of it refer to the new birth or whether they refer to two births—physical birth and rebirth respectively.

The second construction has the force of saying, "Not only does a man have to be born physically to be acceptable to God—even if he is a physical son of blessed Abraham, but he must be born spiritually as well." "Born of water" thus labels physical birth either because water is a reference to the male semen or because it signifies the amniotic fluid in the water sack surrounding the unborn baby.

We think this approach unlikely for several reasons. (a) Pairing water and Spirit occurs several times elsewhere in Acts 2:38, Titus 3:5, in the accounts of Jesus' baptism (Mt. 3:16; Mk. 1:9-10; Lk. 3:21-22; Jn. 1:32-33) and in Christian baptisms like Acts 9:17-18 and 10:44-47.

(b) In Titus 3:5 "regeneration" means "new birth" if the word in the Greek is broken down into its constituent parts. It serves as an equivalent for "born again" in John 3:3.

(c) Jesus calls for rebirth in 3:3 so that 3:5 appears to be a restatement designed to correct Nicodemus' intervening confusion. What he designates "born again" in 3:3 equals "born of water and Spirit" in 3:5, and "born of the Spirit" in 3:6 and 8 (cp. "born/begotten of God" in 1:13; James 1:18; I Jn. 2:29; 3:9). Thus Jesus' remarks stand over against Nicodemus' misunderstanding, not inclusive of it. In contrast, "to be born of water" in this view would signify the same thing as "born of flesh," which Jesus denies in 3:6 (cp. 1:13).

(d) The text does not say "not only born of water but also of spirit," as if viewed in distinction like the two births of 3:6 by flesh and by Spirit. "Born of water and Spirit," in fact, are conceptually united in the Greek by being objects of the same preposition.

(e) It seems trite to say "You have to be born to enter the kingdom of God," especially since this ruler's mind needed to be turned away from physical birth instead of turned toward it and since Jesus puts this phrase in a statement of warning, urgency, or necessity: "Unless a person is born physically and spiritually he cannot enter the kingdom of God."

(f) Finally, not only would it seem trite, but we wonder whether it is true; note that Paul even says that "flesh and blood *cannot* inherit the kingdom of God" (I Cor. 15:50). Inheriting the kingdom that comes from above in his conception does not even include physical things like being born from below. Peter agrees when he speaks of Christians as "having been begotten again, not from corruptible seed, but from incorruptible [seed] through the living and abiding word of God" (I Pet. 1:23).

We agree that the above reasons may not individually or collectively prove our preference in strict terms, but the passage may certainly be understood in harmony with our conclusions reached elsewhere. The first construction of John 3:5, in which both parts apply to the new birth, has four variant interpretations of "born of water": the Old Testament ceremonial washings, John's baptism, washing of the word, and Christian baptism. Only the last two make room for the Spirit's involvement, for John's baptism and the Old Testament cleansings specifically lacked that dimension (Jn. 7:39; Acts 1:4-5; 2:4, 33; 19:1-5), but it occupies the center of attention in the text of John 3. Identifying "born of water" with Mosaic washings also does not do justice to Nicodemus' need to do something he was not already doing.

"Born of water" as "washing of the word" takes its cue from Ephesians 5:26: ". . . in order that he might sanctify [the church] having cleansed [it] by the washing of water with the word." John 3:5 comes to mean that men are born again by being born of the cleansing word and of the Spirit. Ephesians 5:26 does not, however, really equate water and word and may itself refer to Christian baptism. The likelihood of water referring to the message is at best no stronger than a baptismal reference especially since baptism and the Spirit combine in a number of passages elsewhere (Acts 2:38; 8:12-19; 10:44-48; 11:15-16; 19:1-7). Jesus' conversation with the woman at the well of Sychar (Jn. 4:13-14) evidently connects water imagery with the Spirit (cp. 7:37-39). If so, then John 3:5 would have to be translated something like "born of water *even* Spirit" or the text would be saying in effect "born of Spirit and Spirit." "Even" is not a very natural rendering in this setting.

Baptism as an outward sign of an inward grace interprets particular texts by employing at least five concepts: baptism *in* remission of sins, faith of the sacrament, salvation by calling, baptism as occasion, and baptism in the Holy Spirit. They are aspects of one general position that feels compelled to put water baptism after forgiveness in order to avoid merit. Therefore baptism is said to be in forgiveness, the faith of the sacrament being the only aspect of the whole that God regards in bestowing his grace. In salvation baptism in water can be the *time when,* but the *basis of* is baptism in the Holy Spirit, an act that Jesus does. Calling on the Lord replaces baptism in water as the overt act that leads to salvation.

However cogently the idea "outward sign of an inward grace" may be put, it does not comfortably bear the weight of New Testament data. The law of parsimony suggests that, all things being equal, the less complicated view is more likely the correct one. It appears to us that a goodly number of special conceptual moves must be made in order to harmonize particular baptism texts with the assumed understanding of faith and works in Paul. The procedures are sufficiently complex to warrant re-examination of this fundamental matter in comparison with the alternative view proposed on that issue in our study.

Second, we must look at the relationship between baptism and the *gift of the Spirit* in the first alternative view of Christian baptism. Much of what belongs here has been covered in the last chapter's comments on baptism in the Spirit since Spirit baptism normally replaces water baptism as having to do with forgiveness. Most of those comments dealt with *when* salvation comes in relation to Spirit baptism. *What* baptism in the Spirit is needs to be addressed more directly followed by further notations on the time of occurrence.

What the Spirit needs to do for and with a man depends on the nature of man. Since the overall structure of thought in the first alternative view of baptism contains the element of total depravity, the work of the Spirit can be looked upon as having two aspects. The first is an enabling act by which a person in his depravity is brought to the point where he can exercise free will to accept or reject the gospel. This aspect of divine operation is usually considered to be something God's Spirit does for all men to bring them to moral responsibility. If this step is included in the Spirit's work, it has no correlation particularly with baptism since it must occur even before a fruitful hearing of the gospel is possible. Man's total depravity is eradicated to the point where conditional election can be the case. Christ's death was intended for all men who would accept it, but God's grace can be resisted by men.

The continuing presence of the Spirit energizes a person to overthrow temptations and besetting sins. How this quickening is accomplished may not always be understood the same way, but often it is conceived of as an operation performed directly on the very capacities of a man's nature instead of being an interpersonal activity. It tends to have the character of miracle rather than influence. Consequently, the present view of the Spirit's work with the believer often leads to the doctrine of perseverance of the saints. God commits himself to keeping the believer from facing trials he cannot endure or to enabling him to endure the ones that God does not remove. We have preferred to think of the Spirit's assistance on the model of interpersonal influence as the primary function directed toward the person himself together with providential control directed toward the person's circumstance. Any work of the Spirit beyond these two dimensions has to be left to conjecture. That view of the gift of the Spirit that associates that gift with water baptism differs from our position, then, only in the special operations it supposes are performed upon the nature of man itself.

We must speak also to the view that takes baptism in water and in the Holy Spirit as separable, and therefore, distinct events because scripture does not seemingly record a consistent relationship between them. To our knowledge only one clear example may be found where the coming of the Spirit *preceded* baptism: the household of Cornelius. In this one instance, however, a significant peculiarity may readily explain the presumed anomaly. For the first time the gospel was being preached to non-Jews; even the evangelist entertained enough doubt about the legitimacy of the enterprise that the venture required God's manifest leading. The gift of his Spirit to these Gentiles provided an unmistakable indication that as Gentiles they were acceptable to God and could be received as brothers without first being circumcised (cp. Acts 15:7-11, 13ff.).

Therefore, included in this dispensation of the Spirit was a defense for the Gentile mission. Thus apologetics was added to salvation in the Caesarean episode. In order to supply apologetic force that would result in Peter's acceptance of Cornelius' family, the distinctive mark of the body of Christ was dispensed prior to baptism into the body of Christ so Peter would have confidence about administering it. It also had to involve miraculous manifestation so it could be seen.

Even here we need not dispense with baptism as a standard prerequisite to the gift of the Spirit. Although the gift chronologically preceded the baptism, it could still have been dispensed on the basis of foreknown identification with the Jewish Messiah in Christian baptism so that logically the completion of initial obedience would still precede the gift. For this reason it is frankly safer to base our interpretation of baptism on teaching about its meaning than to draw conclusions from events not exhaustively explained. Not even this conceptual rearrangement is required, however, since God can grant his blessings in the manner he deems appropriate to special circumstances without thereby contradicting standard procedure or destroying the meaning of this ordinance.

Another case of receiving the Holy Spirit before baptism has been urged in the case of Saul of Tarsus. Acts 9:17 has Ananias laying his hands on Saul with the words, "The Lord sent me . . . in order that you might receive sight and be filled with the Holy Spirit." Subsequently Saul was baptized. It is not clear, however, that the imposition of hands was for both benefits. The parallel account in Acts 22:13 associates the imposition only with the receiving of sight. In Acts 9 it is not necessary to take 17b as an explanation of 17a. The giving of the Spirit may have its association with the baptism that immediately followed.

Acts 8:1-24 and perhaps Acts 19:1-7 could appear at first glance to be examples where the coming of the gift of the Spirit *succeeded* baptism. In both cases "receive the Spirit" describes what happened (8:17, 19; 19:2) and matches the words of gospel promise given at Pentecost: ". . . and you will receive the gift of the Holy Spirit" (2:38). We suspect, however, that there is a difference in the meaning of the expression or, to put it more exactly, a difference in the dimension of receiving the Spirit in these cases that are seemingly separable from water baptism.

First, an additional act is involved in all cases where "receiving the Spirit" succeeds baptism. Peter's promise is conditioned simply on repentance and baptism. Luke does not mention in Acts 2 any conjoined or additional procedure of prayer and the imposition of hands. The laying on of hands, however, occurs at both Samaria and Ephesus.

Second, miraculous gifts are always involved in those cases where "receiving the Spirit" follows water baptism. Peter's promise speaks only about the gift of the Spirit; he gives no indication that in and of itself the acceptance of Jesus as Messiah brings miraculous gifts. In Acts 19, Paul dispensed miraculous gifts inasmuch as the twelve prophesied and spoke with tongues. Although the account in Acts 8 is not so precise, we gather that Peter and John were dispensing miraculous gifts in connection with the laying on of hands. Simon the sorcerer "*saw* that through the laying on of the apostles' hands the Holy Spirit was being given" (8:18). Having the Spirit in personal relationship would not be a visible occurrence. Simon had seen Philip's miracles and was baptized (8:13), hence his interest as a former sorcerer in the miraculous occurrences that followed the intrusion of the gospel into his world. The terminology "receive the Spirit" may be the same where hands are imposed and prayers offered, but what exactly it means is not the same.

Third, there appears to be a pattern of dispensing miraculous gifts for ministry through the laying on of the apostles' hands. We have in Samaria and Ephesus a pattern reminiscent of Paul's words to the Romans: "For I long to see you that I may impart to you some spiritual gift to the end that you may be established" (1:11). Based on his usage of "spiritual gift" in I Corinthians 12-14, the statement in Romans appears to include miraculous dispensations. The apostle evidently made it his practice in confirming the believers to impart such gifts for edification and evangelism. Needless to say, if they are gifts that were imparted or given in such a manner, they are again miraculous in origin if not in nature. The only exception would be gifts of position, such as elder or deacon, in which case the imposition of hands would be ordination, or appointment to an office.

Fourth, at Ephesus Paul's very approach to the twelve disciples of John suggests that he had in mind something beyond the stated benefits of accepting the Messiah. According to the teaching of Acts 2:38 these men would already have received the Spirit in the non-miraculous sense if they had been baptized with Christian baptism. Even within Acts 19 itself it seems evident that Christian baptism by itself brings the gift of the Holy Spirit so that no additional procedure was customary or required. Not having heard whether the Spirit was given meant to Paul that these men had not been baptized in Christian baptism because he immediately questions them about their baptism when they indicate their unawareness of the Spirit's coming. Paul was not seeking to give them *the* gift of the Spirit, but to give them *a* gift of the Spirit. When he asked them whether they had "received the Spirit" when they believed, he meant, we take it, "received a miraculous measure of the Spirit." What he ended up doing was what he originally intended to do when he first met them. Therefore Acts 19 as well as Acts 8 deals with the miraculous gifts of the Spirit bestowed by a separate act rather than the *ordinary gift* of the Spirit himself bestowed at baptism.

Fifth, a view of separableness between water and Spirit baptism as standard procedure means there are two distinct baptisms. We note, however, Paul's declaration in Ephesians 4:5 that there is one baptism. His theme from 2:10 forward has been the unity of believers in Christ especially in light of the Jewish and Gentile origin of the mixed community to whom he speaks. That unity among believers shows itself in the establishment of one body of them, rather than a Jewish and a Gentile one, or rather than one for every group of people that might distinguish itself from others. One baptism applies to all these groups, and it is *one* baptism that applies to them all.

For those who see the gift of the Holy Spirit as separable from water baptism, the expression "baptism in the Holy Spirit" refers to the same thing essentially as "gift of the Holy Spirit" when applied to all Christians. If "gift" and "baptism" describe the same Holy-Spirit event, then baptism in the Spirit is separable from baptism in water. All Christians then receive two baptisms, one by promise and the other by command. If it is also standard procedure in scripture to speak of the Holy-Spirit event as "baptism" (which seems to be the view held in much current literature), and if this baptism is standard experience for all Christians, then the question must at least be raised how likely it would be for Paul to speak of *one* baptism for all Christians. We would expect him to say that there is one Lord for all, one faith for all, two baptisms for all, etc. It appears to us more natural to affirm one of two other options—either that the expression "baptism in the Holy Spirit" means something not standard experience for all Christians or that it means something in standard experience that is inseparable from the event water baptism so that Paul can include it under the one caption "baptism."

Conceivably, one might suppose that the "one baptism" of Ephesians 4:5 was itself baptism in the Holy Spirit, it being Paul's point that what Peter observed at Cornelius' house was indeed the case: the Gentiles received the same gift as the Jews did in the beginning (Acts 11:17). This interpretation is both unlikely and irrelevant. It is *irrelevant* because it does not avoid the problem raised about the one baptism. The interpretation has simply understood this "one baptism" as baptism in the Spirit, which as a distinct event leaves baptism in water to make the second baptism administered as standard practice to all Christians. That water baptism was so administered would be denied by few.

Interpreting 4:5 as baptism in the Spirit is *unlikely* because (a) the clear cases of this usage are comparatively few and are always instances when the modifying phrase "in the Spirit" accompanies the word "baptism"

(Mt. 3:11; Mk. 1:8; Lk. 3:16; Jn. 1:33; Acts 1:5; 11:16; and perhaps I Cor. 12:13). No usage of "baptism" without the accompanying phrase is indisputable, to say the least, particularly when, for reasons previously noted, virtually all lone usages must be inclusive of water baptism. (b) The close parallel between Ephesians and Colossians renders in favor of water baptism since Colossians 2:12 includes water baptism.

In the view being analyzed, we may observe that as to *time* the gift of the Spirit comes to the believer on the occasion of his faith rather than at his baptism. As to *character* the gift of the Spirit is an enabling presence that includes energizing the abilities unto Christian virtue in addition to adjusting the environment to aid and protect the believer and in addition to influencing him interpersonally.

The starting point for this first alternative interpretation of baptism has been to regard it as logically after forgiveness of sins, yet associated with forgiveness. This association is made at the visible, or outward, dimension of that identification with Christ who saves; that is, baptism in water has particularly to do with church membership. Baptism is ideally coextensive with saved people, but after the fact; similarly the visible church is ideally coextensive with the invisible church, but after it. As baptism might be only a meaningless ritual springing from a sham faith, so also membership in the visible church might not correspond with salvation. Ideally and intentionally, however, there is in this view no difference between the number in the invisible church (those really saved) and in the visible church (those viewed by men as saved), and there is no difference between the number who have saving faith and who receive baptism. Nevertheless, *baptism* and the *visible church* into which it brings a person logically follow *faith* and the *invisible church* respectively, and salvation is figured relative to true faith, which works. Baptism then is associated with salvation only insofar as it is associated first with entrance into the visible church, which is in turn coextensive with the invisible church.

As a result when it comes to church membership the difference between our view and this one is that we have placed baptism logically prior to both invisible and visible church membership. This is because we have placed it prior to salvation as well as church membership. We have felt no particular need to divide church membership into visible and invisible dimensions as regards salvation precisely because in constituency there is no intentional or *ideal* difference between them.

Although the distinction is understandable, valid, and *real*, the New Testament never teaches about baptism in terms of that distinction. Church discipline fills the gap of distinction between invisible and visible church.

The very least to be said here is that one must not construe the intended meaning of baptism in any fashion that would imply an ideal difference between invisible and visible church. That difference results from a breakdown in practical operations, not in theoretical relationships. In its best form the alternative view of baptism agrees that no ideal distinction exists. Let it be observed that salvation is never thought of in the Bible as disjoined from its visible expression so as to make room in the doctrine of baptism for a meaning that depends on that difference.

Baptism as an outward sign of an inward faith connects baptism with only the third aspect of our position because it by-passes forgiveness and the gift of the Spirit and focuses only on the outward manifestation of church membership. Baptism into the visible church is at one with outward acts not reckoned in God's salvation. Inward faith is unto salvation just as the invisible church is the group of those actually saved.

A couple of points need to be raised on baptism as primarily for church membership and therefore as an act of witness. (a) Such a meaning for baptism does not exhaust the associations with baptism in the scripture. Emphasis in the New Testament falls on a much broader range of things: riddance from sin, commitment to a new way of living, and receiving the Spirit in addition to entrance into the body. In fact, visible church membership receives the least attention of the three. (b) Such a meaning for baptism creates an unnatural division between faith and obedience, inner and outer, dynamic and formal. In New Testament thought these dimensions form one whole so that bifurcations no longer obtain that once prevailed in the degenerate Mosaism of Jesus' day.

Summary Statement

This first alternative view of baptism differs from our position in placing baptism logically after salvation. It is viewed as a necessary act of obedience that reflects outwardly a person's previous salvation; it witnesses to the world a person's identification with Jesus Christ.

271

Chapter Eighteen

TWO OTHER VIEWS OF BAPTISM

Our positive study concluded that in baptism we identify with Jesus Christ, in consequence of which identification God forgives sin, gives his Spirit, and adds to his church. Such an arrangement places baptism in water logically ahead of the benefits God dispenses. *Baptism is unto forgiveness of sins.* We felt comfortable with this flow of thought because it harmonized with our findings on the meaning of faith and works. Saving "faith" is trust in action, or non-inherent result, because faith trusts that God will regard the believer as righteous. "Works" is inherent result because the action itself produces the result—righteousness. Our present task looks at two other views of baptism that differ from the one sympathetically proposed. These two interpretations understand the meaning of baptism to be such that it may be validly administered to infants and young children who do not yet believe.

Baptism for Original Sin

The second alternative interpretation of baptism is that *baptism is unto the forgiveness of original sin.* The view can include the position we originally advocated. Baptism unto remission of sins meant for us baptism unto remission of *personal* sins. Since at least the third century, forgiveness of original sin has also been attached to this Christian ordinance. The attachment contributed to the institution and perpetuation of infant baptism because the lack of personal guilt in infants was replaced by guilt incurred through Adam's sin. So intense has been this attachment of original guilt that prenatal baptism has been practiced in the case of difficult births that might lead to the loss of unborn life.

In general we deny the doctrine of "original sin" in any sense that leads to eternal condemnation before God. Original sin means the guilt of the human race as a race. We contend that God does not give *personal* condemnation because of purely *corporate* guilt. We are not *physically* born into a *spiritual* relationship. Even as a Jew does not have standing with God because of physical descent from *Abraham,* so also none of us lack standing with God because of physical descent from *Adam.* We are not born spiritually into Adam any more than Jews were spiritually born into Abraham. What is of flesh is flesh. If we all were regarded as born into Adam who sinned, then we all are now regarded as born into Second Adam who obeyed God and replaced First Adam. We may be said to be in Adam, but in any sense that affects eternal destiny we get into him by doing as he did; we likewise get into Christ by identifying with him by faith and aspiring to do as he did. Jesus Christ is the second Adam, who replaces First Adam as appointed head of the race. Whatever we may have lost in Adam through no fault of our own we regain in Christ through no virtue of our own.

Scripture never says that baptism is for the forgiveness of original sin. Such a view is an inference based on another inference that men are guilty unto spiritual death because of Adam's sin according to passages like Romans 5:12ff. That passage teaches, however, that the spiritual life that comes from Christ's righteousness is in principle coextensive with the physical death that came from Adam's sin. As surely as a man dies physically by being a descendant of Adam he lives spiritually by being a descendant of Christ. The basis of original guilt-to-hell is not adequate; therefore it needs no refutation.

Nevertheless we may go on to say that contrary to original guilt the Bible teaches that righteousness and sinfulness have application only to the person who does them: "the wickedness of the wicked shall be upon himself" (Ezek. 18:20; Lev. 18:5; Deut. 24:16). Furthermore, there is no example of infant baptism to imply that original guilt is being forgiven—a position to be argued in the chapter on the candidate for baptism.

Often bound up with baptism for the forgiveness of original sin is the idea that the *gift of the Spirit* regenerates the recipient of baptism so he is able to believe and grow in the faith, especially when applied to infants. Regeneration means here that spiritual abilities are given to replace the hereditary inability to do righteousness. Adam's sin not only brought guilt upon all his lineage, but caused a fallen nature to be inherited by them as well. Birth has the double function of bringing each descendant of Adam into a human race alienated from God by *corporate* sin and of passing on biologically the fallen nature that leads to *personal* sin. "Baptismal regeneration" forgives any personal sin already committed as well as original sin and then serves as the occasion for receiving the Holy Spirit's enablement to obey the commandments of God. God's grace is "infused" so that within the person is an enabling power to do good.

Church membership comes to the candidate for baptism in much the same way as we affirmed before. The prominent difference lies in the possibility that such membership may extend to infants and small children as well as adults.

This second alternative view of baptism conceives of the rite as designed to rid the person from original sin.

Baptism as a Sign of Previous Grace

Positive description

The third alternative view is that *baptism is an outward sign of a logically previous inward grace;* baptism is most directly for the purpose of identifying a person with the visible Christian community. In our own view baptism has most directly to do with identifying a person with Jesus Christ unto salvation and then unto the Christian community. In the third alternative view baptism is for identification with the visible expression of an *external covenant;* in the first alternative view baptism was for identification with the outward expression of an *internal covenant.*

In its broadest sense baptism means the same in the third alternative view as it does in the first alternative view, but it ends up being different because the visible community with which baptism identifies is not so much a believers' community as a birthright community. The birthright community ideally is supposed to become identical with the believers' community. For these two views baptism must mean something different in each case, however, to allow qualifying for the covenant in the one instance on the sheer basis of birthright or ownership and in the other instance on the basis of belief. Birthright means that membership in the covenant automatically extends to offspring of present members. Ownership means that in a slavery culture bondservants qualify for membership ostensibly aside from any commitment to pertinent values and beliefs. According to the present view the New Covenant has retained much of the character of national Israel with its outward associations through the flesh.

Because of this more national character of the covenant, the only thing that necessarily precedes baptism is God's grace and that only in the logical rather than chronological sense. Logically previous means that God's grace precedes baptism only in theory, while chronologically the dispensing of that grace may occur later in time. The regenerating grace of God and whatever other gracious acts are included will come to the individual in God's own time whether during infancy, at puberty, in

274

old age, or at any point along the way. Baptism is administered in anticipation of that later dispensation of grace and subsequent faith.

If God's grace does not even chronologically precede baptism, man's subsequent faith is not chronologically before it either. Furthermore, the faith of the individual is usually conceived of as logically after baptism because according to another part of the total theological system nothing a person does has anything to do with God's saving him. The basis upon which the ordinance is administered can be simply the Christian identity of the parents. Membership in the church operates much as did citizenship in national Israel. The descendants of believers had anticipatory right to inclusion in the body; so also it is in the church.

Objections to the third alternative view

Obviously the meaning of baptism correlates with the nature of the New Covenant and with candidacy for entering it through baptism. These two considerations in turn connect up with the degree of similarity between the Old and New Covenants and between their respective signs—circumcision and baptism.

Spiritual nature of the New Covenant. We comment on the nature of the two covenants in order to make inferences about the distinctions in the meaning of their signs. Fundamentally the issue appears to be whether baptism relates more directly to salvation or to the church. We conceive of the New Covenant as a spiritual relationship that becomes visible as the church; as such it contrasts with the Old Covenant, which centered on a visible nation that was called to be spiritual. The first alternative view creates a less significant contrast than we have made between baptism and circumcision because it associates baptism with the visible church and in so doing agrees with the third alternative view.

In highlighting the contrast between the Old and New Covenants, we note first (1) *a difference between the presence of a national aspect in the covenant.* We affirm the non-political nature of the new people of God. Jesus testified at his trial before Pilate that his kingdom was not of this world or his disciples would have been fighting to keep him from being delivered to the Jews (Jn. 18:36; cp. Mt. 26:52). Thus the church was not established, perpetuated, or spread by military means. He even refused to accept the crown offered to him by Jewish patriots who wanted him to be a political Messiah (Jn. 6:15). The constituency of the church is not based on the flesh, but is figured according to promise (Rom.

275

9:8-9), and the means of reception is by faith instead of circumcision (Rom. 3:21—4:16).

The New Testament contains no provisions for geographical location, racial identity, political organization, or military operation. It is assumed throughout that the church will be like leaven permeating the societies it enters (Mt. 13:33). Its theater of operation is the uttermost parts of the world, all the peoples, every creature. The church of Jesus Christ was not established, promoted, or spread by force, but by proclamation. For these reasons it is a spiritual kingdom within us or among us (Lk. 17:20-21); it is interpersonal.

We see the political nature of the Old Covenant even in the original Abrahamic stage of it because in it God promised the patriarch a lineage and a land for the lineage (Gen. 12:1-4; 17:1-8). Later, when the progeny had multiplied to the point where final formalization could occur, God gave through Moses the law for this constitutional theocracy. In it was contained civil legislation, military provision, judicial regulation, and other matters that pertain to a political nation. This all provided a context into which Messiah would eventually come and subsequently bless all the families of the earth.

While the Old Covenant had a national element, it was not limited to national concerns. The spiritual element was present inasmuch as the ultimate purpose of establishing it was universal blessing, and the law later was annexed to the original promise as a way of defining, restraining, multiplying, and sensitizing to, transgression (Gal. 3:19; Rom. 5:20). To the father of the nation the Lord said in the confirmation of the covenant, "Walk before me and be perfect" (Gen. 17:1). Israel originally had no monarchy, but had Yahweh himself as king with natural leaders raised up among the federation of tribes as need arose (I Sam. 8).

The conjoined national and spiritual components of Israel nevertheless gave logical priority to the national element. The logical priority of the national aspect is shown in the legitimacy of (a) physical birth as a basis for induction into citizenship. *Physical descent* served as the sole and sufficient criterion for administering circumcision, which was the sign of the covenant and the citizenship token of the nation. Offspring were circumcised regardless of beliefs as made evident by the fact that they were regularly to be circumcised on the eighth day (Gen. 17:10-12). Never at any time was faith or commitment to the ideals of Israel made prerequisite to administering the covenant sign to physical descendants

276

of Abraham, *at whatever age* it may have occurred. Ishmael was thirteen when Abraham circumcised him at God's command (Gen. 17:10, 23-25; cp. Ex. 4:24-26). Similarly, at Gilgal Joshua circumcised all the Israelite males up to forty years old because the rite had been neglected during the wilderness peregrinations (Josh. 5:2-9). Ishmael's circumcision shows that it was *applicable even to those who were not of the chosen line* of descent from Abraham (Gen. 21:12; Rom. 9:7); Isaac presumably circumcised Esau as well as Jacob even though God later set Esau aside as heir (Gen. 25:23; Mal. 1:2-3; Rom. 9:13). This consideration shows that circumcision more particularly identified a person with Abraham, with whom God made the covenant, than it identified him with the covenant itself and its provisions—hence the logical priority of national over spiritual concerns in circumcision.

The logical priority of the national element is shown in the legitimacy of (b) slave ownership as a basis for induction into citizenship through circumcision. Beyond physical descent even foreign slaves bought with money were all to be circumcised (Gen. 17:12-14, 27). To buy a slave is not necessarily to convert him. Abraham—to whom this covenant sign was originally given—had enough male slaves and trained men born in his house (318 +) that he could deliver Lot from four kings and their host (Gen. 14:13-16). We wonder whether they all believed in Yahweh and had committed themselves to spiritual ends involved in some manner in the Abrahamic covenant, yet they were circumcised according to the provision. According to Exodus 12:43-51 such slaves could eat the passover along with sojourners if they were circumcised. Inasmuch as passover was a memorial of the exodus, observance of the national freedom holiday could only be appropriately observed by official members of the nation; hence, without circumcision it could not be observed, a fact that welds circumcision to the nation as such. The uncircumcised male was "cut off" from the house of Israel; that is, he had no national citizenship (Gen. 17:14). It is axiomatic that the criteria for membership correspond with the meaning of membership.

Individuals could enter national Israel by birth, and hopefully they would become part of spiritual Israel, but individuals enter the visible church at rebirth because it *is* the elect. Circumcision was first national and then spiritual while baptism is first spiritual and then "national." Circumcision was performed in terms of National Israel, which was to be spiritual Israel. Baptism is performed in terms of Jesus Christ, who

277

will build his church. Those who are being saved are the ones who are being added to the church (Acts 2:41); it is not those who are being added to the church that are being saved. The logical sequence between national and spiritual Israel is the opposite of that between visible and invisible church. National Israel ideally *produced* spiritual Israel whereas the visible church ideally *expresses* the invisible church.

We note secondly (2) *a difference in the reason for lack of congruity between visible and invisible church on the one hand vs. national and spiritual Israel on the other.* The Old Covenant exhibited a difference in the *sequence* of spiritual and national concerns as compared to the church, but ideally there was to be no difference in the *extent* of personnel between National and spiritual Israel; the Old Covenant sign was administered in terms of National Israel. Spiritual Israel was a more restricted number because the education and conversion process that was to follow admission was not always realized. Apostasy meant failure to remain personally faithful, and failure to raise up children to espouse the true religion of their parents meant that many stood under the provisions of the covenant who had no commitment to it. Circumcision into the covenant was nevertheless performed in terms of the ideal, not in terms of the practical, because the national-political part of the covenant allowed such an arrangement to be appropriate. Similarly baptism is performed in terms of the ideal that God calls on men to attain, not in terms of a breakdown of that ideal because of human sin.

Admittedly there is a difference in extent between the visible and the invisible church that can correlate with the distinction between national and spiritual Israel. That difference in both cases is not God's design, but man's deficiency. The meanings of both circumcision and baptism are contemplated with the outer circle instead of the inner circle. In our own presentation we associated baptism (a) directly with salvation, the invisible church, or the inner circle, and secondarily with the visible church. In the second alternative position baptism (b) was associated directly with the visible church, but the church was constitutionally a believers' community only. There is enough theoretical difference between the two schemes pictured below that in the one case baptism (b) can be legitimately administered irrespective of personal faith. That theoretical difference is created by the national-political element in the Abrahamic-Mosaic covenant, an element no longer part of the covenant because it has fulfilled its purpose of bringing the Messiah into the world.

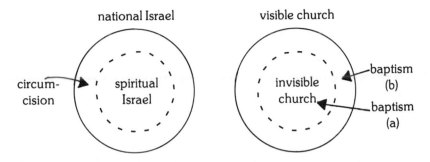

We observe that in broad outlines a loose parallel does exist between the two situations diagrammed, but the spiritual-national incongruity is accounted for differently than is the visible-invisible one. The difference in *extent* between national and spiritual Israel is accounted for by (a) not growing up to espouse the ideals of the fathers, by (b) apostasy from previous beliefs and practice, and conceivably by (c) sham claims of belief and submission to the Mosaic constitution among pagans entering Israel from the outside. The difference in *kind* is that national Israel involved military, executive, geographical, welfare, and other elements more particularly germane to a political entity.

The difference between the visible and invisible church, however, is accounted for only by (b) apostasy or (c) sham conversion. Intergenerational breakdown is eliminated. By being built simply on personal conversion, the amount of difference between the two groups is significantly reduced and then theoretically eliminated by church discipline. In the other schematic, discipline could also theoretically purge out unconverted elements, but the structure of entrance by birth renders that effort much more difficult. It is easier to maintain purity by the positive means of bringing in only those who personally espouse the system, than it is to bring in everyone by birth and then have to eradicate those who do not develop into conformity with the system. There are also additional practical problems like needing obviously negative reasons to eliminate from the body and not being sure how long to wait before expelling so as to give a person fair chance to get properly aligned. Since Israel was a theocracy, expulsion from Israel had to be for extreme reasons because it would mean loss of temporal and political privileges as well; elimination from the church does not, however, remove access to the physical necessities of life provided by the state. For these reasons

279

Jeremiah prophesied the establishment of a new covenant that would produce a pure covenant people because it was founded on personal conversion in the heart and personal knowledge of the Lord (Jer. 31:31-34).

Salvation nature of the New Covenant. Besides the added political dimension in the Abrahamic-Mosaic system, there is also the purely *righteousness character* of the Old Covenant. By contrast the New Covenant has a *salvation character.* The law did not provide for salvation from sin; it provided only for a definition of sin. Again and again the New Testament literature emphasizes the inability of the Mosaic law to obtain salvation for the sinner. In our comment on baptismal candidates we will develop further this theme that baptism into the church must mean something different from circumcision into Israel because the two covenants differ in their connection with righteousness.

A national system that was to be spiritual extends beyond one that is purely spiritual. Since national systems center on this-worldly concerns, they affect a person from birth. Since national entities have application from birth, citizenship is figured from that point on. World views, ethical systems, and value commitments can only come into the picture when a person reaches the age where he can operate in terms of such matters; hence, spiritual citizenship is figured from a later point in life. Because baptism brings us into the church, which is a spiritual nation, it cannot have the meaning and purpose an external rite would have. Therefore baptism cannot be an outward sign of a previous inward grace based on physical descent.

Adult character of New-Covenant membership. Another theme to be addressed specifically under candidacy for baptism is the observation that New Testament examples of baptism are uniformly with adults while Old Testament circumcisions are almost always with infants. While solutions of different kinds have been set forward to explain this phenomenon, we find it striking, to say the least, that baptism should mean the same thing as circumcision when the two rites are not performed on the same subjects according to the examples and teaching material applicable to each ordinance. God's inauguration of circumcision clearly sets forth its application to infants and slaves (Gen. 17:9-14), but neither the inaugural proclamation of baptism nor any other command regarding its administration ever specifies infants as its objects.

Contrast with experience. If the church and Israel are of the same general sort, then in the third alternative view of baptism the assumption must be that all the offspring of elect men and women are themselves also elect. Some interpreters see baptism as the sign of an external covenant because the children of believers *are* regenerate. Their present condition is that of being enabled to grow into Christian manhood. Against this idea we place the clear evidence of experience that children of believers do not always grow into Christian faith and righteousness. Even in scripture itself men like Esau, the sons of Eli, and Absalom grew up from presumably regenerate seed, but did not grow up to faith. Samuel's sons were wicked (I Sam. 8:1-4) and Ishmael was not elect seed.

Others see baptism as the sign of an external covenant because the offspring are *presumptively* regenerate at the time, but may be given that grace at a later time. The faith of sponsors, parents, or the church serves as the interim basis for administering the ordinance. The same examples from scripture and experience still apply. As based on future obedience to the gospel, there seems to be little more reason to suppose such regeneration for the offspring of believers than for offspring of non-believers.

Still others speak of baptism granted to children of believers because they are *conditionally* regenerate. The legitimacy of present administration is conditioned on the child's own future faith, whose coming depends on Christian nurture in the home. But such an arrangement means that earthly circumstance can frustrate the will of God, a position rejected elsewhere in the theology of these same thinkers.

Included in this view of baptism is usually the idea that God elects unconditionally those whom he enables to believe the gospel and live Christian lives without apostasy. The rite is performed on those whom God calls upon to do what their believing parents have done, even though the offspring may not be able to do them because of depravity. He nevertheless calls upon them to do these things because he delights in the obediences commanded. Others whom he elects from outside the hereditary Christian community will receive the sign of the covenant in consequence of personal belief and in consequence of his unconditionally choosing them and enabling them to believe. Even here an unspecified number of spurious conversions, it is often admitted, will come to light as evidenced by failure to persevere to the end. Since his selection is totally unrelated to any virtue or response in the elect, there cannot be any close correlation between salvation and Christian baptism.

However we seek to work out in theory the connection between birthright baptism and salvation by faith, experience blocks the way to the conviction that a uniformity obtains on the regenerate condition of Christian offspring.

Summary

Forgiveness, the gift of the Spirit, and church membership we have placed logically after baptism. In the present interpretation baptism relates most directly to church membership, and church membership correlates with salvation and the gift of the Spirit in a theoretical way though evidently not in a practical way. The real problem for this view comes in finding a way to bridge the gap between the theory of baptism and the practice of administering it to infants without becoming inconsistent with other teachings of scripture, with other parts of the theological system, or with current experience.

Most of what is affirmed in the "theology of baptism" is the same between the third and the first alternative views, but the practice of infant baptism seems to belie the theology advanced for this ordinance. In general the answer has been to appeal to parallels with the Abrahamic-Mosaic covenant and with circumcision that was the sign of that covenant. Therefore in rebuttal it is important to see the difference in the principles on which the two covenants operate, the one being primarily a political covenant unto righteousness and the other being primarily a spiritual covenant unto salvation. These considerations affect the meaning of their initiatory ordinances as well as the candidates on whom the rites are performed.

The three primary views of water baptism may be represented by the accompanying diagram, which shows the relationship of faith and baptism to the logical point when God dispenses salvation from above. All three views of baptism ideally have the same components in the total situation, but the logical relationships between them differ considerably.

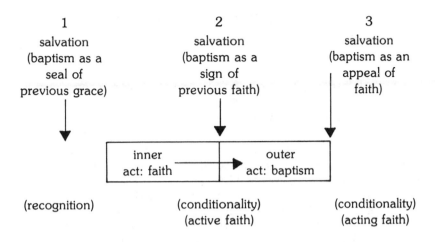

1	2	3
salvation (baptism as a seal of previous grace)	salvation (baptism as a sign of previous faith)	salvation (baptism as an appeal of faith)

inner act: faith	outer act: baptism

(recognition)   (conditionality) (active faith)   (conditionality) (acting faith)

In our own positive statement we have presented baptism as part of the cluster of human responses unto initial salvation. Salvation significance is attached to the cluster level of human response so that emotion,

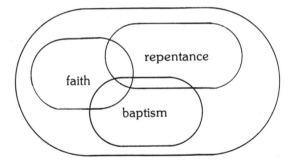

mind, volition, and act equally contribute to the condition for justification. Having baptism occur at a separate time from faith and repentance makes it a less dynamic act, thus leading to ritualism. All the pieces may be present when laid out on an assembly line, but they do not form a car. Parceling up the salvation cluster likewise tends to destroy the functional power of the conversion experience. Baptism ought not be conceptually or chronologically wrenched from its natural setting in this cluster either by delayed baptism or paedobaptism. But this observation involves candidacy for baptism, the subject to which we must now turn.

283

Chapter Nineteen

THE CANDIDATE FOR BAPTISM

Introduction

Curiously baptism has been the focal point of more controversy in the history of the church than one might have supposed. A little reflection, however, will show why so much dissension has surrounded it. Baptism is something to be done, not just something to be understood. An act of obedience cannot easily be left in a state of suspended judgment; something has to be done about it, yet what is done reflects previous decisions about several doctrinal issues.

Theory and understanding surface in the design, or meaning, of baptism because what the rite can mean follows from how one sees the *nature of faith and works in salvation.* Later we will see how the *nature of the church* has implications for who may serve as appropriate administrators. Even the *nature of the trinity* comes into the picture in the controversy about the formula for baptism and about the form of baptism known as triune baptism. The *nature of salvation* comes to the fore in the study of the candidate for baptism in this chapter. All this points up the fact that no clear separation can be made between theory and practice in salvation any more than anywhere else if action is ultimately affected by understanding.

Although other matters could be handled under candidacy for baptism, infant baptism vs. believers' baptism occupies the attention of this chapter. On candidacy for baptism primarily two positions have been maintained: (1) believers' baptism, in which only adults are baptized, and (2) baptism as applicable to believers as well as children of believers. Infant baptism, or "paedobaptism," allows for the baptism of those who have not reached the age of reason, or the age of accountability, when a young person not only understands what salvation entails, but can see the consequences of moral behavior. The following study sketches in ascending order of strength the reasons for believers' baptism and then responds to several points raised in favor of the alternate position.

Believers' Baptism

Uniform precedent for believers' baptism

In all New Testament examples Christian baptism is administered only to adult believers. To put it negatively, no apostolic precedent exists for performing baptism on those who are too young to appreciate the meaning of salvation and the need for it. While sheer silence is not always decisive, a couple of observations make the generalization significant.

Mass conversions. Mass conversions were irrespective of infants. Although men, women, and children are mentioned on occasions where groups of people were present (Josh. 6:21; 8:35; II Chron. 20:13; Jer. 40:7; Mt. 14:21; 15:38; Acts 21:5), general statements on mass baptisms always include men and women only (Acts 5:14; 8:12; 17:4; cp. 8:3; 22:4). Descriptions of the candidates for both Jesus' and John's baptisms show that only adults participated: "those that received the word were baptized" (Acts 2:41); they all *believed*, had all things in common, *sold possessions, worshiped,* and *fellowshiped* daily (2:43-47). "Believers were the more added to the Lord" (5:14; cp. 17:4). The disciples of John were baptized, *confessing* their sins (Mt. 3:6; Mk. 1:5). His baptism was a baptism of *repentance* unto remission of sins (Mt. 3:2; Mk. 1:4; Lk. 3:3; Acts 13:24; 19:4), and he commanded the converts to *bring forth fruits* worthy of repentance (Lk. 3:8-14). John's audience was comprised of the same kind of people as that of Messiah: "I indeed baptize you in water unto repentance, but . . . he will baptize you in the Holy Spirit . . ." (Mt. 3:11). Candidates for John's baptism and Christian baptism were never carried; they always came. In every case the behavior exhibited and required pertained to adults. Parents brought children to Jesus for blessing (Mt. 19:13-15; Mk. 10:13-16; Lk. 18:15-17), but there is no indication that they ever brought them to him, to John the Baptist, or to any of the apostles for baptism.

Household baptisms. Household baptisms also operated irrespective of infants. At least five household baptisms are recorded in the New Testament: the households of Cornelius (Acts 10:44-48; 11:12-18), Lydia (Acts 16:13-15), the Philippian jailor (Acts 16:27-34), Crispus (Acts 18:8, cp. I Cor. 1:14), and Stephanas (I Cor. 1:16; cp. 16:15, 17). At least one of these households surely had a young child in it especially since the households were most likely extended families instead of nuclear ones. A nuclear family has only the parents and children, but an extended family may have grandparents as well as the parents' brothers or sisters with their children. At least some of the New Testament household baptisms additionally involved slaves with their families, which increases even more the probability of young children in them. The presence of children related to the group around Cornelius deserves special emphasis because beyond *slaves* and *kinsmen* there were even close *friends* in this first Gentile audience for the gospel (Acts 10:24).

Not all the household conversions are described with precision, but in most the descriptions are sufficiently precise to preclude children from involvement. In the conversion of *Cornelius' house* the account says that he feared God with all his house (Acts 10:2); that he met with his kinsmen and close friends (24) to hear what God commanded Peter (33); that the Holy Spirit fell on all these hearers (44) so that they spoke with tongues and glorified God (46). Those who received the Holy Spirit were the ones that were baptized (48) and were believers (11:15, 17).

Not much pertinent to our question is said about the conversion of *Lydia's house.* She was evidently not married, but was the head of a home and a business. Paul and Silas went there after release from jail to comfort the brethren in that house as well as others. In the same city the *Philippian jailor's house* was baptized, but those baptized had heard the preaching of Paul and rejoiced greatly (Acts 16:32-34). The *household of Crispus* believed (Acts 18:8). Paul baptized the *household of Stephanas* (I Cor. 1:16), but not long afterward Paul says his household set themselves to minister to the saints (I Cor. 16:15). Thus in every case except the household of Lydia the description of the conversion contains matters not applicable to infants so that they are eliminated from consideration in the record.

Since clearly described household conversions exempt whatever children were in the households, we conclude that in the unclear conversions the same situation obtained. The central consideration here is a matter of language custom. Aside from Christian conversions we find "house" used for situations where not every last person or child is in mind when the word is used. When Jesus healed from afar the nobleman's son (Jn. 4:46-53), the text says that the nobleman "believed and his whole house" (53), regardless of the age of the "child" (*pais*). Samuel's father is said to have gone up to offer yearly sacrifice with "all his house" despite the fact that Hannah and Samuel stayed behind (I Sam. 1:21-22). King David fled from Absalom with "all his house," yet ten concubines remained to take care of the palace (II Sam. 15:15-16). The household idiom appears in Titus 1:11, where Paul exhorts Titus to stop the mouths of gainsayers who were overthrowing whole households by teaching for money things they ought not. Comments

286

like these are made because the leadership of the household or the majority of the house or this house in contrast to other households is under consideration. Certain individuals within the house may not be in the speaker's mind. In the case of household conversions infants are specially eliminated from the matter by description, which has the force of drawing attention to their absence from the proceedings.

The inference is that, although there were children in these households, they were not contemplated in the conversions and furthermore that baptism does not mean something applicable to them because it was not done to them. Household conversions become significant witnesses for adult baptism exclusively, because they are occasions where children are present but are passed over in the call to salvation and baptism. The first reason for not practicing infant baptism is that *there is no apostolic precedent for infant baptism.*

Adult nature of baptism prerequisites

In the previous paragraphs attention was focused on believing, repenting, confessing, fellowshiping, and producing fruit by those who were baptized. We took these actions as indicative of adult behavior with the inference that very young children and infants did not naturally belong to the matters that transpired in the *examples of baptism.*

In the epistles and elsewhere *teaching about baptism* likewise consistently relates to a changed life under grace (Rom. 6:1-14; Col. 2:8—3:17; Gal. 3:22-29; I Cor. 1:10-17); one or more associate acts like faith, repentance, confession (Acts 2:38); or what Peter calls "the appeal of a good conscience toward God" (I Pet. 3:21). John's baptism was so clearly aligned with these factors that it was designated a "baptism of repentance unto remission of sins" (Mk. 1:4; Lk. 3:3; Acts 19:4). In scripture baptism always relates to the dynamic and behavioral aspects of the Christian life.

Baptism does not therefore consist in the physical act itself, but in the physical act within the context of dynamic factors. Without them it is not baptism. At best it is only a putting away of the filth of the flesh (I Pet. 3:21) rather than something pertaining to the cleansing of the filth of the spirit. Baptism stands between a person's two ways of living. As a result the second reason for not practicing infant baptism is that *there is no possibility of doing infant baptism.*

Salvation nature of the New Covenant

Infant baptism, of course, stands alternative to the baptism of believers only. Any meaningful presentation of the latter must occur in this light. Anticipating later particulars of positive arguments, we summarize here the two main conceptual bases that underlie approaches by different religious groups to the defense of infant baptism: (1) the concept of corporate guilt, federal guilt, original guilt, or "inherited" guilt and (2) the righteousness character of the New Covenant. Inherited guilt, etc., contrasts with personal guilt and righteousness covenant contrasts with salvation covenant. A righteousness covenant *defines righteousness* without providing any real solution for correcting unrighteousness. Such was the Mosaic covenant. The Messianic covenant is a salvation covenant inasmuch as it *gives righteousness.*

Priority of guilt. As was argued in the chapter on the significance of baptism, the act is described in the New Testament as a pledge to right-eousness only insofar as it is also a death to sin. If it is a death to sin it must succeed sin. Death to sin could only succeed one's own or someone else's sin. Two things are then evident: (a) at the federal level if inherited sin is denied, as we have done in these pages, then baptism for infants is inappropriate.

(b) At the personal level if personal sin is not reckoned against our record until we understand the commandment, then infant baptism is again inappropriate. That infant sin or guilt is not reckoned as sin is inferred from Romans 7:9: "I was alive apart from the law once, but when the commandment came, sin came to life, and I died." Like Paul we all were personally alive apart from the law at one time, but when we became aware of the commandment we died. This process must take place before "salvation" can be a relevant concept and thus before baptism as a condition to salvation can be a relevant act. Jesus may also imply the safety of children when he says, ". . . in heaven their angels do always behold the face of God" (Mt. 18:10). Before Adam sinned there was nothing required of him or practiced by him that concerned salvation. Sacrificial offerings began afterwards. David said that his dead son could not come to him, but he could go to his son (II Sam. 12:23). If salvation is the nature of the New Covenant, then either inherited or personal guilt must precede entrance into it. Inherited guilt is denied and personal guilt is not reckoned until "the command-ment comes"; therefore infant baptism is doubly inappropriate.

Salvation character of the New Covenant. There is nothing clearer about the New Covenant than its salvation character. In prophecy Jeremiah closed his description of the future covenant with the statement, "I will forgive their iniquity and I will remember their sin no more" (Jer. 31:34; cp. Heb. 8:7 13). The New Covenant has a priest who can really intercede for sinners (Heb. 4:15—8:6) and a sacrifice that can really substitute for sinners (Heb. 9:1—10:18). Although the Mosaic covenant was perfect (Rom. 7:7-12), only the Messianic covenant could *make* perfect (Heb. 7:19, 11; 9:9; 10:1; Acts 13:39; Rom. 3:20; Gal. 2:16; 3:21).

In varying respects baptism is analogous to birth, death-resurrection, cleansing, circumcision, pledge, and initiation; but relative to the prophecy of Jeremiah it is the sign of a new covenant. As such its meaning corresponds to what that covenant signifies. It is a salvation covenant; its sign pertains to forgiveness of sins. If one man does not die for another's sin (Ezek. 18:19-20) and if sins of ignorance are not reckoned against a person (Rom. 7:9), then baptism is irrelevant to little children because no sin has been imputed to them either from themselves or from others. A salvation covenant and its sign have no relevance to those who have no sin. The third reason for not practicing infant baptism is that *there is no need for infant baptism.*

Infant Baptism

The objections to infant baptism above were that there is no *example* of it, no *possibility* of it, and no *need* for it. The positive bases for it are organized below under these same headings.

Examples of paedobaptism
New Testament examples. We objected first to infant baptism because there are no New Testament examples of it. In defense of paedobaptism the lack of examples is handled by three kinds of evidence. The first kind comes from New Testament examples that imply infant baptism. Sympathetic presentations have traditionally included (1) *household baptisms* in the positive evidence for paedobaptism. Earlier we argued that the admittedly strong likelihood of young children in these households in fact negated their inclusion in the baptisms because of the way the candidates themselves are described in all clear cases. There is no

difference in these descriptions whether the household was Gentile (Cornelius) or Jewish (Lydia, Crispus, Stephanas), or whether it was in Palestine (Acts 5:14; 8:12) or elsewhere (Acts 17:4).

Households in scripture are described as doing many things. Besides being baptized, being saved, and receiving mercy (II Tim. 1:16), they are said to believe (Jn. 4:53; Acts 18:8), receive greetings (Mt. 10:12; Phil. 4:22; II Tim. 4:19; cp. Rom. 16:10, 11), not honor prophets (Mt. 13:57; Mk. 6:4), trust in the Lord (Ps. 115:10), put away false idols (Gen. 35:2), be judged (Ezek. 33:20), and to be worthy (Mt. 10:12ff.). Because the presence of children is not necessarily involved in the word "household," Paul commands that deacons be "husbands of one wife, ruling their children and their own houses well" (I Tim. 3:12). In consideration of households in scripture, we must remember that we are dealing with a word, not with a reality so that the real question is how the word is being used. Instead of viewing "house" as necessarily *inclusive of infants* on the principle of solidarity, it appears more natural to view it as often *irrespective of infants* or slaves on the principle of general reference since these are not necessary components of a household.

We have considered the descriptions of the candidates' actions to be a more explicit indication of who was involved than the usage of the word "house." Clear examples occur in which "house" included the children of the home, but in each case what transpired was such as could involve them. "Every male among the men of Abraham's house" was circumcised, even the infants eight days old (Gen. 17:12, 23). Saul threatened to annihilate Ahimelech and all his father's house, which he did to the point of killing the children and sucklings (I Sam. 22:19). Pharaoh permitted the households of Joseph's brothers to come to Goshen (Gen. 45:18-20), which they did "with their little ones" (46:5). In Joshua 5:8 it says, "And it came to pass when they had finished circumcising all the nation that they stayed in their places in the camp until they were healed up." We know from the nature of the case that all the nation does not mean everyone, but only the males; therefore we do not argue from an expression like "all his house" that it means infants and all, but only the believers. The provision for baptism in Acts 2:38-39 contrasts noticeably with the provision for circumcision in Genesis 17:7-14, where the rite was specifically described in infant terms. Context and the nature of the case adjust the general usage of words so that meanings are not static regardless of the subject under discussion.

The absence of infant baptism in the New Testament is sometimes explained by saying that the first century was a *missionary situation*. Adults received more attention because they were the ones to whom the gospel was proclaimed, and the children did not get the attention they would receive in a continuation situation. We doubt that this point, though plausible, accounts for accompanying descriptive elements in the records and the contrasts seen in accounts of non-conversion events where children are mentioned.

Another argument from the New Testament has been taken from (2) Acts 2:39: "For the promise is to you and to your children [*teknois*] and to all that are afar off—as many as the Lord our God will call to him." While paedobaptists have taken "children" to mean the young ones now in your homes, we take it to mean descendants as it does in Luke 3:8, "For I say to you that God is able to raise up offspring [*tekna*] to Abraham from these stones." Even if it means particularly your immediate offspring, it does not have to mean at the age they are now; besides, these offspring God calls, an act inapplicable to infants.

Countering the meaning "descendants" is the contention of many that the first-generation church expected an immediate return of Christ and therefore Peter could not have meant descendants. Implicitly such a view does not agree that inspiration protected the apostles from error in their preaching and writing because Christ did not come within a generation or so unless one says he came dispensationally at A.D. 70 with the formal end of the Jewish state and religion. Paul knew there would be at least a period of apostasy and the appearance of the "man of sin" before the end was to come (II Th. 2:1-12).

(3) *Mark 10:13-16* parallels Luke 18:15-17 and Matthew 19:13-15, where Jesus tells his disciples to let the little children come to him because of such is the kingdom of heaven. Although a passage consistently urged in favor of infant baptism, the text is talking about coming to Jesus for blessing, not for baptism. Furthermore, if the kingdom of heaven is made up of such as these, they have no need to be brought into the kingdom through the initiatory sign of a salvation covenant. The point is not that if they are in the kingdom they have a right to the sign of the kingdom because then all infants and young children are liable to baptism, a point most paedobaptists would not grant.

In this last episode we refrain from making the further objection that Jesus says, "Let them *come*" in contrast to "let them be *carried*." By

291

such comments one commits himself to the validity of baptizing all these children despite their being small enough for him to pick up in his arms. Those who came probably differed considerably in their age and level of awareness of Jesus, but they were not coming to him in a spiritual sense.

Ancient-church examples. A second class of evidence under example is that of the ancient church. We concluded above that apostolic precedent does not include baptism of infants. No denial is made, however, that subsequent to the apostolic age baptism was administered to newborn children from the end of the second century onward. But a prior commitment makes that fact irrelevant because (a) this study allows *tradition* only a confirmatory role in Christian theology. *Sola scriptura* means that "scripture alone" has authority over the human conscience. Practices subsequent to the apostolic era are examples of what was done, but not necessarily precedents for what should be done.

This approach also (b) denies *apostolic succession.* The original apostles were not succeeded by others who took over their offices and perpetuated their authority on earth. James was not replaced after his martyrdom (Acts 12:1-2). Scripture has apostolicity as one of its necessary defining marks; consequently, if apostles had no successors, scripture is not continually being made and precedent is not continuously being set. Scripture becomes the continuing apostolic authority in the life of the church (I Tim. 4:1-6; II Tim. 4:1-8; II Pet. 1:12-21; 3:1-2; Jude 17). Customs not found in scripture have therefore no apostolic authority even if they happen not necessarily to contradict the pronouncements of the New Testament on matters of faith and practice. Our contention is that infant baptism does not fall in the realm of opinion, but stands in contrast to New Testament teaching about baptism.

No final weight is attached to later usages because they do not have approved precedent, that is, apostolic approval. This final authority rests in the *canonical literature* of the New Testament as distinguished from *popular practices* even within the apostolic age itself. While Christ's duly appointed witnesses were still present, aberrant practices and teaching began showing up in various issues. How much more so when their correcting hand no longer directly guided and disciplined the saints. The written word they left behind was intended to serve as the equivalent of their presence, but it was not entirely heeded. Soon afterward, perhaps under the influence of Jewish proselyte baptism as well as pagan rites, impertinent matters in baptism like the temperature

292

of the water, whether it was running or still, whether the candidate was clothed, drinking the baptismal water, and the like crept into the Christian observance. Misunderstanding of salvation led to delaying baptism as long as possible in order to minimize the accumulation of post-baptismal sin that might sever a person from Christ.

We also do not deny that pouring water on the head was substituted for baptism by A.D. 125 or earlier. Whether during or after the apostles' ministry, however, these aberrations were not commanded by them according to the only reliable source of information we have—the New Testament itself. We must go on what the apostles taught more than on what the populace practiced.

Proselyte-baptism examples. The third class of evidence from examples is Jewish proselyte baptism. Proselyte baptism grew out of the Old Testament ceremonial washings, but was not specifically enjoined in the Mosaic legislation. Since the first quarter of the twentieth century, many writers on Jewish baptism have concluded for its pre-Christian origin during the last century B.C. and have drawn attention to the developmental sequence through John's baptism to Christian baptism. Since even the terminology and imagery associated with the practice resemble Christian usage, the inference has been that proselyte baptism renders in favor of paedobaptism because young children and babies of proselytes received the ceremonial bath along with their parents.

The propriety of bringing Jewish proselyte baptism into this question is not particularly affected by the question of its pre- or post-Christian origin. If Christian baptism developed from it or if it developed from Christian baptism, whatever parallels exist between them issue in equally valid or invalid inferences. The crucial point is the difference between the covenants into which the two initiatory rites bring the candidates. First, the Christian covenant is a *salvation covenant* while the Mosaic covenant was a *righteousness covenant*; the law defined righteousness, but it did not grant righteousness. Proselyte baptism as part of the induction into Mosaism was administered according to the same guidelines as circumcision. The objections to be raised later against arguing for paedobaptism from circumcision also apply here to proselyte baptism.

Secondly, the Mosaic covenant was a jointly religious-political system while the Messianic covenant is a purely *religious system*. It is only natural that the national-citizenship aspect of the Old Covenant would affect naturalization in the direction of infant inclusion since political

293

nations and racial identity include flesh-based considerations and impersonal elements in the system. The church lacks these dimensions.

We are persuaded that proselyte baptism was administered to minors because it developed out of the Old Testament lustrations (ceremonial washings) and followed the principles operative in circumcision during the Mosaic era. In turn, neither circumcision nor proselyte baptism would have been performed on minors had it not been for the national, racial, legal, and political elements that Mosaism incorporated above and beyond purely spiritual concerns. Proselyte baptism's striking terminology parallels with Christian baptism—such as death and resurrection, renewal, re-creation, new birth—were true of the spiritual concern in the law, although such language is not used of infants and minors in proselyte baptisms. Jewish proselyte baptisms cannot therefore serve as substitutes for the lack of Christian infant baptisms in the New Testament.

Thirdly, proselyte baptism and Christian baptism were administered to different candidates. Proselyte baptism was performed on non-Jews, but Christian baptism was performed on Jews as well. Developing as it did out of John's baptism, Christian baptism applied to those who could claim Abraham as their physical father. Proselyte baptism of infants was only in the case of those born before their parents' conversion; those born after the parents' conversion were not baptized, but these are precisely and only the ones paedobaptists allow should be baptized. Clearly, proselyte baptism was for induction into national Israel, not for granting a seal to those already in spiritual Israel.

Fourthly, baptized infants who later failed to accept Mosaism personally were regarded as never having been Israelites in the first place.

Possibility of paedobaptism

Family solidarity. We objected secondly to infant baptism because infants cannot do the naturally accompanying actions that make "getting wet" into being baptized. As a first response to this consideration paedobaptists have invoked the principle of "family solidarity." Under this concept the family operates as a unit in faith and baptism. The idea is that a child has the right to the sign of the covenant if he is the offspring of at least one believing parent. One of the more significant passages used in this connection is I Corinthians 7:14: "The unbelieving husband is sanctified in the wife, and the unbelieving wife is sanctified in the brother; otherwise your children would be unclean, but now they are holy." Paul tells the Philippian jailor that if he believes on the Lord Jesus he will be saved and his house (Acts 16:31; cp. 11:14). Jesus said of Zacchaeus, "Today salvation came to this house because *he* is also the son of Abraham" (Lk. 19:9). Family solidarity unto condemnation instead of salvation is also argued from the negative side on the basis of examples like that of Achan in Joshua 7.

The concept involved is comparable to receiving national citizenship. A child born to citizens is automatically a citizen. He has a right to the documents or signs of citizenship that are customary. As he grows up he is taught the values of the society and has the privilege of participating in the processes of the culture. His citizenship continues until such time as he should renounce it by declaration or deed. An alien, however, does not have this privilege of identification. He must consciously accept and commit himself to whatever principles of social intercourse and political process are defined, required, and protected by the nation's constitution. Thus the process is adult in character, requiring activities of which only grownups are capable during the period leading to naturalization as well as in the person's subsequent life as a citizen. He may previously participate in certain aspects of the nation's blessings such as having a job, police protection, or interaction with the members of the nation; but he does not have the status of a citizen so as to vote or participate in public office until after he receives his citizenship papers.

Paedobaptists envision a similar procedure for baptism. A child born to parents who are in the kingdom of God is automatically a Christian. He has a right to baptism as a sign and seal of that citizenship. As he grows up he is nurtured within the church by his parents, godparents, and the believing community around him. His church membership continues until he renounces his faith and is cut out of the olive tree (Rom. 11:20-24). But a child not born of Christian parents must, like the alien, consciously accept the teachings, values, and practices of the kingdom, which means that baptism necessarily becomes a grown-up response preceded and succeeded by behavior appropriate to it. As with naturalization the formal initiation of a candidate is preceded by the catechumenate during which time the candidate receives instruction in the doctrines and usages of the church. An "alien" may participate in certain blessings of the church like study and worship, but he does not have the status of citizen so as to be admitted to holy communion or to hold office in the church until after his baptism.

Baptism-circumcision parallel. As a second response to the impossibility of infant baptism, paedobaptists have invoked the parallel between baptism and circumcision. They see Paul himself correlating the two in Colossians 2:11-12: ". . . in [Christ] you were also circumcised with a circumcision not made with hands in the putting off of the body of the flesh in the circumcision of Christ, having been buried with him in baptism, wherein you were also raised with him through faith in the working of God, who raised him from the dead" (cp. Rom. 2:29).

Since Paul makes the two parallel, baptism is viewed as a replacement of the former sign of the covenant. That former sign encompassed infants of Jewish citizens irrespective of the fact that the children could not assert or verbalize their acceptance and commitment to the law; consequently, baptism is also to be administered legitimately on the basis of the identity of parents already in the kingdom. It serves to identify the child with the Christian community.

Proselyte-baptism analogy. As a third response to the impossibility of infant baptism paedobaptists have invoked the parallel between Christian baptism and Jewish proselyte baptism, which is really an extension of the principles governing circumcision.

Surrogate faith. As a fourth response paedobaptists have invoked the faith of the parents, the sponsors, or the church as a substitute for that of the infant. The appropriateness of such a concept again depends on the preceding notions of family solidarity and the parallel of baptism with circumcision and proselyte baptism. Fundamental to all four of these responses is a distinction between the covenants and so that distinction must be examined carefully.

Infant faith. As a fifth response some paedobaptists have argued for the reality of infant faith. According to this view the infant or little child hears and believes the gospel by the enablement of the Holy Spirit. He is engendered with an incipient faith that is like a seed germinated in the soul. It is not claimed necessarily that scripture indicates such a thing does happen, but it comes as a systematic inference derived from prior conclusions associated with infant baptism. Some passages have been used to confirm infant faith as when Elizabeth said that her unborn child leaped for joy at the sound of Mary's salutation (Lk. 1:44; cp. Mt. 19:14; Mk. 10:14; Lk. 18:16).

Anticipated faith. A final way of bringing faith into the structure of infant baptism is to validate the baptism in anticipation of the future faith. Not the infant's faith or someone else's faith, but the infant's future faith will be applied retroactively to the sign of the covenant. The validity of the present enactment is conditioned on future faith.

Responses to p. uedobaptist evidence

Distinction of covenants. Our fundamental objection to the first four arguments for infant baptism is that *they misconceive the nature of the New Covenant* by failing to subtract from the Mosaic covenant the political element that goes beyond the spiritual concerns of the law and by failing to subtract the fleshly foundation of the Abrahamic promise of a land and lineage through whom the world would be blessed on account of his faithfulness. The nature of the covenant also precedes considerations about New Testament examples because the involvement of children could be inferred from household baptisms, for instance, only if some more preliminary insight created a presumption in favor of including them since they are not specifically mentioned.

The Old Covenant was something with which a person was identified because of physical or legal descent from righteous Abraham, the ancestor of the family. It may be looked upon as having two stages. In its *first stage* it was a land and lineage blessing covenant. According to Genesis 17 the institution of circumcision signified God's covenant to provide Abraham a lineage when he as yet had no child, to give him a land when he as yet was only a sojourner in Palestine, and to bless all the families of the earth when at this point Abraham was not even prominent among them.

To Abraham himself Paul says circumcision was a seal of righteousness by faith which he had in uncircumcision (Rom. 4:9-12) and indicated that God would count him rather than someone else as the father of all who have faith whether circumcised or not. It was not a salvation covenant but a blessing covenant, nor was the covenant at this stage even predicated on the condition of righteousness. The only righteousness discussed was a righteousness Abraham himself had prior to the sign and seal of it (Gal. 3; Rom. 4).

To the descendants of Abraham the seal of circumcision was indiscriminately administered at birth or thereafter aside from personal righteousness, the only qualification being legal inclusion under Abraham. The primary form of this inclusion was physical birth as in the case of Ishmael and Isaac; a second form was servitude in his household, as in the case of "all males in his house" born or bought (Gen. 17:12-13, 27). Circumcision could be a "seal of righteousness" for them only indirectly by marking them as descendants of someone who was righteous and by indicating them as the people through whom the blessings of righteousness would come to the whole world (eventually through the Messiah). By this rite the offspring were recipients in trust of the land God promised to Abraham. No eternal and spiritual relationship to God was bestowed by virtue of this ritual.

There is nothing clearer in the New Testament, however, than the fact that circumcision for physical identification with the father of the race was indecisive, yes irrelevant, to spiritual identification with him. John the Baptist cried, "Do not think to say in yourselves, 'We have Abraham as our father,' for I tell you that God is able to raise up children to Abraham from these stones" (Mt. 3:9; cp. Rom. 9:7-8; 11:17, 20-21). Jesus did not object to the Pharisees' calling themselves sons of Abraham in a physical sense marked by circumcision, but he would not allow them to call themselves sons of Abraham in a spiritual sense because that matter was figured in terms of their actions (Jn. 8:39-40) as was their sonship to God (8:41-44). As with Adam so with Abraham; one does not get into Abraham by birth, but by the behavior of faith. Not passive birth or racial distinction, but active repentance and keeping the commandments of God have importance unto salvation.

There is also nothing clearer than the fact that baptism is the sign of a covenant that brings salvation itself, not temporal privilege or identification with a race of people. Baptism is not a seal of righteousness only to mark a people now through whom righteousness is yet to come. The church is not a flesh-based Israel; it is the body of Christ; it is saved people—a spiritual Israel. It is the kingdom of heaven, not a kingdom of this world.

In its *second stage* the Old Covenant elaborated through Moses formalized a nation and codified in the form of law the definition of righteousness. Circumcision here added the dimensions of formal national citizenship and commitment to the moral, civil, and ceremonial constitution of the theocracy. Circumcision thus obligated a person to righteousness as brought about by works, that is, by keeping the law. Paul for this reason objected strenuously and unyieldingly to circumcising Gentiles, not because circumcision *was a work*, but because circumcision *committed a person to works* by binding him to the law and hence to the righteousness that comes by having to keep it perfectly.

298

Since the covenant was now elaborated in connection with a political nation and its constitution, a child was identified by birth with the ethic of the nation as a baby is in any constitutional nation. He had no choice whether he would be subject to the law of his country. Circumcision became the person's citizenship papers. Without it he was "cut off" from his people, that is, he lost his citizenship (Gen. 17:14). It identified him *with* the righteousness requirement, but not *unto* the righteousness possession. It put him under the perfection requirement instead of delivering him from the imperfection state. Even after identification with the covenant the law had no real provision for salvation from subsequent imperfections so that the formal means by which a person came under the law could not carry the same meaning as baptism, which identifies us with the Perfect One, whose blood continues to cleanse us from all sin (I Jn. 1:7).

As far as this second stage of the covenant was concerned, the law as a way of having righteousness, and physical birth, as a basis for identification with righteousness, were intended only to be temporary measures; for children often depart from the way of their forebears. God added the Mosaic law to the Abrahamic covenant as a righteousness definer (Gal. 3:19) until the Messiah should come as righteousness giver.

Neither the Abrahamic covenant itself nor the Mosaic law built on top of it was unto personal righteousness from unrighteousness. The Abrahamic covenant was not unto righteousness, but unto the bringing about of the basis for it in the Seed (Gal. 3:16). The Mosaic covenant was not unto righteousness, but unto the definition of it. Accordingly, the law anticipated its own abrogation (Heb. 5-10) notably through Jeremiah 31:31-34 (cp. Deut. 18:15 perhaps). God promised to establish a different kind of covenant that would not produce a mixed community, some of whom knew the Lord, others of whom did not, and all of whom had their sins remembered against them.

We say that God committed himself to a new "kind" of covenant in Jeremiah because things were to be different under it in two important respects for our subject: (a) all would know the Lord and (b) their sins would be forgiven. A *birthright covenant* inevitably yields an impure society. The New Covenant helps to avoid that weakness because everyone knows the Lord under it. If everyone knows the Lord in the New Covenant, it must be necessary to know him to get into it; therefore it must be a *believers' covenant*. If the Lord does not remember their sins, then it must also be a *salvation covenant*.

Because it is a believers' covenant, the sign of the New Covenant is administered only to believers; infants cannot believe; therefore they are not baptized. Moreover, if *their sins* are what God forgives, it is a *personal salvation covenant.* The sign of this New Covenant is administered only to those who have sinned, but infants have not sinned; therefore again, they are not baptized.

Preliminary to Jeremiah's prediction he provides a proverbial setting: "The fathers have eaten sour grapes and the children's teeth are set on edge" (31:29; Ezek. 18:2; Lam. 5:7). The prophet denies that representation of divine jurisprudence by affirming the responsibility of the individual for his own sin alone (31:30; cp. Ezek. 18:4, 19-20), which principle appears in the original legislation God gave to Israel: "The fathers shall not be put to death for the children; neither shall the children be put to death for the fathers: every man shall be put to death for his own sin" (Deut. 24:16; II Kg. 14:6; II Chron. 25:4; Ezek. 18:20). In the context of this very principle Jeremiah announces the future inauguration of the New Covenant, which will stand in stark contrast to the popular proverb of his day. The New Covenant is a believers' covenant, a salvation covenant, a personal salvation covenant.

It should be pointed out here that our view of the distinction between the covenants does not argue that the Old Covenant even in its Abrahamic stage was concerned with purely external and temporal matters—and so it could be performed on infants. Rather, the Abrahamic-Mosaic covenant *included* political, fleshly, temporal matters above and beyond spiritual concerns as a setting for them, and because of this inclusion circumcision could be administered to infants. All these elements have been dropped out of the New Covenant because they were secondary, temporal means to primary, spiritual goals in history. Successional lines, hereditary lines, automatic flow of grace, mechanistic and purely legal processes have no place in the new order of things. Messianic baptism is not performed on infants because the elements that would make it appropriate have been subtracted from the covenant.

In our efforts to differentiate between the covenants we want to avoid the impression that they are unrelated and discontinuous. Concern for righteousness gives continuity to the whole sweep of redemption history from Abraham through the church age. Our objection has been to equating the Abrahamic-Mosaic covenant and the Messianic covenant either as to identity or kind. They are not the *same kind of covenant* because the former had a national, political, flesh component beyond the spiritual concerns it addressed and because it was a righteousness covenant rather than a salvation-to-righteousness covenant. They are not the same covenant because the Messianic covenant is called a "new" covenant (Jer. 31:31ff.) and a "second" covenant, the first being taken out of the way to establish it (Heb. 8:7, 13; 10:9). They are different covenants despite the common overall purpose for which God established them.

Distinction of covenant signs. Our comments up to this point have addressed the distinctive natures of the two covenants generally. The points made apply implicitly to family solidarity, baptism-circumcision parallels, proselyte baptism analogies, and surrogate faith. Specific passages warrant attention as well for these concepts individually.

We take up first those points that concern circumcision and its attendant—proselyte baptism. In response to the parallel between baptism and *circumcision*, we note two items on Colossians 2:11-12. First, (a) the two ordinances may be paralleled inasmuch as they are initiation rites, rites of passage, or signs of their respective covenants. In this respect baptism shares a certain likeness to any rite of initiation. Since the covenants differ in kind, however, the initiation rites must differ in meaning. The Old Covenant was a land, lineage, and righteousness covenant; but the New Covenant is a personal salvation covenant. Consequently, entrance into the former could incorporate birthright conditions, but entrance into the latter must be by believers' conditions subsequent to sin and must bear a relation to salvation from sin. It would be allegorizing the comparison, or overdoing the likenesses, to infer infant baptism from infant circumcision because the two covenants do not share the elements that included infant candidates in the previous economy. The tokens of national citizenship apply to infants and young children because national citizenship includes matters that pertain to them. Baptism as a token of spiritual citizenship of a *salvation* covenant does not apply to infants and young children because spiritual citizenship in a *salvation* covenant does not pertain to them. When therefore the national element was subtracted from the covenant and the righteousness element was adjusted to a salvation element, the administration of the initiatory rite was also adjusted to reception only by sinners, original guilt being implicitly denied here. Since the covenants differ, their rites of initiation differ in meaning. Since the meanings are different, the candidates are different.

Secondly, (b) Colossians does not correlate circumcision and baptism particularly. The circumcision Paul describes here is "not made with hands," an expression for divine activity (cp. Job 34:20; Dan. 2:34, 45; 8:25; Mk. 14:58; Acts 7:48; 17:24; II Cor. 5:1; Eph. 2:11; Col. 2:11; Heb. 9:11, 24); hence, he is not speaking of Old Testament circumcision because it was made in the flesh. Inner cleansing is the "circumcision of Christ" in relation to which Paul places a baptism that —in another figure—buries the old to resurrect the new. Christian baptism, then, answers to a figurative circumcision of the heart because the New Covenant is a covenant with the inner man, not a covenant with the flesh (Gen. 17:13-14).

If circumcision were a purely or even primarily spiritual initiation rite, there would have been no need for developing both among the Jews from the beginning (Deut. 30:6; Jer. 4:4; 9:25) and in Paul expressions like "circumcision of the heart" (Rom. 2:29) and "in the spirit" (Rom. 2:29), "circumcision made without hands" (Col. 2:11), and "the circumcision of Christ" (Col. 2:11). Circumcision was validly performed aside from the heart and the spirit (Gen. 17:23) on both infants and slaves. Baptism never receives such a description; it is associated in its descriptions with the inner man and compared to a circumcision without hands. While circumcision *could* involve the spiritual dimension, baptism *must* have that dimension because that is included in Paul's description of what baptism *is*.

Therefore (c) rather than being an argument for baptism as like in nature to circumcision, Colossians 2:11 is an argument against it because the apostle contrasts baptism with circumcision by aligning it with circumcision not made with hands. A rule of exegesis regarding actions is that explanation takes precedence over example because explanation gives clearer meaning. This description of baptism in Colossians carries more finality than all the examples of household baptisms with or without their infants, slaves, and friends. Paul describes what baptism *is* so that the reader is not left to figure out what it is from the examples of it.

As a subpoint we repeat with qualification the common objection that (d) circumcision applied only to males so that baptism cannot have come "in the room of circumcision." Much of what this observation urges lies in the nature of the sign, not in its meaning. It does seem

302

appropriate to note, nevertheless, that a rite limited to males could have been chosen for the sign of a flesh-based covenant because legal and political systems can and do operate more impersonally, less individually, and more in terms of representative heads than dynamic and interpersonal systems do. In the eyes of law or social custom a head can stand for the group in many cases. The difference in the covenants is reflected in this difference between the signs of the covenant.

(e) Paul's objection to circumcision applied only to Gentiles. He raised none against Jewish Christians continuing to observe the rite, and even took Timothy and circumcised him (Acts 16:1-3). Circumcising this young man of mixed blood occurred during the very process of delivering copies of the Jerusalem encyclical that forbade compelling Gentile Christians to be circumcised (Acts 15:22-29). Consequently, Paul's criticism of circumcision was not that it had been replaced by baptism and should not be practiced any longer, but that it meant something inappropriate for Gentiles though not for Jews. Paul's olive-tree illustration shows there is one people of God (Rom. 11:16-24); so circumcision does not bring a person into another people of God. Circumcision, instead of meaning something close enough to be replaced by baptism, meant something in fact exclusive of the Christian faith. Paul's great concern at Antioch, during the conference on circumcision, on the second missionary journey, in Galatians, and elsewhere was not over a simple matter of doing two synonymous signs when they should have been doing only one. To be sure, part of Paul's opposition to circumcision as exclusive of Christian faith was that it identified a person with a system of works, but that is not all. Since he allowed it for Jewish Christians, it must have had another dimension that could continue to have meaning for Jews even after the church was established to promote salvation by faith. If baptism merely came in the room of circumcision, such would not have been the case.

Both the Judaizers and Paul understood this rite as an act of identification with the law of Moses. If for Jewish Christians circumcision could not identify with *righteousness* through law and if it could not for Gentiles identify in any way, then for Jewish Christians it must have identified with *nationality* because this was the only difference left between the two groups. In the Gentile mission Paul was observing the missionary principle of Christianizing rather than culturalizing or nationalizing those of another country. The least that may be said of this situation

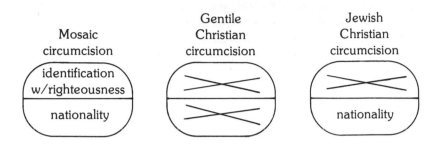

is that the church must be another society besides Israel, a point not granted in the covenant theology that parallels baptism into the church and circumcision into Israel and makes Christians the continuation of the Old Testament kind of people of God. But baptism is not just a sign for entrance into another society like in kind to ideal Israel either; otherwise Paul's criticism of Gentile circumcision would have been to the effect that it was the wrong sign and that baptism should have been performed in place of it. His degree of concern shows that the Judaizing heresy contained more than procedural error; it involved basic misunderstanding about the nature of the church and its role as a continuation of the one people of God. If circumcision identified with national Israel, it could be administered to infants because racial identity and privilege can be predicated on them. The national-identity element in circumcision made the sign applicable to infants, but the New Covenant does not rest on national or racial identity. Consequently, instead of circumcision serving to validate paedobaptism, it precludes it.

In conclusion, baptism was performed on Jews in addition to circumcision and not just on Jewish proselytes. Circumcision among Jews continued with apostolic approval right on into the apostolic age. Arguing that baptism fulfills the previous role of circumcision, paedobaptists overemphasize the spiritual character potentially in circumcision, overdo the "national" character of baptism, and de-emphasize the spiritual character necessarily in baptism.

In passing we say again that *proselyte baptism* does not provide an additional line of argument for infant baptism because it followed the conditions for administering circumcision and because it was not an institution authorized by the Old Testament. In our heart of hearts, we are not certain about the pre-Christian origin of this rite anyway; we have interacted with it only for the sake of argument. One wonders whether the few early—albeit post-Christian—references are in fact talking about the medieval practice or possibly about the initial lustration practiced by first-century Jews.

Personal nature of salvation. The above matters applied to circumcision and proselyte baptism particularly; the matters below concern family solidarity and surrogate faith. We believe that in I Corinthians 7:14 the apostle does not address the spiritual condition in declaring that children of mixed marriages are "holy" rather than "unclean." He means instead that (a) *children of mixed marriages are not illegitimate* (lest someone think there is no legitimate marriage or procreation outside the church or the Christian faith). By "holy" (*hagios*) the apostle does not mean that the children of a Christian parent start out life with a privileged station before God in eternal matters. Similar expressions apply to a non-Christian husband, too: "The unbelieving husband is sanctified in the wife" (7:14a). "Sanctified" (*hagiazō*) carries its most basic meaning of "set apart," not in God or in the church, but in the wife. The children, then, are also holy in that they have an identity, belong, are set apart, not in the church, but in a family unit that provides them a name and gives them standing as family members with whatever privileges that entails. As to the kind of holiness Paul means here, children are not counted holy because one parent is a Christian, but despite the fact that the other parent is not a Christian.

(b) *Spouses of mixed marriages are not defiled or fornicators.* "Sanctified" means spouses are set apart in each other as husband and wife, not set aside in God as saved or covenanted people. Only two verses later Paul reasons that the believing wife might "save" her husband if she continues living with him (cp. I Pet. 3:1-2). His salvation does not come from her believing or he could not later be saved by her influence, yet baptism "now saves us" (I Pet. 3:21); consequently, we cannot suppose that Paul only means that the husband and children become legitimate candidates for baptism with no implication about the husband's salvation—as if the covenant sign only identifies with the Christian community, but has no association with salvation. The covenant is a salvation covenant (Jer. 31:31), the sign of the covenant "saves us" (I Pet. 3:21), and the covenant community is saved people. Paul's subject in the context of I Corinthians 7:14 is not baptism, salvation, or church membership, but marriage and the home and the bearing

305

of conversion upon it. One spouse's becoming a Christian does not invalidate marriage relationships. This-worldly concerns like marital status (7:10-16), slave state (7:21-23), or national identity (7:18-19) do not have to be renounced. "Let each man stay in the calling in which he was called" (7:20; cp. 17, 24). "If he is content to live with her, let her not leave him" (7:10-13).

(c) *The argument from I Corinthians 7:14 would make the unbelieving husband a legitimate candidate for baptism, too.* In harmony with 7:16 paedobaptists elsewhere argue that in the case of adults the dynamic factors of faith and repentance must be present (although that was not necessary but only appropriate for adult slaves in circumcision). Paul does not make the children of believers candidates any more than he makes the unbelieving spouse a candidate, for they are treated alike and described alike in these verses. The reasoning about children evidently does not prove their candidacy because it proves too much.

Besides all this, what unbelieving husband is going to submit to baptism, and how many pagans are going to let their wives have Christian baptism administered to their chilcen? Therefore, (d) *I Corinthians 7 shows that household conversions did not have to include everyone in the home* and that the decision of the father was *not* binding upon all under the solidarity argument.

We have taken holiness in these verses to mean legitimate vs. illegitimate as viewed from a Christian standpoint more than ceremonially unclean vs. ceremonially clean. Ceremonial cleanness operated in the opposite fashion of Paul's pattern in that the unclean defiled the clean (Hag. 2:10-13; Amos 7:17; Isa. 52:1). Moreover in current Jewish thought it had become customary to consider a Gentile unclean as a Gentile. If this principle applied to Paul's concern here, he would have to render the opposite verdict: the believing wife is unclean by virtue of the perpetual uncleanness of the unbelieving husband. The New Covenant does not operate in the realm of ceremonial uncleanness; uncleanness here has a moral sense (Mk. 7:19; Lk. 11:41; Rom. 14:20; Tit. 1:15). We see "holy" used here as in the Annunciation: "the holy [baby] that is begotten shall be called the Son of God" (Lk. 1:35). Mary's son was not illegitimate, but holy.

Holy is always relative to a category. A child is holy, or set apart, relative to a family. People are holy relative to a nation, as in the case of Old Testament children. A person may be holy relative to the church.

In each case, however, the principles that govern the identification are different so that it is not the word "holy" that carries significance, but the defining characteristics of the group in terms of which one is holy or unholy.

Acts 16:31 likewise does not pronounce salvation on other members of a household just because one of them believes. In I Corinthians 7:16 Paul shows that the spouse of a believer still needs salvation. Consequently the Philippian jailor was to understand that he could be saved by putting faith in Jesus Christ and his house could be saved the same way. Salvation through Christ is for all who need it. And so Paul and Silas preached to the jailor *and* to his house (Acts 16:32), baptized the jailor and his house, who rejoiced with his house. Technically, Paul would not have had to preach to all his house if the others could be saved on the faith of the jailor.

Luke 19:9 says of Zacchaeus, "Today salvation has come to this house because he also is a son of Abraham." In keeping with preceding observations, we understand the point not to be that Zacchaeus' whole house was saved on account of his response to Jesus or because of his descent from Abraham, but that salvation came to his house *as an offer* even though he was a hated tax collector because Jesus extended his ministry to all Jews and to Jews only (Mt. 10:6; 15:24-26) as Paul sent first to the Jews (Acts 13:46-47). Furthermore, salvation's coming to this house as a fact would not have to mean to everyone in it or to everyone without belief on the part of the rest. Cases like Zacchaeus' and the Philippian jailor's households we take to be like those of the nobleman, Cornelius, and Crispus (Jn. 4:53; Acts 10:2; 18:8): the rest of the household members participated in the same faith and reverence toward God as the head of the house did. As Paul could not in fact be anathema for his brethren's sake (Rom. 9:3), one person does not function for another in salvation.

The oft-cited example of Achan's family being slain because he had taken spoils of war at the battle of Ai does not necessarily illustrate solidarity. Deuteronomy 24:16 (cp. II Chron. 25:4; II Kg. 14:6) forbade the very kind of thing this execution would have been. Since the spoils were buried inside the family tent, the other family members were party to the deed. It is more likely that the cover up was a family effort than that his innocent children were stoned because he sinned. Furthermore, the execution of the family as a whole would not necessarily speak of

307

their eternal destiny. A convicted murderer converted to Christ might nevertheless be executed without that fact meaning something about eternal state if he genuinely repented meantime.

No denial is made that on the basis of one person's faith blessings might be rendered to another. Mark 2:5 shows that Jesus regarded the faith of the parents in his healing miracles (Mt. 8:10; Mk. 2:5; 9:23ff.). The denial is that forgiveness of sins, salvation, restoration to fellowship with God, or eternal destiny is ever predicated on the faith of others without the faith of the person forgiven. These are matters of inter-personal relationship which by nature cannot be by proxy. Mark 2:5 forms no exception to our generality even though the text says, "Seeing their faith he said to the sick of the palsy, 'Son, your sins are forgiven you.'" The text does not say the palsied man had no faith, but draws attention to theirs.

It is not defensible on the ground of household baptism, I Corinthians 7:14-16, Acts 16:31, and the like, to suppose that the father's faith stands for the whole family unit any more than his disbelief would stand for the whole. The other relatives still have to be saved, according to I Corinthians 7:16. Jesus came to divide mother against daughter and father against son in a religious sense (Mt. 10:34-37; Lk. 12:51-53; cp. 14:26). Their statuses before God are not viewed the same in Christ because he calls for a choice of loyalties: "He that loves father or mother more than me is not worthy of me." Paul teaches that those who are children after the flesh are *not* the children of God (Rom. 9:7-8). Jesus told Nicodemus that what is born of flesh is flesh (Jn. 3:6); except a person is born *again* he cannot see the kingdom of God (3:3). To be born again must mean to be born in a different way, hence, in a way not related to physical birth. Not those who are of *flesh* are sons of Abraham, but those who are of *faith* are his sons (Gal. 3:7). What baptism means as a sign of the covenant becomes illusory and imma-terial if it does not have to do with personal salvation because that is what the covenant itself provides. It is a salvation covenant or it does not solve man's predicament, bring anything beyond what the Mosaic covenant offered, or essentially differ from political systems of this world. Even as circumcision of the heart corresponds with spiritual Israel, so baptism corresponds with the invisible church.

The concept of family solidarity plus surrogate faith relates to circum-cision because both have to do with processes natural to political nations.

The basic unit of political society tends to be the family, while the basic unit of spiritual society tends to be the individual (Ezek. 18). The reason this pattern obtains is that, among other things, "spiritual" means interpersonal. Interpersonal operations function in terms of individuals. It is not surprising then to find circumcision administered to male children of Jewish parentage since the rite bestowed no spiritual status or destiny. But baptism is administered to those who make personal choice relative to restoring personal relationship to God. Concepts of family solidarity fall out of the picture because the New Covenant is not flesh-based, but behavior-based and is not a legal system but an interpersonal one. In an interpersonal system mechanistic process or automatic flow of grace has no place.

This whole cluster of circumcision, proselyte baptism, family solidarity, and surrogate faith has no validity in establishing principles for baptismal candidacy unless the Christian church is like the Jewish nation. Since Jeremiah prophesied a new kind of covenant which is described differently in its fulfillment, we must affirm that the church operates under the auspices of a salvation covenant. Its citizenship comes not from birth, but from rebirth (Jn. 3:3-5). Its practical purity is maintained not simply by the negative process of cutting off disbelievers, but by the positive process of engrafting believers only. It is harder to rid the church of all those who fail to continue in the way they were raised than it is to get rid of apostates from personally chosen commitments. The reason is that under the second construction it is understood to be a purely personal matter where continuous membership depends on continuous positive life quality; in the former construction, automatically being identified with the Christian community implies automatically continuing in that identification unless some pronounced negative move amounts to renunciation of the faith.

We grant that the ideals of a system do not necessarily issue in an ideal expression of the system and that believers' baptism does not necessarily produce a pure Christian community. Apostasy from a personal commitment in baptism or an insincere involvement in the rite can result in a certain admixture of foreign constituency in the visible church. The difference is, however, that when the very structure of the system contributes to diluting the result, it will be doubly weak—because of the system itself and because of further deficiencies in its operation. Church discipline can purify misuse and abuse of the system, but church discipline that has to work against the system, too, will be much more ineffective.

Baptism as the sign of the covenant has to do first with salvation. It does not primarily serve to identify a person with the visible Christian community, but with the invisible person of Jesus Christ whose distinctive act it pictures, participates in, and commits a person to. In the nature of things baptism relates more immediately to salvation than to the church membership that *logically succeeds* salvation. It is subsumed under soteriology (the doctrine of salvation), not just under ecclesiology (the doctrine of the church). Salvation *is chronologically simultaneous with* church membership because they occur at the same time and on the same conditions. By virtue of identification with Christ and the consequent forgiveness of sins and fellowship with the Spirit, the candidate becomes logically thereafter a participant in the group that shares those blessings.

Contentful character of faith. Whatever may be postulated about the Spirit's engendering faith in newborn babies, no positive evidence from scripture or experience indicates that he so enables them to have faith in any way different from a heathen parent's infant. Whatever may be said for infant faith, it is not the kind of faith meant in the command, "Believe on the Lord Jesus and you shall be saved." Faith in salvation matters is consistently described as something that can come by hearing the word of God (Rom. 10:17). It has a content capable of being conveyed by human language and demonstrated in example. Saving faith is not just an ability to trust; it is granted that infants and adults alike have the capacity to do that, but faith in New Testament usage and in salvation connections includes the something believed and the Someone trusted.

Insisting on the contentful nature of faith does not mean rationalizing Christianity into mere statements of ideas and articles of information. It only means that saving faith is not contentless. There is no objection to seeing the Lord "beyond the sacred page," but the encounter with God lies *beyond* the content of the sacred message, not *aside from* it. Knowledge *about* the truth can be conveyed by words and examples in order that knowledge *of* the Truth can be the case. Truth is both conveyed and encountered, which means that there is belief in it and faith in him.

An effort has been made to undergird the notion of infant faith by passages like Luke 1:44, where the unborn child leaped in Elizabeth's

310

womb at the salutation of Mary. Zacharias was told that John would be filled with the Holy Spirit from his mother's womb (Lk. 1:15). The latter expression may be reckoned as heightened expression as when David says, "They go astray as soon as they are born, speaking lies" (Ps. 58:3b; cp. Isa. 48:8). The former is cast in a poetic context that raises one's doubts that Elizabeth believed the six-month fetus knew what was transpiring. His kicking was commented on in terms of Elizabeth's own joy.

Jesus says to let the little ones come to him for to such belongs the kingdom of heaven. Since the kingdom belongs only to those who have faith, infants must have faith. But Jesus is talking about those who can come to him, not about infants. Furthermore, these whom he describes are such as can have faith: ". . . these little ones that believe on me" (Mt. 18:6). The Lord need not have anything more in mind here than is normally meant by faith.

The concern to connect the benefits of baptism with infants has produced yet another way of bringing faith into paedobaptism: it is performed in anticipation of later faith. Anticipated faith as another option causes us to wonder why it would not be better to make the effects of the future baptism retroactive rather than make the future faith retroactive to validate the baptism. God's certainly foreknowing the future faith could place on the infant the salvation benefits in the prospect of later obedience. The preference lies with retroactive baptism because God rather than man is the one who makes the decision about the state of a given infant.

Need for paedobaptism

Lostness outside the church. We objected thirdly to infant baptism because there was no need for it. As a first response to this consideration some paedobaptists invoke the principle that (1) *there is no salvation outside the church.* The obvious question is that if they are not baptized, are they not outside the church? If they are outside the church, are they not lost? Would it not be better to chance a mixed community of believers and disbelievers than to omit some from the saved by not baptizing them into the church?

The first question could be approached two ways because our affirmation has been that children are not lost. They could be regarded as born holy and safe and therefore *born in the church,* so to speak, whether their parents are Christian or not. As they grow they become aware of the teaching of Christianity and they accept it personally or eventually reject it. If they refuse it, they in effect leave the church; if they come to faith, they stay in it. Their personal sins do come along, but they are not reckoned against them until they have matured enough to understand sin and recognize its consequences. At that time they are baptized into formal identification with Christ and consequently his people the church. As a result of their identification they also formally receive forgiveness for those earlier sins they have come to recognize for what they were. Although not reckoned against the young person during the years of growing moral awareness, these sins can now be repented of because he can assume responsibility for them. Children raised in the church never really leave it necessarily; by the time they reach ethical consciousness they also reach faith and repentance, and so are baptized. *This approach conceives of the church as the sum of the safe.*

In favor of this view could be cited Jesus' statement about little children, ". . . for of such is the kingdom of God" (Mk. 10:14; Mt. 19:14; Lk. 18:16). The passage is indefinite, however, as to whether Jesus means that the kingdom is made up of people who are like children or that the kingdom is made up in part by children along with others who share their trusting nature, their humility, their teachableness, and other admirable tendencies. Some might also be inclined to distinguish the kingdom of heaven from the church, the former being a broader category. Moreover, the word "is" may mean description rather than time. The first and eighth beatitudes (Mt. 5:3, 10) stand in a list of future time references: blessed are the poor and the persecuted because "theirs is the kingdom of heaven." "Great is your reward in heaven" uses "is" to express a description whose time is future. Jesus may be anticipating the way these kinds of children will respond to the kingdom when it comes time for them to do so. Colossians 1:2 addresses saints and faithful brothers and then in 3:20 addresses children, telling them to obey their parents. The question, however, is not whether the teaching of scripture is addressed to children, but whether they are in a position of need for salvation from sin. Consequently, the observation does little to solve our problem about whether to view children as being in the church.

Children could also be regarded as *not born in the church.* Instead of viewing them as morally holy, they could be considered ethically amoral until they do anything responsibly good or bad. When they reach spiritual responsibility, like young people in the other construction, they can be saved from the acts they subsequently know were sinful and subsequently assume responsibility for. Babies and children, certain unevangelized heathen, and Old Testament worthies are safe or saved as the case may be, but they are not contemplated in what the New Testament defines as the church. The church is never said to have children in it even in the later New Testament epistles where second-generation Christianity existed. Children are not officially church members and they do not need to be; they participate in the proceedings of worship and study; but they do not vote, hold office, or observe communion. *This preferable approach conceives of the church as the sum of the saved through the gospel.*

The scripture does not clearly affirm that there is no salvation outside the church. It is one thing to say that the church is saved people; it is another to say that it is the only saved people. Salvation does come only through Christ (Acts 4:12), and the church is the body of believers in Christ. The body of Christ is the only agency for spreading the gospel. It is also true that those who reject him do not have salvation. There is a difference, however, between *disbelief* and *unbelief*. There is a difference between those who are outside the church because they have refused the gospel and those who are technically outside the church because they have never heard the gospel. The idea of no salvation outside the church does not have to be affirmed in any sense that applies to our present subject. There may be no *salvation* outside the church, but that does not eliminate *safeness* outside the church.

The real question is not whether children are in the church, but whether they are lost. If infants and minors have no sin on record to be disposed of, baptism as related to salvation is irrelevant for the time being. They are not members of the church, although they are participants in the program of the congregation. *Baptism is not designed specifically for bringing people into the Christian community.* We affirm that they are not lost however we may prefer to view their connection with the church.

A second response by some paedobaptists to the lack of need for infant baptism comes in connection with (2) *the doctrine of original sin*. Two approaches to paedobaptism make it on the one hand a sign related to external covenant privilege in which the person is associated with the visible church. On the other hand paedobaptism is considered a sign related to inward holiness and sanctification. This second meaning is associated with the forgiveness of original sin. By birth itself each person becomes part of mankind which as a group stands apart from God because of Adam's sin. Baptism of infants comes in to remove, not the guilt of personal sin, but the taint of original sin. Depending on the doctrinal framework being used, baptism may also be the occasion when God regenerates the inherited fallen nature so that spiritual awakening and growth can begin.

Original sin is here viewed as a systematic inference that is not true in any sense that would damn a person eternally. Strictly speaking none of us bear *guilt for Adam's sin* though we experience the *suffering from his sin*. We are not born physically into Adam's spiritual condition of estrangement from God; we are born spiritually into him; that is, we get into him, not by birth, but by sin. Since we all have sinned, we are all in Adam; for by sinning as he did we identify ourselves with him and therefore share *the same punishment as he did*, which is essentially alienation from God. Christ as Second Adam replaces First Adam as the representative of our race. After personal sin by which we enter First Adam, in obedient faith we identify with Christ by rebirth unto forgiveness, fellowship with God, and reunion with fellowmen in his body. What as a race we lost in Adam through no fault of our own, we regain in Christ through no virtue of our own. There is both corporate lostness and corporate salvation, but we do not arrive at either condition by physical birth but by personal behavior. *Baptism is not designed for infusing grace into the depraved individual or for delivering him from Adam's guilt.*

If God does not hold against us our own sins of ignorance, why would he hold against us someone else's sins of which we are ignorant? Ezekiel corroborates our expectancy when he makes clear that parents do not die for the children's sins nor vice versa. The soul that sins is the one that dies; guilt is personal (18:14-20; Lev. 18:5). The system of thought that eventuates in infant baptism, however, reckons both guilt and righteousness from one person to another in violation of this fundamental precept. Transferring holiness and guilt from one person to another is artificial and unnatural to an interpersonal system. In John's baptism the people were baptized "confessing *their* sins" (Mt. 3:6). In Christian baptism the call is to "wash away *your* sins" (Acts 22:16). Neither John's baptism nor Christ's is ever in scripture connected with original sin.

314

A point of consistency

Except for the Eastern Orthodox Church paedobaptists have seldom practiced infant communion along with infant baptism. This lack of similarity in the observances of the two ordinances is unexpected in light of (1) *their fundamental connection* as ritual observances bearing relation to identification with Jesus Christ and salvation. Even if one were to associate baptism primarily with visible church membership only, it would appear to be as cogent to argue for the infant observance of the one as for the other. Baptism is identification while communion is re-identification.

This lack of infant communion is unexpected also because of (2) *the similar reasons by which both may be defended.* As circumcision provided a basis for infant baptism, the passover meal provides an equally valid basis for observing the Lord's Supper. If personal understanding does not need to be present for the one, it does not need to be present for the other. If surrogate faith or subsequent faith can legitimize the one, it can legitimize the other. Understanding and faith were not prerequisites for either circumcision or the passover in the Old Covenant. It is axiomatic that a valid form of argument applies to all subjects to which it is amenable.

Responses to the prospect of inconsistency in this matter have included three distinctions: baptism is passive while communion is active; baptism initiates while communion perpetuates; and the one is single while the other is repeated. In regard to the active-passive distinction we wonder where the idea originates that baptism is passive in any sense that affects this present question. While baptism is administered by another, the piece of bread can be put in the communicant's mouth. Getting one's self baptized demands as much activeness as having the communion served. Baptism is not a passive act except perhaps in the paedobaptist formulation, but it has no more reason so to be considered than does communion. That baptism is a single act of initiation points up matters of frequency and function in response to a question about candidacy; these factors do not bear relevance even about function because the functions pertain to the same concern—identification with Jesus Christ.

Paedobaptists do not appear to argue consistently when they object to infant communion because the Lord's Supper requires activities which infants cannot do: remembering the Lord, discerning his body, proclaiming his death, and self-examination (I Cor. 11:23-29). For similar reasons we have objected to infant baptism because infants cannot do what baptism involves: calling on the name of the Lord, confessing sins, putting faith in Christ, repenting of the past, and commitment to a new future. To be sure, baptism is a rite of membership and communion is a rite of worship, but we wonder why membership does not require what worship requires as far as dynamic factors are concerned. If the principle of proxies and biological inheritance are valid in one case, they are valid in the other. The same reasons for not practicing infant communion are the ones we give for not practicing infant baptism.

Infant baptism tears apart the fabric of conversion and spaces the pieces out over years of time, even though there is an attempt to keep all the pieces. The application of water is pulled out of its natural context and moved forward to the time of birth, and the personal commitment element that should have been interwoven with it is delayed until "confirmation," "covenanting," or "first communion." Naturally this procedure creates a problem on the one end for *baptism* because faith is not there; so artificial substitutions like proxy faith, infant faith, or future faith are made. The procedure creates a problem on the other end for *commitment* because what should have been the act of expressing commitment is not there; so another rite is created in confirmation (although Acts 8:4-19; 9:17; and 19:1-7 have been traditionally used as confirmation texts in scripture). To change our figure, living and interdependent elements are killed when they are cut apart much as separating the organs of the organism destroys its life and power. The vibrancy and triumph of Christian conversion is similarly reduced by such inappropriate dissection done without a feel for the dynamic, interpersonal, reconciling process that is formalized into a point in Christian baptism.

Before closing this discussion the reader should be apprised that we have not labored to keep distinct even the broadly different approaches to paedobaptism. In general the argument from original sin represents one position, while circumcision and related solidarity arguments represent another.

Infant baptism arose and was perpetuated by several influences foreign to the Christian message. Among them were proselyte baptism, initiation into the Hellenistic mysteries, the state church notion, and the doctrine of original sin. When these influences are removed, little commends the practice and serious objections oppose it.

316

Vicarious Baptism

Related to candidacy for baptism is the practice of vicarious baptism, a baptism one person performs for the benefit of another. The procedure has taken several forms since early times. In some cases a person has been baptized for another who was infirm; in other cases, a living person was baptized for a believer, or catechumen, who died before coming to baptism; more extreme has been the practice of baptizing living persons for deceased relatives, ancestors, or friends who had no faith at all while they were alive.

Paul's comment to the Corinthians in the first epistle has provided the biblical basis for vicarious baptism: "Otherwise what are the ones baptized for the dead going to be doing? If dead people do not rise at all, why then are people baptized for them?" (I Cor. 15:29). Many interpreters take the verse to mean that in Corinth living believers submitted to baptism on behalf of dead people in order to procure for them salvation and the resurrection. We must interact briefly with this practice and with the meaning of this verse.

Arguments against vicarious baptism

Nature of salvation. On three grounds we deny the validity of baptism for the dead. The first is that salvation is personal. The objections to infant baptism apply equally to vicarious baptism. Even as one person's faith cannot substitute for another's, so also one person's obedience cannot substitute for another's. Salvation is personal in the sense that salvation is individual.

Nature of baptism. Secondly, salvation is personal in the sense that it operates by personal principles instead of legal or natural ones. Baptism does not carry a sacramental significance because its meaning does not rest inherently in it, nor has an automatic meaning been given to it by God. Baptism takes place in the interpersonal framework within which salvation as a whole occurs. This divine ordinance does not have the sort of character that makes it inherently necessary for salvation. Patriarchal and Mosaic saints obtained eternal relationship to God aside from baptism; hence, baptism is not something without which there could be no salvation.

Time of opportunity. Thirdly, prayers for the dead and baptism for the dead both run counter to the evangelical belief that opportunity

317

for salvation applies to this life. Scripture talks about men dying in their sins or in their righteousnesss; a person's final earthly condition becomes his eternal status (Ezek. 18:13, 18, 19, 21-24, 26-28, 31-32; Rev. 2:10). There is no evidence that opportunity for salvation extends beyond death, much less that such salvation could be brought about by the efforts of others, especially if it is apart from belief on the part of the dead. Whatever Paul means by "baptism for the dead," he does not mean that Christians can save dead people by being baptized in place of them.

Alternative interpretations

With first principles so clearly opposed to vicarious baptism for the dead, it is perhaps not necessary to do more than suggest other ways of understanding I Corinthians 15:29. Even that effort must remain tentative because the passage could refer to a localized practice lost to historical memory. A couple of guidelines need to be emphasized: (a) the practice must presuppose the resurrection in order for Paul to bring the charge of inconsistency against disbelief in the resurrection; (b) Paul's comments must have to do with more than immortality of the soul. Greeks and Jews alike believed in a conscious hereafter; the problem in Corinth evidently did not grow out of a denial of eternal existence.

A large number of modern commentators take the position that some Corinthians were in fact practicing vicarious baptism, but they usually add that Paul does not mean to approve of it. Nevertheless, many other interpretations have been offered that combine in different ways the three primary variants in 15:29: (a) whether "baptism" indicates water baptism or something else; (b) what *hyper* ("for") means in this case; and (c) what "the dead" refers to. Some of the more prevalent interpretations hold that Paul is talking about

(1) baptism of suffering (Mk. 10:38; Lk. 12:50) for the dead in sin (Eph. 2:1-10); note the figurative expressions in the immediate context: "die daily" and "fight with beasts";

(2) baptism in blood with a view to (the resurrection of) the dead; by their death amidst persecution the dead had sufficiently obeyed God for him to consider them "baptized" unto Christ and to raise them up unto salvation even though they did not come to water baptism before their martyrdom;

318

(3) baptism above (the graves of) the dead;

(4) baptism out of respect for the dead, who either by their manner of dying or their previous desire for the candidate's baptism and salvation caused these living people to accept baptism later;

(5) baptism with a view to joining dead Christians at the resurrection;

(6) baptism on behalf of (the resurrection of) the dead.

In the above translation of I Corinthians 15:29 we intentionally slanted the wording to describe, if possible, every person's own baptism in water. If vicarious baptism is not what Paul had in mind (albeit disapprovingly), we suggest that this approach may prove beneficial to understanding the apostle's meaning. Without committing ourselves particularly, we express this interpretation in hopes of clarifying the place of I Corinthians 15:29 in Paul's argument for the resurrection.

Paul is trying both to correct and prevent; he seeks to correct those who espouse this erroneous doctrine, but also tries to prevent its far-reaching consequences on orthodox people who are willing to consider resurrection a matter of opinion. They were glorying in their broad-mindedness on this issue (15:31) even as they gloried in the case of the incestuous man (5:2). Paul is saying,

"If you are willing to suppose that resurrection does not happen (15:12) or that it is past already (II Tim. 2:18), under this reconstruction what will the ones baptized be doing when they are baptized? Their baptism is on behalf of the dead insofar as it looks forward to delivering them from the dead by a resurrection like Christ's. The very meaning of baptism controverts the notion that resurrection does not or will not happen. Baptism is an anticipatory act of *eschatological identification* with the risen Lord.

"Baptism is also a present act of *ethical identification* with Second Adam (15:20-28) in that the candidate commits himself to Christ by re-enacting Christ's distinctive act in history (Rom. 6:1-14). This identification involves a conversion that is not so much from living *in* the flesh as it is from living *according to* the flesh; hence, baptism pictures resurrection to a new life style rooted in the realm of the Resurrected One. But there is no reason while in the flesh to live according to a resurrection ethic if there is no resurrection; there is no reason to live according to the ethic of the Resurrected One if he has not resurrected. We may as well live in terms of a this-worldly ethic (15:32). You cannot continue to tolerate non-resurrection beliefs in the church and in your thinking because it leads to non-resurrection practice;

319

and non-resurrection practice in others will corrupt you (15:33). The doctrine of resurrection is not a negotiable aspect of Christian faith."

Vicarious baptism for the dead contradicts the nature of salvation as reconciliation between persons. Whether it happened in Corinth is immaterial. We have offered one alternate interpretation of I Corinthians 15:29 that seems contextually relevant and grammatically appropriate. Perhaps Paul had in mind some other idea, but on grounds of consistency we affirm that he did not intend to affirm the validity of vicarious baptism for the dead.

Summary

Two positions have been taken on the candidate for baptism: believers only or believers and their children. *In favor of believers' baptism* we have observed that in the New Testament only adults are baptized, that only adults can do what accompanies baptism, and that the New Covenant is a salvation covenant. To put these points negatively, infant baptism should not be practiced because there is no example of it, no possibility of it, and no need for it.

In response paedobaptists have sought *examples of infant baptism* in the household conversions despite the descriptions of the candidates as doing what infants cannot do. Also from the ancient church instances are adduced which we deemed irrelevant because they do not constitute apostolic precedent. Proselyte baptism among the Jews is noted as creating presumptive evidence for Christian baptism because proselytes' children were baptized along with their parents, a point again set aside as impertinent since it was practiced as an extension of circumcision principles.

As to the *possibility of infant baptism* an understanding is necessary of the distinction between the Abrahamic-Mosaic covenant on the one hand and the Messianic covenant on the other. The earlier covenant had a political element in it that explains why circumcision was administered to newborn children. Paralleling baptism with circumcision on the basis of Colossians 2:11-12 forgets that the new covenant has shed this political element that made infant initiation appropriate. Besides this, Paul correlates baptism, not with circumcision in the flesh, but with circumcision made without hands. Proselyte baptism of infants does not surprise us since it, too, pertained to entering the Old Covenant politico-spiritual system.

Family solidarity was discounted as the meaning of I Corinthians 7:14 and similar passages either because they do not address spiritual relationships or because they show the rest of the family also involved in the acts natural to salvation. The related notion of proxy faith again has no application to baptism since baptism involves interpersonal matters rather than those legal and political processes that can be by proxy. Infant faith is also set aside because neither scripture nor experience shows us in children such a capacity as having faith in the propositional and interpersonal sense of the word in the New Testament.

The Old and New Covenants differ respectively as (1) righteousness covenant vs. salvation covenant and as (2) a spiritual-political system vs. a purely spiritual system. Therefore baptism as the sign of the New Covenant is primarily (a) soteriological vs. ecclesiological, (b) commitment to Christ vs. witness to the community, and (c) is associated with the invisible church (those really saved) vs. the visible church (the Christian community in the world).

The *need for infant baptism* is associated particularly with the doctrine of original guilt whereby the newborn baby becomes guilty of racial estrangement by being born into a lost race. Our position has been that not by birth, but by behavior we get into First Adam so as to share his fate. We may suffer on account of other people's sin, but our eternal relationship to God is not forfeited by it. Historically the doctrine of original sin combined with the union of church and state to produce a practice for which paedobaptists yet need to find a reason.

In a word, baptism is the initiation rite into a personal salvation covenant and therefore signifies what entering such a covenant means: forgiveness of personal sin.

CHAPTER TWENTY

THE FORM OF BAPTISM: IMMERSION

Introduction

Description of views

In the history of Christian practice two views have been taken of the form of water baptism. The first view is that "baptize" is a specific act—immersion; the second is that it is a general act allowing for different forms. One considers baptism primarily an act; the other considers it primarily a rite. In the former case baptizing is immersing, which gives name to the rite; in the latter case baptizing is performing the initiatory rite. In the last instance baptism may take place by *immersion*, dipping the whole body in water; by *affusion*, pouring water on the person; by *aspersion*, sprinkling water on the head; or perhaps also by making the sign of the cross with water on the forehead, and the like. In the first instance baptism takes place only as immersion of the whole person. The immersion position teaches that baptism as an act *is* immersion and that baptism as a rite is *by* immersion; others say that baptism as an act and as a rite is *by* immersion.

Description of the task

The problem before us calls for locating the center of meaning in the words *baptizō* (*baptize*) and *baptisma* (*baptism*) so we can see how secondary meanings relate to the kernel idea. The center must be located in such a way as to see how other meanings in the cluster can be attached to it by the standard rules for secondary meaning development. The accompanying diagram pictures the question we need to answer. It cannot be overemphasized that our problem is not deciding whether *baptizō* means to dip, or to pour, or to sprinkle. No one contends that *baptizō* means to sprinkle or to pour; it is agreed that if a word means

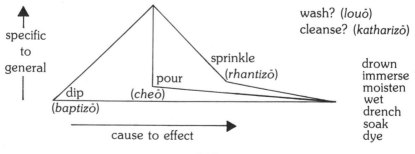

"dip" it cannot mean "pour" or "sprinkle." A word cannot mean parallel actions at the same stage of the language in relation to the same topic. Communication would be impossible if words could mean parallel, mutually exclusive, or opposite things at the same time, even though over a period of time a word like "let" can change from meaning "prevent" to meaning "allow" (KJV Rom. 1:13). Our concern is to decide whether *baptizo* points to the specific action "dip," or whether it refers to a general action like "wash." Of course, the hierarchy of generalization and specificness in a language has more than two "layers" as diagrammed above. The idea of dipping, for instance, is itself a general concept in relation to specific ways of dipping—quickly or slowly, partially or completely, straight down or on a slant, trine or single, etc.; but for the purposes of this study we have only shown the two layers that are primarily at issue in baptism.

In the study of language there are recognized patterns by which words shift their meanings from specific to general ideas or from cause to effect or from general to specific. Our task is to fix the center of *baptizo* so that all its usages in relation to Christian baptism and elsewhere can be accounted for by standard figures of speech figured relative to that center, or locus, of meaning.

Even more precisely our inquiry presses beyond the meaning of *baptizo* and its cognate words and looks directly at the form of the rite of baptism itself. Of course, the meaning of the word is one avenue to discovering the form of the rite, but it is not the only avenue. To put it somewhat differently, the search is not so much for the meaning of the word *baptizo* as it is for the meaning of the word *baptizo* as applied to the ordinance of baptism. Special usages relative to other subjects do not necessarily transfer to this subject; peculiarities here may not crop up elsewhere.

A rite exists prior to the naming of it, and the word exists prior to its application to a rite. Their independent origins cross when the term is applied to the rite. Therefore something must exist in the term that also exists in the rite or nothing would have suggested employing it as a label.

Complicating factors

At least four factors complicate our inquiry. There is (a) the natural difficulty of determining the meaning of a *word* in a language foreign to us and in a culture two thousand years removed from our time. Beyond this problem is (b) the historical development of the form of the *rite* within the church. Plurality of modes in baptism may seem natural because plurality of modes occurs in our present circumstance; what is familiar seems to be right. Furthermore, (c) aspersion is simpler and easier to administer than immersion; an unconscious preference for it on these grounds may help cloud our thinking as we sift through the data. *Practical concerns* can get ahead of exposition and reflection.

Finally, (d) on all hands Christians have recognized that water has no built-in power to cleanse from sin. Because of its *symbolic character* the manner of administration will not enhance or inhibit the water's own ability to eradicate sin. With that realization in the back of our minds, we may find it difficult to muster much energy for investigating the problem. Our only answer can be, however, that since God is obviously the "cleansing Agent" in Christian baptism, we must be sure that we are obeying what he meant for us to do as a condition for dispensing his grace. Consequently, the only motive or motivation we can have for looking into this matter is our gratitude for grace unto his glory.

Proposed method of solution

The structure of our presentation on the action of baptism incorporates two fundamental precepts. The first precept is (1) the necessity of assuming the positive burden of proof. Investigating any subject calls for this method. The rule means that the advocate of a position assumes responsibility for demonstrating the correctness of his position instead of being allowed to call upon others to disprove it. It is conceivable that in the subject before us it may be difficult or impossible to disprove that in New Testament parlance *baptizo* covered an area general enough to include sprinkling and pouring as well as immersion. Therefore if we affirm that *baptizo* does carry a meaning this broad, we take upon ourselves the job of showing that such is the case. In other words, the task is not to prove that *baptizo* meant *only* immerse or that baptism was administered *only* by immersion. The point is where we get the larger idea, not how we get rid of it—how we discover that it means more than immerse, not how we keep it from being bigger than immerse.

The second fundamental precept in our structure of presentation is (2) confirmation by default. This discussion pertains to a narrower vs. a broader view; if the broader view cannot sustain itself, the more restricted position is confirmed by the failure to enlarge it. If affusionists fail to show a case that cannot be assimilated naturally into the immersionist position, the evidence showing that *baptizō* means to immerse becomes evidence showing that *baptizō* means *only* to immerse as far as we can tell.

Meaning of the Word

Classical Greek usage

Since the word antedated the rite, studying the meaning of *baptizō* with its related words serves as a foundation for studying form in Christian baptism. Previous, non-Christian usage in classical Greek can be determined by appeal to classical Greek lexicons. We take this short cut because affusionists do not contest the issue here; consequently, listing primary examples in the Greek poets, orators, and historians seems unnecessary. We subjoin the following summary.

Baptō is the parent of *baptizō*, which uniformly designates "baptize" in the New Testament. *Baptō* means "to dip," with extended meanings like "to wash," "to drown," and "to dye," because they can result from dipping; in this last sense it is always used by Josephus, the first-century Jewish historian. *Baptizō* carries a similar entry in classical lexicons with perhaps the added notion "to overwhelm." We must decide whether the center of the word lies at "dipping," so that the other senses derive from it by effect, or whether it lies at "washing," for example, so that dipping is only a circumstance in washings.

To this query we offer four reasons for locating the center of *baptō* and *baptizō* at the specific and causal level. (1) While *baptō* often means "to dye," *baptizō* is never so used; but they both refer to the same picture. The element held in common must therefore be the more basic one. (2) If we choose any of the effective meanings as a center, we are at a loss to find mechanisms for getting from that center to some of the parallel effects. We cannot imagine a very likely connection between washing and dyeing or drowning. Generalizing or "figurativizing" from the former to the latter would not seem possible. This fact is true because by the nature of the case a word cannot easily mean parallel things without confusion. (3) Ancient Greek lexicons may use *louō* ("to wash") to define *baptizō*, but they never use *baptizō* to define *louō*. In a similar vein Greek lexicons for readers of other languages

325

will give their own word for "wash" as a definition for *baptizō*, but Greek dictionaries of other languages do not give *baptizō* as a definition for a foreign word meaning "wash." Therefore they are not equivalent terms. (4) While *baptizō* and its cognate words are occasionally translated into other languages by words carrying general meanings like "to wash" or effective meanings like "to drench," they are never translated by terms signifying pouring, sprinkling, or any other action naturally parallel to dipping. *Baptizō* must be more specific than *louō*.

Septuagint usage

Moving closer to our area of concern, we enter the Judaeo-Christian circle by examining the most important Greek translation of the Hebrew and Aramaic Old Testament scriptures. Beginning about 250 B.C., a group of Jewish scholars prepared a Greek translation of the Hebrew Old Testament that became known as the "Septuagint" because tradition has it that "seventy" men worked on the project; hence, it is often designated by the numerals LXX. In the thirty-nine canonical books of Hebrew scripture *baptō* appears eighteen times and its derivative *baptizō* only three times, yet from these texts certain observations round out our understanding of the terms as well as elucidate some linguistic principles by which the words adjust according to the situation.

In the first group of passages the action of dipping clearly produces a *complete immersion*. Leviticus 11:32 declares that wooden vessels, as well as skins, sacks, etc., are defiled by dead lizards, mice, and the like. Cleansing is accomplished by dipping or soaking them in water until evening. In one of the two usages of *baptizō* in the Old Testament LXX, Isaiah 21:4 by figurative application translates a Hebrew word meaning "to scare" so that the translation reads, "My iniquity overwhelms me."

In a second group of passages the dipping produces in varying degrees *partial immersions* if not complete ones. At this point we do well to distinguish a difference of connotation between the English words "dip" and "immerse." "Dip" concentrates more on the form of the action as the solid goes down into the liquid; "immerse" speaks more about the effect of being covered over by the liquid when the dipping occurs. "Dip" looks at the total action, stressing the pattern of action through which the solid moves and in consequence often brings in the agency that puts the solid through this pattern and into the liquid. "Immerse" looks at the same total action, stressing the action of the water as the solid is dipped. The same action is occurring under both words; they simply focus on different aspects of it. We suspect that this pair of concepts tends to correspond respectively with *baptō* and *baptizō*; if they do not correspond, then within either Greek word both emphases may appear. At least the idea of *baptizō* "by means of" or *baptizō* "with" does not create a difficulty for immersion, even though "dip with" sounds unnatural; in such cases "immerse with" removes the difficulty.

In the following texts the word *baptō* continues to have the same dipping motion as in Leviticus 11:32, but it is not always clear how total a submersion it produces. Exodus 12:22 calls for the priest to dip a bunch of hyssop in a basin of blood. Similarly in Numbers 19:18 a clean person was to dip hyssop in clean water. Jonathan dipped the end of his staff in a honeycomb (I Sam. 14:27). Hazael suffocated king Ben-hadad of Damascus by dipping a blanket in water and laying it over the sick man's face (II Kgs. 8:15). During a harvest day Boaz told Ruth to come at mealtime and dip her morsel in the vinegar (Ruth 2:14). Job 9:30-31 records the patriarch as saying that even if he washed himself with snow water, God would *plunge* him into the pit, or ditch, or mire.

Three texts speak of dipping the feet. As the Israelites were about to cross into Canaan, the water of the Jordan began to heap up when the feet of the priests bearing the ark were dipped in the edge of the flood waters (Josh. 3:15). In a rather obscure statement about the tribe of Asher, Moses says, "Let him be acceptable to his brothers and let him dip his foot in oil" (Deut. 33:24). In Psalms 68:23 (LXX = 67:24) the psalmist promises that Yahweh will again bring his enemies from Bashan so the Israelites can crush them and dip their feet in the blood of their foes.

At various times the ritual purification of a sin offering required the priest to dip his finger in the collected blood of a bullock and sprinkle it seven times before the veil of the sanctuary (Lev. 4:6, 17). In Leviticus 14:16 the partial nature of the immersion is more pronounced. For the cleansing of a leper the priest was to take a log of oil (approx. 1 pt.) and pour it in the palm of his own left hand and then dip his "right finger" into the oil in his cupped hand.

The most pronounced example of partial immersion comes in another part of the ritual specified for cleansing a healed leper (Lev.

14:6, 51). Two birds were used; one was killed in an earthen vessel over running water; the other was dipped in the blood of the dead bird and let go into the open field. On the basis of Talmudic materials (tractate *Negaim,* chapter XIV, Mishnah 1) it may be possible that the living bird—as well as the cedar wood, hyssop, and scarlet—was dipped in a mixture of the dead bird's blood and the water over which it was killed. Since the house was to be sprinkled seven times with four things (bird, scarlet, hyssop, and wood), perhaps the suggestion has merit although it is not a sure interpretation.

The other two usages of *baptō* appear in Daniel 4:33 (Heb. = 4:30) and 5:21. This figurative usage puts effect for cause when it says that Nebuchadnezzar was dipped in the dew of heaven. The heavy dews of the Near East made him so wet that he looked like he had been dipped in water. In the final reference *baptizō* describes the sevenfold dipping by Naaman the leper in II Kings 5:14.

New Testament non-baptism usage

Baptō, embaptō, baptisma. Later we will take up examples of baptism, but for now we mark non-baptism usages of *baptizō* and certain cognate words used in the New Testament. *Baptō* appears in Luke 16:24 in the words of the rich man: "Father Abraham, have mercy on me and send Lazarus that he may dip the tip of his finger in water and cool my tongue . . . ." In John 13:26 *baptō* twice refers to dipping the sop during the passover meal. Revelation 19:13 speaks of the cloak that was dipped or dyed in blood (covered with blood?). *Embaptō* comes from *en* ("in") plus *baptō*. It is used only in two accounts of the Last Supper to speak of dipping the sop with Judas during the passover meal (Mt. 26:23; Mk. 14:20; cp. *baptō* in Jn. 13:26). The noun *baptisma* never refers to anything in the New Testament except the Christian ordinance, and it seems not to appear in secular settings outside the New Testament. Its meaning therefore will be decided by the conclusions we reach regarding *baptizō*.

Jewish ablutions. Later we will have opportunity to examine more closely the New Testament references to Jewish ablutions. These rituals are mentioned in three books: Mark 7:1-5; Luke 11:38; and Hebrews 6:2; 9:10. They are referred to by a cognate word *baptismos* in Hebrews 6:2; 9:10 and in Mark 7:4. In the latter instance *baptizō* also appears, as it does in another case recorded in Luke 11:38.

The passages in Hebrews have no details that enlighten the reader on the form of these washings. Luke 11:38 does not specify whether a partial or complete bath is meant when it says that the Pharisee was amazed that Jesus "did not first bathe [baptizō] before the meal." Taking a complete bath after coming from the market place seems rather extreme preparation for a meal and that, we take it, may be the very reason Jesus deliberately refused to do it; the burdensome overdemands of tradition had no foundation or precedent in the Mosaic law itself. This mentality of overkill in purification rites and other ritual matters caused Jesus to condemn the religious leaders for their lack of perception in religious matters. Jewish literature describes complete immersions that were part of the tradition of the elders, and these may be what the gospel passages refer to. If so, they confirm the immersion form of the washings.

Matters are somewhat clearer on the washing of cups, pots, and brazen vessels (Mk. 7:4b). Our earlier survey of baptō passages in the Septuagint brought us across references like Leviticus 11:32, where the dipping of small articles was commanded for purification. Two other passages not specifying the action involved are Leviticus 6:28 (= 6:21 in Hebrew and LXX) and 15:12. Even here the tradition of the elders carried matters far beyond the requirements of Moses. Jewish ablutions mentioned in the New Testament add little positive evidence to our understanding of the meaning of baptizō as a word; they rather confirm what we have learned elsewhere.

Baptism of suffering. On three occasions baptizō carries the idea of being overwhelmed in a figurative sense. Jesus tells his disciples, "I have a baptism to be baptized with, and how I am distressed until it will be accomplished" (Lk. 12:50). Jesus asks James and John, "Are you able to drink the cup that I drink or to be baptized with the baptism I am baptized with?" When they say, "Yes," Jesus replies, "The cup that I drink you will drink, and the baptism I am baptized with you will be baptized with" (Mk. 10:38-39; cp. Mt. 20:22, 23). The final usage depends on the meaning of "baptism for the dead" in I Corinthians 15:29: "Otherwise what shall they do who are baptized for the dead? If the dead are not raised at all, why are they yet baptized for them?" If Paul should mean baptism of suffering in an effort to preach the gospel for those dead in sin, then in the tradition of classical Greek usage he associates baptizō with the notion of overwhelming as with a flood. The imagery of immersion still resides in these cases found in a Jewish setting and in the New Testament age itself.

Baptism in the Spirit and in fire. Five times John's baptism in water stands parallel to Jesus' baptism in the Spirit and fire. The first occasion comes in the words of John himself in a summary of his message and ministry: Matthew 3:11; Mark 1:8; and Luke 3:16. The second comes in response to questioning by the religious leaders together with a statement made the next day to the multitudes when he saw Jesus coming: John 1:26, 33. A third time occurs during Jesus' post-resurrection ministry recorded in Acts 1:5. The fourth instance is recorded in connection with Peter's report on the conversion of Cornelius and his household: Acts 11:16. Number five appears in I Corinthians 12:13, when Paul reminds his readers that they were "all baptized in one Spirit into one body." We take it that the baptism in the Holy Spirit refers to the gift of God's Spirit to his Messianic people, an overwhelming experience that engulfs the saved in parallel to the fire of eternal condemnation. Neither experience is secondary or partial; they are ultimate and complete. In this figurative application we still stand within the framework of the original imagery figuratively applied.

Conceptual connections

"Wash," "immerse," "pour," and "sprinkle" distinguish themselves from each other by appearing together in certain texts. We may note the early Christian writing known as *The Didache,* where in chapter 7 (1) *baptizō* stands parallel to *cheō,* which means "to pour." Similarly Leviticus 9:9 says that Aaron "*dipped* his finger in the blood . . . and *poured* out the blood at the base of the altar." (2) A series of passages distinguish "dip" and "sprinkle": "A clean person shall take hyssop and *dip* it in the water and *sprinkle* it on the tent . . ." (Num. 19:18; cp. 4, 7, 8, 10, 13; Lev. 14:6, 51). (3) Other texts show the difference between "dip," "sprinkle," and "pour": "The priest shall *dip* his finger in the blood and *sprinkle* some of the blood seven times before the Lord . . . and *pour* out all the blood of the bullock at the base of the altar" (Lev. 4:6-7; cp. 4:17-18; 14:15-16). (4) "Baptize" differs from "wash" in Acts 22:16: "Arising, be baptized and wash away your sins, calling on his name." Job 9:30-31 says, "If I would wash myself with snow water . . . yet you would *plunge* me in the mire." In all the above examples "baptize" or "dip" translates *baptō* or *baptizō,* while "pour" translates *cheō*, "sprinkle" is given for *rhantizō*, and "wash" renders *louō*. Acts 16:33 states, "He washed their stripes and was baptized—he and all his immediately."

Only in special circumstances do true synonyms appear together in frames such as the above. It should be evident from these characteristic usages that *baptō* or *baptizō* as to action does not equal any of these other words. Were one of the other four meanings substituted for *baptizō* in the examples just cited, the passages would not make sense. If they cannot replace *baptizō*, they do not carry the same meaning as *baptizō*. Therefore we can see by their *conceptual connections* that *baptizō* does not mean the same thing as "wash," nor is it an umbrella term under which sprinkle and pour are subsumed.

When we pass from the New Testament itself, we go from approved precedent to mere example. Nevertheless such writings are profitable for establishing the meaning of the *word*. One sampling from one post-apostolic document makes abundantly clear that the meaning of *baptizō* in relation to Christian baptism was parallel to other modes of applying water rather than inclusive of them. *The Teaching of the Lord to the Heathen by the Twelve Apostles,* mentioned above, is an early Christian writing of unknown authorship and uncertain date, but usually assigned to the first third of the second century. In chapter 7 of *The Didache,* as it is normally called, we find this instruction. After commanding the reader to baptize (*baptizō*) preferably in cold, running water in the name of the trinity, the author proceeds to say, "If you have neither [running or still water], pour [*cheō*] water on the head three times . . . ." We will look at this passage later in more detail, but our only concern here is to point out that *baptizō* parallels *cheō* instead of including it when speaking of the action of Christian baptism.

From scanning background usages in classical Greek, the Septuagint, and the New Testament, we understand that roots in *bap-* contain the word picture of dipping-immersing-overwhelming with possible effective meanings of wash, dye, drench, and the like. Therefore we pass to *examples of the rite* with an expectancy already established from the *meaning of the word.*

New Testament Examples of Baptism

By examining the accounts of baptism in the New Testament, we can observe the *physical connections* present in them and thereby deduce

331

what kind of action occurred in any case sufficiently well described for such a conclusion. Previously we looked for the meaning of a *word*; here we look for the form of the *rite* itself. This method of probing into the form of baptism does not depend entirely on the meaning of *baptizō* because we infer what the word means and what the rite was like by considering the circumstances in which it was done. Many examples of baptism are not sufficiently detailed to let us see what kind of action occurred, but below we look at the ones more clearly described in order to see whether they confirm our expectancy from previous usage of the word.

Candidate in the water

One immersion characteristic found in clear passages is that the candidate went out in the water. The baptism of Jesus himself is an example that calls for attention in this regard. Mark 1:9-11 reads as follows:

> And it came to pass in those days that Jesus went from Nazareth of Galilee and was baptized in [into] the Jordan by John. And immediately, coming up out of the water, he saw the heavens separated and the Spirit descending to [into] him like a dove. And a voice came out of the heavens, "You are my beloved Son; I am pleased with you" (cp. Mt. 3:13-17; Lk. 3:21-22).

At a couple of points the translation is not absolutely certain and so we have bracketed the central meaning of the word *eis* that appears in the original. Only the first bracket bears on the immersion question, but either translation suffices for our purposes. Since the previous part of the sentence speaks of broad geographical areas, we are safer to choose "in" as our rendering. It may seem abrupt to shift so quickly from a large perspective to one so small that the reader's eye is directed to the movement of a body down into the water of the Jordan River.

One conclusion, however, appears to be inescapable: Jesus was out in the water. The text does say "coming up out of the water," not "out of the river." Nevertheless that phrase probably means leaving the river since the same expression in Acts 8:39 is distinguished from the baptism itself (cp. Judith 9:8). Regardless of whether we understand this phrase to mean coming back up from beneath the water or walking back up out of the river, the Lord was in the Jordan when he was baptized. A major reason for the spread of aspersion since the Council of Ravenna in 1311 is the relative ease with which it can be performed. As with most acts, if baptism can be administered by sprinkling, then pouring and immersion will tend to disappear. Since wading out into the middle is less convenient, we may surmise that John deliberately bypassed less troublesome procedures in the effort to do something considered more satisfactory. Walking out into the river does not naturally belong to a pouring or sprinkling circumstance, but it is required for immersion.

Jesus' particular baptism was not one performed in a special way because a generalizing statement about John's baptism occurs in Mark 1:5: "And all the Judaean territory and the Jerusalemites were going out to him and were being baptized by him *in* the Jordan." It was not just in the case of Jesus that the Baptist took the candidate out in the river; it was his general practice.

Administrator in the water

A second immersion characteristic is that the administrator went out into the water with the candidate. The baptism of the Ethiopian eunuch offers a case similar to the baptism of Jesus but with the administrator characteristic made explicit. Acts 8:36-39 reads,

> And as they were going along the road, they came to a certain water [some water], and the eunuch says, "Look, water; what prevents me from being baptized?" And he ordered the carriage to stand still and they both went down into the water—both Philip and the eunuch, and he baptized him. And when they came up out of the water, the Spirit of the Lord took Philip and the eunuch did not see him again because he went on his way rejoicing.

Again we note that going out into the water is appropriate for immersion especially. But this baptism stresses the detail that Philip got in the water with the candidate, an aspect of the whole ritual not naturally belonging to sprinkling or pouring. In sprinkling or pouring the administrator does not get wet.

Abundance of water

Next we look at the familiar statement in the fourth gospel that describes one of the places where John baptized: "And John also was baptizing at Aenon near Salem because there was much water [were many waters] there; and they were coming and being baptized" (3:23).

333

In this citation the abundant supply of water is tied to the reason for John's baptizing at that location. From everything we have in hand the Messiah's herald carried on all his baptizing up and down the Jordan and its tributaries (cp. Lk. 3:3). He baptized Jesus near the Jericho ford in the Jordan. Bethany beyond Jordan is uncertain (Jn. 1:28); but if "Bethabara" is the correct reading, we know a second place in the Jordan Valley where John labored. Aenon is on the Wadi Farah, one of the four main tributaries to the Jordan. "Much water" fits immersion more readily than affusion or aspersion.

Change of location for baptism
A less precise passage, but one nevertheless worth noting, is the account of the Philippian jailor's baptism together with that of all his household. Acts 16:32-34 says,

And they spoke to him the word of the Lord with all those in his household. And having taken them aside that hour of the night, he washed off their wounds; and he was baptized—he and all his house—immediately. And bringing them into his house, he set table, and with his whole house he rejoiced, having put faith in God.

Paul and Silas spoke to the whole household, which leads us to think that the proclamation took place in the jailor's home. After the prisoners' wounds were cleaned, the family went up into his house. The implication seems to be that they left their house meantime, perhaps for the baptism, and then returned to eat and fellowship. While this inference may not be necessary, it must be considered a possibility. If so, pouring and sprinkling must not be in mind because they would not have changed sites in order for the missionaries to administer the baptism. Inhabitants of Jerusalem and Judaea went out to where John had located his baptizing ministry. That point confirms the idea that John confined his baptizing to locations with abundant water supplies.

The generalization appears legitimate that wherever sufficient details are presented for distinguishing between the alternatives proposed in the history of the ordinance, the baptisms were enacted by the dipping motion we expected to see in a rite designated by a word root meaning "to dip."

We feel that the expectancy created by pre-Christian and non-Christian meaning of *words* connected with baptism has been borne out by New Testament examples of the *rite* itself. In all cases where details were sufficient to indicate a likely choice between the alternatives, immersion was the case.

Ancient Translations of the Idea

Studies of ancient New Testament translations have shown that *baptizō* was handled two ways in reference to baptism. (1) Most translated it by a word meaning "dip" or "immerse." Examples of this procedure during the first seven centuries include the Peshitta, one Coptic translation, the Armenian, the Gothic, the Ethiopic, and the Philoxenian Syriac. (2) Others transliterated *baptizō* into their own language. It is perhaps more proper to say that they brought the word into their language, thereby creating a technical term for the name and administration of the ordinance. The Sahidic Coptic, the Basmuric, and the Latin Vulgate adopt this expediency. These languages of course had words meaning dip or immerse, but by using a loan word, they had a specialized word ready-made. Consequently, they did not have to "technicalize" or Christianize one of their own words in order to name the rite—baptism—or refer to its performance—baptize.

If we were to adopt the position that *baptizō* carried a *general* meaning like "wash" or "cleanse" irrespective of mode, we would have to explain how all these translations as well as many later ones came to pick the same *specific* mode when no translation in the Christian era ever opted for any other specific mode like sprinkling or pouring. It seems inescapable that *baptizō* as to action means a relatively specific act—immerse—rather than a general one.

Meaning of the Act

New Testament writers set forth Christian baptism under several metaphors. Ananias compares baptism to (a) *a cleansing* when he tells Paul to be baptized and wash away his sins (cp. I Pet. 3:21). We take it that spiritual cleansing is the most fundamental meaning of baptism because John's baptism as predecessor of Christian baptism was performed in water unto remission of sins. In John 3:5 Jesus speaks of baptism as (b) *a birth* when he says, "Except a person is born of water and Spirit, he cannot enter into the kingdom of God." He does not elaborate very fully what he means by calling baptism a birth; but in addition to its meaning a fresh beginning, perhaps he intended to

335

liken baptism in form to the infant newly born from the moist surroundings of his mother's womb.

According to I Peter 3:21 baptism is similar as a "true antitype" to (c) *the flood*. The two events share the element of salvation brought about by water; the amount of water reinforces the immersion pattern of the ordinance. A loose analogy appears in Colossians 2:11 between baptism and (d) *circumcision*. With circumcision there is the idea of initiation rite, rite of passage, or act of identification. In a similar vein Paul elsewhere allows Christian baptism to serve as a functional equivalent of (e) *the crossing of the Red Sea*. By so doing, the Israelites renounced their sense of belonging to the land of bondage and identified themselves with their divinely appointed deliverer. There may also be a certain formal likeness in that the crossing of the sea involved a wall of water on the left and right (Ex. 14:22). The letter to the Galatians compares baptism to (f) *dressing*: "As many as were baptized into Christ put on Christ" (3:27). Romans 6 adds the metaphor of (g) *crucifixion* when the apostle declares that "our old man was crucified with him that the sinful body might be done away with, in order that we would no longer be in bondage to sin" (6:6; cp. Gal. 2:20; 5:24; 6:14). In the same chapter he also calls baptism (h) *a death, a burial,* and *a resurrection* inasmuch as the old man this time is buried and a new man comes to life (cp. Col. 2:12).

In these several analogies the writers' main emphases fall on the common *meaning* between baptism and those functional equivalents to which various aspects of baptism are likened. In some more than others the reader senses a certain kinship in *form* as well. So it is that immersionists have seen confirmation of their position in Romans 6 when Paul considers baptism (1) a *likeness* (*homoiōma*) of Christ's death and resurrection. Under appropriate conditions the word for "likeness" seems to stress the shape of a representation, it being the term used when Romans 1:23 speaks of exchanging "the glory of the incorruptible God for the *likeness* of an image of corruptible man." Christ was born "in the *likeness* of men" (Phil. 2:7); "the *shapes* [appearances] of the locusts were like horses prepared for war" (Rev. 9:7; cp. LXX Deut. 4:12, 16; Ex. 20:4; Ps. 105:20; Isa. 40:19; Ezek. 1:26; 23:15).

Further confirmation comes in the fact that (2) both death and resurrection are called "likenesses." Perhaps it is not amiss in comparing Christ's death with the form of our baptism to draw attention even to physical details in the likenesses between them: during immersion breathing ceases; the eyes are closed; the hearing does not function; and the person is passively laid down in the watery grave and raised from it again. We feel that this understanding of our obedience more easily carries with the experience of baptism the impression that we are being united with Christ than does affusion or aspersion, where this physical similarity does not help prompt the appropriate sensations. Ritually this likeness of his death combines with the likeness of his resurrection only in the act of immersion. With the burial imagery added to the likeness of his death-resurrection, there is strong confirmation of immersion as the shape of action baptism displays.

While other matters are paralleled to baptism, (3) baptism is never called a *homoiōma*-likeness to any of them. The closest case comes in I Peter 3:21, where baptism is called an *antitypos*-likeness of salvation by the flood. It is hard to say how much Peter may have had in mind the *abundance* of *water* that *separated Noah's family from the sin* of men drowned in the cataclysm, but his attention is more immediately fixed on the similar "salvation" import of the two events. *Antitypos* does not seem to stress appearance and form so much as *homoiōma* does in Romans 6.

While it is satisfactory, of course, to have a likeness simply in *meaning* between our baptism and Christ's death-resurrection, (4) an *added appropriateness* comes if, in fact, there is also a likeness in *form* between the two. Our formal re-enactment of his distinctive act serves especially well as that by which we identify with him who alone died and arose never to die again. In baptism we commit ourselves then to that same degree of obedience to the Father—an obedience unto the last full measure of devotion in the hope of the resurrection. Thus Romans 6 connects our baptism with the death-resurrection of Jesus even as Jesus called his death a baptism and called upon his disciples to commit themselves to that degree of obedience (Lk. 12:50; Mt. 20:20-28; Mk. 10:35-45). In this symbolic death we bury the old sinful identity pronounced accursed by the law (Gal. 3:10; Deut. 27:26), and arise to a new identity pronounced righteous because of him in whose likeness we died therein and rose again. We have also passed from under the jurisdiction of the Mosaic law inasmuch as it included a physical-material-political kingdom that governs this-worldly affairs. We have been released from that law by virtue of our "death"; the law has dominion

337

over a man only as long as he lives (Rom. 6:7, 9; 7:1); we have arisen to the system of interpersonal relationship governed more fundamentally by the love of Christ than by laws of church-state systems. We indeed expect that the form of a rite should correlate well with its distinctive significance, and we see Paul's ethical appeal to baptism in Romans 6 as suggested by the "shape" of the ordinance.

Since the precursor of Christian baptism already established spiritual cleansing as its primary meaning by doing it in water (Mt. 3:6, 11; Mk. 1:4, 8; Lk. 3:3; Jn. 1:26; cp. I Pet. 3:21), we can look upon the element —water—as suggestive of the cleansing aspect of the meaning of baptism. The form of administering the element does not at this point theoretically bear a primary role except insofar as Jewish ablutions may have dictated the special propriety of immersion. But cleansing does not exhaust the meaning of baptism inasmuch as forgiveness of sins comes in a particular connection—relationship to the person and work of Jesus Messiah, most particularly his death-resurrection. At this point the form of administering the symbolic cleansing agent comes into play and directs attention to God's distinctive act in salvation history when in the person of the Son he died and rose again. By participating in that immersion (form) in water (agent), the believer identifies himself with the Sinless One through a symbolic re-enactment of his distinctive act. The sinner is then regarded both as sinless like Christ and committed to Christ unto the same extent of his exemplary obedience to the Father. Baptism as immersion therefore declares not only the idea of spiritual cleansing (element), but the basis and context of spiritual cleansing (form).

Obviously the kind of evidence presented from Romans 6 could not by itself establish immersion as the form of Christian baptism because what is most appropriate is not therefore necessary. Nevertheless once that position has been satisfactorily demonstrated on the basis of other considerations, it is significant to bring this passage into the discussion to round out the presentation from scripture that indeed Christian baptism is each man's death and resurrection, both in meaning and in form. The meaning of Christian baptism as an identification with Jesus Christ is most suggested in immersion in that it re-enacts his distinctive act.

Summary

The case for immersion gets its positive starting point from the original meaning of the term. Its grammatical, conceptual, and physical connections have been those expected from an immersing action. Consequently, classical Greek, the Septuagint, New Testament non-baptism usages as well as extra-biblical literature have testified to the meaning of *baptizō*.

Further evidence came from biblical *examples of the ordinance.* Where the cases of baptism were sufficiently clear, immersion was the action involved as demonstrated by the fact that candidate and administrator went out into the body of water, by the abundance of water indicated when amount is considered, and possibly by the change in location in order to perform the baptism.

Translations of the idea into other languages find the word consistently carrying the idea of dip or immerse throughout the first seven centuries of the Christian era. When the word was not rendered this way in translations of the New Testament, it was used as a loan word in the new language.

Baptism is compared to cleansing, birth, the flood, circumcision, the exodus, the crucifixion, and the death-burial-resurrection of the Christ. The *meaning of the act* most appropriately connects with the last of these because it is a *homoiōma*-likeness and because only this particular *event* has a real connection with the forgiveness of sins symbolized by baptism. In it we find confirmation for the view that baptism as an act *is* immersion and as a rite is *by* immersion.

Chapter Twenty-One

THE FORM OF BAPTISM: NON-IMMERSION

Introduction

In the last chapter we surveyed the structure of evidence for immersion, noting that the alternative view called for indifference as to the "mode" of baptism. This chapter presents the line of thought that issues in that second view. For want of a better term we will frequently designate it "affusion," even though that term specifically refers to pouring. More often than not, fellowships taking the second view do not practice immersion and pouring alongside sprinkling so there is historical propriety in this procedure; besides, those points of evidence that would argue for affusion would in principle argue for sprinkling as well since the choice is a narrower vs. a broader view. "Affusion" in this chapter, then, labels the second view and serves as a caption over pouring, sprinkling, and immersion collectively.

Arguments for the Broad View

Secondary meanings of "bap-" words

The first major step in the argument for the general meaning of *baptizō* comes from the fact that words with the root *bap-* have secondary meanings. We present this fact first in keeping with the historical development of these words. The approach does not provide the strongest or most direct defense for the position, but it supplies a foundation for subsequent arguments from Jewish ceremonial washings and church history. (1) The *extended meanings* of *bap-* purportedly developed in Jewish usage to cover ceremonial cleansings that represented more than one precise form. (2) Christian baptism developed out of the *Jewish lustrations* by way of the baptism of John. (3) *Church history* provides early evidence for pouring, thus confirming the expectancy created by the previous two points of the argument.

Daniel 4:33. As an example of the extended meaning of the root *bap-*, Daniel 4:33 (30 in the Hebrew Masoretic Text) is cited, where Nebuchadnezzar is described as "*wet* with the dew of heaven." The Greek translation of this verse in the Septuagint uses *baptō* to render the Aramaic word *tsaba'*, which means "to make wet." Since the deranged king is said to be "baptized," *baptō* can describe an event whose action was something closer to sprinkling than to immersion; therefore,

Christian baptism can also describe an event whose action is something other than immersion.

These references in Daniel may, on the other hand, be accounted for satisfactorily as examples of putting effect for cause in order to achieve bold expression. Nebuchadnezzar was so drenched by the dew that he was like someone dipped in water. Our comment comes subsequent to establishing satisfactorily from other considerations that *baptō* means "dip." This passage does not controvert that definition, but indeed depends upon it for its forcefulness. We do not go to passages that speak of effect in order to discover the meaning of a word as to its action. That *baptō* designates an action was shown earlier; hence, this usage is figurative relative to that action rather than vice versa.

I Kings 18. A like situation occurs in Elijah's contest with the Baal prophets according to I Kings 18. Origen (c. 185-c. 254) speaks of the episode in his *Commentary on John* 6:13. He uses *baptō* to describe drenching the sacrifice and altar, which was done by pouring water on them. *Baptō* applies to a circumstance accomplished by the action of pouring; consequently, Christian baptism may be accomplished by an action like pouring as well.

Again we can say (a) *effect* is put for cause. The reason for using *baptō* in an effective sense is even more obvious here since Elijah clearly intended to exaggerate as much as possible the difficulty of the miracle. By pouring so much water over the sacrifice, the wood, and the altar, he made them as wet as dipping them in the brook Kishon would have made them. Exaggerated wetness called for exaggerated description of wetness.

(b) The altar and sacrifice standing in the water had the *appearance* of a partial immersion. This element of the account may have contributed to Origen's manner of expression because the prophet had a trench dug around the altar to retain the water poured on it. In picturesque fashion Origen depicted the altar, as it were, partially submerged in the water like the cone of a volcano protruding from the sea.

Beyond effect and appearance (c) John's baptizing may have suggested calling the drenching of the sacrifice a baptism; under this reconstruction Origen would be calling it a "baptism" by *analogy* even as Paul called the exodus a baptism (I Cor. 10:2). Origen is trying to determine why the priests and Levites believed the returning Elijah

341

would baptize (Jn. 1:19-28). Pouring water profusely on the sacrifices is the closest thing that Elijah did that would resemble baptism, but he had *other* people do that; so the question remains why the Levites thought Elijah would baptize [!].

II Kings 5. II Kings 5:1-19 records the healing of Naaman the leper by the prophet Elisha. The Greek translation of 5:10 used *louō* to translate the Hebrew *raḥats* at the point where Elisha said, "Go and *wash* [*louō*] in the Jordan seven times." In 5:14 the narrative continues with the statement, "Then he went down and *dipped* [baptizō] seven times in the Jordan according to the word of the man of God." On all hands it is agreed that *louō* carries the generic meaning "wash," as does also the Hebrew word behind it. Since Naaman obeyed that command *louō* by the act *baptizō*, the latter can interchange with the former as a synonym. *Baptizō* therefore means "wash"; Naaman did not dip himself in the Jordan; and baptism can be performed by as wide a variety of actions as he could have washed himself by.

(a) The word *baptizō* shows what Naaman did, not what *louō* means. *Louō* itself does not specify any mode of washing; but in order to obey the command, Naaman had to employ a mode by doing something specific. That specific thing he did was *baptizō*. We do not have here a case where *baptizō* translates *louō* or defines it; rather, we have a loosely expressed command carried out later by a specific act of obedience. The example therefore presents *no necessary exception* to our view.

(b) The leper had to do something that was countable and could be done *in* the Jordan River. Pouring and sprinkling water on one's self could be counted, but they would not require walking out into the river. Some forms of washing—as with a sponge—would not easily be countable. The example therefore presents *no likely exception* to our view.

(c) We note the dictum explained elsewhere that words used to describe the same thing do not necessarily mean the same thing. If a father tells his son to feed the cat and the son pours milk in a bowl, we do not conclude that "pouring" is a synonym for "feeding." The example of Naaman therefore presents *no possible objection* to immersion.

(d) For the sake of argument we could say that obeying *louō* by *baptizō* as easily shows that Jewish lustrations were performed by immersion rather than by other actions. Since "to wash" (II Kg. 5:10,

342

12, 13) does not specify the form, the leper got the form from known Jewish practice. In this fashion the example could as easily be turned into *an actual objection to affusion.*

(e) A specific action may be referred to by a more general term. Although the action meant is really immersion, it can be referred to by a less precise designation. A good example of this principle appears in Justin Martyr's *Dialogue with Trypho*: "They are led out by us to the place where there is water . . . and . . . they wash themselves with water . . . He that is enlightened is washed." Inasmuch as the candidate is taken to water or a place of bathing, the action involved is immersion; yet Justin uses *louō* to describe the performance of baptism.

(f) We propose a final argument against making *baptizō* a general word on the basis of II Kings 5. *Louō* translates *raḥats* in 5:10, both words meaning "to wash." *Baptizō* in 5:14 translates *tabal*, which means "to dip." If using *baptizō* following *louō* makes *baptizō* mean "wash," then *tabal* following *rahats* makes *tabal* mean "wash"; but everyone admits that *tabal* means "dip."

Appealing to effective meanings of *baptizō* and *baptō* cannot account for the phenomena associated with the terms. If baptism could be for other results like "dye" or "drown," "wash" cannot be the fundamental meaning of *baptizō*; there is no way to start with dye or drown and get to parallel effects of such widely different natures. Again, we say, parallel meanings do not exist for the same word. Therefore the locus of the word must lie at a relatively specific level so that it is in a position to move out various cause-effect lines to these otherwise unrelated ideas.

Jewish ceremonial cleansings

A second major step in the argument for the general meaning of *baptizō* is the idea that Christian baptism derives from Jewish ceremonial cleansings. These purifications included cleansings required by the Mosaic law as well as others contained in the tradition of the elders. The proposition is that *baptismos*, a noun related to *baptizō*, came to be used in a technical sense for this whole set of ceremonial cleansings. Among them were immersions, pourings, and sprinklings so that in Jewish circles the term *baptismos* designated a wider class of actions than just immersion. Christian baptism therefore could as well be aspersion or affusion since the set of cognate words naming it was employed technically as general terms covering these forms of action also.

Preliminary considerations. At least five considerations affect this argument. It is admitted again on all hands that (1) *baptō, baptizō, baptisma,* and *baptismos* all derive from the root *bap-,* which signifies "to submerge." We agree additionally that (2) these words have secondary meanings like wash, cleanse, dye, purify, drown, etc. Furthermore, no one objects to the linguistic principle that (3) words may develop technical usages that go beyond the original word picture in their roots. *Baptō* can mean to dip, then to dye by dipping, then to dye by any action. Such development does not even require a passage of time sufficient for the original meaning of the root to pass from memory. Simultaneously within a language we may have the words "family" and "familiar" without consciously thinking of the one when we use the other; in fact, *familiar* has lost its association with "family" in contemporary English to such an extent that the word "familial" has been generated to mean "pertaining to the family." The only question on this third step is whether the word *baptizō* has gone through this process, a matter we will investigate shortly.

The fourth consideration is (4) whether Christian baptism grew out of the Mosaic and traditional Jewish washings. It may be granted for the sake of argument that Jewish purification rites supplied a background for John's baptism, which in turn led to Christian baptism. Certain disclaimers must accompany such associations, however. Christian baptism differs from John's baptism because the giving of the Spirit did not accompany the latter (Mt. 3:11; Jn. 7:37-39, etc.). Both Christian and Johannine baptism differed from the preceding lustrations in that the former (a) were performed once instead of repeatedly, a difference created by the difference in their meanings. Christian and Johannine baptism (b) were not self-administered as the lustrations were. Furthermore, the two baptisms (c) were for cleansing from spiritual defilement rather than from ceremonial defilement.

The newness of John's baptism as distinguished from traditional and Mosaic lustrations is implicit in the investigation conducted by the priests and Levites when they said, "Why are you baptizing, then, if you are not the Messiah, or Elijah, or the Prophet?" (Jn. 1:25). The newness of John's baptism may also be inferred from the fact that a new word was coined for it—*baptisma.* This uniqueness caused a separate word to be generated that never in extant literature designates any Jewish lustration or any occasion of one. Nevertheless, all distinctions duly regarded, Jewish washings are suggestive of, analogous to, and perhaps typical of, Christian baptism since water is used in all of them for cleansing other than the filth of the flesh.

344

We reserve for later treatment, however, the question (5) whether Christian baptism had its point of departure in Jewish lustrations in such a way as to be considered as included among them or as standing under the same label with them. It is one thing to derive one observance from a class of other observances, it is another thing to include it among them as a parallel item.

The final consideration is the decisive issue: (6) whether the rite of baptism has variant forms. A label may stand over a series of rites that differ in form from one another; that possibility does not indicate that any or all of the individual rites themselves vary in form. The question is not whether the term *baptismos* can serve as a title for a series of rites with different forms; the question is whether Christian baptism, as supposedly one of those rites, can vary in its form. With this preliminary survey we now investigate some particulars of the argument from Jewish lustrations.

Argument from Hebrews. In terms of the preceding introduction we enter the discussion at point 5. *Baptismos* occurs only four times in the New Testament: Mark 7:4, 8 and Hebrews 6:2; 9:10. The only passage that conceivably includes Christian baptism under *baptismos* is Hebrews 6:1-2:

> Wherefore leaving the fundamentals of the Christian message, let us press on to perfection, not laying again a foundation of repentance from dead works and of faith towards God, of teaching about washings/baptisms/ lustrations, and of laying on of hands, and resurrection of the dead and eternal judgment.

Taking our cue from the content of the Great Commission, we might well include Christian baptism among the preliminary elements of Christian belief. Since nothing else in Christianity would seem to qualify as a washing or lustration, the Jewish washings or John's baptism or both could be involved in the plural word "washings." It is not likely that the plural could refer to "baptizings," that is, occasions or acts of baptizing; one would not teach about occasions or acts of baptism. The differences between Christian baptism, John's baptism, Jewish washings, and pagan rites could be the subject of instruction in 6:2.

The next step moves to Hebrews 9:9-10:

> . . . which is a parable for the present time, according to which are offered both gifts and sacrifices that cannot as respects the conscience make the worshiper perfect, being only with meats and drinks and different washings fleshly ordinances imposed until a time of reformation.

345

To this verse is added the observation that in 9:13 the writer talks about "the blood of bulls and goats and the ashes of a heifer sprinkling them that have been defiled." The combination of 9:10 and 13 suggests that a rite administered by sprinkling can be included under the same label that includes Christian baptism in 6:2.

Certain objections need to be raised, however, against the conclusion that these facts show Christian baptism can be sprinkling. First, (a) it is not clear that the sprinkling of 9:13 falls under the scope of the word for "washings" in 9:10. *Baptismos* could simply refer to the lustrations

Jewish purification rites

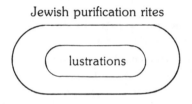

among the larger class of purification rites; the sprinkling of 9:13 can be a purification rite without being a lustration.

The second objection is that (b) variation in the term does not mean variation in the rite. Even if we make the unnecessary identification between 9:13 and 10, it only shows that the term *baptismos* was used technically as a caption for a group of rites with differing forms. It does not show that the baptismal rite itself had differing forms. The accompanying figure assembles the aspects of this question into one picture. In the diagram, "(a)" represents a word picture in the root *bap-*, which all agree was originally a submerging action. One word—*baptisma*—became the label for a rite "(b)" we know as Christian baptism. All

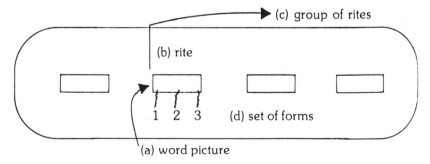

parties also agree that a term can develop a technical usage as in "(c)," where it comes to stand over a group of rites that do not all have the word picture the word originally contained. The reader will note that we have done this very thing with the word "affusion" in this chapter; although it means pouring we have made a technical term out of it to fill the void of a good word for the general view. The point of contention, however, comes at "(d)" in the attempt to conclude that because the word can change, the rite has changed.

Two issues face us here: the meaning of a word and the form of a rite. To demonstrate variation in the one does not demonstrate variation in the other. Showing that *baptismos* can stand over a list of pouring, sprinkling, and immersing rites no more shows that the baptism rite can be by sprinkling than it does that the sprinkling-of-blood rite could have been performed by pouring (Heb. 9:13, 19; Num. 19:14-19). On the basis of the Jewish-lustration argument it would be as natural to perform baptism by some other form as it would to use red-heifer blood instead of water as the element or to self-administer it on the analogy of other lustrations that fall under the heading *baptismos*.

A third objection to the argument from Hebrews is that (c) it does not distinguish what would theoretically be possible on the one hand and what was commanded and practiced on the other. Our subject is not what could have been instituted as the initiatory rite into Christ, but what *was* instituted. We agree that sprinkling or pouring water on the candidate would be appropriate in some respects. The issue here is not one of moral law or inherent necessity, but of positive commandment. "Positive commandment" refers to a specific commandment requiring one way of accomplishing a purpose that could be accomplished by more than one appropriate way.

We must beware of confusing theoretical possibilities with actualities. Many believe that baptism can *in principle* be administered variously even without approved precedent because the meaning would be the same. But the question is not what in principle God could have instituted, but what in principle fulfills God's intention in what he did institute. We need to differentiate between what in theory fulfills God's intentions and what in theory his intentions could have been. Unless we have reason to believe that God's intention was general enough to include dip, sprinkle, and pour, we end up in disobedience. Much of the cogency in the argument for sprinkling and pouring comes from the awareness that one way of applying water has no more inherent power to remove sin than another. But our concern is not relieved, because we want to obey God in his positive commandments as well as in his moral law. Cattle captured in war could conceivably be sacrificed to God, yet God commanded Saul to kill the cattle. Saul lost his kingship over this very issue of positive commandment; we could conceivably lose something, too. Our concern is not theoretical possibility, but divine intention.

A fourth objection to the argument from Hebrews is that (d) *baptismos* never labels the individual rite Christian baptism, nor any other specific rite, for that matter. Hebrews 6:2 at best only includes Christian baptism under *baptismos*; the term *baptisma* refers to the individual rite, whether Christian baptism, John's baptism, baptism to Moses (I Cor. 10:2), or Jewish proselyte baptism. *Baptisma* was a *baptismos.* Both nouns do come from the same root; but if we invoke the principle of technical meanings, it is important to separate the technicalized word from other words related to it. These cognate words do not change with the technical one. The line of reasoning from Hebrews 6 and 9 may be irrelevant because the technicalizing that could have occurred applies to a word never used specifically for Christian baptism.

A fifth objection to the argument from *baptismos* is that (e) the generalized usage may stem from its effect instead of its form. The result of dipping can be cleansing, or purification; the result of sprinkling or pouring can be the same. Since these rites in Judaism shared a common effect, they were labeled by a word that had that effect. Usage as to effect does not show the form of the action or rite itself. Our conclusion is that there is no reason to suppose that any rite fluctuated in such ways suggested for baptism. We would expect a legislated, symbolic rite to have a standard form.

Argument from Mark 7:1-4. Another passage often brought into presentations favoring a general meaning for "baptize" is Mark 7:3-4 (cp. Mt. 15:2; Lk. 11:37-38):

> For the Pharisees and all the Jews, unless they wash their hands diligently to the wrist, do not eat, keeping the tradition of the elders; and (coming) from the marketplace, unless they baptize themselves [*baptisôntai*] they do not eat. And there are many other things that they have received to keep—washings [*baptismoi*] of drinking vessels and copper bowls (and cots).

The parenthesized words "and cots" do not appear in some significant authorities, but their absence or presence does not affect the case in

348

either direction; in regard to the meaning of *baptismoi*, whether written by the author or a copyist, the words presumably do not involve a departure from proper Greek usage or the scribe would surely have noticed his mistake. A few ancient manuscripts also replace *baptisóntai* with *rhantisóntai*, meaning "they sprinkle themselves" or "they get themselves sprinkled." Again the difference, though interesting, probably has little bearing on the meaning of *baptisóntai* since the scribes who penned the alternative reading evidently saw no impropriety in the statement.

The passage is cited because total immersion is thought to be an extreme measure for removing ceremonial defilement. That such was not necessarily the case in the mind of the Jews, however, appears from traditional writings that describe minutely the ceremonial lustrations practiced by them.

The passage is also cited because cots, or couches, or beds—as the word is variously translated—were objects involved in the rites signified by *baptismos*. Since immersing large items strains credulity, it is proposed that the idea in words containing the root *bap-* is wider than immersion. (a) We need not, however, suppose that these beds, or couches were such large affairs. Furthermore, (b) we know from some Jewish writings that larger pieces of furniture were constructed so they could be dismantled for lustrations (see the Talmudic tractate *Kelim* XVIII:9; XIX:1). (c) Even if they were large pieces, the argument from *baptismos* says nothing particularly about the form of the baptismal rite since *baptismos* never names our Christian ritual and since it would only carry such a generalized meaning by technical usage explained above in Hebrews 9.

We see a threefold statement about Jewish purification rites in these verses. At the first level comes the normal washing of hands before meals (Mk. 7:3; Mt. 15:2): *niptó*. The second level has to do with complete baths if the person has been in the market place and runs the risk of ceremonial defilement by touching an unclean person: *baptizó*. In the third level belong lustrations performed periodically on household items: *baptismos*.

The only other New Testament passage related to Jewish washings and baptism is John 3:25-26:

> Then a questioning arose from the disciples of John with a Jew about purification. And they came to John and said to him, "Rabbi, he who was with you beyond the Jordan to whom you have borne witness—behold he is baptizing and all are coming to him."

Obscurity surrounds this episode, but the gist of it appears to be that the purification question concerned the relationship of John's baptism and Jewish purification rites. At least from the contemporary Jewish viewpoint John's baptizing would be associated with Jewish purification ritual, and the question would have to do with why he was baptizing and what was the meaning of his baptism (cp. 1:19-28).

Little can be settled about the form of baptism from this passage because "purification" (*katharismos*) is an even more general term than "wash" (*louo*) and signifies effect with little if any reference to action.

Ecclesiasticus 34:30. As *baptizo* occurs only three times in the Septuagint Old Testament, so also it occurs only twice in the Old Testament Apocrypha. In Ecclesiasticus 34:30 the question is asked, "He that washes himself [*baptizomenos*] after the touching of a dead body, if he touch it again, what does his washing avail?" Numbers 19:11-19 details the procedure for purifying someone who has touched a dead body, and twice in those verses it speaks of sprinkling the water of purification on the unclean person (13, 19). Since sprinkling was the mode of administering the cleansing, the claim is that we have a case of *baptizo* performed by aspersion.

First, it may be questioned whether Ecclesiasticus refers to the whole purification in Numbers 19. The sprinkling occurred on the third and seventh days, but Ecclesiasticus speaks of touching the dead body *again*. According to the provisions in Numbers the person would not be clean until the evening of the seventh day, at which time the body would not be around to defile the person "again."

Secondly, however, if in some sense the author of Ecclesiasticus did have in mind the whole ritual purification of Numbers 19, he did not necessarily use *baptizomenos* to designate that whole cleansing procedure or to name the specific act of sprinkling. The concluding element in the process was bathing on the seventh day. The Septuagint translation of the Old Testament uses the Greek word *louo* ("to wash"), which is one of the secondary meanings of *baptizo* because a person normally submerges himself at least partially when he takes a bath. We suppose it is this particular lustration amidst the whole process that the writer of Ecclesiasticus designates in his usage of *baptizomenos*. At least, it need not be more than that.

Judith 12:7. In Judith 12:7 we find the other reference in the Apocrypha. In this reference *baptizo* appears with the sequential preposition *epi,* which fundamentally means "on" but here must mean "at" since it governs "a fountain of water":

> And she sent to Holophernes, saying, "Let my lord command now that your servant be allowed to go out to prayer." And Holophernes ordered the bodyguards not to prevent her. And she remained in the encampment for three days. And she would go out every night to the ravine Baitulous and baptize/wash herself in the camp at the fountain of water. And when she came up [out of the pool of water?], she asked the Lord God of Israel to guide her way into the raising up of the sons of his people. And entering in pure, she remained in the tent until someone brought her food at evening.

The argument goes that Judith would not have immersed herself in a camp that was full of soldiers; therefore, she must have washed her hands, face, or feet—a washing described by *baptizō.* On the contrary, however, such a washing could have been done in her tent, but she went outside to do it every night. Secondly, her daily observance together with the word "pure" indicates that she was performing Jewish ablutions, which were normally immersions of the body at least in part. In this and other occasions for taking a bath, we do not insist on a total immersion of the body, nor need we do so since examples of partial immersion clearly occur in the usages of this word. Whether total or partial must be determined from the nature and purpose of the particular example of *baptizō.*

Thirdly, going out at midnight suggests that she wanted to avoid being seen. Her place for bathing was, generally speaking, in the camp, which lay in an *aulon,* or valley; but it was specifically located in a *pharanx,* or ravine. The site was evidently a ravine leading off the main valley, which is a natural place for a spring to come out of the hillside. Her privacy resulted from a combination of darkness and seclusion. *Baptizō,* occurring in a setting like this one, provides no difficulty for the immersionist position.

Conclusion on Jewish lustrations. From Hebrews 6:2 it appears that Christian baptism could be classed with Jewish lustrations at least for purposes of comparison and contrast. That these lustrations as a group could be labeled *baptismoi* could also be granted. The evidence does not, however, warrant the conclusion that (a) the category over which *baptismoi* stands extended far enough to include sprinkling and pouring actions as argued from Hebrews 9:13; Ecclesiasticus 34:19; and Numbers 19:11-19. Even if the category were that broad, it does not follow that

(b) any individual rite within the group varies as widely as the group itself. It also cannot be demonstrated that (c) *baptismos* was ever used to label the specific rite of baptism while at the same time serving as a caption for all religious lustrations. Our conclusion is that the Jewish lustrations do not provide a positive basis for the generalized view of the meaning for *baptizō*.

Church history

A third major step in the argument for the general meaning of *baptizō* comes from confirmation in church history. The secondary meanings of *bap-* words and the adaptation of that root to Jewish ceremonial cleansings created presumptive evidence for the legitimacy of sprinkling and pouring. The correctness of that position finds confirmation in the varied practice of the early church.

Examples of affusion. Instances occur as early as the first part of the second century where water was poured on the candidate. Probably the earliest reference comes from the *Didache* cited earlier. *Didache* 7 reads as follows:

> Now concerning baptism, baptize thus: after first repeating all these things, baptize in running water in the name of the Father and the Son and the Holy Spirit. If you do not have running water, baptize in other water; and if you cannot use cold water, use warm. And if you have neither, pour water on the head three times in the name of the Father and Son and Holy Spirit. And before the baptism let the baptizer and the one who is to be baptized and any others who can do so fast. And you must order the one who is baptized to fast for one or two days previously.

After recommending affusion in cases of necessity, the writer goes ahead to use *baptizō* again in a way possibly inclusive of the *cheō* he has just mentioned. If running or other water was not available, preparation by fasting would still presumably be done by both the one baptized and the baptizer. Therefore *baptizō* would end up getting applied to a case of affusion.

In Eusebius' *Ecclesiastical History* 6:43 an account is given of Novatus, who was baptized by aspersion in his sickbed because it was thought that he would die. Upon recovery, however, he was not baptized in the normal way as was expected for entering an order of the clergy. An exception was made in his case; but he later renounced his commitments, not only to the bishopric, but also to Christ.

352

Other cases of "clinical baptisms" appear. In Cyprian's *Epistle* 76, written mid-second century, he answered favorably a question about the validity of aspersion. In support he referred to Numbers 8:5-7; 19:8, 9, 12, 13; and Ezekiel 36:25-26. The case here rests, of course, on the propriety of the comparison, but the fact that he was questioned about aspersion shows that it was not a matter agreed upon among Christians of the first few centuries. Even here it had to do with the sick or feeble, not just anyone, and so Cyprian's response must be understood in that context.

Response to church-history examples. In response to these citations from early church history, we offer several observations. First, (1) we have adopted the principle of *sola scriptura*. "Scripture alone" stands in contrast to scripture plus tradition. The teaching of the Bible provides our only primary basis for belief and practice. For this reason, in arguing for immersion, we did not present even the patristic evidence favorable to immersion. Instead, we reserved that data for countering the affusionist position as argued from early Christian writers. Because we did not accept sub-apostolic testimony as normative for the church, we kept it back to even less than a confirmatory role for immersion. The tradition of the elders during the Mosaic dispensation caused considerable confusion for the Jewish people; the tradition of the church has done the same in the Christian era. One method of avoiding confusion about God's intentions is to restrict the foundation of our confession to the recognized contents of the Christian canon.

Secondly, (2) we have adopted the principle of *approved precedent.* This concept actually restates the previous one because approved precedent is apostolic precedent and apostolicity is a primary criterion for New Testament writings. The New Testament was written by apostles and those who served under them as extensions of their office. Approved precedent emphasizes the *example* of the Lord's apostles while *sola scriptura* draws attention to their *teaching* in written form.

Practices found in the period immediately after the apostolic age do not carry particular weight even though they appear in close historical relationship. While it may be tempting to suppose that early leaders pass on practices of the apostles, we have not allowed their testimony and example to do more than confirm what we know from the apostles directly. According to *Didache* 7 cited earlier as well as other records, several foreign matters were introduced into baptismal practice at an early date: the temperature of the water, preference for running water, disrobing the candidate, baptizing new-born babies, delaying baptism as long as possible. During the first century itself perversions on a number of matters were creeping into the churches despite apostolic presence and disapproval. When we get beyond the primary witnesses of the resurrection and their chosen associates, we get on uncertain ground. Evidence from such sources cannot play a very important role in the thinking of the church.

Thirdly, (3) in the first centuries after the apostolic age *affusion or aspersion occurred only in special circumstances.* We note (a) several statements about the form of baptism. *Didache* specified pouring water on the head three times if baptizing (*baptizō*) was not possible. Toward the end of the quotation translated above, the writer accommodates the term *baptizō* to a non-*baptizō* act; he used the word in the last instance as a label only for the rite. The force of the case is that when the commandment cannot be obeyed, the next best thing may substitute for it; that does not change the meaning of the commandment. Standard procedure is not affected by cases of this sort, nor is the meaning and form of baptism itself altered by substitutions made for the sake of expediency. This example is not one of indifference or general meaning, but one of alteration.

That affusion was not a matter of indifference can be inferred from the following set of statements by Christian writers of different stripes during the first-through-fourth centuries. Arranging these citations in roughly chronological order, we begin with the *Epistle of Barnabas,* an apocryphal work attributed to the companion of Paul and originating during the last quarter of the first century or first quarter of the second. In a description of baptism it says, "This means that we go down into the water full of sin and pollutions, but come up again, bringing forth fruit, having in our hearts the fear [of God] and in our spirit the trust that is in Jesus" (11).

The *Shepherd of Hermas* (c. A.D. 150) contains just one statement directly relevant to the form of baptism: "But this seal is water into which men descend who are bound to death, but ascend who are destined to life" (2:4:3).

Justin Martyr (c. 114-165) writes in his *First Apology* 61, "Then they are led out by us where there is water and . . . in the name of God the Father and Lord of the universe, and of our Savior Jesus Christ, and of the Holy Spirit . . . they are washed with water . . . the one who leads to the washing place [laver] him who is to be baptized calling him by this name alone . . . he that is illuminated is washed." Here "wash," or "bathe," means the baptismal act, which a person is led away to water in order to do. Perhaps Justin uses "wash" because he has in mind Isaiah 1:16-20 to which he refers. At any rate, "leading away" favors an act that requires a substantial amount of water, or it would be brought to the candidate.

Tertullian (c. 160-c. 225), who lived in North Africa, has several baptism references in which he uses a form of the Latin word *tingo*, meaning to dip or immerse. In *Concerning Baptism* 2 the person baptized is dipped down into the water, and amid the utterance of some few words is sprinkled and then rises again. In 4 he also says that we are not "dipped in those waters that were in the beginning." A little later he adds, "There is no difference, then, whether a person is washed in a pool, a river, a fountain, a lake, or canal, nor is there any difference of consequence for those whom John immersed in the Jordan or Peter in the Tiber." Other uses of *tingo* for "baptize" appear in 11 and 12. In the work *Against Praxeas* 26 he says, "And indeed not once only, but three times according to the several names we are immersed into the several persons."

Cyril (c. 315-386), bishop of Jerusalem, in *Catecheses* 17 (written about A.D. 350) offers an especially distinct picture of baptism: "For as he that goes down into the water and is baptized is surrounded on all sides by water, so the apostles were baptized all over by the Spirit. The water surrounds the body externally, but the Spirit incomprehensibly baptizes the soul within."

Ambrose (c. 340-397), bishop of Milan, in *Concerning the Sacraments* recounts a baptism: "You were asked, 'Do you believe in God Almighty?' You said, 'I believe.' And thus you were immerged; that is, you were buried."

With Chrysostom (c. 347-407), bishop of Constantinople, we are reminded that other vocabulary was developing for *baptize* and *baptism*: *kataduō*, to submerge; and *ananeuō* to emerge; *anaduō*, to emerge upwards; as well as other related words. In his *Baptismal Instructions* 25 he comments, "After this anointing the priest makes you go down into the sacred waters, burying the old man and at the same time raising up the new, who is renewed in the image of his Creator."

355

Besides the above statements about baptism and examples of it, (b) several comments get their origin from the burial picture for baptism in Romans 6 and Colossians 2. Dionysius Areopa, for example, in *Concerning Ecclesiastical Structure* 2 says, "Properly the total covering by water is taken from an image of death and burial out of sight." Also on the imagery noted in Romans 6 the First Council of Toledo issued the following statement on baptism in A.D. 400: "For immersion in the water is like a descent to the grave, and again emersion from the water is a resurrection."

Athanasius (c. 296-373), bishop of Alexandria, speaking even of infant baptism, explains the meaning of baptism: "To immerse [*kataduō*] a child three times in the pool and to emerse [*anaduō*]—this shows the death . . . ." Basil the Great (c. 330-379), bishop of Caesarea, declares in *Concerning the Holy Spirit* 15,"By three immersions [*katadusis*] and by the like number of invocations the great mystery of baptism is completed."

In addition to the earlier quotation from Chrysostom, we find in *Baptismal Instructions* 11, "Baptism is a burial and a resurrection. For the old man is buried with his sin and the new man is resurrected, being renewed according to the image of his Creator." Gregory of Nyssa (c. 330-c. 395) in *Concerning the Baptism of Christ* explains, "Coming into water, the kindred element of the earth, we hide ourselves in it as the Savior did in the earth."

In the fourth-century production called *The Apostolic Constitutions* 3:17 it says, "Immersion [*katadusis*] denotes dying with Christ; emersion [*anadusis*], a resurrection with him." Damascenus in *The Orthodox Faith* 4:10 comments similarly, "Baptism is a type of the death of Christ for by three immersions baptism signifies . . . ."

Chrysostom again writes on John 3, "For when we immerse our heads in the water as in a sepulchre below, the old man is buried and wholly sunk once for all; then as we emerge again, the new man rises again" (*Homily* 25:2). Augustine (354-430), bishop of Hippo in Africa, says, "Rightly are you immerged three times who have received baptism . . . for that thrice-repeated submersion [*submersio*] expresses a resemblance of the Lord's burial."

Besides the direct statements about immersion and the teaching about baptism in the imagery of Romans 6, the crude practice of disrobing candidates witnesses to the same. The custom gained in uniformity as the early centuries wore on. Chrysostom of Antioch, Ambrose of Milan, and Cyril of Jerusalem describe the custom. Since nakedness does not pertain to pouring or sprinkling on the head, setting aside modesty to perform immersion testifies to a strong commitment to the latter.

We cannot help noting also that the Eastern Orthodox communions have always maintained the practice of immersing even infants. The Greek Orthodox Church in particular, we suspect, has found it quite unnatural to their own language to describe a pouring as *baptizō*.

Summaries on church history. We have found two main departures from standard practice, the first being *clinical baptisms.* The "clinici," as they were called, who had water poured on them while severely sick in bed, were usually barred later from priesthood if they recovered. There were evidently two reasons for this stricture: (a) the sincerity of their conversion was suspect because of its circumstances; in earlier times it may also have been that (b) their baptism was considered abnormal because of its form.

The other possible departure is *baptizing the head,* but that expression need not mean just the head. Studies of this historical question reveal that it was not in fact until the Council of Ravenna in 1311 that official sanction was given by the Western Church to the practice of affusion and aspersion.

From church history we observe the following generalizations about Christian baptism: (1) immersion was standard procedure except in cases of necessity, where water was poured on the person. (2) Threefold immersion was practiced even with infants when that practice gained in popularity later. (3) The Greek Orthodox Church practices immersion unto this day. (4) On the form of baptism the issue in the centuries immediately after the apostolic era was not what *baptizō* meant or what was performed as standard procedure, but whether substitutions in cases of expediency were valid. Novatus' not being baptized in "regular" fashion after recovery from sickness reinforces this point. (5) Since many authors under varying circumstances and from different places over a long period of time are gathered together in such a survey, we would not assume an exact uniformity of viewpoint and practice on their part; but it does not appear that early Christian practice particularly reinforces affusion as standard procedure for formal identification with Christ.

357

Arguments Against Immersionism

If we correctly perceive the proper structure of the argument for immersion, the responsibility of the affusion position consists in finding data that will not readily fit with the immersionist position. For reasons expressed along the way, the above *arguments for affusion* have not proved satisfactory; we turn now to *arguments against immersion* to see whether in fact certain pieces of information do not fit that position.

Problems with prepositions

Accounts of the baptism of Jesus and the Ethiopian eunuch contain the clearest statements about the form of the rite. While many who take the general view about form feel free to allow immersion in these two examples, others attempt to demonstrate that it did not necessarily happen even here because the descriptions of the baptisms lack precision. The ambiguity comes from questioning the meaning of three prepositions crucial to the immersionist understanding in these texts: *eis,* meaning "into"; *en,* meaning "in"; and *ek,* meaning "out of." It is alleged that *eis* signifies, not only "into," but also "unto." Likewise *en* means, not only "in," but "at" or "near." Lastly *ek* may mean "away from" in addition to "out of." Jesus went down *to* the water, was baptized *at* the Jordan, and came *away from* the water. The baptism could have been a pouring. Similarly the eunuch got out of the carriage, went to the edge of the water with Philip, and came away again. Without getting lost in detailed matters, we endeavor to assess the validity of these claims because our own positive presentation has laid considerable stress on examples of baptism.

Eis. A general remark on these prepositions is that (a) if they do not respectively mean "into," "in," and "out of," no clearer way of expressing these concepts by way of prepositions can be found in the Greek language. In addition, they each contain word pictures distinctive to themselves. Secondary meanings do develop for all words including prepositions, but (b) secondary meanings are not invoked unless the word picture does not accord well with the nature of the thing discussed. If a word carries significations as different as "unto" vs. "into," some manner of distinguishing them in given statements must be possible or communication could not occur through them. No possibility would ever exist for making clear by prepositions that Jesus, say, went "into," rather than "to," the stream.

We distinguish multiple meanings of the same word by the nature of the subject discussed by it, giving preference to the agreed word picture. Since the water of a river can be entered, the word *eis* means "into" in the accounts of Jesus and the eunuch's baptisms, even though cases arise that require "to" as translations of *eis*. The English word "into" does not always mean "into the midst of"; it may sometimes mean "hard up against," as in the statement, "The car ran into the bridge abutment." We would never suppose, however, that just because it can mean "hard up against" in the right setting, "into" can mean such a thing in the sentence, "The car ran into the river." A bridge abutment cannot be entered, but water can; so we "sort out" the meanings of "into" by the nature of the situation in which it appears, giving precedence to what we know from experience is its basic word picture.

In the situation of a man walking down *eis* the river bank, we say *eis* means "to"; but in his walking *eis* the water, we say *eis* means "into." As surely as "into" means into the water since it can be entered, *eis* means into the water in these baptismal accounts and for the same reason. In a given case we do not have to find a *special reason* for adopting a preposition's fundamental word picture because of the *general reason* that the primary meaning is assumed unless the nature of the case requires otherwise. Providing a reason becomes the responsibility of the one who seeks to use a secondary meaning. The validity of adopting the secondary meaning is not on equal footing with that of adopting a primary meaning.

En. The same linguistic principle applies to *en*. We understand "baptized *en* the Jordan River" (Mk. 1:5) as "baptized *in* the Jordan" rather than "*at* the Jordan" despite the fact that under proper circumstances *en* may be translated "at." If *en* can mean "*in*," that is what it means because "inside-ness" is its word picture; if it cannot mean "in," it signifies "at" or some other related concept appropriate to the circumstance.

In the particular reference Mark 1:5 we understand *en* to mean "in" because a river is something that a person can be in and because baptizing is something that can happen in a river. It is not quite legitimate to question this standard meaning for *en* here by paralleling it with John's baptizing "*en* Bethany" (Jn. 1:28) and "*en* Aenon" (Jn. 3:23). In the first place, (a) the verses in the fourth gospel could be translated "in Bethany" or "in Aenon" inasmuch as a person can be "in" a village and baptizing can occur "in" a village; consequently, no inference may be transferred back to Mark 1:5 to detract from the clarity of that verse. Preferring "at" as a translation of *en* may come from idiomatic expectancy in English rather than from meaning requirements in Greek.

In the second place, (b) the passages in John could be rendered "at Bethany" or "at Aenon," but the reason for that possibility comes from circumstances not present in Mark 1:5. From John 3:23 we learn that the Baptist's reason for baptizing *en* Aenon was that there was much water there. Since the water was not inside the village, it must mean "in (the environs of)" Aenon; that is, "at" Aenon. The reference to baptizing *"en"* Bethany beyond Jordan connects naturally with Mark 1:5, which indicates that his baptizing ministry farther south was in the Jordan rather than in some village nearby or in Jericho. The need for much water (Jn. 3:23) for his baptizing also makes it natural to suppose that John means the Jordan River up by Bethany. There would be more water in the Jordan than in the village so that "at" Bethany might commend itself as a translation of the phrase without doing an injustice to the principle of preference we have enunciated.

As a conclusion on *en* we may translate "at" Aenon and "at" Bethany because of preferred English idiom or because of circumstances suggesting that John's baptizing ministry occurred "in the environs of" rather than "in" these villages. But no such suggestions appear in Mark 1:5 so we prefer "in" the Jordan, especially since the immediately following example of Jesus' baptism has him going into the water and coming out of it again (1:9-10).

On the background of what has been said about *en* in Mark 1:5, we can discuss the use of *en* in the expression "baptize in water." The question has been whether to translate the phrase "baptize *in* water" or "baptize *with* water." Immersionists often prefer the former and non-immersionists the latter. Against immersion *en* is said to carry the idea of means and therefore implies that the baptizing was done by sprinkling or pouring, because the *liquid* is what was "moved."

In favor of the translation "with water" we note that Mark 1:8 and Luke 3:16 omit *en* altogether even though (a) the parallel passage in Matthew 3:11 contains *en* (cp. Jn. 1:26, 33), and even though (b) the associated statements about baptism in the Holy Spirit and fire have *en* (Mk. 1:8; Lk. 3:16; Mt. 3:11; Jn. 1:33; I Cor. 12:13). The absence of *en* before *hydati* ("water") most naturally expresses means; the presence of *en hydati* in parallel accounts with plain *hydati* and in associated statements suggests that with or without the preposition instrumentality is the idea (note *baptō* + gen. in Lk. 16:24 as well).

Earlier in the language means, or instrumentality, would have been covered simply by a special termination on the end of the word for "water" (*hydati*). During the Hellenistic period in the New Testament, Greek was increasing the use of prepositions in addition to these "case endings"; consequently, *en* might appear in front of a word in the instrumental case without changing the idea from instrumentality ("*by means of* water") to location ("*in* water"). Even with this growth in prepositional usage, however, grammarians of New Testament Greek usually say that means is still not commonly expressed by *en;* that preposition usually denotes location or manner.

Our view of this matter is that "in water" or "with water" (or "into water" as in "*eis* the Jordan" for that matter) does not affect the immersionist view. (a) Only Luke 3:16 definitely omits *en* before "water"; textual variants are found later in that verse on "baptize in (by) the Holy Spirit" and also in Mark 1:8 on "baptized in water." It is probably not necessary to suppose that all the references must be understood in a uniform way. As we will note again presently, (b) even parallel passages like Matthew 3:11 and Luke 3:16 do not have to mean exactly the same thing in their corresponding elements. We could be content with allowing the exact sense to shift at the level of precision where we are just now working. If we conceived of the sense as varying in this manner, we would understand the passages with *en* to mean "in" and the ones without *en* to mean "by means of." (c) The decision regarding meaning here depends somewhat on the manner in which the evangelists put their gospels into final form. *Hydati* and *en hydati* may simply be alternative equivalents of the Aramaic word for water plus the prepositional prefix b^e, which has a range of application wide enough to cover means, manner, and location. Consequently, the situation is one in which a language having several precise devices of expression is forced to render an Aramaic particle that has a more general signification. A precise translation must be used to render a general one so that on different occasions different precise Greek expressions can occur; strictly different things are meant because of the requirements of translation.

Regardless of textual reading or translation, however, the issue decides nothing against immersion because (d) water can be conceived of as the means of covering, immersing, or overwhelming a solid. Means does not have to be attached to what moves the solid into the liquid; in fact, the solid does not have to move at all in order for the imagery in *baptô* or *baptizô* to apply. Confirmation of this point comes from non-biblical passages where *baptizô* carries the notion of "overwhelming" (cp. Isa. 21:4 in LXX). "Dipped with water" does grate on English idiom, but "immersed with water" does not; the reason, we suppose, is that "dip" stresses the movement of the solid while, in referring to the same action, "immerse" stresses the movement of the water. Therefore, whether "water" refers to the element or the means seems immaterial as an argument (1) *against* immersion in these expressions.

En hydati and *hydati* also do not require a view of baptism that (2) *includes* immersion, but allows for sprinkling and pouring as well. In this conception *en hydati* would have immersion in mind and *hydati* would be affusion or aspersion. Our comments above on means and on Aramaic equivalency apply here as well so that the idea is not sustained by the data we have to work with.

On the non-immersionist side, however, we wonder whether the question can so easily be left undecided. While it is physically *possible* to walk out into a river or pool and sprinkle or pour water on the candidate, it is not *natural* to do so. Baptism *with* water does not offer so much difficulty for immersion as baptism *in* water offers for pouring and sprinkling.

Ek. In a discussion of *ek* we again invoke the principle of word-picture preference. Coming "*ek* the water" in Mark 1:10 and Acts 8:39 means "out of" rather than "away from." The preposition (*apo*) has the strict idea of going away from, and no reason presents itself for needing to depart the original signification of *ek* in favor of *apo*.

In order to present a reason for preferring "away from" over "out of," affusionists customarily observe that Matthew 3:16 actually puts *apo* in the place where *ek* appears in Mark 1:10 (cp. Acts 8:39). *Ek* must then be a synonym for *apo* in this instance because they replace one another. We suppose, however, that (a) *it would be equally legitimate to argue that "apo" means "out of" in Matthew 3:16 since it parallels ek in Mark 1:10.*

More importantly, (b) words are not synonymous just because two writers use them to *cite the same event.* A description never exhaustively reproduces the reality itself, but selectively notes enough of its features for the listener to grasp the overall nature of the event. (c) *Both*

362

"out of" and *"away from"* are involved. When Jesus came up out of the water and walked on the bank, he both came out of and went away from. Mark notes the first stage of movement; Matthew notes the second.

Furthermore, (d) *apo* and *ek* could be variants that *translate the same Aramaic word.* As in our earlier discussion about *en*, we consider it worthwhile here to remember the Aramaic background of the gospel record and writers. That background could have been an *oral account* crystallized in Aramaic wording by the early witnesses of the resurrection as they told and retold outstanding events of Christ's ministry before it was reduced to written form. Perhaps preliminary *written accounts* such as those mentioned in Luke 1:1-4 underlie the finished forms of Matthew, Mark, and Luke. Regardless of the likelihood of such procedures, it is clear that the original proclamation of the gospel was carried forward by the *Aramaic-speaking followers* of our Lord. Their Semitic mind set necessarily shaped the wording of what they had been recounting in their native language. In preparing oral and written presentations of those things that had been fulfilled among them, they had to transfer their testimony into Greek for circulation in the non-Jewish world. Aramaic had relatively few prepositions so that the ones that did exist expressed more general concepts or a greater variety of meanings. The one preposition *min* covered both "out from" and "away from" and meant simply "from." Greek had no preposition whose word picture was so general; consequently, in order to express leaving a body of water, the speaker was forced to translate his thoughts into more specific ones. Sometimes it was done one way ("out from"); sometimes another ("away from"). Therefore *apo* ("away from") does not have to be a synonym of *ek* ("out from") either because separate parts of the same *event* are being indicated by the two writers or because separate translations of the same *word* are being used.

Another matter related to *eis* and *ek* comes to the surface in the conversion of the Ethiopian eunuch (Acts 8:26-40). Luke recounts his baptism by saying that they both went down into the water and came up out of the water. The point raised against immersion from this account is that Philip as well as the eunuch would have been baptized if "going down into" means immersion and "coming up out of" means emersion. Immersionists, however, differentiate the baptism itself from the going down into, and coming up out of, the water. Indeed it seems impossible to do otherwise since Philip "baptized" the eunuch *after* they both went down and *before* they both came up (8:38-39). Baptism therefore was a separate act performed between the other two. The reason "into" and "out of" hold significance for immersion is that walking out into the water does not fit so naturally with affusion or aspersion.

"Much water." In our positive presentation for immersion we made use of the statement that John baptized "at Aenon near Salem because there was much water there" (Jn. 3:23). Thus we associated the abundance of water with the requirements of his baptism and inferred that it was immersion because affusion and aspersion use comparatively little water. The reason for needing much water, however, has often been assigned to the personal requirements of the crowds who followed him and to the needs of any beasts of burden they had brought along. A supplementing factor is the scarcity of water in Palestine, especially during the dry season, and the strain an influx of people would put on local water supplies. John's sensitivity to these concerns prompted him to choose places where extra demand for water would not work hardship on the local populace. A final factor is the suggestion that "much water" be translated "many waters" understood as "many springs" in keeping with the name "Aenon," an Aramaic plural form meaning "springs." Under this reconstruction we have, not a large body of water necessarily, but several small ones possibly. Presumptive evidence for immersion then falls out of the text.

Many springs nevertheless amount to much water. That the drain-off formed pools sufficient for immersion is not enhanced or hindered by the choice of translations. We may do well to remember that (a) Greek has a word for "spring" so that we would have expected it to be the translation, were springs the idea in the Evangelist's mother tongue.

Furthermore, (b) the Greek plural probably represents a literal rendering of the Aramaic idiom. Four other times John uses "many waters" for "much water" always in the sense of abundance instead of number, and he is the only New Testament writer so to use it (Rev. 1:15; 14:2; 17:1; 19:6). Although "water" (*hydōr*) is often singular in the Septuagint (Gen. 43:24; 49:4; Ex. 7:21, 24; Lev. 11:34, etc.), it occurs several times in the plural with "many waters" as a translation of the Hebrew *mayim rabbim* (literally "many waters"): II Samuel 22:17; (LXX = II Kg. 22:17); Psalms 18:16 (LXX = 17:16); 29:3 (LXX = 28:3); 32:6 (LXX = 31:6); 77:19 (LXX = 76:19); 93:4 (LXX = 92:4); 107:23 (LXX = 106:23); 144:7 (LXX = 143:7); Jeremiah 51:13 (LXX =

28:13); 51:55 (LXX = 28:55). The Aramaic word *mayim* presumably lies behind the Greek *hydata*, whose plural form is less usual in its own language than it is where Jewish idiom has affected Greek usage—as in the LXX. Presumably therefore *polla hydata* represents a literal translation of the Aramaic word, which is always dual. Consequently, we doubt both the idea and the inference from it.

Moreover, (c) the text of John's gospel ties the reason for "much water" to the baptizing rather than to the multitudes. Such a connection would not be impossible to suppose if we had warrant for it; but as it is, the association of water with the hearers' personal needs appears to be arbitrary. What is true as to fact is not necessarily true as to the point being made in a given statement. The feeding of the five thousand and the four thousand remind us that people some distance from home would need food as well as shelter during their stay, but no mention is made of John or Jesus locating their ministries relative to these needs; only water is mentioned in the case of John's work. We prefer to think that the admittedly double use of the water as to fact is a different question from the point the gospel writer makes when he declares that John *baptized* at Aenon because there was much water there.

Arid climate. A less significant argument against immersion comes from the dry climate in Palestine: ready access to enough water for baptism would provide a problem if baptism were immersion. Needless to say, the population of this area took seriously the need to collect water into pools and cisterns during the rainy season. The culture was already accustomed to using water extensively for lustrations and other purification rituals. The ascetic Jewish sect called the Essenes maintained itself on the northwest corner of the Dead Sea at Qumran amidst one of the most desolate regions in the Holy Land; yet they are known for practicing not only initiatory lustrations, but also daily cleansings as well. Water supply either for immersion or concentrated multitudes of people evidently created no insuperable difficulties for the ministry of John the Baptist or of Jesus.

Paul's baptism. According to Acts 22:16 Ananias commanded Paul to arise and be baptized and wash away his sins. The argument is that Paul was baptized standing and therefore was not immersed. Such a comment, however, draws an unwarranted conclusion because (1) "arise" may simply translate the Hebrew interjection *qum*, which is not so much a commandment to get up as it is a commandment to get

365

started. As such the idiomatic expression may be addressed to listeners who are already standing.

Even if "arise" does include getting up—as seems likely from Acts 9:18, (2) it does not mean that he remained standing while he was baptized, or that he did not move to a place where the baptism occurred. "Get up" does not mean get up and stand still; it may mean simply "get up" in preparation for doing something. Immersion is most usually administered from a standing to a submerged and then to a standing position again anyway.

Revelation 19:13. In passing we note an objection formerly raised at times against the proposition that *baptizō* has never been translated "to sprinkle." According to the Greek text of Revelation 19:13 the rider of the white horse wears a "robe covered/immersed/dyed [*bebammenon*] with blood." *Bebammenon* is a perfect participle from *baptō*. In its place this verse contains the form of a word meaning "sprinkle" in some ancient texts: the Latin Vulgate, Bohairic Coptic, Ethiopic, Harclean Syriac, some manuscripts of the Old Latin, and a few early Christian writers. From Greek manuscripts of varying dates we know of at least four different forms of *rhantizō* ("to sprinkle") that replace *bebammenon* at this point; this substitution may have occurred under the influence of Isaiah 63:3.

Whatever the origin of the variant, we obviously have a textual problem instead of a translation possibility. Needless to say, just because a word can replace another without making the sentence into nonsense does not mean the varying words are synonyms; the sentence may not make the same sense when the new word is substituted. We feel then justified in saying that if *baptizō* is general enough to cover for places where the action was really sprinkling or pouring, we would surely expect to find an instance where sprinkle or pour occurs at the point in the translation where *baptizō* occurs in the original.

Baptism metaphors

Objection has also been raised against using Romans 6 in discussions of the form of baptism, and properly so perhaps if the passage has been treated as primary evidence. At any rate, certain objections here must still be set aside. It is noted, for example, that (1) baptism also involves the metaphor of crucifixion, or circumcision, or getting dressed, which does not answer to any form of baptism. Obviously no use of water can picture crucifixion or circumcision and for that very reason neither of these can be meant to describe the form of the ordinance.

It should be clear that (a) when no formal correspondence can exist, no formal correspondence is meant. With death and resurrection, however, a correspondence in form can be meant and, we take it, *is* meant because (b) baptism alone is called a *homoiōma*-likeness of them. Furthermore, (c) the fact that crucifixion has no formal likeness to baptism establishes nothing against another analogy carrying intended likeness to baptism. Finally, (d) among the analogies of baptism only Christ's death-resurrection bears a real relationship to the meaning of baptism. Birth, circumcision, the flood, the exodus, and getting dressed are merely suggestive imageries; they have no actual connection with the forgiveness of sin. Messiah's death-resurrection, however, establishes a real basis upon which the Father wills to view us as sinless like him.

It is also noted that (2) baptism bears a meaning similar to that of the sprinkling of the blood for purification (Num. 19:9, 17-18; Heb. 9:13, 14, 22; 10:22; 12:24; I Pet. 1:2). While objecting to immersionist usage of Romans 6, affusionists themselves argue on the same pattern that the sprinkling of the blood of Christ is for the removal of guilt; hence, baptism can just as easily have a likeness to sprinkling.

As to theory, of course, baptism could have the form of sprinkling in recollection of the Old Testament purification ritual, but that is not the issue. There is an almost endless array of relevant things to which baptism could bear a resemblance, but a rite could not have an endless array of forms and still be perceived as the same rite. We seek to discover whether, out of all the possible rituals God could have enacted, he has specified any one of them as a positive command. Making note of this fact only shows that the argument from baptismal analogies belongs in fact among confirmatory evidences inasmuch as analogy must be preceded by discovering the prior commandment.

If first it could be shown that the word "baptize" found in the prior commandment (Mt. 28:19, etc.) referred to a rite without a form, sprinkling water could serve as a form that bears a meaning similar to the sprinkling of blood. But that contention cannot bear its burden of proof so that the manner of administering baptism cannot be broadened beyond the immersion action that gave name to the rite originally. That baptism is a form as well as a rite named by its form leaves us with only one principle by which to conclude a proper line of thought: we have no right to change the form of a ritual command; baptism is the form as well as the rite that has that form. Baptism *is* said to be a *homoiōma*-likeness to immersion, which in itself might not eliminate an alternative form that reminded us of the sprinkling of blood; but baptism *is not* said to be a *homoiōma*-likeness of the sprinkling of blood —or any other analogy for that matter. We might close by wondering why baptism unto remission of sins would be formally administered in terms of a shadow of the atonement rather than in terms of the substance of the atonement.

Baptism in the Holy Spirit

The expression "baptism in the Holy Spirit" contains the word used to name the Christian ordinance of baptism. Some writers use this observation against the immersionist position. The argument hinges on the fact that "baptism" in the Holy Spirit is also called a "coming upon" when Jesus says, "But you will receive power when the Holy Spirit has *come upon* you, and you shall be my witnesses . . ." (Acts 1:8). Subsequently, twice in Peter's sermon on Pentecost this same event is termed an "outpouring": "I will *pour out* of my Spirit on all flesh" (Acts 2:17; cp. 2:33; Joel 2:28; see also Tit. 3:6; Isa. 32:15; Prov. 1:23). Later in Caesarea, the same apostle addressed the household and friends of Cornelius when the Holy Spirit *"fell on"* all those hearing the word (Acts 10:44; cp. 11:15). To these may be added an imagery related to this phenomena from Ezekiel 36:26: "I will give you a new heart and I will *put* a new spirit *in* you." Four pictures are used to express the union of God's Spirit with man. If "baptism" meant immersion, the other descriptions could not be used because the images are exclusive of each other; if "baptize" is a general word that serves to designate a rite only rather than an action as well, the other terminology for baptism in the Holy Spirit has propriety.

Immersion does bear a parallel relationship with sprinkling and pouring as far as forms of action are concerned. We do not, however, have to put a general-to-specific relationship between *baptisma* and the other two actions in order to call receiving the Spirit both a baptism and an outpouring or falling. Mutually exclusive literalisms can nevertheless be compatible metaphors. "Baptism in the Holy Spirit" obviously denotes a figurative idea, as does "outpouring of the Spirit," "falling of the

Spirit," or " 'inputting' of the Spirit." We do not literally immerse someone in the Spirit or pour the Spirit on him simply because (a) the Spirit
is neither a liquid nor a solid. "Immersing," "outpouring," "inputting"
must be figurative. Language allows us to "mix metaphors," but it
does not allow us to mix literalisms. The reason it does not is that literal
expression minimizes the distinction between the word's image and
the reality's nature, and parallel realities cannot mix; but in figurative
expression there *is* a distinction between the word picture and the
reality pictured. Consequently, we do not have to remove the parallel
relationship (and hence the exclusiveness of the images) by making
one word carry a general picture and the other convey a specific one.

We remove the exclusiveness by making a distinction between the
picture and the thing pictured. The part-to-whole relationship takes
place, not between the word pictures themselves, but between the
word pictures and the reality. Making one word ("baptize") general
and the other ("pour") specific eliminates the mutual exclusiveness
of dipping and pouring by doing something to the meaning of one of
the words ("dipping"). Making them both figurative eliminates the
exclusiveness by making both into figurative parts of the same real whole.
We take the latter alternative because the Spirit is not literally water
so that his coming cannot literally be expressed by a form of the application of water. Immersion in the Holy Spirit emphasizes the overwhelming completeness of the relationship with the Spirit. Outpouring
of the Spirit stresses his coming from above us. Falling on us draws
attention to the point-in-time occurrence of the event. Putting the
Spirit in us communicates that his influence permeates us to the level
of our motives, feelings, affections, attitudes, and thoughts, which are
all associated with the "inner man." The lack of cogency in this argument against immersion grows fundamentally out of a failure to distinguish language and reality, and thereafter a failure to appreciate the
added difference symbolic language makes in the usage of words.

Other observations tell against the argument from baptism in the
Holy Spirit. The imageries of pouring, baptizing, and falling upon are
simply figurative expressions that address different aspects of the total
event. We know this, not only because the Spirit is not a liquid, but
because (b) the imageries for union with the Spirit are mutually exclusive.
The pouring, inputting, and baptism are not the only figures for this;
Jesus "breathes on" his disciples in John 20:22. Making baptism a
general word will not enable it to incorporate so diverse a figure as

"breathing on." There is no more reason to make "baptize" a general word on the basis of this set of figures than there is to make "pour on" or "put in" general to incorporate the others. Therefore, the "pouring on" and "putting in" are not reconciled with baptize by enlarging the latter, but by recognizing the figurative character of all these expressions. They do not speak of the mode of his coming, but of aspects of his coming to us. The same reality may be set forth *figuratively* under various images without making any of them relate *really* to any other of them. In light of this conclusion, the line of reasoning from baptism in the Holy Spirit has no bearing on our question about the form of water baptism, because baptism is not called a likeness of the outpouring of the Spirit.

For the sake of completeness we add another possible way of understanding the combination of pouring and immersing figures. Above we suggested that pouring and immersing emphasized different *aspects* of the Spirit's coming; here we note that (c) pouring and immersing may look at different *stages* of the Spirit's coming. The pouring speaks of his being dispensed from the Father while the immersing speaks of the subsequent entering of the disciples overwhelmingly into him.

Sprinkling of the blood

Leviticus 14:1-9 and Numbers 19:17-20 describe purification rites for leprosy and for touching a dead body, both of which involved sprinkling. On this background Psalms 51:7 says of actual cleansing from sin, "Purge me with hyssop and I will be clean; wash me and I will be whiter than snow." In a similar application Ezekiel 36:25 promises, "Then I will sprinkle clean water upon you and you will be clean; from all your filthiness and from all your idols I will cleanse you." In a Messianic prophecy Isaiah predicts, "He will sprinkle many nations" (52:15). Moses, David, Isaiah, and Ezekiel represent God as considering sprinkling a suitable manner of depicting purification from sin. Surely sprinkling the blood of the real sacrifice would be appropriate symbolism for spiritual cleansing. Inasmuch as Isaiah predicts that the Servant will actually sprinkle many nations, baptism by sprinkling fulfills the anticipation of the prophet.

Our concern does not have to do with *what can serve* as an appropriate symbol of purification. The blood of the Lamb might be symbolically aspersed on the sinner after the analogy of the hyssop dipped in clean

370

water or in blood. Our object of inquiry, however, is *what God did institute* to symbolize spiritual cleansing through the Messiah. As far as the Suffering Servant prediction is concerned, we agree that only the *meaning* of contact with his blood need be envisioned, not necessarily the *form* of that contact as well. These rituals are *analogous,* but not therefore *determinative* for the form of Christian baptism. Even as the outpouring of the Spirit does not argue for affusion, so also the sprinkling of blood does not argue for aspersion.

Access to water

In our own day churches have baptistries built into the church building, but in New Testament times we suppose there were none of these; yet, the contention goes, we never find people taken to a supply of water large enough for baptism.

On the other hand, however, we never see water brought to the people either, as could be the case with pouring or sprinkling. (a) The problem, of course, is that baptism scenes are not always described with the precision necessary to satisfy our questions about form.

(b) There are cases where water *was* sought. During John's ministry the multitudes went out to be baptized by him (Mk. 1:4-5):

> John the Baptist came in the desert and was preaching baptism of repentance unto remission of sins; and all the Judean country and all the Jerusalemites were going out to him and were being baptized by him in the Jordan River, confessing their sins.

During his ministry he always located himself by sources of water satisfactory for immersion and the people went out to him. This phenomenon qualifies as going to the water. The conversion of the jailor and his household may involve a change of location from his house (Acts 16:32) to the place of baptism (16:33) and then to his house again (16:34). The argument that people were not taken to water appears not to consider adequately these points.

(c) The candidate may not have needed to change locations. The conversion of Lydia and her household occurred at the place of prayer beside a river (Acts 16:11-15). In the household conversions there would be no real need of taking the family elsewhere if they had bathing facilities in their homes, especially in Jewish homes that observed the ritual lustrations of Judaism. This may be true of Paul when Ananias baptized him. These possibilities are strong enough that the argument from location does not reinforce the affusionist position.

The three thousand on Pentecost

On Pentecost according to Acts 2:41 three thousand were baptized after accepting the Christian message. Occasionally the objection has been voiced that so many could not have been conveniently immersed on one day, nor would it have been easy to find enough water for such an undertaking. In recent decades these points have not been reiterated so frequently because some of the pools in and around Jerusalem would have served well the purpose of mass baptism. If its antiquity is sufficient, the Lower Gihon would have been especially appropriate in that it covers some 3½ acres and has terraced sides. The Pool of Siloam mentioned in John 9:7 would be another suitable pool for baptism. Other pools and water supplies in and around Jerusalem would have sufficed.

The time factor also puts no strain on the situation as we know it. The twelve apostles alone could have baptized the whole multitude in a space of four hours or so if it took about a minute for each candidate. Spaced out around the banks of the Lower Gihon, they could have worked simultaneously. Others from among the 120 could also have assisted in the project as well as those previously baptized that day. If two thousand invalids can be bathed in the healing session at Lourdes, surely three thousand able-bodied people could have been baptized in that period of time.

Arguments Against the Broad View

In the previous pages we responded to each consideration as it arose; here we offer some general comments on the view that *baptizō* as to action is indifferent.

Linguistic objection

The first objection to affusionism is a linguistic one: it does not take the fundamental and expected meanings of several words relevant to the subject. It is a revealing thing, we feel, that regarding baptism *baptizō* consistently does not mean "dip," but an extended idea like "wash." *Eis* does not mean "into," but "unto"; *ek* does not mean "out

372

of," but "away from"; *en* does not mean "in," but "at," "beside," or "by means of." An unexpected meaning is too frequently called for, and demanded without a sufficient originating reason for proposing a significance of *baptizō* that creates special considerations. If positive reasons caused us to begin with "wash," it might be different; but without them the resulting problems should in themselves turn us away from this meaning to one for which positive evidence already exists. The cumulative force of needing to appeal constantly to secondary considerations creates the suspicion that something in the affusionist interpretation is unnatural to its setting, especially when the physical circumstances in all clearer examples of baptism are not the kind expected for such secondary meanings.

Symbological objection

The second general objection to the affusionist position is a symbological one: we wonder whether affusionism properly understands the form-meaning composite inherent in a symbolic rite. By its very nature a symbolic rite has form, and baptism is just such a rite inasmuch as it is called a likeness (Rom. 6:5). The wedding ceremony is a rite, but not a symbolic one on the whole; therefore cultures have generated many different forms of it. But observances that bear meaning symbolically require relatively prescribed forms to signify that meaning appropriately. Some natural or historical connection must unite the emblem and the referent. So to speak, a window would not symbolize strength.

In such a vein all the Mosaic institutions were established with particular forms. The animal for a certain sacrifice, for example, was a red heifer without blemish; it could not then be a sorrel horse that was lame. The manner of sacrifice was also specified rather closely. Old Testament purification rituals had set patterns as did those developed in Jewish tradition. Even the tabernacle bore symbolic meaning in its structure so that the Hebrew writer recalls the divine mandate, "See that you make everything according to the pattern that was shown to you in the mountain" (Heb. 8:5; cp. Ex. 25:40). Divine authority rests behind the form as well as the meaning of a symbolic institution.

A symbolic rite has meaning *and* form. It is not likely then that Jesus would institute a symbolic rite without establishing its form; a symbolic rite without a form is a virtual contradiction of terms. From the standpoint of theory we would know that this rite has form as surely as any

373

other one ordained by God, and we expect more precision in the ordinance than water applied by another. Since no form is separately described in detail, the form of the rite is the name of the rite and illustrated in the examples of it.

If, however, such a variety of acts as immersion, affusion, and aspersion can fall under the same label, *baptizō* means any act with water applied by another. In other words, baptism has no form, just meaning; consequently, it is not classed among symbolic rites because they have both. Baptism is not then included among Jewish lustrations—which brings the matter full circle because it was by classifying baptism among these rites that the most likely argument for affusion originated. On the one hand, if it does not mean more than they did, it is not a separate rite; on the other hand, it is more than cleansing from physical defilement (I Pet. 3:21), or even cleansing from spiritual defilement; thus we pass to the next objection.

Theological objection
The third general objection to the affusionist view is a theological one: baptism is a symbolic rite that means more than spiritual cleansing. Part of the reason affusionists feel content with variable form is that they limit its symbolic import to spiritual cleansing. The emphasis therefore falls on the *element* in keeping with the tendency to classify baptism as primarily a spiritualized Jewish ablution. If all it signifies is cleansing, the manner of administering the water does not loom so large. New Testament teaching, however, identifies baptism with the salvation and change related to Christ's death-resurrection; consequently, baptism is not just a spiritual cleansing (water), but a spiritual cleansing done on the basis of the death-resurrection of Christ (immersion). As truly as the cleansing is associated with the *water*, the identification with the Messiah in his distinctive act is associated with the *immersion* in water.

When cleansing considerations dominate, baptism ends up getting connected with Old Covenant types and Jewish traditions: ceremonial ablutions, sprinkling of blood and "clean" water, and the like, which are only shadows of the true and therefore are secondary matters. The death-resurrection of the sinless Messiah, on the other hand, is the substance and fulfillment of what all these prior types anticipated. Baptism then as to form takes on the marks of that to which it draws

374

attention and him to whom it commits us. Our interest is not just in the element, but also in the manner of its application because baptism is not just a spiritual cleansing but a spiritual cleansing connected with the basis for that cleansing. We thus derive confirmatory and presumptive evidence for immersion by noting the identification of baptism with the grave and empty tomb of the promised Messiah.

Conceptual objection

The fourth general objection to affusion is a conceptual one: affusion confuses meaning and form, as well as effect and action. Baptism does symbolize cleansing from sin; but when we would know what to do, there is nothing required except water and someone to apply it. Affusionism has taken the *effect* of baptism and considered it the *form* of baptism; but washing, cleansing, purification, and so on, are not apt to be considered forms. Truly, *baptizō* may mean these things as to effect, but we do not go to examples of effect in order to learn the form of action. The Jewish ablutions to which baptism is compared had particular forms, not just any form. Even if they were all called *baptismoi,* they were not the same in action or effect. If baptism were an example among them, it would still have its own form. Baptism would not itself vary so widely in form as all the rites with which it was classed any more than any of the rest of them would.

Logical objection

The last general objection is a logical one: affusion does not bear its burden of proof. (1) A *word* may come to be put for its effect and then for the effect without reference to the original form of action; there is no positive evidence, however, that such has happened with *baptizō* in relation to Christian salvation. (2) It may be possible to classify Christian baptism among *baptismoi* generally, but it is not evident that *baptismoi* included sprinkling, pouring, or other actions parallel to immersion or partial immersion. (3) Some *examples* of baptism in the New Testament cannot be shown to be immersions, but no clear one is found with any other form to create presumption for such a position on ambiguous ones. (4) It is possible that exceptions to immersion found in the ancient church preserved a legitimate apostolic precedent for special cases, but we cannot ascertain that fact because several other aberrations in Christian practice and teaching existed after, as well as during, the apostolic era. (5) It is possible for forgiveness of sins to be symbolized by the divine ordination of other forms, but we have no indication that God has so ordained them. It appears then that the most that can be said regarding approved precedent for baptismal practice is that affusion could be possible or that it could not be disproved. But we do not practice what cannot be disproved, especially if a positive case for a different position can be presented as all agree from word meaning, New Testament practice, and historical testimony. By default, therefore, affusion is set aside in preference to immersion because the latter can bear its burden of proof.

The structure of thought in affusionism seems to be that it cannot be disproved; the challenge appears to be that immersionism is called upon to eliminate a broad range of actions as possible baptismal forms. Forcing the negative burden of proof onto the immersionist position gives apparent power to arguments that otherwise do not possess it; it attaches unwarranted significance to items traditionally appealed to in presentations favoring affusionism.

This pattern of thinking lies underneath the tendency, for example, to take *unclear New Testament examples of form* as indicating *general meaning* for *baptizō*. It is manifest also in taking the effect of the act as the form of the act. Not assuming the positive burden of proof has also produced the standard statement that first-century baptism was *usually* immersion. Many affusionists agree that there are immersions in the New Testament; the trouble is that these immersions are equal in number to the clear cases of baptismal form. "Usually," then, comes from projecting later patristic practice back into the apostolic era without even adjusting for the difference between standard practice and substitutions due to necessity. "Usually" attempts to take advantage of unclear cases and unapproved cases, but affusionism could profit from such evidence only as confirmation of previous positive evidence.

The problem affusionism must face is its responsibility for getting a place to stand so that plausibility can be attached to secondary meanings, Jewish washings, unclear examples in the New Testament, and exceptions to immersion found in extra-canonical literature from early Christian sources. We keep wondering what brings in the idea that as normative practice the form of baptism is indifferent and that it is general enough to include such disparate acts as sprinkling, pouring, and dipping. *Baptizō* itself does not require a non-immersion meaning; Jewish ablutions do not require it; early Christian practice in cases of necessity do

376

not legitimize it as standard procedure; and we cannot affirm succession to apostolic authority in order to agree with the right of the church to declare it *now* a matter of indifference. We cannot allow the desire for defending non-immersion to come unconsciously from an impulse to accommodate modern practices.

Summary and Conclusion

Three steps comprise the thought structure for the affusionist view. (1) Secondary meanings of *baptō* and *baptizō* include "washing." (2) Christian baptism derives from, and may even be classified among, Jewish lustrations. (3) Church history demonstrates that instances of pouring did in fact occur by the end of the first century or so.

Regarding secondary meanings, the evidence does not demonstrate that *baptō* or *baptizō* came to be used for washing by any mode. As to Jewish purification rites *baptismoi* cannot be shown to cover more than the lustrations performed by complete or partial immersions; even if it did cover all purification rituals, accommodating the *word* does not vary the baptismal *rite* itself. In church history some Christians preferred to substitute affusion in cases of necessity rather than to do nothing or to endanger life.

Besides specific objections to individual items raised against immersion, we offered five general criticisms of non-immersion. (a) Affusion creates the need to take secondary meanings, not only for *baptizō* itself, but for *eis, ek,* and *en,* a set of prepositions whose normal meanings can fit naturally with the circumstances in immersion. (b) Affusion makes baptism less than a symbolic rite by ridding it of form, a necessary characteristic of symbolic rites. (c) By omitting form, affusion represents cleansing from sin rather than cleansing from sin through the death-resurrection of the Sinless One. (d) Affusion confuses the effect of *baptizō* with the action of *baptizō*. Lastly, and most importantly, (e) affusion does not bear its burden of proof, but relies instead on a series of possibilities it presents for immersionism to disprove.

The essence of our problem is whether the word *baptizō* is only a rite so that various actions fall under it, or whether it is an action as well with figurative mechanisms that adjust it upward to generality or outward to effect. We have argued that the latter needs to be chosen in order to accommodate the data available from several relevant sources. The mechanisms we propose are (a) cause to effect—from "immerse" to

"wash"; (b) complete and partial immersion; and (c) changing focuses
—action of the solid (dip) or action of the liquid (immerse).

Taking *baptizō* as a general act like "wash" or "purify" creates a
situation where parallel meanings must be accommodated within the
same word. The general expectancy, however, is that a word does not

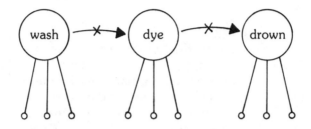

mean parallel things within a set at the same time in the history of a
language. Communication would not be possible if among farm animals
"horse" meant specifically a horse, a cow, or a sheep. If a term covers
all three, it does not and cannot designate any one of them to the exclusion of the others because the others are called the same name.

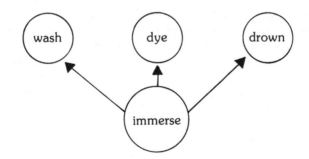

By putting *baptizō* at a causal locus, we can get to all the effective meanings found in relation to the word as well as retain its original word picture.

Our efforts on the form of baptism are disproportionate to other
matters in salvation, but the amount of material has been determined
not just by importance but also by complexity and practical ramifica-
tions for obedience. We are convinced that the cause of Christ would be
appreciably expedited if Christians could agree on the candidate and
form of baptism. Adopting the procedure frequently used in pioneer

missionary areas would enhance the solidarity of witness where Christ and his salvation have been known for centuries. Immersion as baptism has been practiced by many pioneering affusionist groups in order not to throw a stumblingblock before the missionary enterprise. The spirit of that practice would be well to express everywhere, especially if the burden of these last two chapters has come anywhere near to being convincing on this complex topic.

Chapter Twenty-Two

TRINE BAPTISM

Introduction

Two preceding chapters surveyed evidence pertaining to immersion, sprinkling, and pouring as forms of baptism. The present chapter discusses another matter of form in water baptism—whether it has threefold or singular action. Trine, or triune, baptism immerses, sprinkles, or pours three times, once for each member of the trinity. Baptism is one event, but it has three actions. The alternative view performs the action one time only.

Trine baptism relates exclusively to the "baptismal formula" of Matthew 28:19: "Therefore go, make all the ethnic groups disciples, baptizing them into the name of the Father and the Son and the Holy Spirit . . . ." No other biblical text makes such a full statement, and no example of baptism is recorded with sufficient precision to determine whether the apostles administered it in a single or threefold manner. As a result, the biblical argument is fairly well restricted to the wording of the Great Commission according to Matthew.

Arguments for Trine Baptism

The theological argument

The *form* of an ordinance must conform to the *doctrine* of the ordinance. Since the doctrine of baptism is trinitarian, the form of baptism is triune. In this reconstruction the trinity, comprised of Father, Son, and Holy Spirit, consists of clearly distinguishable members all of whom are entered by the candidate in the one event of baptism. The cogency of the theological argument depends on the presupposed view of the trinity and rests upon the fact that all three members are mentioned in Matthew 28:19.

We doubt the propriety of saying that the "doctrine" of baptism is trinitarian. The "trinity" is indeed mentioned here; the proper affirmation, however, is not that the doctrine of *baptism* is trinitarian, but that the doctrine of *God* is trinitarian. The doctrine of baptism is related to God, who is trinitarian. For the sake of argument we could accept the principle stated, in which case we argue that the *doctrine* of baptism has to do with meaning, but meaning does not have a required *form*, because more than one form can contain a meaning. The choice of form, then, rests on authority. Identification with a *triune God* may be indicated by a *single act.* This can happen because *there is not a necessary correlation between form and meaning.*

A ritual cannot incorporate into its *form* everything contained in its *meaning.* Even if we supposed it proper to say the "doctrine" of baptism is trinitarian, that admission would not particularly settle the discussion in favor of triune action. Out of the many interrelated aspects of the rite the question is how much and what the ordinance was intended to convey by its form. The expression involved does not require baptism to mean entrance into each member of the trinity individually. From what Matthew says it is sufficient to view the entrance as an identification with the trinity "corporately" rather than individually. The question is whether the "tri-" or the "-une" part of triune deity corresponds to the form of baptism. The doctrine of baptism relates the act of baptism to *God;* it is a further step to determine whether it relates the act of baptism to the *nature* of God. *There is not an exhaustive correlation between form and meaning.*

The grammatical argument

The present participle. Occasionally an argument for trine baptism is made out of the Greek word for "baptizing" in Matthew 28:19. Present participles, so the argument goes, contrast with aorist participles by indicating linear rather than punctiliar action. The present participle shows that the action of "baptizing" forms a "line" rather than a "point" in keeping with the fact that trine baptism takes a period of time, but single baptism is a one-time act.

The fallacy here comes from equating reality and language. Linear and punctiliar action do not differ in the length of the actual action, but in the way the speaker thinks about the action. Any act may be thought of as in progress (linear) or as a fact (punctiliar); so any act can be referred to by either tense. The only difference, so to speak, is whether the speaker's eye is following the progress of the action or whether his mind simply refers to the fact of its occurrence. "Yesterday I *mowed* the yard" refers to the same event as "While I *was mowing* the yard I got sunburned," but the two verbs do not carry the same meaning. In Matthew the present tense simply shows that the author contemplates the baptizing as in progress.

381

That the present tense does not come from a threefoldness in baptism can be seen from the use of the present tense for John's baptism (Jn. 1:25), which was obviously not trinitarian or triune. Furthermore, the aorist tense describes Christian baptism (Rom. 6:3).

The "-izō" verb element. Another argument from the Greek observes that *baptizō* is an "-izō" verb; the claim is made that such verbs have a frequentative force; that is, they indicate actions involving repetitive action so that *baptizō* (vs. *baptō*) indicates trine baptism. By the time of the New Testament, however, the iterative, frequentative, intensive, and causative ideas formerly associated with this class of verbs had begun to disappear. They are used on occasions where the action is not iterative. The "-izō verbs were proliferating and starting to take over the meanings formerly carried by cognate verbs without this special termination. The "-izō" and "non-izō" forms did not usually stand simultaneously in the language after the earlier, classical period. Again the linguistic argument fails as shown by the control case of John's baptism, which the New Testament also designates *"baptizō."*

The historical argument

The argument stated. Christian writers from the end of the first century onward speak of trine immersion, but single baptism did not supposedly originate until about the fourth century. The earliest reference to trine immersion is probably *Didache* 7. After stating preferred ways of baptizing, the document proceeds to say, ". . . pour water on the head three times in the name of Father and Son and Holy Spirit." Whether the immersion described previously was trine immersion is ascertained only by analogy from the more express description of affusion. In light of the several non-germane matters in this same document, we cannot attribute more legitimacy to trine immersion than we can to the supposed need for running water or cold water in baptism.

The so-called "Apostolic Canons" condemned single immersion and required trine immersion. It is to be observed here that single immersion was also practiced contrary to the trine-baptism position. If these canons were compiled over a long period of time and finalized in the fourth century, the earlier the claim for trine baptism, the earlier the claim for single baptism as well.

The argument qualified. Although these and other extra-biblical testimonies show that the practice of trine baptism was widespread and early in some places, church fathers do not present uniform evidence

382

on this question. While many references to baptism are ambivalent, Tertullian (c. 160-c. 225) writes from North Africa in his *De Corona* 3,

> To deal with this matter briefly, I begin with baptism. When we are going to enter the water, but a little before, in the presence of the congregation and under the hand of the president, we solemnly profess that we disown the devil, and his pomp, and his angels. Hereupon we are thrice immersed, making a somewhat ampler pledge than the Lord has appointed in the Gospel (*The Ante-Nicene Fathers* [Eerdmans], Vol. III, p. 94).

Tertullian gives evidence of the practice, but refrains from agreeing that trine action was commanded in Matthew's gospel. Besides his negative testimony several early references to baptism do not indicate anything specific on mode; consequently, the historical argument does not present decisive testimony.

Objection to the argument. In principle we must set aside appeals to early Christian literature for substantiating views not immediately derivable from the canonical literature of the New Testament. Sub-apostolic and patristic writings may sustain a confirmatory role where primary evidence appears in the Bible. Too many heretical doctrines and practices appeared in the apostolic age itself to allow much credence to subsequent developments that had no correcting and restraining influence from the apostolic office.

This comment shows, of course, that we do not affirm apostolic succession; consequently, we feel no obligation to accept as ecclesiastically authoritative even those later practices and pronouncements that perchance do not contradict previous revelation. Even apostolic succession would establish no sure guideline because uniformity is wanting in the post-apostolic era on this and many other issues. Affirming the protestant principle of "scripture only" contrasts with putting scripture and church tradition on equal footing. Apostolic succession implies the same inspiration and authority for subsequent leaders as is accorded the original apostles in all concerns of faith and practice. Such a concept is belied by the notion of completed canon whose fixed contents were pronounced upon by the ancient councils. We urge the observation that the members, leaders, and conveners of these councils could not with consistency regard themselves as possessing inspiration and authority equal to those New Testament writers from whom they distinguish themselves by putting New Testament writings in a peculiar category and giving them distinctive status. That is not what happened between the prophets and the writings of Moses.

Arguments Against Trine Baptism

In general we feel that the positive evidence for threefold baptism is inadequate because the elements for its defense are either inaccurate, inappropriate, or explainable on other grounds. Since single action requires less precise data, our position is that the less precise wording of Matthew 28:19 argues for single action. The most charitable verdict we can render is that trine immersion broaches a moot question, but we offer some arguments for setting the practice aside.

Theological objections

The most serious consideration relates to the view of the trinity implied by triune baptism. Even on the basis of "ontological trinity," triune action presents a seemingly defective view of the divine oneness. "Ontological trinity" means a threeness in the *make-up of the trinity* itself and stands in greatest contrast to "modal trinity," where the threeness addresses the *functioning of the trinity.* In modal trinity the same One is doing all three activities: "Father" represents one function (creating); "Son" represents another function (redeeming); "the Holy Spirit" represents yet another (sanctifying). In ontological trinity three distinct persons form a corporate oneness wherein the three share the same nature, purpose, and total identification.

In ontological trinity the stress must still fall on the oneness of God as the prior truth, because their interpersonal unity is a larger truth than their individual identity. The twoness-in-oneness of marriage is comparable to the threeness-in-oneness of the Godhead, and for this reason at the most inclusive level man is said to be created in the image and likeness of God (Gen. 1:26-27). Oneness-in-plurality characterizes both orders of being. Tritheism differs from this concept because "three gods" do not share a common purpose and a common identity. The difference between tritheism and trinity is like the difference between a man and a woman on the one hand and a husband and wife on the other.

Trine baptism seems to imply a lack of appreciation for the oneness of God. At least we would not expect that in a situation where Father, Son, and Spirit fulfill complementary roles in the same program, identification through baptism would take place at the individualized level instead of the corporate level. The single form of baptism more appropriately reflects the one meaning of the Father, Son, and Holy Spirit.

The grammatical objections

The singular "name." In keeping with our contention that the primary identity of the trinity lies at the corporate level, Matthew 28:19 says that baptism is "into the name," not "into the names." "The name" emphasizes identity in the Hebrew idiom that often affects expression in the Greek New Testament. "To call on the name of the Lord," for example, does not mean to call on a proper noun; rather, it means "to call on the Lord," but with greater stress upon who and what he is. It exemplifies what is known as "pleonasm," where for emphasis' sake the speaker uses more words than necessary for conveying the basic idea. According to Acts 2:30 God "swore with an oath to [David] that of the fruit of his loins he would set [seed] upon his throne" (cp. II Sam. 7:12-16). "To swear with an oath" means to swear solemnly or emphatically. To call on the name of the Lord is to call on him with special attention to his identity, character, and authority.

Since the formula talks about the name, identity lies at the corporate level instead of at the individual level. "Of the Father," "of the Son," and "of the Holy Spirit" are all three attached grammatically to the same noun. Conceptually, then, the three are here regarded in the aggregate by virtue of individual participation in the same corporate identity. It is into that corporate identity that baptism brings a person. Since the Father, Son, and Holy Spirit always function together in complementary fashion, there is no practical reason for separating them in the candidate's mind by performing acts of individual identification with each member of the Godhead separately.

The single "into." Presumably the action of baptism corresponds with the entrance into that which the action effects. Not only does the text not repeat the name with each member, it does not repeat the entrance by saying "into the name of the Father and into the name of the Son and into the name of the Holy Spirit." Matthew does not picture three entrances, but one; consequently, he apparently means entrance into what is singular here—the corporate identity. To be baptized into any one of the trinity is likewise to be baptized into the other two because

385

they are not only *one* corporate identity, but they are *at one* in purpose and operation.

Other New Testament testimony

Baptism in the name of the Lord Jesus. If mentioning all three members of the trinity warrants the inference that a separate baptismal action corresponds to each one, for the same reason mentioning one member warrants one baptismal action. Acts 8:16 remarks about the Samaritan Christians, "For [the Holy Spirit] was not yet fallen on any of them, but they were only baptized into the name of the Lord Jesus." In Ephesus the twelve disciples of John "were baptized into the name of the Lord Jesus" (Acts 19:5). Paul asks the Romans, "Are you ignorant that all we who were baptized into Christ were baptized into his death?" (6:3). Likewise to the Galatians he says, "As many of you as were baptized into Christ put on Christ" (Gal. 3:27). On Pentecost Peter told the audience, ". . . be baptized in the name of the Lord Jesus . . ." (Acts 2:38). From these texts those who teach "Jesus-only" baptism argue for single action in something of the same way that those who teach trine baptism argue from Matthew 28:19. The lack of consistency in the New Testament wording shows that inferences regarding action are not valid from either set of evidences. A principle of interpretation that cannot be applied consistently should not be applied at all.

The non-trinitarian meanings of baptism. Earlier we objected to absolutely equating the form of an ordinance with the meaning of an ordinance. Trine baptism goes beyond relating baptism to *God* by trying to relate baptism to the *nature of God*; hence, the argument assumes that the form is "two layers deep": (1) that to which it corresponds and (2) the nature of that to which it corresponds.

By parity of reason the interpreter could reach an alternate conclusion by moving to the (2) natures of (1) other things included in the meaning of baptism. Baptism not only communicates *separation from past sins*, symbolized by a cleansing element; it communicates *separation from such behavior* as well as union with other behavioral values. This aspect of the meaning of baptism is compared with burial-resurrection in Romans 6 and Colossians 2. Since (2) the nature of (1) separation-from-sin-plus-union-with-obedience is singular, one could conclude that baptism is a single action even as people are not buried and resurrected three times, or circumcised three times in order to put on Christ three

386

times (Col. 2:11-12; Gal. 3:27). Similarly (2) the nature of (1) appeal-of-a-good-conscience-toward-God (I Pet. 3:21) is singular, as well as (1) the body of Christ into which baptism brings a person (Eph. 2:15-16; I Cor. 12:13). Therefore by trine-baptism interpretative technique baptism is singular.

By such methodology the interpreter puts himself in the position of having to choose which meaning's nature determines the form of baptism and has to generate unrevealed reasons for that choice. Inasmuch as there are different numbers in the natures of the meanings of baptism, it is inherently impossible to satisfy their mutually exclusive demands by the form of this one ordinance. Since trinitarian threeness can be removed by appeal to trinitarian oneness, nothing triune remains of the argument based on the nature of baptismal meanings. That wherein the natures are agreed is singularity so that singularity of action is what we would expect in the form of baptism.

The one baptism. Before leaving the subject of triune baptism, we express dissatisfaction with one argument sometimes used against the view. In Ephesians 4:5 Paul speaks of "one Lord, one faith, one baptism." The last entry has been taken to deny threefold baptism.

While we have not accepted trine baptism as a necessary form of the rite, we have not rejected it because of Ephesians 4:5. The concept of trine baptism is not really that of three baptisms, but of one performed in threefold fashion. Moreover, Paul does not have our question before his mind as he writes. He seeks to affirm the singularity of Lordship, faith, and baptism in contrast to a situation where there would be different lords, faiths, and baptisms for Jews and Gentiles or for some other breakdown of humankind. There is only one baptism in contrast to others, regardless of how many aspects or stages there might be within it.

Triune usage in baptism may not invalidate the obedience of the candidate and so we can leave the issue unchallenged for reasons of fellowship and Christian unity. But for our part trine baptism is not only unrequired, it tends to obscure the very matter it seeks to elucidate, for the primary truth about the "trinity" is oneness instead of threeness, even as the primary truth about marriage is oneness instead of twoness. The concept at least in the minds of the administrator and the candidate should be the one God into whose fellowship baptism brings the believer.

Chapter Twenty-Three

THE FORMULA FOR BAPTISM

Introduction

Divided according to their (1) *sequential prepositions,* three different "formulae" appear in the New Testament descriptions of baptism: (a) baptism *into* the name (*eis to onoma*); (b) baptism *in* the name (*en tōi onomati*); and (c) baptism *on* the name (*epi tōi onomati*). The first is used in Matthew 28:19; Acts 8:16; 19:5; Romans 6:3; and Galatians 3:27 (cp. Acts 19:3[2]; I Cor. 1:13, 15; 10:2; 12:13). The second appears only once: Acts 10:48 (cp. Mt. 21:9; Mk. 16:17; Lk. 10:17; Jn. 14:26; Acts 3:6; 9:27). The third occurs in Acts 2:38.

All three expressions have been regarded as approximate translations of the Hebrew expression *lᵉshem* ("with respect to the name of") so that weighty theological distinctions should not be based exclusively on the Greek sequential prepositions used to render the Hebrew inseparable preposition *lᵉ*. Nevertheless, since the Greek prepositions have more restricted meanings, they may create different shades of meaning through the very process of translation from Hebrew. Baptism "*eis* the name" may stress *identification with Christ*; baptism *en* or *epi* may emphasize the *identity of Christ* in terms of whom the ordinance is administered. The interpreter does well, however, not to insist on fine distinctions unless the nature of the particular situation should reinforce them. Inasmuch as both ideas are true, they represent differences that do not make a difference.

Divided according to their (2) *objects,* two different "formulae" are used for Christian baptism: (a) baptism into the name of the trinity (Mt. 28:19) and (b) baptism in(to) the name of Jesus (Acts 2:38; 8:16; 10:48; 19:5; Rom. 6:3; Gal. 3:27). This variance provides the subject of our present chapter because contentions have been made since ancient times that only one or the other represents legitimate baptism. After a brief statement on the "trinitarian formula," the following treatment concentrates on "Jesus-only" baptism.

The "Trinitarian" Formula

The meaning of the formula

Identification. "Baptizing them into the name of the Father and the Son and the Holy Spirit" means first (1) *identification.* The word *into* implies identification by indicating direction toward. The *name* emphasizes identity, as does the *personal object* specified. Elsewhere benefits and states often stand as objects of baptism, but here men are baptized into the personal God.

Identification with the Godhead. Second, the formula means (2) identification with the *trinity.* Baptism (a) identifies with God in his oneness more directly than in his threeness. *Into* is not repeated with each member and *name* is singular. The Great Commission (b) broadens the horizon of interest beyond the Christ who redeems to the Father who forgives and the Spirit who strengthens men to observe everything God commands.

The use of the formula

We agree with the ancient dictum that what is not expressed by word may be present by faith. It is not saying the words, but believing their meaning that validates the performance of baptism. Acts and the epistles give the impression that the original disciples did not consider specific wording essential because they give descriptions rather than formulae. Subsequent to the New Testament era the formalizing mentality progressively crystallized Matthew 28:19 into a test of *validity.* It is not expressly indicated in the New Testament, however, that there need be any verbalization of the meaning of baptism in order to insure that it has meaning. For expediency rather than necessity administrators repeat a description of its significance in order to reinforce *awareness* in the minds of participants. There is no magic in words, but there is meaning in them; that meaning should always be present at baptism.

The "Jesus-only" Formula

Better representation of the trinity

"Jesus-only" baptism is best understood as a response to trine baptism because the latter mode of administering the ordinance stresses the individuality of each member in the Godhead. The primary impetus for the shorter statement comes from the belief that God is essentially a single being. Because of this conception the reaction to *triune* baptism comes as a matter of course; the objection to *single-action* baptism in the name of the trinity is not usually so strong, although there is a tendency to see the alternatives simply as "Jesus-only" baptism and

389

trine baptism. We cannot enter upon an excursus on the trinity, but enough can be said to point toward the solution.

Unitary deity. Again we can say "Jesus-only" baptism is not just a preference for the shorter descriptions of baptism in Acts and the epistles. The real crux of the issue is—at least usually—the view of the trinity. In typical fashion passages on the divine oneness are assembled and understood to mean that God is essentially a single being. The classic text for this position is (1) *Deuteronomy 6:4*: "Hear, O Israel: Yahweh our God—Yahweh is one, and you shall love Yahweh your God with all your heart, and with all your soul, and with all your might." If he is one, there cannot be three of them.

The oneness of God here must contribute, however, toward loving him with all our being. Whether he is a single being or a triune entity is immaterial to loving him. When Genesis 2:24 calls Adam and Eve "one flesh," it does not deny the individuality of the man and the woman. It is preferable, then, to take Deuteronomy 6:4 to mean that Yahweh is the only God there is and/or that he is unique among the gods men have believed in (cp. Deut. 4:35, 39; I Sam. 2:2; Joel 2:27). If God is the only one of his kind and his kind is "full of lovingkindness," we have a reason for loving him with all our self.

Another text is (2) *John 10:30*: "I and the Father are one," said in such a way that the Jewish leaders claimed he was making himself God (10:33). Obviously, however, Jesus could not have meant that he and the Father were the "same one," because he had just said that the Father *gives* the sheep into his hand; so the two, though one, must be distinct. His *reference to Psalms 82:6* shows (10:34-38) that he means the Father and he are "at one," sharing a common purpose and goal and working together.

A little farther along in (3) *John 14:7-10* Jesus says among other things, "He that has seen me has seen the Father." Again he does not mean what his words could conceivably be made to mean because (a) he proceeds to say that he is in the Father and the Father is in him. That same manner of expression comes up again several times in John 17, where he is in the Father and the Father is in him, and he is in the disciples and the disciples are in him (21, 23, 26; cp. 10:38). The formula *a-in-b-in-a* is a Johannine expression for unity, which is the topic of Jesus' highpriestly prayer in John 17. Furthermore, (b) John 14:7-10 could not make Jesus and the Father the same person Philip is "seeing," because Jesus proceeds to say in 14:12 that he is *going to* the Father. In the John 14 passage Jesus means that he and the Father are "at one" in their work; on that account, seeing him is "as good as" seeing the Father.

In general the word "one" in reference to deity means the Father, Son, and Holy Spirit are (a) at one, (b) unique, (c) of the same nature, or (d) the only deity there is in the class of deity.

In order to bring the unitary viewpoint into harmony with the obvious distinction between the Father and Son during his ministry, interpreters favoring one-person deity have proposed that a part of God separated off and incarnated, subsequently returning into the original One like a cup of water dipped from a bucket and poured back into it. How worthy such a model is will need to be evaluated in light of the known nature of God as well as the evidence presented below; for now we may say that such a model concedes enough to make appropriate a trinitarian formula, because all "three" have a part in the salvation that baptism appropriates.

Triune deity. Besides the Great Commission a number of New Testament passages speak of all three members of the Godhead (Acts 2:33; 7:55; I Cor. 12:4-6; II Cor. 1:21-22; 13:14; Eph. 4:4-6; I Pet. 1:2 I Jn. 5:4-8). The clearest Old Testament text is Genesis 3:22: "Man has become like *one of* us" (cp. Gen. 1:26; 11:17; Isa. 6:8). Other references distinguish various pairs of the three persons.

The best way to get at the (1) *distinctness* between the three is to look at events and actions that separate them. (a) The *baptismal account* has the Father speaking from heaven, Christ arising from baptism in the Jordan, and the Holy Spirit descending on him like a dove (Mt. 3:16-17; Mk. 1:10-11; Lk. 3:21-22; Jn. 1:33-34). (b) The *procession of the Spirit* shows Jesus praying to the Father to send another advocate

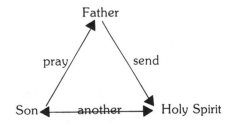

391

(Jn. 14:16; cp. 16:26; 15:26-27; 16:7-15); consequently, the first must be sufficiently distinct from the second to pray to him (cp. Mt. 17:5; Jn. 12:28; 14:6; Rom. 8:26; I Tim. 2:5). The second must be sufficiently distinct from the third to send him (cp. Jn. 15:26; 16:7). The third must be distinct enough from the first to be called "another." There is no way to maintain the idea that the Father, the Son, and the Holy Spirit are three names for the same person *during time*.

As we said above, one answer has been to move the singleness of God to *eternity* past and future; the three may be temporarily distinct, but eternally they are the same person. This move does not seem adequate to handle the "with" passages: "The Word was with God" (Jn. 1:1; cp. 17:5). It leaves one wondering how scripture could even speak of the pre-incarnate Word unless he is identifiable; a cup of water poured back into a bucket of water is no longer identifiable and intentionally so in this concept. We can always admit that our categories of thinking do not apply adequately to the spiritual realm, but there is no reason to appeal to such a notion. These matters that have been revealed in our linguistic and conceptual categories are presumably understandable in terms of this-wordly experiences and/or rational categories. We hasten to add that we do not feel we understand the trinity fully even though we feel we understand it formally.

All these and other special explanations seem quite unnecessary. The ultimate concern in propounding them is to avoid Jewish and Muslim charges that Christianity promotes paganism by teaching a polytheism with three gods. Without attempting a formal rebuttal of everything involved here, we first reaffirm the (2) *oneness* of the trinity as to nature, purpose, uniqueness, loneliness, and corporate solidarity. The pagan deities warred against one another instead of sharing common goals fulfilled through complementary roles. Among them appeared no ethical deity like the unique God of Israel, for they were normally gods of power rather than gods of principle, being made in the image of their human creators. Yahweh is also one in that he is the only Godhead; the ancient pantheons did not exist except in the minds that imagined them. Lastly, God is one at the group level.

Second we affirm the (3) *triunity* of the three even though we cannot offer a model that expresses the concept satisfactorily. With appropriate adjustments perhaps *marriage* comes closest to illustrating plurality in oneness. The Hebrew parallelism in Genesis 1:26 suggests that male and female correlates with the "we" image of God, especially when reinforced by the comment in Genesis 2:24 that the two become one flesh. Of course, since God is spirit, all the fleshly distinctives of marriage fall out of the comparison, leaving plurality at one level transcended by oneness at a higher level. Spouses are not one in the same sense that they are two; therefore, they can be one and two at the same time. Likewise for members of the Godhead.

As with marriage the Father, Son, and Spirit fulfill complementary roles. Their relationship is constant, permanent, and total so that their oneness goes beyond that of a committee, for example. A committee is not always operating; it is not permanent; and its members are involved together only in selected matters. Husband-wife relationship is also like the trinity in that it is interpersonal.

Another, less adequate model is *the ideal nature of the church* for which Christ prayed in John 17 and to which Paul analogized marriage in Ephesians 5. In the Lord's Prayer Jesus asks that the disciples may be one as he and the Father are one (17:22). Citing Genesis 2:24 in the course of his injunctions on marriage, Paul inserts into his discussion a comment on the church: "This mystery is great, but I am speaking in regard to Christ and in regard to the church" (5:32). The implication seems to be that he considers marriage and the church as analogous realities, both of which are elsewhere compared to the Godhead.

Better presentation of biblical usage

The argument. Without unitary trinity, objections to Matthew 28:19 appear to carry little weight. As it works out (1) the trinitarian statement is used only in Matthew's Great Commission. In the six other references baptism is simply in(to) the name of Jesus. That fact is supposed to throw suspicion on the integrity of Matthew's text or the credibility of his statement. Furthermore, it is claimed that (2) the formal and precise nature of the formula reflects a later period in the church when liturgical formalism was developing.

Response to the argument. (a) Manuscript evidence does not suggest any reason for questioning the *integrity of the text.* (b) A New Testament view of scripture excludes any question of the *reliability of the statement.* Questioning credibility does not really set well with the high view of scripture normally associated with "Jesus-only" baptists. Without granting certain presuppositions about gospel origins, a person would have

393

little reason to adopt the conclusion. The gospel records may not give the very words of Jesus on occasions like these, but the point is that our prior commitment to the truthfulness of biblical concepts makes it a secondary issue whether he said exactly these words in expressing his total will for their leadership of the coming kingdom.

Furthermore, (c) *the difference in wording* between Matthew and Acts need not represent *a difference in meaning*. From the nature of the divine unity, to be identified with any one of the Godhead is to be identified with the other two. Therefore, the two "formulae" need not be interpreted in a restrictive or contrasting manner. There is no reason to suspect contradiction between what Jesus commanded his disciples and what they did. Since the trinitarian expression appears in scripture, it surely offers a legitimate description that could serve as a statement at the time of a baptism.

(d) *In Acts "baptism in the name of Jesus" stands in contrast to something parallel* so that it is not contrasted with the longer statement in Matthew. The word "only" is used nowhere but in Acts 8:16: "For as yet [the Holy Spirit] was fallen on none of them, but they were only baptized in the name of the Lord Jesus." "Only" modifies "baptized," not "Jesus." The contrast is between Christian baptism and receiving the Spirit that Peter and John would bestow on them. Similarly baptism in the name of Jesus stands over against John's baptism. To use such occasions as a denial of the Matthaean record supposes the wrong set of contrasts.

Finally, (e) non-Matthaean statements simply *designate* baptism whereas Matthew more fully *describes* it. "Baptism unto Moses" (I Cor. 10:2) or "baptism unto the name of Paul" (I Cor. 1:13-14) is hardly a formula. We may grant that Matthew 28:19 has greater *liturgical potential* because of its structure; it is quite another thing to suppose that it has a *liturgical origin* and was later written back into the mouth of Jesus by an unknown author/redactor. Well-worded statements need not come from liturgical sources. The fundamental mistake in this whole discussion is calling Matthew's statement a "formula" in a strict sense. The fact that it does not appear elsewhere does not mean *later origin* or *liturgical form*, but *descriptive nature*. There is no particular reason it should appear elsewhere because there is no reason baptism has to be described this way. It is as likely that the ritualizing tendencies in religious observance have transformed it into a formula as it is that they created it as a formula.

In summary, Matthew 28:19 describes baptism as identification with the Godhead. It is not the usage of these words, but the awareness of their content that should accompany the Christian rite of initiation. Therefore, it is of little consequence whether the "trinitarian formula" or the "Jesus only" formula is that statement made on the occasion of baptism. For our part, however, we do urge the candidate not to take the view of the Godhead that commonly goes with the plea for Jesus-only baptism.

The elements in the Commission fit appropriately with our concern to highlight interpersonal matters as of the essence of salvation. The Great Commission describes reconciliation between God and man.

Chapter Twenty-Four

THE ADMINISTRATOR OF BAPTISM

Introduction

Although Christendom generally agrees that baptism is not (1) *self-administered,* considerable discussion has occurred over the question of whether it is (2) *a clerical function* or (3) *a general function.* Within clerical function two views have developed: *successionism* makes clerical validity dependent on generation-to-generation connection with the original apostles. *Non-successionism* allows formal ministry to rise spontaneously out of a new group without outside validation by previously ordained ministry. Either way the validity of baptism depends on a proper administrator. As a *general function* baptism gains its validity only from considerations within the candidate.

In questions like administration of baptism the manner of approaching the issue is crucial. Our pattern of thought begins with first principles and attempts to infer properly the nature of the question. Admittedly certain items may not be deducible from first principles because God may have laid down positive commandments about these items. He may have done so for reasons of good order, that is, to avoid confusion or to establish a most appropriate way of doing what could conceivably have been handled several ways. As respects *divine authority* such regulations govern Christian practice as surely as those called moral commandments, even though they are not as important as respects *inherent necessity.* Positive commandments require specific injunctions or clear precedents because the points of concern cannot otherwise be known; they cannot be known because first principles do not imply them. In total perspective the sources of information on administration come indirectly from (a) first principles and directly from (b) teachings and (c) precedent.

Our manner of approaching this issue therefore is as follows: (a) we begin with first principles and carefully deduce what may be legitimately implied by them; (b) then we look for positive commandments or clear precedents that establish anything more explicit. This methodology is particularly crucial because it establishes (1) *the proper use of silence* in interpreting scripture. If, for example, there is no precept or precedent for *unofficial administration* (silence), it means nothing necessarily; the pattern may be due to chance because of abbreviated records about apostolic practice. On the other hand, if there is no precept for *official administration* (silence), it again means nothing because official administration may be implicit in the nature of salvation or the church. Silence can have no place in establishing a position. Where there is silence, conclusions must be *formed from first principles* or, more often than not, *left as matters of opinion.*

Beginning with the nature of salvation and then advancing to positive commandments also establishes (2) *the proper placement of the burden of proof.* Generally speaking, the affirmative bears the burden of proof. In our present question as in so many others, the discussion often bogs down because each position tries to call on the other one to supply evidence that will disprove the alternate view. Calling for evidence that disproves, however, becomes legitimate only if relevant first principles create presumptive evidence for that alternative view. The biblical evidence against many viewpoints is not explicit enough to unseat them; people need not feel any compulsion to accept those viewpoints just because they cannot controvert them successfully. Silence can only confirm what first principles have established in bearing the positive burden of proof.

Non-clerical Baptism

Precept

The first fundamental proposition is that (1) *salvation and therefore the church have a primarily interpersonal nature*; hence, it is not necessary for the administration of salvation to occur after the pattern of a legal process. Since (a) *salvation* is bringing a man back into personal relationship with God, the "transaction" takes place between him and God; it is a two-party process. Nothing needs to be added in order to validate it.

If salvation is interpersonal, then (b) the *church* is a witness to grace, not a channel of grace. The flow of grace goes directly from God to the individual instead of flowing through the church. Church personnel, official or otherwise, testify to the good news; they do not mediate the benefits of it. This pattern holds for proclamation and exhortation (evangelism) as well as for the ordinance of initiation (baptism) and the ordinance of worship (communion). To make grace flow from God through the church to the individual overlays personal salvation with legal operation. From the nature of salvation and the church, we see no first principle for requiring official church action in the performance of baptism.

The second fundamental proposition is that (2) *no point is ever made in New Testament teaching as to who should perform baptism.* The interpersonal character of salvation and the church means that no theological foundation can be laid for official performance of baptismal initiation. Nevertheless, God might choose for the sake of orderliness to go beyond theoretical requirements and institute a class of ministry with this and other responsibilities. Because baptism pertains not only to salvation but also to entering the body of the saved, it is conceivable that the group aspect of this ordinance could legitimize official operation representative of the group.

The New Testament never indicates that administering baptism, communion, or the gospel has been reserved for a special class of Christians, even though certain advantages could perhaps be found in all these cases. This observation contrasts with Old Testament procedures. Only the Levites, for example, could officiate at the altar and perform other official functions of the tabernacle, but in the New Testament practical considerations have not led to a positive commandment on administering baptism. What has no positive basis in scripture cannot be required with divine sanction among the people of God.

At this point it becomes evident how far-reaching the implications are for baptism as part of the salvation process. If it were a church act and yet unto salvation, grace would be flowing through the church. Even if baptism were simply a church act with no salvation implications, it might be appropriate for official representatives of the community to "naturalize" the alien into their group. But since baptism is unto salvation, the church aspect logically follows salvation and therefore cannot be determinative for official administration.

Precedent

By themselves examples of baptism in the New Testament do not settle the administration question. Nevertheless it is worthwhile to note instances of (1) *delegating to others the performance of baptism.* The practice of Paul in *the Corinthian mission* perhaps best illustrates his attitude. Looking back on it later, he was glad he himself had not baptized very many (I Cor. 1:13-17). Evidently he left the task to others; those persons, of course, could have been Silas and Timothy, his original assistants in Corinth (Acts 18:1-17), but the matter is unexplained in I Corinthians.

Another, less certain illustration comes from *the conversion of Cornelius' household.* There are two possible translations of Acts 10:48: "And he commanded them to be baptized . . ."; or, "And he commanded that they be baptized . . . ." The first rendering makes "them" the direct object of "commanded," whereas the second makes "commanded" an indirect-discourse verb and makes "they" the subject of "be baptized." In the latter case his comment would be directed more particularly to the six Jewish brethren who accompanied him from Joppa, and would delegate to them the performance of baptizing. Since they are simply called "brethren" (10:23; 11:12), we have no indication that they were ordained leaders (cp. 15:22-23).

If Peter had his companions perform the baptizing, he was following *the example of Jesus,* who had his disciples perform what was evidently the equivalent of John's baptism: ". . . Jesus . . . was baptizing more disciples than John—although Jesus himself did not baptize, but his disciples [did it] . . ." (Jn. 4:1-2). All three instances imply a certain indifference to administration.

Delegating to assistants or presiding over the ceremony does not have quite the same character as making validity dependent on the administrator. If validity depended on an ordained administrator and there was one present, we wonder what would prompt Jesus, Peter, and Paul to have someone else do it. Possibly under special circumstances official functions may be delegated, but a justice of the peace does not have an assistant perform the wedding ceremony and pronounce the couple husband and wife if he himself is present and able to fulfill his function. In modern church settings where official administration is believed necessary, the performance of baptism is not assigned to a lay member. We wonder, then, how likely delegation could account for these examples unless we assumed all the assistants were ordained as well.

Another observation is that Paul evidently maintained the practice of (2) *not immediately ordaining official leadership in pioneer fields.* On the first tour he and Barnabas delayed appointing elders until the return leg on the journey (Acts 14:23). His last efforts show the same practice in mission situations because he left Titus behind in Crete to organize the churches previously established through their joint efforts

(Tit. 1:5). We are not disposed to believe that the churches had no converts between their founding and their organization; if they did, the practice of immediate baptism tells against postponing the rite until ordained leadership was appointed or came from somewhere else.

A third set of examples falls under the caption of (3) *carrying out spontaneous "lay" missions.* Philip baptized the Ethiopian eunuch and sent him on his way rejoicing, but Luke's account leaves little room for ordaining him to official ministry. One wonders what he did if he converted others in Ethiopia as tradition in fact claims. Those spread abroad by the persecution after Stephen's martyrdom went everywhere preaching the gospel (Acts 8:4). We doubt that there were ordained officials in every cluster that fled. The church at Rome evidently originated from non-apostolic witness, perhaps from refugees of Saul's persecution (Acts 11:19?) or from Roman converts at Pentecost (Acts 2:10). At any rate it strains credulity to believe that all converts of "lay" witness had ordained administrators at their baptism.

Paul's early evangelistic endeavors are recorded in Acts 9:19-25. Immediately upon his conversion he proclaimed in the synagogues that Jesus was the Son of God. "His disciples" mentioned in 9:25 shows that his efforts were fruitful. He hardly received ordination at such an early date, and there is no hint that official clergy baptized his converts. This occasion probably demonstrates as well as any that the necessity of official administration never occurred to the minds of first-century Christians.

New Testament precedent does not indicate that baptism was performed only by ordained clergy. This finding accords with previous observations from precept that no point is ever made about administrator and that no theological implication establishes a foundation for clerical necessity. Nothing raises baptism above an essentially interpersonal operation between God and the candidate directly. The "administrator" merely assists the candidate in his obedience to God; baptism is the candidate's obedience, not the administrator's bestowal.

Practice

We conclude that any administration is acceptable as long as it provides for the *solemnity* and *meaning* of the event. Frivolousness, perfunctoriness, and ignorance naturally contradict the weighty significance of salvation from sin. Awareness of meaning transforms an otherwise insignificant motion into a worthy act of obedience. The potential perversions of decency and order are avoided by influence rather than authority in accordance with the personal medium in which salvation operates generally.

As a rule those qualified to evangelize are qualified to baptize. The mediation of the gospel and the performance of its rites are in principle of one and the same validity. Presumably the sobriety, concern, and caring attendant to proclamation would accompany the administration of the ordinance so as to avoid frivolousness. The knowledge that would enable valid witness for Christ would bespeak valid baptism unto Christ. Where there is appropriate attitude and proper awareness there is valid obedience.

Clerical Baptism

Precept

Clerical successionism disagrees with our claim that grace does not flow through the church. Three texts are used in defending the concept that God has delegated to the leadership of his kingdom the responsibility and right to dispense and withhold grace. The first text is Matthew 16:18-19:

> And I also say to you that you are Peter and on this rock I will build my church and the grave's gates will not have strength against it. And I will give you [sg.] the keys of the kingdom of heaven and whatever you bind on earth will stand bound in heaven and whatever you loose on earth will stand loosed in heaven.

The second passage is Matthew 18:18:

> Truly I say to you, as many things as you [pl.] bind on earth will stand bound in heaven and as many things as you loose on earth will stand loosed in heaven.

A third statement comes from John 20:21-23:

> Jesus then said again to them, "Peace [be] to you." Even as the Father has sent me, I also send you. And having said this he breathed on [them] and said to them, "Receive the Holy Spirit. If you forgive the sins of certain ones, they stand forgiven to them; if you hold certain ones' [sins] against them, they stand held against [them]."

Therefore grace is at the disposal of the apostolic office and those to whom that right has successively devolved over the centuries. Baptism falls within the scope of retaining and remitting sin.

401

The Matthew 16 reference stands at the center of an age-old controversy on the role of Peter and the apostolic office represented by him as "first among equals." The question is whether "the rock" refers to Peter, to Christ, or the content of Peter's confession. There is, of course, no impropriety in speaking about the apostles as *historically* the foundation of the church (Eph. 2:19-22); the problem comes in making their office *theologically* the foundation of the church so as to make divine grace in principle dependent on the limitations of human awareness.

The use of the keys is a second matter in Matthew 16 that does not have to mean that the apostolic office—and by implication other clerical offices—has the authority and responsibility of clerical absolution whether baptismal or confessional. Absolution, or forgiveness, of sins is a divine prerogative. Using the keys need not mean more than the proclamation of the Good Confession so that men's sins are bound or loosed upon them by virtue of their response to the gospel proclaimed.

Matthew 18:18 recounts a similar episode with all the apostles later. The binding and loosing on this occasion is associated with the process of church discipline (18:15-17; cp. I Cor. 5:1-8) and with the assurance of answered prayer (18:19-20).

John 20:23 replaces binding and loosing imagery with forgiving and holding sin against someone. The context mentions commission to mission and so may be sufficiently understood in reference to forgiveness through response to proclamation. Jesus evidently means that God forgives enemies when we forgive them enough to tell them the good news unto their salvation (Acts 7:60; Lk. 23:34). Jesus' appearance to the ten on this occasion occurs in a room the apostles had locked for fear of the Jews; he breathes on them, saying, "Receive the Holy Spirit." Perhaps in this act and in these words he is getting at the proper attitude, spirit, and boldness necessary for witnessing their convictions and experiences to their enemies. Later this very thing came to pass when previously fearful men, locked behind these closed doors, stood boldly in the temple on pain of death to give "their witness" (Acts 4:1-13) and to speak comfortingly to people who had executed their beloved Master (Acts 3:17-21). Under this reconstruction Jesus means that ministers in effect are retaining men's sins if they do not proclaim to them the gospel by which men can be saved.

402

In the Great Commission Jesus directed to his special disciples the commandment to perform baptism, but this observation hardly demands clerical baptism. The obvious problem is that an argument that "proves too much" does not prove even what it seems to show. By parity of reason the Lord could be understood to mean that all facets of evangelism were restricted to apostolic, or at least clerical, fulfillment. In principle forbidding anyone to preach except ministers educationally qualified makes as much practical sense as forbidding others to baptize.

The retention or absolution of sins cannot ultimately rest on human agency or be limited to human pronouncement. All sin is against God even though it is also against fellowmen. The one offended must do the forgiving. To these basic principles the texts brought forward in defense of clerical absolution make no clear addition so as to justify either confessional or baptismal absolution from sin. Validity of baptism does not depend on more than the persons involved, for no belief or practice is binding if positive evidence is lacking.

Precedent

In all cases where the administrator's clerical status is known New Testament baptisms were performed by ordained personnel. Although the generalization may be admitted, its significance is doubted. First, the New Testament records concentrate by and large on Christian leaders who with propriety could be classified as "clergy" in the modern sense. Exceptions to this generality turn out to have unknown status rather than known, non-clerical status. Without a precept to create the necessary generalization, these unclassified examples remove the legitimacy of any inference for clerical baptism.

Second, the generalization about clerical baptism has no more cogency than one about clerical proclamation. Nearly all the evangelistic efforts noticed by the New Testament came from "ordained" messengers. Certain exceptions may have occurred in missions resulting from persecution, but there is no more reason to suppose lay missions in these cases than there is to suppose lay baptism. The nature of the case is really what causes a person to conclude for lay missions in these instances, and the nature of the case is really what causes a person to conclude for lay baptism as well.

From precept and precedent combined we note that there are no cases of sending for an administrator of baptism. In contrast to Old

WHAT THE BIBLE SAYS ABOUT SALVATION

Testament priesthood regulations, there is no precise statement to the effect that one of the responsibilities of the ministry is to perform the baptism of converts. We have also found no clear line of thought from first principles. Third, the critical point was not—and is not—*whether* official leadership did the baptizing, but *why* they did it. It would be aside from the issue even if all baptisms were clerically administered in New Testament records. The concern in this study is the theological one—how baptism must be administered. For example, if Philip had called Peter and John to come down from Jerusalem and baptize his converts in Samaria, it would not prove he was ineligible to perform the baptisms; it might have been that he wanted to show both the Samaritans and the Jews that this previously outcast group was acceptable into the one kingdom of heaven. Having recognized Jewish leaders from Jerusalem perform the baptism would have demonstrated clearly what needed to be known by everyone involved. Other baptisms may have been clerical, not because it was theoretically necessary, but because it guaranteed propriety in the situations described.

Practice

Guaranteeing propriety has indeed been advanced as the very reason for practicing clerical baptism in non-successionism. It keeps down incidents of baptizing people not ready as yet and cases of improper attitude and procedure. While such a concern is commendable, the solution demonstrates overkill. Practical measures will suffice that stop short of lawmaking in interpersonal processes. To limit baptizing to clergy may communicate as unhealthy a view of baptism as the extreme against which it overreacts.

Conclusion

Precepts among first principles do not carry us beyond interpersonal process in baptism. *Precedent* leaves the matter indecisive without a prior theological foundation; New Testament examples could conceivably be accounted for by either clerical or non-clerical presuppositions. *Practice* dictates that propriety rather than law govern the performance of this rite. Any procedure as to personnel that fosters appropriate attitude and proper awareness is approved in the non-clerical administration of this important and meaningful event.

Chapter Twenty-Five

THE IMPORTANCE OF BAPTISM

The forms of religion are never so important as the meaning attached to them. Nevertheless, since ritual acts embody and convey meaning, they take upon themselves a practical importance more commensurate with their theological significance. Therefore, we bring our materials on baptism to a close by summarizing the things that indicate its importance.

The Persons Commanding Baptism

The importance of any activity comes in part from the persons that command it. Christian baptism derives importance primarily from the fact that (a) *Jesus Christ* himself commissioned the apostles to include it as an integral part of their evangelistic mission (Mt. 28:18-20; Mk. 16:15-16). Baptism cannot then be regarded as an afterthought or a negotiable matter. Baptism was administered later by the apostles under his authority. (b) *The apostles* included this ordinance in their proclamation from the very first (Acts 2:38; 10:48). (c) Even the *Holy Spirit* is associated with baptism because under his influence the scripture came into being, not only as a record of past example, but as a norm, guide, and precedent for future faith and practice.

Every student of the New Testament recognizes the facts just noticed, but their importance can be appreciated more when set in contrast to other alternatives. Christian baptism, for example, does not merely carry forward a custom of the church. It did not originate under the influence of respected men in the venerable past. Its hallowed character does not arise from its ecclesiastical antiquity, but from its divine origin; consequently, its function and importance do not come from the security sensed in identification with the *past*.

Christian baptism also does not merely mark identification with a group in the *present*. It is not a rite of passage that gets its authority from the mechanics of social process. Christian baptism gets its primary authority from a *person* who is not just a dead founder, but a present, living Lord.

The Significances of Baptism

The candidate expresses several important concerns by his baptism. Most inclusive among them is that (a) he desires to identify with Jesus

Christ whose distinctive act is re-enacted in water baptism (Mt. 28:18-20; Acts 8:16; 19:5; Rom. 6:3; Gal. 3:27; Col. 2:12). (b) He pledges himself to the resurrected life guided by values, purposes, and goals transcendent to the flesh he buries in this watery grave; whereupon he resurrects to live anew and from above (Rom. 6:1-14; Jn. 3:3-8). In Christian baptism (c) the candidate formally appeals to God for salvation (I Pet. 3:21; Acts 22:16). Finally, we may say that (d) he dies to perfect law-keeping as a basis for relationship with God (Col. 2:11-15).

The Consequences of Baptism

We have found four consequences especially promised in connection with obedience in Christian baptism. Fundamental to the other three is the Father's acceptance of our identification with Christ (Rom. 6:3, etc.). When we identify ourselves with Christ, God accepts that identification. In consequence of that identificaton, he grants forgiveness of sin (Acts 2:38; 22:16), the gift of the Spirit (Acts 2:38; 5:32; 8:16; 19:1-5), and entrance into the church, or church membership (I Cor. 12:13). Baptism formally culminates initial salvation and has importance accordingly.

The Occasions Including Baptism

We consider it noteworthy that our Lord considered baptism important enough to include in (a) the Great Commission, which summarizes what is *done* in evangelism even as the kerygma in I Corinthians 15:3-4 summarizes what is *said* in evangelism. A person's final words carry special significance and his hearers assume he has chosen weighty matters in his farewell remarks.

At each stage along the way in fulfilling their commission, the disciples brought baptism into the event as a culmination of initial presentation. (b) Pentecost occasioned the first proclamation of the gospel in its historic reality, and Peter set forth baptism as one of the terms of the Messianic covenant (Acts 2:38). When the gospel took its second step and went to (c) Samaria, Philip baptized the believers (Acts 8:12-13). Peter carried the gospel one step farther when he preached to (d) Cornelius' household, who were the first Gentile converts. They, too, were baptized (Acts 10:47-48). Even those who had been (e) John's disciples were later baptized in the name of Jesus (Acts 19:1-7).

The Frequency of Mentioning Baptism

Perusing a concordance on the words "baptize" and "baptism" gives some indication of its relevance to the Christian enterprise. On sheer word count "baptism" occurs more frequently in the New Testament than "repentance" and its related words. Baptism is mentioned in every conversion account in the book of Acts with a possible exception in the case of Sergius Paulus, who "believed" (Acts 13:12). A topic of such frequent mention could hardly be peripheral to Christian practice.

The Example of Jesus in Baptism

Jesus' example of submission and humility encourages every person who would identify himself with the program of God in history. Even though—as John himself observed—Jesus did not need John's baptism for any forgiveness of sins, he submitted to it anyway as an act of identification with the program of God being carried on through the Baptist's ministry. On account of his example no one could ever suppose that such ritual procedures as Christian baptism are dispensable because only the spiritual aspects of religion have real value. Neither could anyone ever presume to be above obedience in baptism as if it were beneath his dignity or too demeaning to his station. Obedience in Christian baptism is surely not "too much trouble" if Jesus was willing to walk over seventy miles to be baptized by John in the Jordan. If Jesus calls all men to take up their cross and follow him, nothing short of willing submission is appropriate in following his example in fulfilling all righteousness.

The Doctrinal Issues Enmeshed in Baptism

Another reason considerable debate has centered on baptism is that at least five salvation-related issues surface there. The *candidate for baptism* touches on the relationship of the group to the individual. Particularly involved is the concept of inherited guilt, or original guilt, which provides one argument for infant baptism. Infant baptism relates also to the nature of the church, that is, whether identification with

407

the church through this act operates on purely spiritual and therefore personal principles or whether the church is such that faith of parents and congregation can serve by proxy to legitimize baptism prior to personal accountability. Furthermore, baptism for the dead involves the character of an ordinance, that is, whether a ritual act is inherently necessary for a spiritual benefit.

The *administrator of baptism* brings up the flow of grace, that is, whether grace flows directly from God to the individual or whether it flows through the church by virtue of a clergy that officially represents the church.

Tied up with the *significance of baptism* is the nature of faith. At issue here is whether "faith," particularly in Pauline literature, refers only to inner activity or whether outer activity is also included with the inner under a conditionality relationship between human response and divine grace.

Even the nature of the trinity gets brought into the picture because some have argued that the trinitarian *formula for baptism* in Matthew 28 misleads most people into tritheism and should be replaced with baptism in the name of Jesus. Trinity also figures into trine baptism, the alternative against which Jesus-only baptism is posited.

Our verdict on each of the theological issues associated with baptism hinges on the interpersonal character of Christian salvation. In all cases the difficulty originates from moving salvation out of the interpersonal domain into legal, locative, quantitative, and natural categories. Any importance attached to baptism, therefore, must be seen in its larger interpersonal setting.

In light of the above observations, Paul's words to the Corinthians do not depreciate the importance of this ordinance: "Christ did not send me to baptize, but to preach the gospel" (I Cor. 1:17). Instead of putting Paul at odds with the Great Commission, we prefer to understand two thrusts to the verse. First, in 1:14-17 he uses "baptize" to mean "to perform baptism." I Corinthians 1 has to do with divisions at Corinth that centered around prominent personalities. In this connection Paul expresses his relief that providentially he himself had not baptized more of the Corinthians than he did, because they might have used that as another reason for identifying themselves with him instead of Christ (1:13).

Second, his comment may have the force of a limited negative: "Christ did not [so much] send me to baptize as to preach the gospel."

If so, it compares with Jesus' comment to the seventy when they returned from their mission throughout Palestine: "Do not rejoice that the spirits are subject to you, but rejoice that your names have been written in heaven" (Lk. 10:20). Presumably Jesus wanted them to rejoice more because of their salvation than over their successes at exorcism. For Paul the proclamation of the gospel took priority over administering baptism, regardless of its importance to the believer.

Balance is the key to proper presentation on this and other subjects included in Christian doctrine. While baptism is not the end-all and be-all of the gospel, neither is it immaterial, dispensable, or negotiable in the offer of salvation. We seek sensitivity in perceiving the proper stress to be attached to this re-enactment of the most singular event in the history of divine effort toward human salvation—the death, burial, and resurrection of our Savior.

Part Six—Perseverance in Salvation

Chapter Twenty-Six

ASSURANCE OF SALVATION

Introduction

Salvation may be regarded descriptively as to the way it was accomplished and how it is applied. Salvation may also be regarded dynamically as to its ongoing certainty. One aspect of this certainty is the objective foundation and continuation of salvation: *security*, or preservation. A second aspect is the relationship of Christian living to ongoing salvation: *perseverance*. A third aspect is the subjective confidence about being saved: *assurance*. The first centers on God while the other two center on us.

In this chapter we attempt to balance together those elements that most affect the sense of assurance: the basis, content, time, and means of assurance. In the following two chapters we assess two other views of ongoing salvation that emphasize in the first instance the perseverant life and in the second the objective framework.

Basis of Assurance

The assurance of salvation lies more in God than in ourselves. This fact is the case because he has more to do with our salvation than we do, and because what he does is more important, more ultimate, and more decisive. He is pre-eminent before salvation and in its continuation.

Messiah's work

Although the fact is a truism in Christian thought, in the Father's eyes Messiah's (1) *atonement* suffices for the salvation of sinners. According to Hebrews 10:1-14 the Father did not regard animal sacrifice as adequate or appropriate for the removal of human sin. The writer quotes Psalms 40:6-8 to that effect and comments, "We have been sanctified through the offering of the body of Jesus Christ once for all" (10:10).

Notably this text does not call attention to sufficiency for initial delivery so much as it does to sufficiency for permanent cleansing. So to speak, that Messianic work not only absolved sinners from individual sins or from sins over a specific period of time, it sufficed for categorical change, the removal of sinners from the classification "sinners" into the

410

group of "the sanctified ones." The writer of Hebrews infers from their annual repetition that animal sacrifices did not accomplish what the one-time offering of the Messiah gained—deliverance from consciousness of sins. His point is not that sinners are delivered from awareness of what sin is or what it can do to a person; he means that because of Messiah's one sacrifice sinners have no more consciousness of being looked at as sinners.

Hebrews speaks from a legal point of view and therefore looks at the change from sinner to saint as a permanent categorical change. I John makes much the same point but as a continuous active process because the writer speaks from a behavioral and interpersonal point of view: "The blood of Jesus his Son cleanses us from all sin" (I Jn. 1:7). We are conscious of having sins (I Jn. 1:8, 10), but not conscious of having sins held against us (Heb. 10:3). Understanding these things helps assurance of salvation because the basis of our standing with God stands sure.

Because of the sufficiency of Messiah's blood we have confidence that the Accuser cannot sustain what would otherwise be a legitimate case against us. Our imperfection brings us under the curse of God's law (Gal. 3:10-12) and in effect would transfer our citizenship to the realm of darkness. But the blood of Christ intervenes to deliver us:

> Now is come salvation and power
> and the kingdom of our God
> and the authority of his Messiah
> Because there has been cast down the Accuser of our brethren
> who accused them before our God day and night,
> And *they* conquered *him* through the blood of the Lamb
> and through the word of his testimony (Rev. 12:10-11a).

Because of the Lamb that was slain, Satan has no right to us, and our foundation in God stands firm having this seal: "The Lord knows them that are his" (II Tim. 2:19; cp. Jn. 10:3, 14, 17).

The notions of permanent cleansing in Hebrews 10 and continuous cleansing in I John 1 come close to being synonymous with the second major aspect of Messiah's work, which we call (2) *intercession*. Messiah's highpriestly function comes in for unique emphasis in Hebrews. In general, chapters 5-7ff. are an exegesis of Psalms 110:4: "The Lord swore and will not repent himself, 'You are a priest forever after the order of Melchizedek'" (cp. 2:17-18). The priestly role of Messiah

411

presupposes his sacrificial role so that what saved once and for all becomes foundational for what continues to save at all times. One aspect is categorical while the other is continual; the first removes the sin while the second removes sins. In either case we have bold assurance in drawing near to God through Messiah (4:16; 7:19, 25; 10:1, 22).

God's power

Because of the blood of the Lamb, Satan has no right to us, but he also has no power over us. The first way in which God's power creates assurance is that (1) by it *we conquer death*. No one can snatch us out of his hand since the Father is greater than all (Jn. 10:28-29). The original setting for the statement of this fact involved a confrontation between Jesus and the religious leaders, who failed in their attempt both to argue with the Lord and to stone him for blasphemy. Official religious leaders could not act successfully to overthrow Jesus' disciples inasmuch as God was on his side. This principle held true later even at Calvary, for by the resurrection Jesus was declared with power to be the Son of God (Rom. 1:4). The same is true today; though men might think they are doing God service by putting us to death (Jn. 16:2) if they are allowed to do so, there is no implication that God has abandoned us for being out of favor with him; it gives no indication of eternal destiny or being forsaken by the Father (Rom. 8:31-39; cp. Mt. 27:46). Our assurance accompanies us to the grave because of the hope of our own resurrection.

The second way God's power creates assurance is that (2) by it *we escape demon possession*. After Jesus exorcised Legion from the Gadarene demoniac, the man wanted to go with the Lord to the west coast of the Sea of Galilee. He was instructed, however, to return to his house and tell what great things the Lord had done for him (Lk. 8:26-39). One motive for wanting to remain with his benefactor may have been to have protection against being repossessed. If so, his fears could be allayed because Christ's power would protect him wherever he was. We infer from this exorcism in Jesus' name that a Christian need not fear demon possession contrary to his own will. We rest assured that the Lord who casts out demons can keep them out.

A third way God's power gives assurance is that (3) by it *we avoid overwhelming temptation*. God does not allow more temptation than we can bear; he provides a way of escape so we can endure it (I Cor. 10:13).

412

His protection can come by controlling our environment or by enhancing our strength to endure what the environment contains. The inference is that whatever comes has been allowed to come so that by letting it come God is giving us a vote of confidence that we can handle it. We are assured therefore of salvation because God has the power to deliver from death, demon possession, and overwhelming temptation.

God's willingness

Not only is God able, but he is willing to save us. He who is not willing that any *sinner* should perish (II Pet. 3:9) may be expected to do everything sufficient to keep a *saint* from perishing. Paul says as much in Romans 8:32, "He who did not spare his own Son but delivered him up for us all, how shall he not also with him grant us all things?" It is not in character for God to abandon us as evidenced by the great lengths to which he has gone in bringing us to himself to begin with.

God's immutability

In more than a few traditional assurance passages, the unchangeableness of God serves as part of the foundation for confidence. In Hebrews 6:17-18 the writer encourages his readers by recalling the oath taken by Almighty God when he made covenant with Abraham:

God, being minded to show more abundantly to the heirs of the promise the immutability of his counsel, interposed with an oath that by two immutable things [omnipotence and oath], in which it is impossible for God to lie, we have a strong encouragement, who have fled for refuge to lay hold of the hope set before us.

We inherit that promise made to the patriarch because we have set our hope on Jesus through whom we became spiritual descendants of faithful Abraham. It is no surprise that Hebrews, written to encourage assurance, incorporates into its material every topic with respect to which God takes an oath in the Old Testament. When God interposes with an oath there is double surety.

With perhaps greater emphasis on the interpersonal dimension of the assurance situation, faithfulness serves as another way of saying immutability. Paul included faithfulness in his encouragement to the Corinthians: "God is faithful who will not allow you to be tempted above what you are able to bear" (I Cor. 10:13). Over time God can be trusted

413

not to change like the fickle gods of the heathen who were driven by desire instead of committed to values. They were gods of power, but God is a God of principle as well. With him there is consistency between promise and fulfillment. I John 1:9 says, "If we confess our sins, he is faithful and just to forgive us our sins and to cleanse us from all unrighteousness" (cp. I Th. 5:24; II Th. 3:3; Heb. 2:17; 3:2; 10:23; 11:11; I Pet. 4:19). He is consistent in his love inasmuch as the same love that saved also preserves from undue temptation. All aspects of his total action with us and for us harmonize with one another.

Thus God's consistency exists (a) over time between promise and fulfillment and (b) throughout various aspects of his total plan and operation for us. Consistency also holds true (c) between members of the trinity. In conjunction with the famous statement "No one will snatch them out of my hand," Jesus speaks of his unity with the Father: "I and the Father are one" (Jn. 10:30). In the previous verse he likewise says, "No one can snatch them out of the Father's hand." Earlier in the gospel Jesus emphasizes the harmonious relationship of the Father and the Son in establishing salvation: "Everything that the Father gives me will come to me, and him who comes to me I will certainly not cast out" (Jn. 6:37). Later Jesus speaks to the apostles about the harmonious relationship of the Son and the Spirit in continuing salvation: "I will ask the Father and he will send you another advocate . . . the Spirit of truth; . . . he abides in you and will be with you" (14:16-17; cp. 16:12-14). The self-consistency, unchangeableness, and immutability of God establish the certainty out of which assurance can grow.

God's love

Much of what has been said about the basis for assurance can be subsumed under divine love. In Romans 8:31-39 the apostle Paul makes love the organizing center for assurance of salvation. Answering the question "Who shall separate us from the love of God," he speaks of (a) God's power: "If God is for us who is against us?" (31). "Who will lay anything to the charge of God's elect? God is the justifier" (33). The long list of opposing forces presents nothing that can keep us from being more than conquerors through him who loved us (35-39). (b) God's willingness and (c) self-consistency also come in for notice: "He that did not spare his own son but delivered him up for us all, how shall he not also with him grant us all things?" (32). (d) The sufficiency of Christ's work of atonement and intercession is noted: "Who is he that condemns? It is Jesus Christ who died, yea rather was raised from the dead . . . who also intercedes for us" (34). If an omnipotent, immutable God loves us in Jesus Christ, we certainly can have an assurance of salvation based more in him than in ourselves.

Our experience

Although our assurance rests more in God than in ourselves, it does rest in ourselves. We know, for example, that (1) we have believed and repented of past sin and that faith and repentance continue to characterize us before God. From a more formal standpoint we know that (2) we have committed ourselves to Jesus Christ in Christian baptism. To a certain extent a parallel can be drawn here between salvation and marriage; we know we are married because we took our vows in the wedding ceremony. Even those who reject baptism as a rite of passage into Christ illustrate the felt need for a clear "time-when" for salvation because they substitute another rite in its place to serve the same function: asking Jesus into your heart.

I John 3:18-21 firmly roots assurance in active love, by which "we know we are of the truth." When we conduct ourselves according to his commandments, we not only abide in him, but have assurance that we abide in him. Certainty of salvation comes from knowing that (3) we are doing what he commands (cp. II Tim. 2:19a + c). According to this passage in John, action is a more reliable indicator of salvation than our heart is (3:20). Even so our conscience and feelings can still play a part: "Beloved, if our heart does not condemn us, we have boldness toward God" (3:21). As long as we put feelings after obedience and active love, there is assurance because (4) we feel assured. Assurance of salvation correlates with the fact of salvation so that feeling assured serves as a confirmatory reason for continuing to feel assured of salvation.

We also know that (5) we are sincere. Although sincerity perhaps belongs under feeling, the affective dimension, or the emotional aspect of our nature, we give it a separate listing because of its importance. Even in salvation itself God evidently distinguishes between sins of sincere ignorance and willful disobedience (Acts 26:9; 17:30; 14:16; Rom. 3:25; I Tim. 1:13). Sins of sincere ignorance are not reckoned, and they are forgiven upon repentance when the ignorance is removed (Num. 15:22-29; Lev. 4; 5:14-19; 22:14). We take it therefore that

415

our sincerity counts for something with God if in our intent to do his will we misperceive what he means. Needless to say, however, sincerity ceases to be sincerity when we presume upon it or when we neglect honest efforts at removing ignorance. Naturally such a view of the value of sincerity in salvation has implications for assurance of salvation. There is a certain comfort in realizing that God plays fair with us as long as we play fair with him in salvation.

In speaking as we have about our own activity, we are referring to experience, not as a basis for salvation, but as a basis for the assurance of salvation.

Content of Assurance

The assurance of salvation has more to do with deliverance from sin than deliverance from sinning. Perfect Christian living before God is the goal: "Be therefore perfect as your heavenly Father is perfect" (Mt. 5:48; cp. Lev. 11:44-45; 19:2; 20:7; I Pet. 1:15-16). We call it the goal simply because it is never the achievement. I John 1:6-10 cites the fact that Jesus' blood gives *continued cleansing* from all sin as we confess sin; if we claimed to have no sin we would be liars. There is also the continued need for Christ's *intercession* (Heb. 7:25, etc.). Constantly we are exhorted to *growth* in Christ, which must mean we have not yet attained the ideal (cp. Phil. 3:8-16, etc.). In scripture itself we find *examples of sin* in Christian people like Peter (Gal. 2:11-13). The ideal has never changed, but the difference between performance and perfection is always made up by forgiveness; of this we are sure.

Protection

In avoiding sin we must be careful about what we expect from *him.* Expectancy corresponds with assurance in that assurance does not come if expectancies err. Although we have warned against expecting to live perfectly, we must also emphasize that God makes provisions to move us toward perfect living. He promises *protection* from conquest (Jn. 10:28; Rom. 8:31-39) and overwhelming temptation (I Cor. 10:13a), which are conditions in the environment.

Empowerment

He also promises *empowerment* to cope with life: sometimes the way of escape is through the fire (I Cor. 10:13b). This psychological strength is associated with the work of the Spirit and the indwelling of the Son. Ephesians says,

416

. . . I bow my knees to the Father . . . that according to the wealth of his glory he might give to you to be strengthened through his Spirit in the inner man, that Christ might dwell in your hearts through faith that you, being rooted and grounded in love, might be strengthened to apprehend with all the saints what is the breadth and length and height and depth and to know the love of Christ that surpasses knowledge in order that you might be filled with all the fullness of God (3:14-19).

This benefit addresses the condition in the self rather than the condition in the environment.

In Christ we have been delivered from the state of sin, that is, the state of estrangement from God. The focus is not directly on automatic deliverance from acts of sin. If we sin, we do not fall out of the state of relationship with him. We need not agonize therefore over post-baptismal sins as if the conversion process needed to start all over again. There is no reason to delay baptism as long as possible in order to take away the problem of later sins. We have no fear that some unconfessed sin would keep us from heaven if death should remove us before we had occasion to request forgiveness. The *attitude* of commitment to Christ together with the gift of a *state* of salvation relieves us of perfection fulfillment as a basis of maintaining relationship with God through Christ.

Guidance

In avoiding sin we believe that God promises sufficient *guidance* for us to know what he expects from *us*. We could infer this point from his not reckoning sins of legitimate ignorance (Acts 17:30). His general will for all Christians is laid down in scripture. On the surface of it we see no reason to suppose that God has any more specific will for individual Christians; that is to say, his general will for all men is his specific will for my life, and I am free and responsible to make a contribution to the needs that present themselves from every quarter. If his will for me is any more specific than what I can discover from his general will, that will have to be imparted to me by further divine effort. We need not worry about what God wants us to do if he has not clearly made it known.

Furthermore, we do not have to know that he is directing us in some special way even if he is; we will end up doing what he wants even if guidance is unawares. In general we do not assume that God has picked out a special task and place for each person at each point in time; but if he has, the following dictum always applies: to the extent that God's will is specific his guidance is explicit. We have assurance that "his divine

417

power has given us all things that pertain to life and godliness through the knowledge of him who called us by his own glory and virtue" (II Pet. 1:3). Anything beyond this must be communicated to each one of us as clearly as it was to those God specially called to specific tasks in Holy Writ.

Generally speaking we are assured primarily of interpersonal blessings and secondarily of those items that may come in consequence of harmonious relationships. Our health may be no better; our wealth may be no greater; but what is guaranteed is a quality of interpersonal relationship with God and man because we have been delivered from sin and are being delivered from sinning. The discrepancy between perfection and performance comes from the fact that God's grace is resistible after salvation as well as before it. Though grace is sufficient for perfection, it is not efficient for perfection.

Time of Assurance

The assurance of salvation lies in the present more than in the future. Since assurance is something we experience, it has to do with the present time. Moreover, it is our conviction that a correlation exists between the human basis of assurance and the sense of assurance. As our responses unto initial salvation are conditions for applying Christ's blood to our sinful status, so also our continued faith and obedience are conditions for continued cleansing from all sins. Whether we continue to be in Christ depends then on whether we continue in the obedient faith that serves as the continuing condition for that status. It may be true that years down the road we may depart the faith, but we need not worry now about such an unforeseeable eventuation.

Some Christians are persuaded that once any person's salvation has occurred it cannot be lost. The reason it is viewed as irreversible is either (a) that God protects irresistibly from falling or (b) that he never withdraws his salvation even if there is a falling. We contend that these alternatives detract from assurance rather than enhance it, as usually believed. Under the first alternative, lack of perseverance supposedly indicates lack of genuine conversion originally. Such an arrangement detracts from present assurance because we cannot know now whether we will persevere to the end. We cannot distinguish ourselves from others who began as well as we did, but later apostatized to show presumably the lack of genuineness in their original faith. That lack of

418

genuineness was not perceivable before so that our faith may also not be genuine although we cannot perceive that now. Under the second alternative, assurance diminishes because we cannot distinguish ourselves from others who have never made any profession; a Christian faith that makes no difference has no power to create a sense of assurance that there is any reason for a difference to exist. In the interest of assurance, therefore, we state the case from scripture that salvation can be lost.

Hebrews 10:26-39

More than any other book in the Bible, Hebrews directs itself to the issue of losing salvation. It is actually a word of exhortation (13:22) sent to Christians who needed encouragement not to forsake their calling. Of the several places where apostasy comes fully into view, 10:37-39 is perhaps the clearest text because it is least subject to certain interpretative distinctions systematically employed in such passages by those convinced that apostasy from actual salvation never happens. Although the section covers 10:26-39, we quote only 10:37-39:

> "For yet a very little while
> the coming one will come and will not delay;
> And my righteous one will have life by faith,
> And if he turns back,
> my soul has no delight in him."
> But we are not of turning back unto destruction, but of faith
> unto the obtaining of life.

We cannot suppose that (a) the person discussed is not really saved, because he is described as "my righteous one." Furthermore, in the preceding context the person has been sanctified by the blood of the covenant (10:29).

Neither can we suppose that (b) the turning back was incomplete or that the reversion had only to do with loss of abundance rather than status or with punishment rather than destruction. The person described "turns back," a point which the Hebrew writer interprets by saying "turn back to destruction." In the immediately preceding context he also mentions the fearful expectation of a destruction worse than death (26-29).

419

Furthermore, we cannot suppose that (c) dispensational distinctions affect the apostasy issue, because 10:37-38 quotes Habakkuk 2:3-4 from the Mosaic dispensation and applies it to the principles of operation in the Christian dispensation. It will not do to allow for apostasy under the Old Covenant, but not under the New. If the writer quotes a passage from a former dispensation and applies it to the present age, he must be assuming that the dispensational distinction is not a difference that makes a difference.

Lastly, we cannot suppose that (d) warnings of this kind are hypothetical, but never become real in the experience of a Christian. The author does separate himself and his readership from such as he contemplates when he says, "But we are not of turning back unto destruction, but of faith unto the obtaining of life." Those whom he has in mind, however, could be joined by his readers if they do not heed his warnings. To say that the readers are not of them that turn back is not to say that there can be no such thing as turning back. Not only do people not warn others about what cannot happen, but the author here would be stating a falsehood if in fact there is no such thing as a righteous one turning back to perdition. Whenever a punishment—like perdition—is specified, the sin must be possible; no one prepares a punishment for an unreal potentiality.

The careful reader will discern that the quotation from Habakkuk used in Hebrews 10 departs considerably from the Old Testament verses as they appear in our modern translations of Habakkuk. This variance stems from the practice in Hebrews of loosely quoting the Septuagint Greek version rather than the Masoretic Hebrew text of the Old Testament, which normally lies behind our English translation. The Septuagint was a pre-Christian Greek translation that enjoyed considerable popularity during the first century A.D. The Masoretic text we use today is a standardized Hebrew text prepared by the Masoretes, who preserved the oral tradition about technical points in the Hebrew Old Testament text. Their work flourished during the sixth through tenth centuries. The Septuagint was obviously prepared from Hebrew manuscripts that had a textual tradition divergent from the Masoretic text. Which text most accurately preserves the original wording of the prophet does not materially affect our concerns here because the Hebrew writer clearly accepts as true the statement as he presents it: if the Lord's righteous one turns back to perdition, the Lord has no pleasure in him.

Hebrews 6:4-8

After a word of reproof for lack of progress in understanding (5:11—6:3), the writer of Hebrews comments in the following manner:

> For it is impossible to renew again to repentance those who have once been enlightened and have tasted of the heavenly gift and become partakers of the Holy Spirit and have tasted the good word of God and the powers of the coming age, and then fall away, crucifying to themselves the Son of God again and openly putting him to shame (cp. "fall away" in Gal. 5:4; II Th. 2:3; I Tim. 4:1; Heb. 4:1; 12:15; II Pet. 3:17).

On the positive side the persons in view experience enlightenment; taste of the heavenly gift, the word of God, and the powers of the coming age; and partake of the Holy Spirit. All these marks identify them as Christians. On the negative side they fall away, crucify the Son of God to themselves, and put him to an open shame. These acts categorize them with those who originally crucified him in public nakedness.

Those who originally rejected him, however, did not perhaps stand in even so great a jeopardy because at least they did it ignorantly (Acts 3:17; 13:27; 26:9; Lk. 23:34; I Cor. 2:8; cp. Jn. 15:21), and sins of ignorance are either forgiveable or not reckoned (Acts 17:30; I Tim. 1:13; Rom. 5:13; cp. Num. 15:22-26; Deut. 19:1-10). The ones of whom the Hebrew writer speaks are enlightened (6:4; 10:26) so that their final rejection would be willful (10:26) and their fate worse than death (10:28-31). By combining Hebrews 6 and 10, we observe the following about the ones contemplated in the epistle: they are sanctified by the blood of the *Son* and then trample it under foot and recrucify him; they partake of the *Spirit* and then insult him.

Loss of Esau's birthright

In 12:15-17 the writer of Hebrews warns his readers again about falling short of God's grace. Such falling he compares with Esau's selling his birthright for one meal. This example is evidently chosen because birthright bears suggestive likeness to the spiritual heritage available to the sons of God. As surely as Esau could repudiate his right of primogeniture, the Christian can forfeit his eternal reward and his place in the church of the firstborn (12:23).

The exodus example

Chapters 3-4 in Hebrews take up a theme originally expressed by Psalms 95:7-11, which makes a comparison between the exodus and salvation. The comparison shows that deliverance from bondage does not necessarily mean obtaining God's rest. When Jude 5 and I Corinthians 10:1-13 are placed alongside Hebrews 3-4, the total picture becomes one in which leaving the bondage of Egypt was finalized at the crossing of the Red Sea; the crossing identified the Israelites with Moses' leadership and formalized them into a nation (I Cor. 10). They soon received their constitution at Sinai; but instead of remaining faithful till they had conquered Canaan, they fell into disobedience and lost Palestine and more. Having saved a people out of Egypt, God destroyed them that disbelieved (Jude 5).

The spiritualizing of this great event in the history of national Israel serves to exhort unto diligence lest anyone fall in the same example of disobedience (Heb. 4:11). Egypt answers to the bondage of sin. Crossing the Red Sea equals "baptism" (I Cor. 10:1-2), and moving along the journey to Canaan corresponds with the period of nourishment through "Christ" (10:3-4). To be saved from bondage is not to receive eternal rest because a period of time intervenes; between those events a person may fall by the wayside instead of persevering to the end. The ones who fail to remain faithful to the end do not enter their eternal rest. The Israelites were saved "from" but not "unto"; we also may be saved from but not unto.

The "if" condition

In Hebrews, as well as elsewhere, inheriting eternal life is contingent on continued faith. We are the house of God *if* we remain faithful to the end (3:6, 14; cp. 6:11). God directs his goodness toward us *if* we continue in his goodness; otherwise we will be cut off (Rom. 11:22; cp. Jn. 15:6, 7, 10, 14). Paul exhorts the Galatians not to grow weary in well doing because they will reap in due time *if* they do not give out (6:9). Christ will present us holy, without blemish, and unreprovable *if* we continue in the faith (Col. 1:23). On the negative side Hebrews 2:3 says, "How shall we escape *if* we neglect so great a salvation?" The one that endures to the end is the one that will be saved (Mt. 10:22; 24:13; I Cor. 15:2; Heb. 10:38; Rev. 2:10), and he will reign with Christ (II Tim. 2:12).

Destruction for fruitlessness

Land. After describing a person who has the Spirit and then crucifies the Son, Hebrews specifies a destiny of destruction which it likens to the burning of a field. The writer adjusts the figure somewhat by making the reward a blessing so the punishment is a curse as well as a rejection and a burning. The nature of the illustration means that application cannot be carried through strictly since ground cannot be destroyed or rewarded like people. Ground itself cannot be burned. Speaking of it as rejected and burned is as close as the writer can come.

We wonder whether the writer may be using the word "ground" as a metonymy standing for the ground with everything produced by it. The harmony between producer and produced means that poor ground produces poor crops or, more exactly here, no crops at all. What is true of its produce is true of itself. Since thorns and thistles are no good, the ground itself is no good. Therefore the ground is rejected and cursed, being put to no further use; the produce is burned. In the rejection, cursing, and burning, the illustration is being modified by activities that are done to what the terms in the illustration signify, instead of being done to the terms themselves. The point of burning is not that of purification, but of destruction because rejection of the ground heads the list of actions taken relative to it. In this general regard of fruitfulness we could also bring in the parable of the sower (Mt. 13:3-9, 18-23).

Trees. John the Baptist warns his Jewish audience that trees which do not bear good fruit will be cut down and cast into the fire (Lk. 3:7-9). In the parable of the barren fig tree a vineyard owner and his vine-dresser agree to cut down a fig tree if it bears no fruit after it is fertilized (Lk. 13:6-9). In the Sermon on the Mount Jesus says, "Every tree that does not produce good fruit is cut down and thrown into the fire" (Mt. 7:17). A related figure is Paul's olive tree in Romans 11.

Vine. In John 15:1ff. his relationship to the disciples Jesus compares with a vine and its branches. The Father is the husbandman who takes away every branch that does not bear fruit. Exhorting his disciples to remain in him, he "fudges the figure" a little by telling them that if they do not remain in the "vine," they are thrown out of it and burned like dead branches. The burning of the useless branches is not for purification, but for destruction. Purifying is covered elsewhere in the vine figure when the Father cleans the fruitful branches. The application of all these fruitlessness figures seems obvious: when the Christian life style does not correspond to the Christian expectancies, the unfruitful person is removed from his place among the saved. No character, no status; loss of character, loss of status.

423

Ezekiel's warnings

Remaining faithful till death highlights an important truth in all dispensations: a man's final condition determines his eternal destiny. Ezekiel makes this point especially clear when he teaches on the one hand that a man's previous transgressions are not held against him if he turns from them and keeps the Lord's statutes (18:21-23; 33:14-16, 19). On the other hand he says, "When a righteous man turns from his righteousness and commits iniquity . . . he will die in his sin, and his righteous deeds which he has done will not be remembered" (3:20; cp. 18:24-26; 33:18). Even though God should say to the righteous, "You shall surely live," if the righteous person trusts in his righteousness and commits iniquity, he will die in his sins (33:13). The person is called "righteous" and promised life, yet he will die in his sins. According to this prophet it is as possible to turn from righteousness to wickedness and die as it is to turn from wickedness to righteousness and live (33:12). A righteous man becoming a sinner is as possible as a faithful city becoming a harlot (Isa. 1:21). A person's ultimate end does not depend on, say, the percentage of his life he lived righteously, but on his condition before God at the conclusion of his years. If that final condition is wickedness, it does not matter whether he was wicked all along or righteous for a while and wicked thereafter; he will die in his sins. If apostasy were impossible from a practical standpoint, there would be no particular reason to emphasize the point that a man's final condition determines his eternal destiny.

Removal from the olive tree

In Romans 11, Paul depicts the people of God as an olive tree with the patriarchs as the root and faithful Israelites as the branches. Arguing that God has not cast off his people, the apostle regards the one people as spiritual Israel so that Gentiles who turn to Christ are like wild olive branches grafted into Israel. Unfaithful Jews are broken out to make room, so to speak, for Gentile sons of Abraham by faith.

The possibility of apostasy enters the picture when Paul declares that his Gentile readers, who were originally grafted into the tree, may be broken off again if they do not continue in the goodness of God. Natural and wild branches both stand in the olive tree by faith; those that fall receive the severity of God by being cut off (11:20-24). As their grafting in pictures salvation, so also their removal again pictures loss of salvation.

424

Removal from the Book of Life

Being in the Book of Life means being saved (Rev. 13:8; 17:8; 20:12, 15; 21:27; Phil. 4:3; Dan. 12:1; cp. Lk. 10:20; Heb. 12:23). It is of interest then that removal from the Book of Life is contemplated in some scriptures.

To the church at Sardis the writer of Revelation promises that the Lord will not blot out from the Lamb's Book of Life the names of those who overcome (3:5; Ps. 69:28; cp. Ex. 32:32; II Pet. 2:3). The natural implication is that he will blot out the names of those who do *not* overcome. There must be such a thing as blotting out. There would be little consolation in the saying that because of their overcoming he would not blot out their names if indeed he also would not blot them out if they did not overcome. In a contrast between overcoming and not overcoming, the not blotting out must contrast with blotting out.

The dog and sow example

Recalling the proverb about the dog and sow, Peter comments on escaping the defilements of the world through the knowledge of the Lord and Savior Jesus Christ. Becoming entangled and overcome again makes people worse off than before: "'the dog returning to his own vomit' and 'the sow that was washed to wallowing in the mud'" (II Pet. 2:22; Prov. 26:11). Those whom the apostle envisions had been defiled by the world, had escaped, and then returned to those defilements again (20-21); they had been bought by the Master, but had then denied him and brought swift destruction on themselves (2:1; cp. I Tim. 1:19; 4:1). This whole situation reminded Peter of being led astray by false prophets in the old dispensation (2:1) and of the angels who fell from their original estate unto condemnation (2:4; cp. Jude 6). Similar warnings about the destructive results of false teachers appear in I Timothy 4:1 (cp. 1:19) and the book of Jude.

Paul's concern about himself

Writing to the Corinthians, Paul compares his Christian self-discipline to that practiced by men training for the games. He explains his daily effort in this regard by saying, ". . . lest in some way, having preached to others, I myself would be rejected" (I Cor. 9:27). In 9:22 he spoke of becoming all things to all men in order to save some. Everything he did was for the purpose of becoming a partaker of the reward of the gospel (23); his purposeful striving in spiritual exercise anticipated an incorruptible crown. It would be ironical that, having made his efforts to save others, what he offered to them he himself would not possess in the end. He would, so to speak, be "disqualified" from partaking of that incorruptible crown he had made available to the whole Mediterranean world.

Paul's concern lies with the eternal rewards of the gospel, not so much with the temporal values of it. In respect to the games the subject of his thinking is what comes at the *end* of the race, not what comes along the way. The eternal dimension comes in under the expression "incorruptible" *crown*. His "preaching to others" (9:27) was for their *salvation* (9:22); consequently, his jointly partaking thereof (9:23) has to do with salvation, not just with the sense of well being that a person has when he is spiritually "in shape." Since his being rejected, disqualified, or unacceptable stands in contrast to preaching to others (9:27), it must stand in agreement with jointly partaking of salvation. We take it then that Paul considered it possible even for himself to lose salvation if he did not maintain the quality of life God calls upon his servants to demonstrate.

"In vain"

Three "in vain" passages provide another, albeit, less certain basis for the doctrine of apostasy. Paul says in I Corinthians 15:1-2, "Now I make known to you, brothers, the gospel that you received, in which also you stand, by which also you are saved if you hold fast with the word that I preached to you, except you believed in vain." In this statement the apostle regards the Corinthians as saved people, yet he speaks of their believing in vain so that no profit regarding eternal salvation would come from their belief; thus apostasy would be assumed. It may be possible, however, to suppose Paul assumes their salvation when he makes his first comments and then adds parenthetically the closing comment as a qualifier if he was in error on that point. "Believe" in that case would be a belief short of commitment as the word is used in James 2.

Elsewhere in the Corinthian correspondence Paul uses a related expression similarly translated "in vain": "And working together with him, we entreat also that you not receive the grace of God in vain" (II Cor. 6:1). The apostle does not speak of receiving the word as in

426

belief without commitment; he speaks of receiving grace in a salvation setting and then goes on to speak of his enduring trials for the faith.

Twice in Galatians Paul uses the same "in vain" expression. "I fear for you lest somehow I have labored for you in vain" (4:11). "Did you suffer so many things in vain, if indeed it has been in vain" (3:4). Paul's labor would be in vain if the Galatians fell away; their suffering would also be in vain if they left the faith. That none of the Galatians had been genuinely converted seems most unlikely under the circumstances; there was no question about relationship to Christ until the Judaizing teachers came and confused them. Our verdict here depends partially on how the apostle views them elsewhere. More important, however, is whether he viewed apostasy as possible aside from any consideration of his readers particularly. That he did so seems sufficiently clear from his great distress over Judaizing influences.

As far as God is concerned he saves us permanently when he saves us, but that permanent salvation rests on continued faithfulness. We do well to heed the warning of Jude: ". . . the Lord, having saved a people *once and for all, afterwards* destroyed those that did not believe." Continued salvation presupposes the same attitude that was presupposed in initial salvation.

Means of Assurance

The assurance of salvation derives from growing in personal and interpersonal activity in Christ. Assurance of salvation refers to the sense of certainty we have about our good standing with God through Jesus Christ. There is both the fact of continued salvation and our sense of certainty about that fact. The former pertains to security in salvation itself while the latter has to do with the assurance of salvation. The first section of this chapter surveyed the main components in the objective certainty of salvation. The next section argued that separating present status from final condition makes the present assurance more certain. This section makes some practical comments on the dynamics of assurance.

Growth

In the section on the possibility of apostasy we centered our presentation on the book of Hebrews. Written as it was to warn the readers

427

about this possible eventuation, Hebrews provides a rather systematic treatment of matters that bear as well on solving the apostasy problem. In its overall structure the book alternates paragraphs of encouragement with blocks of teaching material related to perseverance. The general point throughout is that *continued growth is the safeguard against apostasy.* This principle holds true in the sense that a person who is continually growing will continue to *be* saved. It holds true also in the sense that a growing person will continue to *feel* saved. The freshness of new discoveries in Christ keeps the focus of attention on the things of Christ both as to fact and as to feeling. Christian living brings its own justification for continued Christian living with the result that *continued growth brings a sense of assurance.*

Underneath everything said on standing firm is the idea that pressing on to perfection provides the safeguard against apostasy. In other words Hebrews recommends dealing with the problem before it becomes a problem, and makes use of the fact that there is greater stability in movement than in stillness. A bicycle balances more easily while it is moving. A top will stand up as long as it keeps spinning. Such imageries remind us that inactive faith will lose its stability, too.

The law of all living things is that what does not grow will die. If our Christian life quality now is no more advanced than it was three to five years ago, its vibrancy will probably not continue and we will lose interest in it. Progress provides its own motivation to continue to progress, as any experienced dieter will tell you. As long as measurable weight loss occurs, a person can keep hanging in there; but once the pattern snaps and attention wanders to other things, old eating habits resume and the dieter drifts back into the very condition he was overcoming. As with dieting so with spiritual discipline; the process of apostasy is usually a drifting away (Heb. 2:1) instead of a cascading over the brink. Likewise its reverse is more often a slow climb than a vault into the heights. The secret to the whole matter is continued progress on the long haul so that from time to time as we look back to see how far we have come, definite progress is obvious from the vantage point we have gained.

Doctrinal growth

Perseverance by continued growth is a formula that the Hebrew writer urges on his readers in two respects. The first of the book has to do with *growth in understanding* and pervades about nine and a half

428

chapters. In 5:11-14 he rebukes the brethren for not understanding even "the rudiments of the first principles of the oracles of God," and then proceeds to discuss at length several points derived from Psalms 110:4, which in turn leads into concepts based on Jeremiah 31 and Psalms 40: the superiority of Messiah's sacrifice, priesthood, and covenant. The original audience of this treatise needed to understand more adequately the temporary character of God's previous revelation to the fathers and its preparatory role that led to the full and final revelation in the Son. Without confidence that their present commitments were in fact correct as shown by the previous revelation itself, these early believers left themselves open to temptations that could draw them back into former beliefs.

In our own day we have advantages that leave us without excuse if we depart the faith because conflicting philosophies have destroyed our equilibrium. The New Testament has now been fully written so that we no longer have to rely on oral communication of the word. The printing press has made it possible for everyone to own a personal copy of what God has spoken to us in his Son. Modern translations have largely removed the Bible from its associations with another era by expressing the truth in words more easily able to be understood. Tools for Bible study are readily available so that it is relatively easy to grow in our knowledge of Christian doctrine.

Knowledge, however, is not virtue and there is more to the New Covenant than a set of beliefs. Christianity is not so much a philosophy to be believed as it is a religion to be lived. Since there is more to it than truths understood, steadfastness to the end requires more than increase in learning. Not only so, but information has a way of getting stale over time if it is not combined with dynamic factors.

Interpersonal growth

For this reason the Hebrew writer devotes the last three and a half chapters to encouraging *growth in interpersonal activity.* As to the activity aspect Christianity is an art—the art of living. It is something like playing the piano. As far as knowing is concerned, I know where all the notes are on the instrument and which ones need to be combined to make chords. I could even learn the best fingerings for running different scales. In terms of music theory, I might be able to understand what notes ought to be in the left hand and right hand to create the most pleasing sound. With all that, however, I am not and would not be a pianist. Understanding all the right things does not make me a Christian either, nor does it provide all the ingredients necessary for "holding fast the beginning of our confidence firm to the end" (3:14).

On the interpersonal side we must remember that "the Son" came to "give his body" so "a new covenant" could be established where men's "sins would be remembered no more." Sin's removal means that now we can "draw near to the throne of grace with boldness" while realizing that the Author of our faith has brought many other sons into glory as well; consequently, we relate vertically to God above and horizontally to our brothers who are in the world. The activity commended in Hebrews is not just keeping busy, but keeping busy with people. Physical activity, of course, has a therapeutic value of its own; but though bodily exercise may profit a little, it does not especially profit against apostasy. The sphere of the activity must be people.

Spread through the last section of Hebrews are three forms of inter-personal activity mentioned by the writer. The first is (a) *fellowship with the faithful*. In a passage often cited to encourage worship attend-ance, the readers are admonished "to provoke each other to love and good works," especially in anticipation of special trials that lie ahead. Assembling with the faithful makes exhortation possible for us, too. Not only are we known by the company we keep, but we become like the company we keep. If such is the case for evil, it can also be a mechanism used for good.

A second form of interpersonal activity is (b) *imitation of the faithful*. In an extended section on faith several Old Testament saints are selected in order to point out the effects of their trust in God. This "great cloud of witnesses" culminates in "the Perfecter of our faith" to whom the faithful look for inspiration and guidance. Even among contemporary saints there are those whose issue of life calls us to imitate their example. Noticeably it is an imitation drawn forth by considering the "issue" of their life. The self-destructive elements in certain behavior only become evi-dent over time. By following the example of people who have produced quality lives on the long term, we will be able to hold firm permanently.

A third form of interpersonal activity is (c) *service to all mankind*. "Love of the brethren" must continue, but so must "showing love to strangers." Such activity establishes a point of contact with unbelievers so that love can flow through it to draw them to the faith. The benefit in view here, however, is not so much for the strangers as for the one who shows love to them. The surest way to confirm ourselves in the faith is to be instrumental in extending it to those outside the faith. Our own growth comes in being the author and perfecter of other men's growth.

The good life does not just happen; it is planned. The new life in Christ does not automatically continue either, for it is still subject to detracting and distracting influences in the world around. So to speak, the river of life empties into the lake of fire; self-preservation demands that we not drift along effortlessly with the current trends. Continued progress is the necessary safeguard against apostasy. That growth must have the dimensions specified in the book of Hebrews: understanding, activity, and personal relationship.

Intrapersonal growth

Our presentation on perseverance so far has followed the emphases of the presentation in Hebrews. It remains for us to set this matter in its larger context. *Perseverance* is active continuation to the end. The writer of Hebrews specifies *sanctification* as the means by which perseverance occurs: growth displaces death. *Assurance* is largely feeling saved. Therefore persevering in salvation and continued assurance of salvation go hand in hand. The bases of assurance are also the means to it. There are also two dimensions in which sanctification unto assurance actually occurs: within a person and between persons. We seek to explain these more systematically in the following paragraphs.

If perseverance is action and assurance is feeling, then assurance is controlled and maintained like any other feeling. Knowing, feeling, and doing interrelate in such a way that each affects the other. From personal experience each of us can verify that our emotions grow out of our thinking and doing. Thinking as a part of knowing contributes to doing perseverance and feeling saved, not only according to Hebrews, but also according to Paul when he says in Philippians to think on things true, honorable, just, pure, lovely, of good report, virtuous, and praiseworthy (4:8-9). The power of positive thinking is not to be underestimated in its effects on how we feel and therefore on how assured we feel about our salvation.

But neither Hebrews nor Philippians stops with thinking or knowing. They both pass on to interpersonal activity, for the Philippian Christians were to do what they saw in Paul. Then it is that "the God of *peace*" would be with them. If how we feel arises from what we do and think, then we can deliberately make use of this fact in strengthening assurance. The three functions feeling, knowing, and doing are arranged in that ascending order as far as their ability to be willed is concerned. Since willing a feeling is especially difficult and since feelings arise from thinking and doing, we can will our feelings indirectly by willing to do and to think. Because assurance is a feeling, we can enhance it by willing to do spiritual exercises like prayer, scripture reading, fasting, fellowship with the faithful, imitation of their lives, and service to all mankind (cp. I Jn. 3:18-20). As we grow in these personal and interpersonal activities, we will grow in confidence about salvation.

The interrelationship between knowing, feeling, and doing is covered by the concept of reciprocation, which becomes a description of growth in assurance. Reciprocation refers to processes where A affects B, which turns around and affects A. All growth processes operate in a setup where two or more poles act back and forth on each other. Christian growth and Christian assurance come under this format. According to our previous pages reciprocation occurs in two respects: within the individual and between individuals—intrapersonal and interpersonal. Within the individual the two poles are inner and outer with inner

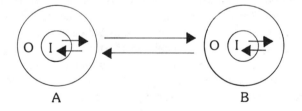

A   B

comprising thinking, feeling, willing, and the like while the outer has to do with overt activity. "Out of the abundance of the heart the mouth speaks" (Lk. 6:45), a statement that traces the inner to outer movement. "Where your treasure is there will your heart be" (Mt. 6:21), a saying that tells how the outward action of giving, etc., shapes the affections of the inner man. What we think and feel affects what we do, which in turn deepens our understanding and affection so that greater works are done, etc.

The same reciprocating pattern occurs between persons who influence one another in a growth of Christian oneness and witness. Love displayed to another triggers in him the love he returns to the first person. We love him who first loved us (I Jn. 4:19), and we love others because he first showed us love (I Jn. 4:21). The beginning point can be either inner or outer and with person A or person B, but once begun it affects the other pole unto a continuing growth. Perseverance and assurance both result from the process because the means of the first equal the means of the second.

Speaking as we have on the "mechanics" of assurance, we address the subjective awareness more than the objective status. These procedures do not so much produce the salvation as the sense of salvation. What we feel and what actually is may not coincide so that the lack of feeling saved does not tell against our being saved any more in fact than our feeling saved speaks for our salvation. Assurance is a derivative matter that depends on understanding of the faith and on performance of its demands. Our confidence is in him who saves, and it is appropriate that we feel what in fact is true; consequently, we may draw upon resources that foster this aspect of abundant life.

Inner witness of the Spirit

Conceptualizing assurance as the product of human functioning stands in contrast to assurance conceived of as *direct miraculous implantation*. The "inner witness of the Spirit" means under our reconstruction an *indirect natural effect* produced in us by obedience to the Spirit's directives for bringing assurance; that is, assurance comes from the Spirit's influence, not from his miracle. When we are thus led by the Spirit in putting to death the deeds of the body, we experience a sense of adoption, crying out, "Abba, Father" (Rom. 8:12-15). Paul states to the Romans in 8:16, "The Spirit himself testifies with our spirit that we are children of God." The passage could mean that the Spirit testifies, not *to* our spirit, but *with* our spirit *to* the Father. In this case the passage does not directly pertain to our subject. If, however, the point is something like "sharing witness with" our spirit, then Paul associates our certainty of divine sonship with the agency of the Holy Spirit. Our point, however, is that he does not necessarily have in mind a mystical experience, the mechanics of which are wholly unknown to us. We perceive that influence satisfies the requirements of assurance.

The interpretation of Romans 8:16 does not become an ultimate concern because whether the sense of assurance is connected with the

433

Spirit or derived from normal psychological processes, the effect is the same as long as the inner witness comes indirectly. If it is indirect divine operation, the two conceptualizations approximate each other except that inner witness has a larger scope because it ties back into the Spirit's originating influence for assurance.

When the inner witness means direct functioning, however, practical dangers develop because a correlation *must* exist between the sense of assurance and the fact of security if the Spirit directly creates that assurance within us. Under that construct the lack of assurance must mean the lack of security so that the lack of constancy in the sense of assurance becomes in itself a basis for not having assurance; insecurity thus feeds on itself. For this reason I John 3:18-20 says action takes precedence over feeling as a basis for assurance. In fact, our loving acts for the brethren become a basis for controlling the feeling of our hearts: "Hereby [loving in deed] we . . . shall assure our heart before him" (19). Assurance does breed greater assurance (3:21) and lack of it tends to reinforce itself, but the important thing to remember is that this tendency is normal behavior we experience, not communication we receive.

We attribute periods of uncertainty to the usual vagaries and instability of human emotion. Such a view has the effect of greater assurance because uncertainty does not necessarily mean anything more real than emotional fluctuation means in matters aside from salvation. The assurance of salvation cannot be a fundamental reason for assurance or the lack of assurance becomes a reason against it. Assurance and salvation correlate, but the correlation is not always one to one. "True religion and undefiled" is doing something before it is feeling something. Feelings only confirm salvation. Therefore behavior is a better barometer of spiritual condition than feelings are.

Summary

Ideally assurance of salvation correlates with actuality of salvation. Since the *basis of salvation* stands sure, it contributes to our feeling saved for sure. On the positive side Messiah's atonement and intercession suffice for initial and continued relationship to God. By his unchanging power and love he strengthens us to cope with temptation to desert the Lord and deny the faith. On the negative side God protects us against forcible conquest and demon possession even while he

434

controls our environment to guard us against overwhelming temptation. Even as the basis of salvation is a basis of assurance, so also our responses to that basis figure into assurance. Faith, repentance, commitment in baptism, and continued obedience serve to bolster and confirm assurance because a life of obedience necessarily corresponds with the status of salvation. God's provision for perseverance is as sufficient as his provision for salvation. Therefore our assurance is more in God than in ourselves.

A proper understanding of the *content of assurance* also has implication for our sense of assurance. God gives sufficient guidance to make us certain of his will for us. In this we are assured of deliverance from sin but not from sinning, for God's grace is resistible to our own shame and destruction.

As for the *time of assurance* it is comforting to know that we do not have to hold our confidence in abeyance until the end of the course in order to see whether our beginning was genuine. The possibility of apostasy means that we can separate our present status from our status decades hence. Falling from the faith can explain instances where Christian character has been set aside even though it seemed as genuine as our own. Such apostasy, however, casts all the blame on us because we fall away despite God's sufficient provision for our perseverance.

In many respects the bases of assurance are also the *means of assurance*. Growth in sanctification guarantees both perseverance and assurance. All growth occurs by reciprocation between two or more poles. Assurance grows by reciprocation between inner and outer man and between men. Growth and therefore assurance is triggered outside us by an act of love to which we respond in love. By our will to respond we deepen the inner affections and thoughts which in turn produce greater active love directed at other men and to God above, who influenced the whole process of change between and within us to start with.

435

Chapter Twenty-Seven

PERSEVERANCE OF THE SAINTS

Introduction

Positions on apostasy

Our treatment of continuation in the Christian faith combined absolute assurance in God with less than absolute certainty in ourselves for future faithfulness. That treatment corresponds with one of three approaches taken toward a person who turns behaviorally away from his Christian commitment. As part of the total picture outlined in the previous chapter we have maintained that (1) the person was saved but now is lost. The position examined in this chapter is that (2) the person was never truly saved in the first place as shown by his failure to continue to the end. Some believe that (3) the person was saved and is still saved later despite his behavioral departure from the Christian life—a view examined in the next chapter.

As contrasted with the first position the other two are not equally objectionable. The second approach agrees with the first in that it considers the person lost in the end; the intervening status is different, but in such a way as to be academic in respect to his eternal destiny. The last doctrine, however, is decidedly more objectionable because salvation status is divorced from righteous behavior despite the fact that the whole point of salvation is to get rid of the sinful behavior that caused separation from God in the first place. It appears to forget that an interpersonal relationship is involved here and proceeds as if salvation is a kind of mechanical, impersonal, legal process. Such a concept fosters the insensitivity to sin that lies at the heart of all that the gospel attempts to accomplish in the world.

Terminology on apostasy

On one side of the picture we speak of *apostasy*, or *falling away*, by which we mean the denial of the faith once affirmed both intellectually and behaviorally and the faith to which commitment was at one time made. A distinction needs to be made between apostasy and *backsliding* because in the latter instance the person has lost for a time some degree of his earlier zeal for righteousness, but has not given up his beliefs or his faith in Christ to such an extent that God rejects him. It corresponds with the difference between grieving the Spirit (Eph. 4:30; cp. I Th. 5:19) and doing despite to the Spirit (Heb. 10:29). Of course, the difference is one of definition that may be affirmed doctrinally despite uncertainty about a given person's experience.

"Apostasy" is often defined to mean falling away from high exposure to the gospel and perhaps a keeping of its ethic and believing of its teaching without any decisive commitment to the person of Jesus Christ. "Apostasy" is sometimes defined also as a falling from grace (Gal. 5:1-4) in which one falls from Christian liberty into legalistic observances and feelings about the necessity of doing good works to maintain sonship with the Father; such a person has begun to put a false significance and necessity on his actions, but he has not been thereby thrust out of salvation status. Christians may lose their rewards of Christian living and their testimony to others, but not their status. We will be using apostasy, however, to mean falling out of the state of salvation.

On the other side of the picture, where apostasy is denied we find the expressions *eternal security, once saved always saved,* and *once in grace always in grace.* Such labels lack the emphasis of the preferable one, *perseverance,* because it draws attention to the believer's need to remain faithful in a practical sense. Without this stress a person may be tempted to fall into a kind of "antinomian" thinking, where the way he lives afterwards has no affect on his continued relationship to God as if he does not have to "obey God's law" if he has the status of God's son. Some writers prefer *preservation* as an even better term because it gives priority to God's activity in a man's continued faithfulness. *Security* is often used to indicate the certainty of a believer's continued salvation in distinction from *assurance,* which is personal confidence about salvation.

Marriage can serve again to illustrate three possibilities following initial salvation. *Apostasy* resembles the case where an errant spouse backslides in the responsibilities and conduct natural to marriage. Deterioration gets to the point where one divorces the other. *Perseverance* is like a case where the faithful spouse can keep shedding influence to help keep the other one from being lured into practices that destroy the marriage. *Security* may be compared to the situation in which the husband totally strays from behavior becoming to a husband, but his wife does not divorce him; they are separated, but not divorced.

Priority of positive evidence for perseverance

The perseverance model is taught because students of scripture believe the Bible teaches it, not necessarily because of any desire to remove the need to be responsible in Christ or to lessen the high calling to which salvation commits us. Advocates of perseverance are well aware of the material on apostasy incorporated into the previous chapter, but they have pre-understandings based on other scriptures that require them to consider apostasy secondary to the primary truth of perseverance. Those pre-understandings must be examined in order to have a meeting of honest minds on the issue.

In order to solve any difference of viewpoint like this one, there must be the usual application of the principle that *the burden of proof rests on the affirmative.* Many incorrect ideas are difficult, if not impossible, to disprove because relevant materials may not have been written so as to divert the reader away from those concepts. The *burden of proof is borne by primary proof,* not confirmatory evidence. *Evidence that leads only to one conclusion is primary proof;* evidence that can fit with more than one conclusion does not prove any of them. At this point in the discussion the perseverance model needs to assume the positive burden of proof by presenting data that does not fit with the apostasy possibility. It needs to show that the fact of perseverance is a more fundamental truth than the possibility of apostasy, and it needs to show that fact in such a way as to include the evidence we have surveyed regarding apostasy.

Reasons for the Perseverance Model

God's promise to protect

Against overwhelming temptation. The most likely line of defense for perseverance is that God freely promises to keep us from apostasy that could happen because of temptation *in harmony with our wills.* Even without a systematic a priori from which it derives, Christians know perseverance is true because scripture positively teaches it. Our conviction is that among the passages normally cited, (1) I Corinthians 10:13 has the best claim on establishing the view. The others must assume this one for their background in order to gain validity: "God is faithful who will not allow you to be tempted above what you are able to bear, but will with the temptation also provide the way of escape."

If God provides for dealing with temptation to this extent, the inference appears to be that a man will never stumble so as to fall. The Lord will strengthen him by exhortation, will enable nature, or will restrain Satan to keep the power of enticement at a manageable level. Job's life serves as a good example of this model for preservation. He resisted temptations that would have snatched him out of God's hands by getting him to curse God (Job 1-2). (a) An implicit assumption, however, is being made in the inference that a man *will* bear what he *can* bear. Paul's statement falls on the heels of the exodus analogy in which the Israelites were saved from Egypt. They were able to endure the privations of the wilderness and rise to the demands of the conquest, but most of them did not in fact do so. In addition, (b) the promise about God's faithfulness follows a verse warning against falling: "Therefore let him that thinks he is standing watch out lest he fall" (I Cor. 12:10). God does provide protection against overwhelming temptation that would draw us away in conformity with our wills through enticement. Providing protection differs from guaranteeing protection if the situation involves a choice on the part of the one protected.

(2) A similar description of the Christian experience comes from one reading of I John 5:18: "We know that everyone begotten by God does not practice sinning, but the One begotten by God keeps him and the evil one does not touch him." An alternative form of the original text says, ". . . but the one begotten by God keeps himself and the evil one does not touch him." If the first reading is adopted, the verse teaches that Jesus keeps us so that Satan does not touch us in such a way as to destroy characteristic Christian living. Keeping him, however, does not require a keeping that is essentially divine causation alone; that is, it is not an enablement or change of the abilities or capacities so that we will always do the right. It can be an interpersonal keeping in which the divine supply of influence is sufficient while the human response to the influence may prove less than adequate because it was less than what was potential.

Whereas I Corinthians 10:13 promises God's provisions, I John 5 describes their operation in the practical Christian life. First, we notice that the text does not say the evil one "*cannot* touch" us (5:18), but that he "*does* not touch" us. Second, since it says "*does* not touch," we need to decide whether this pattern is uniform or characteristic. Third, we must consider whether "being born of God" is more decisively a matter of *correlating with,* or *causing,* "Satan's not touching us." If the one who has been born of God stays in the Son, he will be kept so that Satan does not touch him. If he "stands born" (perfect participle) of God, he does not practice sinning, not *because* he is born of God, but *in keeping with* that fact.

439

Correlation rather than cause is preferable since (a) the context describes something that can be seen by a brother. The point is that a brother may be recognized by the absence of sin practice so that correlation between righteousness and being born of God is sufficient for these verses.

This consideration from the immediate context relates to another consideration from the general context of the letter that forms one non-perseverance understanding of 5:18: (b) gnosticism was unconcerned about moral behavior as relevant to salvation (cp. 3:10). Being born of God has a visible aspect in the behavior of the Christian, a condition in I John set in contrast to gnosticism. Greek philosophy viewed spirit as good and matter (including flesh) as evil. This dualism underlay gnosticism, where secret "knowledge" formed the basis of salvation, and salvation meant deliverance from the realm of flesh, not from the guilt of sin. Therefore, behavior had little to do with the concerns of salvation in the gnostic sense. People of this persuasion had found their way into the early churches and were trying to assimilate Christianity into their philosophical religion. Of course, they were destroying Christianity in the process of that attempt. John's epistles as well as Colossians and several other New Testament books were written among other things to warn their readers against this heresy. Naturally they strongly emphasize the behavioral element as a necessary aspect of the Christian experience. The behavior of those born of God contrasts then with the irrelevance of behavior in gnostic thought. Consequently, correlation rather than cause is again the concern of the verse. If the cause of not sinning (an internal matter) does not necessarily come into the picture here, then being protected from external forces may be sufficient meaning when it says that the Son "keeps" him in such a way that Satan does not "touch him" (cp. Jn. 17:11-12, 15; II Th. 3:3).

While the application to gnosticism in (b) above may follow properly from (a), another sequence from (a) seems preferable because it lies more on the surface of the immediate context of 5:18 and obvious parallels elsewhere in I John. Being in Christ means that the blood of Jesus Christ cleanses us from whatever uncharacteristic sins do crop up in our lives (1:7-9). Such "sin not unto death" is the sin for which the Begotten One gives us forgiveness when we ask (5:16). "Giving him life" (5:16) equals "the evil one does not touch him" (5:18). The

440

blood of Jesus Christ keeps us from the domain of the Evil One when we do not make a practice of sinning. The keeping by the Begotten One lies logically before the characteristically sinless life, aspiration for which is the condition for being kept from deliverance into Satan's kingdom; the keeping has generally to do with keeping us from Satan's dominion, and has specifically to do with removing occasional sin from our record so as to make it continually appropriate to remain sons of God. Paul teaches that God's goodness keeps us in the olive tree, but we have to keep ourselves in that goodness or we will be trimmed out of the tree (Rom. 11:22).

Against overwhelming force. A second cluster of passages used in defense of perseverance says that God freely promises to keep us from being forcibly overwhelmed *contrary to our wills.* (1) One such passage used in support of perseverance is John 10:28: "And I give them eternal life, and they will certainly not perish forever, and no one will grab them out of my hand." Especially on the background of I Corinthians 10:13 this popular verse is taken to mean that no one will snatch them out of his hand either by virtue of temptation or by force. While grabbing away "indirectly" by temptation makes sense, it is not necessarily the sense that Jesus had in mind. The strict picture is that of snatching them away by force, in which case it would be contrary to the will of the one who held them in his hand as well as contrary to the will of the one who was snatched away. Grabbing away would be done directly by a third party, not indirectly through temptation.

Without a background supplied from I Corinthians 10:13, this verse in its own background stands aside from the perseverance issue. Jesus is carrying on a running argument with the Jewish leaders who oppose him and seek to suppress his ministry. They are in sympathy with efforts to seize upon the Old Testament concept of the Messianic kingdom and adapt it to their present political concerns. Jesus' point in his rebuttal is to contradict and offset their attempt to overwhelm him and his followers by making him look bad in their eyes. He means that they do not accept him for who he is because they stand outside his circle of followers by virtue of prior commitments to goals and aspirations antithetical to his own. In keeping with their commitment to their own program, they do not believe in him and in his program. His followers on the other hand hearken to him and come to him and no one will stop them; neither will anyone snatch them away from him after they come because in attempting to do so they would be fighting against God (cp. Acts 5:33-39) with whom Jesus is at one in his purposes. The truth of his claim of identification with the Father is illustrated by their inability to stone him for claiming that identity. Consequently, the passage moves in the plane of protection against forces used against his followers, not temptation to yield to enticement.

Earlier we said that I Corinthians 10:13 is the most likely basis for perseverance because more than any other passage it may address the matter of protection against being lead away in accordance with our will, that is, through enticement. Snatching by enticement is not a necessary reconstruction of Jesus' words in John 10:28-29, however.

(2) John 6:39 has also come into the discussion in support of the perseverance contention: "And this is the will of the one who sent me: that everything that he has given me I should not lose any of it, but should raise it up at the last day." Accordingly Christ keeps everything God gives him, and resurrection in him is guaranteed.

A difficulty presents itself for such an interpretation in light of the case of Judas Iscariot. In the highpriestly prayer of John 17 Jesus speaks of the Father's giving his disciples to him (17:6) and that while he was with them he was keeping them in the Father's name. Then he adds, "I guarded them and no one of them perished except the son of perdition in order that the scripture might be fulfilled" (Jn. 17:12). Jesus may have had in mind only the physical dimension of protection here since at the release of the disciples in Gethsemane the gospel writer recalls this verse parenthetically (18:9). Nevertheless, the situation illustrates again in the use of language the difference between guarding and protecting from external attack on the one hand and from desertion on the other. Jesus protected his followers from arrest and execution by Jewish authorities, but he did not protect Judas against suicide. Similarly, keeping and guarding us spiritually against forcible natural or supernatural overthrow by powers can be a different benefit from one that would guarantee against spiritual suicide.

(3) Romans 8:35-39 lists a large number of things that cannot separate us from the love of Christ: tribulation, anguish, persecution, famine, nakedness, peril, sword, death, life, angels, principalities, things present, things future, powers, height, depth, any other creature. As a statement of fact the passage means that any or all these things give no indication that Christ no longer loves us. As a statement of promise

442

the passage means that Christ's love moves us to endure all these things and that love previously and continuously demonstrated is sufficient to engender perseverance strong enough to endure them. As a statement of pledge it means we commit ourselves not to let any of these things separate us from that love. It is important to see that love is the only means of enablement Paul mentions here.

Romans 8:35-39 follows 31-34 in which third persons have no power against us (31), lay nothing to our charge (33), or condemn us (34). The conclusion follows that we need not fear their forcible intervention against us contrary to our wills. Furthermore, in that God "freely gives us all things" (32) and Christ makes intercession for us, we have sufficient resources that we *can* endure anything present or future which would seek to draw us aside through our wills; whether we *will* endure depends on whether we do what we can. Sufficient resources do not guarantee satisfactory results. Though it may include temptation through our will, the emphasis of this text falls on forcible separation contrary to our will. This point seems also to be the point from other considerations noted below under Jesus' mediatorial reign.

(4) I Peter 1:5 likewise declares that we are protected by the power of God through faith unto a salvation ready to be revealed in the last time. We suppose the apostle means that the power of God protects against external forces, and it does so for each one of us if we put our trust in that protection. Another passage of similar import is Revelation 3:10: "Because you have kept the word of my steadfastness, I will also keep you from the hour of trial." Jude 24 says, "And to him who is able to keep you free from stumbling and to make you stand blameless before his glory with exceeding joy . . . ." II Thessalonians 3:3 promises, "The Lord is faithful who will establish you and guard you from the evil one."

Against Satan's claim to us. Jesus' intercessory role both on earth and in heaven has normally buttressed the case for perseverance. Not long before his own arrest in Gethsemane Jesus told Peter, "Simon, Simon, behold Satan asked to sift you like wheat, but I prayed for you that your faith would not fail. And when you get turned around, strengthen your brothers" (Lk. 22:31-32). On the basis of John 11:42 the conclusion is drawn that the Father always gives Jesus his requests: "And *I* knew that you always hear me . . . ." Messiah's heavenly role of intercession receives much attention in Hebrews 4:14—9:28 as well as in Romans 8:34 and elsewhere.

We doubt nevertheless that statements about the efficacy of Christ's mediatorial acts can sustain the position that everything for which he prayed will necessarily come to pass without any qualification whatever. Such a view no more follows from the fact that he prays for our salvation than that all men will be saved in the first place because the Father himself desires it (II Pet. 3:9). There is always the additional consideration in his will that all men are to be saved because they freely decide to come to him; similarly, there is the further consideration in God's will that all men continue to be saved because they freely decide to stay with him. In both cases God has willed to qualify his preferences for us by our own will for ourselves. We again invoke the principle applied against perseverance in I Corinthians 10:13 that there is a difference between what we can do and what we will do. God may at Christ's request provide those circumstances that make us able to endure, but we may not in fact endure. Jesus' prayer for providing those circumstances does not alter the matter of perseverance. Jesus' prayer for Simon eventuated in Simon's godly repentance, but universalizing what worked for Peter presupposes the doctrine of perseverance rather than proves it.

That all Jesus' prayers are answered affirmatively appears also to be an overstatement. The highpriestly prayer in John 17 includes a request for the unity of all his followers. In the present circumstance of division among us, we feel uneasy about the positive fulfillment of that prayer. There can be no consolation here from appealing to the unity of the saved in the fact of their being saved. Jesus did not mean the invisible unity of the body of Christ which it has by definition and nature; he meant the visible expression of it on earth because the purpose of that unity is that the world may believe that the Father sent him (17:21). This unity we do not have. His prayer therefore was not answered affirmatively on this particular issue any more than anyone else's prayer will be answered affirmatively if it involves the contrary free choice of those for whom the prayer is offered.

Messiah's mediatorial reign and intercessory priesthood in Romans 8:31-39 depicts our security against outside forces. Tribulation, persecution, angels, other creatures, etc., have no inherent power to separate us from God so that we do not infer from difficulties that God cannot protect the ones he loves from the experiences Paul lists. The apostle initiates this paragraph with the questions "Who is against us?"

444

"Who will lay anything against God's elect?" "Who is he that condemns?" "Who/What will separate us from Christ's love?" Satan cannot accuse us before God any more successfully than he accused Job, for the Father with or without Jesus' prayer put a boundary on Satan's trial of that patriarch (Job 1:6—2:10). World rulers may indict us, yet in Christ we are guiltless before God. The security of the beloved consists in protection from all external circumstances directed against our status; Paul does not handle in this section the separate question "Can a man be drawn away by his own lust to a sin unto death?" James seems to think so (1:12-18).

Furthermore, the expression "the love of Christ/God" does not mean the love that we have for Christ, but the love that he has for us (Rom. 8:35, 39). The paragraph makes clear that otherwise ambiguous point by the statement in 8:37: ". . . we overwhelmingly conquer through him that loved us." Consequently, these verses do not state the *fact of security* from having our love for God grow cold (Mt. 24:12) even though they might imply a *pledge to endurance*.

In Hebrews the priesthood of Christ emphasizes the forgiveness of sins. Satan elsewhere is called an Accuser: "For the Accuser of our brothers has been cast down, the one who accuses them before our God day and night. And they conquered him on account of the blood of the Lamb and on account of their testimony, and they did not love their life until death" (Rev. 12:10-11; cp. Zech. 3:1). All the inadequacies, weaknesses, and sins of those in Christ are "covered by the blood" so that no room remains for Satan to badger God in order to get us because of our imperfection and sinfulness (I Jn. 1:8). The Hebrew writer depicts the situation as one in which the readers take the initiative, for he exhorts them to draw near to God through Jesus the Messiah in time of need. To intercede for those who seek God differs substantially from interceding to keep them from being able to fall. The intercessory work of the Messiah—or the Holy Spirit for that matter—must be kept within the basic interpersonal character of the God-man relationship.

God's promise to perfect

The previous pages addressed the preventive ministry of God for our preservation. Here we address the positive ministry of God for our perfection. Whereas the former line of thought emphasized the truth about God's protection from external temptations and forces, the

445

present line of thought stresses the increased enablement to cope with those forces and temptations. He does not work only unto our original deliverance from the state of sin (justification), but also unto our continued growth in the conquest of the practice of sin (sanctification). If he did not withhold his Son for our original deliverance from sin, he will not leave us orphans (Jn. 14:18), but will give us his Spirit for continued conquest over sin. "He who began the good work in you will bring it toward completion until the day of Jesus Christ" (Phil. 1:6). "So, my beloved, even as you have always obeyed, not only in my presence, but so much more in my absence, work at your salvation with fear and trembling; for the one who works in you both willing and doing his good pleasure is God" (2:12-13). "And the God of all grace who called you into his eternal glory in Jesus Christ will perfect, confirm, strengthen, establish you after you have suffered a little" (I Pet. 5:10).

Passages of encouragement, comfort, and exhortation do not particularly have to do with necessary perseverance of the saints except on the supposition of irresistible grace. That God dispenses his grace in such a way that it cannot be refused by the people who need it does not appear to have biblical support at least as a universal principle of divine operation. Regardless of what Stephen meant by it, he could at least accuse the religious leaders of the first century and their predecessors: "You stiff-necked and uncircumcised in heart and ears, you always resist the Holy Spirit; as your fathers did, so do you" (Acts 7:51). It might be conceivable that the first Christian martyr meant grace was resistible in cases where God allowed the resistance, but such an answer only preserves the concept of irresistible grace from a possible objection; it does not make clear the positive basis on which it rests. We simply affirm here without elaboration that irresistible grace derives from the philosophical viewpoint that God could not be sovereign if his creatures had free moral agency. In contrast we affirm that sovereign means only that God by his omnipotence *controls* every event in history, not that he by his creativity necessarily *programs* every event in history. Regarding initial and continued salvation his will is not that he wants to save some or all men, but that he wants to save all men who will respond to his sufficient evidence and exhortation. He allows the resistance of his grace unto the just condemnation of all those who do so. Irresistible grace must undergird all texts on continued assistance in order to obliterate the distinction we made originally between what

446

a man can do and what he will do. If we can resist sufficient grace for perseverance, we will not necessarily persevere despite the tendency to do so.

The manner in which God preserves through enablement may be seen from Philippians 1:6 7: "Do not be anxious in anything, but in everything by prayer and supplication with thanksgiving let your requests be made known to God. And the peace of God that surpasses understanding shall guard your hearts and your thoughts in Christ Jesus." Anxiety in heart and thought is displaced by the peace of God; peace comes from prayer and thanksgiving. This kind of preservation tends to be the case in direct proportion to the degree of God-consciousness resulting from spiritual exercises. God gets the credit for the inner peace and psychological strength because it is he who is the subject of that consciousness. God, however, is not particularly doing something to the individual who is being strengthened, and he need not do anything. The person keeps himself (Jude 21) by keeping himself in the love of God, and the love of God keeps him (Jude 24) because he keeps himself conscious of it. Such preservation through enablement does not function irresistibly unto necessary preservation.

Romans 14:4 says, "Who are you that you judge another's servant? To his own master he stands or falls. Yes, he shall be made to stand, for the Lord is able to make him stand." Instead of this being an indication of irrestible perseverance, it shows only that God continues to regard as his own servant someone whom we may regard as errant because he differs from us on matters of opinion. In his sovereign freedom and principled exercise of grace God is able to regard him as his own despite his misunderstanding some things about God's expectancy of him.

God's predestination

According to Romans 8:29 God foreknew and has predestined individuals to eternal salvation. Advocates of perseverance argue that if a person fell from salvation it would prove God's foreknowledge and predestination wrong. Paul only traces through the broad sequences in the eternal scope of salvation. God's foreknowledge and predestination in the case of apostates would include their apostasy as well as anything else they did. To foreknow something means only to foreknow what it is at the moment being foreknown; any preceding changes along the way would also be foreknown along the way.

The Christian's assurance

A final reason for believing in perseverance is the assurance of salvation. Knowing that there is no possibility of lostness assures the believer of his destiny. One objection to the assurance argument is (1) that it misconstrues the character of assurance. Assurance is a present sense of certainty that arises from present experience and understanding. It does not have to be based on the logical certainty that a statement can have, but on the psychological certainty an experience can give.

A second objection to the assurance argument for perseverance is (2) that because of the practical circumstances of life the doctrine of perseverance creates the adverse effect. The intent behind defending it is to enhance assurance in believers, but from both experience and scripture we have questions raised about those who do not carry through on their commitment to Jesus Christ. To *scriptures* like Hebrews 10:24-39 and to examples like Judas the common response from the perseverance position is that the lack of genuine conversion becomes manifest in this very lack of perseverance. Assurance reduces for the Christian because of the things that perseverance allows someone to do without really being saved, including exorcisms. In *experience* we know of people who, as far as we can see, possessed as genuine a zeal as we presently do. If their apostasy shows the lack of genuine conversion, then certainty can come only when we have finished the course. Therefore present assurance diminishes because it cannot be separated from possible future delinquency.

One's assurance is no better under perseverance than under apostasy. A believer's psychological certainty under perseverance is as greatly stunted by uncertainty about the genuine nature of present faith as it is stunted under apostasy by uncertainty about future faith. In fact, we would contend that present assurance about present faithfulness is easier to have than present assurance about future faithfulness. Under apostasy present assurance is not lost or stunted; a groom does not feel insecure about his present love for his bride just because he understands that twelve years later it can grow cold. He does not need a statement from an omnipotent God to tell him that his love will never fail in order for him to have certainty about the genuineness of his present love. Our psychological assurance will continue as we continue to live and move and have our being in God and among his people, and as we continue to grow in the faith.

(3) Using perseverance to argue for assurance confuses the fact of perseverance with the sense of assurance. The irreversibility of salvation could indeed enhance assurance if it were not for the distinction between objective and subjective truth. The hitch in the doctrine of the perseverance of genuine faith is the problem of coming to know that we in fact have that genuine faith. Instead of basing assurance objectively on the teaching that salvation is irreversible, we have been content to base it on the fact that salvation is eternal. When God gives it, he gives it permanently as far as he is concerned; we may prove faithless, even though he is faithful. Personal responsibility replaces whatever advantage would purportedly be gained under the doctrine of perseverance.

Arguments Against the Apostasy Passages

Evidence supporting the doctrine of apostasy has come under the close examination of scholars who say that truly converted people will not fall away and be lost. Their pre-understanding has caused them to formulate ways of assimilating that evidence into their total presentation in such a way that it makes continued salvation more primary than apostasy.

Impossible possibility

The concept labeled "impossible possibility" is one mechanism brought to passages and experiences appearing to teach that apostasy can occur. "Possibility" means that as far as our own capacities are concerned falling away is quite real. "Impossibility" means that God makes up the differences between what we can handle and what the situation demands of us. As far as we are concerned it is possible to fall, but God makes it an impossibility by refusing to let Satan have us even as Jesus prayed so that Satan could not have Peter (Lk. 22:31-32). Presumably God will restrain Satan's activity or enhance our ability to cope with him.

When texts of scripture warn against falling away, the biblical writer is encouraging us in our frailty aside from any consideration of the divine assistance that will in fact compensate for it in varying degrees. When we wonder why passages of warning were written if no real possibility exists for apostasy, the answer comes that such warnings exemplify yet another way by which God exerts himself to insure our perseverance. Consequently, he not only guarantees our perseverance

449

by *restraint of Satan* on the one hand and *increase of ability* on the other, but also by the *influence of scripture,* preaching, and fellowship. The warning texts of scripture were written to give exhortation, and exhortation was given because it has real power to aid us in our weakness.

God first chooses exhortation instead of removal of temptation or miraculous regeneration because it is appropriate that we should live godly lives in the face of pressures to the contrary. Moreover, the less stupendous the assistance the more glorious God's praise.

While the notion of the impossible possibility has some apparent cogency, it does not do justice to the scriptures involved bcause more than exhortation comes out of these warnings. There are specified consequences for not heeding the warnings. Willful sin after the knowledge of the truth leads to punishment more severe than death (Heb. 10:26-31). Refusing him who warns from heaven allows no escape from the shaking of heaven and earth because God is a consuming fire (Heb. 12:25-29). Drifting away from the great salvation spoken through the Lord leads to recompense greater than what was received by those who disobeyed the word spoken through angels (Heb. 2:1-3). Since specified consequences are to occur, the author of such warnings would simply be declaring falsehoods were it the case that through one safeguard or another God prevents the believer from "shrinking back to perdition." Such an arrangement certainly did not prevail in the previous economy from which the Hebrew writer argues on the pattern of lesser to greater in the new economy. The passages in point do not specify simply what would be appropriate punishment for apostasy; they say they will happen to apostates. The impossible-possibility device could at best only apply to *passages that do not specify punishments for apostasy.*

Uncommitted believers

A second conceptual device for handling passages and experiences apparently illustrating apostasy is to regard the persons addressed as not genuinely saved people. The warnings issued to them serve to urge them on into genuine profession and life. Warnings about consequences under this conception bode real dangers because present progress has not brought true conversion so that they have no guarantee of the gift of perseverance. "Apostasy," then, is redefined because falling away cannot mean falling away from salvation; so it means falling away from some previous degree of progress toward salvation. The dangers for them derive, not from having left salvation, but from leaving more than ordinary opportunity for faith; and God renders severity of judgment in direct proportion to opportunity for faith. This "uncommitted-believers" device can be applied to *passages that specify punishments for apostasy.*

Hebrews 6:4-6. The general context of Hebrews supposedly discourses about such unsaved people (note 2:1-4; 3:7—4:13; 6:4-6; 10:19-39). Concerning those in 6:4-6 it is sometimes said that their enlightenment was intellectual only and that their tasting of the heavenly gifts, the good word of God, and the powers of the coming age was merely superficial and external. They had not internalized; they had only tasted. Enlightenment and experience fell short of commitment. They were like the ten spies who ate of the fruit of Palestine, but did not conquer the land of promise (Heb. 3-4; Num. 13-14); the readers here had only spied out spiritual Canaan and heavenly Zion (Heb. 12:22).

At first glance such an interpretation may have apparent value, but closer scrutiny reveals its inaccuracy. In different places throughout Hebrews (a) the hypothetical people in view are described as *partakers* of the Holy Spirit, the distinctive feature of a Christian. Partakers do not have mere acquaintance with, but are *in* what they partake of. This is clear from the usage elsewhere in Hebrews: Jesus partook of flesh and blood because the children partook of the same (2:14); the holy brethren are partakers of the heavenly calling (3:1); those who hold fast to the end are partakers of Christ (3:14); babes are partakers of milk (5:13); all men are partakers of parental discipline (12:8).

(b) *Taste* is also misused under the proposed interpretation. In 2:9 the author speaks of Christ's tasting of death for every man. Even outside Hebrews with perhaps one exception (Mt. 27:34) "taste" does not stand in contrast to swallow or consume, but stresses the perception of the experience (Mt. 16:28; Mk. 9:1; Lk. 9:27; 14:24; Jn. 2:9; 8:52; Col. 2:21; Ps. 34:8; I Pet. 2:3). If anything, the passage means the very opposite of not experiencing the blessings of Christian living.

(c) *Canaan* does not represent initial salvation, but answers to the ultimate salvation of heaven according to the usage of Psalms 95 in Hebrews 3-4. The scope of God's displeasure with the Jews covered

451

forty years, not just the two years of travel up to the time of Kadesh-Barnea. As elsewhere in the New Testament this sequence of events parallels the Christian life from conversion till heaven: crossing the Red Sea was their baptism (I Cor. 10:1-2), and they were saved from Egypt (Jude 5); eating the manna was their partaking of Christ (I Cor. 10:3-4); entering Canaan would have been their entrance to heaven, but by their unbelief they *fell* in the wilderness (Heb. 3:17). Consequently, the readers of Hebrews are encouraged not to *fall* in the same example of disobedience and unbelief (4:11). The wilderness peregrinations correspond to the earthly Christian life during which we may also apostatize. The Israelites had faith to cross the Red Sea, but not to conquer their Canaan rest. Christians may have faith to leave the bondage of sin, but when the going gets rought they may return in heart to the flesh pots of Egypt, forgetting the taskmaster's whip. Today is the day of perseverance; afterwards comes rest; hence, "today" is the period in the desert, and "rest" is Canaan. Therefore, eating the grapes of Canaan does not correspond with a superficial acquaintance with the benefits of salvation prior to commitment because that application would have to do with this life. If such partaking refers to anything related to this subject, it refers to partaking of the Holy Spirit during salvation as the earnest of an inheritance we may meantime refuse to conquer.

(d) *Enlightened* appears again in 10:32, where it is joined with a description of the readers which includes their suffering joyfully the spoiling of their possessions knowing that they had a better and more abiding possession. It appears on the basis of this connection as well as the word "partakers" that 6:4-6 cannot be disjoined from the readers so as to apply to hypothetical possibilities that will never become real for them.

(e) *The readers of Hebrews themselves* elsewhere receive descriptions befitting saved people. We recognize in this comment that the author distinguishes the people of 6:4-6 from the recipients of his letter (cp. 10:39; II Cor. 13:5; Acts 8:22), but the warnings he issues here and periodically throughout the book must have some relevance to their situation or there was no need to write them (cp. terms common to 10:32-34). The "Hebrews" were babes (cp. I Cor. 3:1) that should have been grown-up enough to teach (5:11-14); they were sons enduring discipline (12:3-13). They are addressed as brothers (2:12; 3:1,

6; 10:19; 13:22, 23) who have fled to Jesus for refuge as an anchor for their soul (6:18-20). Continually the Hebrew writer identifies himself with his readers by the words "we" and "us" (2:1-4; 10:39; 12:1, etc.). Terminology like this is inappropriate for informed but uncommitted people. Consequently, both the Hebrews themselves and the hypothetical people in view have Christian characteristics ascribed to them; to the Hebrews warnings are given on the basis of the declaration that the hypothetical people can lose their salvation.

Hebrews 10:26-39. Concerning those described in Hebrews 10:26-39 we observe that the author says they received a knowledge of the truth and were sanctified by the blood of the covenant. Now they are treading the Son of God underfoot, counting that blood a common thing, and doing despite to the Spirit of grace. Their punishment will be worse than death. The righteous person is said to shrink back to perdition. When we read these two key sections of Hebrews reflectively, we wonder how an author could make it any clearer that he is describing a Christian who has turned his back on Christ unto his own destruction.

It does not help the difficulty here to distinguish the readers of Hebrews from those described in 10:26ff., even though 10:39 does say, "We are not of them . . . ." He does not mean "we Christians," but we the readers plus the writer. This verse is a word of exhortation like 6:9: "But, beloved, we are persuaded better things concerning you . . . ." "We Christians do not shrink back to perdition" would be an interpretation that contradicts 10:29 because in that verse those who have been sanctified by the blood of the covenant do in fact face a punishment worse than death. A punishment worse than death could not be the mere chastisement of a Christian because of his faults and failures.

At this point we sense the awkward exegetical stance in which the doctrine of perseverance puts the interpreter. By necessity some of the most outstanding aspects of the Christian experience must be assigned to unregenerate people. It seems incredible especially to speak of having the Holy Spirit to the point of miracle and yet not be saved (Heb. 6:4-6; cp. Mt. 7:22-23).

Acts 8:4-24. Simon Magus in Acts 8:4-24 is sometimes cited as an example of this very situation. He did indeed believe and was baptized, but the idea that he received a miraculous measure of the Spirit when Peter and John came down is not warranted. We doubt that Luke means to say that the apostles' hands were laid on everyone. That this dispensation was selective may be reflected in the statement that the Spirit had "fallen on *none* of them"; it was after the imposition of hands that Simon "thought to obtain the gift of God with money." The record does not make clear whether he tried to buy the miraculous gift dispensed to the Samaritans or whether he sought another gift, one that would give him the right to transmit what both they and he had received.

Even if we were to suppose that he was a recipient of the recent miraculous dispensation in Samaria, Peter's words of refusal need not imply he had *never left* the "gall of bitterness" and "the bond of iniquity" in the first place. This apostolic visitation may itself have been the occasion of his downfall. The little word "perhaps" may also show that Peter did not conclude anything about his *present* lost or saved condition. Only by assuming perseverance could we get the idea that men previous to salvation may possess endowments promised to believers.

The exodus wanderings. The three New Testament examples that spiritualize the wilderness wanderings follow in the tradition of Psalm 95. Interpretations guided by the perseverance concept have regarded as unsaved those paralleled to the wanderers. We commented earlier, however, in connection with Hebrews 6 that (a) Canaan represents heaven, not the saved state. Furthermore, (b) Jude 5 speaks of salvation once and for all time from Egypt followed by destruction of unbelievers. He applies it to the readers who need to contend earnestly for the faith because ungodly men have crept in among them and turned God's grace into lasciviousness. Their influence could be destructive to the believers. Even angels, Jude observes, lost their proper habitation irreparably (6).

I John 2:19. This passage has been used to support the idea that any who depart the faith were never in it in the first place: "They went out from us, but they were not of us; for if they had been of us they would have remained with us, but they went out so that they made it manifest that they were not of us." More precisely, however, the text does not speak of their leaving the faith, but of leaving the fellowship. Therefore the writer is not necessarily addressing the question of apostasy at all because apostasy would have preceded the withdrawal. If he is not describing apostasy, then he is not saying that it is recognized by abandoning fellowship or that it is defined as leaving what was never really entered. Leaving the fellowship shows that these antichrists found no identity there. How they came to the point of finding no identity lies beyond the writer's concerns. Perhaps they never experienced true conversion and eventually left; but perhaps they did really believe, only to be influenced later by heretical teachers who turned them aside from the truth and they eventually left (cp. Tit. 1:10-16). Since the text fails to say they were "never of us," we do not know that. The writer cannot be made to speak of more than their condition at the time of departure. John's point is that this desire to leave illustrates the mechanism of self-cleansing: when someone is or becomes other than what the group stands for he will leave the group. The apostle simply observes an important process in group dynamics.

Matthew 7:22-23. Unlike I John 2:19 the Sermon on the Mount contains the word "never": "Many will say to me in that day, 'Lord, Lord, we prophesied by your name, didn't we, and cast out demons by your name, and by your name did many powerful works?' And then I will confess to them, 'I never knew you; depart from me, you workers of lawlessness.'" The view here is (a) that Jesus never knew these people even though they were performing signs and wonders. Since having the Spirit is the mark of the Christian, we would not expect to find unconverted people having the Spirit in such a fashion that they could perform exorcisms; so we anticipate finding some other framework that more satisfactorily makes sense of the passage. It could be (b) an emphatic negative. It would appear more likely to suppose (c) that these people only thought they were casting out demons and doing mighty works. On another occasion Jesus asks the Pharisees by what power their followers cast out demons (Lk. 11:19), not meaning that they did so, we assume, but because they thought so or claimed so. Of the several tacks listed here, this one is perhaps best. Less likely is the suggestion that (d) in some cases they thought they were doing miracles by divine power, but were doing them by demonic power.

Another approach is to say (e) that God was operating through the office, which was held by people themselves reprobate. God honored the functioning of the ruling and priestly offices held by Pharisees and Sadducees, but would not save them at the judgment. A couple of doubtful parallels have sometimes been cited in the persons of Balaam (Num. 22-24) and Caiaphas (Jn. 11:47-53). Divine operation through an office held by a reprobate is conceivable in cases where miraculous manifestation is not involved (cp. Mt. 23:1-3ff.), but supernatural

455

demonstration carries apologetic force and therefore approval of the claim of the miracle worker (Mk. 2:1-12); consequently, the moral test applies (Mk. 9:38-40; cp. Judges 13-16). We suggest that Caiaphas simply said more than he realized while Balaam's repentance was accepted (Num. 22:34; contrast 14:40; I Sam. 15:24; Mt. 27:4; Heb. 6:6?). In Matthew 7:22-23 we would prefer affirming apostasy to having to affirm miraculous manifestation by unregenerate men.

A final reconstruction of Matthew 7:22-23 is (f) that Jesus' words reflect an effective proleptic viewpoint. He projects his viewpoint to the judgment day and regards these prophets as always being what they turned out to be; in effect, having never begun is the same as apostasy. There may be a certain amount of parallel with Jesus as the master of the house, who said, "I do not know where you are from" (Lk. 13:25, 27), despite the fact that he ate and drank with them and taught in their streets (13:26). Actually, of course, he "knew" where they were from (Jn. 8:23, 44).

Hebrews 3:14. How natural the effective proleptic viewpoint fits with the context of Matthew 7:15-23 one must judge for himself, but the concept is intriguing in Hebrews 3:14, 6: "For we have become partakers of Christ if we hold fast our original confidence firm to the end"; ". . . whose house we are if we hold fast our boldness and boasting of hope." In 3:6 we could conceivably regard "whose house we *are*" as (1) futuristic present, as if to say, "whose house we will be" (cp. futuristic presents in Mt. 17:11; 24:43; 26:2, 18; 27:63; Lk. 3:9; 19:8; Jn. 4:21, 23, 25, 35; 8:14, 21; 10:15; 14:2, 3; etc.). We also might take the "are" as (2) a descriptive present rather than a temporal present so as to say, "We are God's house if we hold fast" because as such God's house holds fast; were it not to persevere, it would show itself not to be God's house (cp. I Cor. 15:2).

In Hebrews 3:14 the descriptive sense has less likelihood because the verb is a present perfect: "we have become" or "we are become." It is better regarded as (3) an effective proleptic statement. From the viewpoint along the way a person may now be in a saved state despite the fact that he will fall out of grace and be lost. From the projected viewpoint he is in fact out of grace so that in anticipation of his latter end he may already be viewed in God's eyes as fallen and spoken of as lost. Along the way God may give him the blessings of Christian life, dispense the Spirit, forgive his sins, and so on. The Father goes ahead and acts toward us now in a manner appropriate to our condition now, though he knows it will not last. It is like Jesus' going ahead and calling a Judas because he is a good man at the time even though he knows the latter end; for he deals with him in terms of where he *is*, not where he will be. For consistency's sake God operates within time although he stands above time. From his standpoint above time God may regard the saints as saved; in speaking to us within time God normally addresses us in terms of our viewpoint in time. As far as any practical consequences are concerned, a son who is disinherited is *looked upon* as never having been a son in the first place: he receives no inheritance.

Under this reconstruction the present status becomes a matter of temporal viewpoint. It allows for the future apostate to have the Spirit and the blessings of the Christian experience while at the same time allowing that present saint to be regarded as lost in the mind of God as he presently beholds the future. This conceptualizing mechanism avoids the unlikelihoods that perseverance must adopt in order to accommodate itself to the data of scripture. As one alternative, interpreters find themselves needing to deny the salvation status of believers who partake of the Holy Spirit, taste the powers of the age to come (Heb. 6:4-5), perform exorcisms (Mt. 7:22-23), and are sanctified by the blood of the covenant (Heb. 10:29). The other primary alternative for interpreters is to continue affirming the salvation status of people who count the blood of the covenant an unholy thing and do despite to the Spirit of grace (Heb. 10:29-30). In terms of time men apostatize, but in terms of eternity they do not.

Removal from the Book of Life. According to Revelation 3:5 the one who overcomes will not be blotted out of the Book of Life (cp. 22:19; Ex. 32:32; Ps. 69:28). Not being written in the Book means eternal destruction from God (Rev. 13:8; 17:8; 20:12, 15); written in it means salvation (Rev. 21:27; Lk. 10:20; Phil. 4:3; Heb. 12:23; Dan. 12:1; Mal. 3:16-17; cp. Isa. 4:3; Ezek. 13:9). As with all other cases of warnings either those addressed are unsaved so that the warnings are real or they are saved and the warnings are hypothetical.

We say again that the hypothetical concept has no place in any case where consequences are mentioned because it could not be other than misrepresentation. Interpreters favoring preservation agree by saying that as to fact vs. as to statements real consequences must be aimed at

457

people uncommitted to what they know or even believe. In offering warnings to their readers, the authors of the New Testament are not operating in facts but in statements. The writers do not distinguish between real threats to the uncommitted and hypothetical threats to the committed because as authors they do not know the real condition of those to whom they write (note Acts 8:22; I Cor. 15:2; Gal. 3:4; 4:11). Moreover they suspect a mixed readership in this regard. When we read their writings, then, we read them theoretically, says the advocate of perseverance; and when we do, we interpret the given statement in light of what we know about the more fundamental truth—that the committed are the preserved and the uncommitted are the threatened.

To the above set of thoughts we agree as far as it goes, but it fails to settle the issue, not only because we feel that the pre-understanding about perseverance nowhere finds solid foundation, but because it fails to observe in texts like Hebrews 6 and 10 or Revelation 3:5 that the biblical writers do in fact regularly distinguish their readers from their statements or make their statements conditional with respect to them. Revelation here says, "I will certainly not blot *his* name out of the Book of Life," not "I will certainly not blot *your* name out of the Book of Life." Even something like the latter could be conveyed by a human writer by putting it in a conditionality context. Hebrews 6:4-6 states the point of apostasy descriptively by saying, "Those who were once enlightened . . . ," and then moves back to direct address in 6:9: "But beloved we are persuaded of better things of you . . . ." Such a distinction does not have the effect of saying, "Now of course what I have just said has no application to you." That would weaken the power of the exhortation. It means, rather, "I am expressing confidence in you to encourage you not to do what is quite possible, which is of course the reason I am warning you about it. You need to do those things now that will keep you from drifting further away."

Pointing out 6:9 in response to apostasy in Hebrews 6:4-6 performs no relevant expository function because we are not denying that the author of Hebrews stops short of pronouncing on the destiny of the Hebrews. Pointing out that no one is actually said to be blotted out of the Book of Life performs no expository function either, because we do not deny that. Our concern comes from the status of the theoretical persons that fall away in Hebrews or get blotted out of the Book in Revelation. In Hebrews the descriptions are simply too Christian for application to non-Christians; here in Revelation what it means to be in the Book of Life is too obviously salvation status to be applied to the unsaved. Theoretical vs. real raises a false issue to replace the correct one: theoretical possibility of apostasy vs. theoretical impossibility of it, The theoretical possibility thereof seems inescapable.

Being blotted out of the Book of Life raises a point about Judas. When the seventy returned from their evangelistic tours, Jesus responds to their enthusiasm over exorcisms, "Nevertheless in this do not rejoice —that the spirits are subject to you, but rejoice that your names are written in heaven." If the twelve were included in the seventy, Judas was among them. Revelation 3:5, etc., speaks of being blotted out of the Book. Since it surely refers to salvation status, Judas was in that Book as late as the mission of the seventy. Unless we deny the lost condition of this former apostle, we have a likely example for being in the Book and then removed.

Another text of importance for the Book-of-Life imagery is Revelation 13:8. The American Standard Version, the New American Standard Bible, The Living Bible paraphrase, Today's English Version, and the Revised Standard Version translate the verse, ". . . whose name has not been *written from the foundation of the world* in the Book of Life of the Lamb that has been slain." The Authorized Version, the New International, and others say, ". . . whose name has not been written in the book of life of the Lamb that has been *slain from the foundation of the world.*" The original text is not in doubt on this part of the verse; the question has to do with analyzing the syntax. For our part the prepositional phrase in question ought to be construed with "slain" instead of "written" because "slain" is the immediately preceding element. The grammatical decision is between proximity vs. prominence; "slain" is nearer, but "written" holds a more prominent place in the sentence. While word order does not play nearly so important a role in Greek, we would prefer to think that near position must take precedence over distant prominence in instances where two equally sensible understandings would otherwise be possible and where no inflectional devices would clarify the grammatical connection.

If "not written from the foundation of the world" is preferred, we suggest that (1) the effective proleptic viewpoint of God's foreknowledge applies here to the enumeration of the saved instead of applying to the death of the Savior. Perseverance, however, would interpret the

459

association with "not written" to confirm the position that (2) apostatizing people were never in the Book so that apostasy again means falling away from preliminary progress toward salvation, not from salvation itself. This reconstruction is at variance, however, with the other passages that speak of being removed from the book (3:5, etc.), unless one adopts the unsatisfactory expedient that (3) removal is only a threat which never really occurs. Because of those other passages commentators may look upon the Book as (4) containing everyone's name to start with and dropping each one as he passes the point of withdrawn opportunity; no passage in fact does ever speak about *adding* a name to the register. A couple of difficulties arise with this suggestion because not being in the Book from creation would not allow for any deleting later. In addition, Jesus' comment to rejoice over being written in heaven (Lk. 10:20) surely implies more than merely being alive and not past the point of no return.

The difficulties created by the Book-of-Life passages taken in the aggregate can be resolved in two ways. We can suppose that (a) the figure might not always carry exactly the same force. This consideration would allow the Book to stand for the ultimately saved, the present saved, or the savable, depending on the immediate concern of the author. The "savable" is synonymous with not having yet passed the point of no return. The second option for the solution is to let the contents of the Book mean the same thing throughout, but allow the possibility that (b) there is a shift in the viewpoint from which the figure is used. Throughout all the usages, being in the Book means being saved. Adding and blotting out look at the changing contents as time goes along. Never being in the Book looks at it from the end of time, an eventuation certain and foreknown at the beginning of time.

A textual problem in Revelation 13:8 adds a final element of complexity to this verse. The recent United Bible Societies text of the Greek New Testament has evaluated the manuscript evidence in favor of a singular "whose" instead of a plural one. "Whose name has not been written in the Book" could then modify the "him" earlier in the verse so that the beast would be the one not written in the Book. Even with the uncertain reading "whose" in the singular, the grammatical anamolies elsewhere in Revelation have caused most translations to connect "whose" with "dwellers on the earth" as a kind of individualizing singular. If "whose" modifies "him," then, of course, the verse falls aside from our present discussion entirely.

One impulse is to agree that uncommitted Christians could be the object of some warnings and judgments in scripture. The word "faith" can refer to knowledge plus assent without involving a trust commitment; James 2 evidently uses the word "faith" in this manner. To know the information is not necessarily to believe it is true; to believe the truth is not necessarily to commit ourselves to it. Admittedly the gospel writers may have spoken the way they did, not knowing who among their readers may have needed to move from mere intellectual assent into full faith commitment; their warnings under these circumstances would perhaps not be distinguishable from warning about apostasy from salvation so that interpreting the passages one way or the other comes to a stalemate.

Paul has a statement in I Corinthians 15:2 to the effect that by the gospel we are saved except we believe in vain (cp. Gal. 3:4; 4:11). While the force of the English expression "in vain" could be "with no profit because you later will turn away," the original seems to favor more the notion that there was some inadequacy like believing without counting the costs, believing without making commitment, or believing without sufficient foundation in fact. The verse could serve as a model for what is meant by an inadequate kind of faith. Even if no particular scripture text could be cited, we may still grant the truth of the idea proposed. Applying it to given texts, however, becomes the problem because the marks of those described in passages about apostatizing seem too pronouncedly Christian to be very convincingly handled by appeal to incomplete faith. We do not deny the distinction, but we deny the application of it in these cases.

In this general section on uncommitted members amidst the Christians, we may agree that the condemnation aimed at false teachers should possibly not be listed among passages for apostasy. Jude 4 speaks of such people who evidently were beginning already within the apostolic age to syncretize Christianity with Greek philosophy and pagan religion. That they even acceptably espoused Christianity itself remains uncertain in some cases (cp. II Tim. 2:14—4:4; II Pet. 2; 3:3-4). In the case of the false teachers in II Peter 2 it appears that at one time they were reckoned by the writer as saved: ". . . false teachers . . . denying the Lord who *bought* them" (2:1; cp. Acts 20:28; I Cor. 6:20; 7:23; I Pet. 1:18-19; Rev. 5:9). The false prophets of II Peter evidently correspond to the ones in Jude and perhaps II Thessalonians 2; II Timothy 2-4; and II and III John as well, because Jude says the apostles predicted these false teachers (17-18).

461

Loss of reward and witness

Many passages that speak of loss are taken to mean loss of reward or witness. Reward does not look to the reward of eternal life, but to non-salvation matters like sense of abundance in life or God's approval on the way we have conducted ourselves. Our testimony to others will be lost also when we lack the drawing power of example. For such failures Christians may come under eternal judgment (I Cor. 10:30-32; cp. II Sam. 7:14-15). Most of our treatment of this mechanism we reserve for the chapter on eternal security, but one item or so can be examined in the present chapter because perseverance can appeal to this mechanism as well.

According to I Corinthians 9:27 Paul says, "But I keep my body under control and bring it under subjection lest somehow, having preached to others, I myself should become disqualified." While some translations carry "rejected," "castaway," or the like for the last word of the passage, opponents of apostasy prefer "disapproved" as a milder expression so as to make room for continued salvation. God's dissatisfaction with Paul's ministry becomes the concern of the passage.

Such a meaning could be possible though we judge it unlikely. (a) The crown figure applies elsewhere to eternal salvation. In 9:25 the activities of which he speaks lead to an incorruptible crown, an imagery used clearly in II Timothy to describe the eternal reward: "I have fought the good fight; I have finished the course; I have kept the faith. Henceforth there is laid up for me the crown of righteousness that the Lord, the righteous judge, will give me in that day, and not to me only but also to all those who love his appearing" (4:7-8). In II Timothy he speaks of the eternal reward of righteousness, not the earthly rewards of ministry. Surely the "incorruptible crown" in Corinthians means more than God's satisfaction with Paul's ministry.

(b) Context raises another consideration against the alternate proposal. We note first the connection this section has with the loss of life among the wandering Israelites previously saved from the death of Egyptian bondage (I Cor. 10:1-13). Although earlier in chapter 9, the apostle did talk about the reward of satisfaction he sought in preaching the gospel without support, since 9:23 he has adjusted his emphasis toward exhortation to salvation at the end of the course. "Save" in the end of 9:22 triggers this exhortation. He now talks of becoming a partaker of that gospel's reward that he shares with others—whether as a minister or not.

462

General objections to the perseverance model

Insufficient biblical base. All the passages brought up in defense of perseverance have some inadequacy that removes them from the possibility of providing the positive evidence required. A list of the possible mechanisms of perseverance presupposed by these texts includes (1) restraining the level of temptation, (2) influencing increased motivation to endure temptation, (3) regenerating our nature (?), (4) forgiving our failures, (5) protecting against forcibly carrying us away contrary to our wills, and (6) God's not turning his back on us later by giving us away. While in theory we could affirm all six mechanisms as operations of divine grace tending toward spiritual preservation, we confess our doubt about the concept of natural regeneration at least as a uniform necessity.

The problem with these six devices is not so much the identity of them, as it is the proper use of them. The first major problem in applying the mechanisms is (a) reading passages on *sufficient protection* as if they spoke of *efficient protection.* We find insufficient reason for believing that restraining temptation, enhancing motivation, and regenerating nature operate to the extent of irresistibility. A distinction needs to be made between general tendency and absolute uniformity and between sufficiency and actual causation.

The second major problem is (b) applying the mechanisms to the passages involved. Advocates of perseverance read statements on protection against third parties as protection against ourselves. But what would prevent hauling us off contrary to our will does not prevent enticing us away in conformity with our wills. There are many "keeping" passages in the New Testament, but we look here at only a couple of them to illustrate the several nuances of meaning in the general idea of keeping.

According to II Timothy 1:12 Paul felt confident that Jesus Christ was able to keep unto "that day" what he had committed to him. The meaning in this passage seems not to pertain to preventing his apostasy in his imminent martyrdom, but with something beyond this life. The apostle had committed into Christ's hands his basis for standing with God, and he would not be disappointed by Christ's inability to accomplish that end. First, Paul's confidence lay in his certainty that God had appointed Christ rather than any other as the one to be identified with in order to receive eternal sonship with the Father. Secondly, his confidence lay in the certainty that such identity would suffice unto righteousness against the Accuser who would seek title to the imperfect because they had not measured up to God's standard—perfection. Thirdly, Paul's confidence lay in his certainty that being in Christ afforded safety against any forcible detachment from God. We understand the "keeping passages" as referring to the word of Christ that Paul had in mind in II Timothy 1:12; consequently, it is subsequent to the committing of it to Christ and therefore something that has to do with matters aside from the person's own decisions about commitment. "Being kept by the power of God" is a keeping through faith (I Pet. 1:5); when we keep faith he keeps us rather than turning us away and keeps us rather than let Satan lay claim to us.

Another passage that receives considerable attention in the study of perseverance is John 6:37-40. Here the Son "keeps" those the Father gives him. The context highlights two senses in which the Son keeps men. The first sense of keeping—which does not receive enough attention in discussions on security—is found in 6:37: "He that comes to me I will certainly not throw away." In this case keeping contrasts with being thrown away. Jesus does not get tired of us and toss us aside. The second sense of keeping comes in 6:40: "And this is the will of the one who sent me: that I should not lose anything of all that he gave me and that I should resurrect it in the last day." In this case keeping contrasts with losing. "Losing" must carry the idea of "letting get destroyed," which involves forces or persons besides Jesus and the one given to him. Such "not losing," however, does not include the decision on the part of the one given to leave the safety of the Son. That conclusion is clear from 17:12 and 18:9 where Jesus kept and guarded them and "lost" none of them, but Judas was "lost." The significant point is that Jesus did not "lose" him, yet he was lost. Therefore at least in Johannine usage "keeping" and "not losing" does not include personal choice to leave Jesus. It may be important to add that Judas is said to have been given to Jesus so that there is no room for supposing that Jesus' keeping and not losing did not include Judas because he was never given to Christ. We conclude that a person can be lost despite the will of the Father (6:39) and the safety of the Son (17:12).

Our task in interpretation is to refrain from putting artificial restrictions upon the meaning of biblical words and statements. The human language used by God in scripture must be allowed to have its normal fluid character: "The One begotten by God keeps him" (I Jn. 5:18);

"Keep yourselves from idols" (I Jn. 5:21); Jesus will "keep what is committed to him" (II Tim. 1:12); "Keep the good thing . . . by the Holy Spirit" (II Tim. 1:14); "Keep yourselves in the love of God" (Jude 21); "Now to him who is able to keep you from stumbling . . ." (Jude 24). Many passages give only one aspect of the total picture or do not make clear which aspect they are addressing (I Cor. 1:8; Prov. 24:12). The problem in interpreting the "keeping passages" may be solved by distinguishing the sense in which "being kept" may be meant. As a total picture we propose that (1) we keep ourselves by putting ourselves in his care; that (2) God keeps us by enablement and protection to the point that we are able to bear up; that (3) we keep ourselves by bearing it; that (4) he keeps us from the claim and capture of Satan if we bear it; and that (5) he keeps us instead of casting us away, which would be to go back on his promises.

The constant combination of exhortation and promise finds explanation, we feel, in the conclusion that exhortation applies to (1) and (3) and that promise applies to (2), (4), and (5). The problem in synthesizing the biblical data about perseverance is one of deciding which is prior— God's keeping us or our keeping ourselves, that is, the problem of which is the basis of the other.

Apparent incoherence. We have a difficult time understanding (1) why God would dispense his grace irresistibly to those saved through Jesus Christ when he did not do so before men needed salvation. Surely "the grand plan of the ages" must be more ultimate than restoring human fellowship with God because he could have avoided the need for that program by gracing man irresistibly in the beginning. On the surface of it all we struggle to imagine why God would protect a saved person from falling when he did not protect man from falling in the first place. The eternal will of God is of course inscrutable, but we believe scripture does not provide a positive basis on which to build this position, a position which is also not deducible from first principles. In so saying, we deny the validity of the philosophical undergirdings on which we feel the doctrine really rests. If perseverance actually does come from philosophical rather than biblical presuppositions, it is fair to raise the issue of consistency because the position must stand on its merits. We can at least see how much loss of abundant human life and divine honor could have been avoided had God acted before the Fall as perseverance feels he operates after restoration. Philosophically it would appear more

465

acceptable to suppose that the problem of evil became a reality because God willed to bestow on some of his creatures the increased dignity of free moral agency. Evil became a real result of a divine blessing. Freedom has not been absolute, but has been sufficient that a man could reject God from a state of innocence; we believe that he can do so from a state of salvation for whatever reason he could have rejected him in a state of innocence.

Perseverance is defended by two theological persuasions—by those who believe God chose individuals unconditionally and by those who believe his election was conditional. Conditional election requires sufficient free moral agency to avoid the doctrine of particularism. To advocates of the second position a second inconsistency arises: (2) man has effective free moral agency to reject God before salvation, but not afterwards; grace is resistible before he experiences redemption, but not resistible when he is in Christ. If anything, under the redemptive motive, we would expect it to be the reverse.

Perseverance position A originally resulted from a systematic line of thought that begins with what we will call "unconditional sovereignty," an inadequate term meaning that at least subsequent to the Fall of Adam God's exercise of control over history is not ultimately conditioned on anything in the creature but only on the good pleasure of his own will. When we enter the picture at the point of man's need for salvation, we find a flow of thought that has been traditionally summarized under the letters T U L I P. Man has Total depravity, by which is meant that in all aspects of his nature and relationships sin has had an effect to such an extent that he has no ability to respond to God. Next comes Unconditional election, meaning that no act on man's part was taken into consideration when God before times eternal chose whom he would save. No act could be taken into consideration because man had no ability (as stated in the previous step) to perform any act of righteousness for meeting that condition and also because God acts sovereignly. Christ died to provide Limited atonement, that is, an atonement limited in its intent to the ones God had unconditionally designed to save. At the time of proclamation God provides Irresistible grace parallel to the preaching of the word so that the person elected will in fact respond unfailingly to the message. Lastly, Perseverance of the saints guarantees the permanent faithfulness of the believer. In this system of thought perseverance at the end follows deductively from the "unconditional sovereignty" and Total depravity on the front end of the system.

On the subject of perseverance we propose a point of consistency to this construction in that man in the state of grace was free to reject God before the Fall, but is not free to reject him now in the state of grace after salvation. Adam was able and allowed to fall. In the history of Christian thought few (that is, supralapsarians) have been consistent enough to affirm that, in order to maintain unconditional sovereignty, man had no free will even prior to the Fall. The reason, obviously, is that if such were the case, God would not only be responsible for evil in the world, but he would be the cause of it. We would suppose it more consistent to have exercised irresistible grace before the Fall if in fact God deemed it appropriate to his eternal will to operate in relation to man after that fashion.

In reaction to this line of thought a second one developed that sought to make adjustments on the previous one. Augustine of Hippo (354-430) formulated the first one and was followed especially by John Calvin (1509-1564) during the reformation in the fifteen hundreds. Shortly thereafter a group called the Remonstrants led a revolt against the former system because they felt it degraded man into an automaton, did not represent scripture in certain respects, and led to quietism and fatalism. In an effort not to change any more than had to be changed, they left in tact some of what they sought to adjust. Rejecting "unconditional sovereignty," they took the center out of the T U L I P without removing the ends: T (U L I) P. The Total depravity was then eradicated by a "common grace" for all men, not just the elect, but eradicated only to the point of ability to respond to the message; hence, it was not Irresistible grace any longer. It was not Unconditional election or Limited atonement either because by enablement man could fulfill the condition of faith that God required; and so it was a matter of exercising free will to accept Christ. The atonement could then be understood as intended for all men but applied to all men who willed freely to believe.

Under this new construction, perseverance position B was retained, but without the Unconditional election, Limited atonement, and Irresistible grace that previously had stood ahead of it. The point of this rather lengthy digression is to demonstrate that this newer approach lost the systematic advantage afforded by the older reconstruction. Now perseverance could not be argued on the consistent principle that divine grace as such is always irresistible. Perseverance position B now had to rest solely on direct biblical testimony, which we have previously endeavored to show does not have sufficient clarity of itself to guarantee that doctrine. Now, in fact, it creates at least an apparent inconsistency by letting the sinner have free will to accept, but not letting the saint have free will to reject. The circumstance of the saint—which is presumably higher—ends up having lower dignity than the sinner because he does not have free will. We would propose that dropping out the U L I is not enough; the T (uli) P needs to fall out as well.

Yet a third inconsistency develops among some theologians of the dispensational type because they may agree that (3) man has free will to fall from grace in the Mosaic dispensation, but not under Christ. For some reason not able to be specified, God has simply decided that in Christ salvation does not reverse. More can be said about this construction in the following chapter about eternal security.

Determinism. We confess that we see no way short of sheer determinism to have absolute certainty of the perseverance of a saint. A God who would have to resort to determinism in order to keep a man committed to him is a lesser God. Such a God could never have any more glory from men than he could receive from the operations of the laws of nature. Both man and God are reduced in such a scheme of things— God is reduced because he cannot get man to remain faithful without determining him, and man is reduced because he is wholly determined. If we are nothing more than stimulus-response creatures, we would hardly be in the image of the God of the Bible. Beyond whatever ambiguity can be credited to inexactness in human language in relevant passages, the difference of interpretation here derives mainly from the dissimilar views of man brought to the texts by the interpreters—dissimilar specifically in the conception of free will. For many, free will means the ability to lay hold on the good option set before us, and so the theologian speaks of "freedom for" and "freedom from." "Freedom from" removes whatever shackles hold the will in bondage so that there is "freedom for" apprehending what previously could not be reached for. As a total picture of human acts of will, such a notion is quite amenable to the concept of stimulus-response, where the organism will behave in a given way under given conditions.

In the confines of this presentation we cannot pursue the subject of *free will* even adequately, but we can point out descriptively that the views presented above do not incorporate *choice* in the sense of choice between alternatives. They only provide for responding to the option presented by God, not the choosing between options. In order for God to have the guaranteed result perseverance, we would have to respond the way God wants so as to preserve us, or perseverance of the saints could not be an eventuation guaranteed ahead of time. Although such a view of man accords well with much psychological and sociological presupposition in modern secular research, we feel compelled to set it aside as a final principle because it leads necessarily to manipulation, to irresponsibility, and to God as the ultimate author of sin. We agree that significant tendency exists in this direction, more even than we are wont to suppose, but we must stop somewhere short of a one-to-one correlation between a set of circumstances and a set behavioral response in moral matters. Man can live by rational values, not just by physical drives.

The stimulus-response model for human nature leaves no room for our distinction between what we *can* do and what we *will* do, but we have not viewed man as a stimulus-response creature. Therefore we do not feel that restraining temptation, influencing motivation, and regenerating nature will guarantee preservation because they do not mean we will in fact resist. Free will is the ability to choose between alternatives; it is the ability to refrain from acting when all the requisites for acting are present. Adequate protection against apostasy does not give actual protection against it because we may choose the easier way out.

We hasten to point out that our objection from determinism does not prove perseverance false and it is not calculated to do so. Our objection at most has only the force of challenging consistency in biblical interpretation. Perseverance B affirms free will in the preconversion state against passages as likely to argue against it there as the passages cited for postconversion perseverance are likely to argue against free will here. Perseverance A affirms free will in pre-Fall Adam, but not in restored man; if it does not affirm free will in pre-Fall Adam, it makes God the efficient author of evil. Our own understanding considers the positive scriptural foundation inadequate and confirms this inadequacy with an appeal to inconsistency.

The nature of faith. Our previous entry regarding determinism in human nature relates to another difficulty in the view of man taken by many who espouse perseverance and security: the theory of natural, or ontic, depravity. Natural depravity means that man's failure to lead the ideal life is explained by a biologically based, hereditary lack, or "privation." By birth he receives the "fallen nature," which guarantees

469

that he will become a sinner. Conversion involves the renewal of the ideal human nature Adam supposedly possessed before he fell. As a result the hearer can now have genuine faith because genuine faith can only issue from regenerate human nature. (a) Genuine faith corresponds to a kind of ontic nature.

It is our opinion that the concept of miraculous regeneration has contributed much to the "feel" of permanence about genuine faith. This underlying predisposition has caused many interpreters automatically to read texts on God's enablement and protection to mean absolute certainty against apostasy. Without this presupposition a number of other options come into the discussion as exemplified by our responses above.

Cautiously we offer another critique of some discussions about faith in salvation. It appears from the way comments are often made that (b) faith and the word "faith" are not distinguished. The problem here presents the old difficulty of confusing language and reality. Our point in this observation is to highlight the fact that faith *itself* is something subject to degrees so that it is not easy to speak of it as an all-or-nothing matter. The *word* "faith," however, is there or not there. Much thinking about faith itself seems to proceed as if it is a black-and-white, either-or kind of thing that can then be treated like the once-and-for-all thing perseverance pictures *genuine* faith to be. Our preference has been to speak of *acceptable* faith, and to regard acceptable faith as being of such a degree as to express itself in obedience. Thus the difference becomes one of the degree of faith rather than the kind of faith.

Obviously faith may be looked upon as increasing by degrees to the point that intellectual assent changes to active commitment, but even here the situation is not one of mere sequence from assent to action. There is a back-and-forth relationship between the two so that assent is in turn more certain as a result of the action performed because of that assent. Understanding, assent, and commitment therefore are not a straight-line causal series, but a reciprocating set that reinforce each other. This process of inter-reinforcement is what provides the mechanism for growth in faith. Understanding leads to assent, which leads in turn to commitment, each of these "stations" themselves being matters of degree. Active commitment clarifies experientially what was understood partially to begin with, and that enlightened viewpoint increases the certainty of the mental assent.

470

For simplicity and brevity's sake we usually pass over the complexity of this process by referring to "genuine faith," almost as if it were a discrete entity. Language then shapes our perception of the reality as well as reflects the nature of reality. The word, however, in this case refers not so much to a completed reality, but to a process that grows toward the ideal in all dimensions involved. By speaking of faith, however, as if it were a discrete reality, we ready our minds for accepting the notion that it can be a one-time given and a once-and-for-all possession, which means perseverance. Putting this observation together with a one-time miracle on human nature, we find the double key to the perseverance mind set that understands scripture rather convincingly, given its presuppostions. Aside from these substructures, nevertheless, the case for perseverance loses its clinching quality.

Warnings

There is a frequent criticism of perseverance that is often made in relation to scriptures that warn about the consequences of apostasy. The criticism is that such warnings cannot have any real power for people who also know that by promise they cannot apostatize. This objection, however, forgets that commentators of the opposite persuasion do not consider the people described in Hebrews 6, etc., as saved people who have no worry about apostasy. For those who believe in perseverance apostasy refers, not to loss of salvation, but to turning away from making commitment to Christ after exposure to the gospel and belief of it. Of course, if these warnings are understood as applying to saved people as they may be in the doctrine of eternal security, the criticism has significant value.

Appreciated emphases of perseverance

While the view is not accepted as a proper reflection of the complete biblical teaching on this subject, some emphases in the doctrine of perseverance may be appreciated. (1) Perseverance draws attention to the fact that *eternal* salvation is given now. Salvation does not "wear out" (Jn. 3:15-16, 36; 5:24; 6:39-40, 47; 10:28; 17:2; Acts 13:48; Rom. 6:23; I Pet. 5:10; etc.). It is not a process and does not need to be renegotiated periodically. When God justifies us it is a permanent justification as far as he is concerned. Like marriage our salvation does not have to be renewed annually. We have no more consciousness of

471

sins (Heb. 10:1-4). Neither is God fickle in giving salvation, taking away tomorrow for no reason what he has granted today; salvation is for "keeps." On the other hand whether marriage avoids divorce poses a different question; likewise whether apostasy is possible broaches a new issue. A company sells a piece of merchandise with the intent of giving it permanently to the one who buys it, but the repossession clause is activated if the terms of possession are not met. Salvation does not have to be renewed like a driver's license, but it is also not like a high school diploma that remains valid despite the fact that a graduate may have forgotten everything it stands for.

A second point of appreciation is that (2) perseverance roughly corresponds with the truth that true conversion tends to be permanent. Being lost and saved again three times in one week is psychologically foreign to what is meant by conversion and salvation. Perseverance unties the status of salvation from the fluctuations of our emotions and ties it to the power of God and our obedience of the gospel. The correspondence between true conversion and perseverance is no more absolute, however, than the correspondence between proper child raising and perseverance (Prov. 22:6).

Thirdly, (3) perseverance certainly underscores our assurance that no one can take us away from God contrary to God's will or ours. Like the Gadarene demoniac we need not fear that the physical absence of Jesus leaves us open to the overwhelming power of demonic forces. We have freedom to go fearlessly to tell people what great things he has done for us. At the ascension Jesus did not abandon his disciples like orphans in the world; he sent us another Advocate to be with us— his Spirit (Jn. 14:18). That assurance also applies to protection against Satan's accusing us to God because of our imperfection.

Fourthly, (4) perseverance retains the necessity of maintaining the Christian life. As soon as we separate our standing with God from our living before him, we have become little better than the false teachers of apostolic days who let their Greek philosophy lead them to believe that the actions of the body have no bearing on the purity of the spirit. God is interested in more than just our status under him; he has a vested interest in our growth into the image of his Son, not only for his own glory, but for our abundance.

Chapter Twenty-Eight

ETERNAL SECURITY

Reasons for the Eternal Security Model

Much of what has been said in the previous chapter to defend perseverance applies also to the case for security, but eternal security goes beyond perseverance by teaching that a one-time, heartfelt commitment to Christ remains unconditionally effective. The status of anyone who has confessed the Lord does not alter because of a returning to his former way of life nor, according to some, because of an intellectual abandonment of Christian beliefs. To be sure, it is said, there are losses that such a "carnal Christian" incurs. He loses (a) his Christian witness so that he cannot lead other people to Christ by his own Christ-like example, and he brings reproach on Christ's body the church. He also loses (b) his abundant life so that he no longer experiences the better quality of life possible in Christ. (c) His liability to punishment also increases, but salvation does not correspond with Christian faith and practice. He loses his sanctification, but not his justification.

Salvation by faith

The primary reason for advocating eternal security comes from a misunderstanding of salvation by faith. Paul's teaching that we do not earn salvation by what we do is reversed to imply that we also do not merit condemnation by what we do. If outward actions could make a difference in whether we remained in a saved status, our continued salvation would be by works and not by faith. In initial salvation we would begin by faith, but in continued salvation we would be perfected by works. Paul criticizes such a scheme when he says to the Galatians, "Are you so foolish? Having begun by the spirit, are you now finishing by the flesh?" (Gal. 3:3). "Galatianism" refers to the concept of salvation by faith plus preservation by works of the flesh. It formed part of the Judaizers' teaching so relentlessly opposed by the apostle. If apostasy implies Galatianism, eternal security must be the case.

Loss of witness and abundance

According to Paul's building imagery in I Corinthians 3:10-17, Jesus Christ is the foundation of the temple of God, and each man builds on it with materials that have differing degrees of durability. To those who espouse eternal security the text means that the life quality built up by the living stones of the edifice may be carnal and fleshly, but the persons themselves will be retained in good standing before God despite their loss of abundance in life and witness to others.

Analogy to physical sonship

Salvation themes are set forth under several images related to sonship. Christians are said to be "born again" so that they are sons of God. Jesus spoke of the prodigal son who went into the far country and wasted his inheritance only to return in repentance and be reinstated in the life of the household. While he resided in the faraway land, he was still the son of his father. As physical sonship is a once-for-all-time relationship established at birth, so also spiritual sonship is a once-for-all-time relationship established at rebirth.

Analogy to national Israel

Tracing through redemption history from Abraham until today, advocates of security observe that the nation of Israel was divided and its Northern and Southern Kingdoms were allowed to fall into captivity. God did not, however, cast off his people at any time, even when they refused their Messiah (Rom. 11:1). "The gifts and the calling of God are not repented of" (Rom. 11:29). Consequently, when God calls a person and gives him salvation, the gift is not withdrawn at a later time even for unfaithfulness any more than the election of Israel was withdrawn during times of unfaithfulness. Chastisement may be experienced, but not disinheritance.

Pressure of compassion

A much more practical reason for eternal security stems, we believe, from the very down-to-earth circumstance of death. Our genuine desire to comfort loved ones of the deceased may create an unconscious pressure to reconstruct biblical understanding of the fate of those with highly questionable credentials. Broadening the scope of what backsliding can cover becomes the rational justification for the inclination of the heart.

Responses to Security Arguments

Action vs. works

The first response to the doctrine of security is that it misunderstands what Paul means by "works." Fundamentally we agree with eternal security in its call for recognizing the same relationship between human acts and salvation in both entering and maintaining salvation. The doctrine of eternal security arises, however, from not properly defining "works" in the sense Paul normally uses the term. "Works" does not contrast with "faith" as outer vs. inner action. Instead "works" are acts whether inner or outer that produce perfect righteousness, while "faith" stands for acts inner plus outer that meet the terms of pardon. The two words address kinds of relationships between acts and results (causality vs. conditionality), not kinds of acts themselves (outer vs. inner). Man's responses are necessary for salvation, not because they cause it, but because God commands them as conditions for his giving salvation. This conditional relationship between inner-plus-outer response and initial salvation is the same as it is between inner-plus-outer response and continued salvation.

Even as there is symmetry between pre- and post-salvation acts relative to salvation, there is also symmetry between acts unto salvation and acts unto subsequent condemnation; conditionality applies to both sets. This sameness must be true or we are locked into Mosaism or Galatianism in the first set and merit or perfectionism in the second. Under conditionality one good act or attitude does not make us absolutely perfect or keep us that way any more than one bad act or attitude makes absolutely imperfect. As one act does not save us, so one act does not damn us. We do not deal in absolutes either in election or reprobation, salvation or apostasy; the reason is that the system in which we stand is primarily interpersonal, not legal. The person God always stands between our act and the result he wills to give both in justification and apostasy; therefore there is not a one-for-one relationship between a sin and a condemnation because as he gives in respect to salvation he forgives in respect to condemnation.

For this reason also perfectionism, the opposite extreme of eternal security, does not have to be the case after justification; repentance is what God calls for in his forgiveness relative to his Son. After salvation we sin from time to time and are forgiven on request because post-baptismal sins are also cleansed by the blood of Christ (I Jn. 1:7-9). Now, of course, if we begin presuming on the grace of God, not caring how we act or not trying to live appropriately to our righteousness status, there comes a point for each of us where God draws the line and we lose our relationship with him. Attitude looms large in this system of things.

475

Loss vs. lost

For our part the eternal security position misidentifies the building materials in I Corinthians 3:10-17 as personal life qualities or acts (3:1-5?) instead of seeing them as converts or other contributions to the growth of the building (3:6-8). Paul speaks of the works of ministry, not of the acts of members. He laid Jesus Christ as a foundation and called the Corinthian Christians God's building. The building units represent converts (here as well as everywhere else the sanctuary figure is used: II Cor. 6:16; Eph. 2:19-22; I Pet 2:3-6). Other men follow the wise master builder, not by putting themselves in the building, but by putting others into it as he did. Their problem in evangelism may have stemmed from using wisdom rather than power (3:18-20; cp. 1:18— 2:16), so that their method drew men to themselves or to more prominent ministers whom they emulated (3:21-23ff.) rather than to Christ. The building had weak places in its construction as a result.

The fiery test of time or the final judgment would destroy combustible material like wood, hay, and stubble. In so doing, it would not be burning off the dross from each member's life, but would be the destroying of members or features of the church brought in by wisdom and competition. The converts would not stand the test, but the minister himself would be saved.

Even if we have overly restricted Paul's meaning, the text does not necessarily eliminate apostasy. At most, it speaks only of people caught up in competitiveness and wisdom who have remained babies instead of growing up (3:1-3; 4:6; 13:11; 14:20; Eph. 4:14; Heb. 5:12-14; cp. I Cor. 8:1-13). They may end up doing and teaching in such a way as to be least in the kingdom of heaven (Mt. 5:19-20; cp. 11:11; 25:40, 45; Lk. 7:28). That they are least in the kingdom by doing such things is a different issue than whether they can get worse than the degree of acceptability Paul talks about here.

Physical vs. spiritual sonship

The argument from sonship represents an interpretation pattern known as "allegorizing the comparison." Every parable, metaphor, comparison shares some characteristics with that to which it is compared, but not everything about the one side of the comparison corresponds to something on the other side. Physical and spiritual sonship have in common such particulars as similarity between "father" and "son," closeness of relationship between them, the fact that the first gives beginning to the second. The birth imagery gets at the matter of starting all over again with a new orientation and viewpoint (Jn. 3:3-8; II Cor. 5:17; Tit. 3:5; I Pet. 1:23) and thus equals the figure of resurrection (Rom. 6:1-14).

Pushing the parallels beyond the intended likenesses changes a metaphor or parable into an allegory. Parables, metaphors, or comparisons have some aspects alike, but an allegory ideally makes everything correspond between the figure and the reality. "Allegorizing the comparison" pushes the number of correspondences beyond what the author intended in making the comparison. The interpreter's task focuses on discovering from the author how many aspects of likeness he means to convey to the reader.

In inferring eternal security from the parable of the prodigal son, for example, interpreters allegorize the comparison when they say that the prodigal was still a son while he lived in the foreign country. We surely are not to believe that the prodigal was still a spiritual son during this time just because he sustained physical sonship with his father. By its very nature physical sonship remains irreversible, but spiritual sonship is reversible because Adam, the son of God (Lk. 3:38), fell from walking with God. The parable of the prodigal son and other usages of physical sonship imagery cannot serve as evidence for the irreversibility of spiritual sonship.

It is an offense to spiritual sensitivity to suppose that the unrepentant prodigal was acceptable to his father while he lived riotously with harlots and wasted his inheritance. Even the parable of the prodigal son itself indicates that he "was dead and became alive again, was lost and became found" (Lk. 15:24, 32). The elder brother represents the Pharisees while the prodigal son represents the publicans and sinners (15:1-2). In the parables of Luke 15 Jesus teaches that the Father is more pleased by the repentance of sinners than by the relatively more holy lives of people like the Pharisees who thought they needed no repentance. We do not legitimately infer that the Pharisees of Jesus' day were also in a saved condition just because they could be represented in this parable by the elder brother.

Actually, the parable does not suit the discussion of apostasy because it deals with first-time lostness rather than second-time lostness. We have all gone into the far country; salvation corresponds with returning to the father. Apostasy would parallel leaving for the far country a second time, a matter beyond the scope of this story.

477

If for the sake of argument we wanted to counter the doctrine of eternal security based on physical birth, we could legitimately say that a physical son may be disinherited from legal sonship; therefore spiritual sons may *lose* their justification (legal standing) because they have lost their sanctification (life quality). Paul even said to the Galatians that he was having birth pangs until Christ could be reformed in them again (4:19). Birth pangs could easily suggest that the Galatians were needing to be reborn. If the same imagery can yield opposite inferences, the inferences stand aside from the reason for using that word picture.

In the minds of many, physical sonship has more relevance to eternal security than it has from our perspective. The reason is that sinful behavior is thought by many to be caused by a natural sinful bent inherited biologically from our first parents after the Fall. Conversion includes among other things the remedying of this deficiency; it is called "regeneration." This correction of the principal cause of sin is an essentially miraculous alteration. Such a framework adds plausibility to the notion that, once corrected, man's natural deficiency no longer exists to turn his aspirations and faith away from God.

For our part natural depravity has no clear biblical foundation as a separate item of doctrine, and it is not needed as a systematic requirement to fill in the unanswered question of why all men have sinned—Adam sinned without having such a fallen nature. In our mind without the natural depravity presupposition there is little reason to use the irreversibility of physical sonship as an argument for the irreversibility of interpersonl relationship, which is what salvation is.

National vs. spiritual Israel

Under conditionality comes also a consideration of Paul's statement, "The gifts and calling of God are not repented of" (Rom. 11:29, cp. 2). The relevance of Paul's words to perseverance and security presupposes two points: (1) that the statement constitutes a universal principle in divine operation; and (2) that God's gifts and calling are always unconditional.

On the first point in this context we should remember that in Romans 11 the apostle is not elaborating a basic point in systematic theology. He is discussing the relationship of Israel to the Gentiles during the gospel age and says the Jews are in one sense enemies and in another sense beloved and elect (11:28). In the one case they are enemies of Gentile Christians because of their disbelief, and in the other they are beloved because of their fathers. Then in 11:29 the apostle affirms the permanence of their calling and gifts. He means that as a nation Israel has not been replaced by the Gentiles, because to Israel corporately as a nation God has made a permanent commitment from which he has not turned away. In fact, the Gentile believers are pictured even in the church age as grafted into the Jewish olive tree whose root is holy (16). The root is the fathers (11:28) Abraham, Isaac, Jacob, Moses, Joshua, and David. It was to Abraham that God made eternal promise, and it was to David as the theocratic, dynastic head that God gave eternal rulership over Israel (II Sam. 7:12-16). The apostle tells his predominantly Gentile readership to regard themselves as grafted into this nation. There is therefore one people of God, the people that has not been cast off by him (11:1).

Yet in the same discussion Paul also says that "they fell" (11:11b, 12), suffered loss (11:12), and have been "cast off" (11:15). He can say in one respect that they *have not* been cast off and in another respect that they *have* been cast off because in the first instance he is speaking corporately and in the second instance he is speaking individually. This observation brings up *the second point in this context* regarding perseverance: God's gifts and promises are sometimes conditional even though the gifts and promises per se are not repented of. They may be withdrawn from the individuals to whom they were made because they were gifts and promises held out permanently but applied or withdrawn as conditioned on the faith of those benefited. In the case of Israel there was the corporate level and the individual level. Matters were settled at the corporate level because God made eternal promises to Abraham and David in terms of whatever consideration he wished to bring into that promise; actually it was the faith of these men that prompted him to make those eternal promises that had to do with the corporate identity of who would be God's special people. At the individual level membership in the corporate identity is conditioned on personal faith. Those who do not have faith are broken off (11:17, 19, 20, 21, 22).

As to the special people therefore, at the individual level membership in the corporate body is an "unrepented-of gift" conditioned on faith; that is, it is never withdrawn as long as the individual believes. At the

479

corporate level the identity of the special people is a settled matter; there is no condition for the continuation of the gift to Abraham of considering him the father of the faithful. The Jewish branches that had no faith were trimmed out of the olive tree so that in fact only a remnant of Israel is still in its own tree (Rom. 9:27-33; Isa. 10:22-23). Gentiles were put into the tree by faith. Inasmuch as the branches represent faithful individuals and inasmuch as Paul is addressing first-generation Gentile Christians, apostasy rather than perseverance inheres in this chapter: if men do not continue in God's goodness by continuing to have faith, they will be cut off (11:22).

Inconsistency

Eternal security creates inconsistency with other doctrines and practices of its adherents. As an example of *practice* we may note believers' baptism. The doctrine of eternal security normally obtains among those who teach and practice the baptism only of adult believers. One of their central arguments against paedobaptism has been that it fills the visible church with people who bear no resemblance to the ideal for which the church stands. Infants that do not grow up to espouse the faith personally nevertheless bear the identifying mark of baptism and visible church membership. We wonder how really different the situation is when eternal security produces the same effect by continuing to affirm the salvation status of people in the neighborhood who have turned their backs on everything the church stands for.

As an example of inconsistency in *doctrine* we note in some writers especially an unusual combination between what is attainable without gaining salvation and what is allowable without loss of salvation. They will allow the unconverted person to be enlightened, to taste of the powers of the age to come, to taste of the Spirit, and to perform miracles and exorcisms by his power. On the opposite side of the issue they will allow the converted Christian to lose his place in the grapevine (Jn. 15:2), walk in darkness (I Jn. 1:6), or lose intellectual confidence in the truth of the gospel, and yet be saved. If the unregenerate can do so much without receiving salvation, we wonder why the regenerate can do so little and get by with it.

False alternative

Security posits a false extreme as the alternative view. Presentations favoring eternal security often feature a contrast with frequent repetition of salvation, lostness, and re-salvation. In this respect we agree more with eternal security because it is not psychologically natural to move in and out of faith and commitment to Christ every month or so. Assurance of salvation certainly is more certain than that.

Principally two ideas have contributed toward belief in a recurrent saved-lost-saved pattern. The first is the *doctrine of perfectionism,* which teaches that by the Spirit all sinful acts can be eradicated from the life of the Christian. Should some besetting sin continue to plague a person, he can infer that he has not been saved and sanctified or that he has fallen out of it. The second idea is the *doctrine of the inner witness of the Spirit* by which is meant the sense of assurance itself, which is presumably supplied by the Spirit that we are children of God (Rom. 8:16). If that sense is not present, the inference is that the fact is absent as well. We prefer to recognize that our emotional or affective dimension needs to be brought under the Lordship of Christ, but it is too unstable to serve as reliable evidence of salvation. Too many other things affect our feelings for us to suppose that God's Spirit is always the only influence on them for the Christian.

Similarity to antinomianism

In Paul's day some teachers evidently tried to argue that since we are not saved by our works, then it does not—as regards salvation— matter what we do. Gnostics put a little different twist to this point by conceiving of salvation as deliverance from a state of being, particularly from the confines of material existence. Knowledge, not virtue, became the means of deliverance and therefore the focal point of interest. Since action is a function of the material body, moral behavior in the use of the bodily members was "immaterial" to salvation. Again behavior had no bearing on the essential concern—relationship to God. Security amounts to much the same thing because how Christians conduct themselves has no effect on status with God so that Christian behavior is divorced from Christian standing.

Value of warnings

Cautiously we raise a criticism of eternal security which stems from portions of the Bible that admonish the reader to faithfulness because of the punishments for disobedience. Warnings about destruction make little impression on a person who believes that destruction cannot come

481

to the saved. In our chapter on perseverance we observed that the criticism carries no weight because the proponents of perseverance regard these passages (a) as addressed to the uncommitted, not to the saved. In this chapter on security we observe that the criticism also has no weight because the proponents of security regard these passages (b) as referring to chastisements, not condemnation. Under either view then the substance of the objection can be accepted, but it has no affect on the issue. The only way for the apostasy advocate to profit from the warning passages is to show either that Christians are being described in the first case or that eternal punishment is meant in the second.

Our objection to security lies mainly in its overextension of a principle that is in itself true: post-baptismal sins do not necessarily cast us out of Christ. Security is theoretically the opposite extreme of perfectionism. In light of the larger question about sins after salvation, the real problem is finding a way to avoid perfectionism while avoiding security as its logical alternative. The suggestion we make is to step aside from concern with *amount of righteousness* and substitute *aspiration for righteousness.* Christians affirm the ideal, but accomplish less than the ideal; divine forgiveness compensates for the difference—if repentance continues to authenticate commitment to that ideal. Growth becomes the concern both objectively and subjectively. Objectively as long as we are aspiring to be full-grown people, God forgives failure and keeps considering us to be in Christ; subjectively, by growing, we have the feeling of assurance that we are in Christ, especially if we understand how the objective dimension of the situation is being viewed in God's eyes. Perfectionism can frustrate; security can destroy. But to reject the one is not to accept the other because neither format makes the interpersonal category primary in its thought. Perfectionism brings in *nature* by speaking of re-generation, and security brings in *legality* by speaking of unconditional status. Personal commitment to the person of Christ replaces successfully accomplishing everything we aspire to do for him.

Eternal destinies

In regard to the pressure to comfort relatives at the loss of loved ones, we sense that being non-committal is insufficient because people can observe the different way we speak about obviously saintly brothers at such a time. The only way we see out of this dilemma is to be non-committal in all cases while speaking the unapplied truth that the hope of heaven removes the sting of death.

482

Counterproposals by Eternal Security

Several counterproposals against apostasy texts received attention in the chapter on perseverance: the impossible possibility, uncommitted believers, and loss of reward and witness. These three mechanisms are calculated to explain biblical statements that can sound as if apostasy is meant. In addition to them we mention three more interpretation mechanisms used in literature defending security.

Dispensational distinctions

Most of our presentation about perseverance and security so far has been directed toward theologians who operate out of the framework of covenant theology. They stress continuity in the purpose and modus operandi of God. Others who work from dispensational theology allow more discontinuity between the Old and New Testaments. Writers of this latter persuasion sometimes add dispensational distinction to the list of devices by which to set aside passages apparently teaching the possibility of apostasy for Christians.

According to this theory anything addressed to Israel has no necessary application to the church and therefore to the question of perseverance or apostasy in the Christian dispensation. Under the law there could be apostasy, but not under the gospel. Passages affected by this approach include Ezekiel 18 and 33, exhortations in the teaching of Jesus purportedly directed to Israel rather than to the church (Mt. 10:22; 24:13; Mk. 13:13), and Paul's figure of the olive tree in Romans 11.

As an impression about the theory of salvation and divine grace, we wonder (a) what possible motive there could be for preservation in the church that would not apply equally in the case of Israel, especially since the law was only added to grace until the Messiah should come (Gal. 3:19). We contend that salvation in both eras operates the same way fundamentally. (b) Even though by *theory* salvation would have to be by works under the law, in *fact* those under the law were not saved by the law, but by faith (Hab. 2:4). (c) Salvation under the first covenant actually came to Israelites retroactively from the death of Christ just as much as salvation under the second covenant actually comes to Christians proleptically from the death of Christ: "And on account of this he is mediator of a new covenant in order that, a death having taken place for the redemption of transgressions under the first covenant, they that have been called may receive the promise of the eternal inheritance."

(d) Furthermore, there are verses in the Old Testament that can as legitimately argue for perseverance as passages in the New. David says, "Restore me to the *joys* of my salvation" (Ps. 51:12); he does not ask for his *salvation* back after the Bathsheba incident. Making distinctions in the mode of retaining salvation in the different dispensations seems artificial when the real basis and mode of appropriating salvation are identical in all dispensations. (e) The New Testament texts that teach about apostasy sometimes do so on the basis of Old Testament passages; for example, Hebrews 3-4, etc., from Psalms 95; or II Peter 2:20-22 from Proverbs 26:11. Hebrews 10:38-39 from Habakkuk 2:4 affords a particularly significant passage because its clarity overrides the interpretative options frequently introduced against apostasy passages. According to it the "righteous one" can shrink back to perdition, a concept accepted by the Hebrew writer as not only true for the age of Habakkuk, but for his own age as well. If an interpreter sets aside the Old Testament passages because they are in another dispensation and admits they teach apostasy, by implication he creates a cul-de-sac for himself when it comes to their New Testament applications.

(f) The olive tree of Romans 11 cannot be handled dispensationally to avoid its testimony against eternal security, because it mixes Jews and Gentiles in the one olive tree. The Gentiles do not form part of Israel nationally in any sense Paul addresses in Romans. He is concerned with Israel as ideally what it should have been, that is, Israel spiritually. The apostle pictures his work among the Gentiles as coming in the tradition of Israel so that the one people of God is continuously defined by one principle—standing as God's people by faith. The Gentiles, who originated historically outside Israel, were by faith grafted into Israel, where the status for true Israelites also depended on continued faith. Both Israelites and Gentiles can be taken out of that tree if their faith does not continue.

Assorted verbal distinctions

The interpersonal character of salvation becomes obscured by purely verbal distinctions. The prodigal son is said to have lost his relationship to his father but not his sonship. What is salvation but relationship? Such word-based distinctions show lack of perception about the subject under discussion. Salvation is positive relationship to God; even the unregenerate are related to God if all we mean is something like relationship by creation. The prodigal was supposedly lost and found, not lost and saved; but salvation is pictured as finding. *Confessing* is said to be the way the regenerate returns to God while *believing* is the way the unregenerate is saved, but sinners under John the Baptist were baptized unto remission of sins, confessing those sins.

Hypothetical consequences

Another security mechanism for handling passages on apostasy is to interpret them as speaking about the theory of things. "You who would be justified by the law are severed from Christ; you fell from grace" (Gal. 5:4). Paul's point according to this reading is not that the Galatians have in fact fallen from grace, but that justification by law and justification by Christ mutually exclude each other; to be in one system necessitates being out of the other. The Galatians did not really understand the inconsistency of what they had done; they were not intending to deny grace in listening to the Judaizers' message. Their fall from grace was a loss of liberty because now they were faced with the burden of maintaining the rigors of Mosaic requirements.

We could grant that Paul is not necessarily pronouncing condemnation on his readers, but only means to have them understand what serious doctrinal and psychological complications arise from favorably responding to Judaizing influences. Saying, however, that they could not fall from grace positionally is quite another matter, especially when in many texts about apostasy the author specifies punishments to which apostates are liable. In order to have any useful application, the "only-in-theory" mechanism must be limited to passages that do not specify punishments for apostasy.

The hypothetical idea then does not apply to a passage like Hebrews 10:26-39, where the author warns about the grave consequences of counting as a common thing the blood of the covenant by which we have been sanctified. Some commentators consider statements like these to be exhortations based more on the response of love than that of fear. The statements would be exhortations in the sense that knowing what *ought* to happen to us spurs us on because of overwhelming gratitude to redouble our efforts in Christian living, even when we know full well that no loss of salvation will come to us—yea, *because* we know that; the most that could come is chastisement instead.

485

While this idea makes some sense, it does not reflect the teaching of the passage. The text does not say, "Of how much more severe punishment do you think a person *ought* to be judged worthy," but, "of how much more severe punishment do you think he *will* be judged worthy . . . ?" Furthermore, in this particular reference the punishment is significantly greater than being executed without compassion on the word of two or three witnesses. Chastisement hardly belongs in the company of such dire threats. Just because the writer of Hebrews distinguishes his readers from the *hypothetical people* he describes (6:9; 10:39) does not mean he was speaking of *imaginary consequences*; by this distinction he only expresses his confidence that for his readers this real possibility will not become their fate because they will respond to his "word of exhortation" (13:22).

Impossibility of renewal

In discussions about apostasy the impossibility of renewal to repentance usually comes up (1) *as an ad hominem argument in interpreting experience*. Experience provides examples of people who have behaviorally rejected Christ and later returned to repentance. If advocates of the doctrine of apostasy appeal to case studies to bolster their position, they must also accept behavior as indicating that people are renewed to repentance. Behavior of repentance, however, is at variance with scripture that denies renewal: "For it is not possible for those once enlightened . . . , having fallen away, to renew to repentance" (Heb. 6:4-6). If anyone takes the apostasy position, he must be consistent and agree that after apostasy re-salvation is impossible. Supposing that such a conclusion is not acceptable to advocates of apostasy, defenders of security feel justified in maintaining their view.

The doctrine of apostasy, however, is not derived from experience, but from the testimony of scripture. If case studies are used, they are brought in for illustrative purposes, not as instances of apostasy. They serve only to help set the issue before the mind. Someone who presumably has been in Christ may fall and then renew his commitment years later, but reading this pattern with certainty is not possible because *we* know neither his heart nor God's attitude toward him. There are several possibilities: he may not have had genuine faith to start with; he may or may not have really been rejected by God; or he may have repented without God taking him back; his second repentance may not be genuine.

Non-apostasy positions limit the possibilities for looking at this kind of situation. Belief in perseverance locks us into denying the genuineness of all conversions that do not last—insofar, of course, as we can tell. Belief in security locks us into affirming the continued salvation of apostates. But if apostasy can occur, we do not have to affirm either option. By distinguishing doctrine from application, we can say that judgment belongs to God, but his principles of judgment allow for actual condemnation in such cases because of apostasy.

The impossibility of renewal to repentance also comes up (2) *as a consistency argument in interpreting scripture.* Supposedly, the Bible teaches as clearly that no renewal can follow apostasy as it teaches there can be apostasy. In experience we see people renewed to repentance seemingly in contradiction to scripture. Defenders of security therefore feel justified in looking for another interpretation of apostasy texts.

Since scripture cannot be in error here, three things must be true: (a) experientially, behavior cannot have a place in the discussion either to illustrate apostasy or argue against security; (b) theologically, behavior has nothing to do with status after its establishment; and (c) hermeneutically, the disparity between scripture and experience may be explained by taking Hebrews 6:4-6 hypothetically regarding renewal and therefore regarding apostasy, too: "It would be impossible to renew to repentance those who were once enlightened . . . and then fell away . . . ."

The hypothetical interpretation, however, does not do justice to the grammar of the text. Such an idea would surely be carried by a "potential optative" construction in Greek, but Hebrews 6:6 does not contain that construction. Furthermore, the disparity of scripture and experience does not have to be explained by going to a hypothetical situation that never really occurs. Hypothetical vs. real can be replaced by doctrine vs. application of doctrine. It is one thing for scripture to teach the doctrine that apostasy *can* occur; it is another thing for us to make application in particular cases. We do not want to confuse (a) being unable to say when drifting has gone too far with (b) being unable to drift too far. The reason that scripture does not clearly state the apostate condition of particular people is not that such apostasy does not really happen, but that the writers were cautious not to say more than they knew. In this respect we could note that Peter tells the Samaritan sorcerer to pray if *perhaps* the thought of his heart would be forgiven (Acts 8:22; II Cor. 13:5; Heb. 10:39; I Jn. 5:16).

487

According to eternal security, passages about apostasy discount the idea that behavior has nothing to do with the status of salvation after its establishment. That idea cannot be used to explain the variance between Hebrews 6 and observable behavior. The notion of hypothetical statement appears to make the passage pointless for the original readers. We prefer the third option: experience cannot bear a decisive role in the discussion of apostasy, perseverance, and security. As a result we say that a real distinction exists between backsliding and apostasy, but it is one that exists clearly only in the mind of God in specific cases. Our responsibility is to continue efforts at restoration because we do not know whether a person has gone over the line (Gal. 6:1; James 5:19-20; Jude 22-23).

By turning to other passages, we could make a fairly strong case for agreeing with the challenge that once apostasy has occurred its reversal cannot occur. For one thing, from the standpoint of (a) *legal theory* sinners would have no complaint, if after freely being saved by God's grace in fact, they were irreversibly rejected when they willfully rejected him. For another thing, other (b) *passages* could mean the impossibility of renewal. Sinning "willfully," or "with a high hand," could not be atoned for by sacrifice (Num. 15:30-31; I Sam. 3:10-14; Heb. 10:26-27). Blaspheming or insulting the Holy Spirit does not receive forgiveness in this age or the next because it is an "eternal sin" (Mt. 12:31; Mk. 3:29; Lk. 12:10; Heb. 10:29). There is also the sin unto death for which we do not pray God's forgiveness (I Jn. 5:16).

Several (c) *persons* could conceivably illustrate apostasy although, of course, most of these instances are not decisively clear as far as eternal destiny is concerned. The Hebrew writer in 12:15-17 finds some potential parallel between his readers and Esau who sold his birthright irretrievably (Gen. 25:27-34). King Saul (and his dynasty) was rejected from being king over Israel because he did not "devote" the spoils of conquest as God had told him (I Sam. 15; cp. Num. 14:40). The same fate came to the house of Eli the priest, whose sins would never be expiated by sacrifice or offering (I Sam. 3:10-14). Judas provides a most interesting case as noted earlier. He held a position among those "given" to Christ, yet he is called "the son of perdition" (Jn. 17:12; 6:39; 18:9; Acts 1:25). He repented, saying as did Saul, "I have sinned" (Mt. 27:3-5; cp. I Sam. 15:24-34); but it was unto self-destruction rather than to reformation of life (Mt. 27:3-5; Acts

1:18-19). Hymenaeus and Alexander made shipwreck concerning the faith and Paul delivered them to Satan (I Tim. 1:19-20; cp. Mt. 18:15-20 ASV; I Cor. 5:1-13). Philetus denied the resurrection as a future event (II Tim. 2:17-18). Demas forsook Paul, having loved this present world (II Tim. 4:10); his departure, however, may have been from Paul because of fear of persecution. Hymenaeus, Alexander, and the incestuous man of I Corinthians 5 may all represent cases of church discipline, which can be lifted (II Cor. 2:5-11).

Our impression, however, is that a passage like Hebrews 12:16-17 need not clearly mean more than the fact that opportunity for salvation or its renewal ultimately ends (cp. Mt. 25:1-13; Lk. 13:23-27; etc.). A difficulty arises in the particular instance of Hebrews 12:16-17 because the text does not specify whose repentance Esau could not find a place for, his own or his father's. If his own repentance is meant, the point would be that tears caused by fear, frustration, or failure accompanied an all-out effort on his part to bring himself to be genuinely sorry; but he just could not bring himself to feel sorrow for his previous weakness. If his father's repentance is meant, the point would be that Isaac determined not to reverse the decision on birthright even after he realized Jacob had deceived him into granting it to him. We favor the second interpretation because the point at issue in the Old Testament account is the birthright, not Esau's repentance. The assumption is not that if only Esau could have repented he would have received back the birthright; there is no suggestion that lack of repentance was what kept the birthright in his brother's hand. Under the assumption that his own repentance is what could not be found, the spotlight falls on Isaac making a decision about the genuineness of Esau's tearful pleading. We take it that Isaac had "closed the book" on the birthright question much as God had done when he rejected Saul as king over Israel (I Sam. 15). The genuineness of repentance in either one of these cases is immaterial to the decision already irreversibly made.

We would be surprised if Hebrews 6 meant that God would refuse to renew the apostate to a state of repentance if he sought it in repentance. A point of unalterably rejecting the sinner does come finally, but we usually place it at the time of his death. Conceivably *on occasion* God may advance that point into the lifetime of the person, but we would be surprised if *as a general rule* God refuses to renew apostates to the state of repentance if they repent.

489

Our conclusion ought to be that God's unwillingness to accept them back into a state of repentance is relatively rare and that those irretrievably cast out have uniformly reached the point where behaviorally they cannot really be sorry they sinned. *On occasion* men are irreversibly rejected prior to death. *As a rule* men who have experienced the Christian faith and turned away cannot behaviorally be influenced to be sorry for their sin.

Three main proposals have been made for the meaning of "impossible to renew to repentance" in Hebrews 6:4-6. The *perseverance interpretation* says that when a person gets close enough to the Christian faith to experience all the blessings mentioned in 6:4-5, he innoculates himself against genuine repentance if he turns back before bringing his initial experience to the point of commitment. Unsaved people are envisioned here. The *security interpretation* says that when a person experiences the blessings of 6:4-5, he puts himself in a position where he cannot bring himself to repentance if he then turns back from the faith. Saved people are in view, but only hypothetically. The *apostasy interpretation* is the same as the perseverance position except that it is saved people who are contemplated here as losing their salvation.

From the apostasy standpoint several sets of issues need to be treated in order to answer the renewal question in Hebrews 6. The first factor is the translation of the *participle "crucifying."* Strictly translated 6:4-6 reads, "It is impossible for those who were once enlightened . . . to renew to repentance, recrucifying to themselves the Son of God and exposing him to public ridicule."

Participles in Greek cover for a wide range of ideas so that here *time* has sometimes been supplied: "It is impossible . . . while they recrucify to themselves the Son of God . . . ." The implication from the participle is that when they stop "recrucifying" him they can be renewed to repentance. "Stopping that recrucifying," however, would seem to be synonymous with "bringing to repentance." What would a person be doing in getting another person to stop recrucifying without it being a renewing of him to repentance? The temporal notion seems unlikely.

Cause has also been supplied: "It is impossible . . . seeing that they recrucify to themselves the Son of God . . . ." Their recrucifying is looked upon as the reason they cannot renew to repentance either in the sense that recrucifying has irretrievably hardened them or in the sense that

God refuses to restore them to the status of repentance because of their recrucifixion of his Son. The implication from the participle is that they cannot be renewed to repentance.

Co-ordinate circumstance appears to be the safest translation. It simply marks the fact that their recrucifying attends their not renewing to repentance, and no more explicit connection unites the two acts. The implication from the participle is unclear as to whether renewal to repentance can ever happen.

The second factor in the interpretation of 6:6 is whether *repentance* is behavioral or stative. By this differentiation we mean whether "repentance" refers to an act performed by the apostate or whether "repentance" serves as a label for the saved condition of a man. In terms of the statement in 12:17 it is like the difference between Esau's trying diligently to bring himself to repentance rather than trying to bring his father to repentance in giving him back his birthright. The difference has to do with the reason a saved condition is forever forfeit. In the one case it is because of inability to repent, while in the other it is because of God's unwillingness to take a person back. What will not keep a man in Christ is not likely to bring him back to Christ.

The third factor in 6:6 is whether the writer means a *general rule or an absolute uniformity*. For our part it would be sufficient for him to mean that behaviorally a person tends not to be able to come back to repentance if he has experienced all the blessings that Christian faith affords and still turns away. In a tendential sense nothing additional remains with which to draw him beyond what was not sufficient to keep him in the first place. Were he only exposed to the faith superficially, the case might be otherwise. In practical ministry we often find it easier to convert someone bereft of any real acquaintance with the Lord than to renew a former Christian hardened by the deceitfulness of sin.

For Hebrews 6:6 our inclination is to suppose the writer is speaking behaviorally in such a way as to leave open the possibility that an apostate might repent on occasion but not as a usual result. The further truth that God cuts off option even before death may also be clear from other passages, but in all such cases it would appear that genuine repentance is not the case, genuine repentance being distinguished as what followed Peter's denial vs. Judas' betrayal or David's sin vs. Saul's disobedience.

The following considerations create presumption in favor of behavioral impossibility of repentance as the tendency after apostasy. (a) Romans 11:23-24 pictures God regrafting in the olive tree branches that had been broken off. Paul may serve as a prime example of such a pattern. (b) James 5:19-20 speaks of a brother who has erred from the truth and been converted by another so as to be saved from death (cp. Jude 22-23). (c) The ideal relationship between church discipline and apostasy argues for the possibility of renewal since excommunication can be reversed. More will be said on this matter presently. It may even be significant to note that (d) repeated forgiveness is advocated between men so that it must be a principle of operation in the divine model of righteousness. Jesus tells his disciples in an admitted hyperbole that if a brother sins against another person seventy-seven times, the other person should forgive him if he repents (Mt. 18:21-22; cp. Gen. 4:24). We have a difficult time imagining why God would refuse second repentance when he accepts first repentance.

The question that still remains under this interpretation is whether the point of apostasy equals the point of irretrievableness. If we make station #3 the same as station #4, the inference seems to be that all

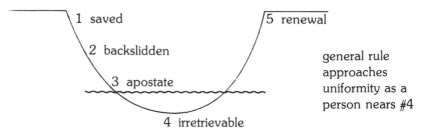

retrievable people belong to the backslidden group instead of the apostate one. As a result all such people remain in a saved conditon prior to their renewal despite their lack of any visible indication of commitment. Taking this approach comes close to affirming the security position in counting as saved people those who bring reproach on the Christ by whom they are presumably saved in the interim before their restoration. The difference lies in allowing for some to go on into a state that cannot be reversed.

Consequently, we make the following suggestion simply for the sake of consistency. There comes a time when a person crosses the invisible line and God no longer considers him a son, that is, a time when he is lost. "Not able to be renewed to repentance" increases from a tendency into a uniformity as a person passes from lostness to irretrievable hardness. If he has crossed the line at #3, he is lost until he makes confession and is reinstated; if he has not crossed the line, he is also forgiven on request. Whether he has crossed the line is academic as far as how his deficiency or his lostness is remedied. Whether he has crossed the line is also academic as far as the efforts and responsibilities of fellow Christians are concerned.

The values of our suggestion are that (1) in terms of theory one would not be bound to say that anyone able or allowed to return was nevertheless in the state of salvation previous to the return. Secondly, as said earlier, (2) some passages of scripture suggest renewal after apostasy is a possibility on occasion. *Romans 11:23-24* speaks of unfaithful Israelites being grafted back into their own olive tree if they do not continue in their unbelief, "for God is able to graft them in again." It is just possible perhaps that the apostle is speaking loosely enough that those grafted in are from a period of time later than the ones cut off or are at least other than precisely the same individuals removed in the beginning. This possibility does not appear to have so strong a likelihood as a reference to the same individuals as were broken out of the tree (cp. 11:30-31). James 5:19-20 and Jude 22-23 may be additional passages suggesting renewal.

Thirdly, (3) there is a consistency in the pre-apostate backsliding by degrees and the post-apostasy hardening by degrees. Before apostasy a person drifts by degrees down to the point where God has drawn the line for him. That drifting by degrees continues right on to the extreme of total hardening if we separate the point of apostasy from the point of irretrievableness.

Fourthly, (4) the structure of this model parallels the structure of church discipline. Although the body of believers may conceivably be inaccurate in their disfellowshiping an errant brother, the general ideal remains true that fellowship in the body visible ought in theory to correspond with membership in the body invisible, which is saved people. Paul enjoined the Corinthians to exercise church discipline against the incestuous man in I Corinthians 5:1-13. The apostle writes again in II Corinthians 2:5-11, whether of the same case or another, to reinstate the disciplined person. This "delivery to Satan" (I Cor. 5:5) was not merely for church purity, but for the benefit of the disfellowshiped man: ". . . for the destruction of the flesh, that the spirit may be saved in the

493

day of the Lord Jesus." Paul similarly "delivered to Satan" Hymenaeus and Alexander "that they might learn not to blaspheme" (I Tim. 1:20). Paul instructed the Thessalonians to have no company with anyone disobedient to his epistle "to the end that he may be ashamed" (II Th. 3:14, 6). In the mouth of Jesus the apostles were instructed to follow a similar procedure which, after first and second admonitions, meant the offender was viewed as a publican and a Gentile (Mt. 18:15-20; cp. Tit. 3:10-11); God promises to stand behind such decisions among his people (Mt. 18:18; 16:19), assuming of course that they are correct in their decision. Other passages relating to disfellowship for church purity or correction are Romans 16:17-20; Galatians 1:8-9; II Thessalonians 3:6, 14; II John 10.

The first parallel between lostness-renewal and disfellowship-reinstatement appears in God's standing by the decision to disfellowship; here (a) disfellowshiping a brother in Christ corresponds with disinheriting a son of God. If the parallel is valid it gives us insight into the kinds of behavior that would characterize a former brother now to be regarded as apostate and disfellowshiped; Paul suggests discipline for the practice of fornication, covetousness, idolatry, reviling, drunkenness, and extortion (I Cor. 5:11). This second parallel appears in the primary motive of church discipline: "that he may be ashamed," "that he might learn not to . . . ," and to destroy the flesh that the spirit may be saved.

The second parallel is that on successful completion of the discipline the person is forgiven; (b) here the reinstatement by Christians corresponds with the renewal in Christ. Paul says that whomever the Corinthians forgave he also forgave "in the person of Christ" (II Cor. 2:10). The third parallel appears in the fact that (c) in both church discipline and renewal to repentance there are varying degrees of failure to renewal; in case of failure the person is permanently viewed as a "publican and Gentile" by Christians and as a reprobate by Christ. Here his end is the same as one never saved; he has committed blasphemy of the Holy Spirit, willful sin, and sin unto death, and occupies the situation of a man impossible to the renewed unto repentance.

We have not elected to rely on an appeal to the difference between divine and human agency for answering the renewal question in Hebrews 6:6. Man may not be able to renew his fellow to repentance, but God could. Presumably God would renew the apostate by providentially giving him experiences beyond what a fellowman could provide. There seems, however, to be no positive basis within the text for being sure that the Hebrews writer means that renewal is impossible just from the standpoint of human agency and so we do not rely on it as a sure method for understanding renewal in this passage.

The irretrievable condition mentioned in Hebrews 6:6 we regard as the full end of backsliding and apostasy, which extreme is approached by degrees from the saved condition (#1), through the backslidden condition (#2), across the invisible line of apostasy from salvation (#3), to irretrievableness (#4). The manner is described elsewhere by the Hebrew writer as a degree matter: drifting and neglect (2:1, 3). The *cause* of the growing tendency toward irreversibleness is the deceitfulness of sin that hardens the heart (3:12-13). From #3 to #4 "impossible to renew" goes from general rule to absolute uniformity. On the three factors originally listed we conclude: "Crucifying the Son of God afresh" is a co-ordinate circumstance; repentance is behavioral; and "impossible to renew" goes from tendency to uniformity.

Summary of Perseverance and Security

The previous two chapters have summarized interpretations proposed for passages teaching the loss of salvation. These explanations often appear to us strained and gratuitous, but the commentators are required to harmonize them with the prior position they feel compelled to take in favor of perseverance and security. Therefore the most natural dialogue between exponents of apostasy and perseverance begins with examining the positive evidence for God's promise to secure the believer's continued faithfulness. This approach we have tried to reflect by positive evidence for perseverance and security put first so that it has a chance to stand on its own merits.

On one side of the issue stands evidence purportedly favoring perseverance: (a) God's promises to protect and perfect those in Jesus Christ, (b) predestination, and (c) Christian assurance. In addition (d) salvation by faith is thought to favor security together with analogies drawn from (e) physical sonship and (f) God's relationship to national Israel.

Of the passages cited in defense of the view, we have regarded I Corinthians 10:13 as perhaps the most likely positive evidence for

495

perseverance, noting however the difference between what we *can* endure and what we *will* endure. In general the passages offered in favor of perseverance are inadequate because of one or another entry in this *summary of distinctions applicable to perseverance passages*: (1) general rule vs. absolute uniformity, or tendency vs. actuality; (2) sufficiency vs. efficiency, or irresistibility; (3) viewpoint along the way vs. proleptic effective viewpoint; and (4) defense against third parties vs. protection against ourselves. Protection against third parties has two subpoints: (a) our protection in Christ against any claim the Accuser might lay against us because of our imperfection and (b) protection against demonic forces that would overtake us contrary to our wills. Other passages pertain to subjects different from that to which advocates of perseverance apply them.

On the other side of the issue stand passages favoring the possibility of apostasy from salvation. We centered our positive presentation on Hebrews 10:38-39 with the inference that similar passages in that book make a similar point. Elsewhere in both testaments texts with varying degrees of clarity confirm the possibility of apostasy. In the accompanying diagram we provide a *summary of mechanisms applied against these apostasy passages*. In some cases it is conceivable that those described as "apostatizing" were (1) uncommitted believers, but no amount of legitimate capitulation can accommodate under this category men described as "sanctified" by the blood of Christ, "partakers of the Holy Spirit" to the point of performing exorcisms, or as "my righteous one." The notion that the (2) old dispensation differed in this respect

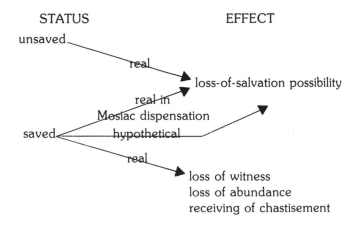

from the present age seems gratuitous; but if for the sake of argument that point were granted, it would not change the sufficiency of New Testament evidence for apostasy. The (3) hypothetical concept has no place here, especially in the several instances where consequences are specified, because scripture would be speaking falsehoods. The (4) loss of witness, reward, abundance, or freedom is true as to fact, but not satisfactory as to the passages involved; fruitless grapevine branches are not cut off and burned for purification, but for destruction.

The nature of man also figures into the apostasy issue. Regeneration is an unrepeatable experience inasmuch as once human nature has been restored it is not reversible. This one-directional change tends to foster the notion of "once-for-all-ness" in salvation because the ability to do good has been permanently restored. The model for perseverance stands then on how we understand two general factors: (a) the nature of man and (b) the nature of God's relationship to man.

In the total schematic involving apostasy, the pattern seems to be salvation that backslides to the point of crossing into apostasy. The general rule is that behaviorally repentance does not come to one who has turned his back on Christ, a rule that approaches uniformity as the person sinks farther and farther toward the depths of irretrievableness.

Perseverance and assurance emphasize an important truth in the total scheme of redemption, but they become false when made into absolutes. In presenting the case for preservation, we separated perseverance and security even though they may be regarded as two aspects of one position. The separation was made because some interpreters allow security to eclipse perseverance in their thinking. As a result the importance of Christian living is lost in respect to salvation, but scripture does not countenance a separation between salvation status and salvation behavior. Whether intended or not, such thinking in effect destroys the whole point of what Christianity seeks to address: the separation from God because of sinful behavior.

The important truths here are that beyond our conversion God gives continued assistance to our further improvement, and that we have continued responsibility for our continued security in Christ. Here as elsewhere in the general subject of salvation, its interpersonal character must stand clear so that perseverance and security are not reduced to God's activity by making nature and law the decisive factors. Perseverance is not therefore accomplished by stimulus-response mechanisms; security is not accomplished by irrevocable legal pronouncement.

Perseverance is such that choice is not lost, and security is such that behavior is not immaterial. Continued salvation is fundamentally interpersonal.

Part VII—INDICES

SELECT BIBLIOGRAPHY OF BOOKS

Included below are some of the more prominent books dealing with various aspects of salvation. Generally, periodical literature has been omitted because of space considerations. Access to articles in serials may be gained through the standard indices for religious periodical literature: *Index to Religious Periodical Literature, Religious and Theological Abstracts, New Testament Abstracts, Old Testament Abstracts, Christian Periodical Index, Religious Index I, Religious Index II, Social Sciences and Religion Periodical Index*, or *Index to Dallas Theological Library Periodicals*.

Commentaries and primary tools have also been omitted because their contribution to salvation studies comes in connection with specific passages or words that may be consulted as desired. Items listed in the bibliography cover a wide range of viewpoints, so the student can read sympathetic presentations from many positions. Asterisks indicate especially significant works.

I. General Works

Anderson, Robert. *Redemption Truths*, Kregel, 1980.

*Arminius, Jacobus. *The Works of Arminius*. 3 vols. Baker, [1853] 1977.

*Aulén, Gustav. *The Christian Faith*. Muhlenberg Press, 1948.

*Berkhof, L. *Systematic Theology*. Eerdmans, 1949. 4th rev. and enl. ed.

Boice, James M. *Awakening to God*. Vol. III of *Foundations to the Christian Life*. InterVarsity, 1979.

_____. *God the Redeemer*. Vol. II of *Foundations to the Christian Life*. InterVarsity, 1978.

_____ (ed.). *Our Savior God: Studies of Man, Christ, and the Atonement*. Baker, 1980.

Bray, Gerald. *Holiness and the Will of God: Perspectives on the Theology of Tertullian*. John Knox Press, 1979.

Brents, T. W. *The Gospel Plan of Salvation*. Nashville: Gospel Advocate, 1928.

*Buswell, James O. *A Systematic Theology of the Christian Religion*. 2-vols-in-1. Zondervan, 1962. Reformed tradition.

*Calvin, John. *Institutes of the Christian Religion*. Trans. by Henry Beveridge. 2 vols. Eerdmans, 1964.

*Chafer, Lewis S. *Systematic Theology.* 8 vols. Dallas Theological Seminary, 1948.

Christopher, Hiram. *The Remedial System.* College Press, [1876].

Cooper, David L. *Man, His Creation, Fall, Redemption, and Glorification.* Los Angeles, Cal.: Biblical Research Society, 1948.

Cottrell, Jack. *Being Good Enough Isn't Good Enough.* Standard Publishing, 1976.

*Cullman, Oscar. *Salvation in History.* Trans. by Sydney G. Sowers. Harper & Row, 1967.

*Denney, James. *The Christian Doctrine of Reconciliation.* London: James Clarke & Co., 1959.

Edwards, Jonathan. *The History of Redemption.* Evansville, Ind.: Sovereign Grace Book Club, 1959.

Gill, John. *Complete Body of Doctrinal and Practical Divinity: A System of Evangelical Truths Deduced from Scripture.* 2 vols. Baker, [1839] 1978. Reformed.

González, Justo L. *A History of Christian Thought.* 3 vols. Abingdon, 1970-1975.

Green, E.M.B. *The Meaning of Salvation.* 1965.

*Henry, Carl F.H. *God, Revelation, and Authority.* 4 vols. Word, 1976-1979.

Hodge, Archibald A. *Systematic Theology.* Eerdmans, 1946.

Horne, Charles M. *Salvation.* Moody Press, 1971. Well-organized overview of salvation from the historic Calvinistic perspective.

Johnson, E. Ashby. *Saved—from What?* John Knox Press, 1966.

Kevan, Ernest F. *Salvation.* Baker, 1973.

Kuyper, Abraham. *Principles of Sacred Theology.* Trans. by J. Hendrik De Vries. Baker, 1980.

Lyonnet, Stanislas; Léopold Sabourin. *Sin, Redemption, and Sacrifice: A Biblical and Patristic Study.* Rome: Biblical Institute, 1970.

Macquarrie, John. *Principles of Christian Theology.* Scribners, 1977. rev. ed.

Micklem, Nathaniel. *The Doctrine of Our Redemption.* 1947.

Milligan, Robert. *The Scheme of Redemption as It Is Revealed and Taught in the Holy Scriptures.* St. Louis, Mo.: The Bethany Press, 1957.

*Moody, Dale. *The Word of Truth: A Summary of Christian Doctrine Based on Biblical Revelation.* Eerdmans, 1981.

Morgan, G. Campbell. *The Bible and the Cross.* Baker, 1975.

*Morris, Leon. *The Apostolic Preaching of the Cross.* Eerdmans, 1965. 3rd ed.

Owen, John. *The Forgiveness of Sin: A Practical Exposition of Psalm 130.* Baker, 1977.

Pink, Arthur. *The Doctrine of Salvation.* Baker, 1975. Strongly Calvinistic.

*Pinnock, Clark H. (ed.). *Grace Unlimited.* Bethany Fellowship, 1975. Arminian.

Pruitt, Raymond M. *Fundamentals of the Faith.* P.O. Box 3000, Cleveland, Tennessee: White Wing Publishing House and Press, 1981. A general work by the Kansas bishop for the Church of God of Prophecy, a movement that does not as yet have an extensive literature.

Purkiser, W.T.; Richard S. Taylor; Willard H. Taylor. *God, Man, and Salvation: A Biblical Theology.* Beacon Hill, 1977. Arminian.

Sauer, Erich E. *The Dawn of World Redemption.* Trans. by G.H. Lang. Eerdmans, 1951.

_____. *The Triumph of the Crucified.* Trans. by G.H. Lang. Eerdmans, 1951.

Shedd, William G. T. *Dogmatic Theology.* Klock & Klock, 1979. Calvinistic.

Smith, C. Ryder. *The Bible Doctrine of Salvation.* Epworth Press, 1946.

*Stevens, George B. *The Christian Doctrine of Salvation.* Scribners, 1905.

Thiessen, Henry. *Introductory Lectures in Systematic Theology.* Eerdmans, 1949.

Van Til, Cornelius. *Common Grace and the Gospel.* Presbyterian & Reformed, 1972.

Verity, G.B. *Life in Christ.* Seabury, n.d.

Ward, Ronald A. *The Pattern of Our Salvation: A Study of New Testament Unity.* Word, 1978.

*Warfield, Benjamin B. *The Plan of Salvation.* Eerdmans, 1935. Reformed.

Wells, David F. *The Search for Salvation.* InterVarsity, 1978.

II. Need for Salvation

A. Sin

*Anselm of Canterbury. *Why God Became Man, and The Virgin*

501

Conception and Original Sin. Trans. with notes by Joseph M. Colleran. Magi Books, 1969.

Atkinson, David. *Homosexuals in the Christian Fellowship.* Eerdmans, 1981.

*Berkouwer, G.C. *Sin.* Trans. by Philip C. Holtrop. Eerdmans, 1971.

*Brunner, Emil. *Man in Revolt.* Westminster, 1979.

Cherbonnier, Edmund. *Hardness of Heart: A Contemporary Interpretation of the Doctrine of Sin.* Doubleday, 1955.

De Rosa, Peter. *Christ and Original Sin.* Milwaukee, Wis.: Bruce Publishing Co., 1967.

Drakeford, John. *A Christian View of Homosexuality.* Broadman Press, 1977.

Dubarle, André Marie. *The Biblical Doctrine of Original Sin.* Trans. by E.M. Stewart. Herder & Herder, 1964.

*Edwards, Jonathan. *Original Sin.* Yale University Press, 1970.

Finney, Charles G. *Guilt of Sin.* Kregel, 1975. Sermons.

Greeves, Frederic. *The Meaning of Sin.* Epworth Press, 1956.

Haag, Herbert. *Is Original Sin in Scripture?* Trans. by Dorothy Thompson, 1969.

Hutchinson, George P. *The Problem of Original Sin in American Presbyterian Theology.* Presbyterian & Reformed, 1972.

Jaspers, Karl. *Man in the Modern Age.* Doubleday, 1957.

Menninger, Karl. *Whatever Became of Sin?* Hawthorn Books, 1973.

Moxon, R.S. *The Doctrine of Sin.* Epworth Press, n.d. Argues for the psychological transmission of sin, in which a person continues to operate subconsciously after evolution has equipped him with reason and conscience.

Rondet, Henri, S.J. *Original Sin.* Trans. by Cajetan Finegan. Alba House, 1967. A Jesuit scholar's history of the doctrine of inherited guilt as taught from the time of Augustine to the present.

Smith, H. Shelton. *Changing Conceptions of Original Sin.* Scribners, 1955.

Stein, Edward V. *Guilt: Theory and Therapy.* Westminster, 1768.

*Tennant, F.R. *The Concept of Sin.* England: Cambridge University Press, 1912. Sin is defined in terms of an animal ancestry of man.

*_____. *The Sources of the Doctrine of the Fall and Original Sin.* N.Y.: Schocken Books, [1903] 1968.

Trueblood, Elton. *The Predicament of Modern Man.* Harper & Row, 1944.

502

Venning, Ralph. *The Plague of Plagues*. London: Banner of Truth Trust, 1965.

B. Nature of Man

*Augustine. "On Free Will." Trans. by John H.S. Burleigh. *Library of Christian Classics*, VI:102-217. London: SCM Press, 1953.

*Barth, Karl. *Christ and Adam: Man and Humanity in Romans 5*. Trans. by T. A. Smail. Macmillan, 1957.

*Berkouwer, G.C. *Man: The Image of God*. Trans. by Dirk W. Jellema. Eerdmans, 1962.

Boston, Thomas. *Human Nature in Its Fulfilled State*. London: Banner of Truth Trust, 1964.

*Cairns, David. *The Image of God in Man*. London: Collins, 1973. rev. ed.

*de Chardin, Teilhard. *The Phenomenon of Man*. Trans. by Bernard Wall. Harper & Row, [1959] 1965.

Dickinson, Curtis. *Man and His Destiny*. 2313 Rancho Lane, Alamogordo, New Mexico 88310: by the author.

*Edwards, Jonathan. *Freedom of the Will*. Yale University Press, [1754] 1957.

Farrer, Austin Marsden. *The Freedom of the Will*. London: A. & C. Black, 1958.

Gerstner, John H. *A Primer on Free Will*. Presbyterian & Reformed, 1982.

Kemp, E.W. (ed.). *Man: Fallen and Free: Oxford Essays on the Condition of Man*. Hodder & Stoughton, 1969.

*Landmann, Michael. *Philosophical Anthropology*. Trans. by David J. Parent. Westminster, 1974.

Lee, Francis N. *The Origin and Destiny of Man*. Presbyterian & Reformed, 1974.

*Luther, Martin. *On the Bondage of the Will*. Baker, [1525] 1981.

*Machen, J. Gresham. *The Christian View of Man*. London: Banner of Truth Trust, [1937] 1965.

MacKay, Donald M. *Human Science and Human Destiny*. Inter-Varsity, 1979.

Moltmann, Jürgen. *Man: Christian Anthropology in the Conflicts of the Present*. Fortress, 1974.

*Neibuhr, Reinhold. *The Nature and Destiny of Man.* 2 vols. Scribners, 1941-1943.

*Orr, James. *God's Image in Man and Its Defacement in the Light of Modern Denials.* Eerdmans, 1948.

Pannenberg, Wolfhart. *What Is Man? Contemporary Anthropology in Theological Perspective.* Trans. by Duane A. Priebe. Fortress, 1970.

Pink, Arthur. *Gleanings from the Scriptures: Man's Total Depravity.* Moody Press, 1969.

Rupp, E. Gordon; P.S. Watson (eds.). *Luther and Erasmus: Free Will and Salvation.* Westminster, 1978.

Rychlak, Joseph F. *Discovering Free Will and Personal Responsibility.* New York: Oxford University Press, 1979.

Stacey, W. David. *The Pauline View of Man.* London: The Macmillan Co., 1956.

Tyrell, Francis Martin. *Believer and Unbeliever.* Alba House, 1974.

Verduin, Leonard. *Somewhat Less Than God: The Biblical View of Man.* Eerdmans, 1970.

Warren, Virgil. *The Implication of Divine Self-Consistency for the Doctrine of Natural Depravity: A Biblical-Systematic Approach.* University Microfilms, 1977.

III. Basis and Scope of Salvation

A. Grace

*Augustine. "A Treatise on Nature and Grace." Trans. by Peter Holmes and Robert Earnest Wallis. *A Select Library of the Nicene and Post-Nicene Fathers of the Christian Church,* V:115—51. Eerdmans, 1956.

Booth, Abraham. *The Reign of Grace.* Eerdmans, 1968.

Crawford, C.C. *What the Bible Says About Grace.* College Press, 1982.

Hordern, William. *Living by Grace.* Westminster, 1975.

Hughes, Philip E. *But for the Grace of God.* Westminster, 1965.

Ryrie, Charles C. *The Grace of God.* Moody Press, 1963.

Smith, Charles R. *The Bible Doctrine of Grace and Related Doctrines.* Epworth Press, 1956.

*Torrance, Thomas. *The Doctrine of Grace in the Apostolic Fathers.* Neo-orthodox.

Watson, John. *The Doctrine of Grace.* Hodder & Stoughton, 1900.

Whitley, William T. (ed.). *The Doctrine of Grace.* 1931. A historical survey from the New Testament through the sub-apostolic, reformation, and post-reformation eras.

B. Atonement

*Abelard, Peter. *Commentary on Romans* in *A Scholastic Miscellany: Anselm to Ockham.* Vol. X of *Library of Christian Classics.* Ed. and trans. by Eugene R. Fairweather. London: SCM Press, 1956. The original exposition of the moral influence theory of the atonement.

*_____. *Epitome of Christian Theology.*

*Anselm of Canterbury. *Cur Deus Homo?* ["Why God Became Man"] in *A Scholastic Miscellany: Anselm to Ockham.* Vol. X of *Library of Christian Classics.* Ed. and trans. by Eugene R. Fairweather. London: SCM Press, [1098] 1956. A seminal exposition of the satisfaction theory of the atonement.

*Aulén, Gustav. *Christus Victor: A Historical Study of the Three Main Types of the Idea of Atonement.* Trans. by A.G. Hebert. Macmillan, 1954. An exposition of the dramatic theory of the atonement.

*Baillie, Donald M. *God Was in Christ: An Essay on Incarnation and Atonement.* Scribners, 1948.

Banks, Robert. *Reconciliation and Hope: New Testament Essays on Atonement and Eschatology Presented to L.L. Morris.* Eerdmans, 1974.

Barnes, Albert. *The Atonement.* Bethany Fellowship, [1860] 1980.

Barth, Karl. "The Judge Judged in Our Place." *Church Dogmatics.* IV/1. Edinburgh: T. & T. Clark, 1956.

*Berkhof, L. *Vicarious Atonement Through Christ,* 1936.

*Berkouwer, G.C. *The Work of Christ.* Trans. by Cornelius Lambregtse. Eerdmans, 1965.

*Bushnell, Horace. *The Vicarious Sacrifice.* Scribners, [1866] 1903.

Campbell, J. McLeod. *The Nature of the Atonement.* London: James Clarke & Co., 1859. 4th ed.

Cave, Sidney. *The Doctrine of the Work of Christ.* Cokesbury, 1937.

Crawford, Thomas J. *The Doctrine of Holy Scripture Respecting the Atonement.* Baker, 1954.

*Culpepper, Robert H. *Interpreting the Atonement.* Eerdmans, 1966.

505

An especially helpful summary of views along with a positive statement.

Dale, Robert W. *Theory of the Atonement.* London: Congregational Union of England and Wales, 1914. 26th ed.

*Denny, James. *The Death of Christ: Its Place and Interpretation in the New Testament.* London: Hodder & Stoughton, 1911. rev. ed.

DeVaux, Roland. *Studies in Old Testament Sacrifice.* University of Wales Press, 1964.

Forsyth, Peter T. *The Cruciality of the Cross.* Eerdmans, [1909] 1966.

_____. *The Work of Christ.* Naperville, Ill.: Allenson, 1958.

Fuller, Daniel P. *Easter Faith and History.* Eerdmans, 1965.

Fuller, Reginald H. *The Mission and Achievement of Jesus.* Naperville, Ill.: Allenson, 1965.

Gaffin, Richard B., Jr. *The Centrality of the Resurrection: A Study in Paul's Soteriology.* Presbyterian & Reformed, 1978.

Grant, F. W. *The Atonement.* Loizeaux Brothers, 1956.

Grensted, Laurence W. *Short History of the Atonement.* Manchester: University of Manchester, 1920.

Grotius, Hugo. *Defense of the Catholic Faith on the Satisfaction of Christ Against Faustus Socinus.* Trans. by F. H. Foster, 1880. The government view of the atonement.

Guilleband, H.E. *Why the Cross?* London: InverVarsity, 1964.

Hegre, Theodore A. *Three Aspects of the Cross.* Bethany Fellowship, 1960.

Hicks, F. C.N. *The Fullness of Sacrifice.* London: Macmillan & Co., 1930.

*Hodge, Archibald A. *The Atonement.* Baker, [1868] 1974. Calvinistic.

Humphreys, Fisher. *The Death of Christ.* Broadman Press, 1978.

Knox, John. *The Death of Christ.* Abingdon, 1958.

Krummacher, F. W. *The Suffering Saviour.* Moody Press, 1947.

Kuiper, Rienk B. *For Whom Did Christ Die? A Study of the Divine Design of the Atonement.* Eerdmans, 1959. Reformed.

Kurtz, Johann H. *Sacrificial Worship in the Old Testament.* Trans. by J. Martin. Klock & Klock, 1980.

Lang, George H. *Atoning Blood, What It Does and What It Does Not Do: An Exposition of the Truth of Atonement as Taught in the Holy Scripture.* Wimborne, England: by the author, 1955.

Lawlor, George. *When God Became Man.* Moody Press, 1978.

Lightner, Robert Paul. *The Death Christ Died: A Case for Unlimited Atonement.* Regular Baptist Press, 1967.

Long, Gary D. *Definite Atonement.* Presbyterian & Reformed, 1977.

Marsh, Frederick Edward. *Why Did Christ Die?* Zondervan, [1921] n.d.

*Marshall, I. Howard. *Work of Christ.* Zondervan, 1970.

Mikolaski, Samuel J. (ed.). *The Creative Theology of P. T. Forsyth.* Eerdmans, 1969.

Moberly, R.C. *Atonement and Personality.* London: John Murray, [1901] 1924.

*Morris, Leon. *The Cross in the New Testament.* Eerdmans, 1964.

Mozley, J.K. *The Doctrine of the Atonement.* Duckworth, [1915] 1947.

*Murray, John. *The Atonement.* Presbyterian & Reformed, 1962.

_____. *The Free Offer of the Gospel.* Presbyterian & Reformed.

*_____. *Redemption — Accomplished and Applied.* Eerdmans, 1955.

North, Christopher R. *The Suffering Servant of the Lord in Deutero-Isaiah.* Oxford University Press, 1950.

*Owen, John. *The Death of Death in the Death of Christ.* London: Banner of Truth Trust, [1852] 1963.

Paul, Robert S. *The Atonement and the Sacraments.* Abingdon Press, 1965.

Rashdall, Hastings. *The Idea of the Atonement in Christian Theology.* Macmillan, 1935.

Ringgren, Karl H. *Sacrifice in the Bible.* Lutterworth Press, 1962.

Ritschl, A. *The Christian Doctrine of Justification and Reconciliation.* E.T. 1902.

Robinson, H. Wheeler. *The Cross of the Servant.* Westminster, 1955.

*_____. *Redemption and Revelation.* Harper & Brothers, 1942.

Rudisill, Dorus P. *The Doctrine of the Atonement in Jonathan Edwards and His Successors.* Poseidon Books, 1971.

Smeaton, George. *The Doctrine of the Atonement as Taught by Christ Himself.* Winona Lake, Ind.: Alpha Publications, [1871] 1979.

Socinus, Faustus. *De Jesu Christo Servatore.* [1594]. The example theory of the atonement.

_____; et alii. *Racovian Catechism.* [1605].

Stibbs, Alan M. *The Finished Work of Christ.* London: Tyndale Press, 1964. 2nd ed. Interacts with the theory that Christ continuously offers himself to make men acceptable to God.

Taylor, Vincent. *The Atonement in New Testament Teaching.* 1945. 2nd ed.

* _____ . *The Cross of Christ.* London: The Macmillan Co., 1956.

_____ . *Forgiveness and Reconciliation.* 1946. 2nd ed.

* _____ . *Jesus and His Sacrifice.* London: Macmillan & Co., 1948.

Turretin, Francis. *The Atonement of Christ.* Trans. by James R. Willson. Baker, [1859] 1978. 2nd ed.

Ullmann, Carl. *The Sinlessness of Jesus.* Edinburgh: T. & T. Clark, 1882.

Ward, Wayne E. *The Drama of Redemption.* Broadman Press, 1966.

*Warfield, Benjamin B. *The Person and Work of Christ.* Baker, 1950.

Whale, J.S. *Victor and Victim.* Cambridge: At the University Press, 1960.

C. Universalism

Campbell, Alexander; Dolphus Skinner. *A Discussion of the Doctrines of Endless Misery and Universal Salvation in an Epistolary Correspondence.* College Press [1840].

Fudge, Edward W. *The Fire That Consumes.* P. O. Box 1311, Falbrook, Cal.: Verdict Publications, 1982.

Heppenstall, Edward. *Salvation Unlimited: Perspectives in Righteousness by Faith.* Washington, D.C.: Review & Herald, 1974.

*Murray, John. *Imputation of Adam's Sin.* Presbyterian & Reformed, 1977.

*Shedd, William G.T. *The Doctrine of Endless Punishment.* Klock & Klock, 1980.

That Unknown Country, or What Living Men Believe Concerning Punishment after Death Together with Recorded Views of Men of Former Times. Springfield, Mass.: C.A. Nichols & Co., Publishers, 1889. An important collection of articles on all sides of the universalism question.

Vandervelde, G. *Original Sin: Two Major Trends in Contemporary Roman Catholic Interpretation.* Amsterdam: Rodopi N.V., 1975.

IV. Application of Salvation

A. Election

*Berkouwer, G.C. *Divine Election.* Trans. by Hugo Bekker. Eerdmans, 1960.

Custance, Arthur C. *The Sovereignty of Grace.* Baker, [1979] 1981. Reformed Perspective.

Daane, James. *The Freedom of God: A Study of Election and Pulpit.* 1973.

Hals, Ronald M. *Grace and Faith in the Old Testament.* Augusburg, 1980.

Jocz, Jakob. *A Theology of Election.* Macmillan, 1958.

Johns, Kenneth D. *Election: Love Before Time.* Presbyterian & Reformed, 1976.

*Pannenberg, Wolfhart. *Human Nature, Election, and History.* Westminster, 1977.

Rowley, H.H. *The Biblical Doctrine of Election.* Lutterworth Press, 1950.

*Shank, Robert. *Elect in the Son.* Springfield, Mo.: Westcott Publishers, 1970.

Sundquist, Ralph R., Jr. *Whom God Chooses: The Child in the Church.* Westminster, 1973.

Thornwell, James H. *Election and Reprobation.* Presbyterian & Reformed, 1961.

B. Predestination

*Augustine. "A Treatise on the Predestination of the Saints." Trans. by Peter Holmes and Robert Earnest Wallis. *A Select Library of the Nicene and Post-Nicene Fathers of the Christian Church,* V:493-519. Eerdmans, 1956.

Bertocci, Peter A. *Free Will, Responsibility and Grace.* Abingdon, 1957.

Best, W.E. *Free Grace Versus Free Will.* Baker, 1977.

*Boettner, Loraine. *The Reformed Doctrine of Predestination.* Eerdmans, 1948.

Bray, John S. *Theodore Beza's Doctrine of Predestination.* Nieuwkoop, The Netherlands: DeGraff Publishers, 1975.

Buis, H. *Historic Protestantism and Predestination.* Presbyterian & Reformed, 1948.

*Calvin, John. *Concerning the Eternal Predestination of God.* Trans. by J.K.S. Reid. London: James Clarke & Co., [1552] 1961.

*Clark, Gordon H. *Biblical Predestination.* Presbyterian & Reformed.

——————. *Predestination in the Old Testament.* Presbyterian & Reformed.

D'Angelo, Edward. *The Problem of Freedom and Determinism.* University of Missouri Press, 1968.

Davidson, Francis. *Pauline Predestination.* London: Tyndale House, 1946.

Farrelly, Mark J. *Predestination, Grace, and Free Will.* Newman Press, 1964.

Fisk, Samuel. *Divine Sovereignty and Human Freedom.* Loizeaux Brothers, 1973.

Garrigou-Lagrange, Reginald. *Predestination.* Trans. by Dom Bede Rose. Herder & Herder, 1939.

Klooster, Fred H. *Calvin's Doctrine of Predestination.* Baker, 1977.

Maurey, Pierre. *Predestination and Other Papers.* John Knox Press, 1957.

*Pannenberg, Wolfhart. *The Idea of God and Human Freedom.* Trans. by R.A. Wilson. Westminster, 1973.

Verghese, T. Paul. *The Freedom of Man: An Inquiry into Some Roots of the Tension Between Freedom and Authority in Our Society.* Westminster, 1972.

C. Faith

*Baillie, Donald M. *Faith in God and Its Christian Consummation.* Faber & Faber, [1927] 1964.

Conner, Walter T. *Faith of the New Testament.* Broadman Press, 1940.

*Machen, J. Gresham. *What Is Faith?* Eerdmans, [1925] 1962.

*Moule, Handley C.G. *Faith: Its Nature and Works.* N.Y.: Cassell & Co., 1909.

D. Repentance

*Chamberlain, W.D. *The Meaning of Repentance.* College Press.

Colquhoun, John. *Repentance.* London: Banner of Truth Trust, [1826] 1965.

Finney, Charles G. *True and False Repentance.* Kregel. 1975. Sermons.

E. Baptism

Adams, Jay E. *Meaning and Mode of Baptism.* Presbyterian & Reformed, 1975.

Aland, Kurt. *Die Sauglingstaufe im Neuen Testament und in der Alter Kirche.* Munich: Kaiser-Verlag, 1961.

Althaus, P. *Was ist die Taufe?* Göttingen: Vandenhoeck, 1950.

*Augustine. "A Treatise on the Merits and Forgiveness of Sins and on the Baptism of Infants." Trans. by Peter Holmes and Robert Earnest Wallis. *A Select Library of the Nicene and Post-Nicene Fathers of the Christian Church,* V:11-78. Eerdmans, 1956.

Aylsworth, N.J. *Moral and Spiritual Aspects of Baptism.* College Press.

Bailey, D.S. *Sponsors at Baptism and Confirmation.* London: S. P. C. K., 1952.

Barth, Karl. *Die Kirchliche Lehre von der Taufe.* Dritte Augflage, Theologische Studien, Heft 14. Zürich/Zollikon: Evangelischer Verlag, 1947.

Barth, Markus. *Die Taufe: ein Sacrament?* Zürich: Evangelischer Verlag, 1951.

Baxter, Richard. *Plain Scripture Proof of Infant Church-Membership and Baptism.* London: Robert White, 1651.

*Beasley-Murray, G.R. *Baptism in the New Testament.* Eerdmans, [1962] 1973. Includes helpful bibliography.

_____. *Baptism Today and Tomorrow.* London, 1966.

*Berkouwer, G.C. *The Sacraments.* Trans. by Hugo Bekker. Eerdmans, 1969.

Bridge, Donald; David Phypers. *The Water That Divides.* InterVarsity, 1977.

Briney, J.B. *The Form of Baptism.* College Press.

Bromiley, Geoffrey W. *Baptism and the Anglican Reformers.* London: Lutterworth Press, 1953.

_____. *Children of Promise: The Case for Baptizing Infants.* Eerdmans, 1979.

*Campbell, Alexander. *Christian Baptism with Its Antecedents and Consequents.* Standard Publishing, 1887.

* _____, and N.L. Rice. *A Debate Between Rev. A. Campbell*

511

and Rev. N.L. Rice on the Action, Subject, Design, and Administrator of Christian Baptism; also on the Character of Spiritual Influence in Conversion and Sanctification and on the Expediency and Tendency of Ecclesiastical Creeds as Terms of Union and Communion. Lexington, Ky.: A.T. Skillman & Son, 1844.

Carr, Warren. Baptism: Conscience and Clue for the Church. Holt, Rinehart & Winston, 1964.

*Carson, Alexander. Baptism: Its Mode and Subjects. Kregel, 1981.

*Cullman, Oscar. Baptism in the New Testament. Westminster, 1978.

*Dale, James W. An Inquiry into the Usage of BAPTIZO and the Nature of Johannic Baptism as Exhibited in the Holy Scriptures. Philadelphia: Presbyterian Board of Publication, 1871.

England, Stephen J. The One Baptism: Baptism and Christian Unity with Special Reference to Disciples of Christ. St. Louis, Mo.: The Bethany Press, 1960.

Flemington, W.F. The New Testament Doctrine of Baptism. London: S. P. C. K., 1953.

Foschini, Bernard M. " 'Those Who Are Baptized for the Dead.' I Cor. 15:29." The Catholic Biblical Quarterly. XII (1950), 260-76, 379-88; XIII (1951), 46-78, 172-98, 276-83.

Gilmore, A. Baptism and Christian Unity. Judson Press, 1966.

Haley, J.J.; B. Butchers. Are Infants Scriptural Subjects for Christian Baptism? Is Baptism for the Remission of Sins? College Press.

Jarrel, W.A. Baptizo-Dip-Only: The World's Greek Scholarship. Rt. 1, Box 283, Splendora, Texas: Splendora Sales, n.d. 2nd ed.

*Jeremias, Joachim. Infant Baptism in the First Four Centuries. Westminster, 1960.

*Jewett, Paul K. Infant Baptism and the Covenant of Grace: An Appraisal of the Argument That As Infants Were Once Circumcised, So They Should Now Be Baptized. Eerdmans, 1978. Special section on the propriety of infant communion. Bibliography.

Kirtley, James A. The Design of Baptism Viewed in Its Doctrinal Relations. Cincinnati: George E. Stevens & Co., 1873.

Lawson, James G. Did Jesus Command Immersion? College Press.

Leenhardt, F.J. Le Baptême Chrétien. Neuchâtel: Delachaux & Niestlé, 1944.

*Moody, Dale. Baptism: Foundation for Christian Unity. Westminster, 1967.

Morris, Henry M., III. *Baptism: How Important Is It?* Denver, Col.: Accent Books, 1978.

*Murray, John. *Christian Baptism.* Presbyterian & Reformed, 1977.

Pusey, Edward B. *Scriptural Views of Holy Baptism.* London: J. Parker, 1867.

Quinter, James; N.A. M'Connell. *A Debate on Trine Immersion, the Lord's Supper, and Feet-Washing.* Cincinnati: H.S. Bosworth, 1868.

Schlink, E. *Die Lehre von der Taufe.* Dritte Auflage. Theologische Studien, Heft 14. Zürich/Zollikon: Evangelisches Verlag, 1947.

Schneider, J. *Die Taufe in Neuen Testament.* Stuttgart: W. Kohlhammer Verlag, 1952.

*Stuart, M. *Is the Mode of Christian Baptism Prescribed in the New Testament?* Nashville: Graves and Marks, 1855.

*Walls, William. *The History of Infant Baptism.* I. London: Griffith, 1705. A seminal work on the history of Christian baptism.

Warns, Johannes. *Baptism: Studies in the Original Christian Baptism.* Trans. by G.H. Lang. Klock & Klock, [1957] 1980.

White, R.E.O. *The Biblical Doctrine of Initiation.* Eerdmans, 1960.

Zwingli, Huldreich. *De Baptismo.* Trans. by G.W. Bromiley. Vol. XXIV of *Library of Christian Classics.* Westminster, 1953.

F. Regeneration

*Burkhardt, Helmut. *The Biblical Doctrine of Regeneration.* Trans. by O.R. Johnston. InterVarsity, 1978.

Charnock, Stephen. *The Doctrine of Regeneration.* Baker, 1980.

Holliday, John F. *Life from Above: The Need for Emphasis on Biblical Regeneration.* London: Marshall, Morgan & Scott, 1957.

G. Conversion

Citron, Bernard. *New Birth: A Study of the Evangelical Doctrine of Conversion in the Protestant Fathers.* Edinburgh: The University Press, 1951.

*Lloyd-Jones, D. Martyn. *Conversions: Psychological and Spiritual.* InterVarsity, 1959.

Moberly, J.C. *The Atonement and Personality.* London: John Murray, [1901] 1924.

H. Justification

Ashcraft, Morris. *The Forgiveness of Sins.* Broadman Press, 1972.

Barth, Markus; Verne H. Fletcher. *Acquittal by Resurrection.* Holt, Rinehart & Winston, 1964.

*Berkouwer, G.C. *Faith and Justification.* Trans. by Lewis B. Smedes. Eerdmans, 1954.

Boehl, Edward. *The Reformed Doctrine of Justification.* Eerdmans, 1946.

*Buchanan, James. *The Doctrine of Justification: An Outline of Its History in the Church and of Its Exposition from Scripture.* Baker, [1867] 1977.

Calvin, John; Jacopo Sadoleto. *A Reformation Debate: Sadoleto's Letter to the Genevans and Calvin's Reply with an Appendix on the Justification Controversy.* Trans. by Henry Beveridge. Baker, 1976.

*Denny, James. *The Christian Doctrine of Reconciliation.* N.Y.: George H. Doran Co., 1918.

Graham, Billy. *How to Be Born Again.* Word, 1977.

Horn, Robert M. *Go Free!* InterVarsity, 1976.

*Küng, Hans. *Justification: The Doctrine of Karl Barth and a Catholic Reflection.* Westminster, 1981.

Mackintosh, H.R. *The Christian Experience of Forgiveness.* 1927.

Owen, John. *The Doctrine of Justification by Faith.* London: Banner of Truth Trust, [1677] 1959.

Redlich, E. Basil. *The Forgiveness of Sins.* Edinburgh: T. & T. Clark, 1937.

*Taylor, Vincent. *Forgiveness and Reconciliation.* London: Macmillan & Co., 1941.

V. Consequences of Salvation

A. Sanctification

*Berkouwer, G.C. *Faith and Sanctification.* Trans. by John Vriend. Eerdmans, 1952.

*Fowler, James W. *Stages of Faith: The Psychology of Human Development and the Quest for Meaning.* Harper & Row, 1981.

Hulme, William. *The Dynamics of Sanctification.* Augsburg, 1966.

Lindstrom, Harold G. *Wesley and Sanctification: A Study in the Doctrine of Sanctification.* Epworth Press, 1950.

Marshall, Walter. *The Gospel-Mystery of Sanctification.* Oliphants Press, [1692] 1956.

Moule, H.C.G. *Christ and Sanctification.* London: Pickering & Inglis, n.d.

*Orr, James Edwin. *Full Surrender.* London: Marshall, Morgan & Scott, 1964.

Prior, K.F.W. *Christian Doctrine of Sanctification: The Way of Holiness.* InterVarsity, 1967.

Ryle, John C. *Holiness: Its Nature, Hindrances, Difficulties, and Roots.* Kregel, [1879] 1956.

Schaeffer, Francis A. *True Spirituality.* Wheaton, Ill.: Tyndale House Publishers, 1971.

Scroggie, W. Graham. *Salvation and Behavior.* Kregel, 1981.

B. Perfectionism

*Augustine. "A Treatise Concerning Man's Perfection in Righteousness." Trans. by Peter Holmes and Robert Earnest Wallis. *A Select Library of the Nicene and Post-Nicene Fathers of the Christian Church,* V:153-76. Eerdmans, 1956.

Chadwick, Samuel. *The Call to Christian Perfection.* Beacon Hill, 1943, 3rd ed.

Cox, Leo. *John Wesley's Concept of Perfection.* Beacon Hill, 1964.

Flew, Robert N. *The Idea of Perfection in Christian Theology.* N.Y.: Humanities Press, [1934] 1968.

Franklin, S.A.M. *A Critical Review of Wesleyan Perfection.* Cincinnati: The Methodist Book Concern, 1866.

Kepler, Thomas S. (ed.). *Christian Perfection as Believed and Taught by John Wesley.* Cleveland, Ohio: World Publishing Co., 1954.

*Murray, Andrew. *Be Perfect.* Bethany Fellowship, 1965.

Peters, John L. *Christian Perfection and American Methodism.* Abingdon, 1956.

515

Sangster, William E.R. *The Path to Perfection*. Hodder & Stoughton, 1943.

Simpson, A.B. *Wholly Sanctified*. Harrisburg, Va.: Christian Publications, Inc., 1925.

*Warfield, Benjamin B. *Perfectionism*. Baker, 1958.

*Wesley, John. *A Plain Account of Christian Perfection*. Beacon Hill, 1966.

C. Healing and the Atonement

Baxter, James D. *Divine Healing of the Body*. Zondervan, 1979.

Grant, Brian W. *From Sin to Wholeness*. Westminster, 1982.

*Kelsey, Morton T. *Healing and Christianity in Ancient Thought and Modern Times*. Harper & Row, 1973. Includes bibliography.

Lapsley, James N. *Salvation and Health: The Interlocking Processes of Life*. Westminster, 1972.

Linn, Matthew; Dennis Linn. *Healing Life's Hurts: Healing the Memories Through Five States of Forgiveness*. Paulist Press, 1978.

*Lovett, C.S. *Jesus Wants You Well*. Baldwin Park, Cal.: Personal Christianity, 1973.

*MacNutt, Francis. O.P. *Healing*. Notre Dame, 1974.

Mayers, Charles W. *A Look at the Modern Healing Movement*. Brethren Missionary Herald Books, 1979.

Mayhue, Richard L. *The Biblical Pattern for Divine Healing*. Brethren Missionary Herald Books, 1979.

Oden, Thomas C. *Guilt-Free*. Abingdon, 1980.

Phillips, J.B. *Making Men Whole*. Word, 1977.

Pitts, John. *Faith Healing: Fact or Fiction?* Hawthorn Books, 1961.

Rogers, Jack; R. Mackenzie; L. Weeks. *Case Studies in Christ and Salvation*. Westminster, 1977.

Stapleton, Ruth C. *The Experience of Inner Healing*. Word, 1976.

Thompson, Murray. *Grace and Forgiveness in Ministry*. Abingdon, 1981.

D. Liberation Theology

*Armerding, Carl E. (ed.). *Evangelicals and Liberation*. Presbyterian & Reformed, 1977.

Cobb, John B., Jr. *Process Theology as Political Theology.* Westminster, 1982.

Hatch, Nathan O. *The Sacred Cause of Liberty: Republican Thought and the Millennium in Revolutionary New England.* Yale University Press, 1977.

Kirk, J. Andrew. *Liberation Theology: An Evangelical View of the Third World.* John Knox Press, 1979.

Migliore, Daniel L. *Called to Freedom: Liberation Theology and the Future of Christian Doctrine.* Westminster, 1980.

*Moltmann, Jürgen. *The Crucified God: The Cross of Christ as the Foundation and Criticism of Christian Theology.* Harper & Row, 1974.

Ogden, Schubert M. *Faith and Freedom: Toward a Theology of Liberation.* Abingdon, 1979.

Runyon, Theodore H. (ed.). *Sanctification and Liberation in Light of the Wesleyan Tradition.* Abingdon, 1981.

VI. Perseverance in Salvation

Anderson, Earl. *The Eternal Security of Believers.* Dallas: American Guild Press, 1956. A dispensational defense of eternal security.

*Augustine. "A Treatise on the Gift of Perseverance." Trans. by Peter Holmes and Robert Earnest Wallis. *A Select Library of the Nicene and Post-Nicene Fathers of the Christian Church,* IV:521-52. Eerdmans, 1956.

Barker, Harold. *Secure Forever.* Loizeaux Brothers, 1974.

Berkhof, L. *The Assurance of Faith.*

*Berkouwer, G.C. *Faith and Perseverance.* Trans. by Robert D. Knudsen. Eerdmans, 1958.

Chafer, Lewis. *Salvation.* Zondervan, [1917] 1965. A good source for seeing how dispensational premillennialism affects the interpretation of passages related to apostasy.

Chatham, Joe. *Treatise on Eternal Security.* Cleveland, Tenn.: White Wing Publishing House, 1976.

Glaze, R.E. *No Easy Salvation: A Careful Examination of the Question of Apostasy in Hebrews.* Broadman Press, 1966. A response to Dale Moody's defense of apostasy.

*Gromacki, Robert G. *Salvation Is Forever.* Moody Press, 1974.

Hobbs, H.H. *How to Follow Jesus.* Broadman Press, 1971.

Ironside, H.A. *The Eternal Security of the Believer.* Loizeaux Brothers, 1924.

_____. *Full Assurance.* Moody Press, 1937.

Lassiter, Perry. *Once Saved . . . Always Saved.* Broadman Press, 1975.

*Marshall, I. Howard. *Kept by the Power of God: A Study of Perseverance and Falling Away.* Bethany Fellowship, 1975. 2nd ed.

*Owen, John. *Hebrews: The Epistle of Warning.* 8-vols-in-1. Kregel, 1973.

Purkiser, W.T. *Security: The False and the True.* Beacon Hill, 1956.

*Shank, Robert. *Life in the Son: A Study of the Doctrine of Perseverance.* Springfield, Mo.: Westcott Publishers, 1961. 2nd ed.

Strombeck, J.H. *Shall Never Perish.* Moline, Ill.: Strombeck Foundation, 1964. 9th ed. Sympathetic presentation of eternal security.

GLOSSARY OF SALVATION TERMS

An asterisk (*) indicates another entry related to the subject involved.

Ablutions. Ceremonial cleansings and washings prescribed in the Mosaic law and later elaborated by Jewish practice. They existed for the removal of ceremonial defilement. Same as *ceremonial washings and *lustrations.

Absolution. In Roman Catholic theology absolution is a judicial pronouncement by a priest in remitting mortal sins committed after baptism. Absolution presupposes *contrition, or repentance, on the part of the sinner; it *infuses power to conquer the practice of sin and removes guilt in the eyes of God and the church. Such *sacerdotal practice goes beyond officially confirming that God has cleansed a penitent who has already approached God directly; absolution accomplishes the cleansing itself by virtue of an authority Christ has invested in the clergy that mediates grace from God to man. Absolution is argued from Matthew 16:19; 18:18; and John 20:21-23.

Absolve. To pronounce *absolution.

Absolutism. A view of moral behavior that sees right and wrong as growing out of the originating purposes of a transcendent being so that there is abiding truth here as elsewhere. Although there is room for personal and social preference as long as they do not contravene the purposes of the Creator, the framework of morality lies objective to the individual and the human race. Contrasts with *situation ethics, or *situationalism.

Acceptilation. A view that regards the value of Christ's sacrifice as deriving from God's arbitrary acceptance of it for the salvation of sinners. Accordingly his death had no intrinsic worth in making salvation possible. Cp. the *Moral influence theory of the atonement.

Actual grace. In traditional theology a kind of grace that evidently pertains to environmental stimuli strengthened to such a degree as to cause response in the person or added to his environment so as to accomplish his act by stimulation. Distinguished from sanctifying grace, which enables the person to perform righteous acts by virtue of an alteration in the soul itself. See *Efficacious grace and *Sufficient grace, two forms of actual grace.

519

Actual sin. Sin that is done in contrast to sin that is reckoned or imputed. See *Imputation and *Sin.

Actual universalism. Same as *unrestricted universalism. See *Universalism.

Adoption. A figure used to describe bringing man back into relationship with God. See *Salvation.

Advocate. A Johannine designation used both of the Spirit (Jn. 14:16, 26; 15:26; 16:7) and of the Christ (Jn. 14:16; I Jn. 2:1). An alternate translation for *"comforter" or *"paraclete" (Gr. *paraklētos*). It describes the Spirit and the Christ in their mediatorial function, being likened unto one who pleads another person's case in a court of law.

Affusion. A term used strictly as a synonym for "pouring" as a form of *baptism. Contrasts with *aspersion and *immersion. On occasion "affusion" is used to include both pouring and sprinkling. Same as *infusion.

Age of accountability. An indefinite time in the development of the person when he not only realizes the difference between right and wrong, but can understand the consequences of his behavior and can be held responsible for his actions in a practical sense. No specific time can be given because of the varying rates of development from person to person. Normally, this "puberty of the soul" has been correlated with "puberty of the body." The concept is of importance among the Jews because it corresponds with *bar mitzvah* and among *paedobaptists because it defines the time of *confirmation or first communion. Among adult baptists the age of accountability marks the earliest time for appropriate obedience in *Christian baptism. Same as "age of reason."

Age of reason. Same as *age of accountability.

Alien baptism. Baptism performed by an administrator outside the religious fellowship evaluating the validity of its administration.

Amyraldianism. Named after the French theologian Moïse Amyraut (1596-1664). The most distinctive characteristic of his Reformed theology is the reversal of the decrees regarding Christ's death and election. In the standard Reformed theology of John Calvin and his followers God decreed who were elect and then decreed Christ's death to save them. Amyraut put Christ's death logically prior to the election process. Amyraldianism thus created a *"hypothetical universalism" that sounded to Reformed theologians rather much like the "potential universalism" of *Arminianism. Actually, of course, it was only an *atonement *sufficient for all,* instead of one potential for all; but the sufficiency logically "existed" for a "time" before the elect were chosen; consequently, it is not exactly the same idea as sufficiency; and inasmuch as it was not dependent on human response, but on the subsequent choice of God alone, it was not the same as potential universalism. Also called "Amyraldism."

Amyraldism. Same as *Amyraldianism.

Anabaptists. Members of a growing movement in Europe during the Reformation that were so named because they insisted on adult *believers' baptism. From the viewpoint of *paedobaptists this practice was "re-baptism," or "ana-baptism."

Anakephalaiōsis. A Greek word meaning *"recapitulation."

Andover hypothesis. The theory based primarily on I Peter 3:18—4:6 that after death and prior to the final judgment the previously unevangelized will have opportunity for salvation through Christ. See also *Universalism.

Annihilationism. The belief that, because the human soul is in itself immortal, God exerts positive effort to put it out of existence if he decides not to save a person eternally. The sinner passes out of existence in contrast to enduring eternal torment (*eternalism) or having continued option for salvation after death (*restorationism). Equals *conditional immortality except that in the latter the human soul is not viewed as naturally immortal.

Anthropomorphism. The application of human characteristics to other than human beings. In theology and biblical studies it refers to the application of human characteristics to God and perhaps other members of the spirit world.

Antinomianism [*anti,* against + *nomos,* law]. The belief that man's relationship to God has no connection with obedience to *moral law. This idea has had two sources in Christendom. One derives from a misunderstanding of the Pauline doctrine of *salvation by *faith; the argument is that if actions do not save, it does not matter what a person does. Another source is the gnostic influences in Christian theology; since spirit is good and matter is evil, human salvation becomes a concern over *knowledge of how to free the spirit from the confines of the flesh. Rather than a concern over right behavior it is a concern over being. Because actions are done by the flesh, which cannot touch the spirit, deeds done by the body are of no importance. *Recognition, *merit, and *conditionality represent three other patterns of logical relationship between human action and human *righteousness. Same as "libertinism" and "lawlessness."

Apokatastasis. A Greek word signifying a form of *universalism, associated historically with Origen of Alexandria (185-253), in which all souls will be brought back to God through a process of *purification after death. Akin to *restorationism.

Apostasy. (a) A complete falling away from the salvation status, being a stage beyond *backsliding, the latter idea applied to people who have not yet *grieved the Spirit to the point of rejection from divine sonship. (b) In the doctrine of *perseverance and especially in *eternal security, apostasy is often made synonymous with backsliding and is more often viewed as falling away from a high exposure to the gospel which, if thus refused, cannot later be genuinely accepted (cp. Heb. 6:4-6). (c) In the context of eternal security "apostasy" often means backsliding, particularly with reference to falling from Christian liberty to legalistic feelings about the necessity of maintaining good works.

Apostate. In the state of *apostasy or a person who has apostatized.

Apotheôsis. A Greek word used to mean *"deification."

Arminianism. Historically a system of theology named for the Dutch theologian Jacobus Arminius (1560-1609). It contrasts doctrinally and historically with *Calvinism in that the former affirmed *conditional election, universal possibility in the intent of the *atonement, as well as the resistibleness of *grace, all three of which John Calvin denied. In modern usage Arminianism also includes more definitely the possibility of *apostasy after *salvation.

Aspersion. A term used to refer to "sprinkling" as a form, action, or mode of baptism, thus contrasting with *affusion and *immersion.

Assurance. The sense of confidence about one's *salvation status before God. In Reformed theology assurance is regarded as an essential element of genuine faith. Elsewhere it is a derivative element of faith and tends to correlate with *faith, but its relationship is not necessarily one-to-one with genuine faith.

Atonement. "At-one-ment" is a word picture for bringing God and man back into fellowship, or "oneness." Usually "atone" and "atonement" stress the objective basis Christ laid in making such union possible. The *scope of the atonement has to do with the range of those for whom it was intended; see *Definite atonement, *Particularism, *Limited atonement; *Actual universalism, *Hypothetical universalism, *Potential universalism, and *Universalism.

The *manner of connection* between Christ's death and man's salvation brings up the theories of the atonement such as *dramatic theory, *example, *governmental theory, *moral influence, *ransom, *satisfaction, and *vicarious atonement.

See also *Efficiency of the atonement, *Sufficiency of the atonement; *Acceptilation, *Necessity of the atonement; *Expiation, *Propitiation; and *Socinianism.

Attrition. The sorrow for sin that arises from fear of punishment for it or from a feeling of repugnance toward it. Differentiated from *contrition. See also *Repentance.

Augustinianism. A system of philosophical theology characterized most fundamentally by an ontological definition of good and evil. Good is form and evil is the lack, or privation, of form relative to a pristine standard. Personal *sin arises from disordered being inherited from Adam and Eve, the parents of our race. *"Original sin" refers to this privation in human nature that resulted from their original act of sin and led to *total depravity for each person.

Authentic existence. Living in the conscious realization of ultimate reality including the awareness of God's knowing existence, and functioning in conformity with the revealed purposes of God for history and human life. See also *Eternal life.

Autosoterism [*autos*, self; *sōtēria*, salvation]. The concept of "self-salvation." Cp. *Merit.

Backsliding. A lessening of the quality of personal Christian living that comes short of complete *apostasy from the state of *salvation. Backsliding causes a loss of the experience of abundant living and a loss of witness, and may even incur temporal chastisement of a psychological, if not physical, sort.

Baptism. The first aspect of baptism as a total event is baptism as a symbolic act of personal identification with Jesus Christ in consequence of which identification God forgives sins, grants the fellowship of his Spirit, and adds to his *church; that is to say, there are three uniform consequences of identification with Jesus Christ given at the time of baptism: *forgiveness of sins, *gift of the Spirit, and *church membership. Other consequences are not necessarily uniform; they are potential but not always actual at least in this life.

Baptism is a formal ordinance administered by one person to another by immersing the latter under water and raising him again in pictorial representation of the distinctive act of the Sinless One—death, burial, and resurrection. Baptism is done in the context of penitent *faith as a commitment to the person and will of Jesus Christ for his life. Relative to Christ and his church baptism is a rite of passage and initiation.

A second aspect of the total baptism event is *baptism in the Spirit, the second benefit of water baptism as listed above. Whereas water baptism is administered by another man, Spirit baptism is formally viewed as administered directly by Christ on the occasion of obedience in water baptism. In this terminology Spirit baptism equals the indwelling gift of the Spirit Christ promised not only to his church corporately, but to each person in it individually for fellowship and motivation to bold proclamation and personal growth.

Baptism for the dead. An expression peculiar to I Corinthians 15:29 in Paul's defense of the resurrection. Many have thought Paul referred to a custom in Corinth while others have advanced a number of interpretations for the phrase. Because of the personal and individual character of Christian *salvation and because opportunity for salvation from sin does not continue beyond the boundaries of this life, whatever the meaning of I Corinthians 15:29, it does not indicate that God intends for living men to submit to this ordinance in order to save dead sinners. See *Vicarious baptism.

Baptism in the Holy Spirit. An expression found in Matthew 3:11; Mark 1:8; Luke 3:16; John 1:33; Acts 1:5; 11:16 and I Corinthians 12:13 usually in reference to the baptism of Jesus vs. that of John. (a) "Baptism in the Holy Spirit" evidently serves as a synonym for *"gift of the Spirit" and refers to the recurring arrival of the Spirit in each person; it is *the establishment of interpersonal relationship* between the Spirit of God and the individual man. The expression originated perhaps from the Johannine baptismal setting from which the Baptist predicted the added and distinctive work of Messiah in terms of John's own work. Perhaps the terminology was suggested by the fact that baptism in the Spirit occurs at the time of baptism in *water. The "over-whelming" character, greatness, and importance of the event may have further contributed to the coining of the term. Outside the gospels and Acts it is replaced by other expressions like *gift of the Spirit, *earnest of the Spirit, and *sealed with the Spirit. Miracle is a non-essential and variant element under this usage of the term.

(b) A second view of "baptism in the Spirit" restricts it terminologically to the event of Pentecost in Acts 2 together with a secondary dispensation on the household of Cornelius in Acts 10(-11). Under this approach the referent of the term differs significantly from the previous definition even though the sum total of the realities involved in salvation are the same. Here it indicates only *the initial arrival of the Spirit in the church* (represented by its apostolic leadership), the Cornelius episode being a special extension of that original event to make clear that the church into which the Spirit came was to have more than a Jewish constituency. Again miraculousness is not of the essence of the event even though miracle occurred in visible demonstration of the fact that the outpouring was in fact taking place and even though the effects of the event were miraculous.

(c) "Baptism in the Spirit" is used in a third manner that presupposes *natural depravity and refers to *an enabling gift* that makes *sanctification (spiritual growth) possible or that (d) accomplishes sanctification if "sanctification" means *the second definite work of grace.

Baptism of blood. An expression designating the martyrdom of a believer who for whatever reason had not yet submitted to Christian baptism. His faithfulness in the face of persecution to the point of death was considered a functional equivalent of commitment to Christ in water baptism. A term usually used in historical theology.

Baptism of desire. The desire for baptism that would cause obedience to the ordinance if circumstances would allow; in traditional theology it was regarded as a functional equivalent of actual baptism.

Baptism of fire. The baptism in fire is referred to in John the Baptist's predictions about the Messiah's work (Mt. 3:11-12; Lk. 3:16-17). (a) Because the expression occurs in connection with burning chaff and fruitless trees, John evidently meant the fire of *hell (cp. Mt. 25:41). (b) Many understand "baptism in fire" to refer to *purification (cp. Rev. 1:15), but the fire meant in John's prediction destroys, not purifies. (c) The baptism of fire is sometimes associated with the tongues of fire that appeared over the apostles' heads on Pentecost as a phenomenon accompanying the baptism in the Holy Spirit (Acts 2:1-4). The appearance of fire on that occasion again seems to be aside from the destruction topic present in John's original prediction.

Baptism of suffering. Used in Mark 10:38-40; Luke 12:50; and perhaps I Corinthians 15:29 to refer to the persecution physical, psychological, and social that men endure on behalf of Christ and the gospel.

Baptismal character. In historical theology a mark (Gr. *sphragis*) put on the human soul itself at the time of *baptism and of such a sort that it remains even on an *apostate in *hell.

Baptismal font. A container for the water used in *baptism. Originally constructed below ground level for adult baptism, but later built above ground for greater ease in baptizing infants. The font may stand in a separate building or any place in the church building that makes for convenient gathering at baptisms.

Baptismal regeneration. A designation with highly diverse significations particularly because of the uncertain import of "regeneration." (a) "Baptismal regeneration" has been used to designate the idea that *forgiveness of sins is granted at the time of water baptism or further that forgiveness is conditioned on obedience in water baptism. Other more complex ideas have also been added including (b) the notion of regenerating the relationship between man and God in a *sacramental sense whereby the effect is automatic instead of one brought about directly by the will of God. Furthermore, (c) it has been used to name, not only the regenerating of the relationship, but the regenerating of the ability of the person to believe and have faith. The biblical texts

526

primarily involved are John 3:5; Acts 22:16; Ephesians 5:26; and Titus 3:5 (cp. I Pet. 3:21). See also *Depravity.

Baptistery [bap' tis-ter-y]. The building or part of the church building in which *baptism is administered. Also spelled "baptistry."

Baptistry. See *Baptistery.

Barthian universalism [Bart'i-an]. An *objective universalism in which all men stand in actual relationship to God as far as the Father is concerned; on the subjective side, however, the sinner may conceivably never come to accept his acceptance. Also called "Christological universalism."

Bath of regeneration. A reference to *water baptism in Titus 3:5. See *Washing of regeneration.

Beatific vision [bē-a-tif' ic]. A powerful sense of the real presence of God. In mystical thought other more supernatural dimensions have been added from time to time. Related to *authentic existence.

Believers' baptism. The baptism of adults who believe. Contrasts with *paedobaptism, where the validity of the *ordinance does not depend on the previous *faith of the candidate, but either on his later faith (proleptic faith) or on the faith of the parents or the believing community (surrogate faith).

Blasphemy. A railing out against someone whether human or divine. Blasphemy may include behavior that in effect insults God or rebels against him.

Blasphemy of the Holy Spirit. An expression used on only one occasion in biblical history (Mt. 12:31-32; Mk. 3:28-30; Lk. 12:10). The only sin in the New Testament specifically said not to be forgiven either in this world or the next although a similar implication seems to obtain regarding *"willful sin" in Hebrews 10:26 and *"sin unto death" in I John 5:16. Why blasphemy of the Spirit is any less forgivable than blasphemy of the Son is not explained; perhaps it is that giving the Spirit represents God's final effort at human redemption, and the Spirit had not been given when Jesus used the expression (Jn. 7:39).

Since it is called a *blasphemy, this sin perhaps involves spoken sin as distinguished from one of neglect or non-verbal misbehavior. If so,

527

it would appear not to be directly equatable with characteristic *sin unto death, that is, sin that continues until physical death occurs. It would be a particularly vicious railing out against the Spirit. Against limiting this sin to a verbal one is the case of *"sin with a high hand" in Numbers 15:30. In that context "doing anything with a high hand" is called "blasphemy."

It may perhaps be identified with "insulting the Spirit of grace" (Heb. 10:29), although such an identification does not explain why blasphemy of the *Son* is forgivable. It is not said to be a sin limited either to unsaved or previously saved. "Blasphemy of the Holy Spirit" is popularly called "the unpardonable sin."

Blasphemy of the Holy Spirit is one of several "terminal sins": *sin with a high hand, *"impossible to renew to repentance," *sin unto death, *willful sin. They evidently do not have the same precise reference even though they may be related attitudinally.

Blood atonement. A name for the work of Christ that draws attention to the fact that his death was a violent one; he did not expire from disease or old age. His perfect obedience to the will of the Father he carried to the point of voluntary self-sacrifice to God's purposes for his life.

Bondage of sin. A twofold limitation in which sin first has caused the person to be in a *stative* bondage before God from which he cannot escape. Secondly the past *practice* of sin has created a psychological bondage which by his own strength he finds it difficult to overcome. In Christ therefore there is both a once-for-all deliverance from the state of sin and a continuing deliverance from the practice of sin.

Bondage of the will. (a) The practical power of sin as habit that keeps men from fulfilling even their resolves to do good. To overcome it, they receive the interpersonal, motivational influence of the real presence of God. (b) In Calvinistic and Lutheran thought especially, bondage of the will is more than the psychological drag of past sin-habit on present resolve; it includes the natural incapacity to will a good act, a problem that needs supernatural and miraculous correction rather than natural influence.

Born in sin. On the basis of Psalms 51:5 (cp. Jn. 9:34) and Romans 5:12ff., theologians have often taught that a child is lost by virtue of the very fact that he is born. Birth brings him into a race which as a race is lost; furthermore, birth transmits to the child the depraved nature that will unavoidably bring about his own personal *sin. See *Original guilt.

Calling. The third element of the *ordo salutis* in Romans 8:29-30. (a) *Salvation comes about through calling the person by the gospel. Essentially, "calling" emphasizes the fact that salvation originates from beyond ourselves; we are invited to participate by him who originated the possibility of return to fellowship with him. Preaching the gospel issues the invitation to salvation.

In addition to this "general calling," as it is termed, (b) many conceive of a special, or "effectual calling." Effectual calling is not simply a calling that has been responded to; it is one in which, parallel to proclamation, there is a supernatural operation of the Spirit that irresistibly causes the hearer to respond favorably to the message. The need for this second aspect of calling comes from presupposing that man naturally has no ability to accept the message because he is *totally depraved and therefore insensitive to spiritual matters. See *External calling.

Calvinism. So called because of its leading spokesman, John Calvin of Geneva, Switzerland; actually much of the Calvinistic system harks back to Augustine of Hippo (354-430). Calvinism contrasts with *Arminianism. Six points make up the framework of historic Calvinism: *inscrutable sovereignty, *total depravity, *unconditional election, *limited atonement, *irresistible grace, and *perseverance of the saints.

Capricious sovereignty. Unprincipled *sovereignty as distinguished from ethically consistent use of the right to choose. *Gods of power* might exercise capricious sovereignty inasmuch as they—like men—are governed by lust; the God of the Bible is a *God of principle* who exercises his power consistently with his *promises. Contrasts then with *principled sovereignty. See "Sovereignty."

Carnal man. See "Man."

Cat grip. An expression that views *salvation as something in which the person is entirely passive in that he does not even contribute to the choice of whether he is saved. It contrasts with *"monkey hold." See also *Irresistible grace and *Monergism.

Catabaptist. One who is opposed to *baptism.

529

Catechumenate. A structured period of Christian education, developed early in the history of the church, in which the catechumen (student) learned the elements of the faith prior to his official entrance into the church at baptism.

Ceremonial law. A classification of commandments, used especially in Old Testament studies, that has to do with religious ritual, such as sacrificial regulations, performance of the temple duties, observance of special days, etc. It contrasts with *civil law and *moral law, or *moral commandment.

Ceremonial washings. Same as *ablutions.

Christocentrism. Same as *Christomonism.

Christological universalism. Same as *Barthian universalism.

Christomonism. A term used in describing Barthian theology because Christ is the only reprobate man as well as the only elect man; Christ is the electing God and the elect man. Same as "Christocentrism."

Church. In New Testament usage the church equals the body of Christ. According to Matthew 16:18-19 a close relationship—if not identity—exists between the church and the kingdom of heaven/God (Mt. 19:23-24; 4:17 + Mk. 1:15). Perhaps terminologically "the church" is "the kingdom of God" now, with Israel and the eternal state being other stages of the kingdom. In Romans 11:15-32 Paul correlates the church with spiritual Israel. The church may be described as the sum of those saved through the gospel.

Traditionally a practical, if not theological, distinction has been made between the *visible church people see as the church and the *invisible church, which consists of those actually saved in God's eyes. *External covenant correlates with visible church and *non-communicant membership, being a "political," or structural, definition of the church and having no *salvific implications. *Internal covenant correlates with *invisible church and *communicant membership. See also *Church membership and *Covenant.

Church discipline. A process for correcting disorderly church members. An outline for it is provided in Matthew 18:15-18. Examples of church discipline occur in I Corinthians 5:1-8; II Corinthians 1:23—2:11; I Timothy 1:20. The procedure includes personal confrontation, confrontation with witnesses, and public exposure to the congregation for purposes of dismissal from the identity of the group and social control of inappropriate behavior. See also *Deliver to Satan and *Excommunication.

Church membership. Having status in the *church, or body of Christ. Church membership, visible and invisible, is logically the third uniform consequence of identification with Jesus Christ. Some paedobaptist communions especially distinguish between *communicant and *non-communicant membership, which corresponds respectively with *invisible and *visible church. In biblical usage church membership is always universal church membership.

Circumcision. A fleshly rite normally performed on the Jewish male at the age of eight days and having the significance of formally identifying him with the Abrahamic-Mosaic *covenant. Circumcision served as the functional equivalent of citizenship papers for national Israel. In Colossians 2:11-13 Paul calls baptism a circumcision without hands insofar evidently as it is the event that formally identifies a person with the Christian covenant.

Circumcision of the heart. An expression suggested by the rite of circumcision in which excess skin was removed from the male genital organ. Spiritualizing this rite, both Old and New Testament writers speak of circumcision of the heart as a way of referring to removing flesh-based values and practices. The person comes to be governed, not by the desire for material things, but by values transcendent to the flesh; more precisely, he comes to be governed, not by abstract values, but by the will of the person of God, whom he loves with his whole heart.

Civil law. A classification of commandments, used especially in Old Testament studies, that has to do with the political operations of national Israel. They include directives on the manner in which the king was to fulfill his office, regulations about warfare, statutes about inheritance, etc. It contrasts with *ceremonial law and *moral law.

Class predestination. The idea that as a group those in Christ are destined to eternal fellowship with God while those who are outside of him are destined to eternal separation from God. Class predestination is distinguished from *individual predestination, which goes on to affirm that the destiny of each individual person has been predetermined by

531

God. See *Predestination, *Conditional predestination, *Foreordination, *Double predestination.

Cleansing. A figure under which *forgiveness of sin is set forth. In Old Testament studies it also included the idea of removing ceremonial *defilement.

Clinical baptism. Baptism administered to people near the point of death.

Clinici [clin-ee' see]. People baptized near the point of death; so called because they were in bed (Gr. *klinē).*

Comforter. See *Advocate.

Commercial theory of the atonement. Same as the *satisfaction theory of the atonement.

Common grace. Grace extended to all men in distinction from grace bestowed selectively on some men.

Communicant church membership. In *paedobaptist communions a *church membership not only of the *visible church, but also of the *invisible church. Communicant membership often comes at a time of *confirmation and personal experience.

Compulsion. In philosophy compulsion refers to external force that causes someone to act. It contrasts with *necessity, which refers to internal causation. The concepts were applied by John Calvin to *depraved man as part of his effort to exonerate God from being the author of *sin.

Concupiscence [cŏn-cū' pis-cence]. Inordinate desire arising from the bodily senses. For Augustine of Hippo concupiscence represented the essence of *sin and derived from fallen nature inherited from Adam.

Condignity. Requirement as from a debtor. Applied to *grace in response to human actions performed by regenerate men through dependence on the Holy Spirit.

Conditional baptism. Baptism administered to those whose baptism is doubted to be valid. It is so called because of the introductory statement: "*If* thou art not already baptized, I baptize . . . ."

Conditional immortality. The belief that sinners pass out of existence after death instead of being eternally separated from God in hell (*eternalism) or allowed endless opportunity for coming back into divine fellowship (*restorationism). The human soul is not immortal, but immortable, that is, able to be made eternal by God's continuously sustaining its existence. At death—or perhaps at the judgment—God withdraws his sustaining power and the person/soul simply ceases to exist. Equals *annihilationism except that in the latter the soul is viewed as having natural immortality so that a positive act of destruction is required for its non-existence.

Conditional predestination. The determination of a person's destiny on the basis of foreseen response to the conditions for that destiny. Corresponds with *permissive predestination and contrasts with *unconditional predestination. See *Predestination.

Conditionality. An aspect of Paul's concept of faith. Conditionality describes the relationship between an act of faith and a result and is in a situation characterized by five marks: a dependent person who can do nothing decisive about his situation, a sovereign who is under no moral obligation to assist him, the sovereign's free promise to help, an obedience predicated on the dependent, and a result bestowed by the sovereign. The obedience of the dependent does not produce the result, but only meets the sovereignly stipulated prerequisites on the background of which it is bestowed.

   Conditionality does not speak of a quality or condition in the needy person, but of the manner of connection his actions have with the result granted by another. Within the category of conditionality vs. cause, etc., attitude rather than amount of obedience serves as the direct basis for initial and continued salvation. Obviously, attitude must be to the extent of obedience or it would not be known or recognizable; attitude correlates generally with characteristic obedience vs. perfect obedience. The sufficiency of characteristic obedience vs. perfect obedience is the difference between grace and merit as a basis for relationship with a righteous God.

   Conditionality contrasts with *antinomianism, *merit, and *recognition.

Confession. (a) The admission of *guilt with a view to *forgiveness. An expression to the offended party that by *repentance a person has dissociated himself from his past behavior. (b) In Roman Catholic usage confession is required through a priest for all *mortal sins and encouraged for *venial sins. The failure to do so brings damnation. Confession in this sense is derived from John 20:21-23. See also *Penance.

Confirmation. The act of personal commitment to Jesus Christ, which was originally an aspect of the *baptism event. In the course of church history, the administration of water baptism was separated from confirmation and moved back to the time of infancy, bringing about confirmation as a separate rite that "confirmed" the validity of the infant's baptism.

Confirmed in holiness. The doctrine that after death or the final judgment a person will no longer have the ability to *sin against God. See also *Second definite work of grace.

Congruism. The belief that God extends *grace to men in conformity with those events most advantageous to its success.

Conscience. The innate human capacity for sensing *guilt or innocence relative to a learned standard of behavior. Conscience is innate as an ability possessed by humankind, but not as a content; that is, right and wrong are not inbred instincts so much as the learned behavior of one's environment together with rational and affective conclusions reached during experience.

Contrition. A sorrow for *sin motivated by a love for God. Is distinguished from *attrition.

Conversion. Emphasizes the change of life style that is part of the whole *salvation reality.

Conviction. The sense of certainty about *sin and therefore the need for *salvation through Christ.

Co-operating grace. A kind of divine provision in which the human *will acts freely through that provision in accomplishing the result. Contrasts with *operating grace.

Corporate salvation. Salvation regarded at the group level. At this level Christ replaces Adam as the one with whom men identify unto salvation. Contrasts with individual, or personal, salvation. See also *Predestination.

534

Cosmic redemption. The redemption of the non-personal creation to appropriate relationship with the Creator. Contrasts with personal redemption, or *soteric reconciliation. See also *Regeneration.

Covenant. A mutual contract between two parties governing the relationship between them and setting forth the responsibilities of each party to the other. God's relationship to Israel is set forth under this form with the prediction in Jeremiah 31:31ff. that God would establish a new covenant with his people. Hebrews draws upon this prediction, but shifts the Greek word *diathēkē* from covenant to *testament in Hebrews 9:15-20, thus showing that these concepts are only models, or ways of thinking of the process of establishing and continuing divine-human relationship. See *External covenant and *Internal covenant.

Declared will. Same as *revealed will.

Decrees. A term referring to God's *sovereign decisions in eternity past, particularly those regarding the death of Christ and *election or *reprobation.

Decretive will [dē-crē′ tiv]. Same as *hidden will.

Defilement. A real or ceremonial taint as measured respectively by *moral law or *positive commandment (ceremonial law). The state of impurity by reason of mixing the person or thing with that which is common, or with that which is not distinctively set aside to a specific task, purpose, or relationship. Defilement centers on the concept of mixture with something foreign. Related to the ideas of impurity, taboo, uncleanness; consequently, the removal of defilement draws upon rituals that involve washing or separation.

Definite atonement. The view that Christ's death was intended to secure the actual *salvation of a definite number *("numerus clausus")* in contrast to a *potential atonement for all or an actual salvation of all. Same as "particularism" and "limited atonement," although the latter term is not preferred by Calvinists because Calvinism approaches the scope of the atonement without presupposed expectancy, which is not the case with "limited" atonement.

Deification. (a) In pagan religions the exaltation of a man into the status and character of a god or his absorption into deity. (b) In early Christianity the term was occasionally employed to express *glorification.

535

Deliver to Satan. An expression found in I Corinthians 5:5 and I Timothy 1:20 referring to the exercise of *church discipline, or *excommunication.

Depravity. (a) A description of man's characteristic manner of behaving relative to God's will for his life; depravity here is a *way of acting.* (b) Beyond behavior traditional Christian theology has posited natural, or ontic, depravity, by which is meant the innate *constitutional inability to do good.* (c) Psychological depravity is the *drag of past failure on present resolve* (habit), the generalized functional weakness of will that does not always keep the satisfaction of bodily drives and material desires within the proper channels, and the social failure to project consciousness from one's own viewpoint to the viewpoint of others so as to qualify personal behavior by the needs of others.

(d) Total depravity refers to the *all-pervasive effect of *sin* in the human person. "Total" does not mean men are as bad as they could be, but that sin has negatively affected all aspects of man and his relations. Traditionally, total depravity has been viewed as biologically transferred from generation to generation as distinguished from being originated anew in each person because of social influence and viewpoint of consciousness directed toward pervertible bodily and psychological drives.

Determinism. A situation in which there is only one real possibility. No other options exist; there is a necessary, one-to-one relationship between what is and what will come of what is. Determinism may be accomplished by direct exertion of external power or internal limitation of ability.

Disobedience. Conscious failure to follow a command.

Divination. In Eastern Christian mysticism divination refers to religious union with God; also known as *theôsis or *theopoiêsis.

Do despite to the Spirit. Same as "insult the Spirit"; see *Apostasy, *Blasphemy of the Holy Spirit, and *Grieve the Holy Spirit.

Double predestination. (a) The doctrine that both *reprobation of the wicked and *predestination of the elect were decided in God's mind before times eternal. Double predestination involves a positive act on God's part in regard to both the saved and the lost; hence, the terminology "double" predestination is most appropriate to a *supralapsarian position and to conditional predestination, because in these positions God's foreordination is equally positive for both the saved and the lost. Contrast in this regard *single predestination.

(b) In Barthian neo-orthodoxy this simultaneous predestination of parallel groups has been replaced with sequential predestination; predestined lostness is followed by predestined salvation, thus producing objective *universalism.

Dramatic theory of the atonement. A view described by Gustav Aulén (1879-1977) in his *Christus Victor.* Although the work was intended as a reinterpretation of Martin Luther's view of atonement, it really set forth an independent statement on the meaning of Christ's death and resurrection. With greater attention to the resurrection Aulén saw Christ's death primarily as making possible his resurrection in triumph over the powers of evil. See *Atonement.

Earn salvation. See *Merit.

Earnest of the Spirit. A Pauline expression occurring in II Corinthians 1:22; 5:5; and Ephesians 1:14. The presence, guidance, empowerment, and intercession of the Spirit is regarded under this figure as a kind of divine downpayment to man of the rewards of *salvation. The Spirit is God's pledge to fulfill the rest of his promises about the future.

Effectual calling. See *Calling.

Efficacious grace. In Roman Catholic theology a kind of *actual grace that operates through the consenting human will in such a way that it guarantees the effect God desires. The efficacy of such *grace may depend on the nature of grace itself or upon the nature of the recipient viewed in his foreseen circumstances. Contrasts with *sufficient grace as another kind of actual grace.

Efficiency of the atonement. Efficiency of the atonement contrasts with *sufficiency of the atonement. Although Christ's death is sufficient for the salvation of all men, it becomes efficient only for those who believe.

Egocentricity. Self-centeredness. A style of existence whose governing principles issue ultimately from one's personal perspective without proper qualification by divine prerogative or the needs of fellowmen corporate or individual. See *Egocentrism and *Situationalism.

Egocentrism. The structural fact that all reality is seen from the view-point of the individual perceiver. Proper functioning requires the projection of consciousness over behind the eyes of fellowmen and necessitates conscious effort to curtail personal desire in preference to the transcendent will of God and the needs of corporate man. See *Egocentricity.

Election. The divine choice of who is saved. Theologians have differed on whether election is conditioned on prior human response to the Christian message. Election contrasts with *reprobation within *double predestination.

Eternal life. Meaningful, endless existence that begins during this life when a person is reconciled to God. See *Authentic existence.

Eternal security. Emphasizes the safety of the saint in God's hands. Usually, however, the expression technically refers to the belief that a person who has a heartfelt conversion experience is permanently saved even if he later reverts to his former manner of life. Contrasts with *perseverance and *apostasy.

Eternal sin. According to Mark 3:9 an eternal sin is so called because God will never *forgive it.

Eternalism. The belief that the wicked are permanently and irretrievably separated from God. Eternalism contrasts with *conditionalism, *universalism, and *restorationism.

Eudemonism [ū-dē' mon-ism]. A theory of ethics that defines right behavior by what brings a sense of well-being. Eudemonism is actively living by reason. Also spelled eudaemonism [ū-dī-mon-ism].

Evil. The opposite of *good. In the case of good as a form of being, evil becomes specifically the lack, or "privation," of form relative to the pristine standard before the *Fall.

Ex opere operato. See *Opus operatum.

Example theory of the atonement. A view of Christ's work propounded by Faustus Socinus (1539-1604) in his *De Jesu Christo Servatore.* Also known as *exemplarism and *Socinianism.

Excommunication. Formal dismissal from the fellowship of the *church and the right to participate in observance of the Lord's Supper. "Greater

538

excommunication" also deprives the person of public and private social relationship and of all other prerogatives except *Last Rites. Excommunication stresses the purification of the church while "church discipline" stresses the correction of the disorderly member.

Exemplarism [ex-em′ plar-ism]. A view of the *atonement in which the value of Christ's work derives from its motivational influence on men to follow his example in moral living and divine service. Also known as the *moral influence theory or the *subjective theory of the atonement. See *Atonement and *Example theory of the atonement.

Exomologesis [ex-ō-mol-ō-gē′ sis]. A full, public *confession of *sin. Also used to designate the whole process of reinstating an excommunicated person back into the *fellowship of the *church.

Expiation. A translation of *hilasmos,* used in some versions since the King James (1611) and the American Standard (1901) in place of *"propitiation." "Expiation" indicates the covering of a sin, or crime, while *"propitiation" means the appeasement of wrath.

Extent of the atonement. Same as *scope of the atonement.

External calling. The call to the unsaved issued through the proclamation of the gospel. Contrasts with *effectual call, which indicates the secret operation of the Spirit parallel to the proclamation in order to energize the sinner and make him irresistibly able to respond positively to the message. See also *Efficacious calling and *General calling.

External covenant. A covenant with God by virtue of membership in the *visible church through *infant baptism, but not necessarily membership in the *invisible church, that is, not in *internal covenant relationship with God. Under this arrangement the *church is viewed as being like national Israel, where the political element was not necessarily complemented by the spiritual element. *Baptism brings the candidate into the visible church, into the external covenant, into *non-communicant church membership, and is done on the basis of parental membership; *confirmation is often viewed as bringing a person into internal covenant relationship with God. See also *Communicant church membership.

Extreme unction. (a) Based on Mark 6:13 and James 5:14-15, extreme unction originally meant a ritual for bodily healing and spiritual comfort.

539

(b) Subsequently it became one of the seven *sacraments in the Roman Catholic Church. Thereupon extreme unction assumed a more decisive emphasis on the forgiveness of the unforgiven *mortal and *venial sins of the dying person. As a sacrament its validity does not depend on the consciousness of the person. Along with *penance, the eucharist, and the apostolic benediction, extreme unction is part of *Last Rites.

Faith. A term used with somewhat different emphases in the New Testament. (a) James 2 uses it with a stress on *mental assent.* (b) Paul adds the elements of *trust* and *commitment.* An act of faith as commitment is an act of *identification.* As to its relationship to results, faith involves *conditionality.* In its relationship to knowledge, it involves *revelation.* (c) "Faith" in contemporary usage often designates a religion, as in "the Christian faith." See *Faith only, *Inchoate faith, and *Vicarious faith.

Faith only. (a) The Pauline doctrine that justification is by *faith in contrast to being by *works or by faith and works together as the apostle employs these two terms in Romans and Galatians. *Salvation is by an *attitude* of trust in God for being viewed as righteous and an *aspiration* to be perfectly righteous like Christ in contrast to *being* righteous, or *accomplishing* moral perfection. Salvation by faith only is a faith that expresses itself in obedience and a faith to the extent of obedience, even characteristic obedience, but the obedience is not perfect and it is a *condition, not a cause, of salvation.

(b) Sometimes "faith only" is used to describe the belief that *salvation is by faith only so as to eliminate *baptism from being logically prior to *justification. Faith only contrasts with *Galatianism and *synergism.

The Fall. In Genesis the original disobedience of Adam and Eve. According to historical theology the Fall involves not only the loss of *innocence and consequent fellowship with God together with specific punishments enumerated in Genesis 3:9-24; it included a loss of ability to do *good, that is, *total depravity, with the result that all Adam's descendants have biologically received a depraved nature. By the Fall the human race as such became estranged from God so that to be a person is to be a lost person.

Fall away. See *Apostasy.

Federal man. Man conceived of as represented by, and included in, Adam in such a way that Adam's *guilt and punishment equally and legally apply to all those thus included in him. Individual men are like cells of the total organism. Adam is like the first cell that divided by fission again and again until mankind as a whole is formed into one large "mass of perdition."

Federal theology. A systematic theology that includes the concept of *federal man.

Fellowship. Interpersonal relationship between God and man or between men. "Fellowship" is consistently used to translate the Greek word *koinōnia*, whose imagery is that of having in common, or sharing. "To be in fellowship with" is often used to mean agreeing sufficiently that personal association and co-operation in worship and ministry can take place. Originally a general word for shared relationship, "fellowship" becomes a quasi-technical term for relationship based on common association with Christ.

Fideism [fē' day-ism]. A designation for the view that the human intellect does not have the capacity to apprehend divine matters. Consequently, fideism exhibits an aversion to rationalism and a preference for feelings and the affective dimension of man.

Filled with the Spirit. (a) An expression used in scripture to preface some specific act by God's man; as such it may designate only a surge of motivation to speak or act for God (Lk. 1:41, 67); or it may include supernatural inspiration in some cases (Acts 4:8, 13). (b) A second usage indicates a person's increased characterization by the values and characteristics of the Spirit (Eph. 5:18). (c) In pentecostal circles it commonly carries an implication of supernatural agency exerted directly on the human capacities and abilities so as to bring about the improved life quality that results from the Spirit's work.

Flagellants. Men who in medieval times and afterwards publicly scourged themselves in *penance processions. The object was to instill *repentance in the observers and aid in the *contrition of the participants.

Foreknowledge. The first element of the *ordo salutis* in Romans 8:29-30. (a) God's foresight of man's faith that serves as the basis for *predestination. This definition understands God's knowledge of the

541

future as intuitive, direct, and without means (*scienta visionis*). (b) In the Reformed theology of salvation God's foreknowledge is by virtue of predestination, a definition that in effect reverses the chronological order of Romans 8:29-30. At the same time foreknowledge gets redefined as "setting regard upon." Here any foreknowing in the sense of (a) above is a knowledge based on a *decree. (c) Foreknowledge could be by the perfect knowledge of nature (*scienta media*). (d) A less precise form of foreknowledge comes as *scienta fide,* a knowledge based on a person's character. Foreknowledge (a) and (d) allow for free choice on the part of creatures.

Forensic justification. Same as *legal justification.

Foreordination. Same as *predestination.

Forgiveness. The act of separating a person's past act from one's attitude toward the present person. Forgiveness separates the offender from his past offense in the mind of the forgiver, while *repentance and *confession separate the offender from his past in his own mind. Forgiveness does not eradicate the past, but it eradicates it from the present so that it no longer affects the relationship. Forgiveness of sins is logically the first uniform consequence of identification with Jesus Christ. See also *Baptism.

Formal sin. An act that is sinful in itself and known to be sinful by the person when he did it. Contrasts with *material sin.

Free moral agency. See *Freedom of the will.

Freedom of the will. A person's ability to choose between alternatives, not just to apprehend the one "option" that lies before him. Freedom of the will intends to deny the notion that *total depravity eliminates the ability to choose to do *good, or to respond to good. It affirms the lack of necessity for a supernatural operation of the Spirit on the ontic ability of man before the human person can accept the gospel message and begin to live the Christian life.

Freedom of the will does not necessarily assume that a person can do good as easily as he can do evil, but that he can do good under the awareness of what good is and with the interpersonal influence of other Christians as well as God's presence to motivate him to that end. Some who believe in total depravity postulate a supernatural operation of

542

God's Spirit on each person at some time during his life so that subsequently he has a freedom of the will he did not previously possess. Freedom of the will contrasts with a stimulus-response view of man's highest capacity and is opposed to the idea of irresistible divine influence. See also *Bondage of the will.

Galatianism. The idea opposed in Galatians that men are initially saved by *grace, but maintain *salvation by *works. Paul's antagonists seemed to think that Messiah's death served as a basis for the *forgiveness of past *sin, but that continued salvation status depended on keeping the Mosaic *law. Evidently they did not clearly understand the perfection requirement laid down by the law and the practical impossibility of "continuing to do all" God has commanded.

General calling. Correlates with *eternal calling, which is issued to all men in contradistinction to *effectual calling performed only upon the *elect. See also *Calling and *Eternal calling.

Gift of the Holy Spirit. "The gift of the Spirit" is the interpersonal relationship with God's Spirit that is established at the time of *conversion and *baptism (Acts 2:38); also called "the indwelling *gift of the Spirit." The Spirit himself is the gift. "A gift of the Spirit" means a gift received from the Spirit, which may include a natural ability (now transformed into a gift of the Spirit by being brought under the Spirit's control; Acts 4:29; Rom. 12:7-8), a natural characteristic (Mt. 19:11-12; I Cor. 7:5-7), or a supernatural endowment (I Cor. 12:28). The gift of the Holy Spirit is logically the second uniform consequence of identification with Jesus Christ. See also *Baptism and *Baptism in the Holy Spirit.

Gifts of the Spirit. Gifts that the Spirit gives in distinction from the gift that the Spirit is.

Glorification. The last element in the *ordo salutis according to Romans 8:29-30. Glorification lies future to the earthly existence (II Cor. 4:17), even though the anticipation of it transforms the person during his time of anticipation (I Pet. 5:1; I Th. 2:12). Besides general references like Romans 5:2 and Colossians 1:27, glorification in Philippians 3:21 and I Corinthians 15:42-43 specifies the transformation of the body from corruptible to incorruptible. Thus glorification refers to exaltation of kind, state, and status relative to the characteristics of man in his present condition.

543

Godparents. See *Sponsors.

Good. (a) Description of a behavior or act figured relative to a standard. In this usage the act is *a discrete good* because it is viewed on its own individual merits as evaluated by the *law, *conscience, nature, etc.

(b) A *circumstantial good* is an act viewed in relation to the whole life, in which case "there is none that does *a good.*" The good act of the good moral man is good, but to no avail *soteriologically because that good act in the context of others that are sinful means that the *perfection requirement remains unachieved. Often this concept is perverted in popular theology to mean that *every* act of an unregenerate, unsaved person is itself not a *discrete good* because perhaps some unconscious evil motive perverts anything and everything such a person does. This supposition overdoes the lack of goodness in the lost and does not correlate with the psychological experience of the unconverted in many cases. The *act* may be pleasing to God without thereby making the *person* pleasing to God.

(c) *Characteristic good* sees the overall pattern of behavior relative to a standard in contrast to looking at individual acts contextualized in imperfection. In this sense Paul means it when he quotes Psalms 14:1, etc., to the effect that "there is none that does *good*" (Rom. 5:9-20).

(d) In historical theology good has been defined not in relation to action alone, as in the above three entries, but as also inclusive of being. Good is a description of the form of being, especially in the Augustinian philosophy that has undergirded Western theology since the fifth century. See in this regard *Depravity. See also *Righteousness.

Governmental theory of the atonement. A view of the atonement set forth by Hugo Grotius (1583-1645) in *Defense of the Catholic Faith on the Satisfaction of Christ Against Faustus Socinus.* Christ's death manifests God's justice more than satisfies his justice.

Grace. A benevolent disposition toward others that goes beyond withholding just punishment (*mercy) to bestowing positive good. See also *Operating and *Co-operating grace; *Sufficient and *Efficacious grace; *Prevenient grace; *Common grace; *Actual grace; *Habitual, or *Sanctifying grace; *Infused and *Imputed grace.

Grieve the Spirit. An expression, used by Paul in Ephesians 4:30, that indicates a straining of one's relationship with the Holy Spirit. Evidently not so extreme as insulting, or doing despite to, the Spirit (Heb. 10:29). See *Apostasy and *Blasphemy of the Holy Spirit.

Guilt. That state which comes from breaking a standard of behavior and committing a personal affront against the author of that standard. The feeling of *guilt is the sense of being viewed by another as having acted in a way inappropriate to the relationship.

Theologically, guilt may be *imputed or personal, depending on whether it is reckoned against us from elsewhere (Adam) or characteristic of us by our own actions. Guilt is a characteristic of the transgressor in the eyes of others.

Habitual grace. Same as *sanctifying grace.

Half-way covenant. An arrangement in which an infant with faithful grandparents could be baptized even though the parents were members only by birth rather than by experience; that is, the parents had *noncommunicant church membership, were under *external covenant relationship with God, or had status only in the *visible church. Also called *"Stoddardianism." See *Church membership.

Hamartiology [hà-mär-ti-ol'ō-gy]. The study of the doctrine of *sin.

Healing. A term with a wide range of usage in scripture including not only disease, but correction from *sin (Isa. 53:5), change from *backsliding (Hos. 14:4), making water fit to drink (II Kg. 2:22), etc. In modern usage "healing" often means bringing psychological and emotional wholeness. Especially because of Matthew 8:17, many authors have argued that physical healing is part of the *atonement, because Matthew considers Isaiah 53:4 in the Suffering Servant Poem a prediction inclusive of Jesus' healing ministry.

Three points may be made in associating the atonement with healing. (1) *Psychological and emotional stability* tend to result from removal of *guilt, etc.; this is not to say, of course, that mental illness is necessarily removed by the gospel since organic matters also pertain to emotional health. (2) *Psychosomatic healing* can surely be allowed because the organic disorders involved result from psychological causes, which, if removed, can often be reversed. The further matter of (3) *physical healing* comes with less certainty inasmuch as miracle or special divine providence must enter the picture. Experience and scripture do not guarantee removal of all sickness from God's people, even though answered prayer always makes physical healing a real, albeit not uniform, possibility; in this regard God's *common grace may be sufficient for his people (II Cor. 12:7-9). Some blessings made possible in the atonement may not be experienced until "this corruptible takes on incorruption" (I Cor. 15:53-58). As far as this life is concerned, then, physical healing is one of the non-uniform results of *salvation.

Heaven. The dwelling place of God where the saved spend eternity.

Hedonism [hē'dŏn-ism]. The ethical theory that says *good is what brings pleasure.

Hell. The permanent abode of the unsaved dead. Distinguished from the Roman Catholic concept of *purgatory, which is a temporary place of *purification rather than a permanent place of destruction, punishment, and containment of evil. See *Eternalism, *Heaven, *Limbo, *Restorationism.

Hemerobaptists [hem"e-rō-bap'tists]. A Jewish religious sect similar to the Pharisees except for their denial of resurrection. Called "hemerobaptists" because they regarded daily *ablutions as an essential part of religion.

Hidden will. What God has in himself *sovereignly determined in eternity past. Contrasts with *revealed will, or declared will.

Household baptism. The mass *baptism of a complete household. The New Testament examples occur in Acts 10:23-48; 11:11-18; 16:11-15; 16:25-34; 18:8; I Corinthians 1:16. Of particular interest in the discussion of infant baptism. See *Paedobaptism.

Hypothetical universalism. A kind of *univeralism that was implied by *Amyraldianism inasmuch as it conceived of Christ's death as logically prior to *election, even though the theological system included only a limited number of those to whom God applied the *atonement. Thus the position said more than the traditional *Calvinistic concept that Christ's death was sufficient for all and less than the *Arminian concept that it was potentially for all. Distinguished from *actual universalism, *potential universalism, and an atonement sufficient for all men.

Illumination. According to New Testament usage, probably a general term for awareness of the truth in contrast to pagan darkness or Jewish ignorance of the true nature of the Messiah and his *kingdom. In the early church "illumination" came to indicate *baptism, perhaps as an extension of Hebrews 6:4 and 10:32. In theological parlance a subjective enlightenment by objective revelation, commonly thought of as accompanied by heightened ability to perceive and understand what revelation is saying. In Barthianism *revelation has dissolved into illumination, thus becoming dynamic inspiration.

Image of God. (a) In Genesis 1:26-27 (cp. 5:1; 9:6; I Cor. 11:7; James 3:9; cp. Acts 17:28-29) a natural likeness between God and mankind. The image of God in its broadest sense addresses the correspondence between the threeness-in-oneness of God and the twoness-in-oneness of man. This interpersonal framework determines the need for the other human characteristics commonly listed as elements of the image: rationality, volition, emotion, spiritual nature, self-consciousness, and moral character; note also dominion and responsibility.

(b) Theologically this understanding of the image is called the "Old Testament image" or the "narrow image," a dimension of man not lost in the *Fall, but greatly affected by it. The "New Testament image," or "broad image," has to do with righteous character, which was lost as a fact for Adam and as a potentiality for his descendants because of natural depravity biologically transmitted. Image in the sense of *righteousness is what *salvation through Christ renews (Col. 3:10). Same as *imago dei.*

Imago dei. Same as *image of God.

Immersion. A term used to designate that action of * baptism in which the candidate is totally submerged under water and brought up again. Meaning strictly to dip into the water in distinction from being brought up from it, immersion designates in common usage both the immersion and emersion involved in the dipping action. It contrasts with *aspersion and *affusion. See also *Tri(u)ne immersion.

Implicit faith. What a person has when he does not believe simply because he has had no opportunity to accept the Christian message. For theological purposes those who are of the sort as would believe

547

if they had opportunity are treated as if they believed, or treated in terms of what they would do.

Imposition of hands. Same as *Laying on of hands.

Imputation. (a) Reckoning something to someone as distinguished from their actually being it or having it. Imputing occurs in the mind of the viewer while characteristics and acts occur in the person himself. (b) Imputation in theological use is applied to God's reckoning Adam's descendants as guilty for Adam's act. Thus imputed guilt contrasts with *personal *guilt, which arises from each person's own disobedience to God's *law.

In like manner *righteousness may in the mind of the perceiver be reckoned to a person from elsewhere in contrast to *personal righteousness, which would come from one's own obedience to God's standard of behavior. Thus Adam's guilt and punishment God imputes to his descendants when they identify with him by doing as he did; Christ's righteousness and resurrection God imputes to his disciples when they identify with him by acceptance of him as God's object of identification and by formal identification through Christian *baptism.

Imputed grace. Grace in the mind of God as distinguished from *grace infused into the being of man. Imputed grace regards as righteous, as distinct from grace that enables to be righteous.

Imputed guilt. See *Imputation.

Imputed righteousness. See *Imputation.

Imputed sin. See *Imputation.

Inability. (a) In biblical usage inability comes from practical considerations of either a psychological or circumstantial sort. (b) Historical theology has further developed the doctrine of natural, or ontic, *depravity, which involves a lack of capacity for *righteousness because of disordered human nature. Inability requires a supernatural operation miraculously applied to the disordered being of man itself, or perhaps providentially applied to man's circumstance. Either way man operates in the stimulus-response category of relationship instead of being a person with the ability of choice.

Inchoate faith [in′ kō-āte.]. Elementary or rudimentary faith. An expression applicable to the kind of faith children may have and therefore the kind of faith *paedobaptists often regard as satisfactory for valid Christian baptism. This inchoate faith some theologians regard as even more than (a) the trusting, tractable nature of a child; it is (b) something supernaturally engendered in the soul of the infant by the work of the Holy Spirit so that it grows to adult dimensions and character in much the same way as a seed becomes a tree.

Incorrigible apostasy. A term used to distinguish clearly from *back-sliding inasmuch as *apostasy is often used synonymously with back-sliding by those who deny the real possibility of losing *salvation.

Individual predestination. The idea that God has not only *predestined classes of men to *heaven or *hell, but that he has specified the eternal destiny of each person in those classes.

Indulgences. In Roman Catholic practice a papal *remission of the temporal penalty due to unforgiven sin. The indulgence draws against the *treasury of merit built up by the *supererogation of Christ, Mary, and the *saints. Indulgences are not sold, but in the case of a partial indulgence are obtained by reciting the rosary and doing the act of piety required; in the case of a plenary indulgence the person's soul must be free from any *venial sin. Plenary indulgences grant remission of all temporal punishment due to one's sins; partial indulgences remove some of the temporal punishment for sin.

Indulgences represent one of the more extreme results of misperceiving the nature of *salvation as a quantifiable system ultimately legal and transactional in character. Salvation operates in the realm of attitude rather than accomplishments per se.

Infallible grace. Same as *irresistible grace.

Infant baptism. Same as *paedobaptism.

Infant dedication. A custom that has grown up among non-paedobaptists as a replacement for *infant baptism. Sometimes the formal naming of the child is included along with a solemn parental dedication to raise the young child in the nurture and admonition of the Lord.

Infant faith. See *Inchoate faith.

Infralapsarianism. In Reformed theology the view that considers God's *decree of *election to follow his decree to allow the *Fall of man.

549

Accordingly man was allowed to *sin as a prior circumstance before God made his sovereign, unconditional choice of whom to save and whom to *reprobate. Contrasts with *supralapsarianism. Also known as "sublapsarianism" and "postlapsarianism."

Infused grace. A grace that alters the human capacity for good deeds, standing in contrast to *imputed grace.

Infusion. Same as *affusion.

Inner light. A doctrine associated with the Society of Friends which asserts that by the power of the Spirit each Christian has a source of inner knowledge for God's will and guidance. Inner light goes beyond the doctrine of the *inner witness of the Spirit, which is limited to certitude about one's salvation status. It also goes beyond the Reformed doctrine expressed in the Westminster Confession of Faith 1:4-5 regarding the Spirit's work that causes the elect to recognize what writings speak to them from God, that is, which books are canonical; this concept is limited to the recognition of canonicity. Inner light goes beyond assurance of salvation and certainty about canonicity to the *content* of Christian faith and practice. It goes beyond *illumination, the ability to be enlightened by revelation, to direct revelation itself.

Inner man. See *Man.

Innocence. (a) The state of not being *guilty. (b) Innocence is occasionally differentiated from sinlessness by limiting the former to cases of unawareness.

Inscrutable sovereignty. In Reformed theology the Creator's right and practice of making choices and *predestinating the future unconditionally, that is, without reference to the will of personal creatures. His movements do in fact represent ethical, principled consistency even though they are unfathomable to men and may appear to be *capricious. See *Sovereignty.

Insufflation. In Roman Catholic practice especially, the act of breathing upon a person or thing in order to represent the present influence of the Spirit (cp. Jn. 20:22). Insufflation is associated with exorcism of evil spirits and accompanies *baptism.

Insult the Spirit. Same as "do despite to the Spirit"; see *Apostasy, *Blasphemy of the Holy Spirit, and *Grieve the Holy Spirit.

550

Intercession. Service as a go-between. A priest is said to represent men to God while a prophet represents God to men. (a) Jesus Christ intercedes for men through his death-resurrection as a basis for initial salvation and continued *salvation* (I Jn. 1:9; Heb. 7:25) while (b) the Spirit intercedes for men in *communication* and *empowerment* (Rom. 8:26-27). Christianity has set aside the practice of *sacerdotalism in which (c) official men approach the Father on behalf of the general populace of the kingdom; the *church itself is a kingdom of priests (I Pet. 2:9; Rev. 1:6), and all members of it intercede for one another.

Internal covenant. A spiritual relationship with the person of God that goes beyond official identification with the *visible church. Internal covenant correlates with *invisible church and *communicant church membership. Contrasts with *external covenant. See *Covenant.

Invincible ignorance. An involuntary ignorance of God's *law that cannot be overcome by serious effort; consequently, it is viewed as not being reckoned against the sinner. Contrasts with *vincible ignorance.

Invisible church. Those taken collectively who are actually saved in God's eyes in contrast to the *visible church, which is seen by the world as having identity with him whom the *church presents.

Irresistible grace. Refers to the doctrine that in receiving God's grace unto *salvation the sinner cannot successfully resist the influence of the divine Spirit. The person may resist in the sense that he does not immediately or automatically come to faith, but irresistible grace is infallible grace because it never fails to accomplish that whereunto it is sent. A young child may resist going to his room, but he cannot prevent his father from taking him there when it is time to go to bed. See *Cat grip.

Just. An alternative translation for "righteous."

Justification. The fourth element in the *ordo salutis in Romans 8:29-30. Removal of sin viewed in legal fashion; a legal pronouncement of acquittal. Justification differs from *forgiveness in that the latter stresses the interpersonal removal of sin. Justification is viewed theologically as a categorical matter because it involves a categorical change; it thus differs from *sanctification, which is viewed as a degree matter because it involves a progressive improvement of life quality within the new salvation category, or status. See *Salvation and *Objective justification.

551

Kingdom of God/heaven. See *Church.

Koinonia [koi-nō-nee'ä]. A transliteration of the Greek word normally translated "fellowship."

Lapsi. A term used in the early church for those who denied their faith in times of persecution.

The larger hope. Another designation for *restorationism.

Last Rites. In Roman Catholic pastoral theology, comprised of *penance, the eucharist, the apostolic benediction, and *extreme unction.

Law. (a) In biblical studies the law of God represents most generally the revealed will of God. (b) It is employed in a literary sense of the first five books of the Old Testament (*Torah*) in contrast to the prophets (*Nebi'im*) and writings (*Chetubim*); on occasion "law" includes the whole Old Testament (Jn. 10:34-35). (c) "Law" also refers to the Mosaic legislation and covenant in contrast to the New Covenant given through Christ. Finally, (d) from the nature of provision for righteousness, law contrasts with *faith in God's *grace as two means to *righteousness in God's eyes. The former has a man righteous in God's eyes because he is righteous in fact; the latter has a man righteous in God's eyes because Christ is righteous with whom the person has identified himself and like whom he aspires to be, but does not succeed in being.

Lawlessness. See *Antinomianism.

Lay baptism. Baptism performed by someone other than an ordained official of the *church.

Laying on of hands. An act used in scripture to symbolize the reception of responsibility for an office (Acts 13:3), to impart the/a gift of the Spirit (Acts 19:6), or to represent the application of divine power in healing (Acts 9:17).

Legal justification. Justification in the eyes of the *law as distinguished from *forgiveness, which stresses the element of interpersonal regard.

Legalism. (a) The notion that relationship to God can take place within the framework of *law. (b) In modern usage "legalism" connotes something inflexible, impersonal, and external; it implies a tendency to forget the intent of a statute and thence to apply it in terms of words in

552

matters to which it does not pertain. It often fails, because of abstraction from the lawgiver, to allow consideration of options the law does not specify. In Christianity this consideration becomes significant because God must be recognized as one who can with consistency provide possibilities beyond those to which he has committed himself, a matter important in the case of the honestly ignorant and the unevangelized.

Liberation theology. An approach to *salvation that centers on the relief of oppression and inequality through the employment of political mechanisms. The weakness lies not in its purpose, but in the means of accomplishing its purpose. Insufficient attention is focused on the necessity of internal change not only in the oppressors of this world, but also in the oppressed themselves. Without conversion the overthrow of oppressors only installs a new class of oppressors recruited from the previously oppressed, who tend to perpetuate oppression by the impulse to revenge. Unless self-centeredness is removed from the heart of everyone involved, the efforts will not accomplish even those social ends originally envisioned. Liberation theology exhibits a naive view of man and makes its mistake primarily because it presupposes the this-worldly perfectibility of man—and that from the outside in. Also known as "political theology" and comparable to the older formulation labeled "social gospel."

Libertinism. Same as *antinomianism.

Life. See *Eternal life.

Limbo. In Roman Catholic eschatology a postulated temporary abode for those who died under the Old Covenant; they had to remain there until the accomplishment of Christ's *redemption. Limbo is the permanent abode of unbaptized infants, who are innocent of *personal sin, but guilty of *original sin. Distinct from *purgatory, *hell, and *heaven.

Limited atonement. Same as *definite atonement.

Lost. A manner of describing a person out of relationship with God. He has no ultimate orientation for his life, both objectively and subjectively. Therefore he possesses no ultimate meaning and senses no ultimate meaning. The lost do not experience *authentic existence or the *beatific vision.

Lustrations. Same as *ablutions.

Man. Scripture speaks of man largely in functional, relational, and phenomenological ways in contrast to structural, ontic, or "scientific" terms. *Inner vs. outer man* exemplifies this tendency. "Inner man" seems to refer to the way a person is in his "heart of hearts"; it is the aspiring self as distinguished from the outer, bodily, accomplishing self. In view of the reciprocation between the outer and inner man, the line of demarcation between them cannot easily or satisfactorily be drawn. Romans 7:13-25 correlates the inner man (7:22) with the "I," the "mind," the "self" (7:25), the aspiring self as over against the "flesh" (7:18) and the "members" (7:23).

Natural man and spiritual man of I Corinthians 2:14-16 seem to be defined more along the lines of *viewpoint.* The natural man looks at the world from a non-transcendent position so that his actions are informed by horizontal rather than vertical relationships; he is bereft of the insight, hence, guidance of the non-material perspective, being confined instead to the concerns and promptings of this world. The spiritual man, on the other hand, has received revelation from God and has access to the omniscient viewpoint so that he can examine life and make his decisions about appropriate behavior from a reference point transcendent to the natural order.

Carnal man carries a more negative connotation because it focuses on the self-centered *behavior* that issues from seeing reality more or less from one's own eyes unqualified by needs of other people around or the will of God above. The carnal man is the behavioral result of the natural man's viewpoint.

Natural, spiritual, inner, outer, carnal man all refer to the same ontic being, but describe him functionally and relationally in different ways. Such a comment, of course, stands aside from a *natural depravity view of anthropology together with natural *regeneration, natural *inability, *original sin, and similar concepts that presuppose a fallenness of man that consists in structural, constitutional, congenital weakness sexually transmitted and miraculously removed. Instead, our comments assume a position of *psychological depravity that places sin, not in the category of nature or ability, but in the category of habit, that is, function.

Material sin. An act that is sinful in itself, but is not held against the sinner either because of ignorance or because he acted under extreme duress. Contrasts with *formal sin.

Mediation. Same as *intercession.

Mercy. A benevolent attitude toward others that prompts withholding just punishment. See *Grace.

Merit. Something deserved. In theology meritoriousness means producing the *righteousness that obliges God to view one as righteous. Meritoriousness contrasts with *antinomianism, *recognition, and *conditionality as differing relationships between a person's own behavior and God's viewing him as righteous. Under the *perfection requirement merit has no value for bringing God to view a sinner as righteous, because *salvation presupposes a man's unrighteousness, which by the nature of the case cannot be overcome.

Metempsychosis. The belief that souls move from one body to the next until the process of *purification is complete.

Military theory of the atonement. Same as *ransom theory of the atonement.

Mistake. (a) A non-moral error as distinguished from a *sin, which is disobedience to *commandment; miscalculating distance is a mistake, but drunkenness is a sin. (b) An attempt is sometimes made to correlate sin vs. mistake with intentional vs. unintentional disobedience, usually in the interest of maintaining one's claim to possess Wesleyan *sanctification despite contrary evidence from personal behavior. Although a difference can be recognized between the culpability of an unintentional vs. that of an intentional sin, scripture never so distinguishes them, but calls for *repentance in both cases.

Monergism. That view of *salvation which sees only God as working to bring the sinner back into relationship with God. In historical theology salvation is monergistic in that man does not—and indeed cannot—do anything about his estrangement from the Father. Biblically, salvation is monergistic in the sense that God alone is acting at the point of pronouncing forgiveness and justification upon the sinner. Man has the ability to respond to previous, resistible promptings of the Spirit and calling of the gospel, but his responses (from amid sins) obviously cannot contribute toward the *perfection requirement for fellowship with God. Traditionally monergism contrasts with *synergism. See *Cat grip and *Conditionality.

555

Monergistic. Being done by God unaided.

Monkey hold. An expression that views *salvation as something in which the person co-operates with God in the choice of whether he is saved. It contrasts with *cat grip. See also *Irresistible grace.

Moral commandment. Same as *moral law.

Moral influence theory of the atonement. Christ's life and death serve as a model of motivation to other men to yield up their last measure of devotion to God in conformity with Jesus' teachings. The view is associated primarily with Peter Abelard (1079-1142) in his *Commentary on Romans.* Virtually the same as *exemplarism and *the subjective theory of the atonement. See also *Atonement.

Moral law. A classification of commandments, used especially in Old Testament studies, that has to do with personal and corporate behavior. It includes such matters as love, respect for God and fellowmen, not murdering, not stealing, and the like. Moral law contrasts in this usage with *civil law and *ceremonial law.

In a second, related usage moral law contrasts with *positive commandment. Moral law refers to what is necessary behavior given the purpose for which man exists, Abraham was called, the universe was made, etc. It is regulation that derives from the nature of the case.

Mortal sin. (a) In Roman Catholic teaching a category of *sin based on I John 5:16. Mortal sins are "grave matters" done knowingly and voluntarily. They bring eternal death unless confessed to a priest and removed by *contrition. Contrasts with *venial sin as the second type of *personal vs. *original sin.

(b) In the original context, however, John may not be speaking of a one-time act as the above interpretation infers; he may mean a characteristic sin. "Unto death" may be a temporal expression meaning until— or tending to be until—physical death, hence, characteristic sin, rather than a degree expression meaning "with the result of spiritual death."

Mourner's bench. The bench on which a person kneels when he is *praying through.

Mystical union with Christ. A fluid expression whose meaning depends considerably on the author. The general range of usage fluctuates between a sense of personal relationship with Jesus Christ on the one hand to the distinctively mystical concept of the "flight of the soul to God." "Christian" mysticism has, however, not usually gone the further step in non-Christian mysticism where the person becomes lost in the Ultimate One so that his individual identity is lost.

As a positive statement the expression should probably be used to indicate a real relationship unperceived by the senses. Fundamentally this union, or relationship, is known by *promise* rather than by immediate *perception* or supernatural *product*. This limitation of the concept seems justified by Samson's experience of God's Spirit in Judges 16:20, where he did not know that the Spirit of God had left him. Not knowing the Spirit's absence implies that the absence or presence could not be ascertained directly; this episode confirms the supposition that God in his own nature, that is, unmanifested, is not able to be perceived by human receptors. On this background mystical union with Christ could refer to something in the mind's eye, a subjective *sense* rather than *perception*. It is real insofar as interpersonal relationship with Christ is actual, but the sense of it comes from faith in promises, not from direct stimulation of the human spirit.

Natural depravity. See *Depravity.

Natural man. See *Man.

Necessity. In philosophy necessity refers to internal causation to act. It contrasts with *compulsion, which refers to external causation. Necessity vs. compulsion is a conceptual device used in Reformed theology to avoid the inference that God carries guilt because man's *depravity means he cannot help sinning.

Necessity of the atonement. (a) Necessity of the *atonement means first that Christ did something for us because "something had to be done" (Gal. 2:21); man was in no position to solve his problem for himself. (b) A second usage considers whether *what* Christ did contained any objective value for *salvation that made it necessary above and beyond the purely interpersonal process of *repentance, *confession, *forgiveness (cp. *acceptilation). (c) Theologians often go on to say that what Christ did was *the something* that had to be done; God had no other option for providing a basis for restoring mankind to himself.

Neophyte. A term used in I Timothy 3:6 for someone recently converted. Often translated *"novice."

Non-communicant church membership. A *church membership in some *paedobaptist communions where people are officially members of the *church by *baptism since they were originally born to parents professing Christian *faith. They are members of the *external covenant, but not members of the *internal covenant.

Novice. (a) As a translation of I Timothy 3:6 the word refers to a recent convert; see *"neophyte." (b) In religious orders a novice is someone in a probationary stage between a postulate and full member of the order.

Obedience. Doing the will of a superior.

Objective condemnation. See *Objective justification.

Objective efficacy. A *sacrament has validity aside from the positive qualification of the candidate as long as it is administered properly by an official administrator. This automatic flow of grace does not depend, for example, on consciousness in the case of *extreme unction or personal *faith on the part of an infant in *baptism. See *Sacraments.

Objective justification. A doctrine based on Romans 5:12ff. that whatever men lost in Adam through no fault of their own (objective condemnation) they regained in Christ through no virtue of their own (objective justification). In the mind of God the race was first lost then saved, but actual *salvation or *lostness for eternity is figured individually. Objective justification has no real bearing on a person's destiny.

Objective universalism. See *Barthian universalism.

Once in grace . . . always in grace. Same as *eternal security.

Operating grace. Another expression for *unconditional grace; it contrasts with *co-operating grace, wherein the human will freely takes divine provisions and uses them to accomplish the end desired.

Opus operatum. A term meaning "act done"; it indicates the efficacy of a *sacrament aside from the attitudes of the administrator or candidate. The validity of the act depends on the legal qualification of the minister, the proper order in procedure, and the absence of wrong dispositions on the part of the recipient. Thus in *baptism the characteristics of the thing signified are attached to the symbol itself, and the absence of personal faith in the infant does not negate the validity and efficacy of the *ordinance. This *objective efficacy is the distinctive feature of the *sacraments as over against other means of grace. Also referred to by the phrase *ex opere operato.

Order of salvation. Same as *ordo salutis.

Ordinance. A religious ritual representative, or emblematic, in form. Ordinances are two in number: *baptism and communion, feet-washing being usually subsumed under communion instead of offered as a third ordinance. Unlike *sacrament, ordinance does not include the concept of *objective efficacy.

Ordo salutis. The "order of salvation" Paul lists in Romans 8:29-30: *foreknowledge, *predestination, *calling, *justification, *glorification. The apostle's list represents the chronological (not logical) sequence only of acts in *salvation that occur on the divine side; hence, the list is incomplete and temporal.

Original guilt. In traditional theology *guilt that the race has as a race and a guilt that destines all men to *hell unless it is erased in Christ. In Roman Catholic theology original guilt is eradicated in the *sacrament of *baptism. *Original sin broadens the picture to include the depraved nature transmitted to all of Adam's descendants. Distinguished from *objective condemnation, or *representative guilt.

Original righteousness. The character Adam had before the *Fall; distinguished from *original sin, the inheritable nature he had afterwards.

Original sin. (a) Inclusive of *original guilt, but distinctive in its reference to natural depravity according to usage in traditional theology. Historically, original sin has been often identified with *concupiscence. The doctrine is derived principally from Romans 5:12ff. (b) Since the arrival of the evolutionary framework in modern theology, original sin has been reformulated as the unwillingness of man to forsake the principles of his animal nature after his transcendent nature evolved. The functional equivalent of traditional original sin therefore is the tendency for men to live by instincts and drives rather than by spiritual values.

559

Outer man. See *Man.

Paedobaptism. The baptism of infants, which contrasts with *believers' baptism.

Paraclete. A term used to designate the Spirit of God, being an anglicized form of the Greek word *paraklētos* (Jn. 14:16, 26; 15:26; 16:7; cp. I Jn. 2:1).

Pardon. (a) In general usage pardon equals acquittal in the eyes of the *law. (b) In Roman Catholic usage "pardon" is another term for *indulgence.

Particularism. Same as *definite atonement.

Particularists. Those who believe in *definite atonement.

Passover. The main Jewish feast, celebrated each spring in memory of the "passing over" of the death angel at the death of the Egyptian firstborn (Ex. 12; Deut. 16). In connection with this feast Jesus was crucified; certain analogies then exist between his offering himself and the sacrifice of the passover lamb at this feast time. Jesus instituted the Lord's Supper during the course of this feast (Mt. 26:26-29) as a memorial of the sacrifice he himself was to become the following day (cp. I Cor. 5:7).

Patripassianism [*pater passo,* suffering Father]. The view of the death of Christ that involves the "Father's suffering," not just in the sense that he was sensitive to the agony of the Son's crucifixion, but in the sense that the Father himself was the Crucified One. Patripassianism presupposes no personality distinction between Father, Son, and Spirit so that they are the same being. Compare *Theopaschitic reconciliation.

Patristic theory of the atonement. Same as *ransom theory of the atonement. So called because the view prevailed among the sub-apostolic "Fathers."

Pelagianism. A set of doctrinal positions associated with Pelagius (late 4th-early 5th cent.), an antagonist of Augustine of Hippo (354-430). Pelagianism denied the doctrines of *original sin, *original guilt, *limited atonement, unconditional *predestination, and infallible perseverance, affirming in place of them the ability of man to initiate movement toward *salvation without divine *grace, which comes later. *Freedom of the

560

will meant for Pelagius that men could avoid *sin, and he even went so far as to name biblical examples of men who had succeeded in doing so. Contrasts with *Augustinianism and *Semi-Pelagianism. See also *Calvinism.

Penal substitution theory of the atonement. That view of the atonement in which Christ's death is viewed, among other things, as a *substitution for the sinner's death and punishment. Same as *vicarious atonement, or *substitutionary atonement.

Penance. One of the seven *sacraments in Roman Catholicism. Penance, meaning "punishment," brings *satisfaction for sin by making up for the loss of righteousness through *confession, *absolution, and *reparation. In more ancient times the severity of penance was significantly greater, including fasting, floggings, imprisonment, pilgrimages, and continence (at one time a lifelong requirement of penance). An act of penance is not necessarily germane to the nature of the salvation program; therein lies its distinctness from acts of repentance, for pilgrimages to places do not pertain to interpersonal considerations related to sin and forgiveness of sin. Penance does not involve a second party in the corrective for past sin; it is an effort on his own to fill up a gap in his own record of righteousness; hence, it moves in a system of self-correctiveness, which is merit.

Perfection. (a) Used loosely it refers to outstandingly good men (Lk. 1:6). (b) In Pauline usage it is absolutized in Romans 3:9ff. Perfection is the requirement for fellowship with a holy God. The word picture in the Greek term is that of coming to an end, or goal, hence, completeness or maturity. See also *Perfectionism.

Perfectionism. The doctrine that through the *sanctifying work of the Spirit a Christian has the capacity to live sinlessly. Such perfection does not come distinctively from personal efforts at self-improvement, but results from the gift of a regenerated nature.

Permissive predestination. A concept of *predestination applicable to free-will choices, in which God permits the fulfillment of the creature's free intent to act. Contrasts with *prescriptive predestination and correlates with *conditional predestination. See also *Predestination.

Perseverance. (a) In general, perseverance has to do with remaining

561

faithful to Christ. (b) As a theological expression "perseverance of the saints" means that God irresistibly causes a genuine convert to continue faithful to the end. The lack of perseverance signals lack of genuine *faith. Once a person is saved he will not be *lost because God will enable him to continue in the faith. Perseverance is technically distinguished from *eternal security because the latter tends to dissociate the necessity of continued practical Christian living from the salvation status. Perseverance also contrasts with *apostasy, which allows for the possibility of falling from *grace.

Personal guilt. *Guilt based on one's own actions in contrast to *imputed guilt, which is reckoned against a person from beyond himself.

Personal redemption. Same as *soteric reconciliation.

Personal righteousness. A *righteousness one would have that would be based on his own perfect *obedience to God's *law, in contradistinction to *imputed righteousness.

Personal sin. See *Personal guilt.

Philosophic sin. Sin as measured by reason and nature instead of by divine revelation.

Pietism. A religious movement originating in seventeenth-century Germany under the influence of Philipp J. Spener (1635-1705). Pietism has stressed devotional activities like prayer, Bible reading, fasting, *fellowship, and other activities that foster affective development in contrast to doctrine, philosophy, and the like, which concentrate on the cognitive dimension of man and the Christian faith.

Plenary indulgence. See *Indulgence.

Political theology. Same as *liberation theology.

Positive commandment. A type of commandment that does not derive necessarily from the nature of the case. Positive commandment contrasts with *moral law. If the purpose of God was to create man as a reflection of himself, adultery is inappropriate by the nature of the case and by the nature of man; hence, marital faithfulness falls within the category of moral law. Given the purpose, however, to have men identify themselves with Christ unto *salvation from *sin, *baptism is a "positive commandment" because God could have decided to mark that identification by any number of ritual acts.

Postlapsarianism. Same as *infralapsarianism.

Potential universalism. A view of the *scope of the atonement which understands God's intent to lay a basis for *salvation for everyone. By intent the *atonement included *conditionality. Atonement then is universal as to possibility, but limited as to fact because of personal rejection by many. Distinguished from *hypothetical universalism and *actual universalism.

Pouring. Same as *affusion.

Praying through. The practice of "agonizing in prayer" until a sense of the peace of God comes upon the sinner. It involves the experience of feeling a face-to-face presence with him. Such practice has the strength of encouraging the person to stay with his prayer until a psychological breakthrough has been made and the mental and emotional burden is lifted. The danger is that the one who prays can confuse the subjective sense of breaking through with an objective breakthrough. Objective breakthrough to God implies hesitancy, aloofness, insensitivity, and the like on God's part and creates the feeling that one's own efforts override or precede the efforts of God in reconciliation. It can create the impression that a man is reconciling God rather than God reconciling man.

Predestination. (a) The second element of the *ordo salutis* in Romans 8:29-30. Predestination basically guarantees the meaningfulness of history because it indicates that ahead of time God decided where history was going; the future is not mere eventuation (*futurum*), but intentional goal. (b) In its salvation application, predestination says first that the class of individuals in Christ is destined for eternal *fellowship with God, others being predestined for separation from him. At a more specific level each individual may be said to be predetermined to *heaven or *hell on the basis of foreknown response to the conditions for being assigned to one destiny or the other. Predestination may even be predicated on a free-will choice in a permissive sense, since all choices to act may be prevented if God so wills. Predestination in this sense is the ratification of possibilities originating outside the will of God. Predestination goes beyond foreknowledge by drawing attention to this ratification of willed behavior.

563

(c) In Augustinian, Calvinistic, or Reformed usage predestination denotes an unconditional predetermining in all areas, not only in nature, but in the spiritual destiny of men as well. This system of theology has only *prescriptive predestination, in which God originates all specific acts; *prescriptive predestination is unconditional predestination.

Same as *foreordination. See also *Class predestination; *Conditional predestination; *Double predestination; *Permissive predestination; *Prescriptive predestination, *Single predestination.

Prelapsarianism. Same as *supralapsarianism.

Prescience. Same as *foreknowledge.

Prescriptive predestination. God's determination of a future event in such a way that no alternative is possible. The mechanics of prescription may be through nature, *law, or special divine providence. Contrasts with *permissive predestination and correlates with *unconditional predestination.

Pretermission. Suspension of a positive penalty for sin. Is distinguished from *forgiveness and *remission.

Prevenient grace. A kind of actual grace that "comes before" the acceptance of *salvation and is designed to lead to acceptance and *sanctification. In Augustinian thought prevenient grace is entirely unrelated to human condition or behavior in contrast to subsequent grace, where the human will co-operates with divine agency in producing the result.

Promise. A statement of benefit relative to the future. Promise is the character of all reward because it comes from the grace of another rather than from the efforts of self. Men do not so much come to the future (*futurum*) as the future comes to them (*adventus*). See also *Predestination.

Propitiation. Regards Christ's death as appeasing God's just wrath at *sin and the sinner. Propitiation is directed toward the *person* of God in contrast to *expiation, which is directed toward the *thing* offending God. Based on passages like Romans 3:25; I John 2:2; 4:10. See *Atonement and *Expiation.

Proselyte. A person that converted to Judaism as an adult in contrast to someone born into the Jewish nation and *faith. Thus a proselyte is a Jew by religion, but not by race.

Psychological depravity. See *Depravity.

Puberty of the soul. Same as *age of accountability.

Punishment. *Retribution against a person for the *guilt of his unacceptable behavior. Punishment differs qualitatively from suffering in that pain may not correspond with guilt; consequently, the experience of physical or psychological pain does not imply guilt from sin.

Purgatory. In Roman Catholic eschatology a temporary abode of the dead where saved people *expiate, or make *atonement for, their unforgiven *venial sins. Contrasts with the situation under *restorationism because in purgatory there is no offer of salvation to people in a lost condition at the time of death. Also contrasts with *hell, which is a permanent place of destruction rather than a temporary place of *purification.

The existence of purgatory is defended on the basis of the apocryphal book II Maccabees 12:39-45 (cp. I Cor. 3:11-15). See also *Second definite work of grace.

Purification. A model that pictures *salvation as ridding from foreign elements. In Old Testament studies purification could be ceremonial or real depending on whether *defilement was (a) ceremonial or (b) real. In historical Christian theology purification has been applied to (c) the cleansing of *venial sin in *purgatory (cp. *apokatastasis). (d) A fourth usage found in the Wesleyan and holiness movements regards purification (cp. *baptism in fire) as a process during earthly life whereby the trials and persecutions in human existence and Christian experience have a cleansing effect upon the soul. See also *Metempsychosis.

Quietism. A view of life that condemns human effort and champions passive existence under the all-determining hand of God. Quietism results from the view of *prescriptive predestination in all affairs so that personal responsibility does not exist. The ideal life is to be in what might be called a "nirvana of the will."

Racial solidarity. A view of mankind that sees the human race as one legal unit in such a way that the guilt of Adam applies to all his descendants. Since Adam and Eve were the human race and all the living have descended from them, what applied to them as the race applies equally to the race in all times. By virtue of being the natural head, Adam becomes the legal head as well.

Ransom theory of the atonement. A view of the *atonement based on Matthew 20:28; Mark 10:45; and I Timothy 2:6, in which Christ's death is viewed as a payment for those whom he redeemed. Origen (c. 185-c. 254) was one outstanding spokesman for this view. Also known as the "patristic theory," or "military theory." See also *Redeemer and *Redemption.

Recapitulation. A concept in historical theology developed from Ephesians 1:10. The "summing up of all things in Christ" includes the restoration of lost men to communion with God through Christ, the recapitulation of all previous revelation in the *incarnation, and the reunion of angels as well as men under the headship of Messiah. Also called *anakephalaiōsis.*

Recognition. A term applicable to the belief that human *obedience can have only a *post facto* relationship with *salvation, logically speaking. Contrasts with *merit, *conditionality, and *antinomianism.

Reconciliation. Reconciliation stresses the restoration of interpersonal relationship in the *salvation complex. *Sin broke not only the *law so as to necessitate *justification, but it separated the subjects from the Lawgiver so as to require reconciliation.

Redeemer. A person who pays a ransom and so is said of Jesus Christ in his role as Savior. He "buys back" the *lost. See *Ransom theory of the atonement and *Redemption.

Redemption. An alternate translation of the Greek word rendered "ransom." Redemption pictures the *atonement under the model of buying the freedom of a slave because certain similarities exist between the two realities. Jesus' giving his life roughly corresponds to "buying." The slave situation compares to lostness in sin because in both cases the "bound person" cannot free himself from the situation. In both instances the benefactor is under no legal or moral obligation to relieve the person's situation. See *Cosmic redemption, *Ransom theory of the atonement, and *Regeneration.

Regeneration. A translation for the Greek term in Matthew 19:28 and Titus 3:5. (a) Etymologically signifying "new birth," or "birth again," the word in the first passage refers to the new age after Christ's return (cp. Acts 3:21). (b) The usage in Titus 3:5 recalls a similar expression in John 3:5. In these passages an aspect of salvation is set forth under the imagery of new birth, the central idea evidently being a new start from a spiritual orientation. Both passages evidently relate to *baptism. (c) From this last usage, especially in John 3:5, a third meaning has developed in systematic theology. Regeneration here is not just renewed relationship with God or starting life anew; it is a re-creation of the natural capacities so as to enable response to the gospel and growth in Christian virtue. See *Baptismal regeneration and *Renovation.

Relativism. A view of moral behavior that does not see right and wrong growing ultimately out of the originating purpose of a transcendent being, but out of the preferences of the individual or the social system. Contrasts with *absolutism.

Remission. An alternative translation for the Greek word rendered *"forgiveness." The underlying Greek word picture is that of throwing away the person's *sin. In English "remission" is distinguished from forgiveness in that the latter focuses on the person while the former removes the consequences of an offence such as withdrawn *fellowship. *Pretermission suspends positive penalty.

Renovation. In Reformed theology especially, the effect of a recurrent enablement operative before, in, and after baptism sometimes on the model of external stimulation engineered by God as distinguished from a one-time *regeneration of the human ability itself. Renovation may be lost, but not regeneration.

Renunciation. A formal statement at baptism in which the candidate— or the *sponsor in the case of infant baptism—renounces allegiance to Satan.

Reparation. Compensation for wrongs done against another. The eye-for-an-eye principle in Exodus 21:23-25 establishes the guideline that the repayment should be commensurate with the sin. Same as "restitution."

Repentance. The act by which a person separates himself from his past act. Repentance has both an intellectual and an emotional component, looks forward to *confession and *forgiveness, and anticipates a transformation of behavior. See also *Attrition, *Contrition, and *Penance.

Representative guilt. A personal guilt incurred by a representative. A concept applicable perhaps to Romans 5:12, in which case it would be a guilt Adam incurred upon himself, not upon the race, even though mankind may experience *suffering (not *punishment) as a result of it. See also *Objective condemnation and *Original guilt.

Reprobate. Descriptive of a lost person. A reprobate is one who is not among the *elect.

Reprobation. In the concept of *double predestination, reprobation refers to the act whereby God condemns sinners to eternal punishment either by a neutral act of passing over them in the *election of others or, as in some theologians, the positive act of appointing them unconditionally to eternal punishment. See also *Election and *Double predestination.

Reserved sins. In the Roman Catholic practice of *penance, certain sins are "reserved" for higher levels of the clergy to *absolve.

Restitution. Same as *reparation.

Restorationism. The idea that, because of eternal opportunity for *salvation even after death, all men will eventually be brought back into *fellowship with God. Also known as "the larger hope." See *Apokatastasis, *Hell, *Purgatory, *Universalism.

Revealed will. God's will insofar as it has been known to men or insofar as it is declared in the proclamation of the gospel to unbelievers. Contrasts with *hidden will, or *decretive will. Also called "declared will."

Righteous. Another translation for "just." Cp. *Good and "holy."

Righteousness. (a) In general usage righteousness, or justness, is good moral living according to the *law of God. (b) In more technical usage it means perfection because the law required a person to continue doing everything (Gal. 3:10). Righteousness theoretically could come from doing all the commandments all the time; hence, it would come by *works and would be personal righteousness. Practically speaking, however, righteousness comes from being regarded as righteous in the eyes of God; hence, it comes by trust (*faith) in the *grace of God and is *imputed righteousness. See also *Imputation and *Imputed grace.

Sacerdotalism. The practice of approaching God through the *mediation of a priest as one who carries divine authority in divine-human relations.

Sacramentalism. The belief in, and practice of, using *sacraments as a means of divine *grace; the belief in the objective efficacy of ritual acts. Sacramentalism presupposes that divine grace flows indirectly through the *church rather than directly from God to the recipient.

Sacraments. In Roman Catholic theology ritual acts, seven in number, believed to have *objective efficacy: *baptism, *confirmation, the eucharist, *penance, matrimony, Holy Orders, and *unction. Luther reduced the number from seven to two: baptism and eucharist. In non-technical parlance sacrament does not always include the idea of objective efficacy, or automatic flow of grace, but may simply indicate an outward sign of an inward grace. Sacraments are performed by one person (ordained minister) upon another, never by the person upon himself. Cp. *Ordinance.

Sacrifice. Represents one of the ways in which Christ's death is regarded in the New Testament and predicted in the Old Testament institution of animal sacrifice. Symbolically the capital punishment due to a person for disobedience is borne by the animal and, antitypically, by Christ.

Saint. (a) In biblical usage a holy person, that is, one set aside to a special relationship with God and his will. Contrasts with "sinner." (b) In Roman Catholic practice, one who from among the saints is set apart as especially holy by virtue of certain qualifications examined subsequent to his death.

Salvation. A word used in scripture to cover a wide variety of ills from which men need deliverance including sickness, famine, political oppression, and poverty. (a) In the Christian vocabulary of the New Testament "salvation" means deliverance from *sin and *hell. The concept is expressed under a number of models and has many facets. *Atonement looks at the *work of Christ* on which salvation is based; "sacrifice" is one image employed to describe it. *Substitution indicates one way of looking at the suffering and death he endured as if he were receiving the penalty due to sinners. *Justification pronounces acquittal in a *legal sense* and pertains to the change of state involved. *Sanctification sets the person aside to a special purpose with God. *Expiation regards the sin as covered in regard to the *law. *Remission focuses on the removal of *sin* from the person when God looks on him; *forgiveness is the same thing, but governs the *sinner,* rather than the sin. *Propitiation stresses the removal of God's righteous indignation at *disobedience.
As to *the return from lostness* *redemption views salvation as a

payment for the freedom of a slave. *Adoption pictures salvation as being given status in a family to which one does not belong. *Reconciliation describes renewed interpersonal relationship between God and man. *Conversion marks the change in life style involved. *Regeneration sees this change of state and behavior as a new beginning. *Sanctification in a second sense sees the new life as a process of salvation from the practice of sin. All these together have been called the "similes of salvation."

(b) In the Greek world of the first century "salvation" meant deliverance from the limitations of material and fleshly existence. It had nothing decisive to do with deliverance from the penalty, power, and presence of sinful behavior.

Salvific. Having the value of bringing about *salvation.

Sanctification. (a) In scripture sanctification often appears to address the same event as does *justification except under a different model. Justification views the removal of sin under the legal model so that it is a pronouncement of acquittal; sanctification views the event as setting the person aside to a special relationship with God and his purposes. *Forgiveness stresses the personal act of removing the sin barrier between God and man.

(b) Theologically "sanctification" has become a technical term denoting the process of Christian growth in which God and men work together (*synergism) in Christian development.

(c) A further development comes in Wesleyan theology, where sanctification, too, is considered a crisis occasion instead of a process. Here sanctification refers to a *second definite work of grace where the last vestiges of inbred *sin are removed by the Spirit. Thereafter the person has the capacity to live sinlessly; he has not only been saved, but also sanctified. In Wesleyanism sanctification as well as justification is *monergistic. See also *Confirmed in holiness and *Perfectionism.

Sanctifying grace. A divine gift of ability in the human soul which enables men to perform righteous acts. Also called *"habitual grace."

Satisfaction theory of the atonement. A theory of the *atonement in which the death of Christ is viewed as primarily a satisfaction paid to God; it "satisfied," or made up for, the honor lost to God by man's disobedience; it was a satisfaction of God's demand for justice. Anselm

570

(1033-1109) set forth this view of the atonement in his work *Cur Deus Homo?* See *Atonement and *Salvation.

Save. See *Salvation.

Scope of the atonement. The scope of the atonement has to do with whether God intended for Christ's death to be applicable to all men or only to a specific number whom he *elected without reference to any act or condition present in them. The presence or absence of *conditionality combines with actuality vs. potentiality as two sets of variables applicable to the question of scope. Thus the possible views are *actual universalism, *potential universalism, and *particularism. See also *Amyraldianism, *Definite atonement, *Limited atonement, *Particularism, and *Universalism.

Scruples. Fears that sin has been committed when none has occurred. An impractical overdemand made on one's feelings, motivations, and desires coupled with a quantifying vs. attitudinal approach to measuring sinfulness and *righteousness. Scruples result from the perfectionist mentality applied to Christian living, where in fact the whole message is that personal perfection does not have to be the case when men in attitude and aspiration identify themselves with the Perfect One.

Seal of the Spirit. A manner of referring to the *gift of the Spirit (Eph. 1:13; 4:30; II Cor. 1:22). His presence with us and effects upon us serve as a mark of identification and security before God. See also *Earnest of the Spirit.

Se-baptism. Self-baptism in contrast to baptism administered by another.

Second definite work of grace. In Wesleyan theology the first definite work of grace is *justification, the pronouncement of acquittal, the change into the *salvation status. The second definite work eradicates the *depraved nature so that the person can live a sinless life of perfect love. This *perfectionism allows for sins of ignorance, unintentional sins, and even sins of impulse in the face of temptations that do not give a person time to muster self-control. Second definite work relates to *sanctification. Thus in Wesleyanism both justification and sanctification are *monergistic.

Whereas *confirmed in holiness places the purification from *sin at

571

death, *purgatory places it after death, and second definite work places it before death. See also *Perfectionism and *Sanctification.

Security. See *Eternal security.

Semi-Pelagianism. A doctrinal position usually identified with Roman Catholicism that stands between the optimistic view of *man in *Pelagianism and the pessimistic view of salvation according to Augustinianism. Principally, Semi-Pelagianism adopts the Pelagian idea that man in his *freedom of the will can make initial steps toward *salvation aside from divine grace; but in favor of Augustinianism it moderates significantly the distance he can go in the pursuit of righteousness. Semi-Pelagianism rejects irresistible *grace, infallible *perseverance, and *definite atonement; it adopts *original guilt from Augustine and ameliorates *original sin in the direction of Pelagianism.

Shedding of blood. See *Blood atonement.

Sin. A word often used to translate *hamartia,* whose picture is that of missing the mark. (a) As to its real nature, sin is an action committed against, or omitted from, a standard of behavior. The standard may be God's revealed will, the nature of man that expresses divine will, the conscience of self or someone else. (b) Sin is secondly a state of estrangement caused by sinful acts. (c) Sin may also be a noun carrying the same meaning as the adjective "sinful." In such a case sin is a description of the characteristic behavior and attitude of a person.

(d) In traditional theology sin is not only an act, but a nature; that is, it is a kind of being/nature that produces sinful acts in men; related to *total depravity. See also *Formal sin, *Material sin; *Mortal sin, *Venial sin; *Sin unto death, *Willful sin, *Sin with a high hand, *Eternal sin; *Original sin; *Hamartialogy, *Mistake, *Transgression; *Guilt, and *Innocence.

Sin not unto death. An expression found in I John 5:16-17 referring to a *sin for which a brother may pray. Inasmuch as John goes on immediately to say that "whoever is begotten of God does not sin," a brother's sin not unto death must mean an uncharacteristic sin or one about which the brother does not take an attitude of indifference. Contrasts with *sin unto death. See *Venial sin.

Sin of ignorance. Same as *material sin.

572

Sin unto death. An expression found in I John 5:16 referring to a sin for which a brother is not commanded to pray. Since the "sin *not* unto death," mentioned in the same context, is one that can be committed by a begotten one, "who does not sin" (5:18), "sin unto death" must be characteristic sin or a sin to which the sinner is indifferent. The sin has been understood as "unto death" in one of two senses: a sin that brings spiritual death or sin that lasts till physical death. The former alternative has the weakness of requiring the concerned brother to be able to recognize whether the sin has brought separation from God. It is perhaps easier then to suppose that the writer meant a characteristic sin, one that as far as someone else can see will continue till death or one that arises out of a permanent attitude. See *Mortal sin.

Sin with a high hand. See *Willful sin.

Single predestination. A designation for *predestination most appropriate under *infralapsarian Calvinism inasmuch as God is said to "pass over many in the saving of some." Under such an arrangement God's act of *reprobation is not as positive as his act of *election. The lost are all lost by virtue of their own sin, and only because of unconditional grace do the *elect receive grace. For the lost there is nothing more that God needs to do to secure their lostness, but for the elect he makes positive choice to override their legally appropriate destiny.

The sinner's prayer. Usually the words of the publican or their equivalent found in Luke 18:13: "God, be merciful to me, a sinner." In some evangelical groups the sinner's prayer is regarded as the time-when of salvation; in this usage it becomes something of a formal replacement for Christian *baptism, which in I Peter 3:21 is described as including the appeal of a good conscience toward God. Biblically we would say that the sinner's prayer is an aspect of the baptism event instead of a second event or a substitute for water baptism.

Situation ethics. Same as *situationalism.

Situationalism. The belief that morality does not derive from abiding truth, but from transient circumstance; consequently, there are no principles of behavior that apply to all situations. Also known as "situation ethics."

Social gospel. Contrasts with personal gospel and concentrates on the evils that inhere in the structures of societies themselves.

573

Socinianism. A view of the atonement named after Faustus Socinus (1539-1604) and likewise known as "exemplarism," or the *example theory of the atonement. Close to the *moral influence view of Christ's death.

Sola fide. Same as *solifidianism; see *Faith only.

Sola gratia. "Grace only." Depending on the theological system, "grace only" may mean the originating category for salvation in contrast to personal perfection (*works) or faith plus works (*Galatianism); others use it to mean that all human response in salvation is logically *post facto* (*recognition) in contrast to *conditionality.

Solifidianism. The doctrine of *justification by *faith only, in distinction from justification by faith plus the merit of good *works.

Soteric. Having to do with *salvation. Cp. *Salvific.

Soteric reconciliation. The reconciliation of men to God in contrast to *cosmic reconciliation, which has to do with restoring the non-personal realm to ideal relationship with the Creator. See also *Regeneration.

Soteriology. The study of *salvation, one of the major categories in Christian doctrine parallel to theology proper, eschatology, ecclesiology, and the like.

Sovereignty. As to its *nature* sovereignty is the right to choose, plan, and accomplish one's will. A term applied to God's right to purpose in consistency with his nature and to act consistently within his purposes. The sovereignty of God is a *principled sovereignty rather than a *capricious one inasmuch as he is governed by his own principles rather than by lust. His sovereignty is *inscrutable insofar as "his ways are past finding out" and are unfathomable to the human recognition. Sovereignty is possessed by virtue of creatorship.

As to its *recognition* and use God's creatures can see in his acts the consistency of holy love by which he operates; consequently, divine sovereignty can never become a legitimate means by which to escape the requirements of consistency in the hermeneutical and theological enterprise; that is to say so to speak, sovereignty is a theological category rather than a hermeneutical device. One's doctrinal system is *his* doctrinal system which he therefore bears responsibility to defend; divine sovereignty cannot solve logical contradiction because it is a characteristic

574

of person, not an aspect of proposition. A distinction is made between objective revelation, then, and subjective systematizing of revelation about God and his acts in history. If the sovereignty is not recognizable, it is of no use to define and affirm. In all this, of course, men do not have the right to question God himself in his sovereign acts, but they do have the responsibility to question those interpretations of his words and deeds that eventuate in logical dilemmas.

As to its *maintenance* divine sovereignty is effected through omnipotence. Sovereignty therefore does not eliminate the free-choice origin of an idea or act outside God, for any foreign move can be prevented through his intervention. The concept of sovereignty does not require that the positive origin of all acts must lie inside God. *Conditionality can operate within the structure of sovereignty because in his sovereignty God can will such to be the case.

Spirit(ual) baptism. See *Baptism in the Holy Spirit (a) and (c) for two definitions.

Spiritual Israel. See *Church.

Spiritual man. See *Man.

Sponsors. In paedobaptist communions others besides the parents who participate in the baptism of an infant and assume certain responsibilities in rearing the child in the Christian faith. On behalf of the child, sponsors promise *renunciation of *sin and Satan, faithfulness to Christ, and obedience to his will and his ministers. Same as godparents.

Sprinkling. Same as *Aspersion.

Stoddardianism. So named from Solomon Stoddard (1643-1729), pastor in Northampton, Massachusetts, who defended the idea. See *Half-way covenant.

Subjective theory of the atonement. See *Moral influence theory of the atonement.

Sublapsarianism. Same as *infralapsarianism.

Submersion. A term occasionally used instead of *Immersion.

Substitutionary atonement. See *Vicarious atonement.

Sufficiency of the atonement. Indicates the sufficiency of Christ's death for the *salvation of all men. Contrasts with *efficiency of the *atonement.

Sufficient grace. In Roman Catholic theology a dispensation of divine grace that is sufficient for the effect desired, but does not in fact lead to that result because of inadequate co-operation on the part of the recipient. A species of *actual grace that contrasts with *efficacious grace.

Supererogation. In Roman Catholic theology the doctrine that Christ, Mary, and the saints did more good *works than their personal fulfill-ment of God's will necessitated. The leftovers have been stored up in a *treasury of merit, which other men can draw on for *indulgences and for bringing up to requirement their own amount of works sufficient for atonement of their sins. Works of supererogation are those done beyond what is strictly required so that as to nature they are not just good, but better vs. good.

Supralapsarianism. In Reformed theology the view that considers God's *decree of *election to precede his decree regarding the *Fall of man. The standard criticism of this arrangement is that God becomes the cause of human sin inasmuch as he decrees infallibly that men should sin. For this reason most modern-day Reformed theologians espouse *infralapsarianism instead. Also known as "prelapsarianism."

Synergism. A view of *salvation that sees man and God working together to bring about *reconciliation with the Father. In historical theology salvation has been called "synergistic" if man is allowed to have anything to do about his estrangement from God. Biblically, the concern is whether man can do anything about his lostness. God alone acts in pronouncing justification, but man can meet conditions for that pronouncement without contributing to justification because it is a pronouncement by God only. Inasmuch as perfection is the prerequisite for divine fellow-ship, a sinner obviously cannot alone or together with God produce that result. The perfection is reckoned upon him despite his actually lacking that character. In evangelical theology synergism may be affirmed of the Christian life and growth in sanctification (Rom. 8:28), but not of justification. Traditionally contrasts with *Monergism. See *Monkey hold, *Conditionality, and *Second definite work of grace.

Synergistic. Having the character of *synergism.

Temptation. (a) Objectively, the presentation of stimuli and influences calculated to draw a person aside from his values and purposes (Heb. 4:15). (b) Subjectively, being drawn to stimuli and influences contrary to one's spiritual commitments (James 1:14).

Testament. A model for describing the establishment and maintenance of divine-human relationship. Hebrews 9:15-20 provides the most specific instance of using "testament" as an analogy of *salvation. The particular points of comparison are its coming into force after the death of him who made it and its having provisions for those whom it benefits. Same as "will."

Theodicy. The defense of the existence, holiness, and omnipotence of God in the face of the atheistic argument from the fact of evil.

Theopaschitic [theos + paschō, God suffering]. A terminology regarding the crucifixion that stresses the deity of the Crucified One. May or may not be associated with monarchianism, where Father, Son, and Holy Spirit are the same person. Compare *Patripassianism and *Theopaschitic reconciliation.

Theopaschitic reconciliation. A form of objective *reconciliation as contrasted to subjective reconciliation. Reconciliation is conceived of as moving from the Father through his human Representative toward mankind as opposed to the other way around. The conception of trinity may adjust this concept in the direction of *patripassianism.

Theopoiēsis. See *Divination.

Theōsis. See *Divination.

Total depravity. See *Depravity.

Transactional theory of the atonement. The idea that Christ's work had the effect of placating One who was less merciful than himself.

Transgression. Disobedience referred to under the word picture of crossing a boundary. Cp. *Sin.

Treasury of merit. In Roman Catholic *soteriology a record, or bank, where are stored up the works of *supererogation by Christ, Mary, and the *saints. Inasmuch as they went beyond the call of duty in the kind and amount of their good *works, a less pious man may draw upon their reserves in obtaining an *indulgence.

Tri(u)ne baptism. A form of baptism in which the action is performed three times, once for each member of the trinity (Mt. 28:19). Contrasts with single baptism, where the action is performed only once. The expression is used in reference to *aspersion, *affusion, or *immersion.

Tri(u)ne immersion. A mode of baptism in which the candidate is placed under the water three times, once for each member of the trinity (cp. Mt. 28:19).

Unconditional. Having no *conditions to serve as the basis for divine choice for assistance or positive blessing.

Unconditional election. The third step in six-point *Calvinism, which declares that God's choice of whom he will save does not regard anything in the person chosen.

Unconditional predestination. See *Conditional predestination.

Unction. See *Extreme unction.

Unforgivable sin. Same as *unpardonable sin; often used as another designation for *blasphemy of the Holy Spirit.

Universalism. (a) In Old Testament studies "universalism" refers to the message of the prophets like Jonah who taught that God was the God of all peoples, not just the Jews, and that he cared for their plight and future as truly as for Israelites. (b) In salvation studies, universalism refers to the belief that all men will be saved (*unrestricted universalism) at least eventually (*restorationism; *the larger hope).

(c) Sometimes *particularists refer to unlimited *atonement by the term "universalism" even though it is only a *potential universalism as far as the intended *scope of the atonement is concerned. The tendency to classify potential universalism with *actual universalism comes from a lack of the *conditionality concept in Reformed theology, conditionality being the conceptual mechanism by which potential for all becomes actual for the some who are actually saved. See also *Actual universalism, *Barthian universalism, *Hypothetical universalism, *Potential universalism, and *Unrestricted universalism.

Unpardonable sin. Same as *Blasphemy of the Holy Spirit.

Unrestricted universalism. The belief that Christ's atoning work secured, not only the possibility, but the actuality of the *salvation of all men so that the only *"hell" the wicked will ever endure is the experience of living in a world presently separated from God. This universal salvation at least applies on the objective side—so far as God is concerned, if not on the subjective side (*Barthian universalism). See *Universalism.

Utilitarianism. The view that defines right action as what brings the greatest happiness to the most people. See also *Eudemonism and *Hedonism.

Venial sin. (a) In Roman Catholic theology a category of *sin defined on the basis of I John 5:16. Venial sins are less serious than *mortal sins and do not bring damnation, but only dispose the soul to death. Venial sins need not be confessed to a priest. Contrasts with *mortal sin.

Vicarious atonement. That view of the *atonement in which Christ's death is viewed among other things as a substitute for the sinner's death and punishment. The value of Christ's work is ultimately interpreted in legal and sacrificial categories. This *penal substitution theory is most particularly associated with John Calvin (1509-1564) and is found in Book II of his *Institutes of the Christian Religion.* See *Atonement.

Vicarious baptism. The practice of baptizing one person in place of another either because the latter is infirm or has died. See *Baptism for the dead.

Vicarious faith. The faith of parents, godparents, or the church community that substitutes for personal *faith in the case of *infant baptism and *vicarious baptism.

Vincible ignorance. An ignorance due to one's neglect to learn what would have been able to prevent sin. Guilt is viewed as reckoned against the offender in such cases although it lacks the severity of guilt incurred despite knowledge. Contrasts with *invincible ignorance.

Visible church. The *church that is seen on earth as distinguished from the *invisible church, which is those truly saved. Visible church corresponds to *non-communicant membership and *external covenant.

Washing of regeneration. An alternate translation for *bath of regeneration, or "laver of regeneration" in Titus 3:5.

Washings. Same as *ablutions.

Water baptism. A term used to refer to that aspect of the total event of baptism that contrasts with *Spirit baptism, or *baptism in the Holy Spirit, or *gift of the Spirit. See *Baptism.

Wesleyanism. A set of teaching named for John Wesley. Its distinctive element is the doctrine of the *second definite work of grace.

Will. (a) See *Testament. (b) The *act* of choosing or the *ability* to choose between alternatives as distinguished from the necessary response to an environmental stimulus or the strongest environmental stimulus.

Will of complacency. In Reformed theology the complacent will of God by which he would, for example, let all come to repentance (II Pet. 3:9) if they could; but, of course, since man is *totally depraved and God has *reprobated the non-elect, no one except the elect will come, and God knows that. Will of complacency regards the salvation process from the standpoint of time and does not contemplate the prior decisions of God in eternity past. Contrasts with *will of preterition.

Will of preterition. The eternal will of God decreed before time in eternity past, when he made his choices unconditionally regarding men and their eternal destinies. Contrasts with *will of complacency.

Willful sin. An expression found in Hebrews 10:26 that evidently does not mean simply a sin a person knows he is committing when he does it; the author views it as bringing about eternal judgment or at least the feeling of condemnation in God's eyes. Paul's experience in Romans 7:12—8:1 does not seem to allow for eternal condemnation for failure to live up to the ideals of the inner man in all instances. Therefore, instead of sinning "willingly," probably a stronger action is meant—something like sinning deliberately, belligerently, with abandon, or with the decisiveness of positively turning one's back on God as if he were insensitive to the human predicament or did not keep covenant to protect from misfortune or persecution. Perhaps the same as *"sin with a high hand" (Num. 15:30-31; cp. Num. 14:40-44; Deut. 1:43; 17:12-13) and *"insulting the Spirit of grace" (Heb. 10:29). See also *Blasphemy of the Holy Spirit.

Works. In James 2 works are those outer actions that follow and complete inner action, which James labels "faith." In Romans and Galatians especially, Paul uses "works" to refer to actions that produce the result (*righteousness) as distinguished from faith, which trusts a second party to give the result (righteousness). Works would produce actual righteousness if a person could, in a practical sense, do everything all the time that the law of God required; faith receives imputed righteousness. If a person always did everything God commands, he would be righteous and so God would be obligated to view him as righteous.

In *faith and *grace God graciously views the person as righteous despite the fact that in terms of personal actions he is not perfectly righteous. Works means inherent result.

In theological discussions other meanings are sometimes encountered: actions done with the motive of winning favor from someone, outward behavior bereft of proper motivations, or actions according to the letter of the law without regard to intent of the law.

Works of supererogation. See *Supererogation.

Wrath of God. God's righteous indignation at sin together with the punishment and destruction that he brings about in order to curb and contain disobedience.